AF703130

Sport and Exercise Psychology

Sport and Exercise Psychology

Edited by Amarion Fisher

STATES
ACADEMIC PRESS
www.statesacademicpress.com

States Academic Press,
109 South 5th Street,
Brooklyn, NY 11249, USA

Visit us on the World Wide Web at:
www.statesacademicpress.com

© States Academic Press, 2023

This book contains information obtained from authentic and highly regarded sources. Copyright for all individual chapters remain with the respective authors as indicated. All chapters are published with permission under the Creative Commons Attribution License or equivalent. A wide variety of references are listed. Permission and sources are indicated; for detailed attributions, please refer to the permissions page and list of contributors. Reasonable efforts have been made to publish reliable data and information, but the authors, editors and publisher cannot assume any responsibility for the validity of all materials or the consequences of their use.

ISBN: 978-1-63989-718-6

Trademark Notice: Registered trademark of products or corporate names are used only for explanation and identification without intent to infringe.

Cataloging-in-Publication Data

Sport and exercise psychology / edited by Amarion Fisher.
p. cm.
Includes bibliographical references and index.
ISBN 978-1-63989-718-6
1. Sports--Psychological aspects. 2. Exercise--Psychological aspects. 3. Physical education and training--Psychological aspects. 4. Sports. 5. Exercise. I. Fisher, Amarion.
GV706.4 .S66 2023
796.01--dc23

Table of Contents

Preface

This book has been a concerted effort by a group of academicians, researchers and scientists, who have contributed their research works for the realization of the book. This book has materialized in the wake of emerging advancements and innovations in this field. Therefore, the need of the hour was to compile all the required researches and disseminate the knowledge to a broad spectrum of people comprising of students, researchers and specialists of the field.

Sport refers to a type of competitive physical activity or game that is primarily focused on the utilization, improvement or maintenance of physical abilities and skills. Sport psychology is a field of study which focuses on the intersection of mental well-being and physical activity. It involves the application of concepts from a variety of fields such as psychology, biomechanics, kinesiology and physiology. Exercise psychology is an area of study concerned with the performance analysis of athletes in terms of exercise. It also helps in building a personalized exercise program for athletes in order to enhance their involvement and enjoyment while exercising. This book explores all the important aspects of sport and exercise psychology in the present day scenario. It consists of contributions made by international experts. A number of latest researches have been included to keep the readers up-to-date with the global concepts in this area of study.

At the end of the preface, I would like to thank the authors for their brilliant chapters and the publisher for guiding us all-through the making of the book till its final stage. Also, I would like to thank my family for providing the support and encouragement throughout my academic career and research projects.

Editor

1

Subjective Rank of the Competition as a Factor Differentiating between the Affective States of Swimmers and their Sport Performance

Aleksandra Samełko[1], Monika Guszkowska[2] and Anna Kuk[1]*

[1] *Department of Pedagogy and Psychology of Physical Culture, Józef Piłsudski University of Physical Education in Warsaw, Warsaw, Poland,* [2] *Department of Occupational Therapy, Józef Piłsudski University of Physical Education in Warsaw, Warsaw, Poland*

Correspondence:
Aleksandra Samełko
al.samelko@gmail.com

Purpose: The aim of the study was to establish the differences in affective states of swimmers depending on the subjective rank of the competition and the relationship between affective states and performance in sports competitions of low, medium and high subjectively perceived rank.

Methods: The respondents (n = 31) aged from 15 to 23 years (18.1 ± 2.397) were studied using the psychological questionnaires *Perceived Stress Scale* (PSS-10), *Profile of Mood State* (POMS), and *Positive and Negative Affect Schedule* (PANAS) during sports events. 362 measurements using *POMS* and 232 measurements using *PANAS* before the starts were collected. The significance of intergroup differences was determined using the Kruskal-Wallis test. A stepwise regression analysis was used to determine the emotional predictors of sports results.

Results: Subjective rank of sports competition differentiated significantly anger (chi^2 = 6.826; p = 0.033), confusion (chi^2 = 11.345; p = 0.003), depression (chi^2 = 10.2; p = 0.006), fatigue (chi^2 = 49.394; $p \leq 0.001$), vigour (chi^2 = 11.345; $p \leq 0.001$), positive emotions (chi^2 = 51.233; $p \leq 0.001$), and negative emotions (chi^2 = 11.552; p = 0.003). Regression analysis showed the influence of mood states and positive emotions on the sports result.

Conclusion: The swimmers' affective state changed depending on the subjective rank of the competition. Depression and positive emotional state made it possible to predict the result in medium- and high-rank competition.

Keywords: athletes, emotions, mood, stress, performance

INTRODUCTION

In the search for predictors of efficiency and effectiveness of sport performance, mental aspects are more and more often noticed since in combination with motor skills, they determine sports success (Cogan, 2019). In terms of mental preparation in swimming it is important to strive for an appropriate and reproducible mental state that will ensure the effective performance of a familiar task. Its important element is affective states, which may have positive or negative valence and could influence specific perception strategies (Bless and Burger, 2017).

Affective states are understood as bipolar constructs currently experienced by an individual in response to a direct or indirect interpretation or appraisal of events and stimuli. It is the combination of emotions and moods (Kontaris et al., 2020). Emotion is a more intense mental state than mood, related to physiological responses. It has a shorter duration and is usually triggered by a specific stimulus (Domínguez-Jiménez et al., 2020). Emotions and moods also differ in intentionality, causes, consequences and function. There are many models that attempt to explain the occurrence of pre-competitive emotions (Lane et al., 2012).

In the traditional approach proposed in the iceberg profile by Morgan (1980), links were sought between the negative or positive affective states and the efficiency of an athlete's performance. This model is still used as a theoretical basis in research (Terry and Parsons-Smith, 2019; Han et al., 2020). The results of some more recent studies support the Morgan's findings that experiencing strong positive states with low levels of negative states is conducive to the achievement of high sporting performance and that successful sportsmen and sportswomen experiencing emotions derive energy from both positive and negative emotions (Martinent et al., 2013).

The results of other studies suggest that in order to act effectively, the athlete should provide himself with as much mental energy as possible, acquired from both positive (e.g., joy) and negative (e.g., anger) affective states (Carter and Sachs, 2012). The complex relations between cognitive antecedents and mediators of affective states in sport are also of interest to researchers (Chadha et al., 2019).

Studies have demonstrated the relationships between sport performance and the appraisal of the emotional state rather than the intensity of affective states alone (Psychountaki and Zervas, 2000). Athletes who positively assessed their somatic excitement before taking part in competitions achieved better results than others (Borek-Chudek, 2011).

According to the transactional concept of stress by Lazarus and Folkman (1984), the response to a situation, e.g., a sports competition, depends on cognitive assessment. An athlete may cognitively assess the start of the competition as a threat or challenge. Lepine et al. (2005) argue that the level of stimulation alone is not as important as the individual's perception of the task. If an athlete approaches the difficulty as a challenge, the probability of experiencing positive states increases (Gross and Thompson, 2007). In turn, conscious experiencing positive emotions improves the effectiveness of coping with stress (Tugade et al., 2004). In a competitive situation, stress depends on the situational context, including the rank of the competition (Gracz and Sankowski, 2007). The high rank of the competition can significantly modify the emotional state of the athlete and influence his or her sports result (Bittner et al., 2005).

The intensification of affective states in a sports competition may, therefore, depend not only on the objective rank of the competition (e.g., national championships), but also on its perception and subjective appraisal by an athlete: the significance of a specific competition for a specific athlete and his or her aspirations (Boldizsár et al., 2016).

Participation in the competition which is the most important from a social standpoint is not always the most important for the athlete. To date, studies on the relationships between the rank of competitions and sport performance have most often used objective rank indicators (Jeon, 2019). Assuming that the measurement of affective states before a sports performance is related to sports results, it is worth analyzing the factors influencing the experience of mood and emotions (Patrícia et al., 2019). We will attempt to fill this gap. It cannot be excluded that subjective rank of competition (understood as a sense of start importance of the athletes themselves) modifies the relationship between the affective states and the sport performance (Ihalainen et al., 2017). The subjective rank of the competition may be determined by the competitor's performance aspirations and his or her inner motivations.

The aim of the study was to establish the differences in affective states of swimmers depending on the subjective rank of the competition and the relationship between affective states and performance in sports competitions of low, medium and high subjectively perceived rank.

MATERIALS AND METHODS

The study examined 31 swimmers at the national (Polish) level aged 15 to 23 years (18.1 ± 2.397). All participants gave written consent to participate in the study as required by the Helsinki Declaration.

In order to appraise the mood state, the *Profile of Mood State (POMS)* (McNair et al., 1971) was used, with the Polish adaptation of Dudek and Koniarek (1987). The psychometric properties of the inventory are satisfactory (Cronbach's alpha is in the range 0.74–0.91). The tool has been used many times in the studies of athletes' mood states, starting with Morgan's research (1980). The adjectives form six scales: depression, tension, anger, fatigue, confusion and vigor. The Polish version of POMS contains an additional scale of kindness and has satisfactory psychometric properties (Dudek and Koniarek, 1987).

Positive and Negative Affect Schedule (PANAS) (Watson et al., 1998) with (Brzozowski, 2010) Polish adaptation (2010) was used to study emotional states. The tool contains the scale of positive and negative affect. The reliability of the scale is satisfactory: the Cronbach's alpha ranges from 0.73 to 0.95 depending on the version and type of sample. The validity of the scale is confirmed by the results of factor analysis, cluster analysis, correlations with other tools and intergroup differences.

The *Perceived Stress Scale (PSS-10)* was used to determine the intensity of stress in the period before the competition. The authors of the original version of the test are S. Cohen et al. (1983), whereas adaptation to the Polish conditions was prepared by Juczyński and Ogińska-Bulik (2009). The validity and reliability of the Polish version of the test are sufficient for the purposes of scientific research.

Procedure

The respondents completed the questionnaires in writing. Before the study began, they had received detailed instructions from one of the researchers – a psychologist. Completion of the questionnaires was supervised by three trained assistants.

The actual stage of the study took place during a sports competition. Each sports competition lasted from 3 to 5 days and had two sessions during 1 day. The swimmers were asked to fill in the PSS and POMS during the general warm-up (approx. 1 h before the first start in the morning or afternoon session) in the swimming pool halls.

Moreover, just before (approx. 10 min) each start (race), the swimmers filled out the PANAS questionnaire. Throughout the competition, the assistants observed the athletes in accordance with the minute schedule of starts (set by the event organizer). It happened that one athlete, starting three times in one session, filled out PANAS three times. There were also athletes starting only once in the session, they participated in one measurement with PANAS.

Each of the 31 athletes was therefore tested several times. We obtained in total 232 measurements of mood states (POMS) at the beginning of both sessions of the day (including 164 for men and 68 for women) and 362 measurements of emotional states just before start (PANAS) (248 for men, 114 for women). Due to a small number of respondents, the results of men and women were combined. Previous studies show that women and men – professional athletes do not differ in terms of mental traits important for this study (Olmedilla et al., 2018).

Sports Results

Data on personal bests for a given distance and swimming style were obtained from respondents each time before the beginning of the race. The results achieved in the races were also recorded[1]. The time results were converted in order to compare the times achieved in different styles and distances. The personal record of an athlete was divided by the score obtained in the race and expressed as a percentage according to the formula: (previous personal best / result achieved in the race) × 100. A score of more than 100 means that the athlete achieved a better result than his or her personal best.

Rank of Competition

Each time just before the race (start), after completing the PANAS the athlete evaluated the importance (rank) of a race on the 3-point scale: 1 – *low*, 2 – *medium*, 3 – *high*).

Statistical Analysis

First, the normality of the investigated quantitative variables was checked using the Kolmogorov-Smirnov test. For most of the variables, distributions different from the Gaussian distribution were noted. For this reason, the Kruskal-Wallis test was used to determine the significance of intergroup differences. As the skewness values of the distributions fell within the range of +/− 2, it was considered that regression analysis could be performed. A stepwise regression analysis was used to determine the affective predictors of sports results. The sports result was the dependent variable. As factors, the indices of 7 moods (anger, confusion, depression, anxiety, fatigue, vigor, kindness) were entered into the equation. Regression analyzes were performed separately for races of low, medium and high subjective rank. A regression analysis was also carried out for all races, additionally introducing the rank of race as a factor. Then, analogous regression analyzes were performed with two emotional states (positive-negative) as factors.

[1] The results were publicly available online on the (Megatiming, 2018) website.

RESULTS

The level of stress did not vary significantly depending on the subjective rank of the race (**Table 1**). The swimmers' mood was the worst on the day of the race of low subjective rank (low perceived importance). Respondents revealed the highest level of negative states and a fairly low level of vigor. The highest level of vigor and the lowest level of four negative mood states were recorded on the day of the high-ranked race (high perceived importance).

In the case of emotional states prior to the start of the race, the differences were not so clear (**Table 2**). The level of positive emotions and negative emotions were significantly different depending on the subjective rank of the race. The level of both positive and negative emotions before the race of the high rank was higher than before the race with lower subjective rank (medium and low).

The sports results obtained at the competition of *low* (M ± 98.15, SD ± 2.765), *medium* (M ± 98.93, SD ± 3.244) and *high* (M ± 99.89, SD ± 1.969) subjective rank were also compared. Their variability was found to be statistically significant ($\chi^2 = 30.469$, $p < 0.001$). The swimmers had better results in races which they rated as the most important, whereas lower scores were observed in less important races.

Stepwise regression analysis was carried out to determine whether the affective states are capable of predicting sports results. First, the predictors were searched for in terms of mood states, separately for the results obtained in low, medium and high-ranked competitions (**Table 3**).

In the case of low-ranked races, sports results can be predicted at almost 20% based on the level of fatigue, which is a negative predictor. Two predictors of the results were identified in middle-ranked races: depression and confusion. In the case of high-ranked races, only depression turned out to be a predictor. Mood states allowed for predicting sport performance during competitions that were assessed the athletes as important. Then, additional factor of a subjective rank of the race was added. Two predictors were revealed: depression (negative predictor) and the rank of the race (positive predictor).

It was also verified whether the emotional state just before the race allows for predicting the results obtained in a given race. The results of the race assessed as medium important and important can be predicted in about 5% based on a positive emotional state.

Two predictors were determined after the introduction of an additional factor of a subjective rank of the race. A positive emotional state and the rank of the race allow for predicting the sport result in about 13%. High results should be expected in high-rank races with swimmers experiencing strong positive pre-competition states measured just before the race (**Table 4**).

TABLE 1 | Stress levels and mood depending on the subjective rank of the race.

Rank of race	Low rank (*n* = 30)		Medium rank (*n* = 86)		High rank (*n* = 126)		Kruskal-Wallis test	
Variable	***M***	**SD**	***M***	**SD**	***M***	**SD**	**chi ^{2}**	***p***
Stress	16.50	5.704	16.15	6.276	14.61	7.122	3.927	0.140
Anger	14.77	5.418	13.12	8.215	11.4	8.287	6.826	0.033
Confusion	11.70	4.268	9.99	4.423	8.80	4.728	11.345	0.003
Depression	19.57	9.111	16.15	12.02	13.63	10.184	10.2	0.006
Fatigue	18.70	4.268	13.99	6.762	10.09	6.715	49.394	<0.001
Tension	14.07	5.47	12.94	6.228	13.16	5.885	1.270	0.53
Vigor	13.43	4.321	15.26	5.129	17.42	6.138	11.087	<0.001
Kindness	17.07	5.948	17.56	4.991	17.13	4.733	1.114	0.573

TABLE 2 | The emotional states before the race depending on the rank of the race.

Rank of race	low rank (*n* = 52)		medium rank (*n* = 146)		high rank (*n* = 164)		Kruskal-Wallis test	
Variable	***M***	**SD**	***M***	**SD**	***M***	**SD**	**chi ^{2}**	***p***
Positive emotions	23.06	9.918	27.65	8.431	32.68	7.582	51.233	<0.001
Negative emotions	14.21	5.263	15.11	5.991	16.02	5.399	11.552	0.003

TABLE 3 | Mood states as predictors of sports result.

Rank of race	Predictor	β	R^2	*F*	*p*
Low	fatigue	−0.470	0.193	7.676	0.010
Medium	depression	−0.558	0.107	5.843	0.04
High	confusion	0.370	0.047	7.116	0.009
	depression	−0.235			
All races	depression	−0.265	0.133	18.926	<0.001
	rank	0.214			

TABLE 4 | Emotional states as predictors of a sports result.

Rank of race	Predictor	β	R^2	F	p
Low	–				
Medium	positive emotional state	0.252	0.057	9.281	0.03
High	positive emotional state	0.230	0.047	8.921	0.003
All starts	positive emotional state	0.249	0.133	18.926	<0.001
	rank	0.136			

DISCUSSION

The results of the study confirm our presumption that the subjective rank of competitions differentiates the swimmers' mood. The mood was the best on the day of the high-rank races. On that day, athletes experienced the weakest negative mood states: fatigue, confusion, depression and anger. The level of vigor was the highest at the time. In other studies of swimmers, fatigue by the big amount of training caused a decrease in vigor (Faude et al., 2008). Especially big differences were observed in the level of fatigue: it was much lower before high-ranked races. The results obtained in our study do not question the findings of other researchers (Torres-Luque et al., 2013) concerning the importance of objectively determined rank of competitions (Gracz and Sankowski, 2007).

Swimmers experienced similar intensity of stress before races, regardless of their perceived importance (subjective rank). Differences in the levels of stress in three different conditions were not statistically significant.

Only negative moods were significant predictors of sports results, regardless of the subjective rank of race. The level of depression was a significant negative predictor of sports results obtained during medium- and high-rank races. The importance of this predictor was also confirmed in the analysis for all races. It can therefore be assumed that this mood is a particularly important factor determining the sports result. The relationship between depression and the appraisal of a difficult situation is carried in two directions. On the one hand, depression is likely to affect how an athlete perceives the situation and interprets his or her experiences (Wolf et al., 2015; Sahin et al., 2017). On the other hand, a difficult situation can make the athlete feel depressed.

In our swimmers, the level of emotions before the race, both positive and negative, was the highest in races of the high subjective rank. This confirms the findings of Gracz and Sankowski (2007) that the strength of the emotional experience of athletes depends on the rank of the competition: the higher the rank, the stronger the emotional excitation (Fernández et al., 2020). In similar study it turned out that strong negative emotions do not prevent athletes from achieving high sports results. The highest-ranked swimmers felt the strongest positive and negative emotions during the competitions, simultaneously achieving the highest sports results (Samełko et al., 2018). This confirms the observation of other researchers that both positive and negative emotions release energy, which has a positive impact on sport performance (Martinent et al., 2013). Feeling positive affective states may require more attention from athletes than experiencing negative states (Vast and Young, 2010).

Our results suggest that sport performance of swimmers, regardless of the subjective rank of the sporting event, can be predicted based on negative moods on the day of the competition. It is more likely that mood states, especially depression, affect sports results by modifying the cognitive appraisal of the starting situation and expectations of the result. It is worth noting at this point that their predictive power decreased with the rank of the competition. In the case of competitions subjectively assessed as the most important, the significance of mood as the predictor of sports result measured by the coefficient of determination was the lowest. Furthermore, the positive emotional state felt just before the race contributed to the mobilization of energy, which allowed for faster covering of the distance, but only when the athlete assigned a moderate or high rank to the race.

The study has limitations. The survey was conducted in a small group of athletes in one sport, which significantly reduces the possibilities for generalization of results. The only cognitive factor considered was a subjective assessment of the rank of the race. The authors are aware that the POMS tool is a quite old questionnaire. However, currently conducted research on athletes show justification for using this tool (Adrade et al., 2013; Rice et al., 2017).

FINAL CONSIDERATIONS

Our results suggest that the pre-competitive mood and the emotions are related to performance, which is reflected in other studies (Patrícia et al., 2019). The subjective rank of the race may be a factor modifying the relationship between affective states and results. It seems appropriate to take measures aimed at increasing the ability of athletes to self-regulate emotionally (Doron and Martinent, 2017). Emotions should be an important area of mental preparation (Samełko et al., 2018). This allows for increasing the effectiveness of athletes also in stressful situations (Gross and Thompson, 2007; Church et al., 2017).

PRACTICAL IMPLICATIONS

Based on the results obtained, the following guidelines can be formulated for the coaches and athletes:

1. Increased knowledge of coaches about how the athlete subjectively evaluates the importance of a sporting event may favor the optimization of athlete's preparation for the competition;

2. Athletes should develop their affective awareness to cope better with the performance situation;

3. Coaches should educate themselves in recognizing the affective states of athletes for more effective training and performance during the competition;

4. The objective and subjective importance / rank of the competition should be taken into account by the coach and the athlete in the period of setting goals for the season.

ETHICS STATEMENT

The studies involving human participants were reviewed and approved by the Senate Research Ethics Committee (Józef Piłsudski University of Physical Education in Warsaw). Written informed consent to participate in this study was provided by the participants' legal guardian/next of kin.

AUTHOR CONTRIBUTIONS

AS data collection, research organization and project, and description of the results. MG research methodology, statistical analysis, and description of the results. AK collecting literature and manuscript proofreading. All authors contributed to the article and approved the submitted version.

REFERENCES

Adrade, E., Arce, C., De Francisco, C., Torrado, J., and Garrido, J. (2013). Versión breve en español del cuestionario POMS paradeportistas adultos y población general. *Rev. Psicol. Delporte.* 22, 95–102.

Bittner, E., Nußbaumer, A., Janke, W., and Weigel, M. (2005). Football fever: goal distribution and non-Gaussian statistics. *Eur. Phys. JB* 67, 459–471. doi: 10.1140/epjb/e2008-00396-1

Bless, H., and Burger, A. M. (2017). Mood and the regulation of mental abstraction. *Curr. Dir. Psychol. Sci.* 26, 159–164. doi: 10.1177/0963721417690456

Boldizsár, D., Soós, I., Whyte, I., and Hamar, P. (2016). An investigation into the relationship between pre-competition mood states, age, gender and a national ranking in artistic gymnastics. *J. Hum. Kinet.* 51, 243–252. doi: 10.1515/hukin-2015-0188

Borek-Chudek, D. (2011). "Emotional states and sports achievements of badminton players," in *Studies in Psychology*, eds O. Gorbaniuk, B. Kostrubiec-Wojtachnio, D. Musiał, M. Wiechetek, A. Błachnio, and A. Przepiórka (Lublin: KUL), 109–132.

Brzozowski, P. (2010). *Skala Uczuœ Pozytywnych i Negatywnych, polska adaptacja skali PANAS D. Watsona i L.A. Clark [Polish adaptation PANAS]*. Warsaw: PTP.

Carter, L., and Sachs, M. (2012). In the mood: flow, mood, and the marathon. *Marathon Beyond* 16, 68–79.

Chadha, N., Turner, M., and Slater, M. J. (2019). Investigating irrational beliefs, cognitive appraisals, challenge and threat, and affective states in golfers approaching competitive situations. *Front. Psychol.* 10:2295. doi: 10.3389/fpsyg.2019.02295

Church, H., Rumbold, J. J., and Sandars, J. (2017). Applying sport psychology to improve clinical performance. *J. Med. Teach.* 39, 1205–1213. doi: 10.1080/0142159x.2017.1359523

Cogan, K. D. (2019). Coaching olympic athletes with sport psychology. *Consul. Psychol. J. Pract. Res.* 71, 86–96. doi: 10.1037/cpb0000129

Cohen, S., Kamarck, T., and Mermelstein, R. A. (1983). Global measure of perceived stress. *J. Health Soc. Behav.* 24, 385–396. doi: 10.2307/2136404

Domínguez-Jiménez, J. A., Campo-Landines, K. C., Martínez-Santos, J. C., Delahoz, E. J., and Contreras-Ortiz, S. H. (2020). A machine learning model for emotion recognition from physiological signals. *Biomed Signal. Process. Control.* 55, 101646. doi: 10.1016/j.bspc.2019.101646

Doron, J., and Martinent, G. (2017). Appraisal, coping, emotion, and performance during elite fencing matches: a random coefficient regression model approach. *Scand. J. Med. Sci. Sports* 27, 1015–1025. doi: 10.1111/sms.12711

Dudek, B., and Koniarek, J. (1987). Adaptacja testu Profil of Mood States (POMS) D. M. McNaira, M. Lorra, L. F. Dropplemana. *Przegl Psychol.* 3, 753–762.

Faude, O., Meyer, T., Scharhag, J., Weins, F., Urhausen, A., and Kindermann, W. (2008). Volume vs. Intensity in the training of competitive swimmers. *Int. J. Sports Med.* 29, 906–912. doi: 10.1055/s-2008-1038377

Fernández, M. M., Brito, C. J., Miarka, B., and Díaz-de-Durana, A. L. (2020). Anxiety and emotional intelligence: comparisons between combat sports, gender and levels using the trait meta-mood scale and the inventory of situations and anxiety response. *Front. Psychol.* 11:130. doi: 10.3389/fpsyg.2020.00130

Gracz, J., and Sankowski, T. (2007). *Psychologia Aktywności Sportowej [Sport activity psychology]*. Poznañ: AWF.

Gross, J. J., and Thompson, R. A. (2007). *Emotion regulation. Conceptual Foundations. Handbook of Emotion regulation.* New York, NY: Guilford Publications.

Han, C. S. Y., Parsons-Smith, R. L., and Terry, P. C. (2020). Mood profiling in Singapore: cross-cultural validation and potential applications of mood profile clusters. *Front. Psychol.* 11:665. doi: 10.3389/fpsyg.2020.00665

Ihalainen, S., Mononen, K., and Linnamo, V. (2017). Which technical factors explain competition. *Int J Sports Sci Coach* 13, 78–85. doi: 10.1177/1747954117707481

Jeon, M. (2019). Analysis of point deduction patterns in Taekwondo using association rule learning. *J. Perform. Anal. Sport* 19, 323–330. doi: 10.1080/24748668.2019.1602441

Juczyński, Z., and Ogińska-Bulik, N. (2009). *Narzêdzia Pomiaru Stresu i Radzenia Sobie ze Stresem [Tools for Measuring Stress and Coping with Stress]*. Warsaw: PTP.

Kontaris, J., East, B. S., and Wilson, D. A. (2020). Behavioral and neurobiological convergence of odor, mood and emotion: a review. *Front. Behav. Neurosci.* 4:35. doi: 10.3389/fnbeh.2020.00035

Lane, A. M., Beedie, C. J., Jones, M. V., Uphill, M., and Devonport, T. J. (2012). The BASES expert statement on emotion regulation in sport. *J. Sports Sci.* 30, 1189–1195. doi: 10.1080/02640414.2012.693621

Lazarus, R. S., and Folkman, S. (1984). *Stress, Apprisal and Coping.* New York, NY: Springer.

Lepine, J., Podsakoff, N. P., and Lepine, M. A. (2005). A Meta-analytic test of the challenge stressor- hindrance stressor framework: an explanation for inconsistent relationships among stressors and performance. *Acad. Manage* 5, 764–775. doi: 10.5465/amj.2005.18803921

Martinent, G., Nicolas, M., Gaudreau, P., and Campo, M. (2013). A cluster analysis of affective states before and during competition. *J. Sport Exerc. Psychol.* 35, 600–611. doi: 10.1123/jsep.35.6.600

McNair, D. M., Lorr, M., and Droppelman, L. F. (1971). *Manual for the Profile of Mood States.* San Diego, CA: Educational and Industrial Testing Service.

Megatiming. (2018). *Swimming Site Containing the Results of the Competition Recommended by the National Swimming Association.* Available online at: http://www.megatiming.pl/ (accessed October 1, 2018).

Morgan, W. P. (1980). Test of champions: the iceberg profile. *Psychol. Today* 14, 92–108.

Olmedilla, A., Torres-Luque, G., García-Mas, A., Rubio, V. J., Ducoing, E., and Ortega, E. (2018). Psychological profiling of triathlon and road cycling athletes. *Front. Psychol.* 9:825. doi: 10.3389/fpsyg.2018.00825

Patrícia, B. M., Lopes Verardi, C. E., Müller, D., Filho, P., and Meruss, N. C. (2019). Analysis of mood states, trait anxiety, and state anxiety: a study with athletes before artistic gymnastics competitions. *J. Phys. Educ. Sport* 19, 2234–2240.

Psychountaki, M., and Zervas, Y. (2000). Competitive worries, sport confidence and performance ratings for young swimmers. *Percept. Mot. Skills.* 91, 87–94. doi: 10.2466/pms.2000.91.1.87

Rice, S., Parker, A. G., Rosenbaum, S., Bailey, A., Mawren, D., and Purcell, R. (2017). Sport-related concussion and mental health outcomes in elite athletes: a systematic review. *Sports Med.* 48, 447–465. doi: 10.1007/s40279-017-0810-3

Sahin, M., Sagirkaya, A., Peker, A. T., Bademli, K., Lok, N., and Lok, S. (2017). Relationship with parental psychological control and stress levels in national sports. *Ser. Phys. Educ. Sport Sci. Mov. Health* 7, 480.

Samełko, A., Guszkowska, M., and Gala- Kwiatkowska, A. (2018). Affective states influence sport performance in swimming. *Pol. J. Sport Tourism* 25, 21–26. doi: 10.2478/pjst-2018-0023

Terry, P. C., and Parsons-Smith, R. L. (2019). Identification and incidence of mood profile clusters among sport participants. *J. Sci. Med. Sport* 22, 100.

Torres-Luque, G., Hernández-García, R., Olmedilla, A., Toro, E. O., and Vallejo, N. G. (2013). Fluctuación del Perfil de Estados de Ánimo (POMS) en un periodo competitivo en judokas de élite. *Rev. Psicol. Delporte* 22, 313–320.

Tugade, M. M., Fredrickson, B. L., and Feldman, B. L. (2004). Psychological resilience and positive emotional granularity: examining the benefits positive emotions on coping and health. *J. Pers.* 6, 1162–1187.

Vast, L. R., and Young, R. L. (2010). Emotions in sport: perceived effects on attention, concentration, and performance. *Aust. Psychol.* 45, 132–140. doi: 10.1080/00050060903261538

Watson, D., Clark, L. A., and Tellegen, A. (1998). Development and validation of brief measures of positive and negative affect: the PANAS scales. *J. Pers. Soc. Psychol.* 54, 1063–1070. doi: 10.1037/0022-3514.54.6.1063

Wolf, S. A., Eys, S. A., and Kleinert, J. (2015). Predictors of the precompetitive anxiety response: relative impact and prospects for anxiety regulation. *Int. J. Sport Exerc. Psychol.* 13, 344–358. doi: 10.1080/1612197x.2014.982676

2

Basic Psychological Need Profiles and Correlates in Physical Activity Participation: A Person-Centered Approach

Chunxiao Li[1], Chee Keng John Wang[2], Koon Teck Koh[2*], Kwang San Steven Tan[2], Shern Meng Tan[2], Wee Boon Ang[2], Liang Han Wong[3] and Huat Neo Connie Yeo[3]

[1] School of Physical Education and Sports Science, South China Normal University, Guangzhou, China, [2] National Institute of Education, Nanyang Technological University, Singapore, Singapore, [3] Physical, Sports and Outdoor Education Branch, Ministry of Education, Singapore, Singapore

***Correspondence:**
Koon Teck Koh
koonteck.koh@nie.edu.sg

Guided by Basic Psychological Need Theory, we investigated the combined associations between need satisfaction and need frustration (*i.e.*, need profiles) and their relations with theoretically relevant correlates including mindfulness, physical literacy, physical activity enjoyment, and physical activity. The participants were Singapore-based school students (N = 844, M_{age} = 12.45, SD_{age} = 1.99, boys = 53.1%) who completed a cross-sectional survey. The results of the latent profile analysis identified four distinct need profiles: profile 1–average satisfaction and frustration (n = 364, 44.1%); profile 2–low satisfaction (n = 251, 29.7%), above average frustration; profile 3–very high satisfaction, very low frustration (n = 144, 17.1%); and profile 4–high satisfaction, very high frustration (n = 85, 10.1%). Among these, profile 3 was the most adaptive one; it had the highest levels of mindfulness, physical literacy, physical activity enjoyment, and moderate-to-vigorous physical activity. Experiences of need satisfaction countered the negative effects of need frustration on these correlates. These findings enhance our understanding of students' psychological need experiences and highlight the need for investigating the combined associations between need satisfaction and need frustration.

Keywords: need satisfaction, physical exercise, latent profile analysis, students, wellbeing

INTRODUCTION

Basic Psychological Need Theory (BPNT; Deci and Ryan, 2000), one of the mini-theories in Self-Determination Theory, has been widely used for understanding human functioning (Vansteenkiste et al., 2020). BPNT posits that humans will achieve optimal functioning and well-being *via* the satisfaction of three basic psychological needs. By contrast, frustration of the three psychological needs will lead to human dysfunction and ill-being (Vansteenkiste and Ryan, 2013; Vasconcellos et al., 2019). Although these tenets are widely supported by a wealth of empirical evidence derived from variable-based analyses such as multiple regression, little research has examined the combined associations between need satisfaction and need frustration (*i.e.*, need profiles) and their relations to human functioning (Rouse et al., 2020; Vansteenkiste et al., 2020; Warburton et al., 2020). To address this literature gap, we used person-centered analyses to examine need profiles and their associations with selected theoretically relevant correlates including mindfulness, physical literacy, physical activity (PA) enjoyment, and PA in school students.

Basic Psychological Need Theory posits that humans universally possess three basic psychological needs, which are the needs for autonomy, competence, and relatedness (Deci and Ryan, 2000). Humans satisfy their need for autonomy when they experience control over tasks, while the need for competence is satisfied when humans feel effective and capable of completing valued tasks. Lastly, the need for relatedness is satisfied when humans experience closeness and connection with significant others. According to BPNT, satisfaction of the three basic psychological needs (*i.e.*, "bright side") is essential for growth and positive development of humans. Recent advancements in BPNT have specified a "dark side", in which the three basic psychological needs are actively frustrated or thwarted (Bartholomew et al., 2011). Hence, it is important to differentiate the difference between low need satisfaction and need frustration (Bartholomew et al., 2011; De Francisco et al., 2018). In the latter case, the three basic psychological needs are frustrated when humans are asked to do tasks against their will, experience a sense of failure and low confidence, and experience feeling excluded and rejected by others. Frustration of these needs are found to ensue dysfunction and ill-being, such as low levels of motivation and mental problems (Deci and Ryan, 2000; Vansteenkiste and Ryan, 2013; De Francisco et al., 2018). Furthermore, in comparison to low need satisfaction, need frustration is considered a better predictor of negative outcomes such as burnout, depression, and sedentary time, supporting the different roles of need satisfaction and need frustration in understanding human functioning (Bartholomew et al., 2011; Vansteenkiste et al., 2020; Warburton et al., 2020).

The establishment of the distinct concept of need frustration has spurred research to simultaneously examine need satisfaction and need frustration. However, most of the research so far have only explored this through variable-centered approaches such as multiple regression analysis (Warburton et al., 2020). Although the use of variable-centered approaches can shed light on explaining the relationships between a set of basic psychological needs and related variables, they provide limited information on the combined associations between need satisfaction and need frustration (Rouse et al., 2020). In other words, it is difficult to answer research questions such as "How are need satisfaction and need frustration combined to predict outcomes through the variable-centered approach?" As a supplement to the variable-centered approach, researchers have also employed person-centered approaches such as cluster analysis and latent profile analysis (LPA), focusing on identifying subgroups within a heterogeneous sample based on the shared similarities on a set of variables (Howard and Hoffman, 2018). Specifically, by employing the person-centered approach, we are able to identify subgroups with different combinations of need satisfaction and need frustration scores (*i.e.*, need profiles) rather than "slicing" the participants into different need-related dimensions.

Indeed one proposition of BPNT is that there is an asymmetrical relationship between need satisfaction and need frustration (Vansteenkiste and Ryan, 2013), that is, while the presence of low need satisfaction does not imply the presence of need frustration, the presence of high need frustration necessitates the existence of low need satisfaction. There is, however, little evidence to support this proposition, as most of the studies conducted to identify need profiles are based only on need satisfaction scores (Vansteenkiste et al., 2020). Two recent studies examined need profiles based on need satisfaction and need frustration scores in the contexts of work, sport, and physical education (Rouse et al., 2020; Warburton et al., 2020). Findings from the two studies identified three to five need profiles (*e.g.*, high satisfaction–low frustration profile, low satisfaction–very high frustration profile). While the findings, based on the domains of physical education and sport, provide support to the asymmetrical proposition, it is only partially supported in the work context given the presence of high competence satisfaction–high frustration profile. Therefore, future studies are warranted to investigate this proposition in the work context.

Identification of different need profiles has implications on the understanding of human functioning. For example, Rouse et al. (2020) found that firefighters from more adaptive need profiles (*e.g.*, high satisfaction–low frustration profile) experienced fewer symptoms of anxiety, depression, and stress than those from less adaptive profiles (*e.g.*, low satisfaction–very high frustration profile). Similarly, athletes from more adaptive profiles reported higher levels of well-being and enjoyment in sport training and lower levels of burnout than their counterparts from less adaptive profiles (Warburton et al., 2020). The findings unveiled some relevance of human functioning through experiencing varying combinations of need satisfaction and need frustration. In extension of the existing literature, we examined several need-relevant correlates, which include mindfulness, physical literacy, PA enjoyment, and PA. In addition to the theoretical relevance to the three basic psychological needs, these correlates are also important determinants of physical and psychological health (Raedeke, 2007; Cairney et al., 2019; Kee et al., 2019).

Mindfulness, a dispositional and trainable quality, refers to "paying attention in a particular way: on purpose, in the present moment, and non-judgmentally" (Kabat-Zinn, 2001). Mindfulness is believed to facilitate need satisfaction and decrease need frustration (Schultz et al., 2015). For example, in a PA setting, the receptive and non-judgmental awareness that characterizes mindfulness would help individuals to act in a way that is in line with their inner-value (autonomy), regulate attention and emotions to cope with physical challenges (competence), and attend to social interactions (relatedness). Indeed results derived from the variable-centered approach have indicated positive associations between mindfulness and need satisfaction as well as a negative relationship between mindfulness and need frustration across different contexts (Campbell et al., 2015; Schultz et al., 2015; Li et al., 2019a,b), yet none of the earlier research has examined the links between mindfulness and need satisfaction/frustration through a person-centered approach.

Physical literacy is defined as "a disposition acquired by individuals encompassing the motivation, confidence, physical competence, knowledge, and understanding that establishes purposeful physical pursuits as an integral element of their lifestyle" (Whitehead, 2013). According to the tenet of BPNT, experience of need satisfaction will lead to positive development and functioning, while frustration of basic psychological needs will result in negative outcomes (Deci and Ryan, 2000). In line with this tenet, need satisfaction in physical education was found to positively predict physical literacy in university students (Wang et al., 2020). Similarly, evidence has shown that satisfaction of basic psychological needs is positively related to positive outcomes such as intrinsic motivation, positive affect, enjoyment, and PA across health, physical education, and PA contexts, whereas need frustration is a negative predictor (Gunnell et al., 2013; Huhtiniemi et al., 2019; Vasconcellos et al., 2019). It is worthy to note that the empirical evidence from these studies were mainly based on the variable-centered approach (Vansteenkiste et al., 2020). To our best knowledge, no research examining how the need profiles would relate to varying levels of PA enjoyment and PA has been conducted.

As an extension of earlier research, the current cross-sectional study was undertaken to examine the combined associations between need satisfaction and need frustration (*i.e.*, need profiles) and their relations with theoretically relevant correlates including mindfulness, physical literacy, PA enjoyment, and PA in school students. By employing a person-centered analytic approach while basing on the findings from previous research (Rouse et al., 2020; Warburton et al., 2020), we anticipated that at least two need profiles characterized by differences in need satisfaction and need frustration scores would emerge (*e.g.*, high need satisfaction–low need frustration and low need satisfaction–high need frustration). We, however, did not expect a high need satisfaction and need frustration profile given that they are suggested to be asymmetrical (Vansteenkiste and Ryan, 2013). Finally, we expected that more adaptive need profiles would have a greater level of positive correlates (*i.e.*, mindfulness, physical literacy, PA enjoyment, light PA, and moderate-to-vigorous PA) and a lower level of sedentary time as compared to less adaptive profiles (Rouse et al., 2020; Warburton et al., 2020).

METHODS

Participants

To be eligible for this cross-sectional study, the participants must be fulltime students studying at a public school in Singapore. A sample of 844 school students were recruited from 19 primary schools (n = 384) and 20 secondary schools (n = 460). There were more boys (n = 448, 53.1%) than girls, and there was no gender difference across school levels [$\chi^2(1) = 0.33$, $p = 0.56$]. The participants had a mean age of 12.45 years (SD = 1.99; range = 9–17).

Measures

We used five standardized scales to measure predictors and outcomes of interest. The predictors were six types of need satisfaction and need frustration. The outcome variables were mindfulness, physical literacy, PA enjoyment, sedentary time, light PA time, and moderate-to-vigorous PA time.

Need Satisfaction and Frustration

We adopted the Basic Psychological Needs Satisfaction and Frustration Scale (Chen et al., 2015) to measure the participants' need satisfaction and need frustration in PA participation. The scale has six four-item subscales, with each subscale measuring one type of need satisfaction and frustration (*e.g.*, "I feel confident that I can do things well"). The participants were asked to report their need experiences in PA participation and rate the items using a seven-point scale (1 = not true at all, 7 = completely true). We computed the six subscale scores for further analysis. A higher score would indicate a higher level of need satisfaction and need frustration.

Mindfulness

We employed the Child and Adolescent Mindfulness Measure (Greco et al., 2011) to assess the participants' dispositional mindfulness level. The scale consists of 10 items (*e.g.*, "At school, I walk from class to class without noticing what I'm doing"). The participants provided responses on a five-point scale (0 = never true, 4 = always true). A total mean scale score was computed, and a higher scale score would suggest a greater level of mindfulness.

Physical Literacy

We utilized the Perceived Physical Literacy Instrument (Sum et al., 2018) to measure the participants' physical literacy. The participants used a five-point scale (1 = strongly disagree, 5 = strongly agree) to provide responses on the nine scale items (*e.g.*, "I am physically fit, in accordance with my age"). A mean scale score was calculated. A higher mean scale score would suggest a greater level of physical literacy.

Physical Activity Enjoyment

We borrowed four scale items from the PA Enjoyment Scale (Raedeke, 2007) to measure the participants' PA enjoyment. The participants were asked "How do you feel recently about the physical exercise you have been doing?" Four seven-point semantic scale items were used for responses (*e.g.*, from "I enjoy it" to "I hate it"). A mean scale score was computed, where higher scale scores would represent greater levels of enjoyment in PA participation.

Physical Activity

We used the International PA Questionnaire-Short Form (Craig et al., 2003) to assess the participants' subjective PA level across a week. This nine-item scale records four intensity levels of PA: vigorous PA, moderate PA, light PA, and sedentary time. According to the data analysis guideline[1], sedentary time, light PA time, and moderate-to-vigorous PA time were computed and represented as total minutes per week.

Data Collection

Recruitment of potential participants and data collection took place from March to December 2019. Upon receiving ethics approval from Nanyang Technological University (ID: IRB-2018-12-009) and the Ministry of Education (ID: 39926), an invitation

[1] www.ipaq.ki.se

email was sent to 40 school principals to participate in this survey. Of those invited, 39 school principals agreed to invite their students to participate in this survey. After obtaining the written informed consent forms from 1,066 participants and their parents/guardians, the anonymous survey forms were administered to the participants in a quiet sports hall or classroom. The participants were encouraged to give honest responses. A total of 844 participants completed the survey and were included in the analysis.

Data Analysis

We used the following approaches to clean our data. We identified missing data points in some of the scale items (up to 1.9% in each item) and replaced them using expectation–maximization algorithm. We recoded univariate outliers to the nearest acceptable values ($Z < 3.29$). We did not identify any extreme multivariate outliers based on the results of Mahalanobis distance ($p < 0.001$; 25). Following the data cleaning process, we conducted a series of confirmatory factor analyses to examine the factorial validity of the psychological measures used. We applied the method of maximum likelihood estimation with robust standard errors for correcting bias induced by multivariate non-normality (Satorra and Bentler, 2010). We used comparative fit index (CFI), Tucker–Lewis index (TLI), root mean square error of approximation (RMSEA), and standardized root mean square residual (SRMR) to evaluate model fit. According to Hu and Bentler (1998), values for CFI/TLI greater than 0.90, values for RMSEA less than 0.06, and values for SRMR less than 0.08 are deemed acceptable. Furthermore, we computed internal reliability (Cronbach's α), descriptive statistics (*M* and SD), and bivariate correlations for the major study variables.

Lastly, we used a person-centered approach (*i.e.*, LPA) to identify the optimal number of need profiles. We specified and estimated models with one to seven profiles using the six need satisfaction and need frustration subscale scores (*i.e.*, six need indicators). We used several fit measures to identify the best model: Akaike's Information Criterion (AIC), Bayesian Information Criterion (BIC), Sample-Adjusted BIC (SABIC), Lo–Medell–Rubin Adjusted Likelihood Ratio Test (LALRT), and the bootstrap likelihood ratio test (BLRT). Lower values of AIC, BIC, and SABIC would suggest a better model fit. A statistically significant finding of LALRT and BLRT would suggest that the model (k + 1 profile) is preferred to the model with one less profile (k profile). It is worthy to note that the BLRT result may always be statistically significant (Masyn, 2013). In addition to using these fit indices, we also considered values of entropy and average posterior probability, number of cases in a profile, and interpretability of the model for determining the optimal number of need profiles. Values for entropy higher than 0.60 and values for average posterior probability greater than 0.80 are considered acceptable (Nagin, 1999). A model containing a profile with less than 5% of the total sample was discarded (Masyn, 2013). To increase the interpretability of the six need indicators, we calculated their z-scores. Values of $\pm$0.49 SD were classified as average, $\pm$0.5 to 0.99 SD as high/low, and $\pm$1 SD as very high/low (Rouse et al., 2020).

Following the identification of the optimal number of need profiles, we conducted a series of Wald chi-square test to examine whether the identified need profiles were related to theoretically relevant correlates, including mindfulness, physical literacy, PA enjoyment, sedentary time, light PA time, and moderate-to-vigorous PA time (Asparouhov and Muthén, 2014). We cleaned our data and conducted preliminary analyses using IBM SPSS Statistics 25 (IBM, Armonk, NY, United States). We conducted the confirmatory factor analyses and LPA using *M*plus 8 (Muthén and Muthén, 1998–2017).

RESULTS

Measurement Model

The results of confirmatory factor analysis supported the factorial validity of the psychological measures used. Specifically, the unidimensional model of the Child and Adolescent Mindfulness Measure had an adequate model fit: $\chi^2(24) = 200.37$, CFI = 0.927, TLI = 0.897, RMSEA = 0.079 [90% CI (0.069, 0.090)], SRMR = 0.052. The adequacy of the first-order six-factor measurement model of the Basic Psychological Needs Satisfaction and Frustration Scale was supported: $\chi^2(237) = 600.36$, CFI = 0.949, TLI = 0.940, RMSEA = 0.043 [90% CI (0.038, 0.047)], SRMR = 0.044. The second-order three-factor measurement model of the Perceived Physical Literacy Instrument demonstrated an adequate model fit: $\chi^2(24) = 72.01$, CFI = 0.984, TLI = 0.976, RMSEA = 0.049 [90% CI (0.036, 0.062)], SRMR = 0.024. Finally, the data fit the one-factor measurement model of PA Enjoyment Scale well: $\chi^2(1) = 4.85$, CFI = 0.999, TLI = 0.992, RMSEA = 0.0768 [90% CI (0.018, 0.133)], SRMR = 0.003.

Descriptive Statistics

Table 1 shows the internal reliability estimates, means, standard deviations, and bivariate correlations for the major study variables. The scales/subscales demonstrated adequate to excellent internal reliability with the current sample (α = 0.70–0.95). The participants reported a moderate level of need satisfaction and physical literacy, a slightly below average level of need frustration, an average level of mindfulness, and a relatively high level of PA enjoyment. Over a 1-week period, the participants reported 3,180.71 min of sedentary time, participated in 767.95 min of light PA, and engaged in 449.32 min of moderate-to-vigorous PA. In line with our expectation, need satisfaction subscale scores were positively related to physical literacy, PA enjoyment, and moderate-to-vigorous PA. However, there was a negative and weak association between autonomy satisfaction and mindfulness. The need frustration scale scores, as expected, were negatively associated with mindfulness.

Need Profiles

Table 2 shows the model parameters of LPA. The six- and seven-profile models that contained a group size with less than 5% of the total sample were subsequently dropped. Although all the results of BLRT were significant, the result of BALRT only reached significance in the two-, three-, and four-profile models.

TABLE 1 | Descriptive statistics and zero-order correlations of the study variables.

	α	M (SD)	Scale	1	2	3	4	5	6	7	8	9	10	11
Autonomy satisfaction	0.71	3.67 (0.71)	1–7	–										
Competence satisfaction	0.85	3.67 (0.80)	1–7	0.63**	–									
Relatedness satisfaction	0.84	3.93 (0.77)	1–7	0.53**	0.50**	–								
Autonomy frustration	0.70	2.72 (0.82)	1–7	−0.06	−0.10**	−0.09**	–							
Competence frustration	0.80	2.65 (0.94)	1–7	−0.09*	−0.30**	−0.19**	0.61**	–						
Relatedness frustration	0.81	2.29 (0.93)	1–7	−0.03	−0.07*	−0.28**	0.61**	0.64**	–					
Mindfulness	0.85	2.03 (0.80)	0–4	−0.14**	−0.001	−0.03	−0.31**	−0.44**	−0.34**	–				
Physical literacy	0.89	3.74 (0.71)	1–5	0.45**	0.64**	0.38**	−0.01	−0.18**	−0.02	−0.12**	–			
PA enjoyment	0.95	5.39 (0.71)	1–7	0.30**	0.34**	0.21**	−0.09**	−0.18**	−0.06	−0.04	0.42**	–		
Sedentary time	–	3,180.71 (1523.32)	–	−0.11**	−0.12**	−0.06	−0.01	0.05	−0.02	0.02	−0.13**	−0.12**	–	
Light PA	–	767.95 (925.31)	–	0.001	0.02	0.06	−0.001	0.02	0.04	−0.07*	0.06	0.09*	0.07*	–
Moderate-to-vigorous PA	–	449.34 (421.38)	–	0.18**	0.31**	0.15**	0.01	−0.09**	0.01	−0.05	0.41**	0.27**	−0.09**	0.18**

PA, physical activity.
$^{**}p < 0.01$; $^{*}p < 0.05$.

The four-profile model had relatively lower values of AIC, BIC, and SBIC than the two- and three-profile models. Taking into further consideration factors of interpretability and its acceptable entropy and average posterior probability values, the four-profile model was finally selected.

Figure 1 presents the characteristics of the four-profile model. Profile 3 was the most adaptive profile and was described as "very high satisfaction, very low frustration" (n = 144, 17.1%). In contrast, profile 2 was the least adaptive profile with "low satisfaction, above average frustration" (n = 251, 29.7%). Profile 1 was described as "average satisfaction and frustration" (n = 364, 44.1%). Finally, profile 4 was described as "high satisfaction, very high frustration" (n = 85, 10.1%).

Correlates of Need Profiles

Table 3 summarizes the descriptive statistics for need satisfaction or need frustration and correlates. The four identified profiles differed significantly in mindfulness, physical literacy, PA enjoyment, and moderate-to-vigorous PA (overall Wald $\chi^2 = 5.67–69.03$, $p < 0.05$). The results of pairwise comparisons confirmed that profile 3 was the most adaptive profile, which had the highest levels of mindfulness, physical literacy, PA enjoyment, and moderate-to-vigorous PA. Profile 2 was the most maladaptive profile, which reported the lowest levels in three out of four significant correlates. Unexpectedly, there were no significant differences in sedentary time (overall Wald $\chi^2 = 1.83$, $p = 0.18$) and light PA (overall Wald $\chi^2 = 0.05$, $p = 0.82$) across the four identified profiles.

DISCUSSION

In extension of previous research, we examined the need profiles and their associations with theoretically relevant correlates in Singapore school students. Our findings revealed four distinct need profiles in the context of PA participation, including profile 1–average satisfaction and frustration; profile 2–low satisfaction, above average frustration; profile 3–very high satisfaction, very low frustration; and profile 4–high satisfaction, very high frustration. A more adaptive profile was characterized by a stronger presence of need satisfaction over need frustration (*e.g.*, profile 3), whereas a less adaptive profile was characterized by need frustration prevailing over need satisfaction (*e.g.*, profile 2). Furthermore, the participants from a more adaptive need profile generally reported a greater level of positive correlates than those from a less adaptive one.

In line with our expectations, more than two (*i.e.*, four) distinct need profiles emerged from LPA. The finding is similar to previous studies conducted in the contexts of work, physical education, and sport (Rouse et al., 2020; Warburton et al., 2020). In these studies, three to five need profiles were identified. The contextual differences may have contributed to the varied number of profiles that emerged across these studies. The emergence of several typical need profiles (*e.g.*, high satisfaction–low frustration profile, low satisfaction–high frustration profile), however, suggests that there is a degree of stability and generalizability of the need profiles across the

TABLE 2 | Summary of model parameters for latent profile analysis.

k	AIC	BIC	SABIC	LALRT *p*-value	BLRT *p*-value	Group size ≤ 5%	Entropy	APP
1	12,431.11	12,487.96	12,449.86	–	–	0	–	–
2	11,681.20	11,771.23	11,710.89	0.04	<0.001	0	0.72	0.92
3	10,971.36	11,094.56	11,011.99	<0.001	<0.001	0	0.83	0.92
4	10,789.97	10,946.33	10,841.53	0.01	<0.001	0	0.78	0.88
5	10,671.48	10,861.00	10,733.98	0.61	<0.001	0	0.75	0.85
6	10,589.06	10,811.76	10,662.50	0.21	<0.001	1	0.78	0.86
7	10,505.45	10,761.31	10,589.82	0.17	<0.001	1	0.79	0.87

k, number of profiles; AIC, Akaike's Information Criterion; BIC, Bayesian Information Criterion; SABIC, sample-size-adjusted BIC; LALRT, Lo–Medell–Rubin adjusted likelihood ratio test; BLRT, bootstrapped likelihood ratio test; APP, average posterior probability.

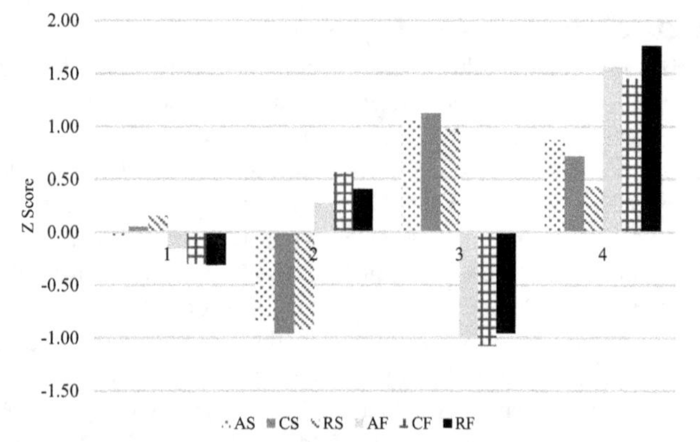

FIGURE 1 | Characteristics of the four-profile model based on the six need indicators. Profile 1 = average satisfaction and frustration (*n* = 364, 44.1%), profile 2 = low satisfaction, above average frustration (*n* = 251, 29.7%), profile 3 = very high satisfaction, very low frustration (*n* = 144, 17.1%), profile 4 = high satisfaction, very high frustration (*n* = 85, 10.1%). AS, autonomy satisfaction, CS, competence satisfaction, RS, relatedness satisfaction, AF, autonomy frustration, CF, competence frustration, RF, relatedness frustration.

contexts. While these typical need profiles provide some support for the asymmetrical hypothesis, there is still limited empirical evidence to fully support this proposition. For example, profile 4 (high satisfaction, very high frustration) was with both need satisfaction and need frustration scores above average, failing to support the asymmetrical hypothesis. The study of Rouse et al. (2020) also found a similar issue (*e.g.*, very high competence satisfaction, high frustration). Hence, more studies are needed to test the asymmetrical hypothesis given the limited empirical evidence for it.

Previous research has shown that different need profiles were uniquely associated with varied levels of correlates such as anxiety, depression, motivation, and life satisfaction (Vansteenkiste et al., 2020). In line with and as an extension to previous research (Vansteenkiste and Ryan, 2013; Rouse et al., 2020; Vansteenkiste et al., 2020; Warburton et al., 2020), each of the four identified need profiles in the present study was found to have unique associations with mindfulness, physical literacy, PA enjoyment, and moderate-to-vigorous PA. However, the identified four need profiles showed no difference in light PA and sedentary behavior. Although mounting evidence shows that moderate-to-vigorous PA leads to multiple health-related outcomes, there is still limited evidence supporting the association between light PA/sedentary behavior and its outcomes (Chaput et al., 2020). Thus, it could be possible that light PA and sedentary behavior are not a sensitive correlate of need profile in comparison to moderate-to-vigorous PA. More studies are warranted to confirm this possibility.

The present findings showed that profile 3 (very high satisfaction, very low frustration) was the most adaptive, which had the highest level of mindfulness, physical literacy, PA enjoyment, and moderate-to-vigorous PA among the four identified profiles. In contrast, profile 2 (low satisfaction, above average frustration) was the least adaptive profile, as it had the lowest levels of mindfulness, PA enjoyment, and moderate-to-vigorous PA. Interestingly, although profile 4 (high satisfaction, very high frustration) had the highest need frustration score, it is still more adaptive than profile 1 (average satisfaction and frustration) and profile 2 (low satisfaction, above average frustration). Further inspection of the need scores across these three profiles indicated that profile 4 (high satisfaction, very high frustration) had the highest need satisfaction score albeit with the highest need frustration score. This would suggest that a high need satisfaction score might be necessary for optimal human functioning. This finding further suggests that high need satisfaction could protect or offset the negative effects of very high need frustration on human functioning. According to Warburton et al. (2020), experiences of high need frustration were less detrimental to enjoyment and well-being when athletes experienced moderate levels of need satisfaction. Thus, experiences of need frustration may not necessarily be maladaptive, and it is important to simultaneously examine the interplay between need satisfaction and need frustration.

Practical Implications

There are significant implications that we can recommend based on the findings and discussion outlined above. The use of the person-centered approach can help practitioners identify student groups that are at risk of dysfunction. In our study, about one-third (29.7%) of the participants was from profile 2 (low satisfaction, above average frustration), the least adaptive profile. To facilitate optimal student functioning, it is recommended to alter the PA environment to reduce students' experiences of need frustration. Furthermore, given the

TABLE 3 | Descriptive statistics for need satisfaction/frustration and correlates.

Variables	Profile 1 Average satisfaction and frustration		Profile 2 Low satisfaction, above average frustration		Profile 3 Very high satisfaction, very low frustration		Profile 4 High satisfaction, very high frustration		Pairwise comparisons between profiles[a]
	M (SD)	*Z*	*M* (SD)	*Z*	*M* (SD)	*Z*	*M* (SD)	*Z*	
Indicators									
Autonomy satisfaction	3.64 (0.52)	−0.04	3.07 (0.54)	−0.85	4.43 (0.44)	1.07	4.30 (0.50)	0.87	–
Competence satisfaction	3.71 (0.57)	0.05	2.90 (0.55)	−0.96	4.57 (0.42)	1.12	4.24 (0.55)	0.72	–
Relatedness satisfaction	4.04 (0.55)	0.15	3.22 (0.67)	−0.92	4.67 (0.44)	0.97	4.25 (0.55)	0.43	–
Autonomy frustration	2.60 (0.58)	−0.16	2.95 (0.62)	0.27	1.91 (0.63)	−1.00	4.00 (0.64)	1.56	–
Competence frustration	2.37 (0.63)	−0.30	3.17 (0.71)	0.56	1.63 (0.52)	−1.08	4.01 (0.64)	1.45	–
Relatedness frustration	2.01 (0.60)	−0.31	2.67 (0.68)	0.40	1.40 (0.50)	−0.96	3.93 (0.69)	1.76	–
Correlates									
Mindfulness	2.14 (0.74)	–	1.94 (0.74)	–	2.30 (0.78)	–	1.42 (0.95)	–	3 = 4 > 1 > 2
Physical literacy	3.77 (0.56)	–	3.24 (0.68)	–	4.24 (0.51)	–	4.24 (0.64)	–	3 > 1 > 2 > 4
PA enjoyment	5.45 (0.64)	–	4.74 (1.43)	–	6.19 (1.32)	–	5.74 (1.63)	–	3 > 4[b] = 1 > 2
Sedentary time	3,153.38 (1411.11)	–	3,418.43 (1683.15)	–	3,064.74 (1441.19)	–	2,792.26 (1538.76)	–	–[c]
Light PA	737.97 (836.70)	–	783.18 (1002.34)	–	795.09 (990.83)	–	805.35 (947.95)	–	–[c]
Moderate-to-vigorous PA	444.99 (421.45)	–	327.53 (372.38)	–	607.57 (445.26)	–	559.55 (405.62)	–	3 = 4 > 1 > 2

PA, physical activity.

[a]*All the differences are significant at the level of $p < 0.05$ (two-tailed) if not otherwise specified.*

[b]*There is a trend that profile 3 has a higher level of PA enjoyment than that of profile 4 ($p = 0.05$).*

[c]*The result of the overall Wald test is not significant.*

protective role of need satisfaction in alleviating the negative effects of need frustration on student functioning, it is more important to enhance the students' need satisfaction. Approaches such as use of non-controlling language that conveys freedom of choice, acknowledging one's perspective, and assisting in identifying realistic goals can be used to prompt need satisfaction (Teixeira et al., 2020).

Limitations and Future Research

Despite contributing to the BPNT literature and providing practical implications, the present study is subject to some limitations. Firstly, we examined need profiles in the context of PA participation with Singapore school students; generalization of our study findings is therefore limited. Further studies should examine the different life domains, countries, and school levels to collaborate and extend the present study findings. Secondly, the use of a cross-sectional survey design prevents us from inferring casual associations between need profiles and their correlates. Future research can use a prospective survey design to examine the predictability of need profiles on the same and additional correlates that are important for human functioning. By employing this approach, we can also examine how need satisfaction and need frustration associate and influence each other. Future research can even use an experimental approach to examine the causal associations. Finally, we exclusively relied on using self-report measures that would potentially bias the results of the study. It is therefore useful for future research to employ objective measures to assess some of the study variables (*e.g.*, use heart rate monitors or accelerometers to measure PA).

CONCLUSION

In summary, our person-centered analyses revealed four combinations of need satisfaction and need frustration in a PA setting (*i.e.*, profile 1–average satisfaction and frustration; profile 2–low satisfaction, above average frustration; profile 3–very high satisfaction, very low frustration; and profile 4–high satisfaction, very high frustration). The identified combinations (need profiles) were strongly related to several correlates, including mindfulness, physical literacy, physical activity enjoyment, and moderate-to-vigorous physical activity. Although the asymmetrical relationship between need satisfaction and need frustration was not fully supported, experiences of need satisfaction countered the negative effects of need frustration on the correlates. These findings enhance our understanding of psychological need experiences. The findings also highlight the need for further investigation of the combined associations between need satisfaction and need frustration, which could provide unique and complementary explanations to human functioning.

ETHICS STATEMENT

The studies involving human participants were reviewed and approved by Nanyang Technological University. Written informed consent to participate in this study was provided by the participants' legal guardian/next of kin.

AUTHOR CONTRIBUTIONS

All authors were involved in manuscript preparation and approved the final version for submission.

ACKNOWLEDGMENTS

The authors would like to thank all the helpers and participants for their contribution in this research.

REFERENCES

Asparouhov, T., and Muthén, B. (2014). Auxiliary variables in mixture modeling: three-step approach using Mplus. *Struct. Equ. Modeling* 21, 329–341. doi: 10.1080/10705511.2014.915181

Bartholomew, K. J., Ntoumanis, N., Ryan, R. M., Bosch, J. A., and Thogersen-Ntoumani, C. (2011). Self-determination theory and diminished functioning: the role of interpersonal control and psychological need thwarting. *Pers. Soc. Psychol. Bull.* 37, 1459–1473. doi: 10.1177/0146167211413125

Cairney, J., Dudley, D., Kwan, M., Bulten, R., and Kriellaars, D. (2019). Physical literacy, physical activity and health: toward an evidence-informed conceptual model. *Sports Med.* 49, 371–383. doi: 10.1007/s40279-019-01063-3

Campbell, R., Vansteenkiste, M., Delesie, L. M., Mariman, A. N., Soenens, B., Tobback, E., et al. (2015). Examining the role of psychological need satisfaction in sleep: a self-determination theory perspective. *Pers. Individ. Differ.* 77, 199–204. doi: 10.1016/j.paid.2015.01.003

Chaput, J., Willumsen, J., Bull, F., Chou, R., Firth, J., Jago, R., et al. (2020). 2020 WHO guidelines on physical activity and sedentary behaviour for children and adolescents aged 5-17 years: summary of the evidence. *Int. J. Behav. Nutr. Phys. Act.* 17, 2–9. doi: 10.1186/s12966-020-01037-z

Chen, B. W., Vansteenkiste, M., Beyers, W., Boone, L., Deci, E. L., van der Kaap-Deeder, J., et al. (2015). Basic psychological need satisfaction, need frustration, and need strength across four cultures. *Motiv. Emot.* 39, 216–236. doi: 10.1007/s11031-014-9450-1

Craig, C. L., Marshall, A. L., Sjöström, M., Bauman, A. E., Booth, M. L., Ainsworth, B. E., et al. (2003). International physical activity questionnaire: 12-country reliability and validity. *Med. Sci. Sports Exerc.* 35, 1381–1395. doi: 10.1249/01.MSS.0000078924.61453.FB

De Francisco, C., Parra, F. J., Arce, C., and Vílchez, M. D. P. (2018). Preliminary empirical validation of the "Basic needs satisfaction in sport scale" with a sample of Spanish athletes. *Front. Psychol.* 9:1057. doi: 10.3389/fpsyg.2018.01057

Deci, E. L., and Ryan, R. M. (2000). The "what" and the "why" of goal pursuits: human needs and the self-determination of behavior. *Psychol. Inquiry* 11, 227–268. doi: 10.1207/S15327965PLI1104_01

Greco, L. A., Baer, R. A., and Smith, G. T. (2011). Assessing mindfulness in children and adolescents: development and validation of the Child and Adolescent Mindfulness Measure (CAMM). *Psychol. Assess.* 23, 606–614. doi: 10.1037/a0022819

Gunnell, K. E., Crocker, P. R., Wilson, P. M., Mack, D. E., and Zumbo, B. D. (2013). Psychological need satisfaction and thwarting: a test of basic psychological needs theory in physical activity contexts. *Psychol. Sport Exerc.* 14, 599–607. doi: 10.1016/j.psychsport.2013.03.007

Howard, M. C., and Hoffman, M. E. (2018). Variable-centered, person-centered, and person-specific approaches: where theory meets the method. *Organ. Res. Methods* 21, 846–876. doi: 10.1177/1094428117744021

Hu, L. T., and Bentler, P. M. (1998). Fit indices in covariance structure modeling: sensitivity to underparameterized model misspecification. *Psychol. Methods* 3, 424–453. doi: 10.1037/1082-989X.3.4.424

Huhtiniemi, M., Sääkslahti, A., Watt, A., and Jaakkola, T. (2019). Associations among basic psychological needs, motivation and enjoyment within Finnish physical education students. *J. Sports Sci. Med.* 18, 239–247.

Kabat-Zinn, J. (2001). *Mindfulness Meditation for Everyday Life.* London: Piatkus Books.

Kee, Y. H., Li, C., Kong, L. C., Tang, C. J., and Chuang, K. L. (2019). Scoping review of mindfulness research: a topic modelling approach. *Mindfulness* 10, 1474–1488. doi: 10.1007/s12671-019-01136-4

Li, C., Kee, Y. H., Kong, L. C., Zou, L., Ng, K. L., and Li, H. (2019a). Autonomy-supportive teaching and basic psychological need satisfaction among school students: the role of mindfulness. *Int. J. Environ. Res. Public Health* 16:2599. doi: 10.3390/ijerph16142599

Li, C., Wong, N. K., Sum, R. K., and Yu, C. W. (2019b). Preservice teachers' mindfulness and attitudes toward students with autism spectrum disorder: the role of basic psychological needs satisfaction. *Adapt. Phys. Activ. Q.* 36, 150–163. doi: 10.1123/apaq.2018-0044

Masyn, K. E. (2013). "Latent class analysis and finite mixture modeling," in *The Oxford Handbook of Quantitative Methods*, ed. T. Little (New York, NY: Oxford University Press), 551–611.

Muthén, L. K., and Muthén, B. O. (1998–2017). *Mplus User's Guide.* Los Angeles, CA: MuthénMuthén.

Nagin, D. S. (1999). Analyzing developmental trajectories: a semiparametric, group-based approach. *Psychol. Methods* 4, 139–157. doi: 10.1037/1082-989X.4.2.139

Raedeke, T. D. (2007). The relationship between enjoyment and affective responses to exercise. *J. Appl. Sport Psychol.* 19, 105–115.

Rouse, P. C., Turner, P. J., Siddall, A. G., Schmid, J., Standage, M., and Bilzon, J. L. (2020). The interplay between psychological need satisfaction and psychological need frustration within a work context: a variable and person-oriented approach. *Motiv. Emot.* 44, 175–189. doi: 10.1080/10413200601113638

Satorra, A., and Bentler, P. M. (2010). Ensuring positiveness of the scaled difference chi-square test statistic. *Psychometrika* 75, 243–248. doi: 10.1007/s11336-009-9135-y

Schultz, P. P., Ryan, R. M., Niemiec, C. P., Legate, N., and Williams, G. C. (2015). Mindfulness, work climate, and psychological need satisfaction in employee well-being. *Mindfulness* 6, 971–985. doi: 10.1007/s12671-014-0338-7

Sum, R. K., Cheng, C. F., Wallhead, T., Kuo, C. C., Wang, F. J., and Choi, S. M. (2018). Perceived physical literacy instrument for adolescents: a further validation of PPLI. *J. Exerc. Sci. Fit.* 16, 26–31. doi: 10.1016/j.jesf.2018.03.002

Teixeira, P. J., Marques, M. M., Silva, M. N., Brunet, J., Duda, J. L., Haerens, L., et al. (2020). Classification of techniques used in self-determination theory-based interventions in health contexts: an expert consensus study. *Motiv. Sci.* 6, 438–455. doi: 10.1037/mot0000172

Vansteenkiste, M., and Ryan, R. M. (2013). On psychological growth and vulnerability: basic psychological need satisfaction and need frustration as an unifying principle. *J. Psychother. Integr.* 23, 263–280. doi: 10.1037/a0032359

Vansteenkiste, M., Ryan, R. M., and Soenens, B. (2020). Basic psychological need theory: advancements, critical themes, and future directions. *Motiv. Emot.* 44, 1–31. doi: 10.1007/s11031-019-09818-1

Vasconcellos, D., Parker, P. D., Hilland, T., Cinelli, R., Owen, K. B., Kapsal, N., et al. (2019). Self-determination theory applied to physical education: a systematic review and meta-analysis. *J. Educ. Psychol.* 112, 1444–1469. doi: 10.1037/edu0000420

Wang, F. J., Cheng, C. F., Chen, M. Y., and Sum, K. W. R. (2020). Temporal precedence of physical literacy and basic psychological needs satisfaction: a cross-lagged longitudinal analysis of university students. *Int. J. Environ. Res. Public Health* 17:4615. doi: 10.3390/ijerph17124615

Warburton, V. E., Wang, J. C., Bartholomew, K. J., Tuff, R. L., and Bishop, K. C. (2020). Need satisfaction and need frustration as distinct and potentially co-occurring constructs: need profiles examined in physical education and sport. *Motiv. Emot.* 44, 54–66. doi: 10.1007/s11031-019-09798-2

Whitehead, M. (2013). "What is physical literacy and how does it impact on physical education?," in *Debates in Physical Education*, eds S. Capel and M. Whitehead (London: Routledge), 37–52.

Influence of Psychological Factors in Federated Futsal and Lifeguard Athletes, Differences by Gender and Category

*Francisco Cano-Noguera, Ricardo José Ibáñez-Pérez, Francisco Cavas-García and Alfonso Martínez-Moreno**

INGESPORTFI Research Group, Department of Physical Activity and Sports, University of Murcia, Murcia, Spain

Correspondence:
Alfonso Martínez-Moreno
almamo@um.es

This research aims to analyse the differences in optimism, resilience, engagement and competitive anxiety as a function of the sport modality practiced in lifeguarding (individual sport) and futsal (team sport); the sport category by age (cadet or youth) and gender. The LOT-R optimism questionnaire, the Connor-Davidson Resilience Scale (CD-RISC-10), the Utrecht Work Engagement Scale (UWES) and the Competitive Anxiety Scale (SAS-2) were applied to a sample of 189 participants (139 men and 50 womwn) aged between 14 and 17 years. The following statistical tests are performed: Cronbach's alpha, Pearson's linear correlation, Student's t-test, Kolmogorov-Smirnov test, Levene's test and multivariate linear regression. The data indicate that there are significant gender differences in total anxiety ($p<0.001$) and all its dimensions (somatic, worry, worry-free), also in optimism and pessimism ($p < 0.001$), as well as in total engagement ($p = 0.051$) and the absorption dimension ($p < 0.001$). When comparing the sample by sport categories, there are statistically significant differences in somatic anxiety ($p = 0.036$) and deconcentration ($p = 0.034$), as well as in LOT-total ($p \leq 0.001$) and pessimism ($p \leq 0.001$). In relation to the sport modalities, lifeguards show more anxiety 38.39 (0.49) and more commitment 4.58 (0.87) while futsal athletes reach higher scores in deconcentration 8.45 (2.29). It is concluded that the variables of commitment and resilience had a statistically significant positive effect, and the category of < 16 years had a statistically significant negative effect, so the lower the category, the higher the optimism.

Keywords: optimism, competitive anxiety, engagement, resilience, sport, federated

INTRODUCTION

Sport research related to stress and well-being factors has been widely developed in recent years (López, 2015; Barbosa and Urrea, 2018), considered as important in different sports (Moreno-Murcia et al., 2006; Cano et al., 2019). Previous studies have highlighted the importance of optimism as a facilitating aspect of resilience (Ferrando et al., 2002; Aranzana et al., 2016; Martínez-Moreno et al., 2020), and competitive stress as a possible inducer of specific development in sport training stages, while also predicting how combinations of other variables could influence the athlete. It is the resilience and optimism of the individual coping strategies, which the athlete uses, that most help him or her (Galli and Vealey, 2008; Fletcher and Sarkar, 2012; García et al., 2014). Some research (Almagro et al., 2011) has indicated the importance of the perceived climate, in training or with peers, of motivation to improve results, as well as the importance of resilience in sport (García et al., 2014). However, they jointly neglect, from a positive point of view, feelings of resilience, optimism and engagement, as well as from a negative point of view, competitive anxiety and perceived stress in sport.

The present study contributes to the literature on psychological elements affecting athletes by examining the competitive context in the disciplines of lifeguarding, individual sport and futsal team sport.

First, the constructs, anxiety, resilience, optimism and engagement are analyzed in the sport domain.

Anxiety, Types and Effects on Sportsmen and Sportswomen

Athletes during competitions are exposed to an environment conducive to generate anxiety symptoms. Anxiety can be defined as a future emotional state characterized by a sense of apprehension, worry and lack of control over one's emotional response (Otto et al., 2010). The term competitive anxiety was coined by Martens (1977) to refer to sport-specific anxiety. Competitive anxiety, which has been examined globally, is now considered an emergent and transient property of the athlete with respect to competition (Anshel, 1995), with two levels of response, which are cognitive and somatic (Ramis et al., 2010). In this direction, Weinberg and Gould (2010) differentiate on the one hand trait anxiety is seen as an acquired behavioral tendency or inclination and is part of the personality or character of athletes. On the other hand, state anxiety is seen as a constantly changing emotional component. These different dimensions of competitive state anxiety may be independently and differentially related to performance (Liştea et al., 2017). Anxiety is considered an endogenous determinant of attention (Castillo, 2009). Therefore, attention should be considered essential as competitive situations will always generate a degree of anxiety in athletes that may affect their performance due to the impairment of the attentional process (Moran, 2012). The study of competitive anxiety is very relevant given its impact -especially when negative- on athletes' performance and has a long history in sport psychology from its beginnings (Smith et al., 1990) to more recent research (Ponseti et al., 2016; González et al., 2017; Castro-Sánchez and Zurita-Ortega, 2019; Castro-Sánchez et al., 2020; Jaramillo et al., 2020; Núñez et al., 2020). Anxiety responses are accompanied by increased physiological arousal, mediated by the autonomic nervous system (Cashmore, 2008). Anxiety in sport has been extensively analyzed in different studies (Hamidi and Besharat, 2010; Correia and Rosado, 2018), as well as in sport performance being of great interest to researchers and coaches (Liştea et al., 2017).

Resilience in Sport

Resilience has become increasingly important in recent years in the field of sport (Zurita-Ortega et al., 2018). According to the theory of Fletcher and Sarkar (2012), based on psychological resilience in Olympic champions, it would be the positive evaluation of the stressful situation shaped by a positive personality, motivation, confidence, concentration and social support, which provide effective decisions and reflections aimed at commitment to the task and increased effort. Therefore, a high level of resilience allows for greater and better adaptation to the euphoria of victory or the disappointment of defeat, using more adaptive coping strategies (García et al., 2014). Being resilient can improve sport performance and vice versa (Chacón-Cuberos et al., 2016). Providing resilience and perseverance leads to greater emotional calm and better planning (Laborde et al., 2017). The capacity to be resilient is twofold, one of which is resilience in the face of conflict, and the other is a positive behavior or attitude toward conflict (Vanistendael and Lecomte, 2002). Together with the optimistic person who has a more adaptive approach to reality than the pessimist (Flórez-Lozano, 2006), we can feel the contribution that optimism makes to resilience (Scheier and Carver, 2003), feeding into it to achieve greater resilience.

Optimism and Sport

Based on the trait theory formulated by Scheier and Carver (1985), optimists are people who have positive expectations and perceptions about their life, while pessimists tend to represent their life negatively and the future as undesirable. Based on Scheier and Carver (2003) guidelines on dispositional optimism, having positive expectations in the face of difficulties increases efforts, and vice versa. Optimism, as a personality construct, is present in athletes and women in pressure situations (Seligman, 2004). When the athlete or woman shows more optimism, she or he presents better sports results and a higher performance (García-Naveira and Díaz, 2010; Londoño et al., 2011). Several studies have pointed out the relationship between resilience and optimism (Yu and Zhang, 2007; Parkes and Mallet, 2011; Souri and Hasanirad, 2011; González-Arratia et al., 2012; Freche, 2013). For Ortín et al. (2013) adolescent handball players with an optimistic profile present less anxiety-state, as well as older players are more optimistic than younger players (García-Naveira, 2008).

Sport Engagement

The above elements or variables, together with engagement, can help or harm athletes if they are not taken into account. Engagement would be a persistent motivational state experienced by athletes in relation to their sport practice and would involve three dimensions: vigor, dedication and absorption. The vigor dimension refers to high levels of energy, high persistence and a strong desire to put effort into training/competition. Dedication is identified with high levels of meaning associated with training/competition, as well as pride and identification with the sport they are playing. Finally, absorption implies high levels of concentration along with the feeling that time is flying by and one is carried away (Schaufeli et al., 2001). Engagement is an optimal state in sport and a type of well-being, which can influence performance as it is one of the components of mental toughness (Crust, 2007). Very little work has applied the study of engagement in the sport domain (Lonsdale et al., 2007b; Hodge et al., 2009; De Freese and Smith, 2013) and it needs to be studied to learn more about how it relates to other aspects (Lonsdale et al., 2007a).

Rationale for the Research

The basis for this research is that some studies have focused on individual sports (Cano et al., 2019), such as swimming, or group sports (Ruiz et al., 2012) such as football. Recently two studies have compared individual and team sports (Reche et al., 2019; Reche-García et al., 2020) but not lifesaving and futsal, which are addressed in this study. It is clear from the scientific literature that individual sports athletes have different characteristics from team sports athletes, in relation to personality (Nia and Besharat, 2010; Raharjo et al., 2018), in terms of the use of mental skills (Kajbafnezhad et al., 2011) in mental toughness (Kumar, 2017) in relation to manifesting anxiety and depression are athletes in individual sports are more likely to present them than those in team sports (Pluhar et al., 2019), in addition in team sports passion profiles are higher than those of individual sports (Kovacsik et al., 2020).

Lifeguarding is based on individual performances with which the participants achieve an individual result and at the same time award points in a ranking to their team, but unlike futsal, there is no collaboration, no joint strategy, no zone defense or collective attack, not even a possibility of verbal communication that takes place in an aquatic environment. Some of the events that take place in the swimming pool are: 200 m hurdles, 100 m combined, 100 m fins, 4 × 50 rescue tube, 4 × 50 hurdles, etc.

Therefore, the working hypotheses will be:

H1, men have less anxiety, commitment and resilience than girls.

H2, youth athletes are more optimistic than cadet athletes.

H3, futsal athletes (collective sport) show lower levels of commitment and resilience than lifeguards (individual sport).

H4, futsal players have less anxiety than lifeguards.

All of the above leads us to the objective of the study, which focuses on finding out the existing differences between lifesaving (individual sport) and futsal (team sport) from a psychological perspective, as well as determining differences in relation to the sporting categories, sex and age of the participants, providing answers to the different hypotheses put forward.

MATERIALS AND METHODS

Design and Participants

A cross-sectional, observational and quantitative design was carried out, selecting the sample in a non-probabilistic or intentional way. The study, **Table 1**, consisted of a total of 189 young lifeguards and futsal players, corresponding to the youth categories, under 18 years of age (16–17) and cadets, under 16 years of age (14–15). Of which 103 participants were lifeguards and 86 futsal players, 50 girls and the remaining 139 men.

Procedure

All the athletes were asked, through their coaches, to collaborate in the research. All the minors, in the lifeguard modality, in the course of the processing of the sports license for the year included a section in which they accepted to participate as sample subjects in possible non-invasive studies that could be carried out. Once informed consent had been obtained from the parents/guardians/legal guardians of the futsal players, all those who wished to participate in the study filled in the questionnaires prior to the celebration of a Spanish championship for the lifeguards and before a league match for the futsal players. Data were collected before the covid-19 pandemic, from the lifesaving athletes, on the day of the competition, in an after-breakfast meeting, all were concentrated in a hotel, and from the futsal players, before the pre-match talk, about 2 h before the lifesaving competition and matches. Their preparation and level of physical work was part of the peak performance phase, taking into account that all participants trained 3–4 h per week. The study was conducted under the guidelines of the Declaration of Helsinki, the design, observational, did not contain any ethical aspects that required prior authorization from the Bioethics Committee of the University of Murcia, Spain.

Instruments

The questionnaire consisted of a total of 54 items comprised of four separate and established questionnaires measuring resilience, competitive anxiety, optimism and engagement, as well as socio-demographic data. Resilience (RS) was measured using the Connor-Davidson Resilience Scale (CD-RISC-10) (Serrano-Parra et al., 2012). The scale has an internal consistency Cronbach's alpha of 0.89 and with a single dimension consisted of 10 statements (e.g., "I know how to adapt to change") with participants responding on a five-point Likert scale, ranging from 0 ("Strongly disagree") to 4 ("Strongly agree").

The Competitive Anxiety Scale (SAS-2) (Ramis et al., 2010) was used to measure anxiety, with an internal consistency using Cronbach's alpha coefficient of 0.83 for the somatic (AS) subscale, 0.78 for the worry subscale (A-C) and 0.73 for the deconcentration (A-D) subscale. It consists of 15 statements preceded by the phrase "Before the competition..." (e.g., "... I find it difficult to concentrate on the match or competition"). Responses were again given on a four-point Likert scale, ranging from 1 ("Nothing") to 4 ("Much"). Somatic anxiety is understood as anxiety that is perceived by the athlete for no apparent reason, worry anxiety as anxiety that can be justified by a specific situation, deconcentration anxiety as anxiety that due to its importance reduces the involvement in the task at hand and total anxiety as the final result of linking all of them together.

Optimism was assessed with the Life Orientation Test-Revised (LOT-R) (Scheier et al., 1994) in its Spanish version (Ferrando et al., 2002), to measure dispositional optimism or generalized predisposition toward expectations of positive outcomes. The LOT-R has good psychometric properties, Cronbach's reliability of 0.70 and 0.69 for optimism and pessimism respectively. The LOT-R questionnaire consists of 10 items (e.g., "In difficult times, I usually hope for the best"), of which four are control items and of the remaining six, three are written in a positive direction (optimistic direction) and three in a negative direction (pessimistic direction) with responses given on a five-point Likert scale, ranging from 0 ("Strongly disagree") to 4 ("Strongly agree"). Likewise, LOT-R Optimism (LOT-O) is understood as the ability of the athlete or woman to have a positive view of situations,

TABLE 1 | Descriptive statistics of the sample.

	n	%
Sex		
Female	50	26.5
Male	139	73.5
Sport		
Futsal	86	45.5
Lifeguard	103	54.5
Category		
Youth	86	45.5
Cadets	103	54.5

LOT-R Pessimism (LOT-P) as the ability to see the negative side of situations and LOT-R Total (LOT-T) as a combination of both. For the sample analyzed, optimism obtained a Cronbach's alpha of 0.79 and for pessimism 0.84.

The engagement questionnaire was the Utrecht Work Engagement Scale (UWES) (Guillén and Martínez-Alvarado, 2014), with a Cronbach's alpha reliability of 0.93 and consisting of 9 items. This questionnaire measures the three dimensions of engagement, which are vigor (UWES-V) (e.g., "I feel energized at work"), dedication (UWES-D) (e.g., "My work inspires me") and absorption (UWES-A) (e.g., "I feel disengaged when I am working"). Each item is answered on a Likert-type scale, ranging from 0 ("Never") to 6 ("Always").

Statistical Analysis

For the descriptive statistical analysis of the sample, the number of cases present in each category and the corresponding percentages of the qualitative variables were obtained. For the quantitative variables, the following descriptive statistics were used: minimum, maximum, mean and standard deviation (SD). Cronbach's alpha was calculated in order to check the reliability of the different scales within this particular sample, and correlations between variables were calculated using Pearson's linear correlation coefficient (r). In addition, for quantitative variables, the t-Student test was performed for the comparisons of means between two groups. Assumptions of normality and uniformity of the variances required for mean comparisons were tested using the Kolmogorov-Smirnov test and the Levene test, respectively. Finally, a multivariate linear regression model was developed to determine the possible effects of sex (male or female), sport modality (lifeguards or futsal) and category (cadet or youth) on the resilience, anxiety and engagement scales. Statistical analyses were performed using SPSS 25.0 for Windows (IBM, New York, NY, USA). Statistical significance was defined as $p < 0.05$.

RESULTS

The mean (typical deviations), Cronbach's alpha reliability indexes, and the correlations between the different subscales of the questionnaires used that address each variable chosen. Internal consistency rates were all higher than 0.79, indicating high reliability.

In **Table 2**, we can see that A-T correlated statistically significantly and positively with A-S, A-C, total engagement (UWES-T), UWES-D and UWES-A dimensions. But negatively and statistically significantly with LOT-O and LOT-P. A-S correlated positively and statistically significantly with A-C, UWES-T, UWES-D and UWES-A and significantly but negatively with A-D, LOT-O and LOT-P. A-C had a positive and statistically significant relationship with UWES-T, UWES-D and UWES-A and was negatively correlated with A-D, LOT-O and LOT-P. The A-D dimension showed a positive and significant correlation with the LOT-O and LOT-P and had a negative correlation with LOT-T, UWES-T, UWES-D, UWES-A and RS.

As for the LOT-R scale, the LOT-T correlated positively and statistically significantly with the LOT-O, UWES-T, UWES-V, UWES-D, UWES-A and RS, however, it correlated negatively and statistically significantly with the LOT-P. The LOT-O dimension was positively and statistically significantly correlated with LOT-P and SR and negatively and statistically significantly correlated with UWES-A. The LOT-P dimension had a negative and statistically significant relationship with the UWES-T, UWES-D, UWES-A and resilience.

The UWES-T showed positive and statistically significant differences with the UWES-V, UWES-D, UWES-A and SR. The UWES-V dimension showed positive and statistically significant differences with UWES-D, UWES-A and RS, and the UWES-D dimension showed positive and statistically significant differences with UWES-A and RS.

Focusing on the differences between males and females in the sample, **Table 3** presents the results of the SAS-2, LOT-R, UWES and RS scales based on gender. There were statistically significant and positive differences in terms of A-T, A-S and A-C, with males reaching higher values, while there were statistically significant and negative differences in favor of females in terms of A-D. LOT-O and LOT-P also showed positive and statistically significant differences in favor of girls. Finally, there were also statistically significant differences in relation to UWES-T, where boys scored higher, as well as in relation to UWES-A, where girls scored higher.

Regarding the sport category variable, higher A-S was found in the juvenile group (<18 years) and higher A-D in the cadets (<16 years), as shown in **Table 4**. The juvenile group scored higher on LOT-T, while the cadets scored higher on LOT-P. There were no differences in any of the engagement dimensions, but the juvenile group had a higher RS ability than the cadets.

When the sample was divided according to sport modality (lifeguard/futsal), there were statistically significant differences between the groups in A-T, and its dimensions, A-S, A-C and A-D, **Table 5**. A-T, A-S and A-C were higher in the lifeguard group, while A-D was higher in the futsal group. There were statistically significant differences in LOOT-T, LOT-O and LOT-P, with the lifeguard group scoring higher in terms of LOT-T, but in LOT-O and the LOT-P, the highest scores were found in the futsal group. In the UWES-T scale, as well as in its dimensions UWES-D and UWES-A, statistically significant differences were found, where the lifeguard group had higher

TABLE 2 | Means, standard deviations, reliability and Pearson's correlation of the scales.

	Mean (SD)	Cronbach's Alpha	A-T	A-S	A-C	A-D	LOT-T	LOT-O	LOT-P	UWES-T	UWES-V	UWES-D	UWES-A
A-T	34.8 (5.66)	0.855	1										
A-S	10.99 (3.1)	0.801	0.892**	1									
A-C	16.66 (3.6)	0.794	0.852**	0.762**	1								
A-D	7.15 (2.36)	0.866	−0.076	−0.338**	−00.483**	1							
LOT-T	15.47 (2.8)	0.835	−0.021	0.092	00.102	−0.327**	1						
LOT-O	6.7 (2.31)	0.791	−0.474**	−0.558**	−0.506**	0.370**	0.484**	1					
LOT-P	3.23 (2.63)	0.845	−0.394**	−0.588**	−0.553**	0.672**	−0.639**	0.364**	1				
UWES-T	4.39 (0.98)	0.811	0.199**	0.266**	0.235**	−0.232**	0.300**	−0.033	−0.348**	1			
UWES -V	4.05 (1.21)	0.859	−0.027	−00.019	0.005	−0.048	0.188**	0.12	−0.095	0.856**	1		
UWES -D	4.48 (1.03)	0.881	0.157*	00.234**	00.205**	−0.243**	0.317**	−0.014	−0.350**	0.935**	0.751**	1	
UWES -A	4.63 (1.14)	0.832	0.401**	00.497**	0.417**	−0.328**	0.289**	−0.200**	−0.483**	0.831**	0.472**	0.716**	1
Resilience	27.51 (4.26)	0.794	−0.121	00.01	−0.026	−0.264**	0.460**	0.254**	−0.266**	0.170*	0.265**	00.162*	.011

A-T, Anxiety Total; A-S, Anxiety Somatic; A-C, Anxiety Concentration; A-D, Anxiety Deconcentration; LOT-T, Lot Total; LOT-O, Lot Optimism; LOT-P, Lot Pessimism; UWES-T, UWES Total; UWES-V, UWES Vigor; UWES-D, UWES Dedication; UWES-A, UWES Absorption. $^{*}p < 0.05$, $^{**}p < 0.01$.

TABLE 3 | Correlations of anxiety, LOT, UWES and resilience in relation to sex.

	Sex		Mean difference	Test *t*-student		*d*
	Men (*n* = 139)	Women (*n* = 50)		$t_{(379)}$	*p*-value	
Anxiety						
Total	38.36 (0.48)	33.53 (6.11)	4.83	5.581	**<0.001**	0.63
Somatic	13.36 (0.48)	10.14 (3.21)	3.22	7.051	**<0.001**	0.80
Concern	18.96 (1.80)	15.83 (3.73)	3.13	5.702	**<0.001**	0.64
Deconcentration	6.04 (1.80)	7.55 (2.41)	−1.51	−4.047	**<0.001**	−0.46
LOT						
Total	15.96 (0.73)	15.29 (3.22)	0.67	1.461	0.146	0.17
Optimism	5.44 (1.15)	7.15 (2.46)	−1.71	−4.74	**<0.001**	−0.54
Pessimism	1.48 (1.31)	3.86 (2.70)	−2.38	−5.984	**<0.001**	−0.68
UWES						
Total	4.62 (0.86)	4.31 (1.01)	0.32	1.965	**0.051**	0.22
Vigor	3.96 (1.21)	4.08 (1.22)	−0.12	−0.618	0.537	−0.07
Dedication	4.71 (0.82)	4.40 (1.09)	0.30	1.8	0.073	0.20
Absorption	5.20 (0.82)	4.43 (1.17)	0.77	4.271	**<0.001**	0.48
Resilience	27.72 (2.96)	27.43 (4.64)	0.29	0.41	0.682	0.05

$p < 0.001$. The bold values indicates statistically significant differences.

scores than the futsal group in these three dimensions. There were no significant differences in the remaining dimensions of the scales.

To determine in LOT-R the effects of the variables sex, type of sport (lifeguard-futsal) and sport category (<18 and <16 years) and anxiety, UWES and RS, a linear regression was performed. The results are shown in **Table 6**, the model was statistically significant $F_{(6;182)} = 14.1$; $p < 0.001$, explaining 31.7% of the explanatory variance. The variables of commitment and resilience had a significant positive effect, and the category of <16 years had a significant negative effect, so the lower the category, the higher the optimism.

DISCUSSION

In sport competition, it is essential to know and control the factors (physical, technical and psychological) that influence performance (Morillo et al., 2016). Going deeper into what Cerin (2003) indicates that the pre-competitive state of the athlete must be analyzed from an interconductual approach to human behavior, which includes other related emotions in addition to anxiety, taking the field model as a reference, looking for relationships with other variables.

The aim of the study focuses on finding out the existing differences between the lifesaving (individual sport) and futsal (team sport) modalities; from a psychological perspective, as well

TABLE 4 | Correlations of anxiety, LOT, UWES and resilience in relation to category.

	Category		Average difference	Test *t*-student		*d*
	Youth ($n = 86$)	Cadets ($n = 103$)		$t_{(379)}$	*p*-value	
Anxiety						
Total	35.36 (5.07)	34.34 (6.09)	1.02	1.237	0.218	0.14
Somatic	11.51 (2.92)	10.56 (3.20)	0.95	2.111	**0.036**	0.24
Concern	17.09 (3.47)	16.29 (3.68)	0.80	1.53	0.128	0.17
Deconcentration	6.76 (2.05)	7.49 (2).55)	−0.73	−2.137	**0.034**	−0.24
LOT						
Total	16.36 (2.20)	14.72 (3.03)	1.64	4.189	**<0.001**	0.47
Optimism	6.79 (2.45)	6.62 (2.20)	0.17	0.501	0.617	0.06
Pessimism	2.43 (2.09)	3.90 (2.85)	−1.47	−3.983	**<0.001**	−0.45
UWES						
Total	4.46 (0.89)	4.33 (1.05)	0.13	0.913	0.362	0.10
Vigor	4.04 (1.17)	4.06 (1.25)	−0.02	−0.088	0.93	−0.01
Dedication	4.55 (0.92)	4.43 (1.11)	0.12	0.771	0.442	0.09
Absorption	4.79 (1.01)	4.50 (1.23)	0.29	1.769	0.078	0.20
Resilience	28.31 (3.89)	26.84 (4.45)	1.48	2.408	**0.017**	0.27

$p < 0.001$. The bold values indicates statistically significant differences.

TABLE 5 | Correlation anxiety, LOT, UWES, and resilience depending on the sport modality.

	Sport		Average difference	Test *t*-student		*d*
	Futsal ($n = 86$)	Lifeguard ($n = 103$)		$t_{(379)}$	*p*-value	
Anxiety						
Total	30.51 (6.03)	38.39 (0.49)	−7.88	−13.219	**<0.001**	−1.49
Somatic	8.13 (2.40)	13.39 (0.49)	−5.26	−21.721	**<0.001**	−2.46
Concern	13.93 (3.31)	18.93 (1.81)	−5.00	−13.17	**<0.001**	−1.49
Deconcentration	8.45 (2.29)	6.07 (1.81)	2.39	7.997	**< 0.001**	0.90
LOT						
Total	14.97 (4.03)	15.88 (0.72)	−0.92	−2.271	**0.024**	−0.26
Optimism	8.27 (2.37)	5.39 (1.17)	2.88	10.866	**<0.001**	1.23
Pessimism	5.30 (2.30)	1.50 (1.31)	3.80	14.233	**<0.001**	1.61
UWES						
Total	4.17 (1.07)	4.58 (0.87)	0.41	−2.89	**0.004**	−0.33
Vigor	4.18 (1.24)	3.95 (1.19)	0.23	1.319	0.189	0.15
Dedication	4.27 (1.20)	4.66 (0.83)	−0.39	−2.627	**0.009**	−0.30
Absorption	4.05 (1.19)	5.12 (0.83)	−1.07	−7.217	**<0.001**	−0.82
Resilience	27.00 (5.49)	27.93 (2.81)	−0.93	−1.503	0.134	−0.17

$p < 0.001$. The bold values indicates statistically significant differences.

as determining differences in relation to the sport categories, sex and age of the participants, responding to the different hypotheses put forward.

On analyzing the correlations of the different scales used in the study, we found a relationship between the level of LOT-T and SR, as well as between the UWES-T and SR. Likewise, we found a negative correlation between the level of A-D and SR, data that support previous studies Trigueros et al. (2020) and Reche et al. (2018). In addition, the study has provided other interesting data such as a correlation between LOT-O level and UWES-D level with SR, supporting previous studies such as Vallarino and Reche-García (2016) with hockey players and Ruiz et al. (2012) with football players; Trigueros et al. (2020) with volleyball players and Reche et al. (2018) with fencers. Similarly, we found a negative correlation between the level of A-D and RS, which was again consistent with the findings of previous studies Reche et al. (2019).

The present data reflected a higher level of A-T and UWES-T in boys, as well as lower levels of A-D and higher levels of LOT-O in girls. Thus, partly corroborating H1, boys have lower A-T,

TABLE 6 | Linear regression.

	B (ET)	Beta	*t*	*p*-value
Sex (Male, Female)	−0.37 (0.47)	−0.059	−0.8	0.425
Sport (Lifeguard, Futsal)	0.53 (0.56)	0.095	0.958	0.339
Category (Cadets, Youth)	−1.17 (0.36)	−0.209	−3.276	**0.001**
UWES	0.63 (0.18)	0.222	3.48	**0.001**
Anxiety	−0.06 (0.04)	−0.129	−1.441	0.151
Resilience	0.24 (0.04)	0.358	5.433	**<0.001**

$F_{(6,182)} = 14.1$; $p < 0.001$; $R2 = 0.317$. The bold values indicates statistically significant differences.

UWES-T and RS than girls. This finding is in line with some previous studies (Martens et al., 1990; Clifton and Gill, 1994) and at the same time does not agree with Reche et al. (2018) and Aranzana et al. (2016) who found no differences between sexes. As for the second part of the hypothesis, it is not corroborated, as girls have higher LOT-O scores, a fact explained by Stach (2006) in sociobiological terms: women, as the mother of the species, must find support mainly in themselves and in their own activities. These data are in opposition to other studies, albeit conducted in the academic field, where Extremera et al. (2007) found that male students showed a stronger optimistic tendency than female students. However, some studies have found that there were no gender differences, for example: Tan and Tan (2014), Aranzana et al. (2016), Hinz et al. (2017), Reche et al. (2018), and Cnen et al. (2020). Furthermore, other authors indicate differences in the interpretation of symptoms in relation to the type of sport and competition experience (Mellalieu et al., 2004). Thus, this variability of data could be marked by the cross-sectional nature and sport modalities of the study, and further longitudinal studies are needed to clarify the nature of these differences.

When analyzing the data according to sport categories: youth (<18 years) and cadets (<16 years), the data show a similar result to previous studies, such as those of Vallarino and Reche-García (2016), who found a higher level of optimism in the under-18 age groups compared to the under-16s. However, other studies, such as Bohórquez and Checa (2017), Sánchez et al. (2012), and Reche et al. (2018), have shown different patterns to the present research, which found higher levels of somatic anxiety and resilience in young people and greater deconcentration and pessimism in under-16s. Kristjánsdóttir et al. (2019) found no significant differences in futsal players related to competitive anxiety or resilience. These results coincide with those presented by Reche-García et al. (2020) where they do not find differences related to the age variables of the participants. In relation to H2, youth category athletes are more optimistic than cadet category athletes, H4 is corroborated. Endorsing previous studies, Vallarino and Reche-García (2016), who found a higher level of LOT-T in groups <18 years compared to <16 years. This difference may be influenced by the fact that cadet athletes, because of their age, have an enthusiastic commitment that represents an individual's feelings of attraction and dedication toward an entity (in this case sport modality) and youth athletes may have a limited commitment that reflects an individual's feelings of obligation and passive responsibility toward an entity (or sport team) (Scanlan et al., 2016). However, other studies, such as Bohórquez and Checa (2017), Sánchez et al. (2012), and Reche et al. (2018), have shown different patterns than the present research, finding higher levels of A-S and RS in younger athletes and higher A-D and LOT-P in <16 years old. Kristjánsdóttir et al. (2019) find no significant differences in futsal players in relation to competitive A-T or RS. These discrepancies between the different studies could be conditioned by the competitive level of the athletes (local-autonomous-national-international), as these levels of competition can enhance and/or generate different responses in the variables analyzed.

When correlating the different scales in terms of sport modality, in A-T, LOT-T, UWES-T and RS, it is the lifeguard athletes who show higher scores than the futsal athletes. Which determines that H3, futsal athletes (collective sport) show a lower level of commitment and resilience than lifeguards (individual sport), H1 is confirmed. Regarding the sport modality and the relationship between collective sport (futsal) and individual sport (lifeguard), we found similar results to previous studies, such as Bohórquez and Checa (2017) and Reche et al. (2018), regarding UWES-T, A-T and LOT-T in individual sports. Likewise, the results of this study reflected a higher level of A-D and LOT-P in futsal participants (collective sport). This is in contrast to previous studies such as those of Sánchez et al. (2012) and Chacón-Cuberos et al. (2016), which found no differences in these variables according to sport modality. This is supported by the main psychological distinction between individual and team sports, which is based on the concept of responsibility (Mroczkowska, 1997), supported by the fact that personal responsibility for the result (positive or negative) is lower in team sports compared to individual sports (Laborde et al., 2016).

We believe that the results presented are due to the specific characteristics of the sports studied. On the one hand, lifeguarding is a sport in which the work is carried out individually but within a team discipline, which we believe reduces the possibility of differences between its practitioners. Whereas, in Indoor Football, the possibility of distributing responsibility among the team, we understand, is the reason for these differences between modalities. As determined by Vallarino and Reche-García (2016) who highlighted the importance of optimism and resilience in hockey players or the study by Ruiz et al. (2012) on football players.

In relation to H4, Futsal players have lower A-T than lifeguards, H3 is endorsed. Since the lifeguard athletes achieved higher scores than the futsal players. Possibly the cause could be as a consequence of the sport modality practiced (individual) as when one realizes that one is unable to achieve a goal it is probably very stressful, as stress occurs when goals become unattainable (Lazarus, 1999). Considering that lifeguarding is performed individually, but, within a team discipline, the athlete is solely responsible for the outcome. Whereas, in futsal, there is the possibility of distributing the responsibility among the different players of the team, we understand that this could be the reason for these differences between the reviewed sports modalities.

The results of the linear regression revealed the importance of the category, the level of UWES-T and the level of SR of the participants. Unlike previous studies, Sánchez-Oliva et al. (2010) or Chacón-Cuberos et al. (2016) that did not emphasize these variables and similar to the studies of Bohórquez and Checa (2017) as well as Reche et al. (2018), in individual sports such as triathlon or team sports such as hockey, which are in line with this study.

CONCLUSIONS

The results of this study provided very valuable information about optimism, anxiety, resilience and the level of commitment of athletes <18 years old and <16 years old, both in lifeguarding and futsal. From the data of this study, it will be possible to establish a better working environment in training and provide psychological work situations so that athletes can obtain greater positive feelings, both in individual and collective sport. Providing coaches and athletes with information on the dimensions analyzed, in order to be able firstly to detect if there are risks in athletes and secondly to prevent them from appearing, with the inclusion in training and/or training of athletes of efficient tools and methodologies in the detection, prevention and reinforcement of concepts such as LOT-T and RS that help athletes and coaches to face them with solvency. Using the present research as a reference, additional future research is needed in other sports, both individual and team, before stronger conclusions can be drawn. Larger sample sizes, longitudinal studies, including pre- and post-competition observation may provide more information on the more concrete effects of these variables on athletes. Such research may also reveal whether the results of the questionnaires are different depending on the athlete's performance in an event.

It is worth noting that higher anxiety and UWES ability was observed in the lifeguarding modality, and higher levels of deconcentration and LOT-R-P were observed in futsal participants.

The study provides insight into the athletes of these two sport modalities on which to deepen future research, generate personalized lines of work and improve performance. We are also aware of the need to continue increasing the sample for future replications, and even generate sport-specific studies and comparing different competitive levels.

Limitations of the Study

With regard to the limitations of the study, firstly, we can point out that the data have been collected through self-reporting. This is a common practice in studies, although it may lead to a bias in the participants' response, exacerbate common variance and artificially increase correlations between variables (Spector, 2006). Secondly, the sample is composed of Spanish athletes, who have their own cultural characteristics; therefore, the results obtained cannot be extrapolated to other samples. It would be interesting to carry out cross-cultural or cross-national studies to verify whether the results of our work are similar to those of other countries.

ETHICS STATEMENT

Ethical approval was not provided for this study on human participants because as it was an observational study and the information was obtained through a questionnaire, in which there was no sensitive information. The ethics committee determined that there was no need for such a report. Written informed consent to participate in this study was provided by the participants' legal guardian/next of kin.

AUTHOR CONTRIBUTIONS

FC-N and AM-M: conceptualization, writing—review and editing, and supervision. FC-N: methodology, writing—original draft preparation, and project administration. FC-G and RI-P: software and visualization. AM-M, RI-P, and FC-N: validation. AM-M: formal analysis. FC-N and RI-P: investigation. FC-G and AM-M: resources. RI-P: data curation. AM-M, RI-P, FC-G, and FC-N: funding acquisition. All authors have read and agreed to the published version of the manuscript.

ACKNOWLEDGMENTS

To Cambridge Proofreading, for their invaluable help with the English of the article.

REFERENCES

Almagro, B. J., Sáenz-López, P., González-Cutre, D., and Moreno-Murcia, J. A. (2011). Clima motivacional percibido, necesidades psicológicas y motivación intrínseca como predictores del compromiso deportivo en adolescentes. *RICYDE. Revista Internacional de Ciencias Del Deporte* 7, 250–265. doi: 10.5232/ricyde2011.02501

Anshel, M. H. (1995). "Anxiety," in *Sport Psychology: Theory, Applications and Issues*, eds E. T. Morris, and J. Summers (Brisbane, QLD: John Wiley and Sons), 29–62.

Aranzana, M., Salguero, A., Molinero, O., Zubiaur, M., Vega, R., Ruiz, R., and Márquez, S. (2016). Influencia del perfil resiliente, optimismo disposicional, estrategias de afrontamiento y carga de entrenamiento en los niveles de estrés-recuperación en nadadores. *Kronos Rev. Univ. Actividad Física El Deporte* 15, 1–12.

Barbosa, S., and Urrea, Á. (2018). Influencia del deporte y la actividad física en el estado de salud físico y mental: una revisión bibliográfica. *Katharsis Rev. Cienc. Soc.* 25, 141–160.

Bohórquez, M. R., and Checa, I. (2017). Psychosocial factors related to the competitive anxiety of sports in training stages. *Cult. Cienc. Deporte* 12, 205–210. doi: 10.12800/ccd.v12i36.951

Cano, F., Montero, C., and Moreno-Murcia, J. A. (2019). Motivación, autoconfianzay experiencia autotélica en deportistas de salvamento y socorrismo. *Rev. Invest. Actividades Acuáticas* 3, 35–40. doi: 10.21134/riaa.v3i6.375

Cashmore, E. (2008). *Sport and Exercise Psychology: The Key Concept, 2nd Ed.* London: Routledge. doi: 10.4324/9780203928097

Castillo, M. D. (2009). *La Atención.* Madrid: Pirámide.

Castro-Sánchez, M., and Zurita-Ortega, F. (2019). Estudio descriptivo de los niveles de ansiedad en deportistas según modalidad practicada. *J. Sport Health Res.* 11, 241–250

Castro-Sánchez, M., Zurita-Ortega, F., Ramírez-Granizo, I., and Ubago-Jiménez, J. L. (2020). Relación entre la inteligencia emocional y los niveles de ansiedad en deportistas. *J. Sport Health Res.* 12, 42–53.

Cerin, E. (2003). Anxiety versus fundamental emotions as predictors of perceived functionality of pre-competitive emotional states, threat, and challenge in individual sports. *J. Appl. Sport Psychol.* 15, 223–238. doi: 10.1080/10413200305389

Chacón-Cuberos, R., Castro-Sánchez, M., Espejo-Garcés, T., and Zurita-Ortega, F. (2016). Estudio de la resiliencia en función de la modalidad deportiva: fútbol, balonmano y esquí. *Retos Nuevas Tendencias Educ. Física Deporte Recreación* 29, 157–161. doi: 10.47197/retos.v0i29.41313

Clifton, R. T., and Gill, D. L. (1994). Gender differences in self-confidence on a feminine-typed task. *J. Sport Exerc. Psychol.* 16, 150–162. doi: 10.1123/jsep.16.2.150

Cnen, T.-W., Chiu, Y.-C., and Hsu, Y. (2020). Perception of social support provided by coaches, optimism/pessimism, and psychological well-being: gender differences and mediating effect models. *Int. J. Sports Sci. Coaching.* 16, 272–280. doi: 10.1177/1747954120968649

Correia, M. E., and Rosado, A. (2018). Fear of failure and anxiety in sport. *Análise Psicol.* 36, 75–86. doi: 10.14417/ap.1193

Crust, L. (2007). Mental toughness in sport: a review. *Int. J. Sport Exerc. Psychol.* 5, 270–290. doi: 10.1080/1612197X.2007.9671836

De Freese, J. D., and Smith, A. L. (2013). Areas of work life and the athlete burnout-engagement relationship. *J. Appl. Sport Psychol.* 25, 180–196. doi: 10.1080/10413200.2012.705414

Extremera, N., Duran, A., and Rey, L. (2007). Perceived emotional intelligence and dispositional optimism–pessimism: analyzing their role in predicting psychological adjustment among adolescents. *Pers. Individ. Differ.* 42, 1069–1079. doi: 10.1016/j.paid.2006.09.014

Ferrando, P. J., Chico, E., and Tous, J. M. (2002). Propiedades psicométricas del test de optimismo life orientation test. *Psicothema* 14, 673–680.

Fletcher, D., and Sarkar, M. (2012). A grounded theory of psychological resilience in olympic champions. *Psychol. Sport Exerc.* 13, 669–678. doi: 10.1016/j.psychsport.2012.04.007

Flórez-Lozano, S. A. (2006). Optimismo y salud. *Jano* 1616, 59–61.

Freche, R. (2013). *Optimism and resilience, as moderated by coping style, on prenatal depressive symptomology and salivary cortisol response to stress (Order N°. 1527372, California State University, Long Beach)* (ProQuest Dissertations and Theses, 139). Available online at: http://search.proquest.com/docview/1509494265?accountid=14555 (accessed February 17, 2021).

Galli, N., and Vealey, R. S. (2008). Bouncing back from adversity: athletes' experiences of resilience. *Sport Psychol.* 22, 316–335. doi: 10.1123/tsp.22.3.316

García, X., Molinero, O., Ruíz, R., Salguero, A., de la Vega, R., and Márquez, S. (2014). La resiliencia en el deporte: fundamentos teóricos, instrumentos de evaluación y revisión de la literatura. *Cuad. Psicol. Deporte* 14, 83–98. doi: 10.4321/S1578-84232014000300010

García-Naveira, A. (2008). El estilo de personalidad en jugadores de fútbol de competición y diferencias en función de la demarcación. *Cuad. Psicol. Deporte* 8, 19–38.

García-Naveira, A., and Díaz, F. (2010). Relación entre optimismo/pesimismo disposicional, rendimiento y edad en jugadores de fútbol de competición. *Rev. Iberoamericana Psicol. Ejercicio Deporte* 5, 45–60.

González, G., Valdivia-Moral, P., Cahón, J., Zurita, F., and Romero, O. (2017). Influencia del control del estrés en el rendimiento deportivo: la autoconfianza, la ansiedad y la concentración en deportistas. *RETOS Nuevas Tendencias Educación Física Deporte Recreación* 32, 3–6. doi: 10.47197/retos.v0i32.50895

González-Arratia, N. I., Valdez, J. L., van Barneveld, H. O., and González, S. (2012). Resiliencia y factores protectores en menores infractores y en situación de calle. *Psicol. Salud.* 22, 49–62.

Guillén, F., and Martínez-Alvarado, J. R. (2014). Escala de compromiso deportivo: una adaptación de la Escala de Compromiso en el Trabajo de Utrecht (UWES) para ambientes deportivos. *Univ. Psychol.* 13, 975–984. doi: 10.11144/Javeriana.UPSY13-3.sesa

Hamidi, S., and Besharat, M. A. (2010). Perfeccionismo y la ansiedad competitiva en los atletas. *Cienc. Comportamiento Soc. Proc.* 5, 813–817. doi: 10.1016/j.sbspro.2010.07.190

Hinz, A., Sander, C., Glaesmer, H., Brähler, E., Zenger, M., Hilbert, A., and Kocalevent, R. D. (2017). Optimism and pessimism in the general population: psychometric properties of the life orientation test (LOT-R). *Int. J. Clin. Health Psychol.* 17, 161–170. doi: 10.1016/j.ijchp.2017.02.003

Hodge, K., Lonsdale, C., and Jackson, S. A. (2009). Athlete engagement in elite sport: an exploratory investigation of antecedents and consequences. *Sport Psychol.* 23, 186–202. doi: 10.1123/tsp.23.2.186

Jaramillo, Á., Mayorga-Lascano, M., and Moreta-Herrera, R. (2020). Ansiedad competitiva y autoeficacia en tenistas de alto rendimiento antes y después de una competencia. *Rev. Guillermo Ockham* 18, 45–54. doi: 10.21500/22563202.4526

Kajbafnezhad, H., Ahadi, H., Heidarie, A. R., Askari, P., and Enayati, M. (2011). Difference between team and individual sports with respect to psychological skills, overall emotional intelligence and athletic success motivation in Shiraz city athletes. *J. Phys. Educ. Sport* 11:249.

Kovacsik, R., Soós, I., de la Vega, R., Ruíz-Barquín, R., and Szabo, A. (2020). Passion and exercise addiction: healthier profiles in team than in individual sports. *Int. J. Sport Exerc. Psychol.* 18, 176–186. doi: 10.1080/1612197X.2018.1486873

Kristjánsdóttir, H., Jóhannsdóttir, K. R., Pic, M., and Saavedra, J. M. (2019). Características psicológicas de las jugadoras de fútbol: habilidades, fortaleza mental y ansiedad. *Rev. Escandinava Psicol.* 60, 609–615. doi: 10.1111/sjop.12571

Kumar, A. (2017). A comparative study of mental toughness between team sports and individual sports. *Int. J. Phys. Educ. Sports Health* 4, 182–184. doi: 10.26524/1542

Laborde, S., Guillén, F., Allen, M., and Watson, M. (2017). The light quartet: positive personality traits and approaches to coping in sport coaches. *Psychol. Sport Exerc.* 32, 67–73. doi: 10.1016/j.psychsport.2017.06.005

Laborde, S., Guillén, F., and Mosley, E. (2016). Positive personality-trait-like individual differences in athletes from individual-and team sports and in non-athletes. *Psychol. Sport Exerc.* 26, 9–13. doi: 10.1016/j.psychsport.2016.05.009

Lazarus, R. S. (1999). *Stress and Emotion: A New Synthesis.* New York, NY: Springer Publishing Company.

Liştea, R., Ducrocq, E., Siminiceanu, A., and Visu-Petra, L. (2017). Getting the butteries to y in formation: a review on the modulating effect of attentional control on motor and visual aspects of sports performance under pressure. *Cogn. Brain Behav.* 21, 249–274. doi: 10.24193/cbb.2017.21.16

Londoño, C., Hernández, L. M., Alejo, I. E., and Pulido, D. (2011). Diseño y validación de la escala de optimismo disposicional/pesimismoEOP. *Univ. Psychol.* 12, 139–155. doi: 10.11144/Javeriana.upsy12-1.dveo

Lonsdale, C., Hodge, K., and Jackson, S. A. (2007a). Athlete engagement: II. Development and initial validation of the athlete engagement questionnaire. *Int. J. Sport Psychol.* 38, 471–492. doi: 10.1037/t50268-000

Lonsdale, C., Hodge, K., and Raedeke, T. D. (2007b). Athlete engagement: I. A qualitative investigation of relevance and dimensions. *Int. J. Sport Psychol.* 38, 451–470.

López, R. (2015). *Relación entre Satisfacción con la Vida y Satisfacción con el Deporte y en Jóvenes Deportistas* (Tesis Doctoral, 359). Available online at: https://accedacris.ulpgc.es/bitstream/10553/13022/2/0707977_00000_0000.pdf.2018 (accessed February 17, 2021)

Martens, R. (1977). *Sport Competition Anxiety Test.* Champaign, IL: Human Kinetics Publishers. doi: 10.1037/t27556-000

Martens, R., Vealey, R. S., and Burton, D. (1990). *Competitive Anxiety in Sport.* Champaign, IL: Human Kinetics.

Martínez-Moreno, A., Ibáñez-Pérez, R. J., Cavas-García, F., and Cano-Noguera, F. (2020). Older adults' gender, age and physical activity effects on anxiety, optimism, resilience and engagement. *Int. J. Environ. Res. Public Health* 17, 1–15. doi: 10.3390/ijerph17207561

Mellalieu, S. D., Hanton, S., and O'Brien, M. (2004). Intensity and direction of competitive anxiety as a function of sport type and experience. *Scand. J. Med. Sci. Sports* 14, 326–334. doi: 10.1111/j.1600-0838.2004.00389.x

Moran, A. (2012). *Sport and Exercise Psychology: A critical introduction*. London: Routledge.

Moreno-Murcia, J. A., Gimeno, E., and González-Cutre, D. (2006). "Efectos del género en la motivación y el estado de flow en deportistas adolescentes," in *V Congreso Internacional de Educación Física e Interculturalidad*, ed E. A. Díaz (Murcia: ICD), 1–29.

Morillo, J. P., Reigal, R. E., and Hernández-Mendo, A. (2016). Relaciones entre el perfil psicológico Deportivo y la ansiedad competitiva en jugadores de balonmano playa. *Rev. Psicol. Deporte* 25, 121–128.

Mroczkowska, H. (1997). Attributive reduction of failure-borne losses in view of team cohesion - analogies and differences in individual versus team competition. *Biol. Sport* 14, 325–332.

Nia, M. E., and Besharat, M. A. (2010). Comparison of athletes' personality characteristics in individual and team sports. *Proc. Soc. Behav. Sci.* 5, 808–812. doi: 10.1016/j.sbspro.2010.07.189

Núñez, A., Ponseti, F. X., Sesé, A., and Garcia-Mas, A. (2020). Anxiety and perceived performance in athletes and musicians: revisiting Martens. *Revista de Psicología del Deporte* 29:21.

Ortín, F. J., De la Vega, R., and Gosálvez, J. (2013). Optimismo, ansiedad-estado y autoconfianza en jóvenes jugadores de balonmano. *Anales Psicol.* 29, 637–641. doi: 10.6018/analesps.29.3.175751

Otto, M. W., Calkins, A. W., and Hearon, B. A. (2010). "Anxiety," in *The Corsini Encyclopedia of Psychology*, eds I. B. Weiner and W. E. Craighead (New York, NY: Wiley and Sons), 1–2. doi: 10.1002/9780470479216.corpsy0073

Parkes, F., and Mallet, J. (2011). Developing mental toughness: attributional style retraining in rugby. *Sport Psychol.* 25, 269–287. doi: 10.1123/tsp.25.3.269

Pluhar, E., McCracken, C., Griffith, K. L., Christino, M. A., Sugimoto, D., and Meehan, I. I. I., W. P. (2019). Team sport athletes may be less likely to suffer anxiety or depression than individual sport athletes. *J. Sports Sci. Med.* 18, 490–496.

Ponseti, F. J., Sese, A., and Garcia-Mas, A. (2016). The impact of competitive anxiety and parental influence on the performance of young swimmers. *Rev. Iberoamericana Psicol. Ejercicio Deporte* 11, 229–237.

Raharjo, H. P., Kusuma, D. W. Y., and Mugiyo, H. (2018). "Personality characteristics in individual and team sports," in *International Seminar on Public Health and Education 2018 (ISPHE 2018)* (Indonesia: Atlantis Press), 92–95. doi: 10.2991/isphe-18.2018.20

Ramis, Y., Torregrosa, M., Viladrich, C., and Cruz, J. (2010). Adaptación y validación de la versión española de la escala de ansiedad competitiva SAS-2 para deportistas de iniciación. *Psicothema* 22, 1004–1009.

Reche, C., Gómez-Díaz, M., Martínez-Rodríguez, A., and Tutte, V. (2018). El optimismo como contribución a la resiliencia deportiva. *Rev. Iberoamericana Psicol. Ejercicio Deporte* 13, 131–136.

Reche, C., Martínez-Rodríguez, A., and Ortín, F. J. (2019). Characterization of the resilience and exercise dependence athlete. *Ciencia Cult. Deporte* 43, 17–23. doi: 10.12800/ccd.v15i43.1395

Reche-García, C., Martínez-Rodíguez, A., Gómez-Díaz, M., and Hernández-Morante, J. J. (2020). Análisis de la resiliencia y dependencia en deportes de combate y otras modalidades deportivas. *Suma Psicol.* 27, 70–79. doi: 10.14349/sumapsi.2020.v27.n2.1

Ruiz, R., de la Vega, R., Poveda, J., Rosado, A., and Serpa, S. (2012). Psychometric analysis of the resilience scale in the sport of football. *Rev. Psicol. Del Deporte* 21, 143–151.

Sánchez, J. C. J., Gómez, R. P., Dueñas, K. G. N., and Gómez-Millán, M. R. B. (2012). Ansiedad y autoconfianza precompetitiva en triatletas. *Rev. Iberoamericana Psicol. Ejercicio Deporte* 7, 113–124.

Sánchez-Oliva, D., Leo-Marcos, F. M., Sánchez-Miguel, P. A., Amado-Alonso, D., and García-Calvo, T. (2010). Relación del clima motivacional creado por el entrenador con la motivación autodeterminada y la implicación hacia la práctica deportiva. *RICYDE Rev. Int. Ciencias Deporte* 6, 177–195. doi: 10.5232/ricyde2010.02001

Scanlan, T. K., Chow, G. M., Sousa, C., Scanlan, L. A., and Knifsend, C. A. (2016). The development of the sport commitment questionnaire-2 (English version). *Psychol. Sport Exerc.* 22, 233–246. doi: 10.1016/j.psychsport.2015.08.002

Schaufeli, W. B., Taris, T., Le Blanc, P., Peeters, M., Bakker, A., and De Jonge, J. (2001). Maakt arbeid gezond? Op zoek naar de bevlogen werknemer [Can work produce health? The quest for the engaged worker]. *De Psychol.* 36, 422–428.

Scheier, M., and Carver, C. (2003). "Optimism," in *Positive Psychological Assessment: A Handbook of Models and Measures*, eds E. S. J. López, and C. R. Snyder (Washington, DC: American Psychological Association), 75–89. doi: 10.1037/10612-005

Scheier, M., and Carver, C. S. (1985). Optimism, coping, and health: assessment and implication of generalized outcome expectancies. *Health Psychol.* 4, 219–247. doi: 10.1037/0278-6133.4.3.219

Scheier, M. F., Carver, C. S., and Bridges, M. W. (1994). Distinguishing optimism from neuroticism (and trait anxiety, self mastery and self esteem): a reevaluation of the life orientation test. *J. Personal. Soc. Psychol.* 67, 1063–1078. doi: 10.1037/0022-3514.67.6.1063

Seligman, M. E. P. (2004). *Aprenda Optimismo*. Madrid: Debolsillo.

Serrano-Parra, M. D., Garrido-Abejar, M., Notario-Pacheco, B., Bartolomé-Gutierrez, R., Solera-Martínez, M., and Martínez-Vizcaino, V. (2012). Validez de la escala de resiliencia de Connor-Davidson (CD-RISC). *Int. J. Psychol. Res.* 5, 49–57. doi: 10.21500/20112084.736

Smith, R. E., Smoll, F. L., and Schultz, R. W. (1990). Measurement and correlates of sport-specific cognitive and somatic trait anxiety: the sport anxiety scale. *Anxiety Res.* 2, 263–280. doi: 10.1080/08917779008248733

Souri, H., and Hasanirad, T. (2011). Relationship between resilience, optimism and psychological well-being in students of medicine. *Proc. Soc. Behav. Sci.* 30, 1541–1544. doi: 10.1016/j.sbspro.2011.10.299

Spector, P. E. (2006). Method variance in organizational research truth or urban legend?. *Organ. Res. Methods* 9, 221–232. doi: 10.1177/1094428105284955

Stach, R. (2006). *Optymizm. Badania nad Optymizmem Jako Mechanizmem Adaptacyjnym*. Cracovia: Wydawnictwo Uniwersytetu Jagiellońskiego.

Tan, C., and Tan, L. S. (2014). The role of optimism, self-esteem, academic self-efficacy and gender in high-ability students. *Asia-Pacific Educ. Res.* 23, 621–633. doi: 10.1007/s40299-013-0134-5

Trigueros, R., Aguilar-Parra, J. M., Álvarez, J. F., Cangas, A. J., and López-Liria, R. (2020). The effect of motivation on the resilience and anxiety of the athlete. *Rev. Int. Med. Ciencias Actividad Fisica Deporte* 20, 73–86. doi: 10.15366/rimcafd2020.77.005

Vallarino, T., and Reche-García, C. (2016). Burnout, resiliencia y optimismo en el hockey sobre hierba femenino. *Cuadernos Psicol. Deporte* 16, 73–78.

Vanistendael, S., and Lecomte, J. (2002). *La felicidad Posible. Despertar en Niños Maltratado la Confianza en sí mIsmos: Construir la Resiliencia*. Barcelona: Gedisa.

Weinberg, R., and Gould, D. (2010). *Fundamentos de Psicología del Deporte y el Ejercicio Físico*. Madrid: Médica Panamericana.

Yu, X., and Zhang, J. (2007). Factor analysis psychometric evaluation of the Conner-Davidson resilience scale (CD-RISC) with Chinese people. *Soc. Behav. Personal.* 35, 19–30. doi: 10.2224/sbp.2007.35.1.19

Zurita-Ortega, F., Chacón-Cuberos, R., Cofre-Bolados, C., Knox, E., and Muros, J. J. (2018). Relationship of resilience, anxiety and injuries in footballers: structural equations analysis. *PLoS ONE* 13:e0207860. doi: 10.1371/journal.pone.0207860

4

The Impact of an Authentic Sports Leadership Program for Coach

Diego Soto Garcia [1], Juan Antonio García Herrero [2], Rodrigo Jesús Carcedo [3†] and Mario Sánchez García [4]*

[1] Department of Physical and Sports Education, Universidad de León, León, Spain, [2] Department of Didactics of Musical, Plastic and Body Expression, University of Salamanca, Salamanca, Spain, [3] Department of Developmental and Educational Psychology, University of Salamanca, Salamanca, Spain, [4] Education Faculty, Pontifical University of Salamanca, Salamanca, Spain

***Correspondence:**
Diego Soto Garcia
dsotg@unileon.es

†ORCID:
Rodrigo Jesús Carcedo
orcid.org/0000-0002-8547-9043

Purpose: This paper studies the effects of authentic sports leadership training on coaches' self-perception of their own authentic leadership, perceived justice, competence, overall self-efficacy, and collective efficacy. Additionally, players' perceptions of their coaches with respect to their authentic leadership, perceived justice, competence, collective efficacy, satisfaction with the coach, and support for basic psychological needs were analyzed.

Design: Twenty-five football and handball coaches were randomly assigned to two groups. Fifteen coaches made up the experimental group that carried out the training leadership program, while 10 coaches made up the control group, carrying out no training whatsoever. A total of 248 football and handball players participated in this study; 136 were led by coaches who participated in the training program, and 112 by coaches who did not participate in the program.

Results: The results of this study indicate that coaches' self-perception is positively influenced after having received training in the variables of authentic leadership, perceived justice, competence, overall self-efficacy, and collective efficacy. Players whose coaches were part of the program perceive them as being more competent as coaches.

Conclusions: The effects of an authentic sports leadership training program are effective for coaches and players alike.

Keywords: sport coaching, identity, influence, self-awareness, football, handball

INTRODUCTION

"He was born to be a leader" or "she is a natural leader" are frequent expressions in different contexts where the figure of a leader is present. In the realm of sports, numerous studies attribute a fundamental aspect of sportsman to the coach (Adie et al., 2012; Balaguer et al., 2012), making him or her one of the most significant actors in terms of team sports performance (Myers et al., 2011). But can good leadership be learned, and is it possible to train coaches in these skills? Northouse (2018), maintains that there is a whole series of beliefs surrounding leadership, which opens the door to the ongoing debate of whether leadership is innate, or conversely, a skill that can be developed by coaches and leaders. As in other social activities, in sports it is assumed that leadership skills can be acquired through training programs (Duda, 2013). Hence, in recent decades there has been a growing interest in the study of leadership models and how to apply them. In many cases, these models have been oriented toward interactions and context (Epitropaki et al., 2017), thus, the coach's influence and how it is perceived by athletes has become increasingly central to various conceptualizations and analyses (Steffens et al., 2016; Epitropaki et al., 2017).

In recent years, there has been a growing interest in studying the relationship between effective leadership and the ethical behavior of the leader (Kaptein, 2019; Gamarra and Girotto, 2021). For this reason, models oriented toward the ethical dimension of team leadership have recently emerged, such as what has been termed "authentic leadership," (Avolio and Gardner, 2005; Gardner et al., 2005a; Moriano et al., 2011). Walumbwa et al. (2008) which posit that authentic leadership comprises four related dimensions: self-awareness, internalized moral perspective, relational transparency, and balanced processing.

Self-awareness refers to the extent which a leader possesses accurate self-knowledge and uses that knowledge to demonstrate he or she is cognizant of their impact on others. Internalized moral perspective pertains to the degree in which a leader's behavior is directed by and is congruent with their personal values and moral standards. It represents a form of self-regulation which allows leaders to engage in ethical conduct even against external pressures. Relational transparency is a leader's presentation of their true thoughts and emotions in an open and transparent manner (vs. being fake or manipulative), while balanced processing is evident when a leader objectively considers and analyzes all relevant information before making decisions (Walumbwa et al., 2008).

Various contextually different studies have shown that authentic leadership is related to the well-being of the leader (Baron, 2012; Gatling and Harrah, 2014; Weiss et al., 2018), additionally improving followers' behavior, satisfaction, and performance (Walumbwa et al., 2008; Caza et al., 2010). In the realm of sports, it has been associated with higher levels of competence and perceived justice on the part of the coach (González-Ponce, 2018), as well as increased satisfaction, enjoyment and cohesion among the team (Bandura and Kavussanu, 2018), as well as greater team cohesion; a relationship mediated by trust and sacrifice (Bandura et al., 2019). A study by McDowell et al. (2018) involving basketball players, the positive team climate presented a mediating effect between authentic leadership and psychological capital and player commitment.

Two of the most influential approaches to sports leadership have been: Leadership Behaviors Model of Sport Leadership (Smoll et al., 1978; Smoll and Smith, 1989) and Multidimensional Model of Sport Leadership (Chelladurai, 1978, 1990, 2007). There have been several programs aimed at training coaches in sports leadership skills which predominantly follow these approaches. One of the pioneers and most widely used is Coach Effectiveness Training (CET), by Smith et al. (1979), which aims to facilitate positive behavior on the part of coaches; likewise, to improve interactions with their athletes. Several studies have supported the usefulness of CET, resulting in more effective coach behaviors and better interactions (Sousa et al., 2008). Based on CET, the Mastery Approach to Coaching (MAC) (Smith et al., 2007; Smoll and Smith, 2009) emphasizes the importance of a task-oriented climate as generated by the coach rather than results-oriented. In this line, the MAC also recommends that coaches avoid post-error punishment and punitive technical instruction (Smoll and Smith, 2010; Vella and Perlman, 2014) in order to facilitate positive athletic behavior and promote a task-oriented climate.

The Transformational Leadership Approach to Coaching (TLAC) is another proposed approach to developing leadership skills. In essence, transformational leaders promote autonomous actions, pursuing the personal growth of athletes, as well as task cohesion, the satisfaction of needs, and intrinsic motivation (Vella and Perlman, 2014). In youth sport contexts, the TLAC has been implemented with the aim of facilitating positive developmental outcomes among athletes (Vella et al., 2012, 2013) and has been employed to facilitate high performance among Olympic athletes as well (Din and Paskevich, 2013).

The convenience of this study is due to the influence that the coach has on the athletes, and also, putting in value the positive effects that authentic leadership has on athletes (Bandura and Kavussanu, 2018), it could be considered transcendent to seek ways to develop this style of leadership and observe the effects on different variables associated with the abilities to lead by the coach and how it affects the athletes.

The objective of this study was to investigate the effect of an authentic sports leadership training program on several variables affecting both the coaches participating in the program and their players. The efficacy of this intervention was tested by both coaches and their players using a before and after study design. Authentic coach leadership, perceived justice, coach competence, and collective efficacy was evaluated by the coaches. The same variables (excluding coach self-efficacy) along with the satisfaction with the coach and perceived need satisfaction was evaluated by the players. As a result, two main hypotheses were developed:

1. From the perspective of the coaches, it is expected that those coaches who received the training program (experimental group) will show a significant increase in the evaluation of their levels of authentic coach leadership, perceived justice, coach competence (total competence, motivation, decision-making, teaching and instruction of skills, and character influence), coach self-efficacy, and collective efficacy after the intervention in comparison with before, whereas no changes will be found in those coaches who did not receive the intervention (control group).
2. From the evaluation of the players, it is expected that those players whose coaches have received the training program (experimental group) will show an increase in their perception of their coach's authentic leadership, perceived justice, coach competence (total competence, motivating, decision-making, teaching and instruction of skills, and character influence), collective efficacy, satisfaction with the coach, and coach support of their basic psychological needs (competence, autonomy, and relatedness).

METHOD

Participants

The training course was offered to all students of the National Degree of Higher Sports Technicians from Spain. A total of 25 coaches agreed to participate, all male, they were randomized;

15 coaches made up the experimental group and 10 coaches made up the control group. The average age of the participants in the experimental group was 36.31($SD = 8.07$), whereas the average age among the control group was 31.72 ($SD = 5.45$). The experimental group had an average of 10.53 years of experience as head coach ($SD = 6.54$), with the control group having had 8.50 average years of experience ($SD = 2.99$).

A total of 248 football and handball players participated in this study, 178 being male, and 70 female; 136 were led by coaches from the experimental group who had received leadership training, and 112 were led by coaches from the control group. The average age of the participants was 17.84 years ($SD = 4.44$). The athletes had an average of 10.45 years of experience ($SD = 4.83$) participating in the sport being played. Finally, all the coaches and the players trained more than 8 h per week and compete in a regional category.

Variables and Instruments

Authentic Coach Leadership

This variable was evaluated according to the Spanish adaptation validated by Moriano et al. (2011) of the Authentic Leadership Questionnaire (ALQ) (Walumbwa et al., 2008). This instrument consists of 12 items. The answer format is a Likert scale from 1 (never) to 7 (always). Following Gadermann et al. (2012) recommendations, internal consistency reliability was calculated using Omega coefficients. Good levels were found for the coaches (before the intervention: $\omega = 0.91$; after the intervention: $\omega = 0.91$) and the players (before: $\omega = 0.93$; after: $\omega = 0.92$).

Perceived Justice

This variable was evaluated using an adaptation of Colquitt's Organizational Justice scale (2001) by García-Calvo et al. (2014a) of which a modification was made in order to measure perceived justice within a sport-specific framework. The instrument consists of 12 items and the response format is a Likert scale from 1 (never) to 7 (always). Internal consistency reliability showed good levels for the coaches (before: $\omega = 0.88$; after: $\omega = 0.85$) and the players (before: $\omega = 0.91$; after: $\omega = 0.91$).

Coach Competence

This variable was evaluated by means of Athletes Perceptions of Coaching Competency Scale II-High School Teams (APCCS II-HST; Myers et al., 2010) validated in Spanish (González-Ponce et al., 2017). There are 15 items in this instrument and four subscales: competence to motivate, decision-making, teaching and instruction of skills, and influence on the player. The response format is a Likert scale from 1 (incompetence) to 7 (full competence). Good levels of internal consistency reliability were found for both coaches (motivate: before: $\omega = 0.63$, after: $\omega = 0.85$; decision-making: $\omega = 0.76$, after: $\omega = 0.77$; teach and instruct: $\omega = 0.89$, after: $\omega = 0.88$; influence: $\omega = 0.77$, after: $\omega = 0.80$), and players (motivate: before: $\omega = 0.78$, after: $\omega = 0.78$; decision-making: $\omega = 0.79$, after: $\omega = 0.84$; teach and instruct: $\omega = 0.79$, after: $\omega = 0.79$; influence: $\omega = 0.70$, after: $\omega = 0.72$).

Coach Self-Efficacy

This variable was evaluated using the Scale of Self Efficacy of Baessler and Schwarzer (1996) based on the Spanish version developed by Sanjuán et al. (2000). This instrument consists of 10 items. The response format is a Likert scale from 1 (strongly disagree) to 4 (strongly agree). Only the coaches gave their responses on this scale. Internal consistency reliability also showed good levels in this case (before: $\omega = 0.84$; after: $\omega = 0.92$).

Collective Efficacy

This variable was evaluated using a scale developed by Leo et al. (2010). This instrument consists of 6 items. The response format is a Likert scale from 1 (poor) to 5 (excellent). Good levels of internal consistency reliability were found for both coaches (before: $\omega = 0.83$; after: $\omega = 0.63$) and players (before: $\omega = 0.71$; after: $\omega = 0.75$).

Satisfaction With the Coach

This variable was evaluated using an adaptation of the Myers et al. (2011) in its Spanish version. This instrument consists of 3 items and represents a reduced version adapted to the Spanish context (González-Ponce et al., 2015). The response format is a Likert scale from 1 (very little) to 5 (a lot). This scale was only responded to by the players. Internal consistency reliability also showed good levels in this case (before: $\omega = 0.80$; after: $\omega = 0.83$).

Perception of Support for Basic Psychological Needs

This variable was evaluated using the Psychological Needs Support Questionnaire (CANPB; Sánchez-Oliva et al., 2013) adapted to the sports context. This instrument consists of 12 items distributed across three dimensions: autonomy, competence, and need for relatedness. The response format is a Likert scale from 1 (totally disagree) to 5 (totally agree). Only players responded to this scale. Again, good levels of internal consistency were observed in the three subscales (autonomy: before: $\omega = 0.81$, after: $\omega = 0.76$; competence: before: $\omega = 0.80$, after: $\omega = 0.77$; relatedness: before: $\omega = 0.87$, after: $\omega = 0.76$).

Procedure

This study was conducted applying a before/after design with an experimental group and a control group. Prior to the intervention, initial questionnaires were administered to all coaches and teams. For the coaches, the questionnaires were administrated outside the sporting context in which they regularly perform their duties as coaches. Conversely, the athletes were taken to the facility where they habitually train and explained the guidelines for completing the questionnaires by the researcher. Any related questions were also addressed at this time. The questionnaires were administered to the athletes collectively, with all members of the team present. The researcher remained on-site and available to the participants at all times should any questions arise. In both cases, the time used by both coaches and athletes was ~25–30 min. For coaches and players in both groups, there was a 7-week period between the first and second administration of the questionnaires.

This study respected the norms of the Declaration of Helsinki. Additionally, the parents of the minors were informed and all participants signed consent forms.

Description of the Program

Authentic leadership seeks to move away from unethical actions, respecting and displaying values that inspire others to join in that direction. According to George (2015, p. 1), "authentic leaders are people committed to meeting the needs of the interest groups they serve, displaying values and self-discipline that inspire others." Our training program was oriented toward this behavior, considering the four dimensions proposed in the Authentic Leadership Questionnaire (ALQ) by Walumbwa et al. (2008): transparency in relationships, internalized morality, balanced processing and self-awareness. The duration of the training program was 15 h divided into four sessions developed within three consecutive days. The structure and contents of the training program took into account the "model for the development of the moral component of authentic leadership" proposed by May et al. (2003). This model consists of three key elements: authenticity in decision-making, authentic behavior, and development of authentic leadership, each of which was present in the training program, especially in sessions 2, 3, and 4. Similarly, in the implementation of the program, "the integral model for the development of the authentic leader and his followers" proposed by Gardner et al. (2005b) was considered. The approach of this model is oriented toward the leader's self-awareness (identity, values and motivations) and self-regulation (balanced processing and transparency in relationships); in particular the contributions of this model were used in sessions 1, 2, and 3 as detailed below. The following table describes the contents and timing of the program.

Program Sessions

Session 1 (4 h). Transparency in relationships. In this session, the program was presented and the relationships that exist in sports groups were developed through inquiry tasks. Tasks were carried out in small groups where the meaning and purpose of relationships and the role of the coach among them were discussed. Communication skills and active listening were developed with the coaches, linking these components to sports environments. Through group dynamics these skills were put into practice, seeking that the coaches could show themselves as they are, without fear of judgments or external evaluations.

Session 2 (4 h). Internalized morality. This session was divided into two main blocks, the first dedicated to the work of the coach's self-awareness (content that was also developed in session 4). Through role play and reflective tasks, the coaches identified their personal values that made sense in leadership with their teams. How to approach ethical behavior and how to maintain authenticity in their conduct from a moral point of view was shared with the coaches through reflective tasks. The second block of this session was aimed at connecting the identity of the coach with the identity and values of his teams. Through role-playing games, everyday situations were put into practice among the teams, the coach being required to recognize frequently recurring moral dilemmas. The worked out was in a way that respected personal values and the identity of the team.

Session 3 (4 h). Balanced processing. Ethical decision-making seeks to objectively examine the variables involved in accepting personal responsibility for actions, results, and mistakes. In this session, the coaches focused on the ethics of decisions made in the teams, seeking to align performance with the value system seen in the previous session. In the same way, information channels and sources of feedback available to the coach were identified (even if they were contrary to his positions). Group dynamics, self-reflective tasks and role-playing games were used where coaches were proposed to commonly experience ethical conflicts with sports teams. Decisions related to authentic leadership were identified as those which respected the relationship between the personal values of the coach and team groups.

Session 4 (3 h). Self-awareness. This session was directly linked to session 2, establishing the identity of the coaches, thus strengthening their values and principles. Similarly, through research tasks, coaches identified the professional areas in which they were most and least effective. In small groups they worked to expose resources and procedures that would allow them to pinpoint the least effective areas. Finally, through group dynamics, coaches shared program highlights and learning reported (see **Table 1**).

Statistical Analysis

In order to study the program's effectiveness, an ANOVA of repeated measurements was conducted with an intra-subject factor (time of measure: before and after the intervention) and an inter-subject factor (experimental and control groups). *Post-hoc* tests of multiple comparisons with the Bonferroni adjustment were also performed in order to analyze significant interactions. In this way, differences between pre- and post-intervention dependent variables within the experimental and control groups, and differences among the same dependent variables between the experimental and control groups at the time of pre- and post-intervention evaluation could be studied. For all analyses, a significance of 0.05 was established for α.

Finally, it should be mentioned that Omega's alpha was used to evaluate the reliability of the scales used. All analyses were carried out with the SPSS 24.0 statistical package (IBM, Armonk, NY, USA).

RESULTS

Coaches

Below are the most relevant results obtained in relation to each of the variables investigated. To evaluate the effectiveness of the program, a series of repeated measurement ANOVAs were performed with an inter-subject factor (experimental vs. control groups) and an intra-subject factor (period of evaluation).

The interaction period of measurement*group was statistically significant (see **Table 3**) for the variables authentic leadership [Wilks' $\lambda = 0.643$, $F_{(1,22)} = 12.21$, $p = 0.002$, $\eta_p^2 = 0.357$], perceived justice [Wilks' $\lambda = 0.724$, $F_{(1,22)} = 8.39$, $p = 0.008$, $\eta_p^2 = 0.276$], ability to teach and instruct skills to players [Wilks' $\lambda = 0.796$, $F_{(1,23)} = 5.89$, $p = 0.023$,

TABLE 1 | Programming, themes, and contents of the authentic leadership program.

Session/duration	Theme	Content
1/4 h	Relational transparency	Team relationships Communication and listening skills
2/4 h	Internalized morality	Identification of personal and group values Relationship of team identity with group values Awareness and shared responsibility
3/ 4 h	Balanced processing	Ethics of decision-making Relationship between personal and group decisions and values Respect for the values and identity of the team in decision-making
4/3 h	Self-awareness	Personal effectiveness analysis Resources for managing effectivity and learning reported

$\eta^2_p = 0.204$], general self-efficacy [Wilks' $\lambda = 0.747$, $F_{(1,22)} = 7.45$, $p = 0.012$, $\eta^2_p = 0.253$] and collective efficacy [Wilks' $\lambda = 0.773$, $F_{(1,23)} = 6.74$, $p = 0.016$, $\eta^2_p = 0.227$].

To interpret these interactions, a series of *post-hoc* tests of multiple comparisons with the Bonferroni adjustment was performed, revealing a significant increase in the levels of authentic leadership ($p = 0.008$), perceived justice ($p = 0.004$), general self-efficacy ($p = 0.005$) and collective efficacy ($p = 0.002$) after the intervention in the experimental group, while no change was found in the control group in these variables. In fact, a significant decrease in this group was observed in the case of authentic leadership ($p = 0.048$). A statistical trend was also found of a marked increase in the ability to teach and instruct skills to players in the post-intervention evaluation in the experimental group ($p = 0.061$), while no variation was observed in the control group.

The interaction period of measurement*group was not statistically significant for the coach's overall competence variable although a clear statistical trend was observed [$F_{(1,23)} = 4.00$, $p = 0.057$, $\eta^2_p = 0.148$]. When a series of *post-hoc* tests was carried out in accordance with Bonferroni's adjustment, a significant increase in the coaches' competence levels was observed within the experimental group ($p = 0.007$), with no change observed in respect to the control group (see **Table 2**, and **Figure 1**).

In addition, no major effect was identified for the period of measurement, however, there was a significant effect for the cluster related to competence to motivate [$F_{(1,23)} = 5.03$, $p = 0.035$, $\eta^2_p = 0.180$] and that of perceived justice [$F_{(1,22)} = 6.07$, $p = 0.022$, $\eta^2_p = 0.216$]. In both cases, the control group (motivational competence: $M = 3.87$; perceived justice: $M = 5.75$) scored higher than the experimental group (motivational competence: $M = 3.32$; perceived justice: $M = 5.28$).

Players

The most relevant results obtained in relation to each of the variables investigated appear below. To evaluate the effectiveness of the program, a series of repeated measurement ANOVAs was performed with an inter-subject factor (experimental vs. control group) and an intra-subject factor (period of evaluation).

The interaction period of measurement* group was statistically significant (see **Table 3**) for the variables: coach's overall competence [Wilks' $\lambda = 0.949$, $F_{(1,80)} = 9.58$, $p = 0.002$, $\eta^2_p = 0.051$], coach's ability to motivate [Wilks' $\lambda = 0.960$, $F_{(1,80)} = 7.43$, $p = 0.007$, $\eta^2_p = 0.040$], decision-making ability [Wilks' $\lambda = 0.975$, $F_{(1,80)} = 4.55$, $p = 0.034$, $\eta^2_p = 0.025$] and ability to positively influence the player's attitude [Wilks' $\lambda = 0.965$, $F_{(1,80)} = 6.48$, $p = 0.012$, $\eta^2_p = 0.035$].

To interpret these significant interactions, a series of *post-hoc* tests of multiple comparisons was carried out in accordance with the Bonferroni adjustment. First, a significant increase in the coach's decision-making ability ($p = 0.027$) was found in the experimental group, while no change was observed in the control group. A significant decrease in the coach's overall competence ($p = 0.007$), the coach's ability to motivate ($p = 0.012$) and to positively influence the player's attitude ($p = 0.023$) was observed in the control group after the intervention, while the experimental group maintained the same levels as prior to the intervention.

The interaction period of measurement* group was not statistically significant for authentic leadership, although a clear statistical trend was observed [$F_{(1,180)} = 3.68$, $p = 0.057$, $\eta^2_p = 0.020$]. The multiple comparison tests post Bonferroni adjustment only detected a statistical trend indicating a decrease in the control group between before and after the intervention ($p = 0.079$), while the experimental group remained the same.

Finally, it is noteworthy that no major effect was identified for the group except in the case of the period of measurement relating to the need for autonomy [$F_{(1,180)} = 5.78$, $p = 0.017$, $\eta^2_p = 0.031$] and competence [$F_{(1,180)} = 4.07$, $p = 0.045$, $\eta^2_p = 0.022$]. In both cases, higher levels were obtained after the intervention (autonomy: $M = 3.51$; competence: $M = 4.17$) compared to before (autonomy: $M = 3.36$; competence: $M = 4.09$) (see **Table 3**, and **Figure 2**).

TABLE 2 | Means and standard deviations of the coaches in the experimental and control groups before and after the intervention, and interaction time of measure*group.

	Before		After		Interactions		Significant interactions	
	Exp. group *M* (*SD*)	Control group *M* (*SD*)	Exp. group *M* (*SD*)	Control group *M* (*SD*)	Time of measure*group *p*	η_p^2	Exp. group	Control group
Authentic leadership	5.21 (0.66)	6.05 (0.34)	5.71 (0.71)	5.63 (0.60)	0.002	0.357	B < A	B > A
Perceived justice	5.02 (0.61)	5.85 (0.31)	5.53 (0.59)	5.65 (0.57)	0.008	0.276	B < A	B = A
Total competence	3.31 (0.48)	3.80 (0.82)	3.65 (0.44)	3.77 (0.51)	0.057	0.148	B < A	B = A
C. Motivation	3.13 (0.65)	3.80 (0.59)	3.51 (0.71)	3.93 (0.70)	0.340	0.040		
C. Decision-making	3.20 (0.54)	3.50 (0.59)	3.42 (0.53)	3.57 (0.58)	0.413	0.029		
C. Teach and instruct	3.30 (0.64)	3.82 (0.31)	3.62 (0.64)	3.52 (0.45)	0.023	0.204	B < A	B = A
C. Character influence	3.53 (0.74)	4.10 (0.38)	4.08 (0.71)	4.16 (0.65)	0.230	0.062		
Self-efficacy	2.77 (0.34)	3.07 (0.39)	3.10 (0.39)	2.95 (0.50)	0.012	0.253	B < A	B = A
Collective efficacy	3.16 (0.42)	3.55 (0.55)	3.60 (0.52)	3.40 (0.44)	0.016	0.227	B < A	B = A

B, Before; A, After.

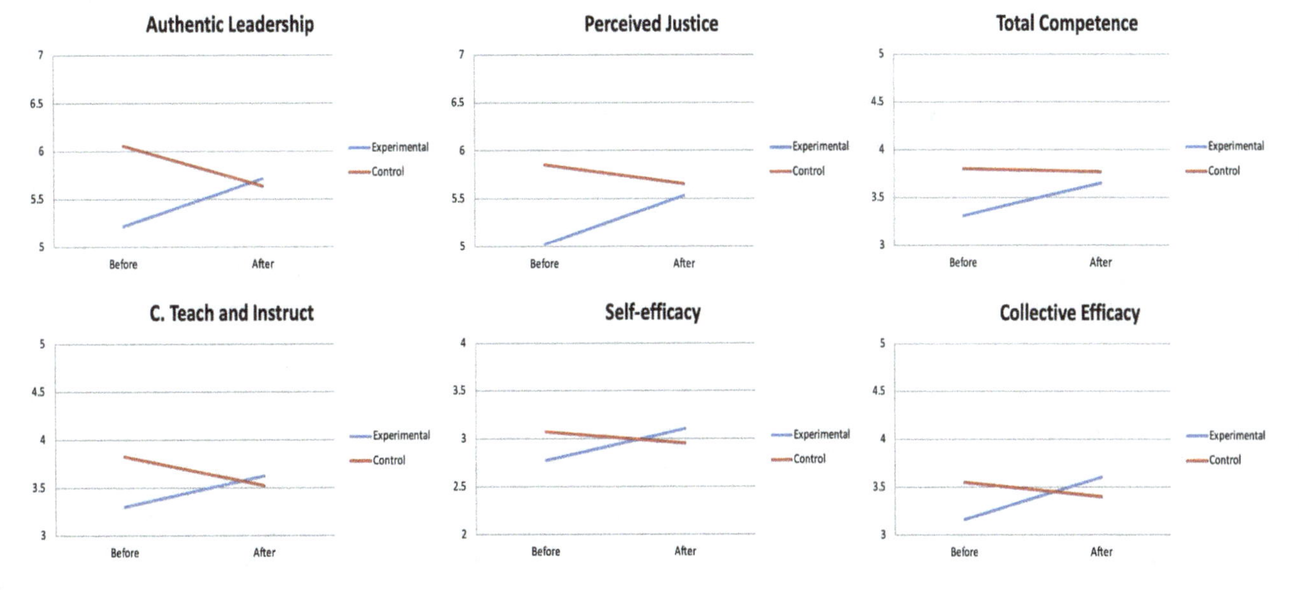

FIGURE 1 | Significant interactions between the time of measure (before vs. after the intervention) and the group (experimental vs. control) for the coaches.

DISCUSSION

Coaches

As results obtained show, the coaches' perception of their own authentic leadership increased significantly for the experimental group, taking into account the before and after measurement period. In the control group, however, self-perception of their own authentic leadership showed a significant decrease. According to the results found in the two groups of coach, the training program had a positive effect on the perception of their leadership style in the experimental group. Results similar to other training programs related to authentic leadership developed in non-sports contexts (Baron, 2012; Fusco et al., 2016; Frasier, 2019).

Paying attention to the relational transparency dimension and the contents developed within the program, it could be considered that communication has an influence on the development of this dimension. Cranmer et al. (2020) relates the coach‘s communication skills to team cohesion and in turn, various studies (Houchin, 2011; González-Ponce, 2018) have revealed positive and significant relationships between authentic leadership and cohesion.

Regarding the development of the internalized moral dimension, role-playing games and reflective tasks that included ethical questioning were used in order to achieve a shared identity that is reflecting the ability of sports leaders to mobilize the efforts of athletes (Slater et al., 2019). The coach's self-perception following the analysis of information related to decision-making and balanced processing could be affected by the contents developed in the authentic leadership program. Since the coach's competence is one of the most determining variables in the performance of sports teams (Myers et al., 2011), it seems

TABLE 3 | Means and standard deviations of the players in the experimental and control groups before and after the intervention and interactions between time of measure*group.

	Before		After		Interactions		Significant interactions	
	Exp. group *M* (*SD*)	Control group *M* (*SD*)	Exp. group *M* (*SD*)	Control group *M* (*SD*)	Time of measure*group *p*	η_p^2	Exp. group	Control group
Authentic leadership	5.35 (0.95)	5.43 (1.02)	5.42 (0.83)	5.27 (0.90)	0.057	0	B = A	B > A
Perceived justice	5.50 (0.83)	5.31 (1.04)	5.42 (0.84)	5.22 (0.94)	0.909	0		
Total competence	3.81 (0.59)	3.93 (0.55)	3.88 (0.56)	3.79 (0.60)	0.002	0.051	B = A	B > A
C. Motivation	3.86 (0.74)	4.02 (0.60)	3.94 (0.66)	3.83 (0.65)	0.007	0	B = A	B > A
C. Decision-making	3.52 (0.54)	3.64 (0.59)	3.66 (0.53)	3.57 (0.58)	0.034	0.025	B < A	B = A
C. Teach and instruct	3.87 (0.69)	3.99 (0.66)	3.85 (0.65)	3.83 (0.68)	0.130	0.013		
C. Character Influence	4.08 (0.68)	4.13 (0.70)	4.16 (0.60)	3.96 (0.70)	0.012	0.035	B = A	B > A
Collective efficacy	3.80 (0.66)	3.69 (0.61)	3.81 (0.69)	3.82 (0.50)	0.179	0.010		
Satisfaction with the coach	4.25 (0.61)	4.16 (0.77)	4.32 (0.65)	4.12 (0.89)	0.286	0.006		
PNS autonomy	3.38 (0.73)	3.33 (0.89)	3.53 (0.79)	3.48 (0.77)	0.995	0		
PNS Competence	4.18 (0.55)	4.15 (0.73)	4.12 (0.64)	4.06 (0.64)	0.786	0		
PNS relatedness	4.25 (0.60)	4.21 (0.69)	4.25 (0.59)	4.19 (0.67)	0.891	0		

B, Before; A, After.

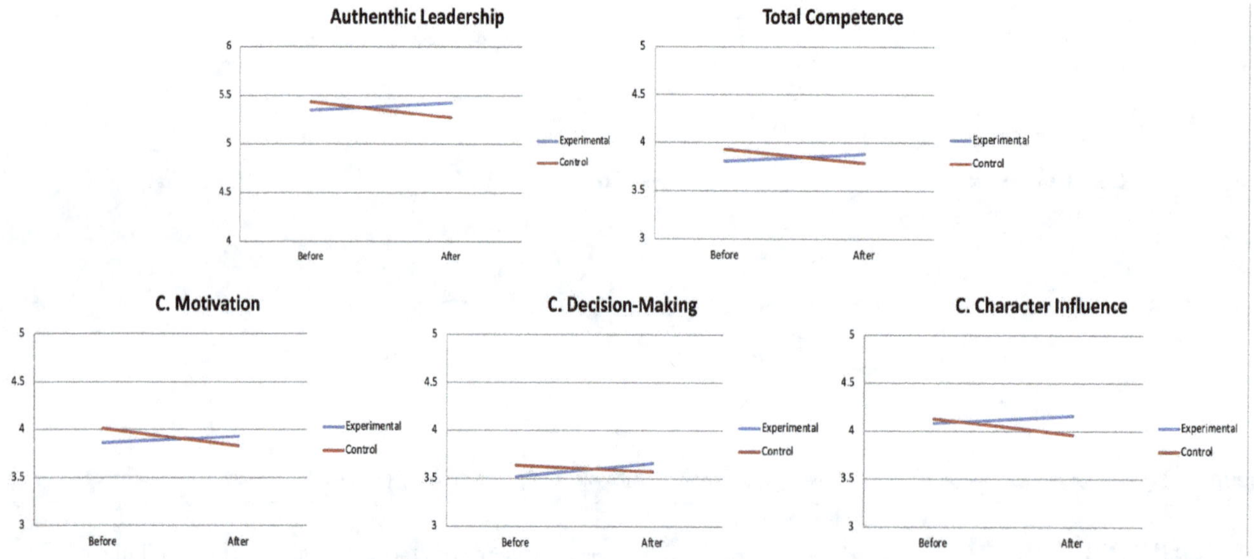

FIGURE 2 | Significant interactions between the time of measure (before vs. after the intervention) and the group (experimental vs. control) for the players.

essential to acquire and develop the coach's self-reflection on their abilities, thus allowing them to evaluate their impact on others.

The significant increase in the perception of authentic leadership of the coach could have effects on the well-being of the coach. A study by Weiss et al. (2018) concluded that that mediated by a reduction in mental exhaustion, authentic leadership lessens the stress of leaders and increases work commitment. In addition, the timing of the training program's administration coincided with the final phase of the season where coaches are subjected to greater pressure in relation to the achievement of objectives, it could be considered that the program could positively affect well-being from the coach. From the perspective of the positive effects that authentic leadership to athletes, Bandura and Kavussanu (2018) conclude in the need to find ways encouraging coaches to adopt authentic leadership. Therefore, it could be considered that a program like the one developed in this study it could be one of those paths.

Other studies in which a leadership skills training program was carried out have evidenced coaches' greater perception of their leadership style and the variables that make it up

(Newin et al., 2008; Vella and Perlman, 2014). With regard to the results obtained concerning the coach's perception of the justice that he/she promotes within the team, the results were significant for the experimental group when taking before and after measurements into account; post-training values being statistically significant. In the control group, no change was observed in terms of the perception of justice being promoted by the coaches. As with other research, coaches felt more confident in their ability to convey the decisions they made (Newin et al., 2008). In different contexts a connection has been made with organizational justice promoted as an important factor in determining leadership style (Gillet et al., 2013). Specifically, authentic leadership has been associated with organizational justice within the business environment (García-Guiu et al., 2015). In the realm of sports, Jowett (2005, 2009) relates a style of leadership and justice promoted by coaches to foster closeness, which includes emotional ties between the coach and his athletes, could facilitate a greater degree of commitment by both parties.

The results obtained after the training program oriented toward authentic leadership meant that the coaches' self-perception of competence, were significant for the experimental group, considering whether the measurement was taken before or after, with higher values obtained after having participated in the training program. No variation, meanwhile, was found for the control group and these results coincide with previous research (Conde et al., 2010; Soriano et al., 2014). When analyzing the subscales into which the questionnaire was divided, it was discovered that the interaction period of measurement* group was significant for the subscale "teaching and instructing skills." For the remaining subscales: "competence to motivate," "competence to make decisions," and "capacity to influence attitude," the interaction period of measurement/group was not significant. The post-training increase occurring solely in the aforementioned subscale ("teaching and instructing skills") may be due to the implementation of the training program on the part of the coaches, and the orientation of these acquisitions toward more procedural aspects that are related to their background (Mesquita et al., 2011b). In this sense, it seems that their assessment of the program has resulted in a stronger appreciation of their own competence in relation to procedural and technical issues. In line with other studies that administered a program with comparable objectives (Smith et al., 2007; Newin et al., 2008), the coaches gained greater confidence with respect to their own competence.

The results obtained for the coaches' self-efficacy were statistically significant for the experimental group when taking into account whether the data was coming from the first or second measurement period. In the control group, no significant modifications were detected regarding perceived self-efficacy between the two sets of data. We believe that the authentic leadership training program modulated the results obtained by the coaches with respect to the perception of their overall self-efficacy. On the other hand, it stands to reason that coaches' perception of self-efficacy may be influenced by their level of training, academic education, or coaching experience (Mesquita et al., 2011a). In this regard, we believe that the program may have generated an increase in coaches' perceived ability to solve problems within their domain. Bandura (2001) emphasizes that the convictions people use to achieve success better predict the perception of their self-efficacy beliefs. In this line, it stands to reason that coaches with higher levels of overall self-efficacy develop more favorable beliefs about their ability to solve problems. In view of the findings, we believe that the contents developed in the authentic training program could have positively influenced the enhanced self-efficacy of the coach. In our work, and also in other studies with similar characteristics (Lee et al., 2002), the training program increased perceived level of general self-efficacy.

The training program oriented toward authentic leadership in terms of the collective efficacy that coaches perceived within their teams indicated a significant increase among coaches who received the authentic leadership program. Collective efficacy is one of the greatest predictors of performance (Feltz and Lirgg, 1998), and in this sense, other studies have linked task-centered and less ego-driven behaviors to higher collective efficacy environments (Damato et al., 2011). In other words, the substantial shift in the values obtained with regard to collective efficacy leads us to believe that the authentic training program implemented alters the coaches' priorities by concentrating their efforts more closely on the task rather than the result. The perception of high collective efficacy is positively related to other relevant variables in team sports performance.

Players

The results obtained with respect to the players' perception of their coach's authentic leadership were not significant for the experimental group. In the control group, a statistical trend was observed which marked a significant decrease in the players' perception of their coach's authentic leadership. It is striking to find the same result among the players in the control group as among their coaches. Both perceived a decrease in the authentic leadership that was developed. It is possible that the incidents that took place within the teams between the two data collection sessions, specifically in this final stretch of the season where relationships tend to deteriorate (García-Calvo et al., 2014b; González-Ponce, 2018), may have generated these results.

Regarding the level of competence that players perceived in their coaches, the results show a significant decrease in the perception of competence in the control group, both in the overall competence, and in two of the subscales of the questionnaire (competence to motivate and competence to influence attitude). For the experimental group, on the other hand, it was found that after the authentic leadership program the players felt that their coaches were more competent in making decisions. It was observed that the authentic training program not only generated an increase in the coaches' perception of self-competence, but that the players under their charge also identified an increase in the coaches' competence (in the subscale decision-making competence). Other studies that administered a leadership program have also found that players reported an improvement in their perception of their coach's competence after he or she had undergone training (Smith et al., 2007; Newin et al., 2008; Urra, 2018). The results in the two groups are therefore noteworthy, given that while the players in the experimental group perceived an increase in the decision-making competence of their coaches, the players in the control group showed a significant decrease in the perception of their coach's competence when he or she had not undergone training.

In terms of perceived justice as reported by the players, the results obtained show no difference between the two periods of measurement in either group. While the coaches in the experimental group perceive themselves to exhibit higher levels of justice, their players do not report the same perception. Regarding collective efficacy perceived by players, the results obtained did not show differences in either group, although other studies in which coaches were trained (Voight and Callaghan, 2001) did in fact reveal an increase in the efficacy perceived by athletes on collective performance.

To conclude, both hypotheses were partially confirmed. In addition, the authentic sports leadership training program had a remarkable effect not only on the coaches, but, for the different variables studied, that effect extended to their players as well.

These findings may have important practical implications. First, this study could be used to guide the organisms in charge of coach training to include leadership as a key aspect. Second, the results of this research should be taken into account by the head coaches of team sports. Likewise, sports clubs and associations could invest more in training programs aimed at developing authentic leadership among coaches as the positive effects involve not only the coaches but also their players. At last, authentic leadership training programs could help coaches and their assistant teams identify possible areas for improvement in their training and development as sports technicians.

Limitations of the Study and Future Research

The sample size regarding coaches was small due to its having been selected from the National Degree of Higher Sports Technicians Schools with the highest level of training in both sports modalities. This helped to make a good selection of reputable coaches. A low power analysis sensitivity was found, but it did not impede that all the interactions time of measure*group showed significant, except for three subdimensions of the competence scale but not for the total score. Also, there was not a follow-up evaluation of the intervention. Future studies should address whether these results hold 6 months, or a year, after the conclusion of the intervention. Finally, the evaluation of the program was carried out exclusively through the application of questionnaires. Future studies of a qualitative nature could study the reasons why this program has been effective. It will also relevant to test the contents and number of sessions necessary for an effective intervention.

CONCLUSIONS

The coach's self-perception of authentic leadership, perceived justice, competence, self-efficacy, and collective efficacy is favorably influenced by the training program. The players also perceive their coach as more competent after the training course. A 15-h intervention program was quite effective with such a short duration. This study highlights the benefit of authentic leadership training in sports coaches.

ETHICS STATEMENT

Ethical approval was not provided for this study on human participants because it fulfilled all the precepts of the Declaration of Helsinki. The participants and their tutors were informed. Written informed consent to participate in this study was provided by the participants' legal guardian/next of kin.

AUTHOR CONTRIBUTIONS

DS: conceptualization, methodology, investigation, resources, data curation, writing—original draft, supervision, and project administration. JG: conceptualization, methodology, software, investigation, resources, writing—original draft, and project administration. RC: methodology, software, formal analysis, writing—original draft, and visualization. MS: investigation, writing—review and editing, and visualization. All authors contributed to the article and approved the submitted version.

REFERENCES

Adie, J. W., Duda, J. L., and Ntoumanis, N. (2012). Perceived coach-autonomy support, basic need satisfaction and the well-and ill-being of elite youth soccer players: A longitudinal investigation. *Psychol. Sport Exerc.* 13, 51–59. doi: 10.1016/j.psychsport.2011.07.008

Avolio, B. J., and Gardner, W. L. (2005). Authentic leadership development: getting to the root of positive forms of leadership. *Leadership Q.* 16, 315–338. doi: 10.1016/j.leaqua.2005.03.001

Baessler, J., and Schwarzer, R. (1996). Evaluación de la autoeficacia: Adaptación española de la escala de Autoeficacia General. *Ansiedad y Estrés* 2, 1–8.

Balaguer, I., González, L., Fabra, P., Castilla, I., Mercé, J., and Duda, J. L. (2012). Coaches' interpersonal style, basic psychological needs and the well and ill-being of young soccer players. A longitudinal analysis. *J. Sports Sci.* 30, 1619–1629. doi: 10.1080/02640414.2012.731517

Bandura, A. (2001). *Guia para La construcción de Escalas de Autoeficacia.* Argentina: Universidad Nacional de Córdoba.

Bandura, C. T., and Kavussanu, M. (2018). Authentic leadership in sport: Its relationship with athletes' enjoyment and commitment and the mediating role of autonomy and trust. *Int. J. Sports Sci. Coaching* 13, 968–977. doi: 10.1177/1747954118768242

Bandura, C. T., Kavussanu, M., and Ong, C. W. (2019). Authentic leadership and task cohesion: The mediating role of trust and team sacrifice. *Group Dyn.* 23, 185–194. doi: 10.1037/gdn0000105

Baron, L. (2012). "Developing authentic leadership through experiential training: an empirical study," in *Academy of Management Proceedings* (Briarcliff Manor, NY). doi: 10.5465/AMBPP.2012.2

Caza, A., Bagozzi, R. P., Woolley, L., Levy, L., and Caza, B. B. (2010). Psychological capital and authentic leadership. *Asia-Pacific J. Business Administ.* 2, 53–70. doi: 10.1108/17574321011028972

Chelladurai, P. (1978). *A contingency model of leadership in athletics.* Tesis Doctoral. University of Waterloo, Ontario, Canada.

Chelladurai, P. (1990). Leadership in sports: a review. *Int. J. SportPsychol.* 21, 328–354.

Chelladurai, P. (2007). "Leadership in sports," in *Handbook of Sport Psychology*, eds G. Tenenbaum and R. C. Eklund (New York, NY: EE.UU: Wiley).

Colquitt, J. A. (2001). On the dimensionality of organizational justice. A construct validation of the measure. *J. Appl. Psychol.* 83, 386–400. doi: 10.1037//0021-9010.86.3.386

Conde, C., Almagro, B. J., Sáenz-López, P., Domínguez, A., and Moreno, J. A. (2010). Evaluación e influencia de un programa de formación orientado a la mejora del clima motivacional transmitido por entrenadores de baloncesto. *Motricidad Eur. J. Human Move.* 25, 165–182.

Cranmer, G., Ash, E., Fontana, J. L., and Mikkilineni, S. D. (2020). Communication for the win: task benefits of coach confirmation in collegiate athletics. *Commun. Q.* 68, 539–559. doi: 10.1080/01463373.2020.1850491

Damato, G., Heard, P., Grove, J. R., and Eklund, R. C. (2011). Multivariate relationships among efficacy, cohesion, self talk and motivational climate in elite sport. *Pamukkale J. Sport Sci.* 2, 6–26.

Din, C., and Paskevich, D. (2013). An integrated research model of Olympic podium performance. *Int. J. Sports Sci. Coach.* 8, 431–444. doi: 10.1260/1747-9541.8.2.431

Duda, J. L. (2013). The conceptual and empirical foundations of Empowering Coaching^{TM}: Setting the stage for the PAPA project. *Int. J. Sport Exerc. Psychol.* 11, 311–318. doi: 10.1080/1612197X.2013.839414

Epitropaki, O., Kark, R., Mainemelis, C., and Lord, R. G. (2017). Leadership and followership identity processes: A multilevel review. *The Leadership Quarterly*, 28, 104–129.

Feltz, D. L., and Lirgg, C. D. (1998). Perceived team and player efficacy in hockey. *J. Appl. Psychol.* 83, 557–564. doi: 10.1037/0021-9010.83.4.557

Frasier, N. (2019). Preparing nurse managers for authentic leadership: A pilot leadership development program. *J. Nurs. Admin.* 49, 79–85. doi: 10.1097/NNA.0000000000000714

Fusco, T., O'Riordan, S., and Palmer, S. (2016). Assessing the efficacy of authentic leadership group-coaching. *Int. Coach. Psychol. Rev.* 11, 118–128.

Gadermann, A. M., Guhn, M., and Zumbo, D. (2012). Estimating ordinal reliability for Likert-type and ordinal item response data: A conceptual, empirical, and practical guide. *Pract. Assess. Res. Eval.* 17, 1–13. doi: 10.7275/n560-j767

Gamarra, M. P., and Girotto, M. (2021). Ethical behavior in leadership: A bibliometric review of the last three decades. *Ethics Behav.* 1–23. doi: 10.1080/10508422.2020.1863799

García-Calvo, T., Leo, F. M., Gonzalez-Ponce, I., Sánchez-Miguel, P. A., Mouratidis, A., and Ntoumanis, N. (2014b). Perceived coach created and peer-created motivational climates and their associations with team cohesion and athlete satisfaction: Evidence from a longitudinal study. *J. Sports Sci.* 32, 1738–1750. doi: 10.1080/02640414.2014.918641

García-Calvo, T., Leon, F. M., and González-Ponce, I. (2014a). Propiedades psicométricas de la escala de justicia percibida en el contexto deportivo. in *IX Congreso Iberomareicano.* Ordem dos Psicólogos Portugueses. Lisbon, Portugal.

García-Guiu, C., Molero, F., and Moriano, J. A. (2015). Authentic leadership and its influence on group cohesion and organizational identification: The role of organizational justice as a mediating variable. *Rev. Psicol. Soc.* 30, 60–88. doi: 10.1080/02134748.2014.987539

Gardner, W. L., Avolio, B., Luthans, F., May, D., and Walumbwa, F. (2005a). Can you see the real me? A self-based model of authentic leader and follower development. *Leadership Q.* 16, 343–372. doi: 10.1016/j.leaqua.2005.03.003

Gardner, W. L., Avolio, B. J., and Walumbwa, F. O. (2005b). *Authentic Leadership Development: Emergent Trends and Future Directions. Authentic Leadership Theory Practice: Origins, Effects and Development.* Amsterdam: Elsevier.

Gatling, A., and Harrah, W. F. (2014). The authentic leadership qualities of business coaches and its impact on coaching performance. *Int. J. Evid. Based Coach. Mentor.* 12, 27–46. doi: 10.3316/informit.781812024191760

George, B. (2015). *Authentic Leadership: Rediscovering.* Harvard Business School. Working Knowledge.

Gillet, N., Fouquereau, E., Bonnaud-Antignac, A., Mokounkolo, R., and Colombat, P. (2013). The mediating role of organizational justice in the relationship between transformational leadership and nurses' quality of work life: A cross-sectional questionnaire survey. *Int. J. Nurs. Stud.* 50, 1359–1367. doi: 10.1016/j.ijnurstu.2012.12.012

González-Ponce, I. (2018). *¿Es importante que es un entrenador sea competente y justo? Evidencias empíricas en equipos de alto rendimiento.* Tesis Doctoral. Universidad de Extremadura. Cáceres. España.

González-Ponce, I., Jiménez, R., Leo, F. M., Pulido, J. J., Chamorro, J. M., and García-Calvo, T. (2015). *En Relación entre lo justo que es el entrenador y la satisfacción de los jugadores. Validación del cuestionario de* satisfacción con el entrenador. En II Congreso Internacional de Optimización del entrenamiento y readaptación físico-deportiva. Sevilla. España.

González-Ponce, I., Jiménez, R., Leo, F. M., Sánchez-Oliva, D., Pulido, J. J., and García-Calvo, T. (2017). Validación al castellano de la escala sobre competencia del entrenador. *Rev. Psicol. Deporte* 26, 95–103. doi: 10.1037/t65985-000

Houchin, G. (2011). *Authentic Leadership in Sports Teams.* The University of Tennessee at Chattanooga. ProQuest Dissertations and Theses.

Jowett, S. (2005). "On repairing and enhancing the coach-athlete relationship," in *The Psychology of Coaching,* eds S. Jowett and M. Jones (Leicester, Reino Unido: The British Psychological Society, Sport and Exercise Psychology Division).

Jowett, S. (2009). Validating coach-athlete relationship measures with the nomological network. *Measure. Phys. Educ. Exerc. Sci.* 13, 34–51. doi: 10.1080/10913670802609136

Kaptein, M. (2019). The moral entrepreneur: A new component of ethical leadership. *J. Business Ethics* 156, 1135–1150. doi: 10.1007/s10551-017-3641-0

Lee, K. S., Malete, L., and Feltz, D. L. (2002). The effect of a coaching education program on coaching efficacy. *Int. J. Appl. Sport Sci.* 14, 55–67. doi: 10.1123/tsp.14.4.410

Leo, F. M., García-Calvo, T., Parejo, I., Sánchez-Miguel, P. A., and Sánchez-Oliva, D. (2010). Interacción de la cohesión en la eficacia percibida, las expectativas de éxito y el rendimiento en equipos de baloncesto. *Rev. Psico. Deporte,* 19, 89–102.

May, D., Chan, A., Hodges, T., and Avolio, B. (2003). Developing the moral component of authentic leadership. *Organ. Dyn.* 32, 247–260. doi: 10.1016/S0090-2616(03)00032-9

McDowell, J., Huang, Y., and Caza, A. (2018). Does identity matter? An investigation of the effects of authentic leadership on student-athletes' psychological capital and engagement. *J. Sport Manage.* 32, 227–242. doi: 10.1123/jsm.2017-0241

Mesquita, I., Borges, M., Rosado, A., and Batista, P. (2011a). Self-efficacy, perceived training needs and coaching competences: The case of Portuguese handball. *Eur. J. Sport Sci.* 12, 168–178. doi: 10.1080/17461391.2010.551413

Mesquita, I., Borges, M., Rosado, A., and Souza, A. (2011b). Handball coaches' perceptions about the value of working competences according to their coaching background. *J. Sport Sci. Med.* 10, 193–202.

Moriano, J. A., Molero, F., and Lévi, J. P. (2011). Liderazgo auténtico. Concepto y validación del cuestionario ALQ en España. *Psicothema* 23, 336–341.

Myers, N. D., Beauchamp, M. R., and Chase, M. A. (2011). Coaching competency and satisfaction with the coach: A multi-level structural equation model. *J. Sports Sci.* 29, 411–422. doi: 10.1080/02640414.2010.538710

Myers, N. D., Chase, M. A., Beauchamp, M. R., and Jackson, B. (2010). Athletes' perceptions of coaching competency scale II-high school teams. *Educ. Psychol. Meas.* 70, 477–494. doi: 10.1177/0013164409344520

Newin, J., Bloom, G. A., and Loughead, T. M. (2008). Youth ice hockey coaches' perceptions of a team-building intervention program. *Sport Psychol.* 22, 54–72. doi: 10.1123/tsp.22.1.54

Northouse, P. G. (2018). *Leadership: Theory and practice.* Thousand Oaks, CA: Sage publications.

Sánchez-Oliva, D., Leo, F. M., Amado, D., Cuevas, R., and García-Calvo, T. (2013). Desarrollo y validación del cuestionario de apoyo a las necesidades psicológicas básicas en educación física. *Eur. J. Human Move.* 30, 53–71.

Sanjuán, P., Pérez, A. M., and Bermúdez, J. (2000). Escala de autoeficacia general: datos psicométricos de la adaptación para población española. *Psicothema* 12, 509–513.

Slater, M. J., Coffee, P., Barker, J. B., Haslam, S. A., and Steffens, N. K. (2019). Shared social identity content is the basis for leaders' mobilization of followers. *Psychol. Sport Exerc.* 43, 271–278. doi: 10.1016/j.psychsport.2019.03.012

Smith, R. E., Smoll, F. L., and Cumming, S. P. (2007). Effects of a motivational climate intervention for coaches on children's sport performance anxiety. *J. Sport Exerc. Psychol.* 29, 39–59. doi: 10.1123/jsep.29.1.39

Smith, R. E., Smoll, F. L., and Curtis, B. (1979). Coach effectiveness training: A cognitive-behavioral approach to enhancing relationship skills in youth sport coaches. *J. Sport Psychol.* 1, 59–75. doi: 10.1123/jsp.1.1.59

Smoll, F. L., and Smith, R. E. (1989). Leadership behaviors in sport: A theoretical model and research paradigm. *J. Appl. Soc. Psychol.* 19, 1522–1551. doi: 10.1111/j.1559-1816.1989.tb01462.x

Smoll, F. L., and Smith, R. E. (2009). *Mastery Approach to Coaching: A Leadership Guide for 24 Youth Sports.* Washington, DC: Authors.

Smoll, F. L., and Smith, R. E. (2010). "Conducting psychologically oriented coach training programs: a social-cognitive approach," in *Applied Sport Psychology: Personal Growth to Peak Performance, 6th Edn.*, ed J. M. Williams (Boston, MA), 392–416.

Smoll, F. L., Smith, R. E., Curtis, B., and Hunt, E. (1978). Toward a meditational model of coach-player relationships. *Res. Q.* 49, 528–541. doi: 10.1080/10671315.1978.10615567

Soriano, G., Ramis, Y., Cruz, J., and Sousa, C. (2014). Un programa de intervención individualizado con entrenadores de fútbol. *Cuadernos Psicol. Deporte* 14, 99–106.

Sousa, C., Smith, R. E., and Cruz, J. (2008). An individualized behavioral goal-setting program for coaches. *J. Clin. Sport Psychol.* 2, 258–277. doi: 10.1123/jcsp.2.3.258

Steffens, N. K., Mols, F., Haslam, A., and Okimoto, T. G. (2016). True to what We stand for: Champions collective interest as a path authentic leadership. *Leadership Q.* 27, 726–744. doi: 10.1016/j.leaqua.2016.04.004

Urra, B. A. (2018). Asesoramiento psicológico a entrenadores en liderazgo deportivo: un estudio de caso. *Rev. Psicol. Deporte* 27, 43–50.

Vella, S. A., Oades, L. G., and Crowe, T. P. (2012). Validation of the differentiated transformational leadership inventory as a measure of coach leadership in youth soccer. *Sport Psychol.* 26, 203–224. doi: 10.1123/tsp.26.2.207

Vella, S. A., Oades, L. G., and Crowe, T. P. (2013). A pilot transformational leadership training program for sports coaches: Impact on the developmental experiences of adolescent athletes. *Int. J. Sports Sci. Coach.* 8, 513–530. doi: 10.1260/1747-9541.8.3.513

Vella, S. A., and Perlman, D. J. (2014). Mastery, autonomy and transformational approaches to coaching: Common features and applications. *Int. Sport Coach. J.* 1, 173–179. doi: 10.1123/iscj.2013-0020

Voight, M., and Callaghan, J. (2001). A team-building intervention program: Application and evaluation with two university soccer teams. *J. Sport Behav.* 24, 420–431.

Walumbwa, F. O., Avolio, B. J., Gardner, W. L., Wernsing, T. S., and Peterson, S. J. (2008). Authentic leadership: Development and validation of a theory-based measure. *J. Manage.* 34, 89–126. doi: 10.1177/0149206307308913

Weiss, M., Razinskas, S., Backmann, J., and Hoegl, M. (2018). Authentic leadership and leaders' mental well-being: An experience sampling study. *Leadership Q.* 29, 309–321. doi: 10.1016/j.leaqua.2017.05.007

5

Aggression Dimensions among Athletes Practising Martial Arts and Combat Sports

Karolina Kostorz [1,2*] *and Krzysztof Sas-Nowosielski* [2]

[1] *Department of Theory and Methodology of Physical Education, The Jerzy Kukuczka Academy of Physical Education in Katowice, Katowice, Poland,* [2] *Department of Pedagogy, Psychology and Sociology, The Jerzy Kukuczka Academy of Physical Education in Katowice, Katowice, Poland*

Correspondence:
Karolina Kostorz
karolciakostorz@o2.pl

Purpose: The main aim of the research was to analyse aggression dimensions among athletes practising martial arts and combat sports.

Material and Methods: There were 219 respondents. The Buss and Perry Aggression Questionnaire (BPAQ) in the Polish adaptation by Siekierka was applied.

Results: Martial arts apprentices turned out to present a statistically significantly lower level of hostility ($p < 0.001$) and of the general aggression index ($p = 0.04$) than combat sports athletes. It turned out that lower level of aggression was noted in female participants (physical aggression ($p < 0.001$), verbal aggression ($p = 0.004$), hostility ($p < 0.001$), and the general aggression index ($p < 0.001$). Analysis revealed that the training experience and the training rank did not differentiated the level of the respondents' particular aggression dimensions.

Conclusions: It would be advisable to perform parallel analyses in other areas of Poland and take into account the respondents' education and place of residence.

Keywords: judo, karate, aikido, wrestling, fencing, aggression

INTRODUCTION

Statistics nowadays indicate an increasing number of crimes involving aggression, such as causing damage to health, engaging in a fight or beating, destroying or damaging property, or robbery crimes, i.e., mugging, extortion, or robbery with violence[1]. Aggression escalation also applies to sport, becoming a subject of growing concern among sports philosophers, pedagogues, and psychologists. It results in progressive dehumanisation and devaluation of sport, manifested in violence on sports pitches and stands (Cynarski and Litwiniuk, 2007; Vertonghen and Theeboom, 2010; Chahal and Chaudhary, 2012). It is worrying that aggression, even under the demands of rules and regulations, sometimes becomes the predominant source of players' excitement, pleasure, and satisfaction, or even the key motive for participating in sports (Krishnaveni and Shahin, 2014). Moreover, aggression combined with the desire to win often pushes athletes into breaching the principles of noble competition and makes fair play forgotten (Graczyk et al., 2010; Vertonghen and Theeboom, 2010; Krishnaveni and Shahin, 2014). Transferring the views of Bandura (2001) to the sports context, one could suppose that if athletes' aggressive behaviours are not punished or, worse, become rewarded (resulting in scoring a point, scoring a goal, winning a medal, or preventing the

[1] Available online at: https://statystyka.policja.pl/st/informacje/57720,Przestepczoscmlodych-ludzi-zwiazana-z-agresja.html

rival from doing so), they will be frequently observed during competitions (Bukowska et al., 2012; Chahal and Chaudhary, 2012). Bukowska et al. (2012) indicate that taking up physical activity can become a way to "clear oneself" of aggression in a socially accepted way. On the other hand, it can reinforce the tendency to react with more aggression in everyday life and strengthen the character traits that are useful in sports competition, but not necessarily in social life, such as bravery or obstinacy (Szmajke and Doliński, 1991; Vertonghen and Theeboom, 2010; Tomczak, 2013). The research conducted so far to investigate this problem has not yielded clear results. In view of the above, it is important to carry out further detailed studies.

It should be emphasised that in its majority, aggression observed in athletes' actions is instrumental in nature: the aim is to achieve non-aggressive benefits by means of aggressive behaviours (Mroczkowska et al., 2008; Klimczak et al., 2014; Martinkova and Parry, 2016). In sport, manifestations of uncontrolled aggression are undesirable for two reasons. They provide young people with negative behavioural patterns, at the same time distorting the image of sport (Mroczkowska et al., 2008), as well as increase the risk of a career-ending injury (Pedersen, 2007). In the case of combat sports, considering the propensity for violent behaviours is not only of cognitive significance because of the dangers associated with the athletes' extensive skills and strength, which can be employed outside the sports arena to use violence, engage in fights, and commit various crimes (Reynes and Lorant, 2001, 2002a,b, 2004; Graczyk et al., 2010; Klimczak et al., 2014; Martinkova and Parry, 2016; Harwood et al., 2017).

The awareness of the factors mentioned above, the inconsistencies in the results of previous studies, were inspirations to conduct our own investigations. There is no doubt that the goals, tasks, and other aspects related to sports competition and recreational practise of traditional martial arts are divergent (Figueiredo, 2009; Martinkova and Parry, 2016), so it was deemed reasonable to analyse aggression dimensions among people practising martial arts and combat sports.

THE PURPOSE OF THE STUDY

The objective of the study was to determine whether there exists a difference with regard to aggression dimensions between respondents and the normative value (Tucholska, 1998), as well as between combat sports fighters and athletes practising martial arts and with the consideration of the training period and degree, and the respondents' gender.

The following research questions were submitted:

1. Is there a statistically significant difference in aggression dimensions between respondents and the normative value developed by Tucholska (1998)?
2. Is there a statistically significant difference in aggression dimensions between athletes practising martial arts and combat sports?
3. Do the factors of gender, training experience, and training rank determine the results of the studied variables, i.e., physical aggression, verbal aggression, angry, hostility and the general aggression index?

Due to the exploratory nature of the research, it was decided to abandon the research hypotheses.

It was expected that the analyses would significantly broaden the scope of the existing knowledge on the subject, thus allowing to obtain important results, especially in the field of humanities, i.e., psychology, sociology, pedagogy, and ethics. Besides, many authors (Tiric-Campara et al., 2012; Kuśnierz and Bartik, 2014; Martinkova and Parry, 2016; Harwood et al., 2017; Basiaga-Pasternak et al., 2020) indicate the scarcity of publications on martial arts and combat sports. It should also be added that the issue of aggression has been extremely rarely raised, especially in the last decade. Undoubtedly, all the above aspects also became an inspiration to perform own analysis.

MATERIALS AND METHODS

Participants and Procedure

The research was performed between March 2017 and November 2017 in sports clubs and sections of martial arts (Pszczynska Martial Art, capoeira, and aikido) and combat sports (judo, wrestling, fencing, taekwondo, and Kyokushin karate) in the Silesia Province in Poland. Nonprobability consecutive sampling was applied in the analyses. After obtaining permissions and support from the club or organisation representatives, researcher approached athletes. Researcher invited potential participants and presented the study aims and conditions. Informed consents were obtained. Those who agreed to participate in the study got the questionnaire with a request to fill it. The respondents were of both genders, at least 15 years old; they had been training martial arts or combat sports for at least 1 year. All individuals submitted a written consent to voluntarily participate in the research. In the case of minors, the consent was obtained from the parents or legal guardians. Over 550 questionnaires were distributed, 243 were collected back. However, some questionnaires were not filled in completely, and these were excluded from consideration. Owing to the above mentioned inclusion criteria and conditions, and lack of complete documentation, results obtained from 219 respondents underwent final analysis. Out of the participants, 113 (51.60%) practised martial arts and 106 (48.40%) were combat sports athletes. Women ($n = 101$) constituted 46.12% of the study group. Their mean age equalled 23.61 years ($SD = 4.83$). Men ($n = 118$) constituted 53.88% of the study group, with the mean age of 24.31 years ($SD = 5.91$). In the analyses, the respondents were divided into two groups depending on training experience: those who had been training for less (107 people) and for more than 5 years (112 athletes). The study also involved analyses depending on the participants' training rank. It was assumed that a high rank meant having at least 3 kyu (3 kup for taekwondo practitioners), and a white and orange colour for capoeira practitioners. In the case of martial arts styles whose representatives took part in the research, this rank is achieved, on average, by individuals after 2.5–3.5 years of regular training. The trainees have high technical skills; they are involved by instructors in conducting parts of the classes, e.g., warm-ups, stretching, etc., and also act as assistants. For combat sports such as fencing and wrestling, the rank of a player was determined by the coach prior to the respondent's completing the questionnaire. The coaches were acquainted with the criteria applied in sporting level assessment, i.e., scores of the official ranking list and the sporting classes awarded for strictly defined achievements. In the statistical analyses, "high rank" referred to respondents who obtained very good (medal zone) or good (places 4–15) sports results in their age categories and achieved a regular increase in their sporting level. These competitors are already included in a specialised training phase. With these criteria, eventually, 94 subjects, including 43 combat sports athletes, had a low rank, and 125 individuals, including 62 martial arts practitioners, had a high rank.

The consent for conducting the research was obtained from the Bioethical Committee of the Academy of Physical Education in Katowice.

Instruments

The diagnostic poll method with the questionnaire technique served to fulfil the assumed aims. A standardised research tool was applied. Aggression was assessed with the Buss-Perry Aggression Questionnaire (BPAQ) (Buss and Perry, 1992) in the version developed by the Amity Institute in Warsaw, Poland (Siekierka, 2005). The tool contains 29 statements designed to evaluate four dispositional components of aggression: physical aggression (e.g., I have threatened people I know.), verbal aggression (e.g., My friends say that I'm somewhat argumentative.), anger (e.g., Some of my friends think I am a hothead.), and hostility (e.g., Other people always seem to get the breaks.). The results for these subscales total the general aggression index of an individual. The task of the respondent was to rank the particular statements using a five-point Likert scale, where 1 meant "does not match my personality at all" and five stood for "fully matches my personality." The questionnaire is characterised by a clear theoretical model and satisfactory psychometric properties (Archer, 2004; Siekierka, 2005; Aranowska and Rytel, 2012). In the study conducted in Poland by Aranowska and Rytel (2012) exploratory and confirmatory models were evaluated among a sample of 3,990 Polish participants (aged from 10 to 79 years). A five-factor structure resulted in the exploratory analysis and five-factor structure showed acceptable fits in confirmatory analyses (with the Cronbach's α ranging from 0.60 for angry to 0.87 for general aggression index).) Measures used to assess the fit of the model to the data took acceptable values, i.e., Root Mean Square Error of Approximation—RMSEA = 0.06; Comparative Fit Index—CFI = 0.86, Normed Fit Index—NFI = 0.85 (Aranowska and Rytel, 2012). Aranowska and Rytel (2012) showed appropriate to high reliabilities for all scales, i.e., Cronbach's α was 0.85 for physical aggression, 0.72 for verbal aggression, 0.83 for angry, 0.77 for hostility, and 0.89 for whole items. In own research, it was obtained indicators of the questionnaire reliability with the Cronbach's α ranging from 0.75 for physical aggression to 0.81 for verbal aggression (**Table 1**). So, it turned out that all scales had satisfactory reliability (John and Benet-Martines, 2000).

The tool also included information for the participants describing the aim and subject of the research, as well as a list of demographic questions, which allowed to obtain data on the respondents' age, gender, training experience, and rank.

Statistical Analysis

The basic analysis of the data employed descriptive statistics for the whole sample, for the groups of martial arts practitioners and combat sports athletes, as well as for the population stratified by gender, training experience, and training rank. The mean (*M*), standard deviation (*SD*), median (*Me*), mode (*Mo*), coefficient of variation (*V*), and skewness (*As*) were calculated. Kurtosis (*Ku*) was used to measure concentration in the study. The distribution was tested for normality with the Shapiro-Wilk W test. Levene's test served to assess the equality of variances. The nature of the variable distributions, Levene's test results, and the sample size ($n = 219$) allowed the use of parametric tests to verify the significance of differences between the tested variables (significance tests for differences in independent samples). The significance level was assumed at $p < 0.05$. In order to compare the levels of the aggression dimensions among the practitioners of martial arts and combat sports with the normative value developed by Tucholska (1998), a significance test called 'Difference between Two Means' was applied, available in the Statistica software. The effect size (*ES*) was calculated (Cohen's *d*) not only whenever statistically significant differences between the examined variables were revealed. It was assumed to be small for values ranging 0.2–0.49, moderate for values ranging 0.5–0.79, and large for $ES > 0.79$ (Rodriguez, 2007).

Based on the data available on the website of the Central Statistical Office in 2018[2], it was assumed that about 101,774 people practise martial arts or combat sports in Poland.

[2]Available online at: https://stat.gov.pl/files/gfx/portalinformacyjny/pl/defaultaktualnosci/5495/13/2/1/kultura_fizyczna_w_polsce_w_2018.pdf

TABLE 1 | Skewness, kurtosis and Cronbach's alpha values.

Studied variable	*As*	*Me*	*Mo*	*V*	*Ku*	*Cronbach's alpha*
Anger	0.17	19.00	19.00	4.71	0.67	0.77
Physical aggression	−0.08	21.00	21.00	9.58	−1.11	0.75
Hostility	−0.60	22.00	23.00	7.65	0.57	0.76
Verbal aggression	0.42	15.00	15.00	5.58	1.04	0.81
General aggression index	−0.22	77.00	78.00	4.88	−1.16	0.79

Source: the authors' own research.

Therefore, it has been calculated[3] that 383 is the minimum recommended size for the own study. At the same time, it turned out that for the sample of 219 respondents, the margin of error was 6.62%. It should be added that in the case of 219 people participating in the own research, the confidence level above 86% was obtained.

The analyses were performed with Microsoft Office Excel 2010 and StatSoft Statistica v. 12.

RESULTS

The study revealed cases of asymmetric (skewed) distributions. However, all variables fell within the range of <-1, 1>, both for the whole sample and irrespective of the type of physical activity undertaken by the respondent, their gender, training experience, and training rank. Thus, it was assumed that the distribution of the studied variable was moderately asymmetric. The kurtosis (*Ku*) for all variables in each group fell within the <-2, 2> range, indicating that the concentration around the mean value was satisfactory (**Table 1**).

In the second step of the analysis, the results of the respondents were compared with the normative value developed by Tucholska (1998) (**Table 2**).

[3] Available online at: http://www.raosoft.com/samplesize.html

A statistically significantly lower level of hostility, and, in the case of the female gender, also of the general aggression index ($p = 0.05$ in one-tailed test; $ES = 0.23$), was observed among women ($p = 0.002$ in one-tailed test; $p = 0.004$ in two-tailed test; $ES = 0.52$ and among men ($p = 0.02$ in one-tailed test; $p = 0.04$ in two-tailed test; $ES = 0.30$) training martial arts and combat sports.

The following analyses considered the type of the undertaken physical activity (**Table 3**).

Martial arts apprentices turned out to present a statistically significantly lower level of hostility ($p < 0.001$; $ES = 0.49$) and of the general aggression index ($p = 0.04$; $ES = 0.28$) than combat sports athletes.

It was very important to implement analyses with the consideration of the respondents' gender (**Table 4**).

It turned out that only the level of anger ($p = 0.75$) did not differentiate women and men. In the remaining cases, a lower level of aggression was noted in female participants. What draws attention is the effect size, which was large with regard to physical aggression ($ES = 0.91$; $p < 0.001$), small in the case of verbal aggression ($ES = 0.40$; $p = 0.004$), and moderate for hostility ($ES = 0.66$; $p < 0.001$) and the general aggression index ($ES = 0.66$; $p < 0.001$).

To answer the question whether the level of aggression dimensions depended on the respondents' training experience or

TABLE 2 | Comparison of the level of aggression dimensions between the respondents' results and the normative value.

Gender	Studied variable	Martial arts and combat sports practitioners		Normative value		*p*-value		Effect size
		M	*SD*	*M*	*SD*	One-tailed test	Two-tailed test	
Women	Anger	19.07	4.05	19.2	4.9	0.42	0.84	0.03
	Physical aggression	18.72	4.26	18.9	5.7	0.40	0.80	0.04
	Hostility	19.52	4.15	21.8	4.7	0.002	0.004	0.52
	Verbal aggression	14.06	2.90	14.5	2.9	0.14	0.29	0.15
	General aggression index	71.38	11.66	74.3	13.4	0.05	0.10	0.23
Men	Anger	19.24	3.78	19.1	4.6	0.41	0.81	0.03
	Physical aggression	22.62	4.29	22.9	6.4	0.35	0.71	0.05
	Hostility	22.25	4.15	23.6	5.1	0.02	0.04	0.30
	Verbal aggression	15.10	2.38	15.7	3.0	0.06	0.11	0.23
	General aggression index	79.20	11.86	81.4	14.8	0.12	0.24	0.17

Source: the authors' own research, with reference to Tucholska (1998).

TABLE 3 | Comparison of the level of aggression dimensions between martial arts and combat sports athletes.

Studied variable	Martial arts		Combat sports		*t*	*df*	*p*-value	Effect size
	M	*SD*	*M*	*SD*				
Anger	19.09	3.87	19.24	3.95	0.28	217	0.78	0.04
Physical aggression	20.38	4.71	21.29	4.65	1.44	217	0.15	0.20
Hostility	19.99	4.28	22.06	4.22	3.60	217	< 0.001	0.49
Verbal aggression	14.45	2.67	14.80	2.69	0.97	217	0.33	0.13
General aggression index	73.91	12.63	77.39	11.95	2.09	217	0.04	0.28

Source: the authors' own research.

training rank, a significance test for differences in independent samples was applied (**Tables 5, 6**).

The presented data imply that neither the training experience nor the training rank differentiated the level of the respondents' particular aggression dimensions.

DISCUSSION

It turned out that in comparison with the normative value developed by Tucholska (1998), a statistically significantly lower level of hostility, and, in the case of the female gender, also of the general aggression index, was observed among women and among men training martial arts and combat sports. The obtained results of own analyses are in line with other authors' outcomes (Wojdat et al., 2017a), who also noticed that regardless of the respondents' gender, the hostility in athletes was lower as compared with the average for the Polish population. Furthermore, a lower level of hostility to the environment was observed in karate, aikido, and taekwondo practitioners (Graczyk et al., 2010). In the same research, only boxers did not reveal a favourable effect of sport on this aggression dimension. These findings corroborate the earlier views of Graczyk (1994). It is worth emphasising that a lower level of hostility is beneficial for health, as confirmed by the research conducted in Finland by Sawicki et al. (2015). It turned out that the sense of hostility was associated with an increased risk of myocardial infarction and stroke, as well as the development of atherosclerotic diseases and diabetes. Additionally, people with high levels of this aggression dimension receive much less social support and face more negative attitudes in their working environment, which contributes to experiencing even more grief, uncertainty, injustice, and suspiciousness. The lower values of this aggression dimension determined both in the presented research and in reports by other authors (Wojdat et al., 2017a) indicate that practising combat sports, mainly traditional martial arts, can satisfy the need for belonging to a social group and contribute to

TABLE 4 | Comparison of the level of aggression dimensions between women and men.

Studied variable	Women		Men		*t*	*df*	*p*-value	Effect size
	M	*SD*	*M*	*SD*				
Anger	19.07	4.05	19.24	3.78	−0.32	217	0.75	0.04
Physical aggression	18.72	4.26	22.62	4.29	−6.72	217	< 0.001	0.91
Hostility	19.52	4.15	22.25	4.15	−4.83	217	< 0.001	0.66
Verbal aggression	14.06	2.90	15.10	2.38	−2.92	217	0.004	0.40
General aggression index	71.38	11.66	79.20	11.86	−4.91	217	< 0.001	0.66

Source: the authors' own research.

TABLE 5 | The level of aggression dimensions depending on the training experience.

Studied variable	> 5 years of experience		<5 years of experience		*t*	*df*	*p*-value	Effect size
	M	*SD*	*M*	*SD*				
Anger	19.10	3.92	19.22	3.90	−0.24	217	0.81	0.03
Physical aggression	21.38	4.74	20.24	4.58	1.79	217	0.07	0.25
Hostility	21.44	4.29	20.52	4.40	1.56	217	0.12	0.21
Verbal aggression	14.92	2.73	14.31	2.60	1.70	217	0.09	0.23
General aggression index	76.83	12.55	74.30	12.12	1.52	217	0.13	0.21

Source: the authors' own research.

TABLE 6 | The level of aggression dimensions depending on the training rank.

Studied variable	High rank		Low rank		*t*	*df*	*p*-value	Effect size
	M	*SD*	*M*	*SD*				
Anger	19.47	3.82	18.74	3.95	−1.37	217	0.17	0.19
Physical aggression	21.27	4.48	20.22	4.81	−1.64	217	0.10	0.23
Hostility	21.45	4.45	20.38	4.25	−1.80	217	0.07	0.25
Verbal aggression	14.61	2.75	14.64	2.64	0.08	217	0.93	0.01
General aggression index	76.80	11.53	73.99	12.89	−1.67	217	0.10	0.23

Source: the authors' own research.

the feeling of confidence about the environment and to showing a friendly attitude to others, mutual cordiality, and kindness. Supinski (1991), after: Tomczak (2013) observed that karate and judo athletes, as well as boxers presented a statistically significantly lower level of aggression than female students of one of the secondary schools in Wrocław. Furthermore, Daniluk et al. (2004) found that national team judo athletes demonstrated low and moderate degrees of aggression as compared with the general population. Budnik (2004) revealed that karate practitioners were characterised by lower aggression intensity than students. In addition, Kuśnierz and Bartik (2014) proved that the practise of combat sports has a favourable impact on fighters; even though ju-jitsu fighters achieved the highest level of physical and verbal aggressions in groups under research, the general level of their aggression was lower than in the case of non-training persons. Mroczkowska et al. (2008) also noticed that in the case of wrestlers, judo athletes, and traditional karate practitioners, the general aggression index was far below the maximum outcome. It should be mentioned, too, that Wojdat et al. (2017a) observed a statistically significant relationship between education and a decrease in general aggression among judo athletes, regardless of gender, with a high determination indicator value. In the control group, this correlation was not implied (Wojdat et al., 2017b).

On the other hand, Szmajke and Doliński (1991) mention the results of studies showing that young people who train 'high contact' sports present a larger tendency toward aggressive behaviours, both in sport and in everyday life, than individuals with no such experience. Jasiński et al. (2002) also noticed that the level of anxiety and aggression was statistically significantly higher in training youth than among young people who had never practised hand-to-hand combat. Other authors also observed that contact sports fighters are more aggressive than contestants in non-contact sports (Chahal and Chaudhary, 2012; Kumar, 2015; Rui and Cruz, 2017). The results of own analyses are also not in line with research conducted by Tomczak (2013). He observed that women and men who practised wrestling or fencing, as well as female judo competitors achieved lower levels of aggression compared with the normative value. In the same study, karate competitors and foil fencers obtained results similar to those of the standardisation group respondents. Tomczak (2013) proved that on exceeding certain values, aggression may even interfere with effective functioning. The author noted negative correlations between physical aggression and the frequency of manifesting the style of planned actions both in judo competitors and in female foil fencers, the style of various actions in female foil fencers, and the effectiveness of sports action in male foil fencers. Tomczak (2013) also indicated that respondents with a higher level of hostility manifested a less diverse style than athletes with a lower average score in this variable. According to Tomczak (2013), a lower level of aggression has more significance in very precise disciplines, such as foil fencing, where special control is required. Furthermore, Wrześniewski (2015) revealed that taekwondo practitioners obtained higher levels of all aggression dimensions than the control group, consisting of physical education and physiotherapy students.

Own research showed that martial arts apprentices presented a lower level of hostility and of the general aggression index than combat sports athletes. Moreover, considering gender and type of the undertaken physical activity, it also turned out that both women and men practising combat sports obtained higher levels of hostility than martial arts respondents. Szmajke and Urbanowicz (2012) indicate that the tendency toward competition is not an inherent trait of human nature but a very strong instinct and that the necessity to engage in competition leads to negative social consequences. According to Aronson (1995), rivalry is not only among the main causes of inter-group prejudices and hostility, of a decline in openness and trust in relationships, but also constitutes a factor strengthening these phenomena. It is pointed out that the very expectation of competition usually leads to attributing negative features, reprehensible motives for action, and biassed judgments to the opponent (Doliński and Szmajke, 1991; Szmajke and Urbanowicz, 2012). What is more, undertaking physical activity, as mentioned in the introduction, can reinforce the tendency to react with more aggression and fury in everyday life (Szmajke and Doliński, 1991). Thus, exercise can strengthen the character traits that are useful in sports fight, but not necessarily in social life. One might suppose that socialisation of anxiety and aggression behaviours based on rigid rules and principles of martial arts statistically significantly decreases their incidence in athletes. These views have been confirmed in publications by many authors (Jasiński et al., 2000; Lu, 2008; Mroczkowska et al., 2008; Krishnaveni and Shahin, 2014; Harwood et al., 2017). Kubacka-Jasiecka and Wrześniewski (2012) claim that although athletes practising martial arts for recreational purposes or participating in combat sports competitions have to self-induce a certain degree of aggression, they do not differ in this respect from individuals engaged in other sports disciplines or physical activities. These authors found average levels of aggression among aikido, karate, judo, taekwondo, and Krav Maga practitioners. Basiaga-Pasternak et al. (2020) proved that competitive and non-competitive combat sports athletes had similar level of all types of aggression. The obtained own results are in line with a study carried out by Budnik (2005), who observed a larger tendency to manifest aggression in sports karate competitors than in respondents practising the traditional form of this discipline. Mroczkowska et al. (2008) also indicated that the general aggression index was statistically significantly lower in people practising traditional karate than in judo athletes and wrestlers. It is worth adding that higher sociability, impulsiveness, and hostile aggression were observed among female basketball players than in female taekwondo practitioners (Litwiniuk and Daniluk, 2009). One should also refer to a study by Graczyk et al. (2010), who found a higher average level of emotional self-aggression in boxers and aikido competitors than in karate and taekwondo athletes. They noted the biggest mean indices of physical self-aggression, hostility to the environment, unconscious aggressive inclinations, as well as displaced and indirect aggression among boxers. These results are very close to those obtained in a prior research performed by Graczyk (1994). Besides, Mazur and Organista (2015) showed that women practising kickboxing and wrestling achieved statistically significantly higher levels of physical aggressiveness than female respondents practising artistic gymnastics and synchronised swimming. The same research revealed that the difference in the total aggression index remained at the trend level, although it should be mentioned that women practising kickboxing and wrestling were slightly more aggressive again. The authors also noted that female wrestling competitors were characterised by a statistically significantly higher average level of suspiciousness and the feeling of guilt than women practising kickboxing. In addition, Vertonghen et al. (2014) found higher levels of physical aggression among kickboxing and Thai boxing athletes as compared with people practising judo, aikido, and karate. In turn, Kuśnierz et al. (2014) did not observe statistically significant differences in physical aggression among capoeira practitioners, boxers, and ju-jitsu competitors. It is worth emphasising that the lowest score was shown in respondents training capoeira, and the biggest average referred to both boxers and the control group, which consisted of high school and physical education students. The authors indicate that contemporary boxers are more prone to aggressive behaviours than previous generations undertaking this type of physical activity. Kuśnierz et al. (2014) proved that the highest mean value for verbal aggression was obtained by non-training respondents, and the lowest by capoeira practitioners. The highest level of anger was noted in the control group, and the lowest in ju-jitsu athletes. In turn, the highest level of hostility was found in the control group and boxers, and the lowest in ju-jitsu competitors. The biggest mean general aggression index was reported for the control group, and the smallest in ju-jitsu athletes. A study carried out by Piepiora et al. (2016) is also worth mentioning. The authors observed that practising different styles of karate, with different rules of kumite, did not differentiate competing athletes in terms of aggressiveness. They noticed that karate practitioners fighting in the semi-contact system (Shotokan karate) presented substantially lower levels of the general aggression index, physical and verbal aggression, and suspiciousness than other competitors in kumite systems. Karate athletes competing in mixed fighting (Shidokan karate) were characterised by significantly higher levels of physical aggression and irritability than those engaged in less violent forms of kumite. Knockdown karate (Kyokushin karate) practitioners tended to have significantly higher overall levels of aggression, both physical and verbal, and suspiciousness than representatives of the semi- contact system (Shotokan karate). Mixed fighting (Shidokan karate) athletes turned out significantly less physically aggressive and irritable than full contact (Oyama karate) fighters and relatively more negative and resentful than those competing in knockdown (Kyokushin karate). It should be emphasised that all the results for competitors and students are presented as average indicators of aggression.

As expected, the own analyses revealed that only the level of anger did not differentiate women and men. In the remaining cases, a lower level of aggression was noted in female participants. What draws attention is the effect size, which was large with regard to physical aggression, small in the case of verbal aggression, and moderate for hostility and the general aggression index. In turn, Wojdat et al. (2017a) noted that among judo athletes, women obtained a statistically significantly lower average only with reference to physical aggression as compared with men. There is no doubt that aggression, especially physical aggression, is one of the functional dimensions for which differences between women and men are indisputable and have been regularly reported in the literature since the 1820s (Hyde, 2005; Rytel, 2011). The observed differences can be explained by biological, social, and evolutionary factors. They can result from the processes of learning aggression; according to the social role theory, gender differences are insignificant in early childhood but they become gradually intensified during childhood as a consequence of the gender role learning process (Rytel, 2011). In addition, as implied by the sexual selection theory, rooted in sociobiology and evolutionary psychology (Rytel, 2011), differences in the level of aggression should emerge early in ontogenesis and reach their highest values in young adults (aged 20–30 years), i.e., at the peak of the reproductive capacity (Archer, 2004, 2009). With reference to the former theory, the higher level of physical aggression in men than in women is associated with the requirements of the social role, while in the case of the latter, it results from the competition in the access to female partners, entailing the need to apply more risky strategies to guarantee a reproductive success. Both theories additionally assume that there are larger differences between males and females in physical than in verbal aggression (Rytel, 2011). The results of our own analyses related to verbal aggression can also be explained by referring to study by Rytel (2011). These authors indicate that for women, the language of conversation is primarily a means to communicate, build relationships, and create bonds. For men, in turn, talking is a way to remain independent and to gain and maintain position in the hierarchical social order. Our results are in line with research performed by Buss and Perry (1992), as well as with the meta-analysis conducted by Archer (2004), which revealed that most studies did not report statistically significant inter-gender differences in the anger variable. Exceptions included a study carried out in England in which a higher average value was observed in women, and an Australian one that revealed an escalation in the aggression dimension among men. It should be noted that Archer (2004) did not provide results concerning the level of hostility. The results of own research do not corroborate the studies in which no statistically significant differences were found between women and men for the aggression dimension (Nakano, 2001; Gerevich et al., 2007). The results of own research are partly in line with a study conducted by Rytel (2011).

Taking into account training experience, own results do not coincide with the outcomes obtained by other authors. Kurpel et al. (2005) observed that in wrestlers, aggression decreased with an increase of competition experience. According to Wrześniewski (2015), practising taekwondo reduces aggressive tendencies, but only after several years of training. Drumińska et al. (2016) revealed a trend toward lower general aggression with increasing training experience in children aged 12–15 years practising judo, taekwondo, and karate. However, in taekwondo athletes, positive correlations were observed between training experience and all aggressive tendencies except physical aggression (Zalech, 2002), and the strongest relationship was demonstrated in the case of verbal aggression. Budnik (2004) noted that karate practitioners with longer training experience were characterised by a higher level of indirect aggression and suspiciousness than athletes with a shorter sporting career. Basiaga-Pasternak et al. (2020) noticed that despite the lack of statistical significance it was noted that the level of almost all types of aggression was higher in the amateurs than in the professionals. It is worth referring to a study performed by Wojdat et al. (2017a), who found a statistically significant relationship between the general aggression index and training experience among judo practitioners. However, it turned out that this correlation was negative in women and positive in men. It is suggested that an increase in the aggression level among athletes with longer training experience can result from frustration caused by lack of sports successes.

Regardless of gender, the own analyses revealed that neither the training period nor the training rank differentiated the level of the respondents' particular aggression dimensions. The obtained results are not in line with studies by other authors, who noted, for example, that practising judo decreased or did not influence the level of aggression (Lamarre and Nosanchuk, 1999; Nosanchuk and Lamarre, 2002). In turn, Reynes and Lorant (2001, 2002a,b); Reynes and Lorant (2004) observed an increase in aggression during judo training and its decrease as a result of karate training. According to these authors, practising combat sports can have a beneficial effect on aggression dimensions, but this can be demonstrated only after a longer period of training; in 10–12-year-old boys, 1 year's training did not yield the desired results (Reynes and Lorant, 2002a,b). Ziaee et al. (2012) implied that karate training had a positive impact on controlling aggression among adolescents, but no such influence was found in respondents practising judo. Attention should also be paid to the worrying results of a study by Rotter et al. (2015), in which a statistically significantly higher mean value for physical aggression was obtained among young people practising sports 3–4 times a week than in their less physically active peers. Among judo and wrestling competitors, a higher level of aggression was observed in athletes from the national team as compared with individuals at a lower training level (Zyto-Sitkiewicz, 1986), which is not in line with research carried out by Skelton et al. (1991), or Daniels and Thornton (1992). It has been indicated that sport engages people with a higher tendency toward physical aggression, and this aggression can only be alleviated with a strong sporting commitment (Reynes and Lorant, 2002a,b; Wojdat et al., 2017b).

On the basis of the results obtained in our own analyses and the research of other authors, it can be stated that aggressive behaviour can be changed, modified, and relieved, but also accumulated through physical activity (Mroczkowska et al., 2008; Vertonghen and Theeboom, 2010; Tiric-Campara et al., 2012; Kuśnierz et al., 2014; Martinkova and Parry, 2016; Harwood et al., 2017). So, these findings provide an important basis to understand personality differences in aggressive-related variables, e.g., assess competitive state anxiety, the level of emotional intelligence, temperamental characteristics.

CONCLUSIONS

Our research allows us to formulate the following conclusions:

1. As compared with the normative value (Tucholska, 1998), both women and men training martial arts and combat sports presented lower levels of hostility; in the case of females, this also applied to the general aggression index.
2. Lower values for hostility and the general aggression index were noted among those practising martial arts than in combat sports athletes.
3. Women demonstrated lower levels of all aggression dimensions, with the exception of anger, for which the difference turned out statistically insignificant.
4. The duration and level of training did not determine the degree of aggression in the respondents.

On the basis of the results obtained in our own analyses it can be stated that regular and with full commitment training combat sports and especially martial arts supervised by a trainer who pays attention to educational aspects and compliance with the rules can become a method of reducing the level of hostility. Martial arts with a centuries-long tradition are regarded in social opinions as a carrier of many desired, moral values and function as an education system for children and young people, not only in Eastern societies. On the basis of the own study, it should be noticed that it is worth introducing elements of martial arts into school physical education and as part of organised physical activity in free time.

It should also be noted that the levels of particular aggression dimensions are not constant, but characterised by a certain dynamics and changeability in a lifetime. The consciousness of these phenomena makes one thus approach any results obtained in a given moment with considerable caution. The results cannot be perceived as final conclusions. Also, because of the sample size, the research presented here should constitute, among others, a starting point for further considerations.

Among the possible areas of expanding this research project, performing longitudinal studies with the application of a cross-sectional and sequential analysis design seems justified. They would aim at determining the changes occurring in the motivational processes, the accepted hierarchy of values, as well as aggressive tendencies, e.g., during a 2-years training cycle. Moreover, as the presented research involved only sports clubs and sections of martial arts and combat sports located in the Silesia Province, it would be advisable to perform parallel analyses in other areas of Poland. It seems that taking into account the respondents' education and place of residence (as divided into the city and the country) would contribute to a more expanded analysis. In this way, the exploration of the subject and the study conclusions could become more comprehensive and more valuable.

ETHICS STATEMENT

The studies involving human participants were reviewed and approved by the Bioethics Committee of the Academy of Physical Education in Katowice (KB/04/2017 as of 13 February 2017). Written informed consent to participate in this study was provided by the participants' legal guardian/next of kin.

AUTHOR CONTRIBUTIONS

All authors listed have made a substantial, direct and intellectual contribution to the work, and approved it for publication.

ACKNOWLEDGMENTS

We would like to thank the coaches and the staff of the karate and judo clubs for their help in conducting this research.

REFERENCES

Aranowska, E., and Rytel, J. (2012). Factorial structure of the Buss-Perry Aggression Questionnaire (BPQA) in Polish population. *Stud. Psych. UKSW.* 12, 135–151. Retrieved from: https://czasopisma.uksw.edu.pl/index.php/sp/article/view/2781 (accessed June 25, 2020).

Archer, J. (2004). Sex differences in aggression in real-world setting: a meta-analytic review. *Rev. Gen. Psych.* 8, 291–322. doi: 10.1037/1089-2680.8.4.291

Archer, J. (2009). Does sexual selection explain human sex differences in aggression? *Behav. Brain Sci.* 32, 249–311. doi: 10.1017/S0140525X09990951

Aronson, E. (1995). *Człowiek, istota społeczna.* Warszawa: Wydawnictwo Naukowe PWN.

Bandura, A. (2001). Social cognitive theory: An agentic perspective. *Ann. Rev. Psych.* 52, 1–26. doi: 10.1146/annurev.psych.52.1.1

Basiaga-Pasternak, J., Szafraniec, Ł., Jaworski, J., and Ambrozy, T. (2020). Aggression in competitive and non-competitive combat sports athletes. *Ido Movement for Culture. J. Martial Arts Anthrop.* 20, 17–23. doi: 10.14589/ido.20.2.3

Budnik, D. (2004). "Agresywność karateków," W: *Korelaty psychologiczne aktywności ruchowej i sukcesów w sporcie. Z badań nad osobowościa sportowców i studentów wychowania fizycznego*, red. M. Mikołajczyk (Warszawa: Polskie Towarzystwo Naukowe Kultury Fizycznej), 88–95.

Budnik, D. (2005). "Karate tradycyjne i sportowe a poziom agresywności adeptów," W *Agresja a kultura fizyczna*, red. J. Supiński (Wrocław: Studia i Monografie AWF we Wrocławiu), 123–129, 79.

Bukowska, K., Marks, M., and Rzetelska, K. (2012). Kategoria wiekowa a poziom agresywności zawodników i zawodniczek kadry narodowej w trójboju siłowym. *Rozprawy Naukowe AWF we Wrocławiu.* 37, 71–80. Retrieved from: https://rozprawy.awf.wroc.pl//articles/RN_2012_37_71-80.pdf (accessed June 25, 2020).

Buss, A., and Perry, M. (1992). The Aggression Questionnaire. *J. Personal. Soc. Psych.* 63, 452–459. doi: 10.1037/0022-3514.63.3.452

Chahal, M., and Chaudhary, P. (2012). A comparative study of aggression behaviour and adjustment variables of sports and non-sports persons. *Int. J. Sci. Res.* 3, 1388–1389. Retrieved from: https://www.ijsr.net/archive/v3i9/U0VQMTQ0MzI=.pdf (accessed June 25, 2020).

Cynarski, W. J., and Litwiniuk, A. (2007). Culture of violence on the example of boxing. *Ido - Ruch dla Kultury.* 7, 84–95. Retrieved from: http://imcjournal.com/images/7/7.9.pdf (accessed June 25, 2020).

Daniels, K., and Thornton, E. (1992). Length of training, hostility and the martial arts: a comparison with other sporting groups. *Br. J. Sports Med.* 26, 118–120. doi: 10.1136/bjsm.26.3.118

Daniluk, A., Litwiniuk, A., and Błach, W. (2004). "Wybrane cechy osobowości a poziom agresji u zawodników kadry olimpijskiej judo," W *Korelaty psychologiczne aktywności ruchowej i sukcesów w sporcie. Z badań nad osobowościa sportowców i studentów wychowania fizycznego*, ed M. Mikołajczyk (Warszawa: Polskie Towarzystwo Naukowe Kultury Fizycznej), 64–69.

Doliński, D., and Szmajke, A. (1991). "Psychologiczne reakcje na sytuacje startowa," W *Psychologia i sport*, ed T. Tyszka (Warszawa: Wydawnictwo AWF Warszawa), 113–152.

Drumińska, E., Wojdat, M., Pujszo, M., and Stepniak, R. (2016). Pedagogical and psychological aspects of prevention of agression at school stage. *J. Educ. Health Sport.* 6, 595–606. doi: 10.5281/zenodo.61003

Figueiredo, A. (2009). "The object of study in martial arts and combat sports research - contributions to a complex whole," W *Martial Arts and Combat Sports - Humanistic Outlook*, ed W. J. Cynarski (Rzeszów: Wyd. Uniwersytetu Rzeszowskiego), 20–34.

Gerevich, J., Bácskai, E., and Czobor, P. (2007). The generalizability of the buss-perry aggression questionnaire. *Int. J. Methods Psychiatric Res.* 16, 124–136. doi: 10.1002/mpr.221

Graczyk, M. (1994). "Symptomy patologii zachowania jako efekty uprawiania pieściarstwa," in *Zjawiska patologii społecznej w sporcie*, ed K. Maroszek (Gdańsk: Wydawnictwo Akademii Wychowania Fizycznego), 54–65.

Graczyk, M., Hucinski, T., Norkowski, H., Peczak-Graczyk, A., and Rozanowska, A. (2010). The level of aggression syndrome and a type of practised combat sport. *J. Combat Sports Martial Arts.* 1, 1–14. Retrieved from: http://medsport.pl/wp-content/uploads/file/journal_of_combat/2010_01/111_Graczyk.pdf (accessed June 25, 2020).

Harwood, A., Lavidor, M., and Rassovsky, Y. (2017). Reducing aggression with martial arts: a meta-analysis of child and youth studies. *Aggress. Violent Behav.* 34, 96–101. doi: 10.1016/j.avb.2017.03.001

Hyde, J. S. (2005). The gender similarities hypothesis. *Am. Psych.* 60, 581–592. doi: 10.1037/0003-066X.60.6.581

Jasiński, T., Kalina, R. M., and Zajac, T. (2000). "Porównanie leku i agresywności młodziezy zróznicowanej rodzajem treningu walki wrecz i innymi czynnikami środowiskowymi," W *Wychowawcze i utylitarne aspekty sportów walki*, eds R. R. Kalina and W. Jagiełło (Warszawa: Wydawnictwo AWF Warszawa), 75–80.

Jasiński, T., Kalina, R. M., and Zajac, T. (2002). "Nasilenie leku i agresywności u młodziezy uprawiajacej rózne formy sztuk walki na tle grupy porównawczej," W *Sporty walki w edukacji dzieci i młodziezy. Perspektywa metodyczna*, eds A. Dabrowski, T. Jasiński, and R. M. Kalina (Płock: Wydawnictwo Novum), 171–183.

John, O. P., and Benet-Martines, V. (2000). "Measurement: reliability, construct validation, and scale construction," in *Handbook of Research Methods in Social and Personality Psychology*, eds H. T. Reis and C. M. Judd (New York, NY: Cambridge University Press), 339–369.

Klimczak, J., Podstawski, R., and Dobosz, D. (2014). The association of sport and violence, aggression and aggressiveness - prospects for education about non - aggression and reduction of aggressiveness. *Arch. Budo.* 10, 303–308. Retrieved from: http://files.4medicine.pl/download.php?cfs_id=753 (accessed June 25, 2020).

Krishnaveni, K., and Shahin, A. (2014). Aggression and its influence on sports performance. *Int. J. Phys. Educ. Sports Health.* 1, 29–32. Retrieved from: https://www.kheljournal.com/archives/2014/vol1issue2/PartA/16.1.pdf (accessed June 25, 2020).

Kubacka-Jasiecka, D., and Wrześniewski, K. (2012). "Agresja i lek w sportach walki," W *Optymalizacja treningu sportowego i zdrowotnego z perspektywy psychologii*, eds J. Blecharz, M. Siekańska, and A. Tokarz (Kraków: Akademia Wychowania Fizycznego im. Bronisława Czecha w Krakowie), 205–232.

Kumar, M. (2015). Study of aggressive tendency among the kabaddi and kho-kho players. *Int. J. Sci. Res.* 4, 2597–2598. Retrieved from: http://www.ijsr.net/archive/v4i7/SUB157043.pdf (accessed June 25, 2020).

Kurpel, R., Zurek, P., and Botwina, R. (2005). "Poziom agresywności a osobowościowe i pozaosobowościowe uwarunkowania sukcesu w zapasach," W *Agresja a kultura fizyczna*, ed J. Supiński (Wrocław: Studia i Monografie AWF we Wrocławiu), 49–57, 79.

Kuśnierz, C., and Bartik, P. (2014). The impact of practice of selected combat sports on signs of aggression in players in comparison with their non-training peers. *J. Combat Sports Martial Arts.* 5, 17–22. doi: 10.5604/20815735.1127448

Kuśnierz, C., Cynarski, W. J., and Litwiniuk, A. (2014). Comparison of aggressiveness levels in combat sports and martial arts male athletes to non - practising peers. *Arch. Budo.* 10, 253–260. Retrieved from: http://files.4medicine.pl/download.php?cfs_id=1343 (accessed June 25, 2020).

Lamarre, B. W., and Nosanchuk, T. A. (1999). Judo - the gentle way. A replication of studies on martial arts and aggression. *Percep. Motor Skills* 88, 992–996. doi: 10.2466/pms.1999.88.3.992

Litwiniuk, A., and Daniluk, A. (2009). "Wybrane cechy osobowości kobiet trenujacych koszykówke i taekwon-do WTF," W *Aktywność sportowa kobiet. Uwarunkowania i skutki,* ed Z. Zukowska (Warszawa: Polskie Stowarzyszenie Sportu Kobiet, 56–62.

Lu, C. (2008). Eastern martial arts and violence prevention: Reversing a stereotype. *Arch. Budo.* 4, 32–36. Retrieved from: http://files.4medicine.pl/download.php?cfs_id=1134 (accessed June 25, 2020).

Martinkova, I., and Parry, J. (2016). The paradox of martial arts - safe combat. Ido Movement for Culture. *J. Martial Arts Anthrop.* 16, 4–10. doi: 10.14589%2Fido.16.4.2

Mazur, Z., and Organista, N. (2015). The level of social aggressiveness in women practising male or female sports. *J. Educa. Health Sport.* 5, 151–164. doi: 10.5281/zenodo.17473%0D

Mroczkowska, H., Kownacka, I., and Obmiński, Z. (2008). Study of the indicators of social aggressiveness in competitors practising combat sports. *Polish J. Sport Tour.* 15, 158–165. Retrieved from: https://pjst.awf-bp.edu.pl/download/Pol_J_Sport_Tourism_15_pp158-165.pdf (accessed June 25, 2020).

Nakano, K. (2001). Psychometric evaluation on the Japanese adaptation of the Aggression Questionnaire. *Behav. Res. Ther.* 39, 853–858. doi: 10.1016/S0005-7967(00)00057-7

Nosanchuk, T. A., and Lamarre, B. W. (2002). Judo training and aggression: comment on Reynes and Lorant. *Percept. Motor Skills* 94, 1057–1058. doi: 10.1177/003151250209400302

Pedersen, D. M. (2007). Perceived aggression in sports and its relation to willingness to participate and perceived risk of injury. *Perceptual Motor Skills* 104, 201–211. doi: 10.2466/pms.104.1.201-211

Piepiora, P., Szmajke, A., Migasiewicz, J., and Witkowski, K. (2016). The karate culture and aggressiveness in kumite competitors. Ido Movement for Culture *J. Martial Arts Anthrop.* 16, 41–47. doi: 10.14589%2Fido.16.2.5

Reynes, E., and Lorant, J. (2001). Do competitive martial arts attract aggressive children? *Percept. Motor Skills* 93, 382–386. doi: 10.2466/pms.2001.93.2.382

Reynes, E., and Lorant, J. (2002a). Effect of traditional judo training on aggressiveness among young boys. *Percept. Motor Skills* 94, 21–25. doi: 10.2466/pms.2002.94.1.21

Reynes, E., and Lorant, J. (2002b). Karate and aggressiveness among eight-year-old boys. *Percept. Motor Skills* 94, 1041–1042. doi: 10.2466/pms.2002.94.3.1041

Reynes, E., and Lorant, J. (2004). Competitive martial arts and aggressiveness: a 2-yr. longitudinal study among young boys. *Percept. Motor Skills.* 98, 103–115. doi: 10.2466/pms.98.1.103-115

Rodriguez, W. (2007). "*Effect size*," W *Encyclopedia of Measurement and Statistics*. ed N. J. Salkind (CA: Thousand Oaks), 300-303, 1. Retrieved from: http://arsmath.org/msl/Library/statistics/common/Encyclopedia-of-Measurement-and-Statistics.pdf (accessed November 12, 2017).

Rotter, I., Kotwas, A., Kemicer-Chmielewska, E., and Watral, A. (2015). Physical activity as a factor reducing aggressive behaviour in adolescents in gymnasium school age. *Pomera. J. Life Sci.* 61, 444–447. doi: 10.21164/pomjlifesci.430

Rui, S., and Cruz, J. F. A. (2017). Unveiling anger and aggression in sports: the effects of type of sport, competitive category and success level. *J. Sport Psych* 26, 21–28. Available online at: http://hdl.handle.net/1822/58138

Rytel, J. (2011). Differences in aggression in Polish men and women in different age groups. *Studia Psychol.* 11, 65–80. Retrieved from: https://czasopisma.uksw.edu.pl/index.php/sp/article/view/2752 (accessed June 25, 2020).

Sawicki, A., Atroszko, B., and Atroszko, P. (2015). "Uwarunkowania i potencjalne konsekwencje cynicznej wrogości w perspektywie edukacyjnej," W *Psychospołeczne aspekty zdrowia*, eds A. Nawrocka, F. Makurat, and R. Breska (Gdańsk: Wydawnictwo Athenae Gedanenses), 51–68.

Siekierka, I. (2005). *Kwestionariusz agresji A. Bussa i M. Perry'ego.* Retrieved from: https://amity.pl/wp-content/uploads/2016/11/kwestionariusz_agresji_is-1.pdf (accessed February 04, 2017).

Skelton, D. L., Glynn, M. A., and Berta, S. M. (1991). Aggressive behavior as a function of taekwondo ranking. *Percep. Motor Skills.* 72, 179–182. doi: 10.2466/pms.1991.72.1.179

Supinski, J. (1991). *Agresja w sporcie, jej determinanty i następstwa społeczno-wychowawcze (Ph.D. thesis).* AWF Wrocław, Biblioteka Główna, Wrocław, Poland.

Szmajke, A., and Doliński, D. (1991). "Dwie strony medalu: negatywne i pozytywne psychospołeczne skutki sportu," W *Psychologia i Sport*, ed T. Tyszka (Warszawa: Wydawnictwo AWF Warszawa), 202–228.

Szmajke, A., and Urbanowicz, M. (2012). The expectation of competition as a moderator of perception and judgment of people: different outcomes of engaging in sport and non-sport competitions. *Rozprawy Naukowe AWF we Wrocławiu.* 37, 81–92. Retrieved from: https://rozprawy.awf.wroc.pl/articles/RN_2012_37_81-92.pdf (accessed June 25, 2020).

Tiric-Campara, M., Tupkovic, E., Mazalovic, E., Karalic, E., Biscevic, M., Djelilovic-Vranic, J., et al. (2012). Correlation of aggressiveness and anxiety in fighteeng sports. *Med. Arch.* 66, 116–121. doi: 10.5455/medarh.2012.66.116-121

Tomczak, M. (2013). *Styl rywalizacji a efektywność działania w sportach walki analiza psychologiczna.* Poznań: Wydawnictwo Akademii Wychowania Fizycznego im. Eugeniusza Piaseckiego w Poznaniu.

Tucholska, S. (1998). Pomiar agresji: Kwestionariusz Agresji A. Bussa i M. Perry'ego. *Studia z Psych. Katolickim Uniwersytecie Lubelskim.* 9, 369–378.

Vertonghen, J., and Theeboom, M. (2010). The social-psychological outcomes of martial arts practise among youth: a review. *J. Sports Sci. Med.* 9, 528–537. Retrieved from: https://www.ncbi.nlm.nih.gov/pmc/articles/PMC3761807/pdf/jssm-09-528.pdf (accessed June 25, 2020).

Vertonghen, J., Theeboom, M., and Pieter, W. (2014). Mediating factors in martial arts and combat sports: an analysis of the type of martial art, characteristics, and social background of young participants. *Percep. Motor Skills* 118, 41–61. doi: 10.2466/06.30.PMS.118k14w3

Wojdat, M., Janowska, P., Pujszo, M., and Stepniak, R. (2017a). A comparative analysis of the level of aggression between female and male judokas society. *J. Educ. Health Sport.* 7, 95–106. doi: 10.5281/zenodo.571449

Wojdat, M., Janowska, P., Pujszo, M., Stepniak, R., and Adam, M. (2017b). Psychological analysis of the level of aggression in the male judokas society. *J. Educ. Health Sport* 7, 59–67. doi: 10.5281/zenodo.375658

Wrześniewski, K. (2015). The effect of taekwondo training on the level of aggression. *Studies Sport Human.* 18, 40–46. Retrieved from: https://sporthumanities.pl/resources/html/article/details?id=168508 (accessed June 25, 2020).

Zalech, M. (2002). Poziom agresywności studentów trenujacych taekwondo. *Kultura Fizyczna* 6, 18–22.

Ziaee, V., Lotfian, S., Amini, H., Mansournia, M. A., and Memari, A. H. (2012). Anger in adolescent boy athletes: a comparison among Judo, Karate, Swimming and Non Athletes. *Iran. J. Pediatr.* 22, 9–14.

Zyto-Sitkiewicz, D. (1986). Osobowościowe wyznaczniki sukcesu sportowego (na przykładzie wybranych dyscyplin sportów walki - judo i zapasów). *Roczniki Naukowe AWF w Warszawie.* 29, 129–148.

6

Differences on Prosaccade Task in Skilled and less Skilled Female Adolescent Soccer Players

Junyi Zhou[1,2,3]*

[1]School of Physical Education and Sport Sciences, Fujian Normal University, Fuzhou, China, [2]Provincial University Key Laboratory of Sport and Health Science, Fujian Normal University, Fuzhou, China, [3]Key Laboratory of Kinesiological Evaluation General Administration of Sport of China, Fujian Normal University, Fuzhou, China

***Correspondence:**
Junyi Zhou
jackychou_1225@126.com

Although the relationship between cognitive processes and saccadic eye movements has been outlined, the relationship between specific cognitive processes underlying saccadic eye movements and skill level of soccer players remains unclear. Present study used the prosaccade task as a tool to investigate the difference in saccadic eye movements in skilled and less skilled Chinese female adolescent soccer players. Fifty-six healthy female adolescent soccer players (range: 14–18 years, mean age: 16.5 years) from Fujian Youth Football Training Base (Fujian Province, China) took part in the experiment. In the prosaccade task, participants were instructed to fixate at the cross at the center of the screen as long as the target appeared peripherally. They were told to saccade to the target as quickly and accurately as possible once it appeared. The results indicated that skilled soccer players exhibited shorter saccade latency ($p = 0.031$), decreased variability of saccade latency ($p = 0.013$), and higher spatial accuracy of saccade ($p = 0.032$) than their less skilled counterparts. The shorter saccade latency and decreased variability of saccade latency may imply that the attentional system of skilled soccer player is superior which leads to smaller attention fluctuation and less attentional lapse. Additionally, higher spatial accuracy of saccade may imply potential structural differences in brain underlying saccadic eye movement between skilled and less skilled soccer players. More importantly, the results of the present study demonstrated that soccer players' cognitive capacities vary as a function of their skill levels. The limitations of the present study and future directions of research were discussed.

Keywords: saccadic eye movement, prosaccade task, cognitive processes, adolescent soccer players, skill level

INTRODUCTION

Eye-tracking methods are widely used in various research domains such as psychology, psychiatry, or sport (Duchowski, 2003). They are popular because eye movement measures are easy to obtain and participants can understand eye movement tasks easily (Noiret et al., 2017). More importantly, eye-tracking methods provide unique means to measure cognitive processes (Thomas et al., 2021). Therefore, eye movement experiments are carried out in different populations in various research domains (Noiret et al., 2018).

Saccade is a rapid eye movement we typically make three times every second (Rayner, 1998). Saccadic eye movements can be characterized by several eye movement measures such as saccade latency (i.e., the time elapsed from the onset of the target to the onset of the first saccade after target onset), saccade velocity (i.e., the velocity of saccade), and saccade amplitude (i.e., the spatial distance between two successive fixations). The prosaccade task is a well-known experimental paradigm that is used to examine saccadic eye movements. In a typical prosaccade task, participants are instructed to fix on a central dot. Then, they have to direct their gaze toward a target dot appearing at the periphery as quickly and as accurately as possible. Research has shown that saccadic eye movements are associated with multiple cognitive processes including processing speed, attention, and inhibitory control (Hutton, 2008; Noiret et al., 2017).

For instance, some previous studies have revealed that the saccade latency needed to trigger a prosaccade in prosaccade tasks varies as a function of the attentional process (Clark, 1999; Pratt et al., 2006; Noiret et al., 2018). Noiret et al. (2017) found that saccade latency is influenced by information processing speed. Moreover, some research on some special populations has suggested that saccade latency variability is a good indicator of attentional fluctuation in saccadic eye movement tasks (Kaufman et al., 2010, 2012). Kaufman et al. (2010) found that patients with Lewy body had greater saccade latency variability than aged controls. Mostofsky et al. (2001) examined the saccadic eye movements of boys with Tourette syndrome. They found that boys with ADHD (i.e., attention deficit hyperactivity disorder) had greater saccade latency variability than boys without ADHD in the prosaccade task. Studies on Alzheimer's disease have shown that patients with Alzheimer's disease had longer saccade latency as well as greater saccade latency variability than healthy senior adults.

The purpose of the present study was to use the prosaccade task as a tool to investigate the difference in cognitive processing underlying saccadic eye movements in skilled and less skilled female adolescent soccer players. Soccer is a game that requires players to process a great amount of internal and external information under pressure within a limited time and react to complex and rapidly changing contexts (Vestberg et al., 2012). Soccer players have to distribute their attention over multiple objects (e.g., moving ball, teammates, and opponents) during games (Ando et al., 2001). Therefore, saccadic eye movement is a critical index for soccer players' performance. Some research has found that eye movement measures vary as a function of skill level in many sports. Ando et al. (2001) revealed that soccer players had shorter visual reaction time than nonathletes when responding to peripheral stimulus, indicating that soccer players had faster visual processing speed. Similarly, Zwierko (2008) found that handball players had shorter response time to peripheral stimulus compared to nonathletes. A recent study showed that cricketers had faster visual reaction times than nonathletes and cricketers' stability of gaze is associated with faster visual reaction time (Barrett et al., 2020). Moreover, some researchers examined the search behaviors of skilled and less skilled soccer players when viewing film of defensive scenarios in soccer finding that skilled players exhibited more fixations, shorter duration, and more fixation locations than less skilled players (Ward and Williams, 2003; Williams and Ericsson, 2005; Williams, 2009; Roca et al., 2011).

In summary, previous studies have shown that there are differences in eye movement tasks among populations with various skill levels. However, to our knowledge, little work has used the prosaccade task to investigate the differences in saccadic eye movements between skilled and less skilled players. Some studies using the prosaccade task only focus on examining the cognitive changes of players caused by head impact exposure in contact and collision sports (Kiefer et al., 2018; Gallagher et al., 2020).

Therefore, the goal of the present study was to examine the potential differences in cognitive processes underlying saccadic eye movements between skilled and less skilled female adolescent soccer players by using the prosaccade task. Based on previous studies, we predict that skilled players would have higher cognitive ability and would thus perform better than less skilled players in prosaccade task. More specifically, we hypothesized that skilled players will exhibit shorter saccade latency, decreased variability of saccade latency, and higher spatial accuracy of saccade than their less skilled counterparts.

MATERIALS AND METHODS

Ethics Statement

This study was approved by the Ethical Committee of the Fujian Normal University. All participants provided their written informed consent to participate in this study. This study was performed in full compliance with the Declaration of Helsinki.

Participants

The G*Power tool (Erdfelder et al., 2009) was used to calculate the sample size in the present study. A statistical power analysis was conducted based on the reported effect size of skill level on saccade latency (mean Cohen's $d=0.817$, from Ducrocq et al., 2016). The result indicated with an alpha level of 0.05; at least 46 participants are required to get a power of 0.80 ($n=23$ in each group). Therefore, we recruited 56 healthy female soccer players from Fujian Youth Football Training Base to participate in our experiment, which met the requirements of statistical power for replicating previous results. Their ages ranged from 14 to 18 years, with an average of 16.5 years. Each player was paid ¥50 for their participation. The experimental design of the present study is a one-way design. Players were assigned into two groups. The skilled player group consisted of 24 skilled players who were determined as Level 1 or Level 2 players. The less skilled player group consisted of 32 less skilled players who were determined as Level 3 or Level 4 players. The levels of players are determined by Fujian Provincial Sports Association according to the latest version of Technical Classification Standards of Soccer Players (2019 edition) developed by Chinese Football Association. **Table 1** reports the age, training years, and the skill level ranking for skilled and less skilled players. Before participants were enrolled in the study, each of them was informed about the study protocol and gave his written informed consent. All participants had normal or corrected-to-normal vision, with no reported color blindness. None of them have suffered from any neurological or psychiatric disorders.

Apparatus

The prosaccade task was programmed in Experimental Builder (SR Research Ltd.). The materials were presented on a 17-inch DELL PC laptop (DELL VOSTRO 15; resolution: 1,920 × 1,080 pixels; refresh rate: 150 Hz). Stimulus was displayed in black (RGB: 0, 0, 0) on a grey background (RGB: 153, 153, 153). Participants were seated at a viewing distance of approximately 58 cm from the computer monitor. A chin rest was used to stabilize the participants' heads. Participants viewed stimulus binocularly, while only their right eyes were monitored. Their eye movements were recorded using an Eyelink Portable Duo eye-tracking system with a sampling rate of 1,000 Hz.

Procedure

The prosaccade task comprised 75 trials. Five of them were practice trials. Each trial began with a fixation cross (1° × 1°) at the center of the screen displayed for 1,000 ms. Then, the target circle (1.2° × 1.2°) was displayed with an eccentricity of ±10° of visual angle in the horizontal plane for 1,500 ms (30 trials for each side), followed by an intertrial interval randomly varied between 800 and 1,200 ms. Participants were instructed to fixate at the cross to ensure that they were looking at the center of the screen when the target appeared peripherally. They were also instructed to look at the target circle as quickly and accurately as possible once it appeared.

Participants were tested individually in a quiet room. After reading the experimental instructions and a brief description of the apparatus, the chair was adjusted to make them feel comfortable, and the eye tracker was calibrated using a nine-point calibration and validation procedure. The maximal error of validation was below 0.5° in the visual angle. At the beginning of each trial, a black circle (0.5° × 0.5°) was presented on the center of the computer screen as drift correction. Once the participant successfully fixated on the black circle, following stimuli were displayed. The prosaccade task lasted about 12 min.

Statistical Analysis

The raw eye movement data were analyzed using Data Viewer (SR Research Ltd.). To ensure the including eye movements data are qualified, following criteria for inclusion were used in analyses (Jazbec et al., 2006): (1) saccades with a latency between 80 and 800 ms is observed, (2) saccade durations must be larger than 25 ms, and (3) saccade amplitude must be greater than 3°. This resulted in a loss of approximately 11% of the trials.

On the basis of these criteria, the following saccade indexes were derived: (1) saccade latency, which was defined as the time elapsed from the onset of the target to the onset of the first saccade after target onset. (2) Variability of saccade latency, which was defined as the standard deviation of saccade latency. (3) Saccade amplitude, which was defined as the spatial distance between the last fixation on fixation cross and the first fixation on target circle. (4) Spatial accuracy of saccade, which was defined as the distance (in degrees of visual angle) between the landing position of the first saccade toward the target circle and the center of the target circle. (5) Peak velocity, which was defined as peak value of gaze velocity (in visual degrees per second) of the saccade. (6) Average velocity, which was defined as average velocity of the saccade.

RESULTS

Independent sample t tests were conducted to compare the difference in each index between skilled and less skilled players (**Table 2**). Skilled players had shorter saccade latency (167.33 ms, SD = 23.32) than less skilled players (184.43 ms, SD = 32.02), $t(54) = -2.21$, $p = 0.031$. Additionally, skilled players had decreased variability of saccade latency (33.89 ms, SD = 10.46) than less skilled players (45.00 ms, SD = 24.30), $t(54) = -2.57$, $p = 0.013$. Skilled players showed higher spatial accuracy of saccade (0.54°, SD = 0.11) than less skilled players (0.60°, SD = 0.08), $t(54) = -2.20$, $p = 0.032$. The saccade amplitude, peak velocity, and average velocity of two groups of players were comparable ($|t|s < 0.91$; see **Figure 1**).

DISCUSSION

In the current study, we conducted prosaccade task to investigate the difference in saccadic eye movements between skilled and less skilled female adolescent soccer players. As we hypothesized, the results showed that the skilled players, as compared to their less skilled counterparts, were faster to saccade to the target appeared peripherally, exhibited less variability of saccade

TABLE 1 | Characteristics of skilled and less skilled adolescent soccer players.

	Skilled players ($n = 24$)	Less skilled players ($n = 32$)	p
Age (years)	16.6 (0.7)	16.4 (0.7)	0.197
Skill level ranking	1.5 (0.5)	3.5 (0.5)	<0.001
Training years	5.29 (0.62)	5.28 (0.58)	0.949

TABLE 2 | Mean (SD) of saccadic eye movement indexes in prosaccade task for two groups of players.

Indexes	Skilled players	Less skilled players
Saccade latency (ms)	167.33 (23.32)	184.43 (32.02)
Variability of saccade latency (ms)	33.89 (10.46)	45.00 (24.30)
Saccade amplitude (°)	9.02 (0.35)	9.04 (0.26)
Spatial accuracy of saccade (°)	0.54 (0.11)	0.60 (0.08)
Peak velocity (°/s)	293.32 (29.56)	285.33 (34.21)
Average velocity (°/s)	176.43 (15.02)	174.80 (12.05)

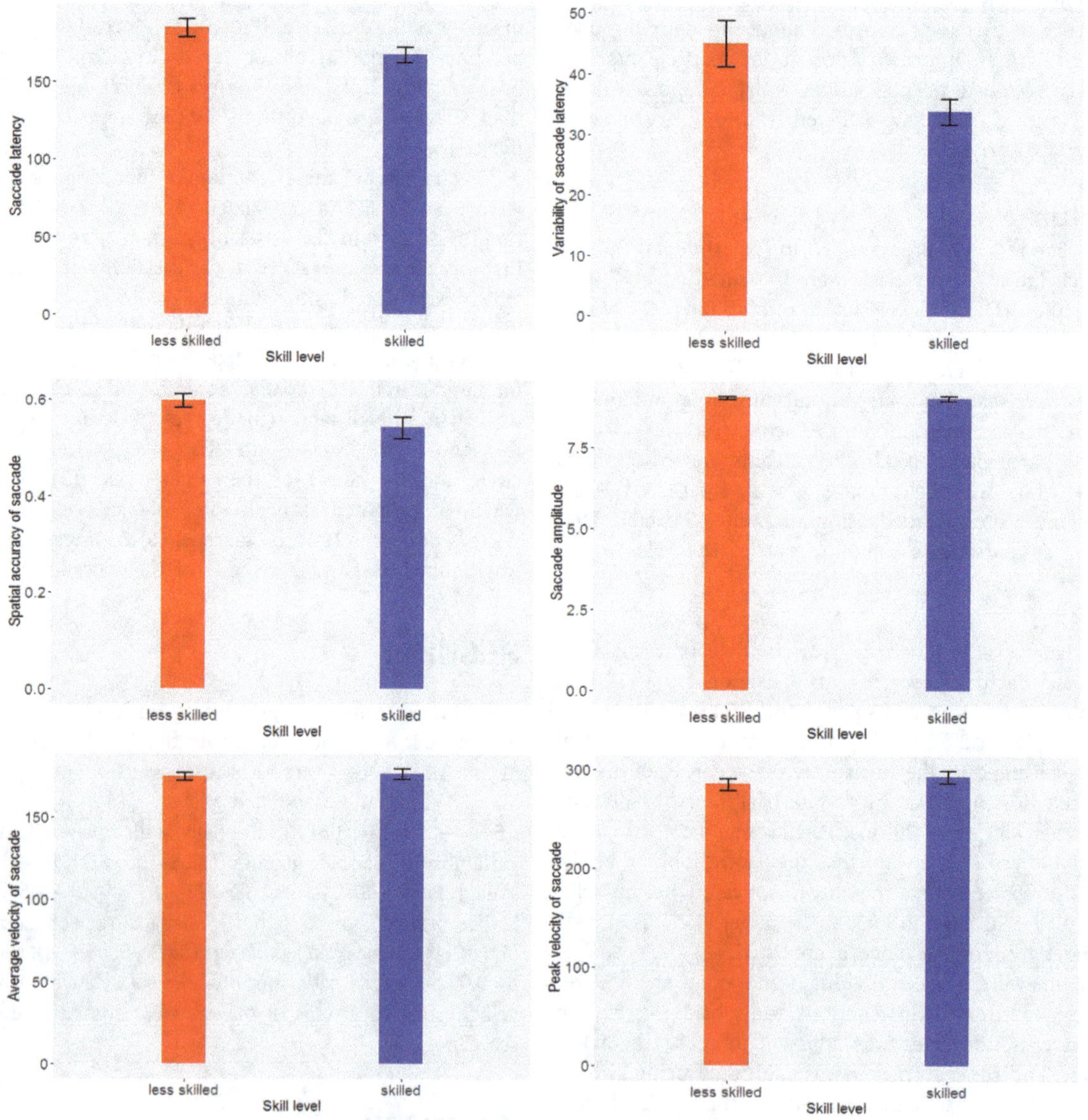

FIGURE 1 | Differences in saccadic eye movement indexes between skill and less skilled players.

latency, and more accurate saccade. Hence, our study supports the view that skilled players have higher cognitive ability and would thus perform better than less skilled players in prosaccade task.

The result that skilled players had shorter saccade latency than less skilled players suggests that skilled players had faster information processing speed than less skilled players. This is consistent with previous studies, demonstrating that saccade latency is influenced by information processing speed (Noiret et al., 2017, 2018) and others showing that saccade latency varies as a function of cognitive function (Coors et al., 2021; Thomas et al., 2021). More importantly, this result is also consistent with studies, demonstrating that players' cognitive capacities vary as a function of their skill levels (Vestberg et al., 2012, 2017; Glavaš, 2020).

Another critical result is that less skilled players exhibited larger variability of saccade latency than skilled players. Kapoula et al. (2010) suggested that variability of saccade latency could be used as a good index of attentional fluctuation in saccadic eye movement tasks. This is due to more attentional lapses caused by more attentional fluctuation in one's attentional system would contribute more longer reaction times in cognitive tasks (Schmiedek et al., 2007; McVay and Kane, 2012; Unsworth and Robison, 2016). This conclusion was supported by several studies, finding that individuals with inferior attentional system had larger variability of saccade latency than their counterparts with superior attention system (Mostofsky et al., 2001; Jazbec et al., 2006; Yang et al., 2013; Kiefer et al., 2018). Taken together, this result may imply that the attentional system of skilled soccer player is superior which leads to smaller attention fluctuation and less attentional lapse.

The result also suggests that skilled soccer players' saccades are more accurate than less skilled soccer players. Previous studies have found that the spatial accuracy of prosaccade is mainly influenced by cerebellar (Ettinger et al., 2005; Optican, 2005; Coors et al., 2021), and the cerebellum, particularly the vermis, plays an important role in the spatial accuracy of saccade (Robinson and Fuchs, 2001; Leigh and Kennard, 2004). Hence, this result may imply that the function of cerebellum of skilled soccer player is superior to that of less skilled soccer. Moreover, this result also implies potential structural differences in brain underlying saccadic eye movement between skilled and less skilled soccer players.

No significant differences were observed in saccade amplitude, peak velocity, and average velocity. For saccade amplitude, previous study found that the saccade amplitude was mainly influenced by target eccentricity in prosaccade task (Petrella et al., 2019). On the one hand, the distance between the peripheral target and the position of the onset of saccade (fixation cross) is constant in the present experiment. On the other hand, all participants in this study had normal or corrected-to-normal vision. Therefore, the absent of significant difference between two groups in saccade amplitude is understandable. For saccade velocity, previous research has demonstrated that the peak velocity was relatively stable (Coors et al., 2021). Sparks (2002) suggested that, from the perspective of neurophysiology, peak velocity is subject to the number of spikes and firing rate of saccadic burst cells. Some researcher suggested that as people conduct approximately 200,000 saccades per day, the saccadic burst cells are continuously trained (Pratt and Welsh, 2006).

Considering that all players in two groups had not suffered any neurological or psychiatric disorders or traumatic brain injury, their nervous system and oculomotor system should be normal and comparable. Therefore, it is also understandable that skilled and less skilled players did not differ in saccade velocity.

The findings of the present study shed some light on understanding of the relationship between saccadic eye movement and skill level in the field of sport and expertise. Besides, these findings supported the results of previous studies, indicating that cognitive ability differed as a function of skill level (Fontani et al., 2006; Brams et al., 2019; Barrett et al., 2020). Furthermore, the present study implies some practical applications for determining or predicting soccer players' skill level and cognitive abilities by analyzing their saccadic eye movements during some eye movement tasks. It would be more economical and convenient for coaches and training instructors to determine a player's skill level using some specific eye movement tasks.

Nevertheless, owing to the restriction of conditions, we should note that the present study has some limitations. For example, the current sample is representative of an adolescent, female, and soccer player sample. It remains unclear whether the results are fully generalizable to adolescent male or adult soccer players' samples. Likewise, it is also unclear whether the results are fully generalizable to players in other sports. Besides, the relatively small sample was used in the present study as was subject to some objective circumstances.

The future studies should include a larger sample to get greater statistical power to detect any differences between groups in cognitive processes on eye movements. Additionally, the current study only explored the differences in saccadic eye movements between skilled and less skilled soccer players using prosaccade task. Yet, growing body of research has shown that antisaccade task is a useful tool to examine fhe differences in inhibitory control and executive unctions among different groups of population (Noiret et al., 2018; Gallagher et al., 2020; Bey et al., 2021; Coors et al., 2021).

Therefore, future research should consider combining prosaccade task with antisaccade task when examining the saccadic eye movements of soccer players.

CONCLUSION

In summary, the results of the current study suggest that skilled soccer players outperform less skilled soccer players on saccadic eye movement in prosaccade task indicating superior cognitive processes underlying saccadic eye movement in skilled soccer players. Overall, the present findings have implications for understanding the relationship between saccadic eye movements and skill level.

ETHICS STATEMENT

The studies involving human participants were reviewed and approved by Academic and Ethics Committee of the Fujian Normal University. Written informed consent to participate in this study was provided by the participants' legal guardian/ next of kin.

AUTHOR CONTRIBUTIONS

ZJ contributed to the conception, design of the study, conducted the experiment, performed the statistical analysis, and wrote the first draft of the manuscript.

ACKNOWLEDGMENTS

The author would like to thank all participants for their cooperation. Special thanks go to Yaojun Chen for her selfless contribution and important support.

REFERENCES

Ando, S., Kida, N., and Oda, S. (2001). Central and peripheral visual reaction time of soccer players and nonathletes. *Percept. Mot. Skills* 92, 786–794. doi: 10.2466/pms.2001.92.3.786

Barrett, B. T., Cruickshank, A. G., Flavell, J. C., Bennett, S. J., Buckley, J. G., Harris, J. M., et al. (2020). Faster visual reaction times in elite athletes are not linked to better gaze stability. *Sci. Rep.* 10:13216. doi: 10.1038/s41598-020-69975-z

Bey, K., Lippold, J. V., Aslan, B., Hurlemann, R., and Ettinger, U. (2021). Effects of lorazepam on prosaccades and saccadic adaptation. *J. Psychopharmacol.* 35, 91–99. doi: 10.1177/0269881120972424

Brams, S., Ziv, G., Levin, O., Spitz, J., Wagemans, J., Williams, A. M., et al. (2019). The relationship between gaze behavior, expertise, and performance: a systematic review. *Psychol. Bull.* 145, 980–1027. doi: 10.1037/bul0000207

Clark, J. J. (1999). Spatial attention and latencies of saccadic eye movements. *Vis. Res.* 39, 585–602. doi: 10.1016/S0042-6989(98)00190-4

Coors, A., Merten, N., Ward, D. D., Schmid, M., Breteler, M. M. B., and Ettinger, U. (2021). Strong age but weak sex effects in eye movement performance in the general adult population: evidence from the Rhineland study. *Vis. Res.* 178, 124–133. doi: 10.1016/j.visres.2020.10.004

Duchowski, A. T. (2003). *Eye Tracking Methodology: Theory and Practice*. London: Springer.

Ducrocq, E., Wilson, M., Vine, S., and Derakshan, N. (2016). Training attentional control improves cognitive and motor task performance. *J. Sport Exerc. Psychol.* 38, 521–533. doi: 10.1123/jsep.2016-0052

Erdfelder, E., Faul, F., Buchner, A., and Lang, A. G. (2009). Statistical power analyses using G*power 3.1: tests for correlation and regression analyses. *Behav. Res. Methods* 41, 1149–1160. doi: 10.3758/BRM.41.4.1149

Ettinger, U., Antonova, E., Crawford, T. J., Mitterschiffthaler, M. T., Goswani, S., Sharma, T., et al. (2005). Structural neural correlates of prosaccade and antisaccade eye movements in healthy humans. *Neuroimage* 24, 487–494. doi: 10.1016/j.neuroimage.2004.08.019

Fontani, G., Lodi, L., Felici, A., Migliorini, S., and Corradeschi, F. (2006). Attention in athletes of high and low experience engaged in different open skill sports. *Percept. Mot. Skills* 102, 791–805. doi: 10.2466/pms.102.3.791-805

Gallagher, V. T., Murthy, P., Stocks, J., Vesci, B., Colegrove, D., Mjaanes, J., et al. (2020). Differential change in oculomotor performance among female collegiate soccer players versus non-contact athletes from pre- to post-season. *Neurotrauma Rep.* 1, 169–180. doi: 10.1089/neur.2020.0051

Glavaš, D. (2020). Basic cognitive abilities relevant to male adolescents' soccer performance. *Percept. Mot. Skills* 127, 1079–1094. doi: 10.1177/0031512520930158

Hutton, S. B. (2008). Cognitive control of saccadic eye movements. *Brain Cogn.* 68, 327–340. doi: 10.1016/j.bandc.2008.08.021

Jazbec, S., Hardin, M. G., Schroth, E., McClure, E., Pine, D. S., and Ernst, M. (2006). Age-related influence of contingencies on a saccade task. *Exp. Brain Res.* 174, 754–762. doi: 10.1007/s00221-006-0520-9

Kapoula, Z., Yang, Q., Vernet, M., Orssaud, C., Samson, M., Dleudonne, B., et al. (2010). Longévité et robustesse de la saccade oculaire automatique chez le sujet âgé sain: Atteinte dans des cas de démence à corps de Lewy. *Psychol. Neuropsychiatr. Vieil.* 8, 295–306. doi: 10.1684/pnv.2010.0228

Kaufman, L. D., Pratt, J., Levine, B., and Black, S. E. (2010). Antisaccades: a probe into the dorsolateral prefrontal cortex in Alzheimer's disease. A critical review. *J. Alzheimers Dis.* 19, 781–793. doi: 10.3233/JAD-2010-1275

Kaufman, L. D., Pratt, J., Levine, B., and Black, S. E. (2012). Executive deficits detected in mild Alzheimer's disease using the antisaccade task. *Brain Behav.* 2, 15–21. doi: 10.1002/brb3.28

Kiefer, A. W., DiCesare, C., Nalepka, P., Foss, K. B., Thomas, S., and Myer, G. D. (2018). Less efficient oculomotor performance is associated with increased incidence of head impacts in high school ice hockey. *J. Sci. Med. Sport* 21, 4–9. doi: 10.1016/j.jsams.2017.06.016

Leigh, R. J., and Kennard, C. (2004). Using saccades as a research tool in the clinical neurosciences. *Brain* 127, 460–477. doi: 10.1093/brain/awh035

McVay, J. C., and Kane, M. J. (2012). Drifting from slow to "D'oh!": working memory capacity and mind wandering predict extreme reaction times and executive control errors. *J. Exp. Psychol. Learn. Mem. Cogn.* 38, 525–549. doi: 10.1037/a0025896

Mostofsky, S. H., Lasker, A. G., Singer, H. S., Denckla, M. B., and Zee, D. S. (2001). Oculomotor abnormalities in boys with Tourette syndrome with and without ADHD. *J. Am. Acad. Child Adolesc. Psychiatry* 40, 1464–1472. doi: 10.1097/00004583-200112000-00018

Noiret, N., Carvalho, N., Laurent, É., Chopard, G., Binetruy, M., Nicolier, M., et al. (2018). Saccadic eye movements and attentional control in Alzheimer's disease. *Arch. Clin. Neuropsychol.* 33, 1–13. doi: 10.1093/arclin/acx044

Noiret, N., Vigneron, B., Diogo, M., Vandel, P., and Laurent, É. (2017). Saccadic eye movements: what do they tell us about aging cognition? *Aging Neuropsychol. Cognit.* 24, 575–599. doi: 10.1080/13825585.2016.1237613

Optican, L. M. (2005). Sensorimotor transformation for visually guided saccades. *Ann. N. Y. Acad. Sci.* 1039, 132–148. doi: 10.1196/annals.1325.013

Petrella, A. F. M., Belfry, G., and Heath, M. (2019). Older adults elicit a single-bout post-exercise executive benefit across a continuum of aerobically supported metabolic intensities. *Brain Res.* 1712, 197–206. doi: 10.1016/j.brainres.2019.02.009

Pratt, J., Lajonchere, C. M., and Abrams, R. A. (2006). Attentional modulation of the gap effect. *Vis. Res.* 46, 2602–2607. doi: 10.1016/j.visres.2006.01.017

Pratt, J., and Welsh, T. (2006). Growing older does not always mean moving slower: examining aging and the saccadic motor system. *J. Mot. Behav.* 38, 373–382. doi: 10.3200/JMBR.38.5.373-382

Rayner, K. (1998). Eye movements in reading and information processing: 20 years of research. *Psychol. Bull.* 124, 372–422. doi: 10.1037/0033-2909.124.3.372

Robinson, F. R., and Fuchs, A. F. (2001). The role of the cerebellum in voluntary eye movements. *Annu. Rev. Neurosci.* 24, 981–1004. doi: 10.1146/annurev.neuro.24.1.981

Roca, A., Ford, P. R., McRobert, A. P., and Williams, A. M. (2011). Identifying the processes underpinning anticipation and decision-making in a dynamic time-constrained task. *Cogn. Process.* 12, 301–310. doi: 10.1007/s10339-011-0392-1

Schmiedek, F., Oberauer, K., Wilhelm, O., Süß, H. M., and Wittmann, W. W. (2007). Individual differences in components of reaction time distributions and their relations to working memory and intelligence. *J. Exp. Psychol. Gen.* 136, 414–429. doi: 10.1037/0096-3445.136.3.414

Sparks, D. L. (2002). The brainstem control of saccadic eye movements. *Nat. Rev. Neurosci.* 3, 952–964. doi: 10.1038/nrn986

Thomas, E. H. X., Steffens, M., Harms, C., Rossell, S. L., Gurvich, C., and Ettinger, U. (2021). Schizotypy, neuroticism, and saccadic eye movements: new data and meta-analysis. *Psychophysiology* 58:e13706. doi: 10.1111/psyp.13706

Unsworth, N., and Robison, M. K. (2016). Pupillary correlates of lapses of sustained attention. *Cogn. Affect. Behav. Neurosci.* 16, 601–615. doi: 10.3758/s13415-016-0417-4

Vestberg, T., Gustafson, R., Maurex, L., Ingvar, M., and Petrovic, P. (2012). Executive functions predict the success of top-soccer players. *PLoS One* 7:e34731. doi: 10.1371/journal.pone.0034731

Vestberg, T., Reinebo, G., Maurex, L., Ingvar, M., and Petrovic, P. (2017). Core executive functions are associated with success in young elite soccer players. *PLoS One* 12:e0170845. doi: 10.1371/journal.pone.0170845

Ward, P., and Williams, A. M. (2003). Perceptual and cognitive skill development in soccer: the multidimensional nature of expert performance. *J. Sport Exerc. Psychol.* 25, 93–111. doi: 10.1123/jsep.25.1.93

Williams, A. M. (2009). Perceiving the intentions of others: how do skilled performers make anticipation judgments? *Prog. Brain Res.* 174, 73–83. doi: 10.1016/S0079-6123(09)01307-7

Williams, A. M., and Ericsson, K. A. (2005). Perceptual-cognitive expertise in sport: some considerations when applying the expert performance approach. *Hum. Mov. Sci.* 24, 283–307. doi: 10.1016/j.humov.2005.06.002

Yang, Q., Wang, T., Su, N., Xiao, S., and Kapoula, Z. (2013). Specific saccade deficits in patients with Alzheimer's disease at mild to moderate stage and in patients with amnestic mild cognitive impairment. *Age* 35, 1287–1298. doi: 10.1007/s11357-012-9420-z

Zwierko, T. (2008). Differences in peripheral perception between athletes and nonathletes. *J. Hum. Kinet.* 19, 53–62. doi: 10.2478/v10078-008-0004-z

7

The Relationship between Big Five and Self-Control in Boxers: A Mediating Model

Guodong Zhang[1], Xin Chen[1], Luxia Xiao[2], Yun Li[1], Bing Li[1], Zi Yan[3], Liya Guo[1] and Detlef H. Rost[1,4]*

[1]Key Lab of Physical Fitness Evaluation and Motor Function Monitoring of General Administration of Sports of China, College of Physical Education, Institute of Sports Science, Southwest University, Chongqing, China, [2]Center for Mental Health Education, School of Psychology, Southwest University, Chongqing, China, [3]Health Sciences Department, Merrimack College, North Andover, MA, United States, [4]Department of Child and Youth Psychology, Faculty of Psychology, Philipps-University Marburg, Marburg, Germany

***Correspondence:**
Guodong Zhang
lygd777@swu.edu.cn

Self-control seems to be the core element for achieving optimal competitive performance, and be of great importance to well-being and healthy development of humans. According to the literature, there exist some correlations between personality traits and self-control. The aim of this study was to shed some additional light on the relationship between the Big Five personality traits and self-control in boxers and investigate self-efficacy as a mediator between the two variables. Two hundred and ten boxers (age: $M = 18.89$, SD = 3.83; amount of boxing practice: $M = 4.93$ years, SD = 3.22; 76 males) of Chinese national athletes participated the study. Results showed a pronounced level of self-control. The higher the competitive level, the higher the level of self-control. There were significant correlations among the Big Five, self-control, and self-efficacy. Self-efficacy mediated the relationship between the Big Five personality traits and self-control.

Keywords: Big Five personality traits, self-efficacy, self-control, mediating effect, boxer

INTRODUCTION

Self-control refers to the phenomenon of people overcoming their natural and automatic tendencies, desires, and behaviors and resisting short-term temptations to achieve long-term goals (Baumeister et al., 2007). It is essential for the well-being and healthy development of humans. Sigmund Freud believed that self-control is a major characteristic of a civilized society (Freud, 1993), while Hare et al. suggested that "the ability to exercise self-control is the key to human success and happiness" (Hare et al., 2009). Good self-control not only prevents drug abuse, criminal offenses, and other undesirable social behaviors, but also promotes the healthy growth of individuals and the harmonious development of society (Moffitt et al., 2011; Tangney et al., 2014). Self-control seems to be the core element for achieving optimal competitive performance (Zhang, 2013; Englert, 2016). Scholars in sport psychology have called for research that "gives a voice" to marginalized groups, which would arguably include boxers (Fisher et al., 2003; Ryba and Wright, 2005; Simpson and Wrisberg, 2013). Boxers should have a pronounced self-control and self-efficacy (Lane, 2006; Yu et al., 2012). Thus, boxing is well suited for applied sport psychology interventions (Schinke, 2007); more emphasis should be put into research on the self-control and self-efficacy of boxers.

Exploring the relationships between self-control, personality traits, and self-efficacy can serve as a starting point for an in-depth study of self-control. Mao et al. (2018) found that openness, conscientiousness, extraversion, and agreeableness were all positively correlated with self-control, and neuroticism was negatively related to self-control. In addition, Vera et al. (2004) believe that self-control is affected by self-efficacy. Most of the existing research on self-control in sporting contexts focused on soccer players, divers, middle-distance runners, and college athletes of all types. There is only limited research on the psychology of boxing in China, especially on the relationship between boxers' personality traits and self-control. This study invited Chinese boxers of national athletes to take part in an examination of the relationship between their personality traits and self-control, and to look for any mediating effect of self-efficacy.

Personality Traits and Self-Control

Previous studies have well documented the relationship between the Big Five and self-control. Neuroticism has a negative correlation with self-control; agreeableness, extraversion, openness, and responsibility are positively related to self-control; self-control is a prerequisite for individuals to adapt to their social environment (Andrei et al., 2014; Coyne and Wright, 2014). In addition, researchers found differences in the relationship between extraversion, openness, and self-control; some studies found that extraversion and self-control had a significant negative correlation (Green et al., 2016), while some others found extraversion was not significantly related with self-control (de Vries and van Gelder, 2013). In the same way, researches on the relationship between openness and self-control had also produced inconsistent results (Andrei et al., 2014; Bazzy et al., 2017). Due to its consistency and stability across languages and cultures (Pilarska, 2018), the Big Five is often used to predict self-control (McCrae and Terracciano, 2005). Therefore, due to the inconsistency of the relationship between Big Five and self-control, and lack of studies among boxers, we hypothesized that 1: Neuroticism is negatively correlated with self-control, while agreeableness, conscientiousness, and extraversion are positively correlated with self-control among Chinese boxers.

Personality Traits and Self-Efficacy

Personality traits are important factors influencing the self-efficacy of individuals (Stajkovic et al., 2018). Studies have linked the Big Five traits and self-efficacy (Judge et al., 2007; Cristina et al., 2018; Coco et al., 2019), for example, neuroticism is negatively correlated with self-efficacy, and extraversion, openness, agreeableness, and responsibility positively correlated with self-efficacy (Judge et al., 2007). Some scholars found that individuals with higher scores of conscientiousness had higher self-efficacy beliefs (Brown et al., 2011). Openness shifts perceptions of demands into challenges to be tackled, broadening task engagement and self-efficacy (Sanchez-Cardona et al., 2012). Research has found that agreeableness can lead to increased self-efficacy (Caprara et al., 2010). Certain researchers have found that individual self-efficacy is positively correlated with extraversion and negatively correlated with neuroticism (Schmitt, 2007). The finding of Djigić et al. (2014) indicated that conscientiousness predicts the self-efficacy of teachers, while Marcionetti and Rossier (2016) believed that conscientiousness, neuroticism, and extraversion are significantly correlated with self-efficacy. Furthermore, Brown and Cinamon (2016) proposed that higher conscientiousness and extraversion, and lower neuroticism, help enhance self-efficacy.

In sports, Wang et al. (2009) found that neuroticism has a significant negative predictive effect on the general self-efficacy of basketball players, while extraversion and conscientiousness have significant positive predictive effects. Based on the existing literature, the current study hypothesized that neuroticism is negatively correlated with self-efficacy, while agreeableness, conscientiousness, and extraversion are positively correlated with self-efficacy in boxers.

Self-Control and Self-Efficacy

Self-efficacy may play a mediating role between personality and self-control. According to Bandura's self-efficacy and self-regulation theories, self-control is affected by self-efficacy, and there was a significant positive correlation between the two (Bandura, 1978). Research found a positive correlation between self-efficacy and self-control (Au, 2015). Graham and Bray (2015) studied self-efficacy as a psychological factor to explain how self-control is performed. Baumeister's analysis showed that self-control requires an individual's own control resources, and self-efficacy complements this resource by acting as a positive emotion (Baumeister, 2002). Yu and Yang's (2008) study concluded that there is an interaction effect between self-efficacy beliefs and self-control behavior.

A large number of researches have shown that there is a positive correlation between self-efficacy and self-control in different population groups (Huang and Yang, 2015). Jones et al. found that self-efficacy and sense of control are important indicators of an athlete's state (Jones et al., 2009). Research shows that self-efficacy had a positive effect on self-control in athletes (Yang et al., 2013). Specifically, self-efficacy mediated the relationship between other psychological traits and self-control among different groups (Wang et al., 2009; Fang et al., 2015). Therefore, the present study further explores whether self-efficacy has a positive effect on self-control in boxers, and whether self-efficacy has a mediating effect between personality traits and self-control. The current study hypothesized: the self-efficacy and the self-control of Chinese boxers are positively correlated; the self-efficacy of Chinese boxers mediates the effects of neuroticism, agreeableness, conscientiousness, and extraversion on self-control.

MATERIALS AND METHODS

Sample

The participants, acquired by cluster sampling, comprised boxers from Chinese national boxing teams as well as teams at several provinces and cities including Shenyang, Hubei, Anhui, Inner Mongolia, Chongqing, and Sichuan. All subjects gave written informed consent in accordance with the Declaration of Helsinki. Permission was obtained from the Southwest University's Human Research Ethics Committee. Prior to answering the items, participants read information about the purpose of the study, implications of participation, and data protection. The information stressed that participation was completely voluntary and anonymous. A total of $N = 230$ questionnaires were distributed, and $N = 210$ valid ones (91%) were returned. Among the participants, $n = 76$ were males (36.2%) and $n = 134$ females (63.8%). There were 79 Level-3 athletes (37.6%), 24 Level-2 athletes (11.4%), 49 Level-1 athletes (23.3%), 45 Master-Level athletes (21.4%), and 13 athletes at the International Master-Level (6.2%). Level-3 is the lowest and the International Master-Level is the highest. The average age was $M = 18.89$ years (SD = 3.83), with the average prior training period being $M = 4.93$ years (SD = 3.22). Fifty participants were under 18 years of age and permissions from their parents were obtained; written and informed consent was obtained from the parents/legal guardians of all non-adult participants. The average time for completing the survey was 20 min.

Procedure

After receiving informed consent from the management, coaches, and athletes of the national team and other sports teams, the questionnaires were distributed to teams at the provincial level or above. The instructions were explained in detail and example questions were provided to the participants, who were asked to read the questionnaire carefully and answer it. The questionnaires were distributed at Jilin Sport University, Wuhan Sport University, Anhui, Inner Mongolia, Chongqing, and Sichuan between the 11th of October and the 9th of November, 2017.

Measures

NEO Five-Factor Inventory

Personality was measured with the validated Chinese NEO-PI-R (Costam and McCrae, 1992; Chen et al., 2016). The NEO-PI-R contains 60 items and is one of the most widely used measures for the Big Five personality traits. The self-report items are rated on a 5-point Likert scale ranging from "strongly disagree (1)" to "strongly agree (5)" and reflect the five higher order domains Neuroticism, Extraversion, Openness to Experiences, Agreeableness, and Conscientiousness. There are 12 items per FFM-FFI domain. A confirmatory factor analysis confirmed the one-dimensionality of the scale (CFA): $\chi^2/df = 1.33$, RMSE = 0.04, TLI = 0.99, GFI = 0.98, CFI = 0.99. The factor loadings of the items ranged between $a = 0.50$ and $a = 0.73$. The internal consistencies of the inventory's five scales were $\alpha = 0.77$ (Neuroticism), $\alpha = 0.76$ (Agreeableness), $\alpha = 0.80$ (Conscientiousness), $\alpha = 0.72$ (Extraversion), and $\alpha = 0.57$ (Openness). The Openness scale was not used furthermore due to its unsatisfactory internal consistency and its cultural unsuitability for Chinese boxers.

Self-Control Questionnaire for Athletes

Self-control was measured by a 24-item, 5-point Likert Chinese scale questionnaire, ranging from "1 = not at all" to "5 = very much"; higher scores indicate better self-control (item example: "In order to complete the training task, I can endure extreme fatigue"). In a previous study, the scale provided a reference for athlete selection (Li and Zhang, 2011). A confirmatory factor analysis confirmed the one-dimensionality of the scale (CFA): $\chi^2/df = 1.15$, RMSEA = 0.03, TLI = 0.97, GFI = 0.92, NFI = 0.87, CFI = 0.98. The factor loadings of the items ranged from $a = 0.49$ to $a = 0.75$. The internal consistency of the questionnaire was good ($\alpha = 0.87$).

Self-Efficacy Scale for Athletes

Based on self-efficacy theory and related theories about competitive sports, Wei et al. (2008) compiled a self-efficacy scale for athletes in intensive sports. This scale consisted of 15 items, such as "I can keep my mind clear and focused during the competition." Each item was measured by a 5-point scale (1 = never been like this; 5 = always so). A higher score indicates a higher self-efficacy. The one-dimensionality of the scale was proved by a confirmatory factor analysis (CFA): $\chi^2/df = 1.07$, RMSEA = 0.02, TLI = 0.99, GFI = 0.96, NFI = 0.95, CFI = 0.99, IFI = 0.99. The factor loadings of the items ranged from $a = 0.43$ to $a = 0.75$. The internal consistency of the scale was good ($\alpha = 0.92$).

DATA ANALYSES

A two-way analysis of variance (ANOVA, LSD-*post hoc* test) was run for testing mean differences. The bias-corrected percentile bootstrap method was used to conduct regression analyses (Fang et al., 2012). To implement this method, we used the Model 4 PROCESS macro for SPSS created by Hayes (2013). Gender, age, years of training, and competitive level were controlled. The 95% confidence intervals of the mediating effects are reported. The statistical significance level was set to $\alpha = 0.05$.

RESULTS

Testing for Common Method Bias

To avoid response bias, some items in the questionnaires were expressed in reverse wording, AMOS 21.0 was used to conduct a CFA, with the common factor of all variables set to 1, and all item variables were used as explicit variables. The CFA results showed that the model fit was low, indicating no serious common method bias. ($\chi^2/df = 2.01$, RMSEA = 0.07, NFI = 0.34, CFI = 0.50, TLI = 0.49, GFI = 0.55, IFI = 0.50).

Self-Control and Self-Efficacy: Group Differences

The averaged item score of the self-control was $M = 3.68$ (SD = 0.49), indicating a relatively high level of self-control among boxers in China. This study also examined the effect of gender and competitive level differences on self-control; the results indicated no significant gender differences ($F = 1.14$,

$p = 0.28$, $d = -0.011$), but a significant main effect of competitive level ($F = 7.81$, $p < 0.01$, $\eta^2 = 0.12$). The interaction between gender and competitive level was not significant ($F = 1.82$, $p = 0.13$, $\eta^2 = 0.04$). The item-based averaged self-control scores of boxers from the five different competitive levels were significantly different. The higher the competitive level, the higher the level of self-control (International Master-Level: $M = 3.92$, SD = 0.62; Master-Level $M = 3.79$, SD = 0.48; Level-1: $M = 3.77$, SD = 0.45, Level-2: $M = 3.83$, SD = 0.49; Level-3: $M = 3.47$, SD = 0.43. The simple analysis showed that the averaged item score of self-control in International Master-Level was significantly higher than that of the Level-3, $p < 0.01$, $d = 0.98$).

The average item score of self-efficacy was $M = 3.50$ (SD = 0.64), indicating that the Chinese boxers' self-efficacy exceeds the theoretical item mean. There was no significant difference between male and female boxers ($p > 0.05$, $d = 0.24$). The mean item scores of self-efficacy among boxers from five different competitive levels differed significantly: the higher the competitive level, the higher the self-efficacy (International Master-Level: $M = 3.81$, SD = 0.76; Master-Level: $M = 3.66$, SD = 0.60; Level-1: $M = 3.53$, SD = 0.58; Level-2: $M = 3.60$, SD = 0.71; Level-3: $M = 3.30$, SD = 0.60). There was a significant difference on self-efficacy between International Master-Level and Level-3 ($p < 0.01$, $d = 0.81$).

Personality Traits, Self-Efficacy, and Self-Control: Correlations

Neuroticism was significantly and negatively correlated with self-efficacy and self-control, while extraversion, agreeableness, and conscientiousness were significantly and positively correlated with self-efficacy and self-control. Self-efficacy and self-control were positively correlated (see **Table 1**).

Testing for Mediation by Self-Efficacy on Effects of Neuroticism, Agreeableness, Extraversion, and Conscientiousness on Self-Control

This study used the Bootstrap method proposed by Fang et al. (2012) and the Model 4 PROCESS macro for SPSS created by Hayes (2013) to conduct mediating effect testing; gender, competitive level, age, and years of training were set as control variables.

Regression analysis showed that neuroticism negatively predicted self-efficacy ($\beta = -0.23$, $p < 0.01$), while self-efficacy positively predicted self-control ($\beta = 0.88$, $p < 0.001$). Neuroticism negatively predicted self-control ($\beta = -0.32$, $p < 0.001$). Extraversion was a positive predictor of self-efficacy ($\beta = 0.17$, $p < 0.001$), while self-efficacy positively predicted self-control ($\beta = 0.78$, $p < 0.001$). Extraversion and self-efficacy were positive predictors of self-control ($\beta = 0.27$, $p < 0.001$). Agreeableness positively predicted self-efficacy ($\beta = 0.26$, $p < 0.001$), and self-efficacy was a positive predictor of self-control ($\beta = 0.77$, $p < 0.001$), as was agreeableness ($\beta = 0.44$, $p < 0.001$). Conscientiousness positively predicted self-efficacy ($\beta = 0.43$, $p < 0.001$), and self-efficacy was a positive predictor of self-control ($\beta = 0.58$, $p < 0.001$), as was conscientiousness ($\beta = 0.47$, $p < 0.001$).

Figures 1–4 present the standardized effects of the paths of neuroticism, extraversion, agreeableness, and conscientiousness on self-control. The bootstrap 95% confidence interval of the indirect effect of self-efficacy did not comprise 0, indicating that

TABLE 1 | Means, standard deviations, and correlation coefficients of personality traits, self-control, and self-efficacy.

	M	SD	1	2	3	4	5	6
Neuroticism	2.94	0.53	1					
Extraversion	3.63	0.49	−0.40*	1				
Agreeableness	3.78	0.46	−0.49*	0.37*	1			
Conscientiousness	3.50	0.48	−0.52*	0.47*	0.54*	1		
Self-efficacy	3.50	0.64	−0.42*	0.48*	0.45*	0.70*	1	
Self-control	3.68	0.49	−0.57*	0.48*	0.68*	0.74*	0.70*	1

**Indicates p < 0.05.*

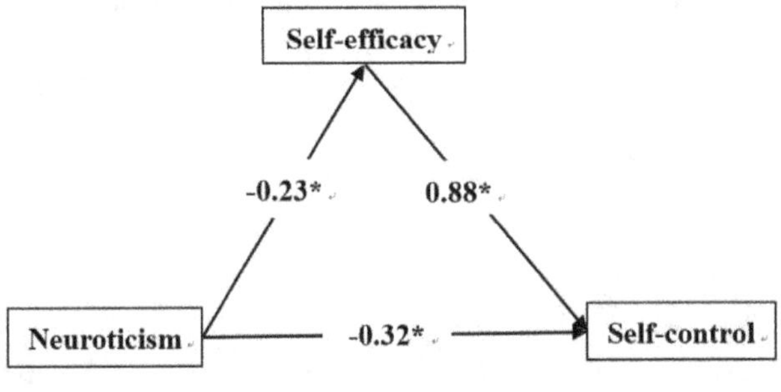

FIGURE 1 | Neuroticism → self-efficacy → self-control. *Statistically significant.

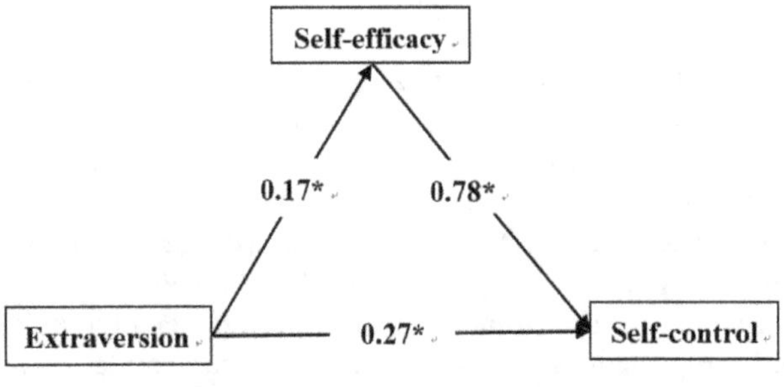

FIGURE 2 | Extraversion → self-efficacy → self-control. *Statistically significant.

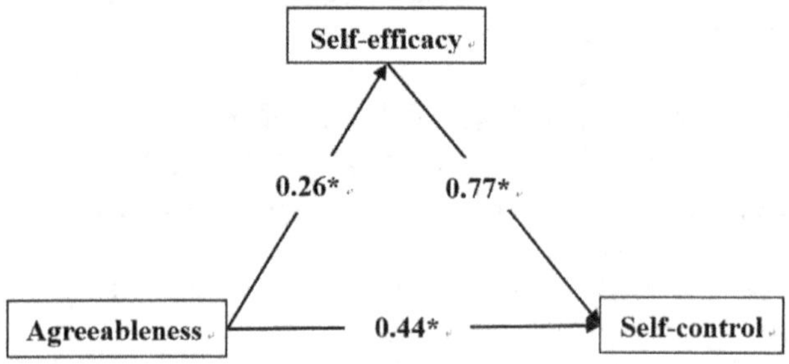

FIGURE 3 | Agreeableness → self-efficacy → self-control. *Statistically significant.

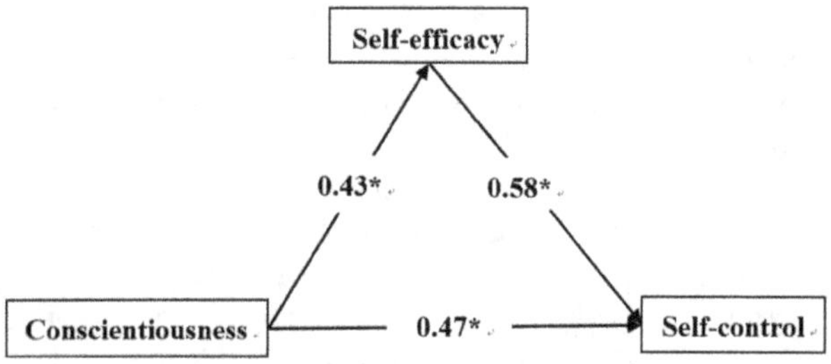

FIGURE 4 | Conscientiousness → self-efficacy → self-control. *Statistically significant.

self-efficacy had a significant mediating effect on neuroticism, extraversion, and agreeableness. Conscientiousness had a mediating effect on self-control. Taking together, neuroticism explained 22% of the change in self-efficacy, extraversion 27%, agreeableness 26%, and conscientiousness 50%. As such, H_4 was confirmed.

DISCUSSION

Direct Influence of Personality Traits on Self-Control

In the current study, there were significant positive correlations between agreeableness, conscientiousness, extraversion, and self-control, and a negative correlation between neuroticism and self-control.

Previous studies have shown that agreeableness, conscientiousness, and extraversion are positively related to self-control (Bazzy et al., 2017), while neuroticism significantly correlated with self-control (Andrei et al., 2014). Based on those studies, the current study assumed that neuroticism is negatively correlated with self-control, while agreeableness, conscientiousness, and extraversion are positively correlated with self-control. These hypotheses are supported and are consistent with the results of Deng and Gao (2015) and Pilarska (2018).

Avoiding injuries and reducing the number of fouls are very important skills for boxers. Self-control is a very important psychological characteristic that influences those skills (Yu et al., 2012). By understanding the mediating relationship between personality and self-control, boxers can not only avoid injuries but also reduce the number of fouls by improving their self-control level and their own skills and tactics (Ba and Zhu, 2008). Song et al. (2009) suggested that boxers should continuously enhance their psychological stability by focusing on the actual combat element of boxing. Therefore, the Big Five factors and the self-control could perhaps be used as psychological criteria to select boxers and the relationship between them is an important first step in order to further boxers. Longitudinal research is needed to evaluate the relevance of these predictors.

The Mediating Role of Self-Efficacy Between Personality Traits and Self-Control

Studies have shown that four of the Big Five factors have indirect predictive effects on self-control through self-efficacy. Theories of self-efficacy hold that the subjective judgment and self-feeling that individuals have about their ability to perform a certain behavior or tasks play an important role in the decision-making process before a behavior is performed (Eastin and La-Rose, 2000). In sporting contexts, scholars have found that the stronger an athletes' self-efficacy, the better their performance in sports as diverse as athletics, tennis, scuba diving, and gymnastics (Vancouver et al., 2002): when athletes perform a task for the first time, their self-efficacy affects their performance (Myers et al., 2004). Other studies have demonstrated that, even despite excellent skills and motivation to win, people with outstanding capabilities are less likely to achieve success if they have poor self-efficacy (Earley and Lituchy, 1991). The present study hypothesized that neuroticism is negatively correlated with self-control, while agreeableness, conscientiousness, and extraversion are positively correlated with self-control; and these hypotheses were supported by the results of this study and are consistent with the results of Zhang (2016) and Marcionetti and Rossier (2016). Moreover, the recent study found that self-efficacy has a significant positive predictive effect on self-control, consistent with the results of Huang and Yang (2015) and Kaida et al. (2006).

The present study also hypothesized that self-efficacy mediates the effects of neuroticism, agreeableness, conscientiousness, and extraversion on self-control. The present study observed four mediating paths, showing partial mediating effects of self-efficacy on self-control for each personality trait variable. Many other researchers have also found that self-efficacy mediates the link between personality traits and self-control, such as Fang et al. (2015) and Stajkovic et al. (2018). Therefore, cultivating and upgrading the self-efficacy of boxers should be emphasized in their training.

LIMITATIONS

Firstly, with the cross-sectional design, no causal relationship could be established. Secondly, the present study focused on the role of self-efficacy in the relationship between Big Five personality traits and self-control, but there are still many other important mediating variables which may influence self-control, such as depression, anxiety, or self-esteem and self-concept, which should also be explored in future research. Finally, the current study focused on Chinese boxers. Further research is needed to figure out whether the results of this study can be generalized to other sports or western cultures.

Despite these limitations, the present study contributes to understand the inherent relationship between big five personality and self-control as well as its possible mechanisms among Chinese boxers. The exploration of the variables can add a fruitful avenue toward the development of knowledge about the processes involved in self-control in sport.

CONCLUSIONS

First, there were significant differences in self-control and self-efficacy among boxers of different competitive levels. Second, there are significant correlations of neuroticism and agreeableness, conscientiousness, and extraversion with self-control, indicating that these four dimensions are direct statistical predictors of self-control. Self-efficacy is positively correlated with self-control. Finally, boxers' self-efficacy mediates personality traits and self-control, indicating that personality traits predict self-control not only directly but also indirectly through self-efficacy. Overall, the mediation effect models constructed in this study had some explanatory power for self-control.

ETHICS STATEMENT

The protocol was approved by the Southwest University's Human Research Ethics Committee. Prior to initiation of the study, all subjects gave written informed consent in accordance with the Declaration of Helsinki.

AUTHOR CONTRIBUTIONS

All authors listed have made a substantial, direct and intellectual contribution to the work, and approved it for publication.

REFERENCES

Andrei, F., Mancini, G., Trombini, E., Baldaro, B., and Russo, P. M. (2014). Testing the incremental validity of trait emotional intelligence: evidence from an Italian sample of adolescents. *Pers. Individ. Differ.* 64, 24–29. doi: 10.1016/j.paid.2014.02.007

Au, E. W. (2015). Locus of control, self-efficacy, and the mediating effect of outcome control: predicting course-level and global outcomes in an academic context. *Anxiety Stress Coping* 28, 425–444. doi: 10.1080/10615806.2014.976761

Ba, Y. M., and Zhu, R. H. (2008). Construction of index system of selecting reserve talent for top notch male boxers of our country. *J. Shanghai Univ. Sport* 32, 89–92. doi: 10.16099/j.cnki.jsus.2008.06.022

Bandura, A. (1978). Self-efficacy: toward a unifying theory of behavioral change. *Adv. Behav. Res. Ther.* 1, 139–161. doi: 10.1016/0146-6402(78)90002-4

Baumeister, R. F. (2002). Ego depletion and self-control failure: an energy model of the self's executive function. *Self Identity* 1, 129–136. doi: 10.1080/152988602317319302

Baumeister, R. F., Vohs, K. D., and Tice, D. M. (2007). The strength model of self-control. *Curr. Dir. Psychol. Sci.* 16, 351–355. doi: 10.1111/j.1467-8721.2007.00534.x

Bazzy, J. D., Woehr, D. J., and Borns, J. (2017). An examination of the role of self-control and impact of ego depletion on integrity testing. *Basic Appl. Soc. Psychol.* 39, 101–111. doi: 10.1080/01973533.2017.1283502

Brown, D., and Cinamon, R. G. (2016). Personality traits' effects on self-efficacy and outcome expectations for high school major choice. *Inter. J. Edu. Voc. Gui.* 16, 343–361. doi: 10.1007/s10775-015-9316-4

Brown, S. D., Lent, R. W., Telander, K., and Tramayne, S. (2011). Social cognitive career theory, conscientiousness, and work performance: a meta-analytic path analysis. *J. Vocat. Behav.* 79, 81–90. doi: 10.1016/j.jvb.2010.11.009

Caprara, G. V., Alessandri, G., Di-Giunta, L., Panerai, L., and Eisenberg, N. (2010). The contribution of agreeableness and self-efficacy beliefs to prosociality. *Eur. J. Personal.* 24, 36–55. doi: 10.1002/per.739

Chen, B. Y., Wan, L., Fang, Y., Yan, L. X., and Lan, J. J. (2016). Interpersonal self-support traits predicting interpersonal trust among undergraduate students: beyond the effects of big five personality. *J. Psychol. Sci.* 6, 163–169. doi: 10.16719/j.cnki.1671-6981.20160624

Coco, M., Guerrera, C. S., Di Corrado, D., Ramaci, T., Maci, T., Pellerone, M., et al. (2019). Personality traits and athletic young adults. *Sport Sci. Health* 15, 435–441. doi: 10.1007/s11332-019-00551-3

Costam, P. T. Jr., and McCrae, R. R. (1992). *NEO personality inventory – revised (NEO-PI-R) and NEO five-factor inventory (NEO-FFI) professional manual.* Odessa, FL: Psychological Assessment Resources.

Coyne, M. A., and Wright, J. P. (2014). The stability of self-control across childhood. *Personal. Individ. Differ.* 69, 144–149. doi: 10.1016/j.paid.2014.05.026

Cristina, P. M., Marinella, C., Tiziana, M., Chiara, M., De Pasquale, C., Gianluca, D. O., et al. (2018). Successfully aging. Choice of life or life that choices. *Acta Med. Austriaca* 34, 107–111. doi: 10.19193/0393-6384_2018_1_18

De Vries, R. E., and Van Gelder, J. L. (2013). Tales of two self-control scales: relations with five-factor and HEXACO traits. *Personal. Individ. Differ.* 54, 756–760. doi: 10.1016/j.paid.2012.12.023

Deng, S. C., and Gao, J. (2015). Big five personality and impulsive buying: the mediation of self-control and sensation seeking. *Chi. J. Cli. Psychol.* 23, 1098–1101. doi: 10.16128/j.cnki.1005-3611.2015.06.033

Djigić, G., Stojiljković, S., and Dosković, M. (2014). Basic personality dimensions and teachers' self-efficacy. *Procedia. Soc. Behav. Sci.* 112, 593–602. doi: 10.1016/j.sbspro.2014.01.1206

Earley, P. C., and Lituchy, T. R. (1991). Delineating goal and efficacy effects: a test of three models. *J. Appl. Psychol.* 76, 81–98. doi: 10.1037/0021-9010.76.1.81

Eastin, M. S., and La-Rose, R. (2000). Internet self-efficacy and the psychology of the digital divide. *J. Compu. Medi. Communi.* 6, 1–13. doi: 10.1111/j.1083-6101.2000.tb00110.x

Englert, C. (2016). The strength model of self-control in sport and exercise psychology. *Front. Psychol.* 7, 824–826. doi: 10.3389/fpsyg.2016.00314

Fang, X., Liu, J., and Zheng, Z. (2015). The relationship among self-supporting personality, self-efficacy and self-control of undergraduates. *Stu. Psychol. Behav.* 13, 500–505. http://psybeh.tjnu.edu.cn/CN/abstract/abstract1456.shtml

Fang, J., Zhang, M. Q., and Chou, H. J. (2012). Mediation analysis and effect size measurement: retrospect and prospect. *Psychol. Devel. Edu.* 28, 105–111. doi: 10.16187/j.cnki.issn1001-4918.2012.01.015

Fisher, L. A., Butryn, T. M., and Roper, E. A. (2003). Diversifying (and politicizing) sport psychology through cultural studies: a promising perspective. *Sport Psychol.* 17, 391–405. doi: 10.1123/tsp.17.4.391

Freud, S. (1993). *New introductory lectures on psychology-analysis* New York: Norton.

Graham, J. D., and Bray, S. R. (2015). Self-control strength depletion reduces self-efficacy and impairs exercise performance. *J. Sport Exerc. Psychol.* 37, 477–488. doi: 10.1123/jsep.2015-0064

Green, J. A., O'Connor, D. B., Gartland, N., and Roberts, B. W. (2016). The Chernyshenko conscientiousness scales: a new facet measure of conscientiousness. *Assessment* 23, 374–385. doi: 10.1177/1073191115580639

Hare, T. A., Camerer, C. F., and Rangel, A. (2009). Self-control in decision-making involves modulation of the vmPFC valuation system. *Science* 324, 646–648. doi: 10.1126/science.1168450

Hayes, A. F. (2013). *Introduction to mediation, moderation, and conditional process analysis: A regression-based approach*. New York, NY: The Guilford Press.

Huang, W., and Yang, Z. (2015). Goal orientation, self-efficacy, and self-control among 3~6 years old children. *Psychol. Dev. Educ.* 31, 547–554. doi: 10.16187/j.cnki.issn1001-4918.2015.05.05

Jones, M., Meijen, C., McCarthy, P. J., and Sheffield, D. (2009). A theory of challenge and threat states in athletes. *Int. Rev. Sport Exerc. Psychol.* 2, 161–180. doi: 10.1080/17509840902829331

Judge, T. A., Jackson, C. L., Shaw, J. C., Scott, B. A., and Rich, B. L. (2007). Self-efficacy and work-related performance: the integral role of individual differences. *J. Appl. Psychol.* 92, 107–127. doi: 10.1037/0021-9010.92.1.107

Kaida, K., Ogawa, K., Matsuura, N., Takahashi, M., and Hori, T. (2006). The relationship between nap habit with self-awakening and generalized self-efficacy. *J. J. Health. Psychol.* 19, 1-9. doi: 10.11560/jahp.19.1_1

Lane, A. M. (2006). Article commentary: Reflections of professional boxing consultancy: a response to Schinke (2004). *Athletic Insight* 8, 85–90. Retrieved from http://www.athleticinsight.com/Vol8Iss3/Reflections.htm

Li, X. Y., and Zhang, L. W. (2011). "The structure and messuerment of self-control of athletes" in *The 90th Anniversary of the Chinese Psychological Society and the National Conference on Psychology*, 639–640.

Mao, T., Pan, W., Zhu, Y., Yang, J., Dong, Q., and Zhou, G. (2018). Self-control mediates the relationship between personality trait and impulsivity. *Personal. Individ. Differ.* 129, 70–75. doi: 10.1016/j.paid.2018.03.013

Marcionetti, J., and Rossier, J. (2016). Global life satisfaction in adolescence: the role of personality traits, self-esteem, and self-efficacy. *J. Individ. Differ.* 37, 135–144. doi: 10.1027/1614-0001/a000198

McCrae, R. R., and Terracciano, A. (2005). Universal features of personality traits from the observer's perspective: data from 50 cultures. *J. Pers. Soc. Psychol.* 88, 547–561. doi: 10.1037/0022-3514.88.3.547

Moffitt, T. E., Arseneault, L., Belsky, D., Dickson, N., Hancox, R. J., Harrington, H., et al. (2011). A gradient of childhood self-control predicts health, wealth, and public safety. *Proc. Natl. Acad. Sci. USA* 108, 2693–2698. doi: 10.1073/pnas.1010076108

Myers, N. D., Feltz, D. L., and Short, S. E. (2004). Collective efficacy and team performance: a longitudinal study of collegiate football teams. *Group Dyn. Theory Res. Pract.* 8, 126–138. doi: 10.1037/1089-2699.8.2.126

Pilarska, A. (2018). Big-five personality and aspects of the self-concept: variable- and person-centered approaches. *Personal. Individ. Differ.* 127, 107–113. doi: 10.1016/j.paid.2018.01.049

Ryba, T. V., and Wright, H. K. (2005). From mental game to cultural praxis: a cultural studies model's implications for the future of sport psychology. *QUEST* 7, 192–212. doi: 10.1080/00336297.2005.10491853

Sanchez-Cardona, I., Rodriguez-Montalbán, R., Acevedo-Soto, E., Lugo, K. N., Torres-Oquendo, F., and Toro-Alfonso, J. (2012). Self-efficacy and openness to experience as antecedent of study engagement: an exploratory analysis. *Procedia Soc. Behav. Sci.* 46, 2163–2167. doi: 10.1016/j.sbspro.2012.05.446

Schinke, R. J. (2007). A four-year chronology with national team boxing in Canada. *J. Sports Sci. Med.* 6, 1–5. doi: 10.1016/j.jsams.2006.07.010

Schmitt, N. (2007). The interaction of neuroticism and gender and its impact on self-efficacy and performance. *Hum. Perform.* 21, 49–61. doi: 10.1080/08959280701522197

Simpson, D., and Wrisberg, C. (2013). Fail to prepare, prepare to fail: professional boxers experiences of training. *Sport Psychol.* 27, 109–119. doi: 10.1123/tsp.27.2.109

Song, Q., Shen, D. D., and Gao, X. F. (2009). Thinking about the actual exertion of combat technique of Chinese boxing players in Beijing olympics-the issue of combined training about Chinese high level professional players. *J. Guangzhou Sport Univ.* 29, 88–90. doi: 10.13830/j.cnki.cn44-1129/g8.2009.05.016

Stajkovic, A. D., Bandura, A., Locke, E. A., Lee, D., and Sergent, K. (2018). Test of three conceptual models of influence of the big five personality traits and self-efficacy on academic performance: a meta-analytic path-analysis. *Personal. Individ. Differ.* 120, 238–245. doi: 10.1016/j.paid.2017.08.014

Tangney, J. P., Boone, A. L., and Baumeister, R. F. (2014). High self-control predicts good adjustment, less pathology, better grades, and interpersonal success. *J. Pers.* 72, 271–324. doi: 10.1111/j.0022-3506.2004.00263.x

Vancouver, J. B., Thompson, C. M., Tischner, E. C., and Putka, D. J. (2002). Two studies examining the negative effect of self-efficacy on performance. *J. Appl. Psychol.* 87, 506–516. doi: 10.1037//0021-9010.87.3.506

Vera, E. M., Shin, R. Q., Montgomery, G. P., Mildner, C., and Speight, S. L. (2004). Conflict resolution styles, self-efficacy, self-control, and future orientation of urban adolescents. *Prof. School Couns.* 8, 73–80. doi: 10.5330/PSC.n.2010-12.240

Wang, Z., Zhang, W., Li, Y. H., Zhang, H., and Hong, P. (2009). The relationship between personality traits, self-efficacy and stress coping styles of woman basketball players. *Chi. Sport. Sci.* 29, 59–64. doi: 10.16469/j.css.2009.11.008

Wei, P., Chen, H. B., and Song, B. P. (2008). Preliminary establishment of sports sense of self-efficacy scale. *J. Xian Physical. Edu. Univ.* 25, 128–130. doi: 10.16063/j.cnki.issn1001-747x.2008.04.030

Yang, L. I., Li, W. Z., and Lian, C. Z. (2013). The theory of challenge and threat states in athletes and self-control in competition. *Adv. Psychol. Sci.* 21, 1696–1710. doi: 10.3724/SP.J.1042.2013.01696

Yu, Y., Hu, Y. H., Zhu, D. P., Gao, P., and Wang, M. (2012). *Research on technical and tactical characteristics model of Chinese men undefined boxing Olympic champion*. Beijing: Department of Science and Education, State Sport Administration. http://cdmd.cnki.com.cn/Article/CDMD-10522-1013327790.htm

Yu, G. Q., and Yang, Z. L. (2008). A research on the implicit effect of self-control. *Psychol. Sci.* 31, 614–616. doi: 10.16719/j.cnki.1671-6981.2008.03.018

Zhang, L. W. (2013). Athletes self-control: important theories and research development. *J. Psychol. Sci.* 36, 515–523. doi: 10.16719/j.cnki.1671-6981.2013.03.004

Zhang, R. P. (2016). Positive affect and self-efficacy as mediators between personality and life satisfaction in Chinese college freshmen. *J. Happiness Stud.* 17, 1–15. doi: 10.1007/s10902-015-9682-0

8

A Systematic Review of Attentional Focus Strategies in Weightlifting

*David L. Neumann**

School of Applied Psychology, Griffith University, Gold Coast, QLD, Australia

***Correspondence:**
David L. Neumann
d.neumann@griffith.edu.au

The way an athlete focuses their attention when lifting a weight has the potential to influence strength development during training and performance outcomes during competition. The effects of attentional focus strategies during weightlifting tasks was investigated through a systematic review. Major databases (SportDISCUS, PsycINFO, Scopus) were searched using key terms relevant to attentional focus and weightlifting and reference lists of identified articles were also searched. Following screening, 16 articles were retained for analysis. The review showed that researchers have recruited experienced and novice weightlifters of both genders in their studies, although male experienced weightlifters are the most commonly studied demographic. Weightlifting tasks have varied from bench press, biceps curls, squats, and leg extensions with some studies using measures of force production against a force plate. The predominant manipulations have been between internal-associative and external-associative foci. An external attentional focus has shown to be beneficial in terms of movement economy as reflected in a variety of outcome measures. The results are interpreted within the framework provided by the Constrained Action Hypothesis and more generally the advantages of an external attentional focus for motor skill learning. An external focus of attention promotes automatic control of actions, thus preventing the motor system being constrained by conscious cognitive control. Implications for informing training programs for athletes and for advising athletes to maximize performance during competition are discussed.

Keywords: attention, weightlifting, concentration, performance, strength training, attentional focus

INTRODUCTION

The action of lifting a weighted apparatus is ubiquitus in sport and exercise. It is used during training to develop muscle strength, muscle mass, and joint strength. It is is also a competitive sport in its own right, as reflected in its Olympic Games status and the formation of national and international governing bodies. The sport of weightlifting requires lifts of the snatch and the clean and jerk with athletes aiming to lift the heavest weight for their division during competition. Other competitive events, often referred to as powerlifting, require the deadlift, squat, and bench press. Weightlifting is also a key component of training for other sports and as part of a physical exercise program. In these situations, there are a multitude of different types of lifts according to the muscles required, equipment used, and the speed, duration, and complexity of the movements.

The physical nature of weightlifting has naturally led to research on physical factors, such as physiology, biomechanics, diet, and injury. Comparatively less work has been conducted on the psychological processes associated with weightlifting. The psychology of weightlifting has been examined from various perspectives, including self-efficacy, intention, and self-regulation behaviors (Rhodes et al., 2017), mindfulness and contemplative movement (Vernon, 2018), and instruction techniques (Milanese et al., 2017). Attentional focus is another psychological factor that has potentially important implications for learning and performance in weightlifting.

Attentional focus, in the context of sport and exercise performance, refers to the process in which the athlete allocates mental resources to cues, stimuli, or states. Attentional focus is commonly classified along one or more dimensions. Nideffer (1976) proposed two dimensions of direction (internal or external) and width (broad or narrow). Stevinson and Biddle (1998) also proposed two dimensions, although they divided attentional foci along task-relevance (association or dissociation) and direction (internal or external). Two dimensional schemes such as these will allow for a particular attentional focus to reflect a combination of the two dimensions. For instance, the task-relevance and direction scheme results in four combinations of internal association (e.g., muscle fatigue, breathing, pain), internal dissociation (e.g., daydreams, mental puzzles, recalling memories), external association (e.g, split times, distance markers, targets), and external dissociation (e.g., scenery, crowd, listening to music).

Subsequent classification schemes have extended upon the task-relevance (or association) and direction dimensions of Stevinson and Biddle (1998). Wininger and Gieske (2010), for example, divided a task-relevance internal foci into bodily sensations, task-relevant thoughts, and self-talk. Brick et al. (2014) used two internal association categories of internal sensory monitoring and active self-regulation. The external association combination has also been conceptualized in different ways, such as a focus on the movement effect (Wulf, 2013). The dimensions or specific categories in a dimension may be more relevant for some types of sports than others. For example, the scheme proposed by Brick et al. (2014) provides an excellent framework for endurance sports like running, cycling, and rowing.

Attentional focus in weightlifting has been largely investigated from the attentional focus strategies of internal association and external association (usually simply referred to as internal and external foci). This approach stems from the influential work by Wulf et al. demonstrating the performance benefits of an external attentional focus over an internal attentional focus in ski-simulator and balancing tasks (Wulf et al., 1998). The external attentional focus benefits were subsequently extended to other motor and sport-related tasks (for reviews, see Wulf, 2007, 2013; Marchant, 2011; Lohse et al., 2012; Wulf and Lewthwaite, 2016). The research has generally shown that focussing away from the body and on the intended movement effect (external focus) produces superior learning and performance outcomes than focussing toward the body (internal focus). Moreover, this effect seems to be due to a relative improvement in performance with an external focus, rather than a relative impairment of performance with an internal focus, because an external focus will typically produce better outcomes than no specific attentional focus instructions.

The benefits of an external focus of attention for motor learning and performance has been reflected in a range of tasks and outcome measures (for details see Wulf and Lewthwaite, 2016). Benefits have been observed in movement effectiveness (e.g., better balance, higher accuracy), movement efficiency (e.g., reduced muscular activity, higher peak force, greater speed, longer endurance), better movement form, and more automatic and fluid movements. The potential for an external focus of attention to enhance movement efficiency is of particular relevance for weightlifting. For example, it may allow an athlete to lift the same weight through less muscular effort. Conversely, and more importantly for competition, it may allow an athlete to lift a heavier weight than would otherwise be possible when no specific attentional focus is adopted.

The present review examined research on attentional focus strategies during weightlifting. A systematic literature review was conducted in which relevant electronic databases were searched using key terms. Search results were screened to yield a final set of articles for coding and analysis. The review aimed to answer the following questions:

1. What types of weightlifting tasks and equipment are used in research?
2. What are the characteristics of the participants who have been studied?
3. What have been the aims, methods, conditions, measures and key findings of research?
4. What theoretical framework has been used to guide the research and interpret the findings?

Following a review of these questions, it was hoped to develop some general principles from what is known about attentional focus in weightlifting. Practical applications and suggestions for research are also offered.

METHODS

The Preferred Reporting Items for Systematic Review and Meta-Analyses (PRISMA) guidelines were followed for the literature search (Liberati et al., 2009), and the rules of inclusion and exclusion described by Meline (2006) were applied. Initially, the SPORTDiscus, PsycINFO, and Scopus databases were searched. The terms used in conducting the search included: ("focus of attention" OR "attentional focus" OR "attentional focusing") AND ("weight lifting" OR weightlifting OR "weight training" OR "strength training" OR "force production" OR "motor control") AND (internal OR external OR association OR dissociation OR associative OR dissociative). The search was not limited by date of publication and included all articles available at time of search (October, 2018). Additionally, to identify articles that may have been missed due to inconsistent use of terms (e.g., "attentional focus" vs. "focus of attention"), the reference lists of

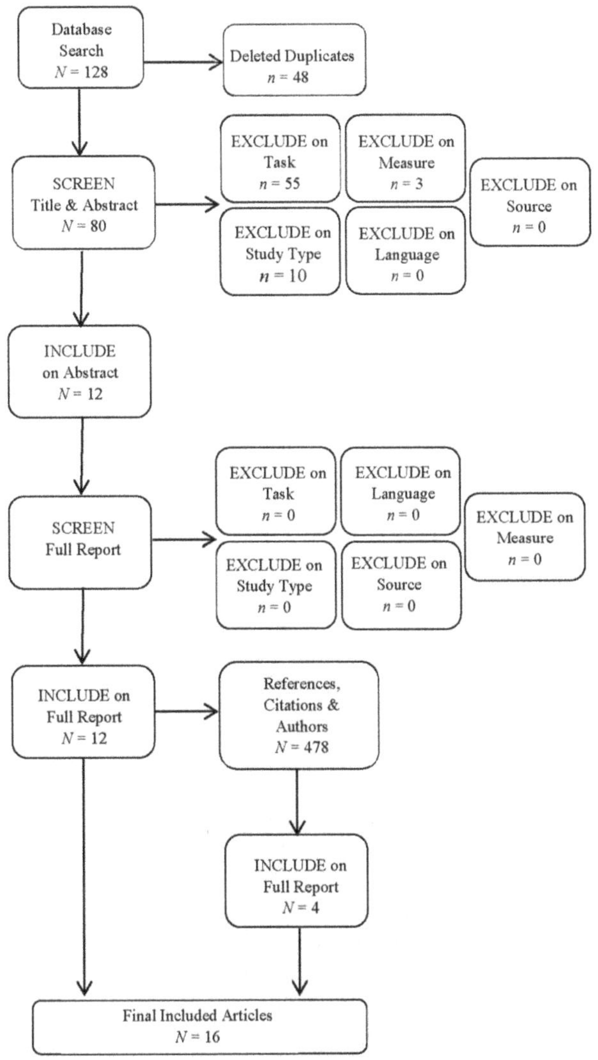

FIGURE 1 | Search results and outcomes of the screening process.

all articles initially selected for inclusion from the database search were examined.

The results from the literature search and screening are shown in **Figure 1**. The database search resulted in 27 articles from PsychINFO database, 46 articles from SPORTDiscus database, and 55 articles from Scopus database, totaling 128 articles. Following the removal of duplicates, this number was reduced to 80 unique articles. Articles were then screened for exclusion or inclusion in a two-step process: title and abstract (step 1) and the full article (step 2). Articles were excluded based on the following criteria: language (not published in English language), source (a dissertation, thesis, abstract only, magazine article, or from a non-peer reviewed source), study type (review, meta-analysis, commentary, letters, or any non-empirical article), did not measure or manipulate attentional foci, did not examine movement against a weight or force plate, or did not include a measure of physical performance or physiological activity.

Following this selection process, a total of 12 articles from the database search, with a further four articles identified following the examiniation of the selected articles reference lists were obtained. As such, a total of 16 articles were included in the systematic review. **Table 1** shows the citation metrics for the articles that were published in journals present in the Scimago Journal & Country Rank database. The mean 2-year impact factor was 1.90 (range 0.968–2.717, $SD = 0.54$), the mean journal h-index was 86.33 (range 42–117, $SD = 22.64$), and seven journals were Q1 ranked. These citation metrics suggest that the journals that published this research were of moderate to high quality. The articles were coded by study characteristics (aims, conditions/groups, outcome measures, and key findings), participant characteristics (sample size, age, gender, weight lifting experience, and location), and task characteristics (exercise/movement completed and equipment used).

RESULTS

Tasks and Equipment Used in Research

The types of weightlifting tasks and equipment used in research on attentional focus strategies are shown in **Table 2**. As can be seen, the bench press (Marchant et al., 2011; Snyder and Fry, 2012; Calatayud et al., 2018a,b; Kristiansen et al., 2018), force plate (Lohse et al., 2011; Lohse, 2012; Lohse and Sherwood, 2012) and bicep curls (Vance et al., 2004; Marchant et al., 2008, 2009; Neumann and Heng, 2011) have been the most commonly used. The bench press and bicep curls are advantageous because they involve relatively simple movements and effectively isolate key muscles. The bench press is also a powerlifting event, and so enhances the real-world relevance of outcomes for competition. The snatch was used by Schutts et al. (2017), which is the only study found in the search to have used an Olympic weightlifting event.

Lohse et al. (2011), Lohse (2012), and Lohse and Sherwood (2012) examined force production when participants pushed with their feet against a force plate. The apparatus allows for the investigation of motor planning (Lohse, 2012), as well as intermuscular coordination (e.g., co-contraction of muscles) and intramuscular coordination (e.g., motor-unit recruitment) under different types of attentional foci (Lohse et al., 2011). The use of a force plate is thus a useful complement to free weights in research. Although not included following the screening process, research has also examined attentional focus effects on muscle activity during a sit up task (Neumann and Brown, 2013), which was a task that did not involve muscular force against any apparatus. There are thus a wide variety of tasks that researchers have used to examine attentional foci at the neuromuscular level.

Participant Characteristics

The characteristics of the participants who have been studied in research are shown in **Table 3**. Most studies have used both male and female participants, with some studies restricting their sample to males only. No studies exclusively used female participants. Although sex does not typically moderate attentional focus effects (but for examples see Becker and Smith, 2013; Flôres et al., 2016; Emad et al., 2017), it is still

TABLE 1 | Publication details of the studies selected for review.

References	Journal name	2-year impact factor	Journal h-index	Quartile
Calatayud et al., 2018a	Journal of sports sciences	2.715	117	Q1
Calatayud et al., 2018b	Perceptual and motor skills	0.989	60	Q4
Greig and Marchant, 2014	Human movement science	1.956	80	Q2
Halperin et al., 2016	Journal of strength and conditioning research	2.340	108	Q1
Kristiansen et al., 2018	Journal of strength and conditioning research	2.340	108	Q1
Lohse, 2012	Human movement science	1.956	80	Q2
Lohse et al., 2011	Journal of motor behavior	1.328	63	Q3
Lohse and Sherwood, 2012	Acta psychologica	1.632	88	Q1
Marchant et al., 2008	Athletic insight	–	–	–
Marchant et al., 2009	Journal of strength and conditioning research	2.340	108	Q1
Marchant et al., 2011	Research quarterly for exercise and sport	2.01	82	Q2
Marchant and Greig, 2017	Human movement science	1.956	80	Q2
Neumann and Heng, 2011	Journal of psychophysiology	0.968	42	Q3
Schutts et al., 2017	Journal of strength and conditioning research	2.340	108	Q1
Snyder and Fry, 2012	Journal of strength and conditioning research	2.340	108	Q1
Vance et al., 2004	Journal of motor behavior	1.328	63	Q3
	Mean (SD)	1.90 (0.54)	86.33 (22.64)	

Citation metrics of 2-year impact factor, journal h-index, and quartile ranking were obtained from Scimago Journal and Country Rank database.

an important empirical question on whether sex differences exist for weightlifting. It is thus recommended that future research include both sexes in research when possible to ensure generalisability of findings and that analyses are conducted to check for sex differences.

Participants have tended to be experienced in weightlifting, although a sizeable portion of studies did not specify the participant experience level. Experienced participants are more likely to be well-practiced and to have develop automaticity in movements. Given the notion that an external focus of attention facilitates automatic motor processes (Wulf and Lewthwaite, 2016) it may be expected that experienced participants are particularly likely to benefit from an external focus of attention than an internal one. Novice participants have also shown learning and performance benefits from an external attentional focus across a range of tasks (Wulf and Lewthwaite, 2016). However, there have been exceptions (e.g., Perkins-Ceccato et al., 2003). In line with the recommendation of Greig and Marchant (2014), further research is needed that tests for differences between experienced and novice participants in attentional focus effects.

Other characteristics of the participants have shown that many studies have recruited undergraduate students or participants aged 20–25 years on average. While some studies have used older samples, these have had a mean age no older than 31 years. Future research could recruit older adult samples to ensure the generality of the findings across a wide age range. Similarly, no studies have recruited younger participants, such as adolescents and children, and it remains to be determined whether study findings can be replicated with a young age group. Most studies have been conducted in Western countries, most noteably the USA, England, and Denmark. Finally, the sample sizes used in research has been relatively small. Samples have varied from 11 to 29 participants with a mean of 17.67 participants. It is recommended that researchers recruit larger samples to ensure that there is sufficient statistical power, to minimize the reporting of spurious findings, and to ensure generality of findings. In summary, reseach has used relatively small samples with participants typically comprised of young males from Western countries who are experienced in the sport of weightlifting.

Aims, Methods, and Key Findings

A summary of the aims, methods, conditions, measures, and main findings in the experiments reported in the 16 studies reviewed is provided in **Table 4**. An external focus of attention has produced lower EMG activity (peak EMG, average EMG, or integrated EMG) than an internal focus of attention in several studies (Vance et al., 2004; Marchant et al., 2008, 2009; Lohse et al., 2011; Lohse and Sherwood, 2012; Greig and Marchant, 2014; Marchant and Greig, 2017). An external focus has also shown superior performance over an internal focus for peak torque (Greig and Marchant, 2014), force production (Marchant et al., 2009; Halperin et al.,

TABLE 2 | Characteristics of the task and equipment used.

References	Task	Equipment
Calatayud et al., 2018a	Bench press	Barbell
Calatayud et al., 2018b	Bench press	Barbell
Greig and Marchant, 2014	Bicep curl	Isokinetic dynamometer (Biodex, System 3)
Halperin et al., 2016	Isometric midthigh pull	Barbell and 9290AD quattro jump force plate
Kristiansen et al., 2018	Bench press	Barbell
Lohse, 2012	Force production—foot pressing	Force plate
Lohse et al., 2011	Force Production—Foot Pressing	Force plate
Lohse and Sherwood, 2012		
Experiment 1	Force production—foot pressing	Force plate
Experiment 2	Force production—foot pressing	Force plate
Marchant et al., 2008	Bicep curls	Isokinetic dynamometer (biodex, system 3)
Marchant et al., 2009	Bicep curls	Isokinetic dynamometer (biodex, system 3)
Marchant et al., 2011		
Exercise 1	Assisted bench press: 40 kg for men, 20 kg for women	Smith machine
Exercise 2	Bench press: 75% of 1-RM	Standard bench and barbell
Exercise 3	Back Squat in high bar position: 75% of 1-RM	Standard barbell
Marchant and Greig, 2017	Leg extension	Isokinetic dynamometer (biodex, system 3)
Neumann and Heng, 2011	Bicep curls	Dumbbell set with changeable disc weights
Schutts et al., 2017	Snatch: 80% of 1-RM	Standard barbell
Snyder and Fry, 2012	Bench press: 50 and 80% of 1-RM	Standard barbell and bench
Vance et al., 2004	Bicep curls--50% of 1-RM	Weighted barbell

2016), reduced pre-movement time in early stages of learning an isometric force production task (Lohse, 2012), accuracy in a force production task (Lohse et al., 2011; Lohse and Sherwood, 2012), more repetitions before failure (Marchant et al., 2011), and better movement kinematics for the snatch (Schutts et al., 2017).

The conditions that may limit the effects of an internal or external focus have also been examined. Lifting at a controlled or explosive speed did not alter the size of muscle contractions as measured by EMG for an internal focus strategy (Calatayud et al., 2018a,b). Moreover, using grips of different width does not interact with the type of attentional foci (internal or external) on EMG activity. In a study on force production, an external focus of attention produced lower EMG than an internal focus at all speeds, but an interaction between focus type and speed was observed for peak torque such that the attentional focus conditions differed in torque only at slower speeds (Greig and Marchant, 2014). The latter findings suggest that lifting speed may influence attentional focus effects.

It is often reported that an external focus is superior than both an internal focus and a control (no instructions) condition and that this is evidence for a beneficial effect of an external focus rather than a relative detrimental effect of an internal focus (Wulf, 2007). Similar outcomes have been reported in weightlifting and force production tasks (Marchant et al., 2008, 2011). However, this finding has not always been found. Both an external and control condition resulted in greater force during an isometric midthigh pull than an internal condition (Halperin et al., 2016). An external focus resulted in more repetitions to failure than an internal focus, but did not differ from a control condition for an assisted bench press (Marchant et al., 2011).

Furthermore, research has not always shown performance benefits with an external focus of attention. No differences between internal and external foci have been observed for time to failure or ratings of perceived exertion for a long duration force production task (Lohse and Sherwood, 2012). In different findings, Kristiansen et al. (2018) reported that both an external and an internal attentional focus produced greater mean and peak EMG amplitude than a baseline condition during a bench press. In the baseline condition, participants performed the lift as they normally would. The authors suggested that the results may reflect that experienced weight lifters were participants and that the use of attentional instructions of any type may have interfered with their normal technique. Another explanation could be that the baseline condition was completed first and performance in the subsequent conditions suffered from fatigue effects. Yet another explanation may relate to the relative high complexity of the attentional focus instructions. For instance, the external focus instructions required participants to maintain the same tempo of the lift as done in the baseline condition

TABLE 3 | Sample size and participant characteristics.

References	*N*	Gender	Age in years (*SD*)	Experience	Location
Calatayud et al., 2018a	18	Male	$M = 31$ (8)	Experienced	Denmark
Calatayud et al., 2018b	18	Male	$M = 31$ (8)	Experienced	Denmark
Greig and Marchant, 2014	25	Both	$M = 23.53$ (1.76)	Inexperienced	England
Halperin et al., 2016	22	Both	$M = 22.5$ (3.3) Range: 17–28	Experienced	Australia
Kristiansen et al., 2018	21	Male	$M = 24.5$ (2.2)	Experienced	Denmark
Lohse, 2012	24	Both	Undergraduates	Unknown	United States
Lohse et al., 2011	12	Both	Undergraduates	Unknown	United States
Lohse and Sherwood, 2012					
Experiment 1	12	Both	Undergraduates	Unknown	United States
Experiment 2	12	Both	Undergraduates	Unknown	United States
Marchant et al., 2008	29	Both	$M = 19.6$ (1.3)	Experienced	England
Marchant et al., 2009	25	Both	$M = 22.72$	Inexperienced	England
Marchant et al., 2011					
Assisted bench press	23	Both	$M = 30.87$ (12.27)	Experienced	England
Bench press	17	Male	$M = 20.82$ (1.42)	Experienced	England
Back squat	17	Male	$M = 20.82$ (1.42)	Experienced	England
Marchant and Greig, 2017	20	Both	$M = 20.2$ (1.47)	Experienced	England
Neumann and Heng, 2011					
Group 1	16	Both	Male: $M = 23.14$ (4.28) Female: $M = 29$ (11.31)	Novice	Australia
Group 2	14	Both	Male: $M = 24.31$ (3.30) Female: 22	Experienced	Australia
Schutts et al., 2017	12	Both	$M = 23.7$ (2.9)	Experienced	United States
Snyder and Fry, 2012	11	Male	Undergraduates	Experienced	United States
Vance et al., 2004					
Experiment 1	11	Male	$M = 26.00$ (6.00)	Experienced	United States
Experiment 2	12	Both	Not provided	Experienced	United States

while also attending to the movement of the barbell and making the move as smooth as possible. The internal focus instructions also referred to moving the barbell as smooth as possible and at the same tempo as the baseline condition, as well as focusing on the pectoralis muscle contractions. These internal focus instructions included some reference to an external focus (move the barbell as smooth as possible). Wulf (2007) has suggested that the use of vague or complex attentional focus instructions may mitigate the benefits of an external focus over an internal one.

To elicit an internal attentional focus, researchers have typically used simple instructions requiring participants to attend to the feelings of the muscle or combinations of muscles primarily involved in the lift. A focus on the primary muscles involved in lifting will increase EMG activity measured from that muscle (Calatayud et al., 2018a). Moreover, a focus on secondary muscles for a lift (e.g., triceps for a bench press) will increase EMG activity of the primary muscle (i.e., pectoralis). However, it should be noted that effects of focusing on a specific muscle may vary across the weights being lifted. Attention to a specific muscle increased activity of the muscle that attention was directed toward when a lighter weight was lifted (50% of 1-RM) but not when a heavier weight was used (80% of 1-RM) for a bench press (Snyder and Fry, 2012).

Instructions used to induce an external focus of instruction have typically required participants to focus on the movements of the barbell, dumbbell, crank handle, or platform (see **Table 4**). Calatayud et al. (2018b) defined an external focus as lifting the barbell in a regular way. However, it may be argued that this instruction did not adequately require participants to focus on the movement effects of the exercise. Further research would be required to evaluate this possibility.

In the only research to examine other forms of attention focus strategies, Neumann and Heng (2011) compared an associative and dissociative focus strategy during a biceps curl task. The study was also unique in measuring heart rate in addition to muscle activity (see Neumann and Thomas, 2009, 2011 for examples of attentional focus effects on heart rate during sport tasks). The dissociative condition required participants to listen to audio of a song whereas the associative condition consisted of listening to audio of a tone that changed in nature based on the EMG amplitude recorded from the biceps muscle. A control condition using no audio and no specific focus instructions was also used. The results showed that EMG, iEMG, and heart rate were lower during the associative strategy than during the dissociative strategy and control conditions. The differences between conditions may reflect a relative benefit of an associative strategy for muscular efficiency. The benefit may reflect that the associative condition had a predominantly external focus (i.e., the effects of the movement on the external audio stimulus). However, the associative condition may have also had an internal

TABLE 4 | Characteristics of the aims, conditions, measures, and key findings.

References	Aims	Conditions	Measures	Key findings
Calatayud et al., 2018a	To investigate the effect of different attentional focus strategies on muscle activity during the bench press at explosive and controlled speeds.	Focus instruction: regular focus (lift the barbell in a regular way), focus on pectoralis (try to focus on using your chest muscles only), focus on triceps (try to focus on using your triceps muscles only) Barbell speed: controlled (2 s rate of descent 2 s ascent), explosive (as fast as possible)	Electromyography (EMG) Contraction duration (for explosive condition)	During the controlled condition, focusing on either the pectoralis or triceps resulted in increased EMG activity in the pectoralis by 6 and 4%, respectively, over using a regular focus. Additionally, in the controlled condition, activity in the triceps increased 4% when a triceps focus was used. There was no difference found in EMG activity or contraction duration between the focus conditions when lifting explosively.
Calatayud et al., 2018b	To investigate the effects of either external or internal focus strategies and varying grip widths on muscle activity during the bench press	Focus instruction: internal for pectoralis (try to focus only on using your chest muscles), internal for triceps (try to focus only on using your triceps muscles), external focus (just lift the barbell in a regular way)	EMG	Significant main effects for attentional focus and grip width for EMG activity in both the pectoralis and triceps muscles (higher during internal focus than external focus), but no significant interactions.
Greig and Marchant, 2014	To investigate the effects of internal and external focusing instructions on force production and muscle activity at varying movement speeds.	Focus instructions: internal (focus on the movement of your arm and muscles during the lift), external (focus upon the movement of the crank hand-bar during the lift). Speed: move the crank at 60°, 180°, or 300° per second.	Force production measured using peak torque Muscle activity measured using EMG	External focus associated with lower EMG in all speeds compared to internal focus. However, an external focus only produced greater torque than in an internal focus when speed was at 60° per second condition. This suggest that focusing instructions may be less effective for explosive movements.
Halperin et al., 2016	To investigate the effect of attentional focus on a force production during an isometric midthigh pull in trained athletes.	Focus instructions: control (Focus on going as hard and as fast as you possibly can), internal (Focus on contracting your leg muscles as hard and as fast as you possibly can), external (Focus on pushing the ground as hard and as fast as you possibly can)	Force measured using Newtons (N).	Both the external focus and control instructions resulted in greater force production than the internal focus instructions (9 and 5%, respectively). This suggests that adopting an internal focus while exerting maximal force hinders performance.
Kristiansen et al., 2018	To compare the effect of internal and external focus with no focus instruction on muscle activity during a 60% 3 RM bench press	Three conditions completed by all participants. Baseline included no focus instructions. External condition instructed participants to focus on the movement of the barbell and that the movement should be as smooth as possible. Internal condition required participants to focus on the contraction of the pectoralis muscle.	Electromyography (EMG)	Both internal and external focus conditions resulted in significantly greater mean and peak EMG amplitudes for 6-upper body muscles compared to baseline, despite all conditions involving the same weight and repetitions. These results suggest that both focus instructions were detrimental to performance. Results could be explained by the fact that participants were experienced lifters and introducing complicated instructions may have interfered with their natural technique.
Lohse, 2012	To investigate the effect of attentional focus on accuracy and pre-movement time during an isometric force production task	Focus instructions: External focus (Mentally focus on the push of your foot against the platform and push harder or less on the platform), Internal focus (Mentally focus on the calf and contract the muscle harder or less)	Accuracy (needed to meet maximum voluntary force [MVC] of either 25% or 50%)	External focus resulted in reduced pre-movement time in early stages of learning, and improved transfer performance (moving from 25% MVC target to 50% MVC target or vice versa) over internal focus.

(Continued)

TABLE 4 | Continued

References	Aims	Conditions	Measures	Key findings
Lohse et al., 2011	To investigate the effect of attentional focus instructions on force accuracy and muscle activity during an isometric force production task	Focus instructions: External focus (Mentally focus on the push of your foot against the platform), Internal focus (Mentally focus on pushing with the muscle of your calf)	Accuracy (target = 30% of maximal force) EMG	Greater accuracy in the external focus condition, and less muscle activity in the tibialis anterior of the calf, but no difference in activity in the soleus. These results suggest that muscles were more efficient and performed better when using an external focus than using an internal focus.
Lohse and Sherwood, 2012				
Experiment 1	To test the effects of attentional focus on accuracy and efficiency at varying levels of muscle contraction	Focus instructions: External focus (mentally focus on the push of your foot against the platform), Internal focus (mentally focus on pushing with the muscle of your calf) Target force: 30, 60, and 100 %MVC. Participants were informed how this force would translate to pounds of force. Force held for 4 second windows.	Accuracy (absolute error: average force across 3 s window with participant's target force subtracted) Cocontraction-ratio (dividing tibialis activity by soleus activity)	External focus produced more accurate force production across all force production targets. Additionally, an external focus reduced cocontraction, suggesting that the muscles performed more efficiently.
Experiment 2	To test the effects of attentional focus on muscle fatigue at varying level of muscle contraction	Focus instructions: External focus (mentally focus on the push of your foot against the platform), internal focus (mentally focus on pushing with the muscle of your calf) Target force: 30, 60, and 100 %MVC. Participants were informed how this force would translate to pounds of force. Participants were required to hold the target force for 60s for 30 and 60 %MVC or until failure for 100 %MVC.	Accuracy (absolute error: average force across 3 s window with participant's target force subtracted) Cocontraction-ratio (dividing tibialis activity by soleus activity) Time to failure (length of holding 100% MVC) Ratings of perceived exertion (for 100% MVC)	Attentional focus had no effect on time to failure, RPE, or accuracy. However, an internal focus of attention resulted in greater cocontraction in early trials, suggesting less efficient muscular coordination.
Marchant et al., 2008	To investigate the effect of attentional focusing on muscular activity during the bicep curl with controlled movement speed	Focus instructions: no instruction, internal focus (focus upon the movement of the arm during the lift), external focus (focus upon the movement of the crank handle during the lift)	Peak EMG Activity Integrated/total EMG activity over 10 repetitions	Peak muscle activity was lower when using external focus than using internal focus and no specific instructions. Total muscle activity was also lower in the external condition than internal condition. These results suggest that the use of external focus resulted in more efficient muscle control.
Marchant et al., 2009	To investigate the influence of attentional focusing instructions on force production and muscle activity during isokinetic elbow flexions.	Focus instructions: internal (focusing internally onto movement mechanics), external (focusing externally onto the outcome of the movement)	EMG Force production (torque)	An external focus of attention results in greater force production and lower EMG activity than an internal focus.
Marchant et al., 2011	To investigate the influence of attentional focusing instructions on muscular endurance in three types of exercises in experienced athletes	Focus instructions: Control (perform as many repetitions as you can before failure), internal (focus on moving and exerting force with your arms/legs), external (focus on moving and exerting force through the barbell)	Repetitions until failure	For the assisted bench press, an external focus of attention resulted in more repetitions before failure than an internal focus, but not for the control instructions. For the standard bench press and back squat, using an external focus of attention resulted in more repetitions before failure than both the internal focus and control instructions.

(Continued)

TABLE 4 | Continued

References	Aims	Conditions	Measures	Key findings
Marchant and Greig, 2017	To investigate the effect of internal focus instructions which emphasize specific muscular activity compared to external focus instructions which emphasize outcome on force and muscle activity during a knee extension task.	Focus instructions: internal focus (focus on muscular activation), external (focus onto the movement outcome)	Force (Peak torque and mean power output) Integrated EMG of vastus lateralis (VL), vastus medialis oblique (VMO), and rectus femoris Ratio of activation for VMO and VL	No difference in torque produced between the focus instructions. External focus instructions resulted in lower iEMG magnitude across muscles than internal focus. Internal focus resulted in greater EMG activity, but not in the specific VMO, suggesting that the internal focus did not result in a selective isolation. Instead, there was a spreading activation effect with elevated activity in muscles not within the focus of attention. Findings suggest that an external focus of attention results in increased muscular efficiency.
Neumann and Heng, 2011	To investigate the effects of an associative and dissociative attentional strategy on muscle activity for a biceps curl	Focus instructions: control (repeat previous lifting technique), dissociative (listen to lyrics of a song playing, and count the occurrence of a word), associative (attend to an auditory tone which varied based on EMG from biceps activity)	EMG and iEMG Heart rate Perceived exertion and exercise satisfaction Movement degrees and velocity	Adopting an associative strategy resulted in lower EMG, iEMG, and heart rate compared to dissociative and control strategies. No difference found in subjective measures of exertion or satisfaction. Movement velocity slower in associative condition than in dissociative or control condition.
Schutts et al., 2017	To investigate the effect of focus of attention on kinematic performance of the snatch	Focus instructions: internal focus (concentrate on moving your elbows high and to the side rapidly), external focus (concentrate on moving the barbell back and up rapidly)	Barbell-cervical-hip angle Vertical/Horizontal barbell velocity Peak elbow velocity	Internal focus resulted in increased elbow velocity compared to external focus. External focus increased horizontal barbell velocity compared to internal. The internal focus also resulted in the athlete squatting under the barbell too soon.
Snyder and Fry, 2012	To investigate the ability of athletes to isolate specific muscles when given internal focus instructions during the bench press	Focus instructions: non-specific instructions, internal (focus on chest muscles), internal (focus on arm muscles)	EMG	Instruction to focus on the chest muscles and triceps muscles increased muscle activity over baseline in these specific areas when bench pressing 50% of 1-RM. At 80% of 1-RM only instructions to focus on chest muscles resulted in an increase in muscle activity over baseline, while instructions regarding a focus on triceps resulted in no further activity over baseline.
Vance et al., 2004				
Experiment 1	To investigate the effect of focus of attention on movement speed and muscle activity during the biceps curl	Focus instructions: internal (concentrate on biceps muscles), external (concentrate on the curl bar)	Angular velocity, EMG and iEMG	Movement was faster and iEMG was reduced in the external focus condition compared to the internal focus condition.
Experiment 2	To investigate the effect of focus of attention on muscle activity when timing is controlled during the biceps curl	Focus instructions: internal (concentrate on biceps muscles), external (concentrate on the curl bar)	Angular velocity, EMG and iEMG	iEMG was reduced when adopting an external focus compared to an internal focus. This was true even with average range and movement time the same between focus conditions.

component due to the audio being directly linked to muscle contraction strength.

Theoretical Frameworks

The beneficial effect on performance of adopting an external focus of attention compared to an internal focus is well-established across a range of different motor tasks, including those that are sport-related (Wulf, 2013; Wulf and Lewthwaite, 2016). The same conclusion has been reached in most, but not all, of studes examining internal and external attentional foci during weightlifting tasks (see **Table 4**). In addition, it has been shown that adopting an associative strategy results in beneficial effects over a dissociative strategy for bicep curls (Neumann and Heng, 2011), which may reflect that the associative condition in the study was largely external in nature.

The benefits of an external focus over an internal focus of attention in terms of reduced muscle activity may be explained by differences in the spread of activation between the two types of foci. In a knee extension task, Marchant and Greig (2017) reported that an internal focus of attention produced higher overall EMG, and that this was not specific to the muscles isolated in the task but that it reflected a spreading activation of increased muscle activity. The authors suggested that this pattern reflects than an external focus of attention results in increased muscular efficiency. A similar interpretation has been made using the measure of integrated EMG (iEMG) (Vance et al., 2004). An external attentional focus has resulted in lower iEMG than an internal focus (Vance et al., 2004; Marchant and Greig, 2017).

Increased muscular efficiency is a key component of the constrained action hypothesis (Wulf et al., 2001), which is one framework in which prior research has been based on. The constrained action hypothesis proposed by Wulf et al. (2001) suggests that adopting an external attentional focus promotes automatic, natural movement control, whereas adopting an internal attentional focus disrupts this automaticity and constrains the neuromuscular system (Wulf, 2013). When an individual focuses on an external cue, it facilitates attention to stimuli distant from their body. This then allows automatic behavior to dominate, improving performance. In contrast, an internal cue constrains motor control, reducing performance. The constrained action hypothesis has since been supported by a number of studies in several different contexts.

Initial evidence for the constrained action hypothesis came from a dynamic balancing task using a stabilometer (Wulf et al., 2001). Participants given an internal instruction were told to focus on their feet and to keep them horizontal, while participants given an external instruction were told to focus on markers attached to the balance platform. Participants underwent 2 days of practice, with each day consisting of seven 90 s balance trials, followed by a retention test on the third day in which no focus instructions were given. Performance was measured on three measures, including reaction time to a dual-task procedure, balance performance, and frequency of adjustments. Participants given the external cue had significantly quicker reaction times, better balance performance, and higher frequency of adjustments. This suggests that those given the external cue experienced lower attentional demands, better learning of balance, and less disruption from voluntary attempts to correct posture, respectively.

McNevin et al. (2003) expanded on these findings in a similar balancing task by introducing different levels of external focus by varying the distance from the body on which participants were instructed to focus. Four groups of participants were instructed to focus on their feet (internal), markers close to the feet (near), markers in the center of the balance platform (far inside), and markers on the outside of the platform (far outside). Findings were similar to that of Wulf et al. (2001) with all three external foci groups performing better than the internal focus group. Additionally, the far inside and far outside groups showed a higher frequency of adjustments, demonstrating the use of more natural automatic motor control.

Most recently, Vidal et al. (2018) investigated the constrained action hypothesis using a standing long jump task with internal and external focus instructions. As expect, participants given an external focus of attention jumped significantly further than those given an internal focus instruction. Additionally, attention instructions affected the movement strategy used by participants, with a difference found in ankle-knee coordination. Those given an internal focus to extend their knees as rapidly as possible showed a jump that recruited primarily knee movement, with minimal hip or ankle movement. In contrast, those given an external focus of trying to jump to cones placed in the distance showed good ankle-knee coordination. These results suggest that the internal focus constrained participants to employing knee flexion, whereas an external focus allowed an automatic coordinated movement pattern between knee and ankle.

The constrained action hypothesis has provided a good explanation of findings from motor tasks as well as weightlifting tasks. Attempts have been made to integrate the hypothesis with other notions of attentional focus effects at the neuromuscular level (see Lohse, 2012; Lohse and Sherwood, 2012). For example, (Willingham, 1999) Control Based Learning Theory of motor control (COBALT) suggests that there are stages of processing that can operate through explicit or implicit modes of control when performing a motor task. Implicit modes are advantageous because they promote automatic selection of spatial targets and automatic movement sequences. An external focus of attention may thus promote implicit control of motor actions and result in better performance. The nodal-point hypothesis (Hossner and Ehrlenspiel, 2010) is another notion with similarities to the constrained action hypothesis. This hypothesis suggests that attention serves to select appropriate actions through the selection of sensory feedback and making ongoing corrections to movements in response to this feedback. This process is faciliated when attention is directed to the effects of movements rather than the movement execution itself. Further research is required to examine the links between the various theories of motor performance within a weightlifting context.

DISCUSSION

The research conducted to date has potentially important implications for training and performance of weightlifting tasks. The increased muscular efficiency and accuracy of force production with an external focus of attention over no specific focus or an internal focus suggests that athletes should adopt an external focus during competition. An external focus may result in superior performance to allow the athlete to lift a heavier weight than may otherwise be possible if attention is directed in other ways. Athletes should practice adopting an external focus when simulating competition during training so that it becomes a component of their competition lifting routine.

Conversely, if increased activation of muscles is the desired goal, there is an argument that athletes should adopt an internal focus of attention. Such benefits of an internal attentional focus would typically exist for training programs that aim to increase muscle growth or strength gains (Marchant et al., 2008). The increased activation of the muscle is likely to be observed in the muscle attended to and to spread to other muscles involved in the lift as suggested by the findings of Marchant and Greig (2017). A similar effect of increased muscle activation might also be observed if athletes adopt a dissociative attentional focus, based on the findings of Neumann and Heng (2011). Whether adopting an internal or dissociative strategy has any actual beneficial effect in training in the short or long term (e.g., increase muscle fatigue more quickly or lead to increased gains in strength) remains to be determined.

An important practical consideration is to determine exactly how the benefits of an external focus of attention for sport performance (or an internal focus on muscle activation) can be achieved in practical terms. The first step in developing effective strategies is to identify what are the key elements that athletes should direct their attention to (Marchant et al., 2008). In research conducted to date, an external focus has been effective when attention is directed to bar or weight being lifted. However, some weight training exercises does not use any apparatus (e.g., unweighted squats, sit ups). In cases when there is no specific implement or object used in a sport, Wulf (2007) suggests analogies and metaphor could be used. Neumann and Brown (2013) had participants direct their attention externally during a sit up task by asking them to focus on making smooth movements without any reference to a body part. For an internal focus of attention, the muscle (e.g., bicep, pectoralis) or the body part (foot, legs) has been commonly used in research as the focal point of attention.

The second consideration is the mechanism by which an instructor promotes an increased attentional focus. The use of instructions, as done in research to date, is the simplest approach and has shown to be effective. Coaches can work with athletes by using instructions to provide clear guidance on how to direct attention effectively. An external focus can be promoted by directing athletes to focus on visual cues like bar movement, the sound of the machine, pushing against the bar, or the end result of the lift. An internal focus can be promoted by instructions that direct athletes to focus on muscle tension, body movements, technique, and form.

Coaches should also provide feedback to athletes to reinforce their learning. Feedback might be enhanced by using additional cues to provide information. For an external focus of attention, this might involve placing markers on the bars or weights, using mirrors, making video recordings, or attaching sensors to the bar or weights to measure movement dynamics (acceleration, velocity, smoothness). For an internal focus, EMG recordings of muscles or movement sensors attached to the body can be used provide visual or auditory feedback to athletes. In addition, athletes should be aware that their own use of "psyching up" or self-talk might need to be modified to ensure that the appropriate attentional focus is used. For example, cue words like "strong" and "powerful" might inadvertently direct the athlete to focus their attention internally and should be modified accordingly during competition.

The third consideration is how to tailor the approach to the specific context. In simple lifts, like the biceps curl, attentional focus instructions are relatively simple because the movement is constrained. However, compound lifts will involve multiple muscles and limbs. In addition, multiple component lifts like the clean and jerk involve discrete movements performed in sequence. Internal focus instructions might need to be varied according to the stage of the lift. Whether external focus instructions need to be varied across the lift remains to be determined. Based on the notion that external attentional focus benefits might result from both intramuscular efficiency and intermuscular efficiency (Vance et al., 2004) the adoption of a single focus may be the most beneficial throughout. For the clean and jerk, for example, the athlete would merely focus on exerting force on the barbell at all stages of the lift. Importantly, when research has examined different types of lifts, the results suggest that the benefits of an external focus of attention may become more pronounced as the movement complexity increases (Marchant et al., 2011). Another important consideration is the amount of weight being lift. Attentional focus instructions may be less effective with higher intensity lifts (Snyder and Fry, 2012). The use of very simple instructions, or just cue words, and extensive practice at lighter weights might mitigate the negative impact of heavy weights on attentional focus effects. Indeed, Schutts et al. (2017) recommends that in general coaching cues for lifting are best if they are short, concise, and specific to the key element being trained.

Exercise psychologists and fitness trainers might also consider appropriate psychological strategies in attentional focus for recreational exercisers. For instance, an external focus of attention may benefit recreational exercisers to adhere to exercise programs. This is because an external focus could draw attention away from negative cues associated with physical exertion and toward positively reinforcing outcomes of the weightlifting exercise (e.g., completion of a rep or set). Research in our laboratory has shown that an external attentional focus has benefits to physical and psychological states during cardiovascular exercise tasks (e.g., Neumann and Piercy, 2013). Moreover, external attentional focus strategies may complement dissociative focus strategies like listening to music, in promoting exercise adherence. An external associative focus may be particularly beneficial given that dissociation can be more difficult to maintain at high levels of exercise intensity. Cognitive strategies like attentional focus may also be integrated with other approaches to promoting physical exercise, like goal setting (e.g., Salehian et al., 2011; Neumann and Honke, 2018).

The studies examined in the present review used weightlifting tasks that were typically of short duration by limiting the number of repetition and sets performed. In considering their findings of less efficient muscular coordination with an internal focus than an external focus, Lohse and Sherwood (2012) suggested that their findings could be relevant to endurance type tasks such as long distance running. It was noted that even a small difference in stride efficiency could be magnified over the course of the entire race due to the high repetitions of the movement. They noted that their internal focus condition produced a trend for shorter time to failure than the external focus condition and that this could reduce performance in endurance running. The benefits of an external attentional focus over an internal attentional focus have been demonstrated in running tasks of short duration (e.g., Schücker et al., 2009; Neumann and Piercy, 2013). However, in a time to exhaustion running task, no difference between internal and external foci was observed in performance or physiological variables (Vitali et al., 2019). Further research is thus required to examine the effects of different attentional foci at the neuromuscular level for endurance tasks and for weight lifting tasks that are performed to exhaustion.

Further research can be conducted to extend upon research regarding the potential benefits of adopting an external (or internal) attentional focus. Importantly, the studies conducted to date have typically been conducted in single-session designs. Thus, the long-term benefits of an external attentional focus remain to be determined. Similarly, transfer effects need to be established to determine whether beneficial attentional focus instructions practiced with one type of lifting exercise in the laboratory will transfer to real world training or competition or to other types of lifting exercises. In addition, it would be worthwhile to examine whether transfer occurs to similar sporting tasks. For example, some sports like shot put and discus, require a short-term maximal muscular effort. It would be informative to examine whether training in an external focus of attention transfers to these tasks (Vance et al., 2004).

The use of new technology to induce attentional foci or that provide additional contexts in which weightlifting can occur requires further investigation. Virtual reality (VR) has emerged as a technology applied to sport (for reviews see Neumann, 2016, 2019; Neumann et al., 2018) and has been most commonly applied to cardiovascular exercises (Murray et al., 2016; Neumann and Moffitt, 2018; Parton and Neumann, 2019) but has also been examined with weightlifting. Chen et al. (2015) examined weightlifting in a virtual environment and found that bicep muscle activity and ratings of perceived workload during bicep curls was higher in the VR condition than a non-VR. These findings may reflect that the VR condition increased an internal attention focus on the mechanics of the movement within the virtual environment. The substitution of a weighted apparatus that participants must move to produce an effect in a virtual environment would be one way to promote an external attentional focus (e.g., completing a deadlift could be translated into virtually lifting a heavy bar to free a trapped virtual person). Physiological measures can also be applied in sport in the form of biofeedback. The study by Neumann and Heng (2011) is an example where muscle activity was translated into an audio signal to direct attentional focus during a biceps curl. In addition, physiological measures other than EMG could be used to examine attentional focus effects on general arousal or emotional reactivity due to the relationship between central and peripheral measures with emotional states (e.g., see Neumann and Westbury, 2011).

CONCLUSIONS

Weightlifting for physical conditioning or sport depends on many physical and psychological factors. Research examining cognitive strategies has shown that performance at the neuromuscular and behavioral level are influenced by the attentional foci that an athlete adopts. To maximize muscular efficiency, an external focus of attention is more optimal than an internal focus of attention or no specific focus in most cases. The challenge remains for researchers to further explore this effect and determine under which conditions it may be magnified. This information will assist in translational research that can allow athletes to reach a higher level of performance than might otherwise be possible.

AUTHOR CONTRIBUTIONS

The author confirms being the sole contributor of this work and has approved it for publication.

ACKNOWLEDGMENTS

The assistance of Brett Parton in the literature search and article collation and screening is acknowledged.

REFERENCES

Becker, K., and Smith, P. J. (2013). Age, task complexity, and sex as potential moderators of attentional focus effects. *Percept. Mot. Skills* 117, 1172–1186. doi: 10.2466/23.25.PMS.117x14z3

Brick, N., MacIntyre, T., and Campbell, M. (2014). Attentional focus in endurance activity: new paradigms and future directions. *Int. Rev. Sport Exer. Psychol.* 7, 106–134. doi: 10.1080/1750984X.2014.885554

Calatayud, J., Vinstrup, J., Jakobsen, M. D., Sundstrup, E., Colado, J. C., and Andersen, L. L. (2018a). Influence of different attentional focus on EMG amplitude and contraction duration during the bench press at different speeds. *J. Sports Sci.* 36, 1162–1166. doi: 10.1080/02640414.2017.1363403

Calatayud, J., Vinstrup, J., Jakobsen, M. D., Sundstrup, E., Colado, J. C., and Andersen, L. L. (2018b). Attentional focus and grip width influences on bench press resistance training. *Percept. Mot. Skills* 125, 265–277. doi: 10.1177/0031512517747773

Chen, K. B., Ponto, K., Tredinnick, R. D., and Radwin, R. G. (2015). Virtual exertions: evoking the sense of exerting forces in virtual reality using gestures and muscle activity. *Hum. Factors* 57, 658–673. doi: 10.1177/00187208145 62231

Emad, M., Neumann, D. L., and Abel, L. (2017). Attentional focus strategies used by regular exercisers and their relationship with perceived exertion, enjoyment, and satisfaction. *J. Hum. Sport Exerc.* 12, 106–118. doi: 10.14198/jhse.2017.121.09

Flôres, F. S., Menezes, K. M., and Katzer, J. I. (2016). Influences of gender on attention and learning of motor skills. *J. Phys. Educ.* 27:e2706. doi: 10.4025/jphyseduc.v27i1.2706

Greig, M., and Marchant, D. C. (2014). Speed dependent influence of attentional focusing instructions on force production and muscular activity during isokinetic elbow flexions. *Hum. Mov. Sci.* 33, 135–148. doi: 10.1016/j.humov.2013.08.008

Halperin, I., Williams, K. J., Martin, D. T., and Chapman, D. W. (2016). The effects of attentional focusing instructions on force production during the isometric midthigh pull. *J. Strength Condition. Res.* 30, 919–923. doi: 10.1519/JSC.0000000000001194

Hossner, E. -J., and Ehrlenspiel, F. (2010). Time-referenced effects of an internal vs. external focus of attention on muscular activity and compensatory variability. *Front. Psychol.* 1:230. doi: 10.3389/fpsyg.2010.00230

Kristiansen, M., Samani, A., Vuillerme, N., Madeleine, P., and Hansen, E. A. (2018). External and internal focus of attention increases muscular activation during bench press in resistance-trained participants. *J. Strength Condition. Res.* 32, 2442–2451. doi: 10.1519/JSC.0000000000002613

Liberati, A., Altman, D. G., Tetzlaff, J., Mulrow, C., Gøtzsche, P. C., Ioannidis, J. P. A., et al. (2009). The PRISMA statement for reporting systematic reviews and meta-analyses of studies that evaluate healthcare interventions: explanation and elaboration. *Br. Med. J.* 339:b2700. doi: 10.1136/bmj.b2700

Lohse, K. R. (2012). The influence of attention on learning and performance: pre-movement time and accuracy in an isometric force production task. *Hum. Mov. Sci.* 31, 12–25. doi: 10.1016/j.humov.2011.06.001

Lohse, K. R., and Sherwood, D. E. (2012). Thinking about muscles: the neuromuscular effects of attentional focus on accuracy and fatigue. *Acta Psychol.* 140, 236–245. doi: 10.1016/j.actpsy.2012.05.009

Lohse, K. R., Sherwood, D. E., and Healy, A. F. (2011). Neuromuscular effects of shifting the focus of attention in a simple force production task. *J. Mot. Behav.* 43, 173–184. doi: 10.1080/00222895.2011.555436

Lohse, K. R., Wulf, G., and Ite, R. L. W. (2012). "Attentional focus affects movement efficiency," in *Skill Acquisition in Sport*, eds N. J. Hodges and A. M. Williams (London: Routledge), 66–84. doi: 10.4324/9780203133712

Marchant, D. C. (2011). Attentional focusing instructions and force production. *Front. Psychol.* 1:210. doi: 10.3389/fpsyg.2010.00210

Marchant, D. C., and Greig, M. (2017). Attentional focusing instructions influence quadriceps activity characteristics but not force production during isokinetic knee extensions. *Hum. Mov. Sci.* 52, 67–73. doi: 10.1016/j.humov.2017.01.007

Marchant, D. C., Greig, M., Bullough, J., and Hitchen, D. (2011). Instructions to adopt an external focus enhance muscular endurance. *Res. Q. Exerc. Sport* 82, 466–473. doi: 10.1080/02701367.2011.10599779

Marchant, D. C., Greig, M., and Scott, C. (2008). Attentional focusing strategies influence muscle activity during isokinetic bicep curls. *Athletic Insight* 10. Available online at: http://www.athleticinsight.com/Vol10Iss2/MuscularActivity.htm

Marchant, D. C., Greig, M., and Scott, C. (2009). Attentional focusing instructions influence force production and muscular activity during isokinetic elbow flexions. *J. Strength Condition. Res.* 23, 2358–2366. doi: 10.1519/JSC.0b013e3181b8d1e5

McNevin, N. H., Shea, C. H., and Wulf, G. (2003). Increasing the distance of an external focus of attention enhances learning. *Psychol. Res.* 26, 22–29. doi: 10.1007/s00426-002-0093-6

Meline, T. (2006). Selecting studies for systematic review: inclusion and exclusion criteria. *Contempor. Issues Commun. Sci. Disord.* 33, 21–27. doi: 10.1044/cicsd_33_S_21

Milanese, C., Cavedon, V., Corte, S., and Agostini, T. (2017). The effects of two different correction strategies on the snatch technique in weightlifting. *J. Sports Sci.* 35, 476–483. doi: 10.1080/02640414.2016.1172727

Murray, E. G., Neumann, D. L., Moffitt, R. L., and Thomas, P. R. (2016). The effects of the presence of others during a rowing exercise in a virtual reality environment. *Psychol. Sport Exerc.* 22, 328–336. doi: 10.1016/j.psychsport.2015.09.007

Neumann, D. L. (2016). "On the use of virtual reality in sport and exercise: applications and research findings," in *Virtual Reality: Advances in Research and Application*, ed Z. Hill (Hauppauge, NY: Nova Science Publishers Inc), 153–182.

Neumann, D. L. (2019). "Competition during sport participation in virtual reality environments and when playing exergames," in *Achievement Motivation: Perspectives, Influences and Outcomes*, ed A. Naomhán (Hauppauge, NY: Nova Science Publishers Inc), 45–74.

Neumann, D. L., and Brown, J. (2013). The effect of attentional focus strategy on physiological and motor performance during a sit-up exercise. *J. Psychophysiol.* 27, 7–15. doi: 10.1027/0269-8803/a000081

Neumann, D. L., and Heng, S. (2011). The effects of associative and dissociative attentional focus strategies on muscle activity and heart rate during a weight training exercise. *J. Psychophysiol.* 25, 1–8. doi: 10.1027/0269-8803/a000011

Neumann, D. L., and Honke, E. (2018). Practice using performance goals enhances basketball free throw accuracy when tested under competition in elite players. *J. Hum. Sport Exerc.* 13, 296–304. doi: 10.14198/jhse.2018.132.05

Neumann, D. L., and Moffitt, R. L. (2018). Affective and attentional states when running in a virtual reality environment. *Sports* 6:71. doi: 10.3390/sports6030071

Neumann, D. L., Moffitt, R. L., Thomas, P. R., Loveday, K., Watling, D. P., Lombard, C. L., et al. (2018). A systematic review of the use of interactive virtual reality in sport. *Virtual Real.* 22, 183–198. doi: 10.1007/s10055-017-0320-5

Neumann, D. L., and Piercy, A. (2013). The effect of different associative attentional focus strategies on physiological and psychological states during running. *Aust. Psychol.* 48, 329–328. doi: 10.1111/ap.12015

Neumann, D. L., and Thomas, P. R. (2009). The relationship between skill level and patterns in cardiac and respiratory activity during golf putting. *Int. J. Psychophysiol.* 72, 276–282. doi: 10.1016/j.ijpsycho.2009.01.001

Neumann, D. L., and Thomas, P. R. (2011). Cardiac and respiratory activity and golf putting performance under attentional focus instructions. *Psychol. Sport Exerc.* 12, 451–459. doi: 10.1016/j.psychsport.2011.02.002

Neumann, D. L., and Westbury, H. R. (2011). "The psychophysiological measurement of empathy," in in *Psychology of Empathy*, ed D. J. Scapaletti (Hauppauge, NY: Nova Science Publishers Inc), 119–142.

Nideffer, R. M. (1976). Test of attentional and interpersonal style. *J. Person. Soc. Psychol.* 34, 394–404. doi: 10.1037/0022-3514.34.3.394

Parton, B. J., and Neumann, D. L. (2019). The effects of competitiveness and challenge level on virtual reality rowing performance. *Psychol. Sport Exerc.* 41, 191–199. doi: 10.1016/j.psychsport.2018.06.010

Perkins-Ceccato, N., Passmore, S. R., and Lee, T. D. (2003). Effects of focus of attention depend on golfers' skill. *J. Sports Sci.* 21, 593–600. doi: 10.1080/0264041031000101980

Rhodes, R. E., Lubans, D. R., Karunamuni, N., Kennedy, S., and Plotnikoff, R. (2017). Factors associated with participation in resistance training: a systematic review. *Br. J. Sports Med.* 51, 1466–1472. doi: 10.1136/bjsports-2016-096950

Salehian, M. H., Rad, A. G., Moghaddam, J. B., Imani, P., and Fazlollahi, S. (2011). Effect of attentional-focus of feedback and goal setting on learning of basketball set shot. *Ann. Biol. Res.* 2, 401–411. Available online at: https://www.scholarsresearchlibrary.com/articles/effect-of-attentional-focus-of-feedback-and-goal-setting-on-learning-of-basketball-set-shot.pdf

Schücker, L., Hagemann, N., Strauss, B., and Völker, K. (2009). The effect of attention focus on running economy. *J. Sport Sci.* 27, 1241–1248. doi: 10.1080/02640410903150467

Schutts, K. S., Wu, W. F. W., Vidal, A. D., Hiegel, J., and Becker, J. (2017). Does focus of attention improve snatch lift kinematics? *J. Strength Condition. Res.* 31, 2758–2764. doi: 10.1519/JSC.0000000000001753

Snyder, B. J., and Fry, W. R. (2012). Effect of verbal instruction on muscle activity during the bench press exercise. *J. Strength Condition. Res.* 26, 2394–2400. doi: 10.1519/JSC.0b013e31823f8d11

Stevinson, C. D., and Biddle, S. T. (1998). Cognitive orientations in marathon running and "hitting the wall". *Br. J. Sports Med.* 32, 229–234. doi: 10.1136/bjsm.32.3.229

Vance, J., Wulf, G., Töllner, T., McNevin, N., and Mercer, J. (2004). EMG activity as a function of the performer's focus of attention. *J. Mot. Behav.*, 36: 450–459. doi: 10.3200/JMBR.36.4.450-459

Vernon, L. (2018). Mind and muscle: considering weightlifting as a contemplative practice. *J. Contemp. Inq.* 5.

Vidal, A., Wu, W., Nakajima, M., and Becker, J. (2018). Investigating the constrained action hypothesis: a movement coordination and coordination variability approach. *J. Mot. Behav.* 50, 528–537. doi: 10.1080/00222895.2017.1371111

Vitali, F., Tarperi, C., Cristini, J., Rinaldi, A., Zelli, A., Lucidi, F., et al. (2019). Action monitoring through external or internal focus of attention does not impair endurance performance. *Front. Psychol.* 10:535. doi: 10.3389/fpsyg.2019.00535

Willingham, D. B. (1999). The neural basis of motor skill learning. *Curr. Dir. Psychol. Sci.* 8, 177–182. doi: 10.1111/1467-8721.00042

Wininger, S. R., and Gieske, D. (2010). Measure of attentional focus: cognitive interviews and a field study. *Athletic Insight* 2, 125–146.

Wulf, G. (2007). Attentional focus and motor learning: a review of 10 years of research. *Bewegung und Training* 1, 4–14. Available online at: https://pdfs.semanticscholar.org/a9e8/f8e69efbfe375d89cf0ff035e3b4f6d4d95f.pdf

Wulf, G. (2013). Attentional focus and motor learning: a review of 15 years. *Int. Rev. Sport Exerc. Psychol.* 6, 7–104. doi: 10.1080/1750984X.2012.723728

Wulf, G., Höß, M., and Prinz, W. (1998). Instructions for motor learning: differential effects of internal versus external focus of attention. *J. Motor Behav.* 30, 169–179. doi: 10.1080/00222899809601334

Wulf, G., and Lewthwaite, R. (2016). Optimizing performance through intrinsic motivation and attention for learning: the optimal theory of motor learning. *Psychon. Bull. Rev.* 23, 1382–1414. doi: 10.3758/s13423-015-0999-9

Wulf, G., McNevin, N. H., and Shea, C. H. (2001). The automaticity of complex motor skill learning as a function of attentional focus. *Q. J. Exp. Psychol.* 54A, 1143–1154. doi: 10.1080/02724980143000118

9

Information Accrual from the Period Preceding Racket-Ball Contact for Tennis Ground Strokes: Inferences from Stochastic Masking

Sepehr Jalali[1], Sian E. Martin[1], Tandra Ghose[2], Richard M. Buscombe[3], Joshua A. Solomon[4] and Kielan Yarrow[1]*

[1]Department of Psychology, City, University of London, London, United Kingdom, [2]Department of Psychology, Technische Universität Kaiserslautern, Kaiserslautern, Germany, [3]School of Health Sport and Bioscience, University of East London, London, United Kingdom, [4]Centre for Applied Vision Science, City, University of London, London, United Kingdom

***Correspondence:**
Kielan Yarrow
kielan.yarrow.1@city.ac.uk

Previous research suggests the existence of an expert anticipatory advantage, whereby skilled sportspeople are able to predict an upcoming action by utilizing cues contained in their opponent's body kinematics. This ability is often inferred from "occlusion" experiments: information is systematically removed from first-person videos of an opponent, for example, by stopping a tennis video at the point of racket-ball contact, yet performance, such as discrimination of shot direction, remains above chance. In this study, we assessed the expert anticipatory advantage for tennis ground strokes via a modified approach, known as "bubbles," in which information is randomly removed from videos in each trial. The bubbles profile is then weighted by trial outcome (i.e., a correct vs. incorrect discrimination) and combined across trials into a classification array, revealing the potential cues informing the decision. In two experiments (both with N = 34 skilled tennis players) we utilized either temporal or spatial bubbles, applying them to videos running from 0.8 to 0 s before the point of racket-ball contact (cf. Jalali et al., 2018). Results from the spatial experiment were somewhat suggestive of accrual from the torso region of the body, but were not compelling. Results from the temporal experiment, on the other hand, were clear: information was accrued mainly during the period immediately prior to racket-ball contact. This result is broadly consistent with prior work using nonstochastic approaches to video manipulation, and cannot be an artifact of temporal smear from information accrued after racket-ball contact, because no such information was present.

Keywords: sports, tennis, occlusion, reverse correlation, anticipatory ability

Elite athletes demonstrate extraordinary ability in their sport of choice. While their sporting acumen may seem like a fundamentally physical attribute, it is in fact scaffolded by a range of cognitive skills that span the sensorimotor pipeline, from perception to action execution (Yarrow et al., 2009). One such skill that has received considerable attention from experimental psychologists is the expert anticipatory advantage.

The expert anticipatory advantage in sports describes a domain-specific benefit that sportspeople exhibit when predicting what is about to happen based on their opponent's current bodily kinematics (as opposed to their opponent's previous action history, which provides a separate cue for predicting current behavior; Mann et al., 2014). This advantage has been demonstrated in experiments simulating a variety of sports, most commonly via temporal and spatial occlusion methodologies (e.g., Jones and Miles, 1978; Abernethy, 1988). Hence, the advantage is widely exhibited, although the extent to which it benefits actual competitive performance remains uncertain (van Maarseveen et al., 2018).

A typical occlusion experiment runs as follows. A sporting scenario is selected, for example, a football (soccer) goalkeeper attempting to save penalties (e.g., Dicks et al., 2010; Smeeton and Williams, 2012). Videos are shot from the sportsperson's (here, the goalkeeper's) perspective, capturing various instances of two or more categories of outcome (for example, penalties struck to the left or right of the goalkeeper). In the actual experiment, participants, often varying in sports expertise (e.g., novice vs. expert goalkeepers) view these videos, attempting to discriminate which outcome will occur on each trial. Critically, the videos are manipulated to exclude some of their visual information. In temporal occlusion, the video is usually terminated early (for example, at or before ball contact), so that only particular sequences of body kinematics are available to guide the response. In spatial occlusion, particular features at constrained spatial locations (for example, the striker's hips) are also removed from the video.

The logic of these experiments is that participants will only be able to perform at above-chance levels if there is information in the video to guide their decision, with performance declining toward chance as this information is systematically removed. Certain sports, such as cricket, have been long-running favorites in the occlusion literature (e.g., Abernethy and Russell, 1984; Müller and Abernethy, 2006; Müller et al., 2006), but occlusion approaches have been applied to sports as diverse as volleyball (e.g., Loffing et al., 2015) and karate (Mori et al., 2002).

Racket sports (e.g., badminton and squash; Abernethy and Russell, 1987; Abernethy, 1990) have been particularly well studied via occlusion techniques. The focus of the current study is the sport of tennis. This sport was among the first to provide evidence of an expert anticipatory advantage, with Jones and Miles (1978) showing that experts were above chance (and better than intermediate or novice players) at guessing the landing position of a serve when the video was stopped 0.042 s before ball contact. Subsequent work has found, for example, that experts extract information from the time when the ball's toss is at its apex onward when predicting spin (Goulet et al., 1989). The temporal occlusion method has also been adjusted slightly to present one of several possible windows of visibility (0.3 s in duration) during service, with above-chance performance for experts when viewing the video for only the 0.3 s immediately before ball contact (Farrow et al., 2005). These temporal occlusion results are supplemented by spatial occlusion studies showing that, for example, experts can still discriminate the direction of tennis serves at above-chance levels following removal of body regions such as the entire lower body, but not when the ball's toss was occluded (Jackson and Mogan, 2007). Experts were also impaired (but to a lesser extent) by removal of the arm and racket.

While the tennis serve is the most straightforward scenario to investigate, ground strokes have also been probed via occlusion methods. With temporal occlusion at ball contact, experts were above chance to discriminate between left/right lobs and passing shots when shutter goggles were used to block vision *in situ* on a tennis court (Shim et al., 2005). More traditional video-based studies have shown that unlike novices, experts could already predict shot direction above chance at −0.12 s relative to ball contact, with further improvements for occlusion occurring at −0.08 and −0.04 s (Rowe et al., 2009). Spatial occlusion work suggests that the arm/racket regions are critical when predicting ground-shot direction (Shim et al., 2006).

Video-based occlusion methods are not perfect, and our knowledge about the expert anticipatory advantage has been supplemented by a variety of techniques. Such techniques include eye tracking to provide information about where sportspeople attend, and animating/manipulating the opponent (e.g., Cañal-Bruland et al., 2011; Ida et al., 2013) including via virtual reality (Vignais et al., 2015). For example, Ida et al. (2013) manipulated the arm/racket angles of computer-generated opponents to successfully influence experts' analogue estimates of the direction, speed, and spin of a tennis serve. In another study, swapping the arm/racket of stick-man representations of an opponent to that of a different shot confused experts trying to predict the direction of ground strokes (Cañal-Bruland et al., 2011). However, here we stay closer to the traditional occlusion approach, but attempt to remedy a possible weakness of the method: its dependency on experimenter decisions regarding exactly what to occlude.

To this end, we utilize a stochastic method of video occlusion borrowed from the psychophysical literature (Ahumada and Lovell, 1971), specifically a form of classification-image analysis (sometimes called reverse correlation) known as bubbles (Gosselin and Schyns, 2001). Bubbles are Gaussian-profiled windows of visibility that reveal the information from an otherwise masked (e.g., uniform gray) display. In the temporal domain, they are rather like the occlusion approach of Farrow et al. (2005), who displayed only a 0.3 s window of information from a video at a time. However, unlike in that study, which utilized a discrete set of nonoverlapping windows as separate conditions, in a bubbles experiment, several bubbles typically appear on each trial and the midpoint of each bubble is chosen at random. Furthermore, their Gaussian profiles remove transients and give the impression of the underlying display being smoothly revealed and subsequently re-masked (see **Figure 1**, for illustration). At the analysis stage, the random bubbles profiles from the different trials are binned by correctness of response and combined to produce a classification sequence. This classification can then be used to highlight the regions from which information must have been utilized to generate correct discriminations.

Although bubbles are typically applied to sparse, tightly controlled psychophysical stimuli, their applicability to a complex real-word scenario like tennis anticipation has been demonstrated

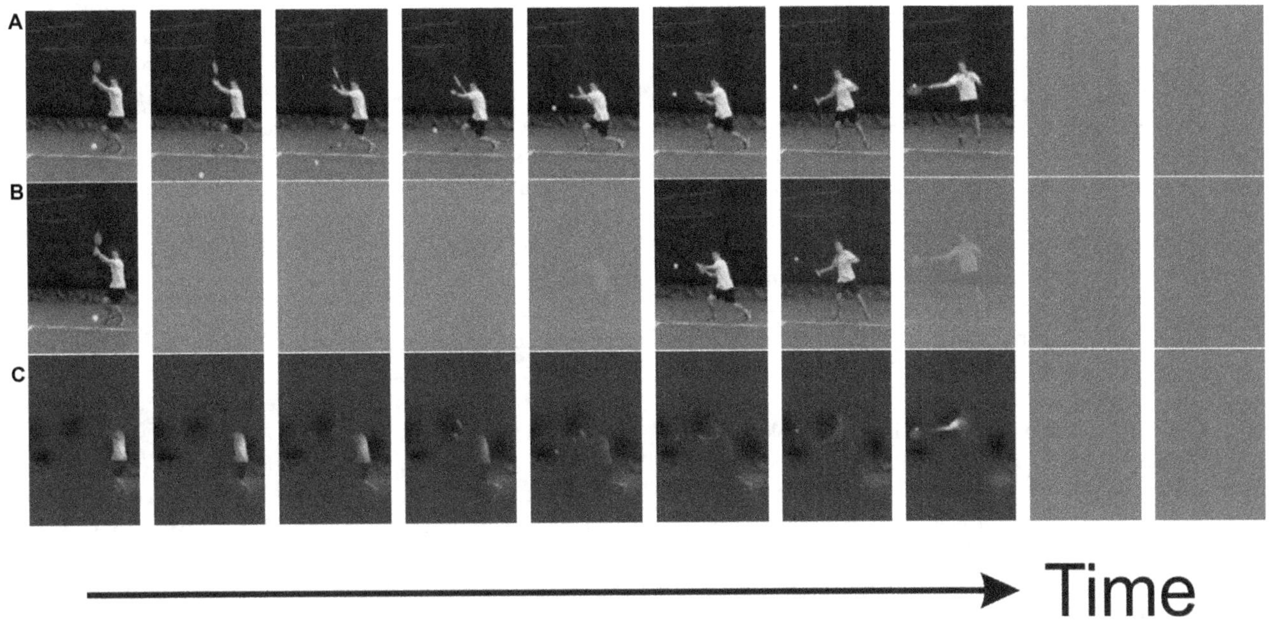

FIGURE 1 | Example stimuli, shown as snapshots from video every 100 ms. **(A)** Video occluded at point of racket-ball contact but with no bubbles manipulation (equivalent to pretest trials here). **(B)** Temporal bubbles permit viewing of entire image, but only at certain times. **(C)** Spatial bubbles permit viewing of only certain regions of the image, but across all (precontact) frames.

recently (Jalali et al., 2018). In that study, we had both novice and competent tennis players view opponents in both service and forehand-groundstroke scenarios. We did not stop the video at racket-ball contact, but the structure of the experiment encouraged participants to respond as quickly as possible while maintaining an acceptable level of accuracy. The bubbles technique proved effective in both the temporal and spatial domains, but it suggested that our participants were primarily utilizing information from the beginning of the ball's trajectory off the racket face rather than their opponent's precontact kinematics. However, the temporal classification sequence did imply possible information accrual just prior to racket-ball contact as well, but this interpretation remained speculative. The reason is that the bubbles technique yields a classification sequence in which very discrete information sources can become smeared (i.e., exaggerated in extent), such that an information source at or just after racket-ball contact might spread back to appear significant in the immediately preceding frames.

Here, we again use bubbles to attempt to find evidence of an expert anticipatory advantage in tennis. Our aim is to quantify the extent of the temporal and spatial regions, prior to ball contact, from which skilled tennis players are able to extract useful information about shot direction, but using a stochastic masking technique (i.e., bubbles). The implementation of the bubbles method does not require any intuitions about information sources, which need to be designed as separate conditions, but rather allows any region of information to emerge in a bottom-up manner. As such, we believe it provides a useful form of methodological triangulation relative to traditional occlusion approaches. However, we made an important change relative to our previous study: We stopped the video at racket-ball contact, with bubbles appearing at random up to that point but no information ever provided afterwards. This change guarantees that any information sources we identify, even if near the point of racket-ball contact, are not the result of the aforementioned temporal smear arising at the analytic stage. We also focus on ground strokes only, without considering services. To presage our results, we find unequivocal evidence for the utilization of kinematic information by competent tennis players, but only for the period immediately prior to ball contact.

MATERIALS AND METHODS

Participants

We utilized a smorgasbord[1] sampling method, attempting to recruit participants with experience playing competitive tennis by various means. Where possible, we recorded their years of experience, current competitive tennis matches per year, and International Tennis Number (ITN), which is an index of their standard of play and ranges from ITN 1 (a player with extensive professional tournament experience and who currently holds or is capable of holding an ATP/WTA ranking) to ITN 10 (a player that is just starting to play competitively). Eleven participants (8 male, 3 female, mean age 30, mean years of tennis experience 13, mean matches per year 48, mean ITN 2.8) were recruited via adverts at London tennis clubs and by word of mouth, and traveled to City, University of London to participate. All completed

[1]This is our own dubious terminology. We originally intended to recruit several separate samples and address additional questions, but recruitment proved more challenging than expected, leading us to form a composite sample.

both temporal and spatial bubbles sessions (see design, below)[2]. We also took the opportunistic step of developing a portable setup and taking it to the National UK University championships, where we recruited participants in their down time between matches (or after they had been eliminated). We tested 22 such participants in total, with 13 completing a spatial bubbles session (8 male, 5 female, mean age 22, mean years' experience 11, mean matches per year 37, mean ITN 2.1) and 13 completing a temporal bubbles session (8 male, 5 female, mean age 22, mean years' experience 10, mean matches per year 44, mean ITN 2.1)[3]. We subsequently took our portable setup to a second lab (at Technische Universität Kaiserslautern) in order to exploit its proximity to an elite school for sport (Heinrich Heine Gymnasium) attended by promising young tennis players and their coaches. We tested 10 such participants (8 male, 2 female, median age 16) who completed both spatial and temporal bubbles sessions[4]. For the German participants, we recorded their "Leistungsklassen" or performance class abbreviated as LK. According to the German Tennis Federation (DTB), the lowest class is LK23 and the highest LK1 consisting of top ranked players in Germany. The German pool had three LK1 players, one LK23 and average of LK 10 (std 8.5). They averaged 7.7 years of experience and 26 competitive matches per year. Finally, from the resulting complete samples of 34 (temporal bubbles)/34 (spatial bubbles) participants, we rejected participants, who were unable to perform the task significantly above chance during bubbles blocks (<55%, yielding binomial $p > 0.05$ that they were simply guessing), but only for our mean classification-array analysis (one of several analyses we ran; see below). We did this because an inability to perform the task makes it impossible for the bubbles technique to retrieve meaningful sources of information. This left final samples of 24 (spatial) and 27 (temporal) participants for mean classification-array analysis. Informed consent was obtained from all participants, who were paid £10 per h (London) and €10 per h (Germany) for their time. Ethical approval was granted by the relevant local Ethics Committees at City, University of London, and Technische Universität Kaiserslautern.

Apparatus and Stimuli

We used the ground-stroke subset of video stimuli from those previously described by Jalali et al. (2018). They were recorded at a tennis club using a tripod-mounted camera (frame rate 120 Hz, frame size 1280 × 720 pixels). Four club coaches/hitters of a good but not elite standard acted as models and were instructed to "hit winners" without attempting explicit deception. They were situated near the baseline and recorded against a largely uniform blue backdrop. They were recorded playing forehand ground strokes (running rightward from a central position to return near the singles side line), directing their shots toward an imaginary receiver's forehand or backhand. To increase image resolution, the camera was positioned at the net, on a line projecting from the filmed player to the imaginary receiver at the opposite baseline (height = 1.6 m, left of center line by 1.25 m).

Videos were first transformed to eight-bit grayscale. Two authors picked a subset of videos that were unambiguous (regarding the direction of the shot – line/cross), relatively homogeneous in terms of the position of the players at the time of ball contact, and lacking in artifactual cues that might allow the videos to be easily remembered for future classification (e.g., an unusual delivery trajectory). In each video, the frame corresponding to ball contact and the position at which the ball struck the racket head on this frame were manually identified for use in the subsequent presentation and analysis (see below).

The experiment was controlled by computers running scripts written in Matlab® (The Mathworks, Natick, U.S.A.) using the Psychophysics Toolbox (Brainard, 1997; Pelli, 1997; Kleiner et al., 2007). Video stimuli were presented via either a cathode-ray tube monitor (for sessions at City, University of London), a short-throw gaming projector (Optoma® GT760; for sessions at Kaiserslautern and temporal sessions at UK university championships), or a MacBook® Pro (spatial sessions at UK university championships). The former two displays had a vertical refresh rate of 120 Hz, while the latter refreshed at 60 Hz, playing a down-sampled video. Only a central 600 × 400 pixel region of each video that excluded irrelevant peripheral information was presented. Displays were presented at around eye level and viewed at an appropriate distance in order to present the opposing tennis player with a height subtending ~4° visual angle (approximating their size as seen from the baseline during actual play). Participants responded by either stepping rightward or leftward, thus lifting the corresponding foot from one of two digital pedals, monitored at 100,000 Hz via a 16 bit A/D card (National Instruments X-series PCIe-6,323; for sessions at City) or by pressing an appropriate arrow key on a computer keyboard (all other sessions).

Design and Procedure

There were two types of session incorporating either temporal or spatial bubbles blocks with participants completing one or both of these sessions, and in some cases up to two additional sessions not reported here (see footnotes 2–4). Each session took around an hour, and consisted of three blocks: One practice, one pretest, and one bubbles block (in that order). During practice, participants viewed small number of videos (between 10 and 24 depending on the experimental location; 50% to forehand, 50% to backhand) containing any of four players (8 possible videos per player) but with a preponderance of videos (70%) from one player and fewer videos (10% each) from the remaining three players, who were saved mainly for the experimental trials (see below). Videos were randomized with replacement.

[2]Most of these participants also completed sessions in which they attempted to guess the direction of serves, but our service stimuli proved extremely difficult to discriminate, thus yielding no conclusive results, and are omitted from our report for concision.

[3]Nine from each group completed just a single block, and four competed both. Some participants failed to report some measures of experience, particularly ITN, so the means are based only on those who responded. Three participants from this group also completed a block using service stimuli, not reported here (see footnote 2).

[4]These participants completed two further blocks with a modified presentation sequence (a fixed rather than random ordering of opponents, to see if experiencing the same opponent repeatedly made them easier to predict) but this change did not generate any clear trend, and these blocks are not analyzed here.

Videos presentations began at −0.8 s relative to racket-ball contact. The practice block constituted a warm-up in which trials terminated at +0.2 s relative to racket-ball contact to provide clear information about the trajectory of the ball off the racket head. By contrast, in pretest and bubbles blocks, videos terminated at racket-ball contact (replaced with a uniform gray screen) or at the time of response if earlier than this.

For these pretest and bubbles blocks, 24 new videos (8 per player, 50% to forehand and 50% to backhand) were selected from the three players seen less often during practice. For the pretest, the videos were presented between one and four times each in a random order, yielding a block of either 24 trials (City and Kaiserslautern) or 96 trials (UK university championships). These differences reflected the fact that City and Kaiserslautern participants typically performed multiple sessions, hence, could have their pretest data combined across them. For the critical bubbles block, these videos were presented further 16 times each in a random order, yielding a block of 384 trials. Participants responded without any deadline. Trials with presentation glitches, that is, where one or more frames were dropped after the −0.2 s time point, were re-randomized and repeated at the end of the block. Feedback about correctness was provided after every trial.

Importantly, during bubbles trials only, the videos were subjected to random masking via the application of bubbles [see **Figure 1**; for videos showing examples of temporal and spatial bubbles, see videos 1 and 2, respectively from Jalali et al. (2018), available at https://www.frontiersin.org/articles/10.3389/fpsyg.2018.02229/full#supplementary-material]. Individual bubbles were combined to generate bubbles profiles in one (temporal) or two (spatial) dimensions. The number of bubbles presented began at 8 or 20 for temporal and spatial sessions, respectively. In principle, this (maximum) number could then be adjusted downward via a QUEST staircase (Watson and Pelli, 1983), varying the number of bubbles in order to try and maintain participants' performance at around 75% correct (i.e., lowering the number of bubbles if the task was too easy). However, as discussed further below, this was never required as the task was very hard even in the absence of any masking. The profile of each individual bubble was that of a 1 or 2-dimensional Gaussian density function, scaled to have unit height. In the temporal sessions, its width (σ) was 3 frames; in the spatial sessions, its width was 12 pixels (vertically and horizontally)[5].

Bubble mean positions were selected at random within a domain extending throughout the relevant space of the video. Bubbles profiles were determined by combining the individual bubbles together. This was achieved by first reflecting bubble magnitudes around 0.5, then multiplying them together, and finally re-reflecting:

$$\text{Bubbles} = 1 - \prod_{b=1}^{B}\left(1 - \text{bubble}_b\right) \quad (1)$$

Pixel intensities were then calculated for display as the mean pixel intensity plus the difference between original and mean intensities multiplied by the Bubbles profile at each point. Expressed in terms of Weber contrasts, pixels were displayed at their original Weber contrasts multiplied by the Bubbles profile.

Data Analysis

The saved Bubbles profiles from each trial formed the starting point in generating classification sequences (temporal conditions) or images (spatial conditions), which reveal the regions from which information supporting a correct response has been extracted. We calculated these classification arrays as per our previous report (Jalali et al., 2018). First, for the spatial condition only, Bubbles were re-centered so that the profile (saved in video coordinates) was translated to a new coordinate frame, centered on the ball at the time of racket-ball contact. Next, for each participant, a weighted sum of (re-centered) bubbles profiles yielded the raw classification array. The sum weights profiles from correct trials positively and profiles from incorrect trials negatively:

$$\text{RCA} = \sum_{c=1}^{C}\text{Bubbles}_c - \sum_{i=1}^{I}\text{Bubbles}_i \quad (2)$$

However, in order to provide more intuitive values for visualizing and combining data across participants, raw classification arrays were normalized to a z-like format. This was achieved via a permutation approach. For each of 2,000 iterations, correct/incorrect labels were randomly re-assigned (without replacement) to individual trials. The means and standard deviations at each point (i.e., each frame and/or pixel) calculated over these 2,000 permutations were used to z-score the classification array. This yielded an array varying around zero with positive values indicating regions of possible information accrual.

In order to draw statistical inferences across large arrays while controlling familywise type 1 error appropriately, data from all participants who were able to perform the task at significantly above-chance levels during bubbles blocks were combined and assessed via both cluster and t_{max} (also known as pixel or single-threshold) corrected permutation tests. These methods, derived from the neuroimaging literature (Blair and Karniski, 1993; Nichols and Holmes, 2002) are standard approaches for solving the multiple comparison problems with large sets of potentially correlated and non-normal data. Our particular implementation is more fully described in Jalali et al. (2018).

We also addressed a prediction particular to the data collected in these experiments, which, unlike typical bubbles experiments, were derived from participants, who rarely achieved 75% correct in a two-choice discrimination. We reasoned that the variability in performance across participants might be utilized in statistical inference. Bubbles are most efficient with 75% correct performance (Gosselin and Schyns, 2001) and would be expected to become less efficient, and thus produce classification arrays more dominated by random noise, with lower levels of discrimination performance. We would therefore expect that for an information-carrying region, there should be a positive correlation across participants between the magnitude of the classification array at that point and discrimination performance. We tested this prediction in a manner exactly analogous to the cluster/t_{max} approach, but using Pearson's r-statistic in place of Student's t-statistic in order to

[5]To speed calculations, each bubble was rounded to zero beyond 4 (temporal) or 3 (spatial) σ from its centre.

formulate cluster and r_{max} corrected permutation correlations. Where t-based tests reveal significant regions of information, r-based tests reveal regions more successfully exploited by better participants. All reported p are two-tailed, unless otherwise noted.

RESULTS

Pretests

In pretest trials, participants saw the videos without degradation, but terminating at the point of racket-ball contact. Pretests were identical in spatial and temporal sessions, and our samples were not fully overlapping between these experiments, so data were collated across all 43 unique participants. Participants showed some ability to discriminate the direction of tennis ground strokes in the absence of information about the ball's trajectory off the racket head (mean proportion correct = 0.632, SD = 0.093) and they did so on average at a level significantly above chance: Modeling these binomial data in the most appropriate way [i.e., with a general linear mixed model (GLMM) with logistic link function, incorporating a random term for the intercept] revealed a fixed intercept term of 0.55, which differed significantly from zero, that is, the null hypothesis of scoring 50% correct ($t_{[42]}$ = 9.25, $p < 10^{-10}$). For the subsets of U.K. participants reporting ITNs (N = 18), years of playing experience (N = 31), or matches per year (N = 27), these variables each were entered as lone predictors in separate GLMMs but failed to significantly correlate with discrimination performance (all $p > 0.29$). However, matches per year did become a significant positive predictor of performance (odds ratio = 1.011, 95% CI 1.004–1.18, $t_{[24]}$ = 3.28, p = 0.003) when an outlying participant (claiming 150 competitive matches per year) was excluded.

Temporal Bubbles

In temporal bubbles trials, videos ran to the point of racket-ball contact, but only those periods revealed by randomly placed temporal bubbles were visible (**Figure 1B**). The Bubbles profiles from each trial were combined with accuracy data to create classification sequences for each participant. The mean z-scored classification sequence across participants is shown in **Figure 2A**, with positive values denoting regions from which information may have been extracted. No frames were significant after t_{max} correction, but a subset of frames (from 86 onwards, that is, from around 0.083 s before racket-ball contact) contribute to a significant cluster (p = 0.013). Cluster-based testing corrects for familywise error on the overall inference that the classification

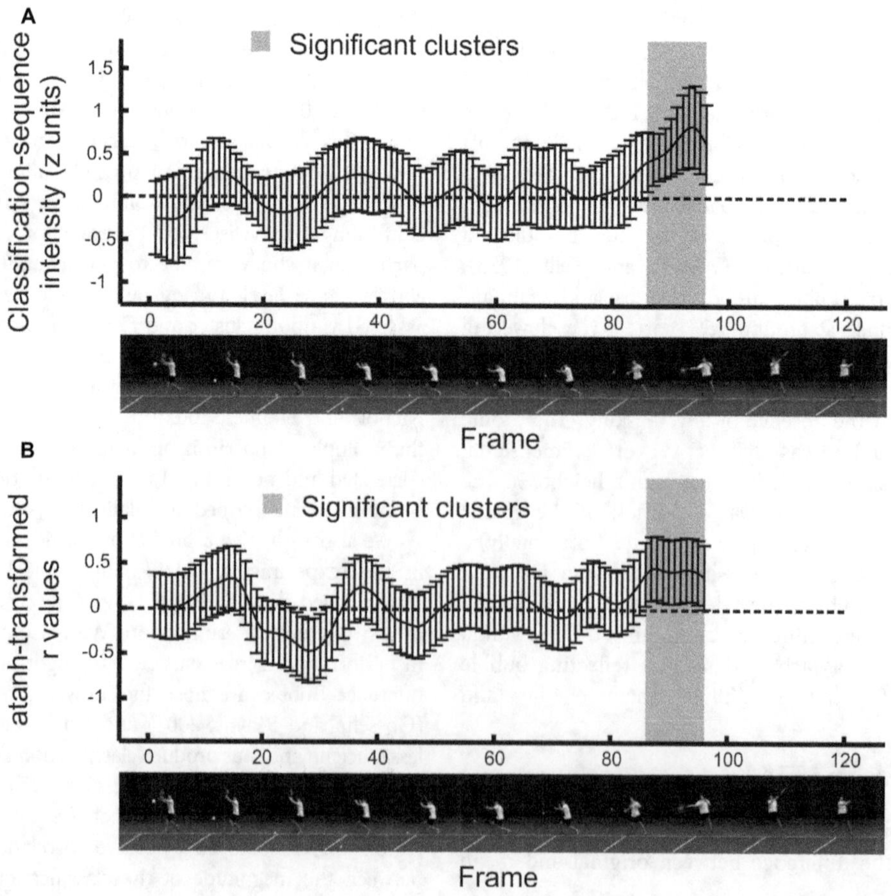

FIGURE 2 | Results from temporal bubbles experiment. Error bars denote 95% confidence intervals. Shaded regions denote significant clusters. **(A)** Mean z-scored classification sequence. **(B)** Correlations between classification sequences and classification performance across participants.

image differs reliably from zero, but does not imply that every point within the cluster is significant (Groppe et al., 2011), particularly in combination with the smoothing effects of bubbles (see Jalali et al., 2018, for further discussion). However, it is clear that some information was successfully extracted from the moment just before racket-ball contact.

Figure 2B shows additional results from a second statistical analysis. Here, instead of assessing the mean classification sequence for just those participants who were still able to perform above chance even during bubbles blocks, we assessed the correlation (for the entire sample of participants) between individual classification sequences and discrimination success. The raw values of r have been transformed to permit the creation of a constant confidence interval, which clarifies where possible clusters emerge. This happens wherever the confidence interval does not include zero, that is, for r values that are significant without any familywise correction. However, these transformed r values retain their basic meaning, in the sense that positive values represent frames where more successful participants (in terms of their ability to do the task) showed more positive classification sequence magnitudes. Our participants varied considerably in their ability to perform the task (between 50 and 75% correct). Because bubbles should be most effective (revealing pronounced peaks at points where useful information is extracted) for participants who approach 75% performance, and much less effective (reflecting mainly noise) for participants who are just guessing, these correlations are informative. Interestingly, the correlation analysis reveals a cluster with the exact same temporal extent as that found in the mean classification image ($p = 0.029$). Of course, these two analyses cannot be considered as independent tests. However, we believe they can sometimes be complementary to one another, as will become clearer in our spatial results.

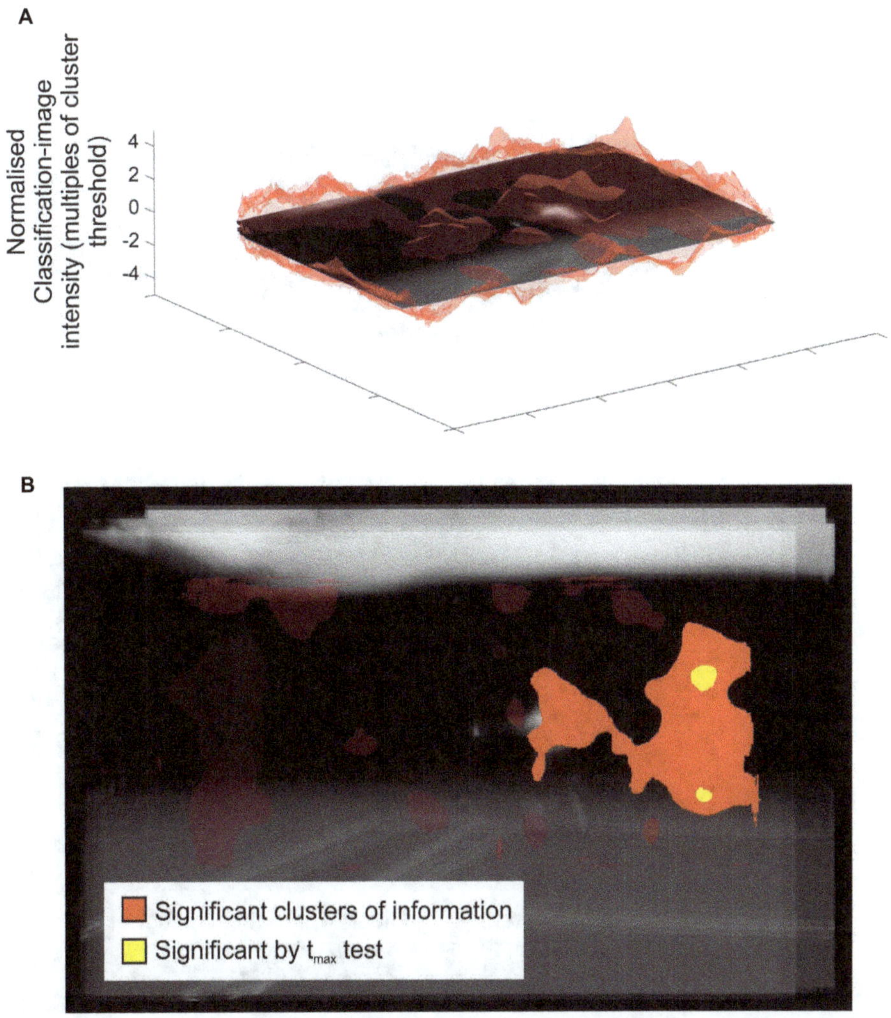

FIGURE 3 | Classification image results from the spatial bubbles experiment. Results are overlaid on an image of the mean of all presented videos for the frames capturing racket-ball contact, centered on the point of racket-ball contact (hence constituent images do not perfectly align). However, the results of the spatial analysis are not specific to any one time point. **(A)** Transparent red peaks denote mean classification-image intensity normalized to the cluster threshold value used in permutation testing (i.e., values more extreme than ±1 formed potential clusters). **(B)** Solid colored regions were significant in cluster/t_{max} permutation testing, suggesting information might have been extracted from this part of the video. Transparent red regions denote nonsignificant clusters.

Spatial Bubbles

In the spatial bubbles task, only particular areas of the video image were visible at random on each trial (**Figure 1B**). Data from our spatial bubbles experiment are shown in **Figures 3, 4**. **Figure 3** shows the mean classification image, along with associated statistical inferences, for participants able to perform the bubbles task above chance. The top part of figure shows the classification image itself, while in the bottom part of the figure statistical thresholding has been applied to reveal a single large significant cluster ($p = 0.0005$). This cluster also incorporates two smaller regions that additionally survive t_{max} correction. This contrast *should* illustrate spatial areas from which visual information was accrued. However, the result is unconvincing. Although the cluster does include a region over the position of the opposing player's body at the time of ball contact, this region only appears within the cluster by virtue of a slim connection to a larger and more pronounced region. The larger region might, at best, be considered to have overlaid parts of the opponent's body at the beginning of the video, when they started their run to intercept the ball. However, this larger region would be inconsistent with the results of the temporal experiment, which suggested that useful information guiding the decision was not extracted until near the time of racket-ball contact.

Our complementary correlation-based analysis is shown in **Figure 4**, which in this case appears somewhat instructive. The format is the same as for the mean classification image shown in **Figure 3** with the raw correlations shown at the top, and statistical thresholding applied at the bottom. However, in this case it is normalized correlation (r) values that are being illustrated and assessed for cluster or r_{max} based significance. No significant clusters were observed, but there is one nonsignificant cluster worthy of mention (one-tailed $p = 0.096$; all other clusters one-tailed $p > 0.36$) which sits over the position of the opponent's body at the time of ball contact. This suggests a trend for those participants better able to discriminate shot duration during spatial bubbles sessions to have classification

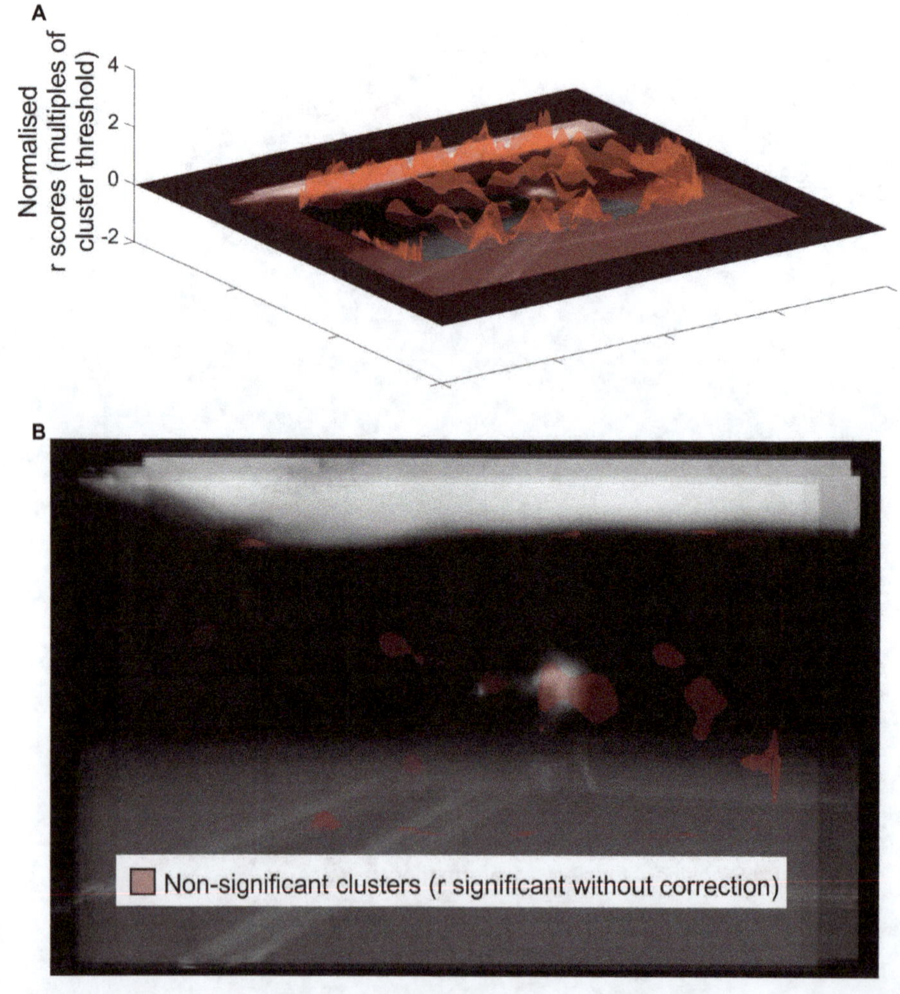

FIGURE 4 | Correlation results from the spatial bubbles experiment. Results are overlaid on an image of the mean of all presented videos for the frames capturing racket-ball contact, centered on the point of racket-ball contact (hence constituent images do not perfectly align). However, the results of the spatial analysis are not specific to any one time point. **(A)** Transparent red peaks denote correlations between classification-image intensities and discrimination performance, normalized to the cluster threshold value used in permutation testing (i.e., values more extreme than ±1 formed potential clusters). **(B)** Transparent red regions denote points where the cluster threshold (representing a significant correlation in the absence of familywise correction) was exceeded, but resulted in only nonsignificant clusters.

images that show stronger peaks in this region. In combination with the data from our analysis of the mean classification image (**Figure 3**), this result suggests that much (or all) of the cluster revealed there may represent a false positive, as it was no more likely to emerge in participants for whom bubbles had a good chance of actually working than it was for participants for whom bubbles could reveal only noise.

DISCUSSION

In our experiments, competent but nonelite tennis players first attempted to discriminate the direction of upcoming forehand ground strokes from videos of a tennis opponent, based only on information available prior to the point of racket-ball contact. On average, they were able to do so, in line with previous reports (Shim et al., 2006; Rowe et al., 2009). Unlike previous reports, we went on to remove additional information using a stochastic approach to video manipulation, by introducing bubbles rather than by applying systematic masking or image manipulation in a particular set of planned conditions. Our main finding was that participants used information from the period immediately before racket-ball contact, specifically within a window reaching back approximately 0.083 s, to perform the direction-discrimination task. Because this information source precedes racket-ball contact, it cannot include the trajectory of the ball off the racket head.

Our temporal results seem fairly consistent with previous reports. For example, Rowe et al. (2009) had tennis experts (broadly comparable to ours in competence, with ITNs of 2–4) judge forehand and backhand ground strokes (going to either the right or left) from videos which could be occluded at between −0.12 and +0.04 s relative to racket-ball contact. They found that experts could predict undisguised shot direction at approaching 75% correct when the video stopped at racket-ball contact, falling to around 60% when models were attempting disguise (c.f. 63% mean performance during pretest here; note that our models were instructed only to "hit winners," but were presented to participants with smaller spatial extents than those of Rowe et al., to be more consistent with typical match viewing). Rowe et al. (2009) also found that experts could still discriminate the direction of ground strokes significantly above chance when the video stopped at either 0.12 or 0.08 s before racket-ball contact, but performed better with occlusion at 0 s. These results imply some accrual from roughly the temporal window we obtained here (in order to show improvement) but also some additional accrual from earlier frames (in order to still be performing above chance). Indeed, a similar study utilizing stick-man graphics in place of videos even found above chance performance with occlusion at −0.24 s, although performance actually then trended worse with occlusion at −0.16, −0.08, or 0 ms (Cañal-Bruland et al., 2011).

Our method was, in principal, well-suited to find the locus of any such early periods of information accrual, because bubbles could appear at any point back to 0.8 s before ball contact. Several possibilities should be considered regarding why we failed to find any such loci, reflecting the various limitations of our approach. The first relates to statistical power. Bubbles are a trial-hungry technique, with typical psychophysical applications using fairly simple stimuli and also very large numbers of trials (Gosselin and Schyns, 2001). This limitation is exacerbated when performance is only a little above chance even in the absence of any bubbles, as was the case here. Indeed, pretest performance suggests that our stimuli were very challenging to discriminate for most participants, so perhaps our stimuli simply did not contain usable information as early as the videos used in other studies, or perhaps it was sufficiently subtle that bubbles could not reveal it.

A second possibility is that information must be integrated over a protracted period, or combined from both of two temporally distinct epochs during early shot preparation, in order to be usable. Such temporally complex cues would still be present in standard temporal occlusion approaches where videos run continuously until a single occlusion point. However, while classification arrays can in principle reveal these kinds of features with enough trials, the bubbles approach is most efficient when the temporal extent of a cue is approximately matched to the temporal extent of an individual bubble (see for example, the simulations presented by Jalali et al., 2018). Note that various suggestions have been made within the bubbles literature to address this issue (Chauvin et al., 2005; Blais et al., 2012) and might be considered in future research on sports.

Regardless of whether there were any earlier information sources that went undetected in our experiment, we can at least assert with confidence that useful information was extracted from our videos immediately prior to racket-ball contact (although, as noted in the methods, we cannot assert that every individual frame highlighted by our cluster test was important). This ability may be learnt through regular match play, generalizing immediately to the particular opponents encountered here. It is also possible that the ability to anticipate was actually learnt entirely during the experiment, given that each stimulus was encountered multiple times. The correlation between pretest performance and matches per year suggests that more regular players are at least quicker to learn their new opponent's kinematic "gives" (or perhaps they are quicker to learn other spurious cues in our videos, although we took steps to minimize these). However, this result must be considered tentative, as it was both exploratory, and relied on the exclusion of an outlying participant.

Our results from spatial bubbles sessions were not compelling and can at best be considered suggestive that our participants may have extracted some information from the torso region of their opponents. This would presumably be during the temporal window revealed by the temporal bubbles sessions, but the experiments are independent so this need not necessarily be the case. The need to apply statistical control across a much larger 2D space, relative to our temporal experiments, may have left our spatial experiment underpowered. We have previously shown that spatial bubbles can be effective with a setup and sample size similar to this one (Jalali et al., 2018), but in that case performance was nearer to 75% correct for all participants. Previous spatial occlusion work with video stimuli has been more conclusive. Shim et al. (2006) used a four-choice task (ground strokes or lobs to forehand or backhand), and found that removing the racket/arm impaired discrimination of videos when viewing was stopped at racket-ball contact. This suggests that these distal regions, which did not emerge in our analysis despite the fact that we centered our co-ordinate frame (and thus maximized power) at the racket head, are in fact important. However, they also observed performance which was still well above chance after these regions had been occluded. Therefore, participants must also have extracted information from other parts of the video, presumably proximal body segments, although the pattern of data was inconclusive in this regard. Indeed, some results from more recent studies using computer graphics in place of real videos suggest primacy for the proximal body: Fukuhara et al. (2017) found that an opponent rendered with a realistic body (but only point-light information for their arm and racket) was better predicted than one with a realistic arm and racket but only a point-light body.

In conclusion, we have replicated classic research showing that skilled tennis players can anticipate upcoming shots based on their opponent's body kinematics. We also used a novel stochastic masking approach in order to highlight the role of the period immediately preceding racket-ball contact in supporting this ability. Although our bubbles approach could in principal have revealed a wider range of information sources relative to traditional occlusion studies (where a limited set of masking conditions must be selected in advance) in practice we have revealed, if anything, fewer such loci. The approach may still have merit, but primarily as a means of methodological triangulation, making an inference based on multiple complementary approaches, such as the temporal result observed here, more secure.

ETHICS STATEMENT

The studies involving human participants were reviewed and approved by Research Ethics Committee, City, University of London, and Research Ethics Committee, Technische Universität Kaiserslautern. Written informed consent to participate in this study was provided by the participants' legal guardian/next of kin.

AUTHOR CONTRIBUTIONS

KY and JS conceived the experiments. SJ coded the experiments and analyses. SM, SJ, TG, and RB ran the experiments. KY drafted the manuscript. All authors contributed to the research design and critically revised the manuscript.

REFERENCES

Abernethy, B. (1988). The effects of age and expertise upon perceptual skill development in a racquet sport. *Res. Q. Exerc. Sport* 59, 210–221. doi: 10.1080/02701367.1988.10605506

Abernethy, B. (1990). Anticipation in squash: differences in advance cue utilization between expert and novice players. *J. Sports Sci.* 8, 17–34.

Abernethy, B., and Russell, D. G. (1984). Advance cue utilisation by skilled cricket batsmen. *Aust. J. Sci. Med. Sport* 16, 2–10.

Abernethy, B., and Russell, D. G. (1987). The relationship between expertise and visual search strategy in a racquet sport. *Hum. Mov. Sci.* 6, 283–319. doi: 10.1016/0167-9457(87)90001-7

Ahumada, A. Jr., and Lovell, J. (1971). Stimulus features in signal detection. *J. Acoust. Soc. Am.* 49, 1751–1756. doi: 10.1121/1.1912577

Blair, R. C., and Karniski, W. (1993). An alternative method for significance testing of waveform difference potentials. *Psychophysiology* 30, 518–524.

Blais, C., Roy, C., Fiset, D., Arguin, M., and Gosselin, F. (2012). The eyes are not the window to basic emotions. *Neuropsychologia* 50, 2830–2838. doi: 10.1016/j.neuropsychologia.2012.08.010

Brainard, D. H. (1997). The psychophysics toolbox. *Spat. Vis.* 10, 433–436. doi: 10.1163/156856897X00357

Cañal-Bruland, R., van Ginneken, W. F., van der Meer, B. R., and Williams, A. M. (2011). The effect of local kinematic changes on anticipation judgments. *Hum. Mov. Sci.* 30, 495–503. doi: 10.1016/j.humov.2010.10.001

Chauvin, A., Worsley, K. J., Schyns, P. G., Arguin, M., and Gosselin, F. (2005). Accurate statistical tests for smooth classification images. *J. Vis.* 5, 659–667. doi: 10.1167/5.9.1

Dicks, M., Button, C., and Davids, K. (2010). Availability of advance visual information constrains association-football goalkeeping performance during penalty kicks. *Perception* 39, 1111–1124. doi: 10.1068/p6442

Farrow, D., Abernethy, B., and Jackson, R. C. (2005). Probing expert anticipation with the temporal occlusion paradigm: experimental investigations of some methodological issues. *Mot. Control* 9, 330–349. doi: 10.1123/mcj.9.3.330

Fukuhara, K., Ida, H., Ogata, T., Ishii, M., and Higuchi, T. (2017). The role of proximal body information on anticipatory judgment in tennis using graphical information richness. *PLoS One* 12:e0180985. doi: 10.1371/journal.pone.0180985

Gosselin, F., and Schyns, P. G. (2001). Bubbles: a technique to reveal the use of information in recognition tasks. *Vis. Res.* 41, 2261–2271. doi: 10.1016/S0042-6989(01)00097-9

Goulet, C., Bard, C., and Fleury, M. (1989). Expertise differences in preparing to return a tennis serve: a visual information processing approach. *J. Sport Exerc. Psychol.* 11, 382–398. doi: 10.1123/jsep.11.4.382

Groppe, D. M., Urbach, T. P., and Kutas, M. (2011). Mass univariate analysis of event-related brain potentials/fields I: a critical tutorial review. *Psychophysiology* 48, 1711–1725. doi: 10.1111/j.1469-8986.2011.01273.x

Ida, H., Fukuhara, K., Ishii, M., and Inoue, T. (2013). Perceptual response and information pick-up strategies within a family of sports. *Hum. Mov. Sci.* 32, 106–120. doi: 10.1016/j.humov.2012.08.002

Jackson, R. C., and Mogan, P. (2007). Advance visual information, awareness, and anticipation skill. *J. Mot. Behav.* 39, 341–351. doi: 10.3200/JMBR.39.5.341-352

Jalali, S., Martin, S. E., Murphy, C. P., Solomon, J. A., and Yarrow, K. (2018). Classification videos reveal the visual information driving complex real-world speeded decisions. *Front. Psychol.* 9:2229. doi: 10.3389/fpsyg.2018.02229

Jones, C. M., and Miles, T. R. (1978). Use of advance cues in predicting the flight of a lawn tennis ball. *J. Hum. Mov. Stud.* 4, 231–235.

Kleiner, M., Brainard, D., Pelli, D., Ingling, A., Murray, R., and Broussard, C. (2007). What's new in psychtoolbox-3. *Perception* 36, 1. doi: 10.1177/03010066070360S101

Loffing, F., Hagemann, N., Schorer, J., and Baker, J. (2015). Skilled players' and novices' difficulty anticipating left- vs. right-handed opponents' action intentions varies across different points in time. *Hum. Mov. Sci.* 40, 410–421. doi: 10.1016/j.humov.2015.01.018

Mann, D. L., Schaefers, T., and Cañal-Bruland, R. (2014). Action preferences and the anticipation of action outcomes. *Acta Psychol.* 152, 1–9. doi: 10.1016/j.actpsy.2014.07.004

Mori, S., Ohtani, Y., and Imanaka, K. (2002). Reaction times and anticipatory skills of karate athletes. *Hum. Mov. Sci.* 21, 213–230. doi: 10.1016/S0167-9457(02)00103-3

Müller, S., and Abernethy, B. (2006). Batting with occluded vision: an in situ examination of the information pick-up and interceptive skills of high- and low-skilled cricket batsmen. *J. Sci. Med. Sport* 9, 446–458. doi: 10.1016/j.jsams.2006.03.029

Müller, S., Abernethy, B., and Farrow, D. (2006). How do world-class cricket batsmen anticipate a bowler's intention? *Q. J. Exp. Psychol.* 59, 2162–2186. doi: 10.1080/02643290600576595

Nichols, T. E., and Holmes, A. P. (2002). Nonparametric permutation tests for functional neuroimaging: a primer with examples. *Hum. Brain Mapp.* 15, 1–25. doi: 10.1002/hbm.1058

Pelli, D. G. (1997). The VideoToolbox software for visual psychophysics: transforming numbers into movies. *Spat. Vis.* 10, 437–442. doi: 10.1163/156856897X00366

Rowe, R., Horswill, M. S., Kronvall-Parkinson, M., Poulter, D. R., and McKenna, F. P. (2009). The effect of disguise on novice and expert tennis players' anticipation ability. *J. Appl. Sport Psychol.* 21, 178–185. doi: 10.1080/10413200902785811

Shim, J., Carlton, L. G., Chow, J. W., and Chae, W. (2005). The use of anticipatory visual cues by highly skilled tennis players. *J. Mot. Behav.* 37, 164–175. doi: 10.3200/JMBR.37.2.164-175

Shim, J., Carlton, L. G., and Kwon, Y. (2006). Perception of kinematic characteristics of tennis strokes for anticipating stroke type and direction. *Res. Q. Exerc. Sport* 77, 326–339. doi: 10.1080/02701367.2006.10599367

Smeeton, N. J., and Williams, A. M. (2012). The role of movement exaggeration in the anticipation of deceptive soccer penalty kicks. *Br. J. Psychol.* 103, 539–555. doi: 10.1111/j.2044-8295.2011.02092.x

van Maarseveen, M. J. J., Oudejans, R. R. D., Mann, D. L., and Savelsbergh, G. J. P. (2018). Perceptual-cognitive skill and the in situ performance of soccer players. *Q. J. Exp. Psychol.* 71, 455–470. doi: 10.1080/17470218.2016.1255236

Vignais, N., Kulpa, R., Brault, S., Presse, D., and Bideau, B. (2015). Which technology to investigate visual perception in sport: video vs. virtual reality. *Hum. Mov. Sci.* 39, 12–26. doi: 10.1016/j.humov.2014.10.006

Watson, A. B., and Pelli, D. G. (1983). QUEST: a bayesian adaptive psychometric method. *Atten. Percept. Psychophys.* 33, 113–120. doi: 10.3758/BF03202828

Yarrow, K., Brown, P., and Krakauer, J. W. (2009). Inside the brain of an elite athlete: the neural processes that support high achievement in sports. *Nat. Rev. Neurosci.* 10, 585–596. doi: 10.1038/nrn2672

10

Pressing Crowd Noise Impairs the Ability of Anxious Basketball Referees to Discriminate Fouls

*Fabrizio Sors [1,2,3], David Tomé Lourido [4], Vittoria Parisi [3], Ilaria Santoro [2,3], Alessandra Galmonte [1], Tiziano Agostini [2] and Mauro Murgia [2]**

[1] Department of Medicine, Surgery and Health Sciences, University of Trieste, Trieste, Italy, [2] Department of Life Sciences, University of Trieste, Trieste, Italy, [3] Department of Medical Area, University of Udine, Udine, Italy, [4] Department of Psycho-Socio-Educational Analysis and Intervention, University of Vigo, Vigo, Spain

***Correspondence:**
Mauro Murgia
mmurgia@units.it

The decision-making processes of referees in sports are affected by many factors, including the pressure of spectators. While the home/visitor bias has been previously investigated, the role of crowd noise has been less studied. In the present study, we investigated how the crowd noise (calm vs. pressing) influence the decisions of basketball referees, when examining videos of potential fouls. In doing so, we also considered the level of competitive anxiety of referees (low vs. high anxiety), as factor potentially interacting with the pressure exerted by the spectators. A 2 × 2 ANOVA (Crowd noise x Anxiety) revealed a significant interaction [$F_{(1,28)} = 7.33$; $p < 0.05$; $\eta_p^2 = 0.21$; power = 0.74], with the highly anxious referees showing poorer performances in the pressing crowd condition [$t_{(14)} = 2.24$; $p < 0.05$; $d = 0.64$]. The results indicate that the crowd noise does not seem to affect the referees' decisions, unless we consider the anxiety. The present findings suggest that the decisions of referees with high anxiety might be more easily influenced by external factors like crowd noise. Based on these results, referees' federations should consider the possibility to develop training protocols dedicated to highly anxious referees, to avoid their decisions from being biased by spectators' pressure.

Keywords: referees, basketball, crowd noise, anxiety, fouls, sport, sound

INTRODUCTION

Within the context of sport psychology research, the different elements that can influence the decisions of a judge or referee have been widely investigated (for a recent review, see Aragao-Pina et al., 2018). In fact, most of the studies that evaluate judgments or identification tasks in sports are related to decisions made by the referees (Plessner and Haar, 2006).

The process of decision-making in referees can be considered as a sequence of social information processing, since the referee is in constant interaction with the athletes and the coaches, and s/he can also be influenced by the people attending the competition, that is, the supporters. The effects of various individual and social phenomena on referees' performance have been studied, namely: the anxiety they experience when performing in competitions (Johansen and Haugen, 2013); their sports and academic training (MacMahon et al., 2007); the coping of stressful situations (Wolfson and Neave, 2007; Page and Page, 2010); the verbalizations of the athletes (Lex et al., 2015) and of the coaches (Souchon et al., 2013); the nationality of the athletes (Dawson and Dobson, 2010; Pope and Pope, 2015); the attentional biases (Pazzona et al., 2018);

the order of events that take place during the competition (Plessner and Betsch, 2001; Unkelbach and Memmert, 2008; Buraimo et al., 2010); the result during matches (Lago-Peñas and Gómez-López, 2016); the condition of playing at home (Pollard, 1986; Boyko et al., 2007; Dawson et al., 2007); the importance of the supporters (Garicano et al., 2005). Altogether, the results of these studies indicate that the task of referees is quite complex and can be affected by various phenomena; among the factors constituting the complexity of refereeing, the psychological factors play an important role and can affect referee's performances to a significant extent.

Regarding the supporters, most studies have focused on the influence that various factors exert on arbitration decisions, such as the number of spectators (Downward and Jones, 2007; Pettersson-Lidbom and Priks, 2010; Picazo-Tadeo et al., 2016), the composition of the crowd, depending on whether they are local or visitors (Dohmen, 2008; Ponzo and Scoppa, 2014), the distance between the field and the stand (Scoppa, 2008; Buraimo et al., 2012), and the noise produced by the spectators (Unkelbach and Memmert, 2010). Although the relevant effect of noise on arbitration decisions was already highlighted by Greer (1983), few studies have evaluated this phenomenon experimentally (Nevill et al., 2002, 2017; Balmer et al., 2007; Unkelbach and Memmert, 2010; Myers et al., 2012).

Balmer et al. (2007) investigated the association between the bias of favoring local football teams by referees with an increase in anxiety and activation in the presence (vs. absence) of crowd noise. The results of the research indicated that, when the crowd noise was present, a bias in favor of the local teams emerged, as well as significant relationships between this bias and the increase of cognitive anxiety and perception of mental effort. The authors suggested that crowd noise is associated with an increase of anxiety and a perception of mental effort, which leads the referees facing this anxiety to take more popular decisions in favor of the local team. Thus, it seems that the referees face a double commitment: on the one hand, to be impartial due to their institutional position; on the other hand, to please the crowd (Sutter and Kocher, 2004). According to Balmer et al. (2007), as the crowd has a more immediate influence, there is a bias in favor of the team playing at home. Sometimes, arbitral inconsistencies can be explained by an avoidance coping strategy. Specifically, when facing difficult situations, referees simply avoid making unpopular decisions by ordering players to continue playing (Nevill et al., 2017).

The explanations related to favoring one team or another are marked by a strong motivational character, which would also allow the opposite outcome. Indeed, referees could show reactance to local supporters because they feel harassed (Unkelbach and Memmert, 2010). For this reason, other types of explanatory theories of the crowd noise influence on arbitration decisions have also been proposed, ranging from Bayesian decision-making models that consider some of the previously mentioned indicators (e.g., playing at home, composition and size of the crowd, number of penalties assigned; Constantinou et al., 2014), to the theory of social influence (Di Corrado et al., 2011). According to the latter theory, referees are governed by the traditional models of conformity with the majority and obedience proposed by Asch (1951) and Milgram (1963). However, this interpretation is not sufficient, according to explanations based on cognitive social theory (Plessner and Haar, 2006; Plessner et al., 2009). Considering the cognitive social theory, social knowledge and the cognitive processing of information are involved when individuals construct their subjective reality (Di Corrado et al., 2011), which in the case of the present study corresponds to the refereeing decisions. These decisions would be similar to those made in a categorization task, where the existence or not of an infraction must be determined.

Within the framework of cognitive research with sports referees, cue learning emerges (Plessner et al., 2009; Unkelbach and Memmert, 2010). This learning is due to the nature of the game in sports such as basketball or soccer, where it is continuous and dynamic, so referees often need to make quick decisions with limited information (Morris and Lewis, 2010). The latter authors point out that referees use temporary contiguity cues as additional sources of information, which are used for the decision-making process. When judging actions such as fouls, not all information is accessible at the same time (for example, limited visual information due to perspective), so concurrent cues such as noise from the crowd can be used (Plessner et al., 2009). Referees can exploit that cue because they learn the correlation between crowd noise and specific criteria in a given situation (Unkelbach and Memmert, 2010). Therefore, the prior experience of the referees with the environmental pressure will influence the signaling or not of an infraction, allowing them to improve the decision making through specific training (Webb et al., 2018). In addition, the signaling or not of an infraction may be conditioned by the anxiety levels of the referees (Balmer et al., 2007).

In the present study, rather than analyzing the effect of the home crowd or the compliance with an arbitration decision based on crowd noise, the aim was to investigate the influence of a calm vs. pressing crowd noise on the ability of basketball referees to discriminate contact situations as regular or not; in particular, in doing so the competitive anxiety characterizing the referees themselves was also considered. On the basis of the aforementioned studies, and considering that participants were not informed about the condition of "local" and "visiting" teams, the research hypotheses were the following: (1) independently from anxiety levels, the ability to correctly discriminate between fouls and non-fouls would be lower in the pressing crowd condition than in the calm crowd condition; (2) considering anxiety levels, the discrimination ability of referees with high anxiety would be more impaired than that of referees with low anxiety in the pressing crowd condition, while no differences would emerge in the calm crowd condition.

MATERIALS AND METHODS

Participants

Thirty male basketball referees voluntarily participated in the experiment. Their age ranged between 18 and 60 years ($M = 27.8$; $SD = 11.8$). They were all active at the time of experimentation, serving as referees from youth leagues to the Italian national second division; their experience ranged between 3 and 35 years

(M = 10.3; SD = 9). Participants were divided in two equally numerous groups—low vs. high anxiety (N = 15 each)—on the basis of the sample's anxiety median score; the two resulting groups were comparable in terms of age (low anxiety: M = 29.3 years; SD = 12.3; high anxiety: M = 26.3 years; SD = 11.1) and experience (low anxiety: M = 11 years; SD = 9.3; high anxiety: M = 9.7 years; SD = 8.9).

All participants had normal or corrected-to-normal vision, and reported no hearing disturbances. Written informed consent was obtained from each participant prior to the beginning of the experiment, in accordance with the Declaration of Helsinki. The experimental protocol was approved by the Ethics Committee of the University of Trieste, and the experiment was carried out in accordance with its recommendations.

Materials

Instruments

The software iMovie and Adobe Audition 3.0 were used to edit video and audio materials, respectively. A laptop computer Dell Inspiron 5559 with a 15.6" LED display was used to test participants. Sennheiser HD 205 II circumaural headphones were used to convey the auditory stimuli. The experiment was programmed with the software E-prime Professional 2.0. The statistical software SPSS 25.0 for Windows was used for data analysis.

Stimuli

The stimuli used for the present experiment were videos of basketball actions containing contact situations; the original audio was removed and replaced with that of a calm crowd and that of a pressing crowd.

The videos suitable for the experiment were selected from an archive of videos used by referee instructors during technical meetings. In particular, three instructors were requested to independently view about 80 of such videos, and to judge whether the specific contact situations were to be considered as fouls or non-fouls; this independent evaluation yielded 17 unanimous fouls and 15 unanimous non-fouls. Out of these, the three instructors were requested to collectively select 10 fouls and 10 non-fouls, by discarding the most evident cases for each category, to avoid the experimental task from being too easy. Then, these 20 videos were edited so that all of them lasted 5 s, being temporally occluded immediately after the contact to be judged.

As concerns the audio, the same three instructors as above were asked to evaluate some tracks extrapolated from videos of basketball matches found online. In **Figure 1** there are the waveforms of the two selected tracks. Beyond the quantitative differences that can be seen in the figure, the two tracks were also qualitatively different. Indeed, the calm crowd track consisted of a continuous background noise of some voices, above which the ball bounces and the players' footsteps were clearly audible. Instead, the pressing crowd track started with a drum noise lasting about 3 s, and then, after few audible footsteps, the crowd started to scream (right after the contacts to be judged by participants). These two tracks were used to replace the original audio of each of the 20 selected videos; as a consequence, the final set of stimuli consisted of 40 videos: 10 fouls with the calm crowd; 10 fouls with the pressing crowd; 10 non-fouls with the calm crowd; 10 non-fouls with the pressing crowd. An example of each can be found in the **Supplementary Material.**

Questionnaire

To measure participants' competitive anxiety, the Sport Anxiety Scale (SAS; Smith et al., 1990) was used. This questionnaire consists of 21 items in the form of statements describing thoughts and feelings that can be commonly experienced before and during sport competitions. With respect to the original version, in the instructions the three occurrences of the term "athletes" were replaced with the term "referees." The answer to each item is to be given on a four-point Likert scale, ranging from "not at all" (1) to "very much so" (4).

The items compose two subscales, i.e., somatic anxiety and cognitive anxiety; the latter can be further divided in two sub-subscales, i.e., worry and concentration disruption. A total competitive anxiety score can also be calculated by adding all the items together. In the present study, we used this total competitive anxiety score, in order to create two groups of participants (low vs. high anxiety).

Procedure and Task

Participants were tested individually in a quiet room. Upon their arrival, they were asked to seat in front of a laptop computer and to wear the headphones; then, the experimenter launched the experimental session. Participants were instructed that their task was to judge whether each contact was a foul or a non-foul, by pressing one of two keys on the laptop keyboard, namely "A" or "L"[1]; in the instructions, no reference was made to the crowd noise.

The experimental session consisted of two blocks, each composed of 20 trials, for a total of 40 trials (corresponding to the 40 stimuli). In each block there were five fouls with the calm crowd, five fouls with the pressing crowd, five non-fouls with the calm crowd, and five non-fouls with the pressing crowd. The stimuli were presented in a randomized order within each block; moreover, within each block the same action was never presented twice (e.g., foul "A" with the calm crowd was presented in the first block, while the same foul "A" but with the pressing crowd was presented in the second block). After each response, there was an interval of 1 s before the beginning of the subsequent stimulus; instead, the interval between the two blocks was of 5 min, to provide participants with an appropriate rest.

Once the experimental session was completed, participants were administered the SAS. The choice to administer it at the end of the protocol rather than at its beginning was made to avoid a possible "triggering" of anxiety-related thoughts/feelings before performing the task, which could have led (some) participants to explicitly focus on the crowd noise as a potential anxiogenic stimulus.

[1]The correspondence between the keys and the answer associated to them was inverted between the two blocks, in order to keep under control any potential effect of the dominant hand.

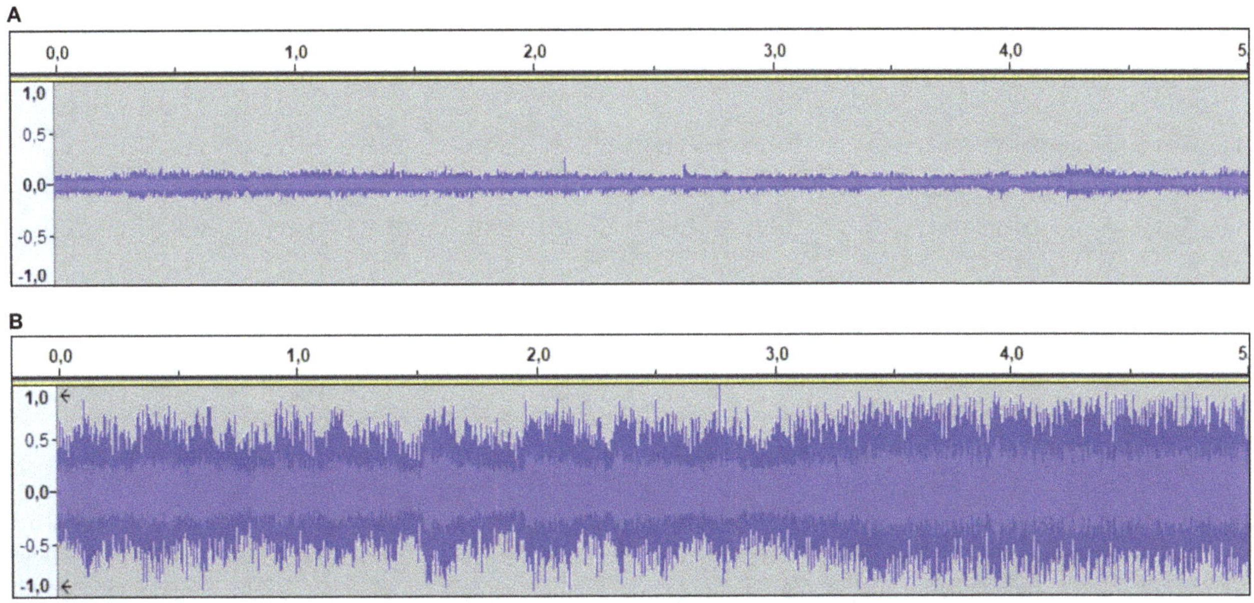

FIGURE 1 | The waveforms of the audio tracks characterizing the calm crowd condition **(A)** and the pressing crowd condition **(B)**.

Statistical Analyses

First of all, the *d'* scores for each participant in each condition—calm crowd and pressing crowd—were calculated, as measures of response accuracy. Subsequently, the competitive anxiety score for each participant was calculated. Then, participants were divided in two equally numerous groups—low vs. high anxiety ($N = 15$ each)—on the basis of the sample's median score. To test the research hypotheses, a 2 × 2 mixed ANOVA was conducted, with crowd noise (calm vs. pressing) as within-subjects variable, and anxiety (low vs. high) as between-subjects variable. Moreover, we conducted planned comparisons between the two groups, in each of the two crowd noise conditions, as well as within each group in the two crowd noise conditions, by means of a set of independent samples *t*-tests, and paired samples *t*-tests, respectively. For the ANOVA, the sphericity assumption was evaluated using the Mauchly test; Greenhouse-Geisser correction for degrees of freedom was applied in case of non-sphericity. The effect sizes were calculated using the partial eta square (η_p^2) (Lakens, 2013), with 0.01, 0.06, and 0.14 considered small, medium, and large effects, respectively. In the case of *t*-tests, effect sizes were calculated using the Cohen's d (Cohen, 1988), for which 0.20, 0.50, and 0.80 are considered small, medium, and large effects, respectively.

RESULTS

The mixed ANOVA did not reveal a significant main effect either for crowd noise [$F(1, 28) = 0.01$; $p = 0.97$] or for anxiety [$F(1, 28) = 0.16$; $p = 0.69$]; however, a significant interaction emerged [$F(1, 28) = 7.33$; $p < 0.05$; $\eta_p^2 = 0.21$; power = 0.74] (**Figure 2**). The set of independent samples *t*-tests revealed no difference between the two groups in the calm crowd condition [$t(28) = 0.81$; $p = 0.43$; low anxiety: M = 0.83, SD = 0.93; high anxiety: M = 1.04, SD = 0.49]; instead, in the pressing crowd condition a marginally significant difference between the two groups emerged [$t(28) = 1.59$; $p = 0.063$; $d = 0.58$; low anxiety: M = 1.14, SD = 0.86; high anxiety: M = 0.73, SD = 0.51]. The set of paired samples *t*-tests highlighted a significant difference in the two conditions for referees with high anxiety, showing lower discrimination ability in the pressing crowd condition [$t(14) = 2.24$; $p < 0.05$; $d = 0.64$]; instead, no difference emerged for referees with low anxiety between the calm and pressing crowd conditions [$t(14) = 1.69$; $p = 0.11$].

DISCUSSION

The aim of the present study was to investigate the influence of crowd noise on the ability of basketball referees to discriminate contact situations as regular or not, also on the basis of their competitive anxiety. Unlike previous studies on similar issues, here the manipulation did not simply consist in the presence vs. absence of crowd noise (e.g., Balmer et al., 2007) or in the variation of its volume (e.g., Unkelbach and Memmert, 2010); instead, to be more realistic, two different tracks were used—one of a calm crowd and one of a pressing crowd—with both quantitative and, most importantly, qualitative differences between them. Moreover, the condition of "local" and "visiting" teams was intentionally not specified to participants, as the phenomenon under investigation was different—more general—than the *home bias* itself. With these premises, and on the basis of previous research mentioned in the introduction, two hypotheses were tested: (1) independently from anxiety levels, the ability to correctly discriminate between fouls and non-fouls would be lower in the pressing crowd condition than in the calm crowd condition; (2) considering anxiety levels, the discrimination ability of referees with high anxiety would be more impaired than

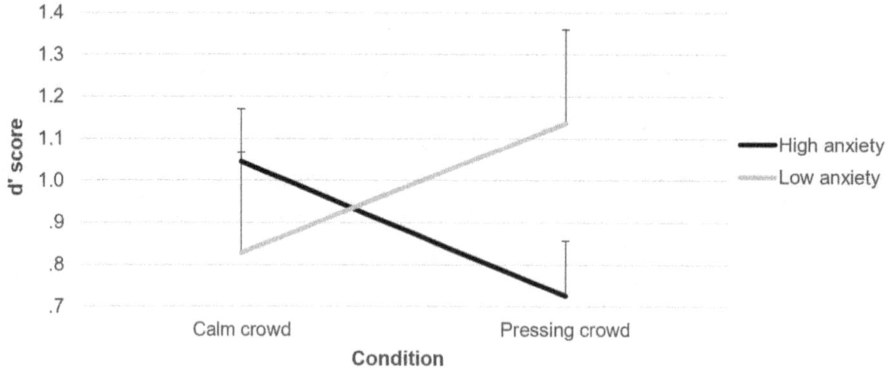

FIGURE 2 | The *d′* scores of referees with low and high anxiety in the calm and pressing crowd conditions. Error bars show the standard error of the mean.

that of referees with low anxiety in the pressing crowd condition, while no differences would emerge in the calm crowd condition.

The results of the experiment seem not to support the first hypothesis, as no difference in fouls discrimination ability emerged between the calm and pressing conditions. The explanation of this outcome can be easily found in the significant interaction between crowd noise and anxiety levels; thus, the overall apparent null effect of crowd noise was actually due to its different impact on participants on the basis of their competitive anxiety. Such an interaction, together with the decreased discrimination ability of referees with high anxiety in the pressing crowd condition, as well as the absence of difference between the two groups in the calm crowd condition, seems to support the second hypothesis. A reasonable explanation of this outcome refers to cue learning, with highly anxious referees being more prone than lowly anxious ones to rely on a salient concurrent cue (like pressing crowd noise), when judging contact situations. However, such a cue can often be misleading or at least ambiguous, thus leading to a poorer performance. Another possible explanation refers to the phenomenon of *choking under pressure*, with more anxious people/athletes being more prone to experience performance decrements in pressing situations (e.g., Otten, 2009). It is also possible to hypothesize a combination of these two explanations: an anxious referee could be performing poorly during a pressing competition, and becoming aware of this s/he could try to improve her/his performance by basing her/his decisions also on crowd reactions, which in most cases would further negatively affect the performance itself. Further studies are needed to deepen the understanding of the mechanisms underpinning the processes that led to the outcomes observed in the present experiment.

An interesting result of the present experiment is the marginally significant difference between referees with high and low anxiety in the pressing crowd condition. Looking at **Figure 2**, it appears quite evident that the trend of referees with low anxiety is opposite to that of referees with high anxiety (as confirmed by the significant interaction). However, for the low anxiety group the comparison between the two crowd noise conditions revealed no significant difference; this is reasonably due to the higher variability with respect to the high anxiety group. Anyway, it appears that the discrimination ability of at least some referees with low anxiety was higher in the pressing crowd condition than in the calm crowd condition; this observation is in line with the phenomenon of *clutch* performances, that is, a performance increase in pressing situations (Otten, 2009), and deserves further investigation to be clarified.

In the present experiment, participants were divided in two groups—referees with low and high anxiety—on the basis of the sample's median score. In future studies investigating similar issues, it would be interesting to use questionnaires/scales with cut-off values, so that participants can be divided in two (or more) groups on more grounded bases. However, existing questionnaires with these characteristics might not suit a specific population like referees, so an alternative solution to make the results more generalizable can be that of expanding the sample size. Another aspect to consider in order to foster the generalizability of the results of future studies is the use of the latest advances in technology, such as virtual reality and/or 3D displays (also for auditory stimuli), as they allow for more ecological experimental settings (Craig, 2013).

Interestingly, the present study significantly adds not only to the literature concerning referees' decision making, but also to the line of research that in recent years is revealing the relevant role of ecological sounds in sports (for a recent review, see Schaffert et al., 2019). Indeed, previous studies highlighted that ecological auditory information can be used by athletes to perceive different features of sport gestures (Murgia et al., 2012; Kennel et al., 2014; Sors et al., 2017), to predict the outcome of opponents' actions (Allerdissen et al., 2017; Camponogara et al., 2017; Cañal-Bruland et al., 2018; Sors et al., 2018), and to improve performances (Agostini et al., 2004; Sors et al., 2015; Pizzera et al., 2017). The present study indicates that the ecological auditory information is somehow important not only for athletes, but also for referees, as it provides them with an additional source of information. Independently from the fact that this information can be useful or misleading, our findings indicate that crowd noise can affect the referees' decisional processes and, consequently, their behavior.

From an applied perspective, the results of the present experiment highlight the importance of referees' competitive anxiety levels in relation with crowd noise. Indeed, while the ability of referees with low anxiety to discriminate fouls does not significantly change with a calm crowd or a pressing one, for referees with high anxiety such ability significantly decreases with a pressing crowd noise, thus determining poorer refereeing performances. Referees' federations should be aware of this phenomenon, as it may influence competitions' results to a significant extent. This does not mean that highly anxious referees should be relegated only to less important matches (where smaller/calmer crowds are expected); rather, federations should consider the possibility to develop dedicated training protocols and/or to include in their staff the figure of the sport psychologist, who could provide specific interventions.

To sum up, the present study highlighted that pressing crowd noise impairs the ability of basketball referees with high anxiety to discriminate fouls. Further research is needed to better understand why this is the case (e.g., which factors cause this bias), as well as whether it replicates also in other sports. Findings should raise the awareness of referees' federations on this and related phenomena, in order to adopt appropriate intervention strategies to avoid competitions' results from being biased by them.

ETHICS STATEMENT

The studies involving human participants were reviewed and approved by Ethics Committee of the University of Trieste. The patients/participants provided their written informed consent to participate in this study.

AUTHOR CONTRIBUTIONS

FS, IS, and MM conceived the idea. FS, DT, VP, IS, AG, TA, and MM designed the study. FS and VP prepared the stimuli. FS, IS, and AG programmed the experiment. FS, DT, and VP collected the data. FS, MM, and TA analyzed the data. FS, DT and MM wrote the first draft of the manuscript. VP, IS, AG, and TA revised the manuscript.

ACKNOWLEDGMENTS

We would like to thank the referees who took part in our experiment for their availability and their suggestions.

SUPPLEMENTARY MATERIAL

Video S1 | Example of foul with calm crowd noise.

Video S2 | Example of foul with pressing crowd noise.

Video S3 | Example of non-foul with calm crowd noise.

Video S4 | Example of non-foul with pressing crowd noise.

REFERENCES

Agostini, T., Righi, G., Galmonte, A., and Bruno, P. (2004). "The relevance of auditory information in optimizing hammer throwers performance," in *Biomechanics and Sports,* ed P. B. Pascolo (Vienna: Springer), 67–74. doi: 10.1007/978-3-7091-2760-5_9

Allerdissen, M., Güldenpenning, I., Schack, T., and Bläsing, B. (2017). Recognizing fencing attacks from auditory and visual information: a comparison between expert fencers and novices. *Psychol. Sport Exerc.* 31, 123–130. doi: 10.1016/j.psychsport.2017.04.009

Aragao-Pina, J. A., Passos, A., Araújo, D., and Maynard, M. T. (2018). Football refereeing: an integrative review. *Psychol. Sport Exerc.* 35, 10–26. doi: 10.1016/j.psychsport.2017.10.006

Asch, S. E. (1951). "Effects of group pressure upon the modification and distortion of judgment," in *Groups, Leadership and Men,* ed H. Guetzkow (Pittsburgh, PA: Carnegie Press), 177–190.

Balmer, N. J., Nevill, A. M., Lane, A. M., Ward, P., Williams, A. M., and Fairclough, S. H. (2007). Influence of crowd noise on soccer refereeing consistency in soccer. *J. Sport Behav.* 30, 130–145.

Boyko, R. H., Boyko, A. R., and Boyko, M. G. (2007). Referee bias contributes to home advantage in English Premiership football. *J. Sports Sci.* 25, 1185–1194. doi: 10.1080/02640410601038576

Buraimo, B., Forrest, D., and Simmons, R. (2010). The 12th man?: refereeing bias in English and German soccer. *J. R. Stat. Soc.* 173, 431–449. doi: 10.1111/j.1467-985X.2009.00604.x

Buraimo, B., Simmons, R., and Maciaszczyk, M. (2012). Favoritism and referee bias in European soccer: evidence from the Spanish league and the UEFA champions league. *Contemp. Econ. Policy* 30, 329–343. doi: 10.1111/j.1465-7287.2011.00295.x

Camponogara, I., Rodger, M., Craig, C., and Cesari, P. (2017). Expert players accurately detect an opponent's movement intentions through sound alone. *J. Exp. Psychol.* 43, 348–359. doi: 10.1037/xhp0000316

Cañal-Bruland, R., Müller, F., Lach, B., and Spence, C. (2018). Auditory contributions to visual anticipation in tennis. *Psychol. Sport Exerc.* 36, 100–103. doi: 10.1016/j.psychsport.2018.02.001

Cohen, J. (1988). *Statistical Power Analysis for the Behavioral Sciences.* New York, NY: Routledge Academic

Constantinou, A. C., Fenton, N. E., and Pollock, L. J. H. (2014). Bayesian networks for unbiased assessment of referee bias in Association Football. *Psychol. Sport Exerc.* 15, 538–547. doi: 10.1016/j.psychsport.2014.05.009

Craig, C. (2013). Understanding perception and action in sport: how can virtual reality technology help? *Sports Technol.* 6, 161–169. doi: 10.1080/19346182.2013.855224

Dawson, P., and Dobson, S. (2010). The influence of social pressure and nationality on individual decisions: Evidence from the behaviour of referees. *J. Econ. Psychol.* 31, 181–191. doi: 10.1016/j.joep.2009.06.001

Dawson, P., Dobson, S., Goddard, J., and Wilson, J. (2007). Are football referees really biased and inconsistent?: evidence on the incidence of disciplinary sanction in the English Premier League. *J. R. Stat. Soc.* 170, 231–250. doi: 10.1111/j.1467-985X.2006.00451.x

Di Corrado, D., Pellarin, E., and Agostini, T. A. (2011). The phenomenon of social influence on the football pitch: Social pressure from the crowd on referees' decisions. *Rev. Psychol.* 18, 33–36.

Dohmen, T. J. (2008). The influence of social forces: evidence from the behavior of football referees. *Econ. Inquiry* 46, 411–424. doi: 10.1111/j.1465-7295.2007.00112.x

Downward, P., and Jones, M. (2007). Effects of crowd size on referee decisions: analysis of the FA Cup. *J. Sports Sci.* 25, 1541–1545. doi: 10.1080/02640410701275193

Garicano, L., Palacios-Huerta, I., and Prendergast, C. (2005). Favoritism under social pressure. *Rev. Econ. Stat.* 87, 208–216. doi: 10.1162/0034653053970267

Greer, D. L. (1983). Spectator booing and the home advantage: a study of social influence in the basketball arena. *Soc. Psychol. Q.* 46, 252–261. doi: 10.2307/3033796

Johansen, B. T., and Haugen, T. (2013). Anxiety level and decision-making among Norwegian top-class soccer referees. *Int. J. Sport Exerc. Psychol.* 11, 215–226. doi: 10.1080/1612197X.2013.773665

Kennel, C., Pizzera, A., Hohmann, T., Schubotz, R. I., Murgia, M., Agostini, T., et al. (2014). The perception of natural and modulated movement sounds. *Perception* 43, 796–804. doi: 10.1068/p7643

Lago-Peñas, C., and Gómez-López, M. (2016). The influence of referee bias on extra time in elite soccer matches. *Percep. Motor Skills* 122, 666–677. doi: 10.1177/0031512516633342

Lakens, D. (2013). Calculating and reporting effect sizes to facilitate cumulative science: a practical primer for t-tests and ANOVAs. *Front. Psychol.* 4:863. doi: 10.3389/fpsyg.2013.00863

Lex, H., Pizzera, A., Kurtes, M., and Schack, T. (2015). Influence of players' vocalisations on soccer referees' decisions. *Eur. J. Sport Sci.* 15, 424–428. doi: 10.1080/17461391.2014.962620

MacMahon, C., Helsen, W. F., Starkes, J. L., and Weston, M. (2007). Decision-making skills and deliberate practice in elite association football referees. *J. Sports Sci.* 25, 65–78. doi: 10.1080/02640410600718640

Milgram, S. (1963). Behavioral study of obedience. *J. Abnorm. Soc. Psychol.* 67, 371–378. doi: 10.1037/h0040525

Morris, P. H., and Lewis, D. (2010). Tackling diving: the perception of deceptive intentions in association football (soccer). *J. Nonverb. Behav.* 34, 1–13. doi: 10.1007/s10919-009-0075-0

Murgia, M., Hohmann, T., Galmonte, A., Raab, M., and Agostini, T. (2012). Recognising one's own motor actions through sound: the role of temporal factors. *Perception* 41, 976–987. doi: 10.1068/p7227

Myers, T., Nevill, A., and Al-Nakeeb, Y. (2012). The influence of crowd noise upon judging decisions in Muay Thai. *Adv. Phys. Educ.* 2, 148–152. doi: 10.4236/ape.2012.24026

Nevill, A. M., Balmer, N. J., and Williams, A. M. (2002). The influence of crowd noise and experience upon refereeing decisions in football. *Psychol. Sport Exerc.* 3, 261–272. doi: 10.1016/S1469-0292(01)00033-4

Nevill, A. M., Hemingway, A., Greaves, R., Dallaway, A., and Devonport, T. J. (2017). Inconsistency of decision-making, the Achilles heel of referees. *J. Sports Sci.* 35, 2257–2261. doi: 10.1080/02640414.2016.1265143

Otten, M. (2009). Choking vs. clutch performance: a study of sport performance under pressure. *J. Sport Exerc. Psychol.* 31, 583–601. doi: 10.1123/jsep.31.5.583

Page, K., and Page, L. (2010). Alone against the crowd: individual differences in referees' ability to cope under pressure. *J. Econ. Psychol.* 31, 192–199. doi: 10.1016/j.joep.2009.08.007

Pazzona, R., Guicciardi, M., and Murgia, M. (2018). The inattentional blindness in soccer referees. *Medicina dello Sport* 71, 216–225. doi: 10.23736/S0025-7826.18.03209-X

Pettersson-Lidbom, P., and Priks, M. (2010). Behavior under social pressure: empty Italian stadiums and referee bias. *Econ. Lett.* 108, 212–214. doi: 10.1016/j.econlet.2010.04.023

Picazo-Tadeo, A. J., González-Gómez, F., and Guardiola, J. (2016). Does the crowd matter in refereeing decisions? Evidence from Spanish soccer. *Int. J. Sport Exerc. Psychol.* 15, 447–459. doi: 10.1080/1612197X.2015.1126852

Pizzera, A., Hohmann, T., Streese, L., Habbig, A., and Raab, M. (2017). Long-term effects of acoustic reafference training (ART). *Eur. J. Sport Sci.* 17, 1279–1288. doi: 10.1080/17461391.2017.1381767

Plessner, H., and Betsch, T. (2001). Sequential effects in important referee decisions: the case of penalties in soccer. *J. Sport Exerc. Psychol.* 23, 254–259. doi: 10.1123/jsep.23.3.254

Plessner, H., and Haar, T. (2006). Sports performance judgments from a social cognitive perspective. *Psychol. Sport Exerc.* 7, 555–575. doi: 10.1016/j.psychsport.2006.03.007

Plessner, H., Schweizer, G., Brand, R., and O'Hare, D. (2009). A multiple-cue learning approach as the basis for understanding and improving soccer referees' decision making. *Progr. Brain Res.* 174, 151–158. doi: 10.1016/S0079-6123(09)01313-2

Pollard, R. (1986). Home advantage in soccer: a retrospective analysis. *J. Sports Sci.* 4, 237–248. doi: 10.1080/02640418608732122

Ponzo, M., and Scoppa, V. (2014). Does the home advantage depend on crowd support? Evidence from same-stadium derbies. *J. Sports Econ.* 19, 562–582. doi: 10.1177/1527002516665794

Pope, B. R., and Pope, N. G. (2015). Own-nationality bias: evidence from UEFA champions league football referees. *Econ. Inquiry* 53, 1292–1304. doi: 10.1111/ecin.12180

Schaffert, N., Janzen, T. B., Mattes, K., and Thaut, M. H. (2019). A review on the relationship between sound and movement in sports and rehabilitation. *Front. Psychol.* 10:244. doi: 10.3389/fpsyg.2019.00244

Scoppa, V. (2008). Are subjective evaluations biased by social factors or connections? An econometric analysis of soccer referee decisions. *Empirical Econ.* 35, 123–140. doi: 10.1007/s00181-007-0146-1

Smith, R. E., Smoll, F. L., and Schutz, R. W. (1990). Measurement and correlates of sport-specific cognitive and somatic trait anxiety: the sport anxiety scale. *Anx. Res.* 2, 263–280. doi: 10.1080/08917779008248733

Sors, F., Lath, F., Bader, A., Santoro, I., Galmonte, A., Agostini, T., et al. (2018). Predicting the length of volleyball serves: the role of early auditory and visual information. *PLoS ONE* 13:e0208174. doi: 10.1371/journal.pone.0208174

Sors, F., Murgia, M., Santoro, I., and Agostini, T. (2015). Audio-based interventions in sport. *Open Psychol. J.* 8, 212–219. doi: 10.2174/1874350101508010212

Sors, F., Murgia, M., Santoro, I., Prpic, V., Galmonte, A., and Agostini, T. (2017). The contribution of early auditory and visual information to the discrimination of shot power in ball sports. *Psychol. Sport Exerc.* 31, 44–51. doi: 10.1016/j.psychsport.2017.04.005

Souchon, N., Fontayne, P., Livingstone, A., Maio, G. R., Mellac, N., and Genolini, C. (2013). External influences on referees' decisions in judo: the effects of coaches' exclamations during throw situations. *J. Appl. Sport Psychol.* 25, 223–233. doi: 10.1080/10413200.2012.713440

Sutter, M., and Kocher, M. G. (2004). Favoritism of agents–the case of referees' home bias. *J. Econ. Psychol.* 25, 461–469. doi: 10.1016/S0167-4870(03)00013-8

Unkelbach, C., and Memmert, D. (2008). Game management, context effects, and calibration: the case of yellow cards in soccer. *J. Sport Exerc. Psychol.* 30, 95–109. doi: 10.1123/jsep.30.1.95

Unkelbach, C., and Memmert, D. (2010). Crowd noise as a cue in referee decisions contributes to the home advantage. *J. Sport Exerc. Psychol.* 32, 483–498. doi: 10.1123/jsep.32.4.483

Webb, T., Dicks, M., Thelwell, R., and Nevill, A. (2018). The impact of referee training: reflections on the reduction of home advantage in association football. *Soccer Soc.* 19, 1024–1037. doi: 10.1080/14660970.2016.1267626

Wolfson, S., and Neave, N. (2007). Coping under pressure: Cognitive strategies for maintaining confidence among soccer referees. *J. Sport Behav.* 30:232.

11

Cognitive Deficits and White Matter Alterations in Highly Trained Scuba Divers

Marinella Coco[1], Andrea Buscemi[2], Valentina Perciavalle[3], Tiziana Maci[4], Gianluca Galvano[5], Antonio M. F. Scavone[5], Vincenzo Perciavalle[6] and Donatella Di Corrado[6]*

[1] Department of Biomedical and Biotechnological Sciences, University of Catania, Catania, Italy, [2] Study Center of Italian Osteopathy, Horus Social Cooperative, Catania-Ragusa, Italy, [3] Department of Educational Sciences, University of Catania, Catania, Italy, [4] Independent Researcher, Catania, Italy, [5] U.O.C. Diagnostic Imaging, Interventional Radiology and Neuroradiology, Garibaldi Hospital, Catania, Italy, [6] Faculty of Human and Society Sciences, Kore University of Enna, Enna, Italy

***Correspondence:**
Marinella Coco
marinella.coco@gmail.com

Nitrogen gas (N2), present in the normal atmospheric air, is a potential source of risk for scuba divers. It seems probable that myelin can represent, in hyperbaric conditions, a preferential site for the accumulation of N2 in central nervous system (CNS). The purpose of this study is to verify whether the practice of the scuba diving is capable to determine a damage of the brain white matter (WM) in a dose dependent manner and, consequently, possible deficiency of their cognitive abilities. For this purpose, 54 professional scuba divers (35 men and 19 women), with at least 2,000 dives in their careers, were studied. Possible alterations of brain WM were evaluated in terms of Fractional anisotropy (FA) by using Diffusion Tensor Imaging, whereas possible cognitive impairments were verified by means of neuropsychological testing, by studying: (1) General mental capability (2) Executive functioning; (3) Visuospatial construction such as Rey Complex Figure; (4) Attention and orientation: (5) Selective attention capacity and processing speed ability; (6) Memory. The results showed alteration of the WM in terms of changes in FA; these alterations, statistically significant but quantitatively quite modest, were mainly observed in the WM of the anterior part of the brain, whereas no differences were observed between left and right hemisphere. The alterations of the WM were associated with changes, also in this case statistically significant but quantitatively quite modest, of the cognitive functions, in particular of those dependent on the prefrontal cortex, such as attention and memory function. The present study leads to the conclusion that repeated dives, even performed in compliance with the current decompression tables, can progressively lead in the CNS to the formation of micro-lesions in the myelin sheet capable of altering the functioning of the neuron.

Keywords: scuba diving, white matter, Fractional anisotropy, neuropsychological testing, sport

INTRODUCTION

Nitrogen gas (N2), present in the normal atmospheric air, is a potential source of risk for scuba divers for two different reasons: during the descent may induce nitrogen narcosis and during the ascent may cause decompression sickness (DCS).

Individuals exposed to increasing N2 pressures exhibit, already at 0.3 MPa, spatial disorientation, altered judgment and impaired neuromuscular coordination (Bennett, 1993), up to the loss of consciousness when the pressure of N2 reaches 1 MPa, a condition related to nitrogen narcosis (Edmonds et al., 1981). The narcotic effect is dependent on to the increase in the partial pressure of N2; the gas in fact, with the increase in pressure, would dissolve in the cell membrane of the neuron (Behnke et al., 1935). In this way, the increased presence of N2 in the cell membrane on the one hand would modify its biophysical characteristics and, on the other hand, the binding of N2 to membrane proteins, would vary their activity (Franks and Lieb, 1994).

It is known that DCS occurs when N2 dissolved in the tissues is released too quickly during decompression, leading to the formation of bubbles that can cause damage to various organs (see Doolette and Mitchell, 2001). The relationship between N2 and adipose tissue is of particular attention in hyperbaric conditions as N2 is five times more soluble in lipids than in water (Weathersby and Homer, 1980; Langø et al., 1996). According to this point of view, the adipose tissue would act as a reservoir for N2, able to accumulate it during the compression phase and then quickly release it during decompression; in fact, it has been shown that the risk of DCS is greater in obese subjects (Carturan et al., 2002).

In the human body lipids are involved in two essential functions: in the form of triglycerides, they are an excellent substrate to be oxidized for producing energy and they are an essential component in the structure of cell membranes. Since the central nervous system (CNS) does not contain triglycerides, brain lipids have been studied to identify roles different from that of energy substrate. Actually, in addition to structural tasks in cell membranes, as myelin, they act as bioMessengers and intervene in cellular signal transduction processes (see Agranoff et al., 1999).

Myelin is a lipid-rich substance that is produced by specialized glial cells, that in the CNS are the oligodendrocytes and in the peripheral nervous system the Schwann cells (see Nave and Werner, 2014). At the level of the axons, the myelin acts as an electrical insulator, favoring the propagation of the nerve impulse at high speed from one node of Ranvier to the other (Waxman, 1980). Lipids represent about 70% of the dry weight of myelin (Norton and Poduslo, 1973), a value that is about twice that measured in the other cell membranes (Chrast et al., 2011).

From a logical point of view, it seems probable that myelin can represent, in hyperbaric conditions, a preferential site for the accumulation of N2 in CNS. However, there are no studies about the possible alterations of myelin in scuba divers, in particular in those that, for professional reasons, perform thousands of dives. It is conceivable, in fact, that a continuous exposure to conditions of high partial pressures of N2 could lead, during the decompression phase, to the formation within the myelin of microbubbles which could compromise the functioning of white matter (WM) in the CNS.

The aim of this study was to verify whether the practice of the scuba diving is capable to determine a damage of the brain WM in a dose dependent manner and, consequently, possible deficiency of their cognitive abilities. Recent literature has documented effects of diving on cognitive functions (Kowalski et al., 2011; Ergen et al., 2017; Howle et al., 2017; Bosco et al., 2018; Verratti et al., 2019). Some of these studies have reported decreased mental flexibility (Cordes et al., 2000), as well as lower verbal memory and intelligence (Hemelryck et al., 2014), sustained attention in divers reporting memory and concentration loss (Taylor et al., 2006), and decrease average response speed (Pourhashemi et al., 2016). Further, we expected that a high number of dives (at least 2,000) with compressed air is able to alter the quality of brain WM, evaluated by using diffusion tensor imaging (DTI), determining cognitive impairments.

MATERIALS AND METHODS

Participants and Procedure

Fifty-four professional scuba divers (35 men and 19 women) in the age range from 28 to 58 years (M_{age} = 40.1 years, SD = 6.08) were recruited for the study. For scuba divers, inclusion criteria were to have performed at least 2,000 scuba dives, with an average of at least 100 dives a year, proven by their personal dive log. Controls were represented by 54 individuals (35 men and 19 women) having the same mean age of divers (mean value 39.7 years ± 7.22 SD). **Table 1** summarizes the main characteristics of both groups. For both divers and controls exclusion criteria were (a) presence of neurological, pulmonary, cardiovascular, or metabolic disease, (b) positive test for thrombophilia, and (c) evidence for patent foramen oval. Prior to the beginning of the study, ethical approval was granted From the first author's university ethics committee. The study obtained ethical permission from the Internal Ethic Review Board - IERB, Department of Education Sciences, Psychology Section, University of Catania (29/11/2018). All participants were informed about the trials of the study and the anonymity of their answers before providing their written consent to participate, in accordance with the Declaration of Helsinki.

TABLE 1 | Characteristics of study participants.

	Male divers (*N* = 35)	Female divers (*N* = 17)	Male controls (*N* = 35)	Female controls (*N* = 17)
Age, years	41.0 ± 6.75	40.9 ± 4.77	38.7 ± 7.51	39.6 ± 6.56
BMI, kg/m^2	25.7 ± 3.18	25.8 ± 3.11	25.4 ± 2.21	25.6 ± 2.85
Immersions	4881.8 ± 2168.13	3841.5 ± 1060.32		

Measures

Neurological and Neuropsychological Assessment

All participants were tested by the same neuropsychologist (T.M.) using a neuropsychological test battery grouped according to major functional category.

General mental capability - Wechsler Adult Intelligence Scale- Revised (WAIS–R; Wechsler, 1981): WAIS–R Full-scale IQ (FSIQ); WAIS–R Verbal IQ (VIQ); WAIS–R Performance IQ (PIQ).

Executive functioning: Trail Making Test (Tombaugh, 2004), Trail A and Trail B; Wisconsin Card Sorting Test, WCST (Berg, 1948).

Reasoning and abstraction- WAIS-R: Similarities (Sims), Comprehension (Compr). Arithmetic (Arith).

Visuospatial construction: Rey Complex Figure (Rey, 1941) scored according to the traditional guidelines developed by Taylor (Spreen and Strauss, 1998): Copy; WAIS-R Block Design, WAIS-R Object Assembly.

Language: WAIS-R Vocabulary (Vocab).

Attention and orientation: Digit Span-forward and backward (Soylu, 2010), Corsi block-tapping test (Kessels et al., 2000) forward and backward.

Selective attention capacity and processing speed ability: Stroop Color and Word Test (Stroop, 1935), score by using the formula originally proposed by Callaway (1959), i.e., time taken to complete the color-word card minus time spent to complete the color card.

Memory: Wechsler Memory Scale–Revised (WMS-R; Wechsler, 1987): Immediate Memory (Logical Memory), Delayed Memory (verbal Paired Association) and Working Memory (Letter - Number Sequencing) were evaluated (Axelrod, 2001). Rey Complex Figure: recall.

Brain Imaging

Scans were performed with conventional techniques and DTI. Along the anterior/posterior commissure line, conventional axial T1-weighted, T2-weighted, fluid-attenuated inversion recovery (FLAIR), and DTI sequences were acquired with a 1.5T imaging system. Acquisition of DTI images were carried out with a single-shot pulsed-gradient, echo-planar imaging protocol (TR8000 ms, TE109 ms, FOV240 mm, matrix128 × 128, section thickness 3 mm). Diffusion gradients were evaluated in 25 non-collinear directions by using 2 b values (0 and 1500 s/mm^2). Duration for DTI acquisition was 8 min and 6 s.

Oval Regions of Interest (ROIs) were positioned bilaterally on images acquired without diffusion gradients (b 0 s/mm^2). Small ROIs of 9–16 pixels (31.64–56.25 mm^2) were located in correspondence of frontal lobe (FL), temporal lobe (TL), parietal lobe (PL), occipital lobe (OL), splenium of corpus callosum (SCC), genu of corpus callosum (GCC), corona radiata (CR), and corticospinal tract (CT) white matter (**Figure 1**).

For each subject, the measures of FA were separately carried out for each side of every white matter region and then averaged across all the sections bilaterally. FA was calculated using the method proposed by Basser and Pierpaoli (1996) on a pixel-by-pixel basis. The scale of FA ranges from 0 (perfect isotropy) to 1 (perfect anisotropy).

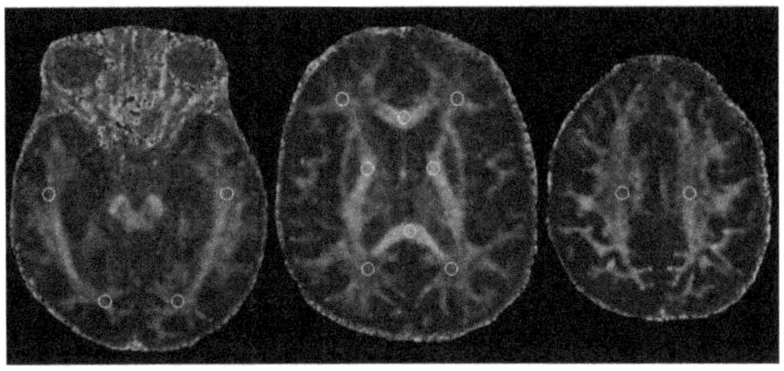

FIGURE 1 | Fractional anisotropy map showing locations white matter Regions of Interest (ROIs).

Statistical Analyses

Differences between the two groups of participants were assessed by one-way analyses of variance (ANOVA) with the nonparametric Kruskal-Wallis test. Voxel-wise group differences in FA were assessed using the ANOVA module in SPM99 followed by group-wise *t*-test comparisons. For these comparisons, significance was determined with a *p*-value of <0.05 (corrected for multiple comparisons at the cluster level) with a seven-voxel extent threshold. Statistical analyses were performed using SPSS v. 23 Statistical Software Package for windows (SPSS Inc., Chicago, IL, United States).

RESULTS

Fractional Anisotropy

The MRI of the brains of scuba divers and controls has highlighted the absence of gross lesions. However, as can be seen in **Figure 2**, if we compared the mean value of FA measured in the 8 ROIs it can be seen that the values measured in correspondence of FL, TL, GCC, CR, and CT were significantly lower in the divers compared to controls. The *post hoc* Dunn's Multiple Comparison Test has been performed (see **Supplementary Table S1**). No difference, however, was detected in correspondence of PL, OL, and SCC. The same figure allows detecting how the same pattern found on the entire sample was observed, without statistically significant differences, both in women and in men. Moreover, the figure shows that it was not possible to highlight statistically significant differences, for the different ROIs, between right and left side.

However, when in scuba divers the mean value of the FA, measured in the different ROIs, is correlated with the number of dives carried out by each of them, a strong negative correlation emerges, as can be seen in **Figure 3**, with the exclusion of SCC as well as of left and right PL and OL. Nor were any gender-dependent differences found.

However, the number of dives obviously increases with increasing age (**Figure 4**) so it is possible that the observed WM anomalies could depend on age and not on the number of dives. To evaluate this possibility, we connected the values of FA with the age of both scuba divers as well

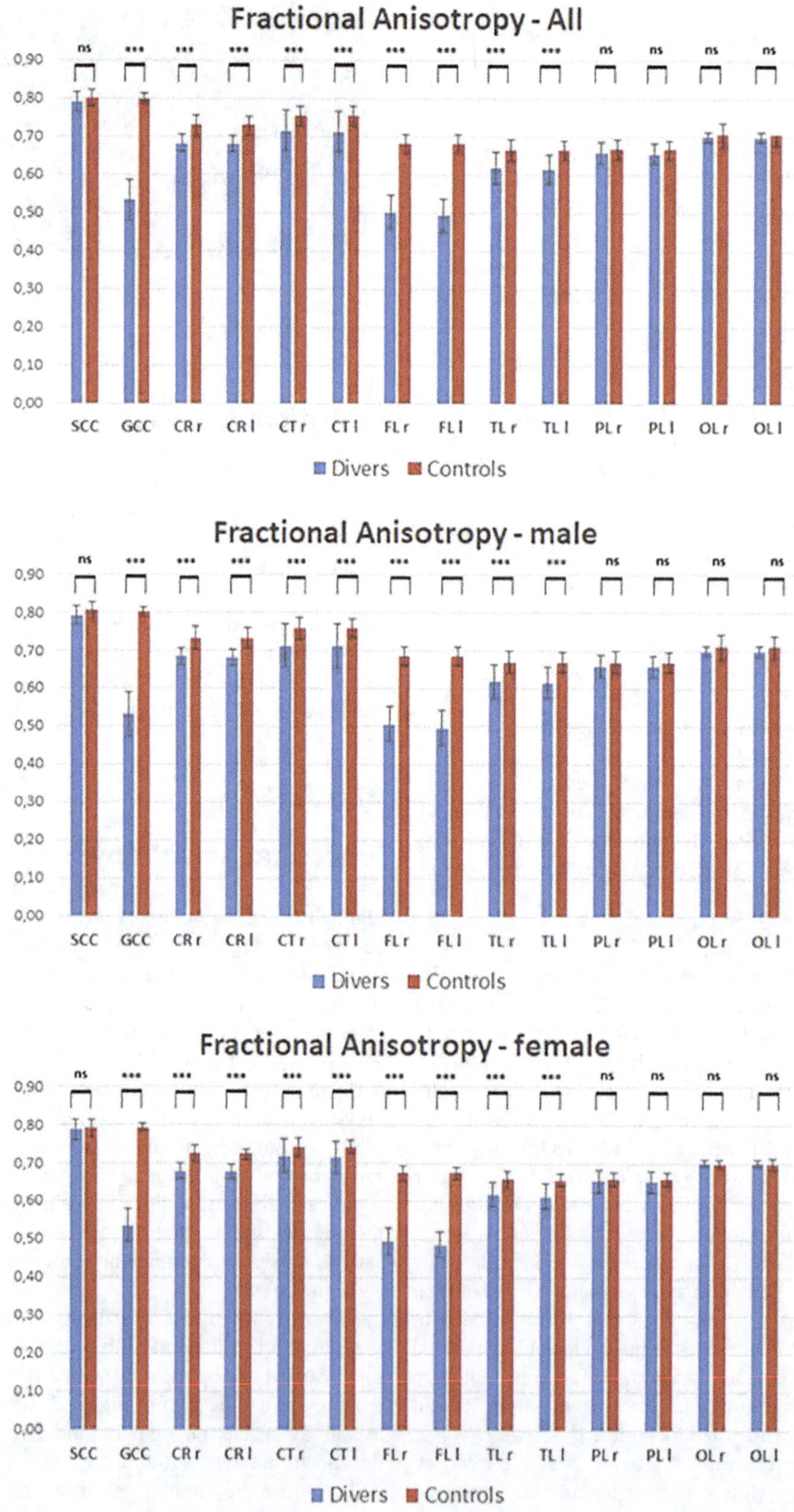

FIGURE 2 | Mean values of Fractional anisotropy measured in scuba divers and controls in correspondence of the 8 ROIs. CR, corona radiata; CT, corticospinal tract; FL, frontal lobe; GCC, genu of corpus callosum; l, left; ns, not significant; OL, occipital lobe; PL, parietal lobe; r, right; SCC, splenium of corpus callosum; TL, temporal lobe. ***$p < 0.001$.

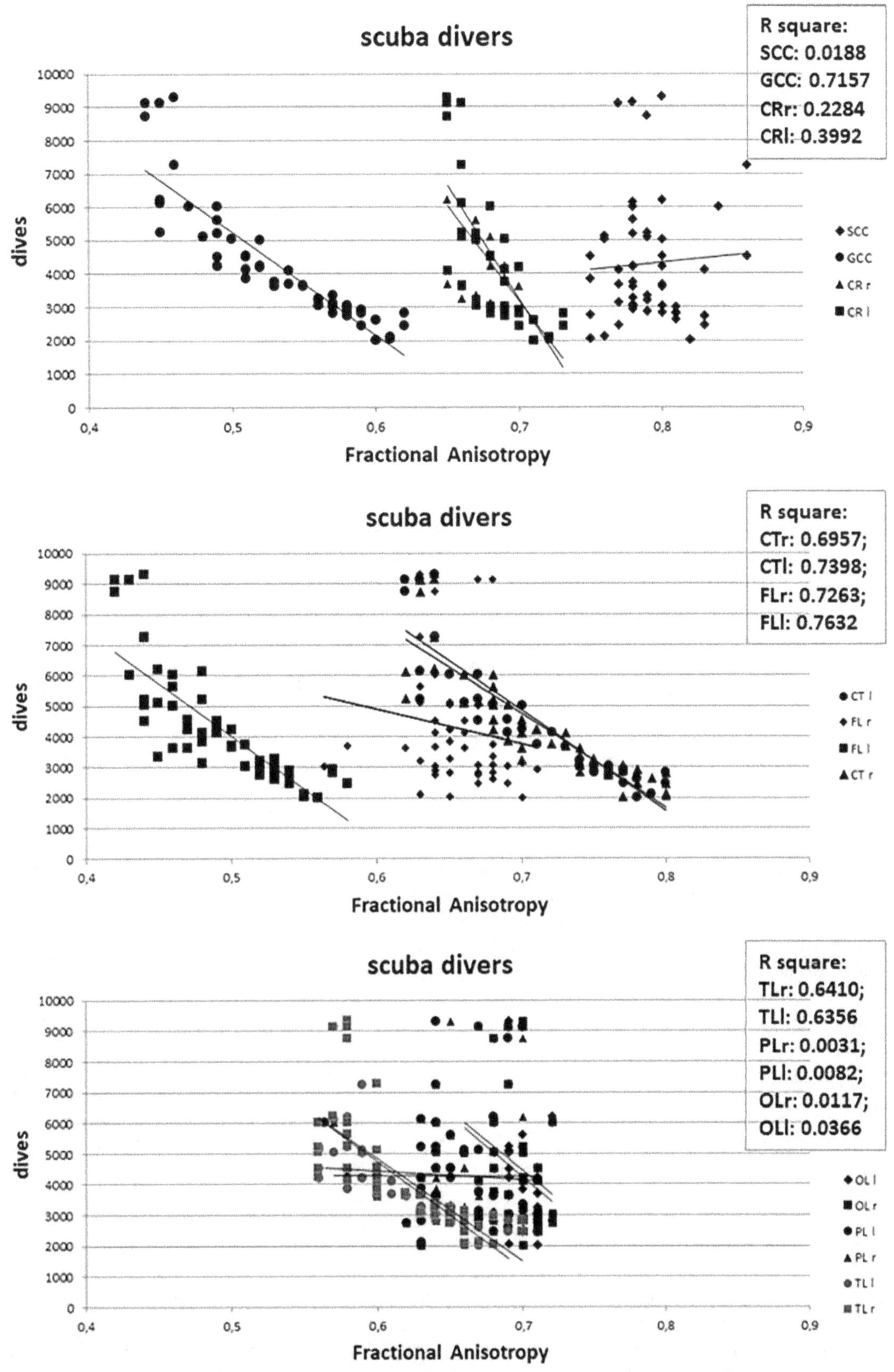

FIGURE 3 | Relation between Fractional Anisotropy and number of dives of divers. Abbreviations as in **Figure 2**.

as healthy controls. However, as can be seen in **Figure 5** where data relating to the left FL are shown, while in scuba divers the values of FA were significantly related with age, the healthy controls did not exhibit any statistically significant correlation. Statistically significant relations were also obtained by relating with age of divers FA values of right FL, GCC, as well as CT and TL of both sides; no relationship between age and FA was detected in controls. Therefore, it is possible to conclude that the changes of FA observed in scuba divers are related to the number of dives and not to age.

Neuropsychological Testing

Data from neuropsychological testing reveal small but significant impaired performances that increases with the number of dives. In **Figure 6** the results obtained for the Ray Complex Figure (top row), for the Corsi tapping test (middle row) and for the Digit Span (bottom row) are reported. The left column shows the relationships between the results obtained in the test and the dives numbers, the center column shows the relationships between the results obtained in the test and the age of the divers, while the right column shows the relationships between the results obtained in the test and the age of the controls.

It is possible to detect that, while in scuba divers there is a significant negative relation between the test's results and both the number of dives and the age, no relation has been highlighted between the test's results and age in the controls. Also in this case, no gender differences were detected (data not shown).

Figure 7 shows the R square values obtained from the correlations, both in scuba divers and controls, between the age of the subjects and the scores obtained in the different neuropsychological tests administered.

As can be seen, in all scuba divers the scores of all the different neuropsychological tests showed correlations with the age of the subjects with R square values that were less than 0.3 only for FSIQ, Trail Making Test Trail A and Trail Making Test Trail B. In the controls, however, there is no correlation between scores in neuropsychological tests and the age of the subjects, with values of *R* square always below 0.1. Nor were any gender-dependent differences found.

DISCUSSION

In recent years a number of studies have highlighted the presence of mild but significant cognitive deficits in scuba divers that have performed a high number of dives (Kowalski et al., 2011; Hemelryck et al., 2014; Ergen et al., 2017; Howle et al., 2017; Bosco et al., 2018; Verratti et al., 2019).

The present study aimed to assess whether underwater diving and compressed air work is capable to induce, in a dose-dependent manner, alterations of the cerebral WM and, consequently, to produce alterations of cognitive functions.

The results showed alterations of the WM both in terms of changes in FA; these variations, statistically significant but quantitatively quite modest, were mainly observed in the WM of the anterior part of the brain; no differences were observed between left and right hemisphere and between women and men.

The alterations of WM were positively related to the number of dives and the age of the divers. In controls, on the other hand, no correlation was found between the FA values of the WM and the age of the participants. This led to the conclusion that the changes of FA are more likely a result of the number of dives and are not due to the possibility that more experienced divers are too likely to be older. The absence of changes in the WM of controls is likely to be dependent on the relatively young age of the subjects (mean value 39.7 years ±7.22 SD), none of which reached 55 years (Chen et al., 2019).

In divers, the alterations of the WM were associated with changes, also in this case statistically significant but quantitatively quite modest, of the cognitive functions, in particular of those dependent on the prefrontal cortex (Coco et al., 2009; Ergen et al., 2017). The results of the present study are in agreement with cognitive deficits previously described in professional scuba divers. In particular, in this research cognitive deficits were found mainly, but not exclusively, in the domain of frontal functions. Kowalski et al. (2011) found delays in reaction time in 25 very experienced divers, compared to 23 non-divers. The findings showed that a lasting cerebral damage possibly develops only after a long diving career consisting of numerous decompressions, and repetitive dives. In addition, their results of the controls suggest that age had no direct influence on reaction times. Investigating long-term effects of diving on cognitive function in 44 experienced scuba divers, Hemelryck et al. (2014) found a worse performance in short-term memory, compared to controls.

The present study leads to the conclusion that repeated dives, even performed in compliance with the current decompression tables, could progressively induce the formation of microbubbles in the myelin, with the result of micro lesions in the axonal sheet capable of altering the functioning of the neuron. Several mathematical models to predict the probability of bubble formation for a given dive profile were proposed; the algorithms constructed on these models are the basis of decompression tables (Parker et al., 1992). Modern dive computers can evaluate in real-time the decompression status and report it to the diver (Lang and Hamilton, 1989). The present results suggest that these mathematical models are able to calculate the formation of bubbles in a short-medium temporal dimension, as in the case of divers who in their life do some hundreds of dives. However, evidently these models cannot predict the slow formation of microbubbles over thousands of dives. In conclusion, this study has shown that in individuals who have made at least two thousand scuba diving with compressed air can be seen modification of the cerebral WM in a dose-dependent manner. These alterations were particularly evident in the FL and in the GCC, without differences of side or gender. It has also been possible to detect that these structural modifications were associated with small but significant cognitive alterations that mainly concerned the executive functions, without gender differences.

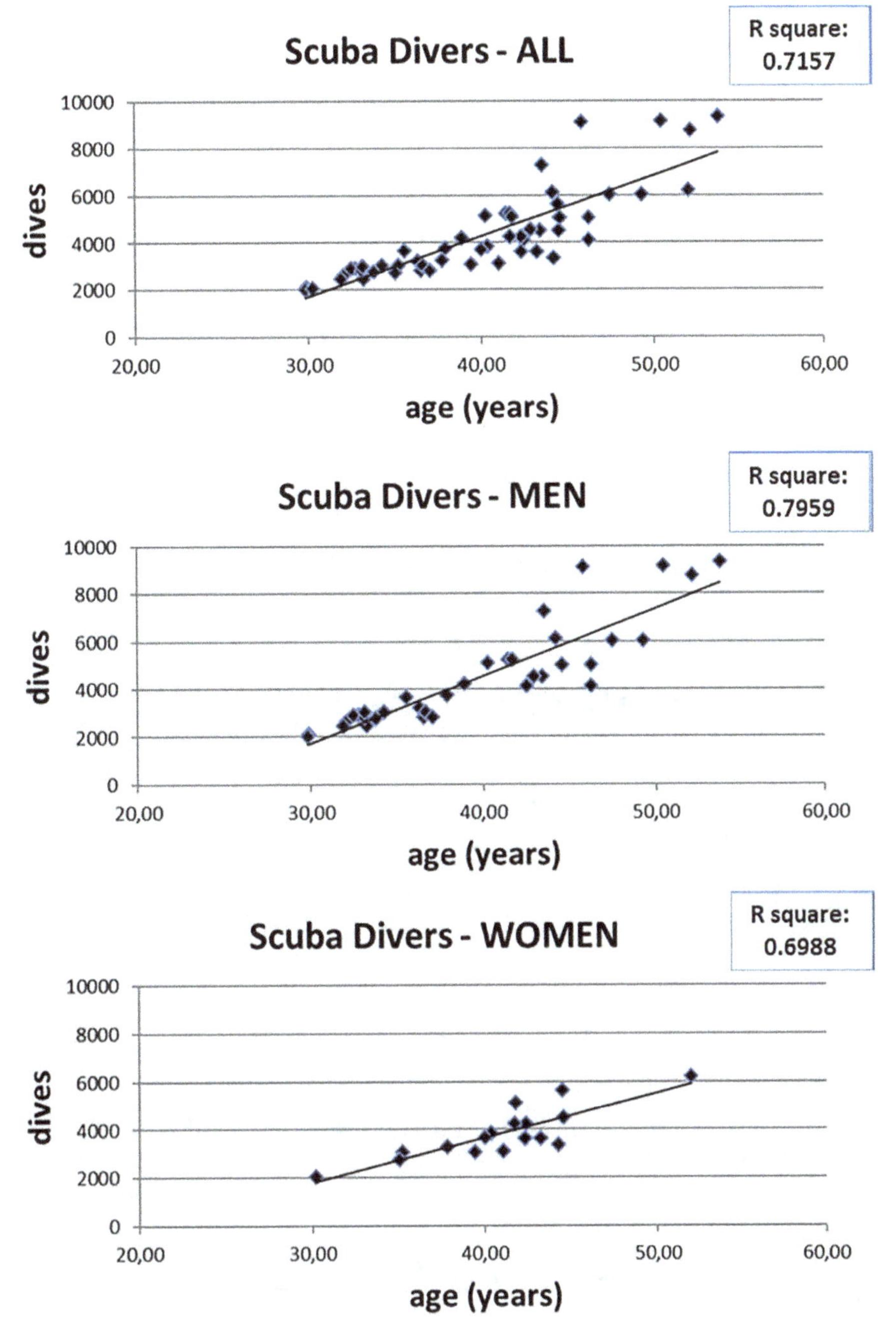

FIGURE 4 | Relation between age and number of dives in scuba divers, as well as in men and women separately.

Despite the gender differences in diver performance still being debated, Brebeck et al. (2017) demonstrated that female divers performed better than male divers on the memory tests, and Pauls et al. (2013) found highest gender differences in non-visuospatial abilities with an advantage for women.

In conclusion, it can be determined that after the diving cognitive response amount is low and it's better that divers instantly refrain from doing something with elevated attention after diving.

Of course, this study has certain limitations. For one, a weakness could be represented by the heterogeneous distribution over the years of their dives. However, these factors will make the achievement of statistically significant differences less likely. Given this heterogeneity, great care was taken to ensure randomization to the control group and experimental groups. Furthermore, in light of the sparse data on female divers, our findings suggest that gender differences in diver performance may merit further investigation.

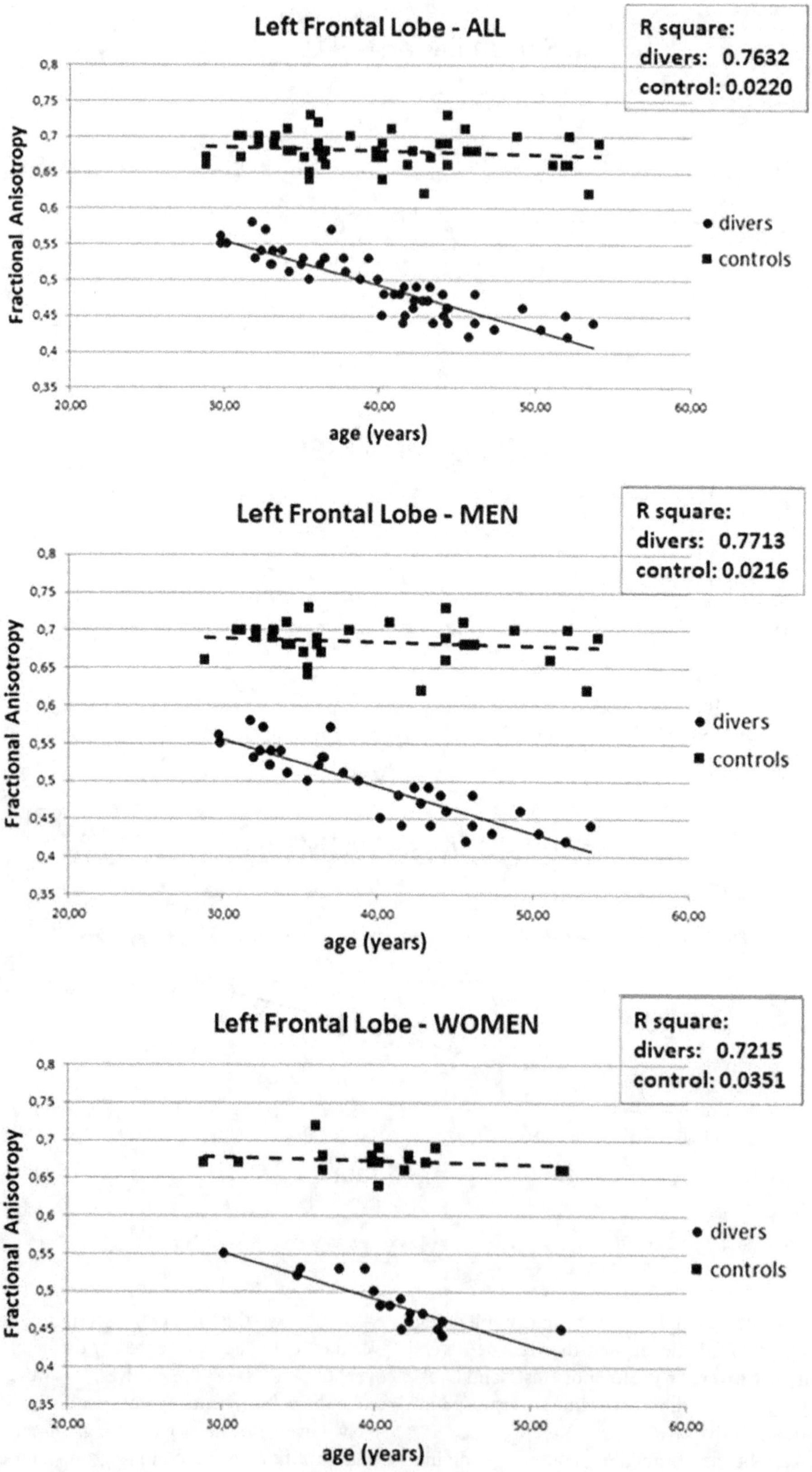

FIGURE 5 | Relation between Fractional Anisotropy and age in scuba divers and controls in left FL.

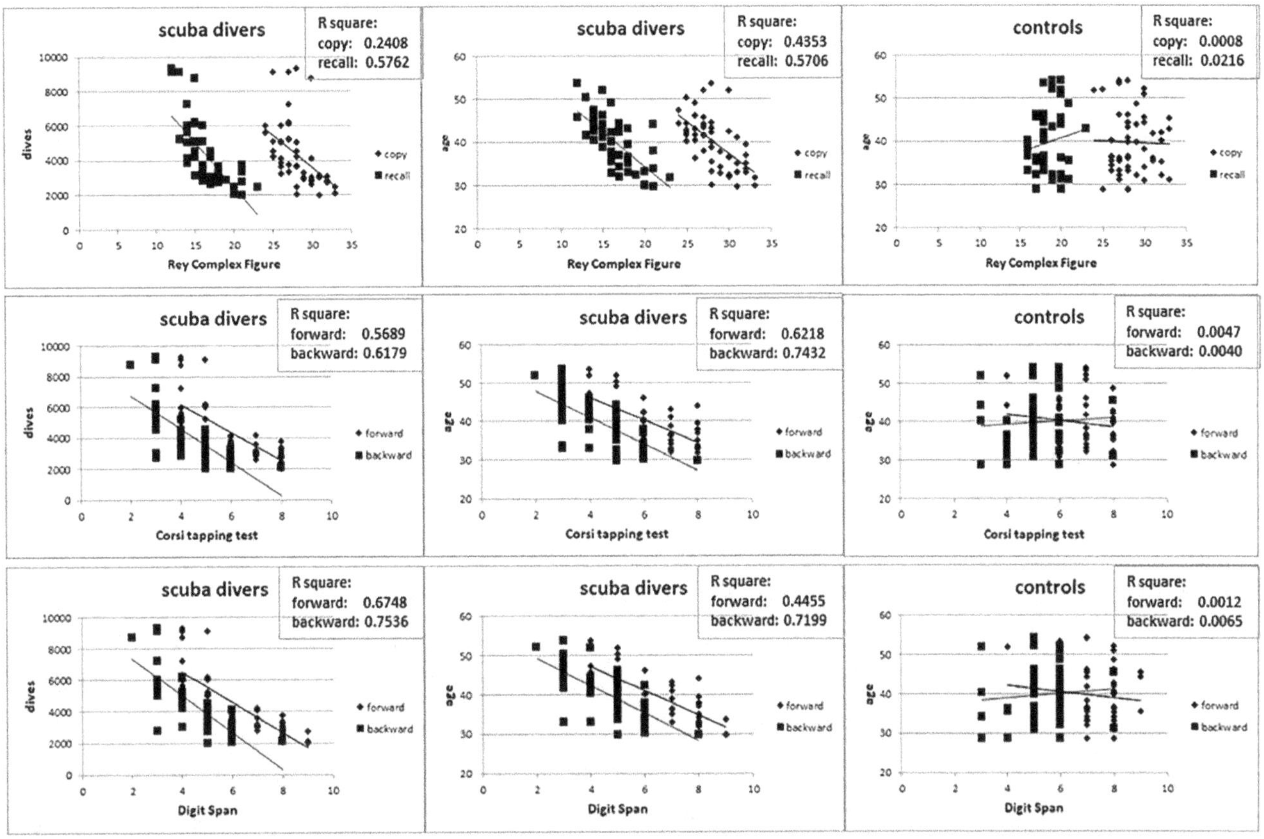

FIGURE 6 | Relation between the results at Ray Complex Figure **(top row)**, Corsi tapping test **(middle row)** and Digit Span **(bottom row)** and the number of dives and age in divers **(left and central columns)** and age in controls **(right columns)**.

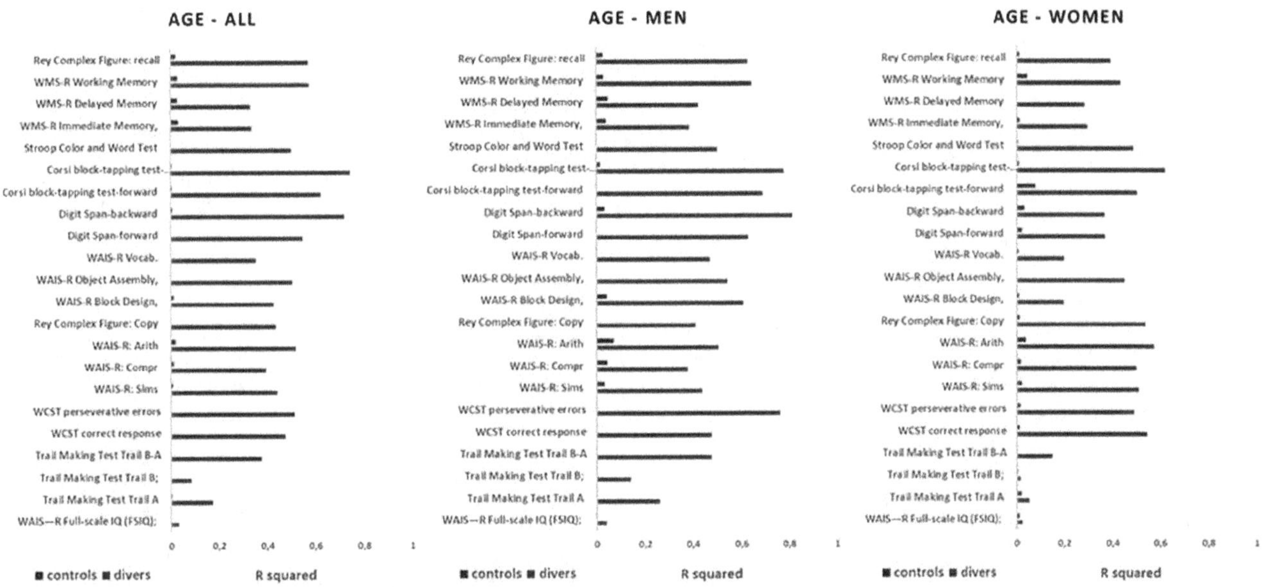

FIGURE 7 | Values of *R* square measured for relations between the results at all neuropsychological tests and the age in divers (blue) and controls (red) in the whole sample (all), as well as in men and women separately.

ETHICS STATEMENT

This study was carried out in accordance with the recommendations of Ethical Committees of our Institutions with written informed consent from all subjects. All subjects gave written informed consent in accordance with the 1964 Declaration of Helsinki. The protocol obtained ethical permission from the Internal Ethic Review Board - IERB, Department of Education Sciences, Psychology Section, University of Catania (29/11/2018).

AUTHOR CONTRIBUTIONS

MC, ViP, AB, and VaP contributed to the conception and design of the study. TM was responsible for neuropsychological testing whereas GG and AS performed the Fractional anisotropy evaluation. MC, AB, DD, and ViP were responsible for data collection and statistical analysis. MC, AB, and ViP was responsible for drafting and finalization of the manuscript. All authors contributed to the manuscript revision and approved the submitted version of the manuscript.

REFERENCES

Agranoff, B. W., Benjamins, J. A., and Hajra, A. K. (1999). "Properties of brain lipids," in *Basic Neurochemistry: Molecular, Cellular and Medical Aspects*, eds G. J. Siegel, B. W. Agranoff, R. W. Albers, S. K. Fisher, and M. D. Uhler (Philadelphia: Lippincott-Raven).

Axelrod, B. N. (2001). Administration duration for the wechsler adult intelligence scale-III and wechsler memory scale-III. *Arch. Clin. Neuropsychol.* 16, 293–301. doi: 10.1093/arclin/16.3.293

Basser, P. J., and Pierpaoli, C. (1996). Microstructural and physiological features of tissues elucidated by quantitative-diffusion-tensor MRI. *J. Magn. Reson. B* 111, 209–219. doi: 10.1006/jmrb.1996.0086

Behnke, A. R., Thomson, R. M., and Motley, E. P. (1935). The psychologic effects from breathing air at 4 atm pressure. *Am. J. Physiol.* 112, 554–558. doi: 10.1152/ajplegacy.1935.112.3.554

Bennett, P. B. (1993). "Inert gas narcosis," in *The Physiology and Medicine of Diving*' eds P. B. Bennett, and D. H. Elliott (London: Saunders Company), 171–193.

Berg, E. A. (1948). A simple, objective technique for measuring flexibility in thinking. *J. Gen. Psychol.* 39, 15–22. doi: 10.1080/00221309.1948.9918159

Bosco, G., Rizzato, A., Moon, R. E., and Camporesi, E. M. (2018). Environmental physiology and diving medicine. *Front. Psychol.* 9:72. doi: 10.3389/fpsyg.2018.00072

Brebeck, A. K., Deussen, A., Schmitz-Peiffer, H., Range, U., Balestra, C., Cleveland, S., et al. (2017). Effects of oxygenenriched air on cognitive performance during SCUBA-diving - an open-water study. *Res. Sports Med.* 25, 345–356. doi: 10.1080/15438627.2017.1314289

Callaway, E. (1959). The influence of amobarbital (Amylobarbitone) and methamphetamine on the focus of attention. *J. Ment. Sci.* 105, 382–392. doi: 10.1192/bjp.105.439.382

Carturan, D., Boussuges, A., Vanuxem, P., Bar-Hen, A., Burnet, H., and Gardette, B. (2002). Ascent rate, age, maximal oxygen uptake, adiposity, and circulating venous bubbles after diving. *J. Appl. Physiol.* 93, 1349–1356. doi: 10.1152/japplphysiol.00723.1999

Chen, Y., Lv, C., Li, X., Zhang, J., Chen, K., Liu, Z., et al. (2019). The positive impacts of early-life education on cognition, leisure activity, and brain structure in healthy aging. *Aging* 11, 4923–4942. doi: 10.18632/aging.102088

Chrast, R., Saher, G., Nave, K. A., and Verheijen, M. H. (2011). Lipid metabolism in myelinating glial cells: lessons from human inherited disorders and mouse models. *J. Lipid Res.* 52, 419–434. doi: 10.1194/jlr.R009761

Coco, M., Di Corrado, D., Calogero, R. A., Perciavalle, V., Maci, T., and Perciavalle, V. (2009). Attentional processes and blood lactate levels. *Brain Res.* 1302, 205–211. doi: 10.1016/j.brainres.2009.09.032

Cordes, P., Keil, R., Bartsch, T., Tetzlaff, K., Reuter, M., Hutzelmann, A., et al. (2000). Neurologic outcome of controlled compressed-air diving. *Neurology* 55, 1743–1745. doi: 10.1212/WNL.55.11.1743

Doolette, D. J., and Mitchell, S. J. (2001). The physiological kinetics of nitrogen and the prevention of decompression sickness. *Clin. Pharmacokinet.* 40, 1–14. doi: 10.2165/00003088-200140010-00001

Edmonds, C., Lawry, C., and Pennefather, J. (1981). "Nitrogen narcosis," in *Diving and Subaquatic Medicine*, ed. C. Edmonds (Australia: Diving Medical Center Publication), 197–208.

Ergen, M., Uslu, A., Caglar, O., Akca-Kalem, S., Cimsit, M., and Gurvit, H. (2017). Evaluation of cognitive performance in professional divers by means of event-related potentials and neuropsychology. *Clin. Neurophysiol.* 128, 579–588. doi: 10.1016/j.clinph.2017.01.007

Franks, N. P., and Lieb, W. R. (1994). Molecular and cellular mechanisms of general anesthesia. *Nature* 367, 607–617. doi: 10.1038/367607a0

Hemelryck, W., Germonpré, P., Papadopoulou, V., Rozloznik, M., and Balestra, C. (2014). Long term effects of recreational SCUBA diving on higher cognitive function. *Scand. J. Med. Sci. Sports.* 24, 928–934. doi: 10.1111/sms.12100

Howle, L. E., Weber, P. W., Hada, E. A., Vann, R. D., and Denoble, P. J. (2017). The probability and severity of decompression sickness. *PLoS One* 12:e0172665. doi: 10.1371/journal.pone.0172665

Kessels, R. P. C., van Zandvoort, M. J. E., Postma, A., Kappelle, L. J., and de Haan, E. H. F. (2000). The corsi block-tapping task: standardization and normative data. *Appl. Neuropsychol.* 7, 252–258. doi: 10.1207/S15324826AN0704_8

Kowalski, J. T., Varn, A., Röttger, S., Seidack, S., Kähler', W., Gerber, W. D., et al. (2011). Neuropsychological deficits in scuba divers: an exploratory investigation. *Undersea Hyperb. Med.* 238, 197–204.

Lang, M. A., and Hamilton, R. W. Jr. (1989). *Proceedings of the AAUS Dive Computer Workshop*. Avalon, CA: USC Catalina Marine Science Center, 231.

Langø, T., Mørland, T., and Brubakk, A. O. (1996). Diffusion coefficients and solubility coefficients for gases in biological fluids and tissues: a review. *Undersea Hyperb. Med.* 23, 247–272.

Nave, K. A., and Werner, H. B. (2014). Myelination of the nervous system: mechanisms and functions. *Annu. Rev. Cell Dev. Biol.* 30, 503–533. doi: 10.1146/annurev-cellbio-100913-013101

Norton, W. T., and Poduslo, S. E. (1973). Myelination in rat brain: changes in myelin composition during brain maturation. *J. Neurochem.* 21, 759–773. doi: 10.1111/j.1471-4159.1973.tb07520.x

Parker, E. C., Survanshi, S. S., Weathersby, P. K., and Thalmann, E. D. (1992). *Statistically Based Decompression Tables VIII: Linear Exponential Kinetics*. Naval Medical Research Institute Report, 92–73. Bethesda, MD: U.S. Naval Research Medical Institute.

Pauls, F., Petermann, F., and Lepach, A. C. (2013). Gender differences in episodic memory and visual working memory including the effects of age. *Memory* 21, 857–874. doi: 10.1080/09658211.2013.765892

Pourhashemi, S. F., Sahraei, H., Meftahi, G. H., Hatef, B., and Gholipour, B. (2016). The effect of 20 minutes scuba diving on cognitive function of professional scuba divers. *Asian J. Sports Med.* 7:e38633. doi: 10.5812/asjsm.38633

Rey, A. (1941). Psychological examination of traumatic encephalopathy. *Arch. Psychol. Geneve* 28, 286–340.

Soylu, F. (2010). Forward/backward digit-span task. *Arch. Neurobehav. Exp. Stimuli* 222. Available at: http://www.neurobs.com/ex_files/expt_view?id=218

Spreen, O., and Strauss, E. A. (1998). *Compendium of Neuropsychological Tests. Administration, Norms and Commentary*, 2nd Edn. New York, NY: Oxford University Press.

Stroop, J. R. (1935). Studies of interference in serial verbal reactions. *J. Exp. Psych.* 18, 643–661. doi: 10.1037/h0054651

Taylor, C. L., Macdiarmid, J. I., Ross, J. A., Osman, L. M., Watt, S. J., Adie, W., et al. (2006). Objective neuropsychological test performance of professional divers reporting a subjective complaint of forgetfulness or loss of concentration. *Scand. J. Work Environ. Health* 32, 310–317. doi: 10.5271/sjweh.1015

Tombaugh, T. N. (2004). Trail making test A and B: normative data stratified by age and education. *Arch. Clin. Neuropsychol.* 19, 203–214. doi: 10.1016/S0887-6177(03)00039-8

Verratti, V., Bondi, D., Jandova, T., Camporesi, E., Paoli, A., and Bosco, G. (2019). Sex hormones response to physical hyperoxic and hyperbaric stress in male scuba divers: a pilot study. *Adv. Exp. Med. Biol.* 1176, 53–62. doi: 10.1007/5584_2019_384

Waxman, S. G. (1980). Determinants of conduction velocity in myelinated nerve fibers. *Muscle Nerve* 3, 141–150. doi: 10.1002/mus.880030207

Weathersby, P. K., and Homer, L. D. (1980). Solubility of inert gases in biological fluids and tissues: a review. *Undersea Biomed. Res.* 7, 277–296.

Wechsler, D. (1981). *WAIS-R Manual.* New York, NY: Psychological Corporation.

Wechsler, D. (1987). *Wechsler Memory Scale-Revised Manual.* San Antonio, TX: Psychological Corporation.

12

Prediction of the Satisfaction with the Student Life, Based on Teaching Competence and Satisfaction with the School

Raúl Baños[1], Antonio Baena-Extremera[2] and María del Mar Ortiz-Camacho[2]*

[1]Department of Physical Education and Sports Science, Autonomous University of Baja California, Ensenada, Mexico,
[2]Department of Didactic of Corporal Expression, Faculty of Education Sciences, University of Granada, Granada, Spain

Correspondence:
Antonio Baena-Extremera
abaenaextrem@ugr.es

The aim of this article was to assess how students evaluate the professional personality competence of physical education teachers in high school and its relation to student satisfaction and student satisfaction with life itself. In line with these aims, this study was completed as a cross-sectional study, which was carried out in a group of 890 physical education students. Of the study group, 50.3% were female and 49.7% were male. The average age was 15.49 years for females (SD 1.79) and 15.00 years for males (SD 2.00). We used a questionnaire featuring the *Physical Education Teacher Competence*, *Intrinsic Satisfaction Classroom Scale*, and *Satisfaction with Life Scale*. The results are presented as descriptive statistics, correlations, and a structural equation modeling analysis showing students' perceived competence, predicted self-determined satisfaction, which in turn corresponds to life satisfaction.

Keywords: teacher competences, classroom satisfaction, life satisfaction, student, physical education

INTRODUCTION

In recent years, diverse research has highlighted the importance of studying the life satisfaction of students, for the academic and personal repercussions that these carry (Méndez-Giménez et al., 2017; Salvador-Ferrer, 2017). For that, several authors (Diener, 1984; Diener and Emmons, 1985; Argyle, 1987) have used the theory of subjective well-being to study the satisfaction of people, identifying two dimensions namely: cognitive and affective dimensions. With this theory, subjective well-being can be understood as a theoretical construct that contemplates the combination of the cognitive process (judgments of satisfaction and dissatisfaction) and two affective processes (positive affect and negative affect) (Diener and Emmons, 1985). On one side, the affective dimension can be identified with emotions and affections, such as worry or boredom among others. On the contrary, the cognitive dimension is related to evaluative judgments of life satisfaction and its specific areas (Diener and Emmons, 1985). In line with this, Campbell et al. (1976) related the cognitive and affective dimensions of the theoretical construct, with life satisfaction and happiness, respectively. A decade later, Diener et al. (2003) synthesized that subjective well-being can be identified with components of life satisfaction, with satisfaction in specific areas of life and with the affect thereof (positive and negative).

On the other side, existing literature shows that school is an important factor determining happiness in teenagers, since they invest most part of their life in the academic environment (Roeser and Eccles, 2000). The relationship between life satisfaction and the diverse variables of school and educations, such as academic commitment (Lewis et al., 2011), perceived academic competence (Suldo and Huebner, 2006), auto efficiency (Maddux, 2002), disruptive behavior (Suldo and Huebner, 2004), and the academic performance (Gilman and Huebner, 2006; Vecchio et al., 2007), have been extensively researched, finding contradictory results regarding this variable.

It has been proven that the satisfaction/dissatisfaction with physical education (PE) predicts a positive or negative satisfaction with school (Baena-Extremera and Granero-Gallegos, 2015) and that music students obtain higher values of life satisfaction than those who study mathematics, geography, or language (Gültekin and Aricioğlu, 2016). This therefore opens up a new field of study, due to the existence of a relationship between satisfaction on several subjects, with the academic environment and even academic performance (Baños et al., 2019).

To understand this relationship, understanding the motivational theories is fundamental. Among these theories is the self-determination theory (Deci and Ryan, 1985), along with the variables that underline it. For example, Granero-Gallegos et al. (2012) found that students with high levels of satisfaction/or those that view PE as a fun subject were highly intrinsically motivated individuals, who valued the effort and work required in PE, with the objective to improve and to give more value to the subject. In line with this, Baños et al. (2017) show that when a student experiences a class situation where fun and/or boredom is promoted, it has a direct influence on the student's performance and can have successful results on their learning process or on the contrary lead to the abandonment of the education system. In this paper, the important role of the professor can be appreciated, as the work design can be a key element in the abandonment or the academic commitment of students (Catano and Harvey, 2011). With this in mind, the influence of the teacher is hugely relevant, as the teacher can have a direct influence on school satisfaction (Baena-Extremera and Granero-Gallegos, 2015) as well as the life satisfaction of a student.

In relation to this, the quality of a students' educational experience is greatly influenced by the teacher's experience inside the classroom (Hill et al., 2003; Yair, 2008; Baena-Extermera et al., 2013) and their teaching skills. However, it is well known that teaching is multidimensional as well as complex (Wang et al., 2011), where teachers face and respond to a series of factors that could affect the students and the teaching-learning process, for example, the characteristics of the course, classroom management, and the teacher-student interaction (Young and Shaw, 1999; Khine, 2005). Therefore, to improve teacher competence, a series of basic competencies should be broken down, with specific and observable aspects for teachers, that help improve the learning process in the classroom (Denyer et al., 2007) and influences related to aspects of motivation and learning. The efficiency of such competences could vary according to each student's personality, some requiring a smart teacher, others a perfectionist, or a careful, encouraging, and loving teacher, but above all, a teacher who has the ability to amuse, enthuse, be affective, open, and caring (Moreno, 2009). Competencies like the knowledge a teacher possesses on the subject, the clarity of their presentation, and how they interact with students as well as creativity are positively related to the satisfaction and motivation of students (Sang et al., 2013). Thus, the way in which a teacher plans and organizes PE classes, adapting to the needs of their students, may influence student satisfaction at school (Baena-Extremera and Granero-Gallegos, 2015).

Considering all the above, the importance of this research lies in studying the influence of a PE teacher's competencies has on student satisfaction. Thus, the hypothesis of this study is that a competent teacher will help students achieve school satisfaction in PE and, at the same time, promote life satisfaction. Considering this hypothesis, the aim of this study is to analyze how a PE teacher's competencies can predict school satisfaction and, in turn, the life satisfaction of secondary school students.

METHODS

Participants

The selection of the sample was of a non-probabilistic type and according to the case on which the students could be accessed. A total of 890 high school (HS) and bachelor (BACH) PE students (442 males = 49.7%, age range = 15.00, DT = 2.00; and 448 females = 50.3%, age range = 15.00; DT = 2.00), belonging to five public and private schools in the Region of Murcia and the Region of Alicante (Spain). In total, 152 students belonged to 1° grade HS (17.1%), 160 (18.0%) of 2° grade HS, 182 (20.4%) of 3° grade HS, 186 (20.9%) of 4° HS, 101 (11.3%) of 1° grade BACH and last, 109 (12.2%) of 2° grade BACH.

Instruments

The following instruments were used to carry out this investigation.

Physical Education Teacher Competence

A validated Spanish version of the *Evaluation of Teaching Competencies Scale* by Catano and Harvey (2011) was used and adapted to PE by Baena-Extremera et al. (2015). The instrument presents eight items that measure the student's perception of the teacher's effectiveness. The students were asked to indicate the degree of agreement with the items, and the responses were collected using a scale of polyatomic items ranging from low (1-2), medium (3-4-5), and high (6-7). The eight constructs that this instrument evaluates are communication, conscience of work, creativity, feedback, individual consideration of the student, professionalism, problem resolution, and social conscience.

Satisfaction With the School

The questionnaire of intrinsic satisfaction was employed and translated to Spanish and validated by Castillo et al. (2001)

from the *Intrinsic Satisfaction Classroom Scale*, by Nicholls et al. (1985), Nicholls (1989), and Duda and Nicholls (1992). This instrument presents eight items that measure the scale of satisfaction with school, with two subscales that measure satisfaction/fun (five items) and boredom with school (three items). The scale was used for the phrase "Tell us your degree of disagreement or agreement in relation with the next affirmations, in reference of all of your school subjects." Responses were collected through a scale of polyatomic items ranging between 1 (totally disagree) and 5 (totally agree).

Satisfaction With Life

The questionnaire used was translated to Spanish and validated by Cabañero et al. (2004) of Diener et al. (1985) and is composed of five items that measure only one factor. This instrument uses a five-point polyatomic scale of items, ranging from (1) totally disagree to (5) totally agree.

Procedure

The design of this work is non-experimental, sectional, descriptive, and predictive. For the development of this study, written informed consent was obtained from the educational centers, teachers, and parents/tutors, and the intention and objectives of the study was provided.

After obtaining the relevant permissions, data were collected. The participants were informed of the study's purpose, the voluntary nature of their participation, and the confidential treatment of their answers. They were told that there were no right or wrong answers and were asked for their utmost sincerity.

The questionnaires were completed in a classroom in about 25–30 min with the same researcher always present and who could be consulted regarding any doubts during the process, respecting the declaration of Helsinki (Helsinki Declaration World Medical Association, 2013).

Data Analysis

An analysis of normality in multiple variants was conducted.

For this, a *normality test based on relative multivariant kurtosis* (RMK) of the PRELIS of the LISREL 9.90 program was conducted. Given the normality, a *Confirmatory Factor Analysis* (CFA) to study the adaptation of such instruments to the samples used in this study was conducted. Multiple reliability and validity indexes were calculated, such as Cronbach's alpha, the compose reliability, and *average variability extracted* (AVE) for each instrument. A correlation analysis between the instruments used was carried out afterwards, as well as diverse models of structural equations, to answer the objective of this study. The calculations were carried out with the statistical package SPSS v.11 and LISREL 8.80.

RESULTS

Analysis of Data Normality

In **Table 1**, we can observe the normality data of the measuring instruments, where finally, the data prove abnormal behavior.

TABLE 1 | Values of the multivariate normality test.

	Multivariant normalized Kurtosis	Mardia-based-Kappa	Higher limit	Lower limit
ECTS	51.2439	0.488	1.027	0.973
SWS	6.5740	0.147	1.034	0.966
SWL	14.788	0.237	1.045	0.955

ECTS, Evaluation of Teaching Competencies Scale; SWS, satisfaction with school; SWL, satisfaction with life.

The values of RMK for the Evaluation of Teaching Competencies Scale ranged from 1.488 and from 1.123 to 1.237 for the satisfaction with school and life satisfaction, respectively.

Confirmatory Factor Analysis

First, the CFA of each instrument to determine the validity and reliability of the sample used in this study was conducted. The results (**Table 2**) were acceptable within the limits established in x^2/gl (Bentler, 1989; Tabachnick and Fidell, 2007), in GFI (Hooper et al., 2008), CFI, IFI, NFI, NNFI (Hu and Bentler, 1995), and RMSEA (Cole and Maxwell, 2003; Chen et al., 2008).

Reliability and Validity Analysis

As some dimensions of the instruments are composed by only a few items, the Cronbach's alpha represents some limitations according to Ventura-León and Caycho-Rodríguez (2017). For this reason and due to the recommendation of Domínguez-Lara and Merino-Soto (2015), the reliability was calculated by the ω of McDonald. Unlike the alpha Cronbach coefficient, it considers the factorial load, which makes the calculus more stable and reflects the true level of reliability without relying on the number of items in the dimension (see Ventura-León and Caycho-Rodríguez, 2017). Values of internal consistency (ω) are acceptable between 0.70 and 0.90 (Campo-Arias and Oviedo, 2008), although Katz (2006) can accept values from >0.65.

In **Table 3**, an analysis of each model is presented: the Cronbach's alpha values, compound reliability, AVE, the average and typical deviation of Evaluation of Teaching Competencies Scale, satisfaction with school, boredom with school, and life satisfaction. As can be observed, all the indexes of reliability, AVE, and all α, which are above the acceptable values according to Dunn et al. (2014) and Hair et al. (2009), emphasize that the compound reliability is considerably more appropriate than the Cronbach's alpha in ordinal scale types because they do not depend on the number of attributes associated with each concept (Vandenbosch, 1996), as the values are more acceptable for each factor.

Correlation Analysis

In **Table 4**, we can see how teacher competence maintains a positive and significant correlation with satisfaction with life (0.119**) and satisfaction with school (0.093**) but remains negative with the ABU. The satisfaction with school presents a negative and significant correlation with the opposite factor

TABLE 2 | Adjustment fit indices of each model.

	x^2	gl	x^2/gl	p	GFI	CFI	IFI	NFI	NNFI	RMSEA
ECTS	60.45	27		0.000	0.99	0.98	0.98	0.96	0.97	0.03
SWS	78.78	19	4.14	0.000	0.99	0.94	0.94	0.92	0.91	0.068
SWL	18.42	5		0.002	0.99	0.99	0.99	0.98	0.98	0.05

x^2, Chi-square; gl, degrees of freedom; p, significance; GFI, goodness-of-fit index; CFI, comparative fit index; IFI, adjustment index; NFI, normalized adjustment index; NNFI, non-normative adjustment index; RMSEA, root-mean squared approximation; ECTS, Evaluation of Teaching Competencies Scale; SWS, satisfaction with school; SWL, satisfaction with life.

TABLE 3 | Scale reliability and convergent validity.

	M	SD	Composite reliability	AVE	α	ω
ECTS	5.49	0.96	0.90	0.50	0.85	0.86
SWS	3.16	0.95	0.83	0.50	0.76	0.80
BWS	2.98	0.85	0.75	0.50	0.69	0.71
SWL	3.54	0.87	0.87	0.57	0.83	0.81

M, mean; SD, standard deviation; AVE, average variance extracted; α, Crombach's alpha; ω, McDonald's omega; ECTS, Evaluation of Teaching Competencies Scale; SWS, satisfaction with school; SWL, satisfaction with life.

TABLE 4 | Correlation analysis between the variables.

	1	2	3	4
1. ECTS	–	0.093**	−0.023	0.119**
2. SATD		–	−0.546**	0.272**
3. ABUE			–	−0.201**
4. SATV				–

*ECTS, Evaluation of Teaching Competencies Scale; SWS, satisfaction with school; SWL, satisfaction with life. *p < 0.05; **p < 0.01.*

on its scale (−0.546**) and positive with satisfaction with life (0.272**). The boredom with school finally correlates negative and significantly with satisfaction with life (−0.201**).

Prediction of Satisfaction With Student Life

In accordance with the objective of this study, different models have been hypothesized to test which would adjust better according to the recommendation of Markland (2007). According to the correlations, the model that better predicted the satisfaction with the student life was approved. The structural regression models were evaluated through the combination of the adjustment indexes previously explained, with their values being x^2/gl = 4.32, GFI = 0.96, CFI = 0.92, IFI = 0.92, NFI = 0.95, NNFI = 0.96, and RMSEA = 0.06. These values adjust perfectly to the acceptable parameters (Bentler, 1989; Tabachnick and Fidell, 2007; Hooper et al., 2008, among others). According with the **Figure 1**, we can observe gamma, beta, lambda-x, lambda-y, and theta delta and theta épsilon values (**Figure 1**). In it, we can appreciate how the Evaluation of Teaching Competencies Scale positively predicts the impact of the satisfaction with school (γ = 0.94), being negative for boredom with school (γ = −0.79), satisfaction with school, predicts at the same time the satisfaction with life in a positive way (β = 0.50), being the prediction of boredom with school (β = 0.05). Finally, the estimated parameters were considered significant when the value associated with value *t* is greater than 1.96 ($p < 0.05$) and all items showed individual reliability values of (λ) > 0.05.

DISCUSSION

The objective of this study was to analyze how a PE teacher's competencies can predict the satisfaction with school, and how these, at the same time, predict the life satisfaction of HS and BACH students. The importance of this research lies in the influence that a PE teacher can generate on the subjective wellbeing of adolescents, not only in the academic field but also in other areas of life. In addition, adolescence is a stage of life that carries profound changes, in which friend and family influences are transformed and where decision-making has a greater impact on adult life (Maršanić et al., 2014). Failing school and even the increasing suicide rate at this stage of life are fundamental aspects of this study, similar to those already mentioned (Kosik et al., 2017).

We emphasize that the three scales, the Evaluation of Teaching Competencies Scale, satisfaction with school and satisfaction with life, obtained viable and reliable results.

The obtained results in this study demonstrate positive and significant correlations between teacher competencies with satisfaction with school and satisfaction with life and had no correlation with boredom with school, although it did find signs of a limited negative relation. These results showed that a PE teacher who is a good communicator, with work and social conscience, a creative and problem resolution capacity, who provides feedback, who has good individual consideration with a student, and who in conclusion is professional, can affect satisfaction not only through fun and how satisfied they are with school but also can also have repercussions in their satisfaction with life. Similar results were found by Kuzmanovic et al. (2013) who showed that students were satisfied when the teacher was available to solve problems, showing consideration, and providing feedback. So, a good teacher is distinguished by his/her students, as a good stimulator, innovator, enthusiastic, with a good sense of humor, and who is self-reflective, and supportive of diversity (Johnstone, 2005; Khine, 2005; Yair, 2008; Delaney et al., 2009).

Satisfaction with school is significantly positively correlated to satisfaction with life; however, it is significantly negatively correlated to boredom with school, and this, at the same time, is significantly negatively correlated with satisfaction with life. Although it has been proven that teenagers who are perceived as happier, learn faster, behave better, and show greater

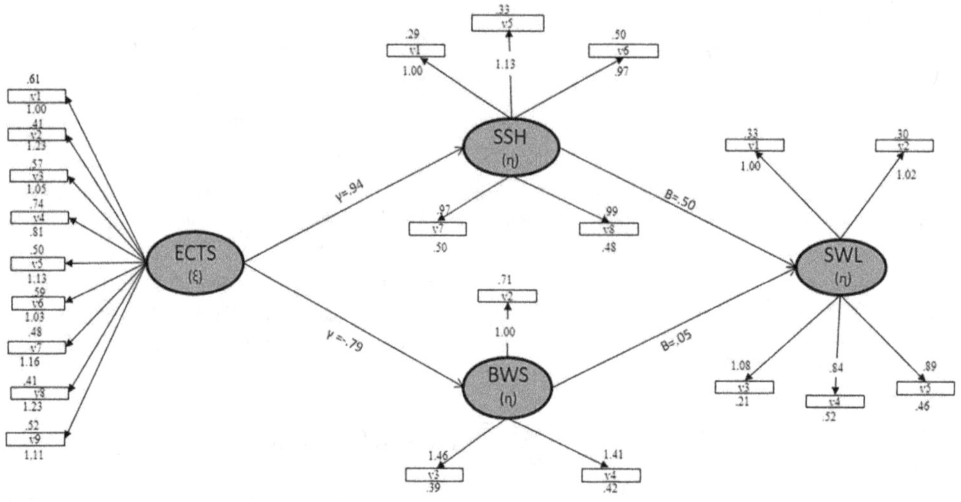

FIGURE 1 | Exogenous variable ECTS (ξ), Evaluation of Teaching Competencies Scale; endogenous bariable SSH (η), dimension of satisfaction with school; endogenous variable BWS (η), dimension boredom with school; endogenous variable SWL (η), satisfaction with life; γ, gamma values; β, beta values.

commitment and academic performance (Noddings, 2003; Ben-Arieh, 2008; Castro, 2011; Baena-Extremera and Granero-Gallegos, 2013; Lyons and Huebner, 2016), the school plays an important role in their subjective well-being, due to the time they spend on academics; therefore, if they find it monotonous and boring, their happiness could be diminished. This input was reflected in the results obtained in this present study, where a student who is unsatisfied at school is related to low levels of satisfaction with life. In line with this, Lyons and Huebner, 2016 found similar results, since students who became bored at school showed less school commitment and more dissatisfaction with their life. Considering this, the correct planning of classroom sessions to avoid monotonous and boring classes is of utmost importance and can increase the levels of satisfaction with life (Quinn and Duckworth, 2007).

In the results of the predictive model, it could be observed how the PE teaching competencies positively predicted the satisfaction with school, and in turn, the satisfaction with life, obtaining similar results to the studies realized by Baena-Extremera et al. (2015). This helped to understand the weight that a PE teacher has on the educative system and on the life of the students, where the difference of being a competent teacher or not, could directly influence the satisfaction or boredom of a student and therefore indirectly influence life satisfaction (Baños et al., 2017). It is also known that the excellence and quality of the institution, as well as the professionalism of the teacher, with traits such as fairness and impartiality, predicts the satisfaction of the student in the classroom and the satisfaction with the teaching quality (Elliot and Shin, 2002) emphasizing the need for good teaching, the setting of clear goals, suitable evaluation methods depending the level of the students, planning of appropriate workload, and having ideal general competencies for teaching (Ginns et al., 2007). However, if teachers do not produce the sufficient impact on their students (Cameron and Lovett, 2015) and the student's perception of the incompetencies of their PE teacher predicts boredom with school, they will not find the prediction of satisfaction with life. These results are important, as an unsatisfied student increases the possibility of failing school or even abandoning school (Elmore and Huebner, 2010) and increases the probability of suicide in teenagers (Singer et al., 2018). For this reason, it is important to have good teaching practices, emphasizing the influence that a PE teacher can have on their students if they are well prepared, avoiding monotonous classes, with organized planning, where the educator gives autonomy to the students and where sessions approach the students' interests (Delaney et al., 2009; Calderón et al., 2013; Lee et al., 2015; Lebrero et al., 2019). By doing this, motivation for PE classes will likely improve (Baena-Extremera et al., 2013), affecting the school and faculty (Aubert et al., 2014), improving the results on the PISA report, alarming on the Spanish education system (Casquero and Navarro, 2010).

Finally, the advances presented in this study with relation to previous research can be summarized. A PE teacher can positively predict the life satisfaction of students through the subject they teach and can especially influences stages where they experience big personal changes, morphological and psychological. Therefore, the original contribution of this study is the impact a PE teacher has not only with regard to the physical activity in a teenager's spare time (Wallhead and Buckworth, 2004; Baena-Extermera et al., 2016) but also on the satisfaction with school and life satisfaction life.

Limitations and Strengths

Future research should consider using different levels and ages and should even consider analyzing these variables in other subjects. Another limitation of this study is its design; a future possibility is to carry out a quasi-experiment, considering the school organization. Nevertheless, the strength of this study is the large number of participants used and the originality of the investigation as very few studies on this topic are present in the current literature.

ETHICS STATEMENT

Ethical review and approval were not required for the study on human participants in accordance with the local legislation and institutional requirements. Written informed consent from the participants was not required to participate in this study in accordance with the national legislation and the institutional requirements.

AUTHOR CONTRIBUTIONS

RB and AB-E conceived the hypothesis of this study and analyzed the data. RB, AB-E, and MO-C participated in data collection and wrote the paper with the most significant input from AB-E. All authors contributed to data interpretation of statistical analysis and read and approved the final manuscript.

REFERENCES

Argyle, M. (1987). *The psychology of happiness*. London: Roytledge.

Aubert, A., Bizkarra, M., and Calvo, J. (2014). Actuaciones educativas de éxito desde la Educación Física. *Retos* 25, 144–148.

Baena-Extermera, A., Granero-Gallegos, A., Pérez-Quero, F. J., Bracho-Amador, C., and Sánchez-Fuentes, J. A. (2013). Motivation and motivational climate as predictors of perceived importance of physical education in Spain. *S. Afr. J. Res. Sport Phys. Educ. Recreat.* 35, 1–13.

Baena-Extermera, A., Granero-Gallegos, A., Ponce-de-Leon-Elizondo, A., Sanz-Arazuri, E., Valdemoros-San-Emeterio, M. D., and Martínez-Molina, M. (2016). Psychological factors related to physical education clases as predictors of students'intention to partake in leisure-time physical activity. *Ciencia & Saude Coletiva* 21, 1105–1112. doi: 10.1590/1413-81232015214.07742015

Baena-Extremera, A., and Granero-Gallegos, A. (2013). Efecto de un programa de Educación de Aventura en la orientación al aprendizaje, satisfacción y autoconcepto en secundaria. *Rev. Ibero. Diag. Ev. - e - Aval. Psicol.* 36, 163–187.

Baena-Extremera, A., and Granero-Gallegos, A. (2015). Modelo de predicción de la satisfacción con la Educación Física y la escuela. *Rev. Psico.* 20, 177–192. doi: 10.1387/RevPsicodidact.11268

Baena-Extremera, A., Granero-Gallegos, A., and Martínez-Molina, M. (2015). Validación española de la Escala de Evaluación de la Competencia Docente en Educación Física de secundaria. *Cuad. Psicol. Deporte* 15, 113–122. doi: 10.4321/S1578-84232015000300011

Baena-Extremera, A., Granero-Gallegos, A., Sánchez-Fuentes, J. A., and Martínez-Molina, M. (2013). Apoyo a la autonomía en Educación Física: Antecedentes, diseño, metodología y análisis de la relación con la motivación en estudiantes adolescentes. *Retos* 24, 46–49.

Baños, R., Barretos-Ruvalcaba, M., and Baena-Extremera, A. (2019). Protocolo de estudio de las variables académicas, psicológicas y de actividad física que influyen en el rendimiento académico de adolescentes mexicanos y españoles. *Espiral* 12, 89–99. doi: 10.25115/ecp.v12i25.2480

Baños, R., Ortiz-Camacho, M. M., Baena-Extremera, A., and Tristán-Rodríguez, L. (2017). Satisfacción, motivación y rendimiento académico en estudiantes de secundaria y bachillerato: antecedentes, diseño, metodología y propuesta de análisis para un trabajo de investigación. *Espiral* 10, 40–50. doi: 10.25115/ecp.v10i20.1011

Ben-Arieh, A. (2008). The child indicators movement: past, present, and future. *Child Indic. Res.* 1, 3–16. doi: 10.1007/s12187-007-9003-1

Bentler, P. M. (1989). *EQS structural equations program manual*. Los Angeles, CA: BMDP.

Cabañero, M. J., Richart, M., Cabrero, J., Orts, M. I., Reig, A., and Tosal, B. (2004). Fiabilidad y validez de la Escala de Satisfacción con la Vida de Diener en una muestra de mujeres embarazadas y puérperas. *Psicothema* 16, 448–455.

Calderón, A., Martínez, D., and Martínez, I. (2013). Influencia de la habilidad física percibida sobre la actitud del alumnado tras una unidad didáctica basada en educación deportiva. *Retos* 24, 16–20.

Cameron, M., and Lovett, S. (2015). Sustaining the commitment and realising the potential of highly promising teachers. *Teach. Teach.* 21, 150–163. doi: 10.1080/13540602.2014.928132

Campbell, A., Converse, P. E., and Rodgers, W. L. (1976). *The quality of American life: Perception; evaluations, and satisfactions*. New York: Russell Sage.

Campo-Arias, A., and Oviedo, H. C. (2008). Propiedades psicométricas de una escala: la consistencia interna. *Rev. Sal. Pública* 10, 831–839. doi: 10.1590/S0124-00642008000500015

Casquero, A., and Navarro, M. L. (2010). Determinantes del abandono escolar en España. *Rev. Educ. Número Extraordin.* 1, 191–223.

Castillo, I., Balaguer, I., and Duda, J. L. (2001). Las perspectivas de meta de los adolescentes en el contexto deportivo. *Psicothema* 14, 280–287.

Castro, A. (2011). Las rutas de acceso al bienestar. Relaciones entre bienestar hedónico y eudaemónico. Un estudio en población Argentina. *Rev. Iber. Diag. Eval.Psicol.* 31, 37–57.

Catano, V. M., and Harvey, S. (2011). Student perception of teaching effectiveness: development and validation of the evaluation of teaching competencies scale (ETCS). *Assess. Eval. High. Educ.* 36, 701–717. doi: 10.1080/02602938.2010.484879

Chen, F., Curran, P. J., Bollen, K. A., Kirby, J., and Paxton, P. (2008). An empirical evaluation of the use of fixed cutoff points in RMSEA test statistic in structural equation models. *Sociol. Meth. Res.* 36, 462–494. doi: 10.1177/0049124108314720

Cole, D. A., and Maxwell, S. E. (2003). Testing mediational models with longitudinal data: questions and tips in the use of structural equation modeling. *J. Abnor. Psychol.* 112, 558–577. doi: 10.1037/0021-843X.112.4.558

Deci, E. L., and Ryan, R. M. (1985). *Intrinsic motivation and self-determination in human behavior*. New York: Plenum.

Delaney, J., Johnson, A., Johnson, T., and Treslan, D. (2009). Students' perceptions of effective teaching in higher education. Paper presented at the Edge Conference, Canada.

Denyer, M., Furnemont, J., Poulain, R., and Vanloubbeeck, G. (2007). *Las competencias en la educación, un balance*. México: Fondo de Cultura Económica.

Diener, E. (1984). Subjective well-being. *Psychol. Bull.* 95, 542–575. doi: 10.1037/0033-2909.95.3.542

Diener, E., and Emmons, R. A. (1985). The independence of positive and negative affect. *J. Pers. Assess.* 99, 91–95.

Diener, E. D., Emmons, R. A., Larsen, R. J., and Griffin, S. (1985). The satisfaction with life scale. *J. Pers. Assess.* 49, 71–75. doi: 10.1207/s15327752jpa4901_13

Diener, E., Oishi, S., and Lucas, R. E. (2003). Personality, culture and subjective well-being: emotional and cognitive evaluations of life. *An. Rev. Psychol.* 54, 403–425. doi: 10.1146/annurev.psych.54.101601.145056

Domínguez-Lara, S. A. D., and Merino-Soto, C. M. (2015). ¿Por qué es importante reportar los intervalos de confianza del coeficiente alfa de Cronbach? *Rev. Cien. Soc.* 13, 1326–1328.

Duda, J. L., and Nicholls, J. G. (1992). Dimensions of achievement motivation in schoolwork and sport. *J. Educ. Psychol.* 84, 290–299. doi: 10.1037/0022-0663.84.3.290

Dunn, T. J., Baguley, T., and Brunsden, V. (2014). From alpha to omega: a practical solution to the pervasive problem of internal consistency estimation. *Brit. J. Psychol.* 105, 399–412. doi: 10.1111/bjop.12046

Elliot, K., and Shin, D. (2002). Student satisfaction: an alternative approach to assessing this important concept. *J. High. Educ. Policy Manag.* 24, 197–209. doi: 10.1080/1360080022000013518

Elmore, G. M., and Huebner, E. S. (2010). Adolescents satisfaction with school experiences: relationships with demographics, attachment relationships, and school engagement behavior. *Psychol. Sch.* 47, 525–537. doi: 10.1002/pits.20488

Gilman, R., and Huebner, E. S. (2006). Characteristics of adolescents who report very high life satisfaction. *J. Youth Adoles.* 35, 311–319. doi: 10.1007/s10964-006-9036-7

Ginns, P., Prosser, M., and Barrie, S. (2007). Students' perceptions of teaching quality in higher education: the perspective of currently enrolled students. *Stud. High. Educ.* 32, 603–615. doi: 10.1080/03075070701573773

Granero-Gallegos, A., Baena-Extremera, A., Pérez-Quero, F. J., Ortiz-Camacho, M. M., and Bracho-Amador, C. (2012). Analysis of motivational profiles of satisfaction and importance of physical education in high school adolescents. *J. Sports Sci. Med.* 11, 614–623.

Gültekin, F., and Aricioğlu, A. (2016). The relationship between the life satisfaction, hope and anxiety of senior students. *J. Coun. Educ.* 5, 57–74. doi: 10.5430/ijhe.v5n2p275

Hair, J. F., Black, W. C., Babin, B. J., and Anderson, R. E. (2009). *Multivariate data analysis.* New York: Pearson Prentice Hall.

Helsinki Declaration World Medical Association (2013). Available at: www.isciii.es/ISCIII/es/contenidos/fd-investigacion/fd-evaluacion/fd-evaluacion-etica-investigacion/Declaracion-Helsinki-2013-Esp.pdf (Accessed August 06, 2019).

Hill, Y., Lomas, L., and MacGregor, J. (2003). Students' perceptions of quality in higher education. *Qual. Assur. Educ.* 11, 15–20. doi: 10.1108/09684880310462047

Hooper, J. D., Coughlan, M. R., and Mullen, M. (2008). Structural equation modeling: guidelines for determining model fit. *Elec J. Bus. Res. Meth.* 6, 53–60.

Hu, L.-T., and Bentler, P. (1995). "Evaluating model fit" in *Structural equation modeling. Concepts, issues, and applications.* ed. R. H. Hoyle (London: Sage), 76–99.

Johnstone, A. (2005). Evaluation of teaching. Higher Education Academy, Physical Sciences Centre, University of Hull. Available at: www.physsci.heacademy.ac.uk (Accessed July 17, 2018).

Katz, M. H. (2006). *Multivariable analysis.* 2nd Edn. Cambridge: Cambridge University Press.

Khine, M. S. (2005). Self-perceived and students perceptions of teacher interaction in the classrooms. Paper presented at the Conference on Redesigning Pedagogy: Research, Policy and Practice, Singapore.

Kosik, R., Fan, A., Mandell, G., Su, T. P., Nguyen, T., Chen, J., et al. (2017). Academic performance in childhood and the risk of attempting suicide as an adult. *Europ. J. Psych.* 31, 73–79. doi: 10.1016/j.ejpsy.2017.03.002

Kuzmanovic, M., Savic, G., Popovic, M., and andMartic, M. (2013). A new approach to evaluation of university teaching considering heterogeneity of students' preferences. *High. Educ.* 66, 153–171. doi: 10.1007/s10734-012-9596-2

Lebrero, I., Alamagro, B. J., and Sáenz-López, P. (2019). Estilos de enseñanza participativos en las clases de Educación Física y su influencia sobre diferentes aspectos psicológicos. *Espiral* 12, 30–39. doi: 10.25115/ecp.v12i25.2286

Lee, H. H., Kim, G. M. L., and Chan, L. L. (2015). Good teaching: what matters to university students. *Asia Pac. J. Educ.* 35, 98–110. doi: 10.1080/02188791.2013.860008

Lewis, A. D., Huebner, E. S., Malone, P. S., and Valois, R. F. (2011). Life satisfaction and student engagement in adolescents. *J. Youth Adoles.* 40, 249–262. doi: 10.1007/s10964-010-9517-6

Lyons, M., and Huebner, E. (2016). Academic characteristics of early adolescentswith higher levels of life satisfaction. *App. Res. Qual. Life* 11, 757–771. doi: 10.1007/s11482-015-9394-y

Maddux, J. E. (2002). "Self-efficacy: the power of believing you can" in *Handbook of positive psychology.* eds. C. R. Snyder and S. J. Lopez (New York: Oxford University Press), 277–287.

Markland, D. (2007). The golden rule is that there are no golden rules: a commentary on Paul Barrett's recommendations for reporting model fit in structural equation modelling. *Personal. Individ. Differ.* 42, 851–858. doi: 10.1016/j.paid.2006.09.023

Maršanić, V. B., Margetić, B. A., Zečević, I., and andHerceg, M. (2014). The prevalence and psychosocial correlates of suicide attempts among inpatient adolescent offspring of Croatian PTSD male war veterans. *Child Psych. Hum. Dev.* 45, 577–587. doi: 10.1007/s10578-013-0426-2

Méndez-Giménez, A., Cecchini-Estrada, J. A., Fernández-Rio, J., Méndez-Alonso, D., and Prieto-Saborit, J. A. (2017). Metas de logro 3x2, motivación autodeterminada y satisfacción con la vida en educación secundaria. *Rev. Psicod.* 22, 150–156. doi: 10.1016/j.psicod.2017.05.001

Moreno, C. (2009). Effectiveteachers-professional and personal skills. ENSAYOS, Revista de la Facultad de Educación de Albacete, 24. Available at: http://www.uclm.es/ab/educacion/ensayos (Accessed January 22, 2019).

Nicholls, J. G. (1989). *The competitive ethos and democratic education.* Cambridge, Mass: Harvard University Press.

Nicholls, J. G., Patashnick, M., and Nolen, S. B. (1985). Adolescents' theories of education. *J. Educ. Psychol.* 77, 683–692. doi: 10.1037/0022-0663.77.6.683

Noddings, N. (2003). *Happiness and education.* New York: Cambridge University Press.

Quinn, P. D., and Duckworth, A. L. (2007). Happiness and academic achievement: Evidence for reciprocal causality. Poster session presented at the annual meeting of the American Psychological Society, Washington, DC.

Roeser, R. W., and Eccles, J. S. (2000). "Schooling and mental health" in *Handbook of developmental psychopathology.* 2nd Edn. eds. A. J. Sameroff, M. Lewis, and S. M. Miller (New York: Plenum), 135–156.

Salvador-Ferrer, C. (2017). Relación entre la gratitud y la satisfacción con la vida en una muestra de estudiantes españoles: el papel moderador del género. *Anales Psicol.* 33, 114–119. doi: 10.6018/analesps.32.3.226671

Sang, C., Ibrahim, Z., and andOwee, T. (2013). An analysis on the relationship between lecturers' competencies and students' satisfaction. *Int. Educ. Stud.* 7, 37–46. doi: 10.5539/ies.v7n1p37

Singer, J. B., Erbacher, T. A., and Rosen, P. (2018). School-based suicide prevention: a framework for evidence-based practice. *Sch. Ment. Health* 11, 54–71. doi: 10.1007/s12310-018-9245-8

Suldo, S. M., and Huebner, E. S. (2004). Does life satisfaction moderate the effects of stressful events on psychopathological behavior during adolescence? *Sch. Psychol. Q.* 19, 93–105. doi: 10.1521/scpq.19.2.93.33313

Suldo, S. M., and Huebner, E. S. (2006). Is extremely high life satisfaction during adolescence advantageous? *Soc. Indic. Res.* 78, 179–203. doi: 10.1007/s11205-005-8208-2

Tabachnick, B. G., and Fidell, L. S. (2007). *Using multivariate statistics,* 5th Edn. New York: Allyn and Bacon.

Vandenbosch, M. (1996). Confirmatory compositional approaches to the development of product spaces. *Eur. J. Mark.* 30, 23–46. doi: 10.1108/03090569610107418

Vecchio, G., Gerbino, M., Pastorelli, C., Del Bove, G., and andCaprara, G. (2007). Multi-faceted self-efficacy beliefs as predictors of life satisfaction in late adolescence. *Pers. Individ. Differ.* 43, 1807–1818. doi: 10.1016/j.paid.2007.05.018

Ventura-León, J. L., and Caycho-Rodríguez, T. (2017). El coeficiente Omega: un método alternativo para la estimación de la confiabilidad. *Rev. Cien. Soc.* 15, 625–627.

Wallhead, T., and Buckworth, J. (2004). The role of physical education in the promotion of youth physical activity. *Quest* 56, 285–301. doi: 10.1080/00336297.2004.10491827

Wang, J., Lin, E., and Spalding, E. (2011). Quality teaching and teacher education: a kaleidoscope of notions. *J. Teach. Educ.* 62, 331–338. doi: 10.1177/0022487111409551

Yair, G. (2008). Can we administer the scholarship of teaching? Lessons from outstanding professors in higher education. *High. Educ.* 55, 447–459. doi: 10.1007/s10734-007-9066-4

Young, S., and Shaw, D. G. (1999). Profiles of effective college and university teachers. *J. High. Educ.* 70, 670–686. doi: 10.2307/2649170

13

Relative Age Effect on Youth Female Volleyball Players: A Pilot Study on its Prevalence and Relationship with Anthropometric and Physiological Characteristics

Sophia D. Papadopoulou[1], Sousana K. Papadopoulou[2], Thomas Rosemann[3], Beat Knechtle[3] and Pantelis T. Nikolaidis[4]*

[1] Department of Physical Education and Sport Science, Laboratory of Evaluation of Human Biological Performance, Aristotle University of Thessaloniki, Thessaloniki, Greece, [2] Department of Nutritional Sciences and Dietetics, International Hellenic University, Thessaloniki, Greece, [3] Institute of Primary Care, University of Zurich, Zurich, Switzerland, [4] Exercise Physiology Laboratory, Nikaia, Greece

***Correspondence:**
Beat Knechtle
beat.knechtle@hispeed.ch

The relative age effect (RAE) on human performance has been well studied in many sports, especially in soccer; however, little information has been available about the prevalence of RAE in volleyball, and its role on anthropometric and physiological characteristics. The aim of the present study was to examine (a) the prevalence of RAE in selected (i.e., to be considered for the national team) and non-selected youth female volleyball players, and (b) the relationship of birth quarter (BQ) with anthropometric and physiological characteristics. Selected (n = 72, age 13.3 ± 0.7 years, weight 62.0 ± 7.2 kg, height 1.72 ± 0.06 m) and non-selected female volleyball players (n = 53, age 13.9 ± 1.1 years, weight 56.4 ± 7.3 kg, height 1.66 ± 0.06 m) performed a series of anthropometric and physiological tests. Twenty-six selected participants were born in the first quarter of the year, 19 in the second, 14 in the third, and 13 in the forth. The corresponding frequency by BQ in non-selected participants was 12, 12, 17, and 12. No association was observed between the number of participants and their frequency by BQ neither in the selected (χ^2 = 2.79, p = 0.425) nor in the non-selected group (χ^2 = 0.64, p = 0.886). Anthropometric and physiological characteristics did not vary by BQ (p > 0.05). The absence of RAE in female volleyball players and the similarities of anthropometric and physiological characteristics among BQ might be due to technical-tactical character of this sport. These findings would be of great practical value for coaches and fitness trainers working with young volleyball players.

Keywords: birth quarter, body composition, human performance, jumping ability, isometric muscle strength

INTRODUCTION

The relative age effect (RAE) on human performance – i.e., the larger prevalence of athletes born in the first months (e.g., first quarter) of the year ("early born") compared to their counterparts born in the last months (e.g., last quarter) of the year ("late born") – has attracted an increased scientific interest during the last three decades considering its relevance for sport performance

(Barnsley et al., 1992) and other domains of human performance (Alsaker and Olweus, 1993). This phenomenon indicated a potential advantage of "early born" compared to "late born" athletes (Duarte et al., 2019). So far, most of the research of RAE in sports has been conducted in soccer (Peña-González et al., 2018; Schroepf and Lames, 2018; Yagüe et al., 2018) and focused on the prevalence of RAE analyzing the distribution of births among months of year. On the other hand, less information exists in female volleyball (Okazaki et al., 2011), which has been one of the most popular team sports in women worldwide (Deaner et al., 2012), and – to the best of our knowledge – no study has ever examined the relationship of RAE with anthropometric and physiological characteristics in this sport.

The findings of existing literature on RAE in volleyball have been controversial so far. An absence of RAE has been observed in Dutch volleyball (Van Rossum, 2006), elite Brazilian adult female volleyball players (Parma and Penna, 2018) and Israeli Division 1 (Lidor et al., 2014). On the other hand, RAE has been shown in the top Japanese volleyball league (Nakata and Sakamoto, 2012), elite Brazilian youth female volleyball players (Okazaki et al., 2011) and female United Kingdom schoolchildren 11–18 years volleyball players (Reed et al., 2017). With an exception, where an over-representation of the last quarters of the year for the whole population in recreational volleyball players was found (Larouche et al., 2010), RAE indicated a higher prevalence of "early born" volleyball players especially in the younger age groups suggesting that RAE was attenuating with age in volleyball. This observation was in agreement with findings in soccer, where RAE was less remarkable in the older soccer players compared to their younger counterparts (Brustio et al., 2018).

Considering the above-mentioned literature on volleyball with some studies observing RAE (Okazaki et al., 2011; Nakata and Sakamoto, 2012; Reed et al., 2017) and others not (Van Rossum, 2006; Lidor et al., 2014; Parma and Penna, 2018), it was suggested that further research on the prevalence of RAE in this sport was needed. Such information would be of great practical interest for volleyball practitioners and policy makers, since an observation of disproportionally high number of "early born" volleyball players would indicate a bias against their "late born" counterparts increasing the risk of drop-outs. This topic was particularly important in adolescence, which was a crucial period for the adherence in sports (Soares et al., 2019). Furthermore, it would be of great practical importance to examine the relationship of RAE with anthropometric and physiological characteristics related to performance in female volleyball players. It has been shown that female volleyball players of high performance level were taller, jumped higher and had larger handgrip muscle strength than their counterparts of lower performance level (Nikolaidis et al., 2015). Also, more successful female volleyball players were taller, lighter and scored higher in standing broad jump and medicine ball throw than their less successful counterparts (Milić et al., 2017). Thus, it would be interesting to examine whether "early born" volleyball players would exhibit superior anthropometric and physiological characteristics compared to "late born." Maturation has been considered previously as a confounding factor of RAE (Peña-González et al., 2018), since early maturers exhibited superior performance than late maturers (Cripps et al., 2016). Therefore, the aim of the present study was to examine (a) the prevalence of RAE in selected and non-selected female volleyball players, and (b) the relationship of RAE with anthropometric and physiological characteristics. Based on relevant research in soccer (Buchheit et al., 2014; De Oliveira Matta et al., 2015), it was hypothesized that RAE would be observed in volleyball players, "early born" would have superior anthropometric and physiological characteristics than "late born" volleyball players, and RAE would have larger magnitude in selected than non-selected volleyball players. For the purpose of this study, "selected" referred to volleyball players who were selected by national team coaches to be considered for the national team of their age group.

MATERIALS AND METHODS

A cross-sectional study design was used in the present research. Birth quarter (BQ), i.e., the quarter of birth, was defined as the independent variable, whereas anthropometric and physiological characteristics were designated as dependent variables. Selected (n = 72, age 13.3 ± 0.7 years, weight 62.0 ± 7.2 kg, height 1.72 ± 0.06 m) and non-selected female volleyball players (n = 53, age 13.9 ± 1.1 years, weight 56.4 ± 7.3 kg, height 1.66 ± 0.06 m) participated in the present study. Selected volleyball players competed in volleyball clubs in Athens. Non-selected volleyball players were members of two youth academies of competitive volleyball clubs from Athens (Greece). All procedures were in accordance with the Declaration of Helsinki as revised in 2008 and approved by the local Institutional Review Board. Participants' parents or guardians provided informed consent prior to exercise testing session. All participants played volleyball at least three years before the study, had three to four training sessions and one official match weekly.

The testing session was carried out during competitive period in indoor volleyball court. It lasted 90 min, and included a supervised warm-up (10 min submaximal running and 5 min stretching exercises) and the following tests in the specific order: weight, height, skinfolds' thickness, sit-and-reach test (SAR), Abalakov jump (AJ), four tests of isometric muscle strength (right and left handgrip, lifting with extended and flexed knees) and 20 m endurance shuttle run test (SRT). Two trials were performed for SAR, AJ, and right and left handgrip test, and the best score was recorded for each of these tests. 1 min break was provided between trials and 5 min break among tests. Although this physical fitness test battery was not sport-specific, e.g., it did not include tests corresponding to movements usually performed in volleyball, the selected tests have been used widely due to their ability to discriminate volleyball players by performance level and playing position (Nikolaidis et al., 2015; Sattler et al., 2015; Brazo-Sayavera et al., 2017; Milić et al., 2017; Paz et al., 2017).

An electronic scale (HD-351 Tanita, Arlington Heights, IL, United States) and a stadiometer (SECA, Leicester, United Kingdom) were used to measure weight and height, respectively. Body mass index (BMI) was calculated using the formula "weight (kg)/height (m)^2." Body fat percentage (BF%) was predicted using the sum of ten skinfolds' thickness (cheek, wattle, chest I, triceps, subscapular, abdominal, chest II, suprailiac, thigh, and calf; skinfold caliper Harpenden, West Sussex, United Kingdom) (Parizkova, 1978). The difference from the age at peak height velocity (Δaphv) was evaluated only in the selected group - because sitting height was measured only in this group - and was used as a measure of maturation (Mirwald et al., 2002). A parameter that was evaluated only in the selected Opto-jump system (Microgate Engineering, Bolzano, Italy) was used to measure AJ, i.e., jumping ability of single vertical jump with countermovement and arm-swing (Bosco et al., 1983). Flexibility was tested by SAR on a box providing 15 cm advantage, i.e., the participant got a 15 cm score when reaching the toes of her feet (Adam et al., 1988). Aerobic capacity was assessed by SRT, a widely used graded exercise test (Adam et al., 1988). Isometric muscle strength was evaluated as the sum of four measures (right and left handgrip test, lifting with extended and flexed knees tests; use of digital handgrip and back-and-leg digital dynamometer; Takei, Tokyo, Japan) and expressed either in absolute (kg) or relative (kg/kg of body weight) values (Heyward and Gibson, 2014).

All variables were expressed using mean and standard deviations. Statistical analyses were carried out on IBM SPSS v.20.0 (SPSS, Chicago, IL, United States) and GraphPad Prism v. 7.0 (GraphPad Software, San Diego, CA, United States). A t test examined differences in all measures between the selected and non-selected group. A chi-square test (χ^2) examined the association of the number of participants by BQ with expected values. Differences in - adjusted for age - anthropometric and physiological characteristics among BQ groups were examined by one-way multivariate analysis of covariance (MANCOVA). In the case of the selected group, the differences were adjusted for both age and Δaphv. The magnitude of the differences was tested by partial eta square, evaluated as small ($0.010 < \eta_p^2 \leq 0.059$), medium ($0.059 < \eta_p^2 \leq 0.138$), and large ($\eta_p^2 > 0.138$) (Cohen, 1988). The relationship among variables was examined by Pearson's product moment correlation coefficient (r), whose magnitude was interpreted as trivial ($r < 0.10$), small ($0.10 \leq r < 0.30$), moderate ($0.30 \leq r < 0.50$), large ($0.50 \leq r < 0.70$), very large ($0.70 \leq r < 0.90$), nearly perfect ($r \geq 0.90$), and perfect ($r = 1.00$) (Batterham and Hopkins, 2006). Significance was set at alpha = 0.05.

RESULTS

The descriptive characteristics of participants are presented in **Table 1**. Twenty-six selected participants were born in the first quarter of the year, 19 in the second, 14 in the third, and 13 in the forth. The corresponding numbers in non-selected participants were 12, 12, 17, and 12. No association was observed between the number of participants and their frequency by BQ neither in the selected ($\chi^2 = 2.79$, $p = 0.425$) nor in the non-selected group ($\chi^2 = 0.64$, $p = 0.886$). In the non-selected group, there was no statistically significant difference among BQ groups on the combined dependent variables after controlling for age in the non-selected group [$F_{(36,\ 104)} = 1.198$, $p = 0.239$, Wilks' $\Lambda = 0.359$, $\eta_p^2 = 0.239$]. In the selected group, no statistically significant difference among BQ groups on the combined dependent variables after controlling for age and Δaphv [$F_{(36,\ 157)} = 0.881$, $p = 0.663$, Wilks' $\Lambda = 0.581$, $\eta_p^2 = 0.165$] (**Figures 1–3**). The relationship of anthropometric and physiological characteristics with age in the non-selected group was shown in **Figures 4–6**.

The relationship of anthropometric and physiological characteristics with age and Δaphv in the selected group can be seen in **Table 2**. Age did not correlate with of the other measures. Δaphv correlated very largely with height, moderately with weight, and with small magnitude with left handgrip muscle strength.

TABLE 1 | Descriptive statistics (mean ± standard deviation) of anthropometric and physiological characteristics of participants.

Variable	Non-selected (n = 53)	Selected (n = 72)
Age (years)	13.9 ± 1.1	13.3 ± 0.7***
Anthropometric characteristics		
Weight (kg)	56.4 ± 7.3	62.0 ± 7.2***
Height (m)	1.66 ± 0.06	1.72 ± 0.06***
BMI (kg/m^{-2})	20.4 ± 2.2	21.1 ± 2.2
BF (%)	21.2 ± 4.1	21.2 ± 4.5
Physiological characteristics		
AJ (cm)	29.2 ± 4.9	30.8 ± 5.0
SAR (cm)	25.7 ± 7.2	24.7 ± 7.4
SRT (min:s)	5 : 22 ± 1 : 24	5 : 00 ± 1 : 17
Isometric muscle strength		
Right HG (kg)	27.2 ± 5.0	29.8 ± 4.5**
Left (kg)	26.2 ± 4.1	29.5 ± 4.3***
Lifting with extended knees (kg)	68.5 ± 12.9	77.1 ± 14.6**
Lifting with flexed knees (kg)	83.7 ± 21.6	90.4 ± 19.0
Isometric strength (kg)	205.6 ± 40.0	227.1 ± 36.6**
Isometric strength (kg/kg of body weight)	3.63 ± 0.43	3.70 ± 0.64

*BMI = body mass index; BF = body fat percentage; SAR = sit-and-reach test; SRT = 20 m shuttle run test; HG = handgrip muscle strength; ***$p < 0.001$, **$p < 0.01$.*

DISCUSSION

The main findings of the present study were that, (a) RAE was not observed in selected and non-selected female volleyball players, (b) anthropometric and physiological characteristics did not differ among BQ groups, and (c) the relationship of anthropometric and physiological characteristics with age varied by performance group with stronger correlations observed in the non-selected than in the selected group.

The absence of RAE in the examined sample of female young volleyball players was in agreement with previous studies in volleyball that did not show any difference on the frequency of BQ groups (Van Rossum, 2006; Lidor et al., 2014; Parma and Penna, 2018). An explanation of the absence of RAE in our sample might be that volleyball has been considered a team sport that did not require exceptional demands in physiological

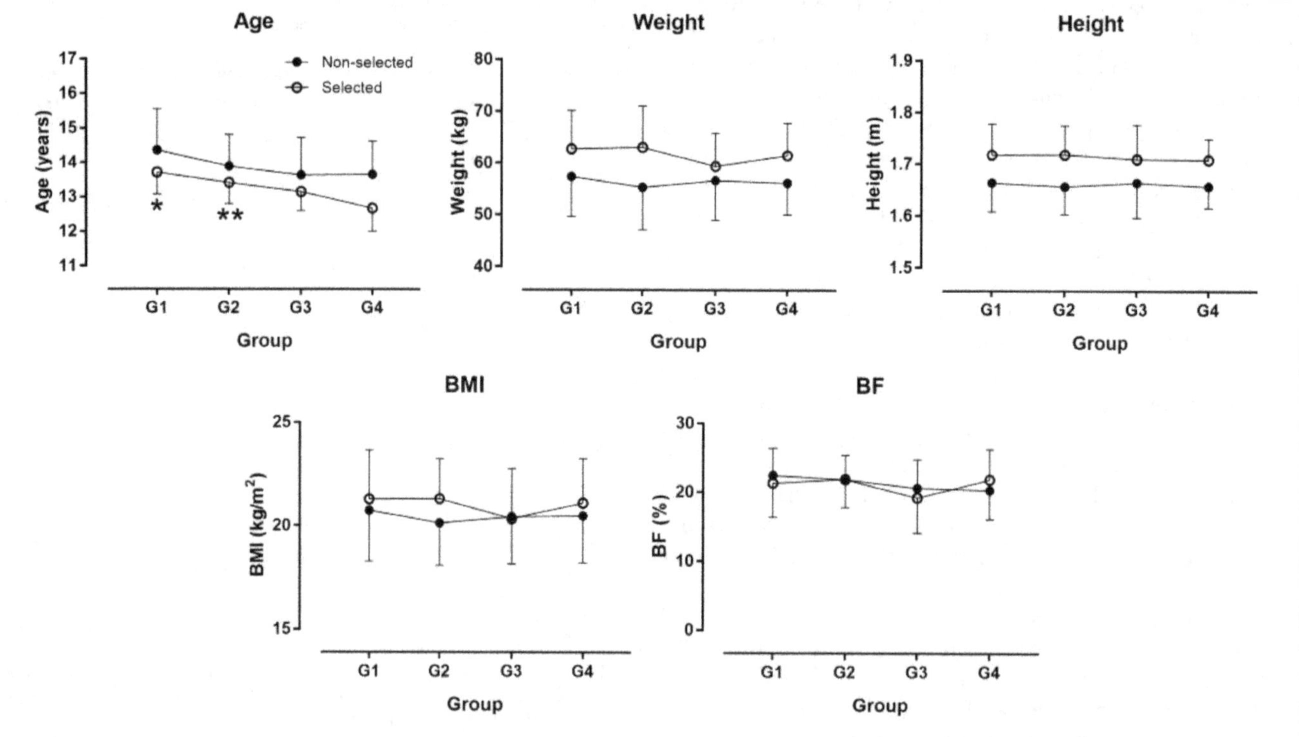

FIGURE 1 | Age and anthropometric characteristics by birth quarter. G1 = born in January, February, and March; G2 = born in April, May, and June; G3 = born in July, August, and September; G4 = born in October, November, and December; BMI = body mass index; BF = body fat percentage. *G1 older than G3 and G4, **G2 older than G4 in selected participants at $p < 0.05$.

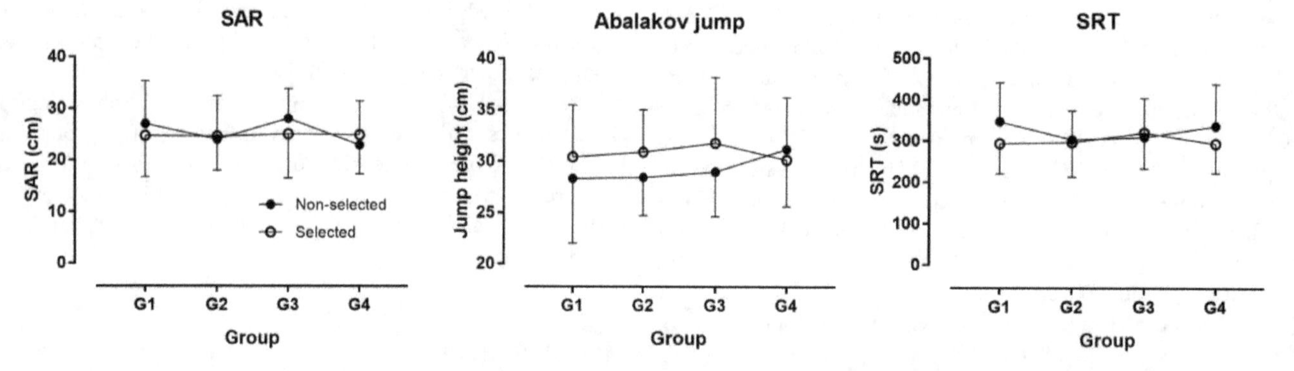

FIGURE 2 | Jumping, flexibility, and aerobic capacity by birth quarter. G1 = born in January, February, and March; G2 = born in April, May, and June; G3 = born in July, August, and September; G4 = born in October, November, and December; SAR = sit-and-reach test; SRT = 20 m endurance shuttle run test. Error bars represent standard deviations.

characteristics (Lidor and Ziv, 2010a) and was characterized by large variability in these characteristics (Nikolaidis et al., 2012). However, it was acknowledged that other studies conducted on this sport (Okazaki et al., 2011; Nakata and Sakamoto, 2012; Reed et al., 2017) observed RAE highlighting the overall conflicting findings in research on volleyball and addressing the need of further research on this topic. Based on the findings of the present study, it might be assumed that sport and human performances without high demands in physiological characteristics – e.g., aerobic capacity, muscle strength and speed – would attenuate the occurrence of RAE.

The absence of RAE in the present study was in disagreement with the existed literature on team sports with high demands in physiological characteristics. For instance, most studies (Korgaokar et al., 2018; Peña-González et al., 2018; Rađa et al., 2018; Schroepf and Lames, 2018; Yagüe et al., 2018; Marques et al., 2019) in soccer have observed an occurrence of RAE, where most soccer players were born in the first quarter or half of the year. Moreover, it has been shown that the number of soccer players born in January would be twice the number of those born in December in the top five European leagues (Rađa et al., 2018). An occurrence of RAE would have implications

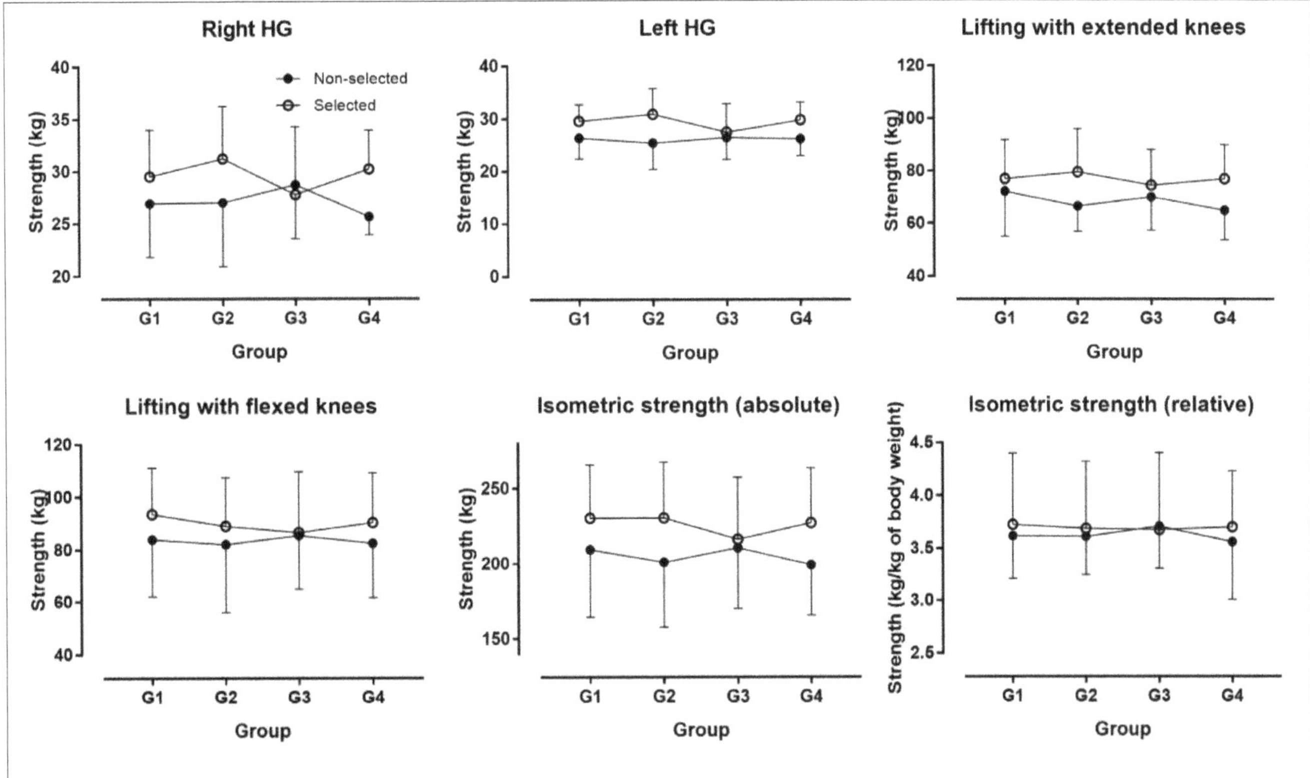

FIGURE 3 | Isometric muscle strength by birth quarter. G1 = born in January, February, and March; G2 = born in April, May, and June; G3 = born in July, August, and September; G4 = born in October, November, and December; "Isometric strength" refers to the sum of the four measures (right and left handgrip strength, lifting with extended and flexed knees. Error bars represent standard deviations.

for talent identification and soccer players' selection and would require action to balance the chances of success for players born in the end of a year (Yagüe et al., 2018). On the contrary, such a bias in talent identification and players' selection should not be a concern in volleyball.

The similar anthropometric and physiological characteristics among BQ were in agreement with the absence of RAE in the present study. This relationship has been examined previously in soccer, where some studies supported an association between BQ and these characteristics, i.e., "early born" showed superior characteristics than "late born" (Pedretti and Seabra, 2015; Altimari et al., 2018), whereas other studies did not observe differences (De Oliveira Matta et al., 2015; Junior et al., 2015; Lovell et al., 2015; Skorski et al., 2016; Peña-González et al., 2018). An explanation of the similar anthropometric and physiological characteristics among BQ might be the role of maturation as a covariate (Lovell et al., 2015; Peña-González et al., 2018).

With regards to the role of chronological age, the findings in the non-selected group showed that weight, height and isometric muscle strength increased with age, whereas BMI, BF and the other physiological characteristics did not. On the contrary, no relationship was observed between age and these characteristics in the selected group. Considering the adolescence as a period with large changes in the characteristics of volleyball players (Lidor and Ziv, 2010b), the variation in the abovementioned relationship by performance level might be partially attributed to the smaller age range of the selected compared to the non-selected group indicating that the former group was more homogeneous than the latter one. In addition, the variation of this relationship when Δaphv – measure of maturation – was considered instead of chronological age, confirmed the important role of maturation during volleyball players' selection (Melchiorri et al., 2017; Nunes et al., 2019), since height (a major determinant of success in volleyball) correlated very largely with Δaphv.

A limitation of the present study was that it was conducted in young volleyball players and it would be needed caution to generalize the findings in adult volleyball players, as it has been observed in other team sports (e.g., soccer) that the prevalence of RAE might vary by age group (Lovell et al., 2015; Korgaokar et al., 2018). Moreover, the administered fitness batter included tests corresponding to important parameters for volleyball performance (e.g., height and jump ability) (Nikolaidis et al., 2015; Milić et al., 2017); however, future studies should include sport-specific tests to mimic volleyball movements. In addition, it was acknowledged that the adopted methodological approach to evaluate maturation based on a combination of anthropometric characteristics and chronological age (Mirwald et al., 2002) provided only a proxy measure. Although this approach has been used widely in research on maturation and team sports performance (Pion et al., 2015; Rubajczyk et al., 2017; Lovell et al., 2019; Rommers et al., 2019), it would be recommended that future studies use laboratory methods (e.g., Tanner scale, hand-wrist skeleton), too. On the other hand, strength of the study was its novelty as it was the first one to examine

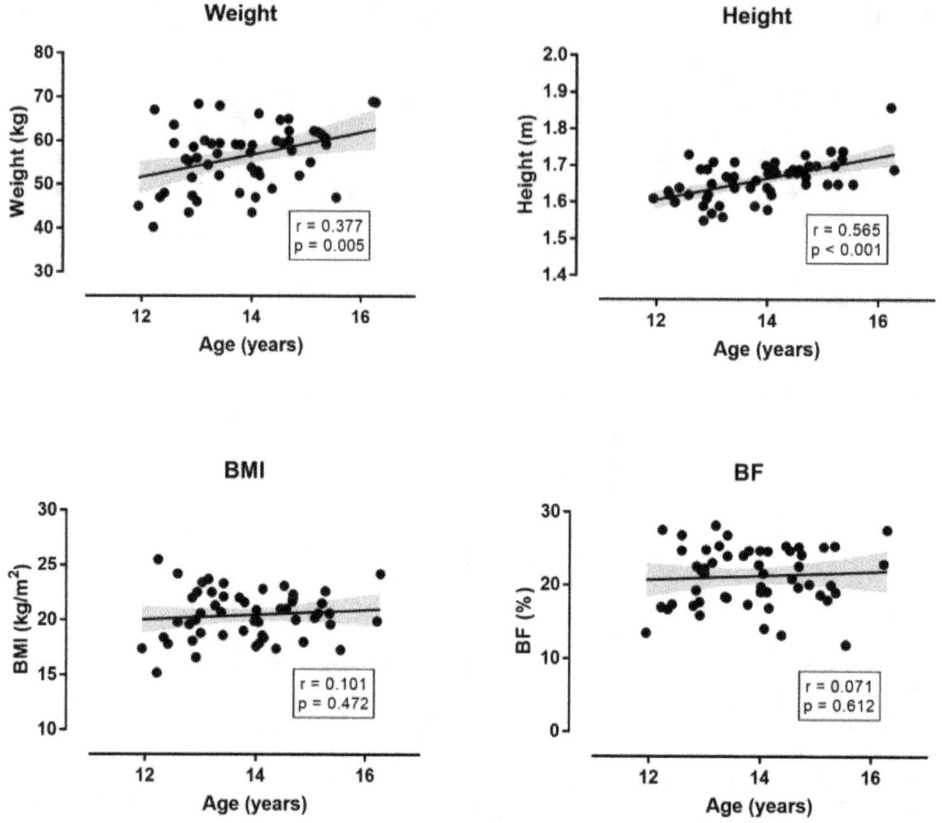

FIGURE 4 | Relationship of anthropometric characteristics with age in the non-selected group (*n* = 53). BMI = body mass index; BF = body fat percentage. The shadow line represents 95% confidence intervals.

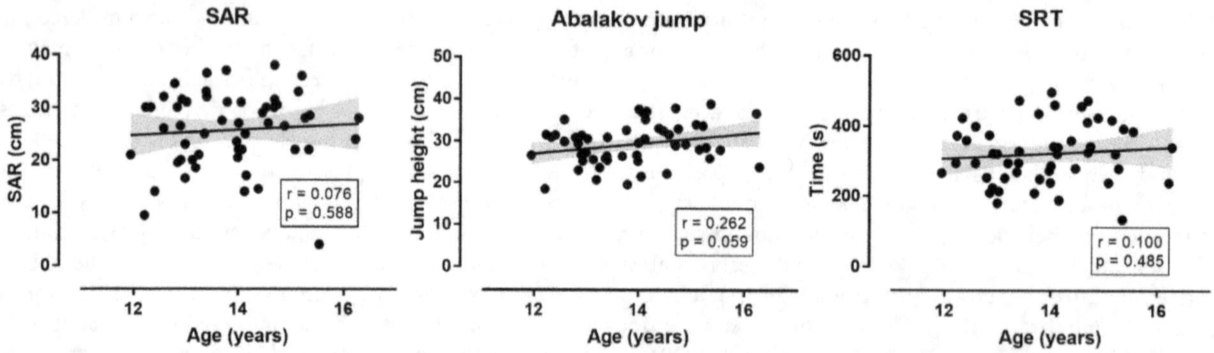

FIGURE 5 | Relationship of jumping, flexibility and aerobic capacity with age in the non-selected group (*n* = 53). SBJ = standing broad jump; SAR = sit-and-reach test; SRT = 20 m endurance shuttle run test. The shadow line represents 95% confidence intervals.

differences in anthropometric and physiological characteristics among BQ of volleyball players. These findings would be of both practical and theoretical importance for practitioners and scientists, respectively. From a practical perspective, it would be suggested that RAE should not be a concern of volleyball coaches and fitness trainers, in contrast with soccer where practitioners should manage the selection bias of their athletes due to the prevalence of RAE. Nonetheless, coaches and fitness trainers should monitor BQ of their volleyball players, especially in the context of players' selection; in case they observed RAE, they should act (e.g., setting individualized fitness goals) to prevent drop-out of potential talents. From a theoretical point of view, the absence of RAE observed in the young volleyball players under examination might imply that human performance not relying on high levels of physical abilities would not be influenced by BQ at young age. Moreover, scientists interested in this topic should examine further the prevalence of RAE and its role on anthropometric and physiological characteristics

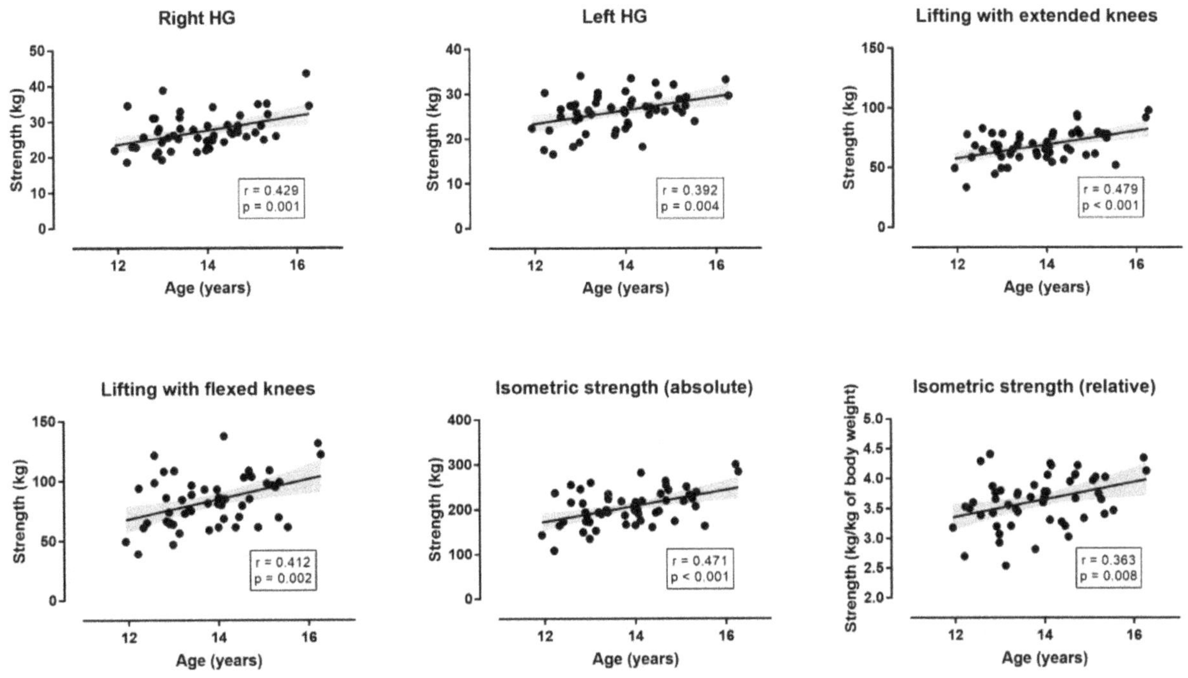

FIGURE 6 | Relationship of isometric muscle strength with age in the non-selected group (n = 53). "Isometric strength" refers to the sum of the four measures (right and left handgrip strength, lifting with extended and flexed knees. The shadow line represents 95% confidence intervals.

especially in sports with more technical than physical demands. With regards to the role of performance level, recently it was observed in soccer that RAE was more prevalent in elite than in non-elite academies (Bezuglov et al., 2019). Thus, future studies should be conducted on the variation of RAE by performance level in volleyball using large sample size to verify this trend.

TABLE 2 | The relationship (Pearson correlation coefficient r) of anthropometric and physiological characteristics with age and difference from the age at peak height velocity in the selected group (n = 72).

Variable	Age	Δaphv
Anthropometric characteristics		
Weight	0.05	0.44***
Height	0.21	0.72***
BMI	−0.08	0.02
BF	−0.13	0.05
Physiological characteristics		
AJ	0.22	−0.02
SAR	0.03	−0.14
SRT	−0.06	−0.09
Isometric muscle strength		
Right HG	0.16	0.21
Left HG	0.11	0.24*
Lifting with extended knees	0.07	0.15
Lifting with flexed knees	0.10	0.17
Absolute isometric strength	0.12	0.21
Relative isometric strength	0.09	−0.10

*BMI = body mass index, BF = body fat percentage, AJ = Abalakov jump, SAR = sit-and-reach test, SRT = 20 m shuttle run test, HG = handgrip muscle strength, Δaphv = difference from the age at peak height velocity. *$p < 0.05$, ***$p < 0.001$.*

CONCLUSION

The absence of RAE in female volleyball players and the similarities of anthropometric and physiological characteristics among BQ might be due to technical-tactical character of this sport. These findings would be of great practical value for coaches and fitness trainers working with young volleyball players.

ETHICS STATEMENT

The studies involving human participants were reviewed and approved by the Institutional Review Board, Exercise Physiology Laboratory, Nikaia, Greece. Written informed consent to participate in this study was provided by the participants' legal guardian/next of kin.

AUTHOR CONTRIBUTIONS

SDP and PN: conceptualization, formal analysis, data curation, and visualization. SDP, SKP, and PN: methodology, validation, investigation, and resources. PN: software. SDP, SKP, TR, BK, and PN: writing – original draft preparation and writing – review and editing. SDP, BK, and PN: supervision and project administration.

ACKNOWLEDGMENTS

The voluntarily participation of all athletes in the present study is gratefully acknowledged.

REFERENCES

Adam, C., Klissouras, V., Ravazzolo, M., Renson, R., and Tuxworth, W. (1988). *The Eurofit Test of European Physical Fitness Tests*. Strasbourg: Council of Europe.

Alsaker, F. D., and Olweus, D. (1993). Global self-evaluations and perceived instability of self in early adolescence: a cohort longitudinal study. *Scand. J. Psychol.* 34, 47–63. doi: 10.1111/j.1467-9450.1993.tb01100.x

Altimari, J. M., Bortolotti, H., dos Santos-Junior, N., Altimari, L. R., and de Moraes, A. C. (2018). Birth month distribution and anthropometric measures of U-15 national elite soccer players. *Revista Brasileira Cineantropometria esempenho Humano* 20, 211–218. doi: 10.5007/1980-0037.2018v20n2p211

Barnsley, R. H., Thompson, A. H., and Legault, P. (1992). Family planning: football style. the relative age effect in football. *Int. Rev. Sociol. Sport* 27, 77–87. doi: 10.1177/101269029202700105

Batterham, A. M., and Hopkins, W. G. (2006). Making meaningful inferences about magnitudes. *Int. J. Sports Physiol. Perform.* 1, 50–57. doi: 10.1123/ijspp.1.1.50

Bezuglov, E. N., Nikolaidis, P. T., Khaitin, V., Usmanova, E., Luibushkina, A., Repetiuk, A., et al. (2019). Prevalence of relative age effect in Russian soccer: the role of chronological age and performance. *Int. J. Environ. Res. Public Health* 16:4055. doi: 10.3390/ijerph16214055

Bosco, C., Luhtanen, P., and Komi, P. V. (1983). A simple method for measurement of mechanical power in jumping. *Eur. J. Appl. Physiol. Occup. Physiol.* 50, 273–282. doi: 10.1007/bf00422166

Brazo-Sayavera, J., Nikolaidis, P. T., Camacho-Cardenosa, A., Camacho-Cardenosa, M., Timón, R., and Olivares, P. R. (2017). Acute effects of block jumps in female volleyball players: the role of performance level. *Sports* 5:30. doi: 10.3390/sports5020030

Brustio, P. R., Lupo, C., Ungureanu, A. N., Frati, R., Rainoldi, A., and Boccia, G. (2018). The relative age effect is larger in Italian soccer top-level youth categories and smaller in serie a. *PLoS One* 13:e0196253. doi: 10.1371/journal.pone.0196253

Buchheit, M., Mendez-Villanueva, A., Mayer, N., Jullien, H., Marles, A., Bosquet, L., et al. (2014). Locomotor performance in highly-trained young soccer players: does body size always matter? *Int. J. Sports Med.* 35, 494–504. doi: 10.1055/s-0033-1353140

Cohen, J. (1988). *Statistical Power Analysis for the Behavioral Sciences*. Hillsdale, NJ: Lawrence Erlbaum Associates.

Cripps, A. J., Hopper, L., and Joyce, C. (2016). Maturity, physical ability, technical skill and coaches' perception of semi-elite adolescent Australian footballers. *Pediatr. Exerc. Sci.* 28, 535–541. doi: 10.1123/pes.2015-0238

De Oliveira Matta, M., Figueiredo, A. J., Garcia, E. S., Wernek, F. Z., and Seabra, A. (2015). Relative age effect on anthropometry, biological maturation and performance of young soccer players. *Revista Brasileira Cineantropometria Desempenho Humano* 17, 257–268. doi: 10.5007/1980-0037.2015v17n3p257

Deaner, R. O., Geary, D. C., Puts, D. A., Ham, S. A., Kruger, J., Fles, E., et al. (2012). A sex difference in the predisposition for physical competition: males play sports much more than females even in the contemporary U.S. *PLoS One* 7:e49168. doi: 10.1371/journal.pone.0049168

Duarte, J. P., Coelho, E. S. M. J., Costa, D., Martinho, D., Luz, L. G. O., Rebelo-Goncalves, R., et al. (2019). Repeated sprint ability in youth soccer players: independent and combined effects of relative age and biological maturity. *J. Hum. Kinet.* 67, 209–221. doi: 10.2478/hukin-2018-0090

Heyward, V. H., and Gibson, A. L. (2014). *Advanced Fitness Assessment and Exercise Prescription*. Champaign, IL: Human Kinetics.

Junior, C. J. S., Palma, A., Imbiriba, L. A., Assis, M. R., and Barbosa, M. A. M. (2015). Relationship between relative age effect and physical characteristics of young soccer players. *Cultura, Ciencia y Deporte* 10, 227–233. doi: 10.1055/s-0031-1287798

Korgaokar, A. D., Farley, R. S., Fuller, D. K., and Caputo, J. L. (2018). Relative age effect among elite youth female soccer players across the United States. *Sport Mont* 16, 37–41. doi: 10.26773/smj.181007

Larouche, R., Laurencelle, L., Grondin, S., and Trudeau, F. (2010). Influence of birth quarter on the rate of physical activities and sports participation. *J. Sports Sci.* 28, 627–631. doi: 10.1080/02640411003587392

Lidor, R., Arnon, M., Maayan, Z., Gershon, T., and Côté, J. (2014). Relative age effect and birthplace effect in division 1 female ballgame players-the relevance of sport-specific factors. *Int. J. Sport Exerc. Psychol.* 12, 19–33. doi: 10.1080/1612197x.2012.756232

Lidor, R., and Ziv, G. (2010a). Physical and physiological attributes of female volleyball players–a review. *J. Strength Cond. Res.* 24, 1963–1973. doi: 10.1519/JSC.0b013e3181ddf835

Lidor, R., and Ziv, G. (2010b). Physical characteristics and physiological attributes of adolescent volleyball players-a review. *Pediatr. Exerc. Sci.* 22, 114–134. doi: 10.1123/pes.22.1.114

Lovell, R., Fransen, J., Ryan, R., Massard, T., Cross, R., Eggers, T., et al. (2019). Biological maturation and match running performance: a national football (soccer) federation perspective. *J. Sci. Med. Sport* 22, 1139–1145. doi: 10.1016/j.jsams.2019.04.007

Lovell, R., Towlson, C., Parkin, G., Portas, M., Vaeyens, R., and Cobley, S. (2015). Soccer player characteristics in English lower-league development programmes: the relationships between relative age, maturation, anthropometry and physical fitness. *PLoS One* 10:e0137238. doi: 10.1371/journal.pone.0137238

Marques, P. R. R., Pinheiro, E. D. S., and Coswig, V. S. (2019). Effect of relative age on the selection of athletes for the youth teams of a soccer club. *Revista Brasileira Ciencias Esporte* 41, 157–162. doi: 10.1016/j.rbce.2018.03.034

Melchiorri, G., Viero, V., Triossi, T., Annino, G., Padua, E., and Tancredi, V. (2017). Anthropometric and performance measures to study talent detection in youth volleyball. *J. Sports Med. Phys. Fit.* 57, 1623–1632. doi: 10.23736/s0022-4707.17.07068-2

Milić, M., Grgantov, Z., Chamari, K., Ardigò, L. P., Bianco, A., and Padulo, J. (2017). Anthropometric and physical characteristics allow differentiation of young female volleyball players according to playing position and level of expertise. *Biol. Sport* 34, 19–26. doi: 10.5114/biolsport.2017.63382

Mirwald, R. L., Baxter-Jones, A. D., Bailey, D. A., and Beunen, G. P. (2002). An assessment of maturity from anthropometric measurements. *Med. Sci. Sports Exerc.* 34, 689–694. doi: 10.1097/00005768-200204000-00020

Nakata, H., and Sakamoto, K. (2012). Sex differences in relative age effects among Japanese athletes. *Percept. Mot. Skills* 115, 179–186. doi: 10.2466/10.05.17.pms.115.4.179-186

Nikolaidis, P. T., Afonso, J., and Busko, K. (2015). Differences in anthropometry, somatotype, body composition and physiological characteristics of female volleyball players by competition level. *Sport Sci. Health* 11, 29–35. doi: 10.1007/s11332-014-0196-7

Nikolaidis, P. T., Ziv, G., Arnon, M., and Lidor, R. (2012). Physical characteristics and physiological attributes of female volleyball players–the need for individual data. *J. Strength Cond. Res.* 26, 2547–2557. doi: 10.1519/JSC.0b013e31823f8c06

Nunes, A., Cattuzzo, M. T., Faigenbaum, A. D., and Mortatti, A. L. (2019). Effects of integrative neuromuscular training and detraining on countermovement jump performance in youth volleyball players. *J. Strength Cond. Res.* doi: 10.1519/JSC.0000000000003092 [Epub ahead of print].

Okazaki, F. H. A., Keller, B., Fontana, F. E., and Gallagher, J. D. (2011). The relative age effect among female brazilian youth volleyball players. *Res. Q. Exerc. Sport* 82, 135–139. doi: 10.1080/02701367.2011.10599730

Parizkova, J. (1978). "Lean body mass and depot fat during autogenesis in humans," in *Nutrition, Physical Fitness and Health: International Series on Sport Sciences*, eds J. Parizkova, and V. Rogozkin, (Baltimore, MD: University Park Press).

Parma, J. O., and Penna, E. M. (2018). The relative age effect on Brazilian elite volleyball. *J. Phys. Educ.* 29:e2942.

Paz, G. A., Gabbett, T. J., Maia, M. F., Santana, H., Miranda, H., and Lima, V. (2017). Physical performance and positional differences among young female volleyball players. *J. Sports Med. Phys. Fit.* 57, 1282–1289. doi: 10.23736/s0022-4707.16.06471-9

Pedretti, A., and Seabra, A. (2015). Relative age effect and its relationship with morphological characteristics and performance in young soccer players. *Revista Brasileira Cineantropometria Desempenho Humano* 17, 367–377. doi: 10.5007/1980-0037.2015v17n3p367

Peña-González, I., Fernández-Fernández, J., Moya-Ramón, M., and Cervelló, E. (2018). Relative age effect, biological maturation, and coaches' efficacy expectations in young male soccer players. *Res. Q. Exerc. Sport* 89, 373–379. doi: 10.1080/02701367.2018.1486003

Pion, J., Segers, V., Fransen, J., Debuyck, G., Deprez, D., Haerens, L., et al. (2015). Generic anthropometric and performance characteristics among elite adolescent boys in nine different sports. *Eur. J. Sport Sci.* 15, 357–366. doi: 10.1080/17461391.2014.944875

Rađa, A., Padulo, J., Jelaska, I., Ardigò, L. P., and Fumarco, L. (2018). Relative age effect and second-tiers: no second chance for later-born players. *PLoS One* 13:e0201795. doi: 10.1371/journal.pone.0201795

Reed, K. E., Parry, D. A., and Sandercock, G. R. H. (2017). Maturational and social factors contributing to relative age effects in school sports: data from the London youth games. *Scand. J. Med. Sci. Sports* 27, 2070–2079. doi: 10.1111/sms.12815

Rommers, N., Mostaert, M., Goossens, L., Vaeyens, R., Witvrouw, E., Lenoir, M., et al. (2019). Age and maturity related differences in motor coordination among male elite youth soccer players. *J. Sports Sci.* 37, 196–203. doi: 10.1080/02640414.2018.1488454

Rubajczyk, K., Świerzko, K., and Rokita, A. (2017). Doubly disadvantaged? the relative age effect in Poland's basketball players. *J. Sports Sci. Med.* 16, 280–285.

Sattler, T., Hadzic, V., Dervisevic, E., and Markovic, G. (2015). Vertical jump performance of professional male and female volleyball players: effects of playing position and competition level. *J. Strength Cond. Res.* 29, 1486–1493. doi: 10.1519/jsc.0000000000000781

Schroepf, B., and Lames, M. (2018). Career patterns in German football youth national teams – a longitudinal study. *Int. J. Sports Sci. Coach.* 13, 405–414. doi: 10.1177/1747954117729368

Skorski, S., Skorski, S., Faude, O., Hammes, D., and Meyer, T. (2016). The relative age effect in elite German youth soccer: implications for a successful career. *Int. J. Sports Physiol. Perform.* 11, 370–376. doi: 10.1123/ijspp.2015-0071

Soares, A. L. A., Kós, L. D., Paes, R. R., Nascimento, J. V., Collins, D., and Gonçalves, C. E. (2019). Determinants of drop-out in youth basketball: an interdisciplinary approach. *Res. Sports Med.* 5, 1–15. doi: 10.1080/15438627.2019.1586708

Van Rossum, J. H. A. (2006). Relative age effect revisited: findings from the dance domain. *Percept. Mot. Skills* 102, 302–308. doi: 10.2466/pms.102.2.302-308

Yagüe, J. M., de la Rubia, A., Sánchez-Molina, J., Maroto-Izquierdo, S., and Molinero, O. (2018). The relative age effect in the 10 best leagues of male professional football of the union of european football associations (UEFA). *J. Sports Sci. Med.* 17, 409–416.

14

Neural Efficiency and Acquired Motor Skills: An fMRI Study of Expert Athletes

Lanlan Zhang[1], Fanghui Qiu[2], Hua Zhu[3], Mingqiang Xiang[4] and Liangjun Zhou[1]**

[1]Department of Leisure Sports and Management, Guangzhou Sport University, Guangzhou, China, [2]Department of Physical Education, Qingdao University, Qingdao, China, [3]Department of Biological Science and Medical Engineering, Beihang University, Beijing, China, [4]Department of Sport and Health, Guangzhou Sport University, Guangzhou, China

***Correspondence:**
Mingqiang Xiang
xiangmq80@163.com
Liangjun Zhou
cxy66662004@163.com

The neural efficiency hypothesis was investigated. Functional magnetic resonance imaging was used to study the differences in brain activity between athletes imagining performing different movements: basketball athletes imagined throwing and volleyball athletes imagined serving. These comparisons of brain activity among athletes imagining movements from their self-sport (e.g., a basketball throw in basketball athletes) versus movements from other sport (e.g., a volleyball serve in basketball athletes) revealed the neural energy consumption each task costs. The results showed better temporal congruence between motor execution and motor imagery and vividness of motor imagery, but lower levels of activation in the left putamen, inferior parietal lobule, supplementary motor area, postcentral gyrus, and the right insula when both groups of athletes imagined movements from their self-sport compared with when they imagined movements from the other-sport. Athletes were more effective in the representation of the motor sequences and the interoception of the motor sequences for their self-sport. The findings of present study suggest that elite athletes achieved superior behavioral performance with minimal neural energy consumption, thus confirming the neural efficiency hypotheses.

Keywords: neural efficiency, motor imagery, motor representation, motor repertoire, task-specific

INTRODUCTION

The difference in physiological characteristics between athletes and nonathletes is an important research field in sports science. Based on the research findings, sport industry can not only understand the physiological mechanisms of high-level athlete, but also improve athlete training and competitive performance. Neural efficiency refers to patterns of more spatially localized or less intense brain activity concomitant with equal or superior performance (Neubauer and Fink, 2009).

Compared to nonexperts, experts routinely exhibit neural efficiency when performing within their domain of expertise (Babiloni et al., 2010; Nakata et al., 2010). However, existing findings are highly variegated and are often inconsistent. Some studies showed that athletes showed increased brain activation when performing motor tasks. For example, badminton athletes showed stronger activation in mirror neuron system than novices during anticipation with videos of shuttle landing (Wright et al., 2011). Basketball athletes showed higher activity in inferior parietal lobule and inferior frontal gyrus than novices in an action anticipation task with basketball free throw (Wu et al., 2013). Expert athletes had greater neural activation than novices in somatosensory and motor planning regions when passively listening to familiar sports sounds (Woods et al., 2014). However, other studies reported that the mind of expert athletes were focused or decreased activation compared with nonexperts. For example, during mental rehearsal of archery, the premotor and supplementary motor areas, and the inferior frontal region, basal ganglia and cerebellum were active in nonarchers, whereas elite archers showed activation primarily in the supplementary motor areas (Chang et al., 2011). This focused and efficient organization of task-related neural networks was also observed in golfers during pre-shot routine (Milton et al., 2007). In another study, table tennis athletes showed less neural activation in task-related brain regions during a go/no-go visual-spatial task (Guo et al., 2017). Athletes also showed less neural activation in prefrontal cortex and insula during affective challenges than controls (Costanzo et al., 2016). These discrepancies may be related to the between-group paradigm (experts vs. novices), which entangles individual differences with neural dynamics. Thus, the use of self-reference could be a better way to probe neural efficiency.

Mentally rehearsing movements has become an important technique in sport and exercise psychology. It can be done from a first- or third-person perspective (Ruby and Decety, 2001). The first-person perspective is reported to be more embodied in the way that it involves kinesthetic representation and evokes motor simulations of one's own body and mainly recruited the left hemisphere (Lorey et al., 2009). In this context, motor imagery is defined as a mental process involving rehearsal or simulation of a given action from a first-person perspective without overt movements (Jeannerod, 1994; Decety and Jeannerod, 1995; Hanakawa et al., 2003). Motor imagery and motor execution have been suggested to be functionally equivalent. At the behavioral level, evidence from mental chronometry suggested that it requires a similar time to imagine a movement or execute it, i.e., so-called temporal equivalence (Decety, 1996; Guillot and Collet, 2005). At the neural level, motor imagery and motor execution involve partially overlapping neural substrates (Grezes and Decety, 2001; Jeannerod, 2001; Grèzes et al., 2003). Specifically, these neural substrates are the supplementary motor area, the premotor cortex, and, in a growing number of studies, the primary motor cortex, the inferior parietal lobule, the basal ganglia, and the cerebellum (Lorey et al., 2009). Besides, complex movements such as ball games are not doable in the confined scanner. Here, the present study was intended to probe the neural efficiency hypothesis using motor imagery as an alternative to motor execution to examine functional differences in the brain activity associated with different tasks.

The anatomical substrate for motor imagery is largely mediated by the parietal-premotor cortical circuit including the inferior parietal lobule, the supplementary motor area, and the postcentral gyrus (Zhang et al., 2018). The parietal-premotor cortical circuit serves its function by building an integrated presentation of actions, objects acted on, and locations toward which actions are directed (Gallese, 2005). In particular, the inferior parietal lobule is a site at which internal models and body representations form (Macuga and Frey, 2011). The supplementary motor cortex has been reported to be involved in motor planning (Hayes et al., 2012; Marchand et al., 2013), while the postcentral gyrus is involved in somatic perceptual processes (Vidoni et al., 2010; Yamashiro et al., 2013; Arce-McShane et al., 2014). Thus, different patterns of functional activation may occur in the parietal-premotor circuit among individuals with different expertise levels while imagining the same movements.

Here, the present study was designed to resolve conflicting findings over neural consumption in sport expert domain by extending previous work in two critical respects. First, motor imagery task of expertise skills was used as test task. Since motor imagery is regarded as largely equivalent in neural level to motor execution, the neural differences found through motor imagery task is likely to reflect the true neural processes of given motor expertises. Second, self-reference and cross validation was used to test the behavioral and the neural differences. To do this, a factorial fMRI design was constructed in which basketball and volleyball athletes imagined throwing a basketball or serving a volleyball. The factorial design enabled self-reference within the group to exclude possible nuisance variables related to individual differences and cross validation between the groups to confirm the effect. These two movements were chose as experimental tasks based on two considerations. On the one hand, many components are kinematically comparable between these two movements. On the other hand, the integration of kinematical components into goal-directed action differs between them. Thus, while both groups of participants performed the same tasks, they had only professionally practiced the movements from their self-sport domain. Therefore, attenuated cortical activity (particularly in the parietal-premotor cortical circuit) along with superior behavioral performance observed while imagining movements from the self-sport compared to those observed while imagining movements from the other-sport would perfectly test the neural efficiency hypotheses.

MATERIALS AND METHODS

Participants

Twenty-four expert basketball athletes (19.2 ± 1.4 years old, age range, 18–21 years old) and 24 expert volleyball athletes (18.9 ± 1.5 years old, age range, 17–22 years old) were studied. All participants were right-handed males (Oldfield, 1971) recruited from the basketball and volleyball teams in Shanghai University of Sport. Basketball athletes had trained 10.7 ± 1.7 h per week for 10.8 ± 1.9 years (range: 8–14 years). Volleyball athletes had trained 9.8 ± 1.3 h per week for 8.5 ± 1.1 years (range: 7–11 years). A typical training week includes 5 days of training (Tuesday to Friday and Sunday) and 2 days of rest (Monday and Saturday). The 5 days of training is made up of 3 days of professional skill training on the court (2:45–5:00) and 2 days of indoor strength training (2:45–5:00). Compared with basketball athletes, volleyball athletes trained for similar intensity as indexed by training hours [$T(46) = 1.95$, $p = 0.06$], but they started their career later as indexed by training years [$T(46) = 5.01$, $p < 0.001$]. Both groups consisted of national first- or second-level athletes who were qualified for provincial or national level competitions. The experimental procedure was approved by the local ethics committee (No. 2018126). All participants provided written informed consent prior to the experiment.

Motor Imagery

To assess participants' general motor imagery ability, the ease of forming visual and kinesthetic images of four basic gross movements (a knee lift, jump, arm movement, and waist bend) was measured with a Chinese translation of Movement Imagery Questionnaire-revised (MIQ-R, Hall and Martin, 1997). Participants rated their ease of imaging on a 7-point Likert-type scale ranging from 1 (very hard to see/feel) to 7 (very easy to see/feel). After the items for each subscale are averaged, a cutoff score of 5 (fairly easy) was used to ensure a participant was eligible for the following motor imagery task.

Field training was applied to all eligible participants on the same day before the experiment to acquaint them with the motor tasks used in the present study, especially the motor task from the other-sport. Basketball throwing and volleyball serving were used as motor imagery tasks. Participants were instructed to use motor imagery from a first-person perspective. For basketball throwing, the participants were instructed to imagine throwing the ball toward the basket after dribbling it three times. To avoid possible fatigue or adaptation effect from a single location, five different locations each were specified for the two tasks. For basketball throwing, the five locations were the central location (the traditional point for free throws) and the other four lateral locations (bilateral to the central location) (**Figure 1A**). All five locations were the same distance from the basket. For the volleyball serve, the participants were instructed to strike the ball, causing it to cross the net after dribbling the ball three times. Similar to the procedure used for basketball throws, we specified five locations on the court as serve locations (**Figure 1B**). All five locations were the same distance from the net. The participants were instructed to perform the motor imagery task while holding the balls

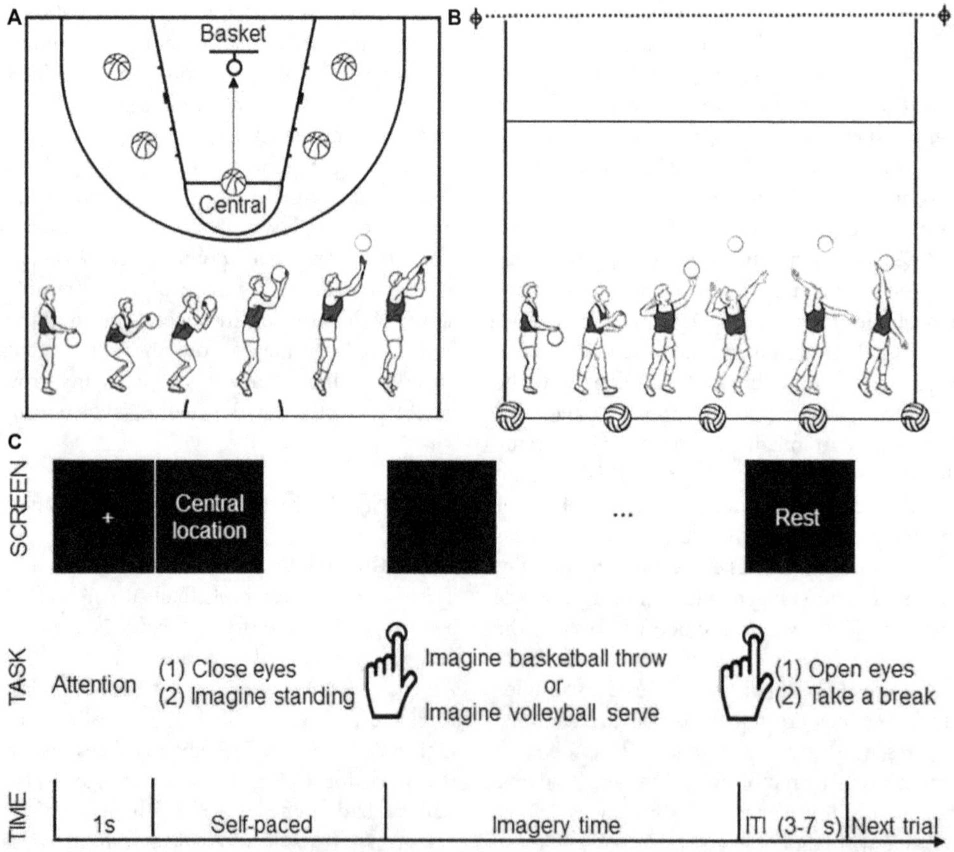

FIGURE 1 | Experimental design. **(A)** The five locations (shown as a basketball) for basketball throws. All five locations were the same distance from the basket (as shown with a circle). The bottom panel shows the decomposed movements required for a basketball throw. **(B)** The five locations (shown as a volleyball) for volleyball serves. All five locations were the same distance from the net (as shown with a dotted line). The bottom panel shows the decomposed movements required for the volleyball serve. **(C)** Time course of the motor imagery trials. During each trial, after seeing a 1-s fixation cross, the participants saw a location instruction. After finishing reading the location instruction, the participants closed their eyes and imagined standing on the specified location. The participants pressed a button to signal that they had started imagining a basketball throw or volleyball serve. The participants pressed the button again when they imagined the ball had left their hand. Following the second button press, a "rest" instruction was presented on the screen, and the participants opened their eyes and took a break. This rest period served as a variable intertrial interval (ITI 3–7 s). Another fixation cross announced the start of the next trial.

as a previous study revealed the importance of implementing task-related motor imagery (Wang et al., 2014).

Behavioral and fMRI measures were performed after field training on two separate days at least 2 weeks apart in a random order. The participants physically performed basketball throws or volleyball serves on the court from each of the five locations. Evidence from existing behavioral studies shows that imagined movements retain the same temporal characteristics as the corresponding executed movements (Sirigu et al., 1995). The execution process of each participant was recorded (Sony PXW-F37, 50 fps) and the durations of motor execution were obtained offline by reading the frame timer of the camcorder. The duration of motor execution was defined as the time between the onset of the first dribble and the offset when the ball left the hand. Three trials were repeated at each of the five locations (for a total of 15 trials) for both tasks. The duration of motor execution required for the total 15 trials was averaged, and the mean value was defined as the execution times for basketball throws and volleyball serves.

The motor imagery time was measured for both groups. Participants performed two runs of motor imagery, including one for basketball throws and the other for volleyball serves. The participants were instructed to mentally rehearse the motor imagery tasks from a first-person perspective with their eyes closed. The motor imagery task was self-paced. Participants pressed a button (E-prime 2.0, Psychology Software Tools Inc., Pittsburgh, PA) with the left index finger to label the beginning and end of their motor imagery task (duration of motor imagery). The instructions resulted in each of the five locations for motor imagery being presented to the participants in random order. Three trials were repeated at each of the five locations (for a total of 15 trials) for both tasks. The 15 trials for both tasks were averaged separately, and the mean values were defined as the imagery time for basketball throws and volleyball serves.

Because both motor imagery and execution are likely to be constrained by the same physical laws (Decety and Jeannerod, 1995; Decety, 1996), a difference in the time required for motor imagery and motor execution tasks may indicate the effects of other physiological factors on the measurement (Sirigu et al., 1995, 1996). Temporal congruence was used as a valid mental chronometry index to evaluate functional equivalence between motor imagery and motor execution (Guillot and Collet, 2005). In the present study, variances in motor time (for both execution and imagery) between the two participant groups were dependent on differences in expertise levels in the self- versus other-sport. The temporal congruence was calculated in the same manner as did in Zhang et al. (2018). A lower ratio score indicates better congruence between execution time and imagery time. Temporal congruence was calculated for each group on each task separately.

Functional Magnetic Resonance Imaging

The experiment was performed using a 2-group (basketball athletes, volleyball athletes; between-participant factor) × 2 task (basketball throw vs. volleyball serve; within-participant factor) factorial design. The experiment consisted of two runs: imagining a basketball throw with a basketball and imagining a volleyball serve with a volleyball. The order of the two runs was counterbalanced among the participants. Each run lasted 6 min, during which 180 volumes were acquired. Each run consisted of 25 trials (5 trials at each location presented in a random order). The participants watched a screen *via* a mirror mounted on the MRI head coil. Time course of the motor imagery trial was illustrated in **Figure 1C**. A 1-s fixation point appearing at the center of the screen indicated the start of a trial. The instruction for one of the five locations was subsequently presented to the participant. Participants pressed a button to mark the beginning and end of their motor imagery (E-prime 2.0, Psychology Software Tools Inc., Pittsburgh, PA). Two adjacent trials were separated by a resting state indicated by a black screen that lasted 3–7 s after the second button press (end of motor imagery). The resting state was used as a baseline measurement. Imaging was acquired using a 3.0 Tesla Siemens Trio Tim MRI scanner with a 12-channel head coil at Shanghai Key Laboratory of Magnetic Resonance. Functional images (repetition time = 2 s, one shot per repetition, echo time = 30 ms, flip angle = 90°, field of view = 240 mm^2 × 240 mm^2, slice thickness = 4 mm, voxel size = 3.3 mm^3 × 3.3 mm^3 × 4 mm^3, slices per volume = 33, volumes for 6 min = 180) were obtained as a gradient echo planar imaging sequence.

Post-scanner Imagery Questionnaires

Immediately after the participants were released from the scanner, the performance of motor imagery tasks was measured with self-evaluation using two questionnaires. The first questionnaire was developed based on that used in Wang et al., 2014 to assess if participants adhered to the experimental protocol. It included four introspective items and was scored on a 5-point Likert-type scale range from 1 (not at all) to 5 (greatly). The first question asked the participants to what extent they have used a first-person perspective during motor imagery. The second question asked the participants to what extent the motor imagery was easily controlled. The third question asked to what extent the first-person perspective motor imagery was clear. The fourth question asked to what extent the ease of performing first-person perspective motor imagery was different between the tasks (basketball throw vs. volleyball serve). The second questionnaire tested the vividness of motor imagery, was developed based on the MIQ-R (Hall and Martin, 1997) and included eight questions related to kinesthetic and visual properties (4 for each) during the motor imagery task. They were rated on a 7-point Likert-type scale ranging from 1 (very hard to see/feel) to 7 (very easy to see/feel).

Data Analysis

Mental Chronometry Test

Temporal congruence was tested with a two-way repeated measure analysis of variance (ANOVA), with the groups (basketball athletes and volleyball athletes) used as the between-participant factor and the tasks (basketball throw, volleyball serve) used as the within-participant factor.

Post-scanner Imagery Questionnaires

The vividness of motor imagery data was also analyzed with two-way repeated measure ANOVA. The use of first-person perspective motor imagery was tested with unpaired t test.

Functional Magnetic Resonance Imaging

The imaging data were preprocessed and analyzed with a general linear model (Friston et al., 1994) using Statistical Parametric Mapping version 8[1] implemented in MATLAB R2013a (MathWorks, Inc., Natick, MA). Preprocessing included slice time correction, realignment, normalization, and spatial smoothing in sequence. Normalization was performed by directly registering the mean functional image to the standard Montreal Neurological Institute template provided by SPM8. The resulting interpolated spatial resolution was 3 mm^3 × 3 mm^3 × 3 mm^3. The functional data were then smoothed with a Gaussian kernel of 6-mm full-width at half-maximum.

The first-level analysis was computed within-participant using an event-related approach in the context of the general linear model. Statistical parametric t-maps were generated for each participant. For each participant, the regressor of interest was defined to characterize cerebral responses to imagery for the four different conditions in the 2 × 2 factorial design. A regressor of no interest was used to model the cerebral responses to a button press. For the motor imagery regressor, onsets were time-locked to the button press that marked the onset of motor imagery, and durations corresponded to the mean motor imagery durations across all imagery trials of the participant. To address the effects of potential contamination by button pressing (Eden et al., 1999), button pressing was included as a condition in the design matrix to model the cerebral responses to button presses. In this way, the regressor of motor imagery would not pick up cerebral responses induced by button press, and this enabled us to regress out the effect of button presses (Bakker et al., 2008). For the button press regressor, onsets were time-locked to the time point each button press was made, and the duration was set at zero. Each effect was modeled on a trial-by-trial basis. Also, the head motion regressors derived from the spatial realignment procedure were included. The rest period was used as the baseline. The contrast images for cerebral responses to motor imagery were compared with those for the rest period and stored for a second-level group analysis.

For second-level group analysis, an SPM8 full factorial model was constructed using a two-way ANOVA model to test whether there were regions showing differences between the two participant groups (between-participant factor) and whether the differences in these regions between the groups were task-dependent. Contrast values for significant clusters were extracted from individual data obtained under the two experimental conditions to conduct correlation analyses. For each group, for each of the two experimental conditions, the mean contrast values and standard errors were calculated to characterize whether the pattern of interaction constituted an effect of expertise. Because there was variance in the duration of motor imagery time (**Table 1**) and that blood oxygenation level dependent (BOLD) signal changes occurred linearly with the duration of neural responses, the mean duration of motor imagery across all trials for each participant was added as a nuisance covariate to ensure that the main results were not affected by interparticipant variation (Dale and Buckner, 1997). Similarly, to make sure the comparability between tasks, the vividness of motor imagery of each participant was also added as a nuisance covariate. The false discovery rate (FDR) approach was used to correct for multiple comparisons (Genovese et al., 2002) at the cluster level with an extent threshold of 15 voxels per cluster (p < 0.05). All statistical maps were overlaid on the CH2 template (Holmes et al., 1998).

TABLE 1 | Duration of motor imagery.

Group	Basketball throw	Volleyball serve
Basketball athletes	4.17 ± 0.22 s	4.18 ± 0.19 s
Volleyball athletes	4.89 ± 0.15 s	4.54 ± 0.16 s

The durations of motor imagery shown in this table were measured during fMRI scanning. The values are expressed as the mean ± standard error of the mean.

Parameter Analysis

For each significant cluster, the Pearson's correlation was tested for all athletes between the behavioral measure (the difference in the temporal congruence of motor imagery between self-sport imagery and other-sport imagery) and the functional measure (the difference in the contrast value between self-sport imagery and other-sport imagery). The threshold for significance was set at p < 0.05.

RESULTS

Expertise-Dependent Behavioral Performance During Motor Imagery

A two-way analysis of variance of temporal congruence revealed a significant interaction between group and imagery task [F(1, 46) = 23, p < 0.001]. Further t-tests revealed that in basketball athletes, congruence between motor imagery and motor execution was higher when imagining a basketball throw than when imagining a volleyball serve (p < 0.001), whereas in volleyball athletes, congruence was higher when imagining a volleyball serve than when imagining a basketball throw (p < 0.01) (**Figure 2A**).

According to the scores on the questionnaire aimed at examining first-person motor imagery, both groups performed the motor imagery task with a first-person perspective without group difference [basketball athletes, 14.92 ± 2.48; volleyball athletes, 15.79 ± 1.92; T(46) = −1.37, p = 0.18].

Two-way analysis of variation of the vividness of motor imagery revealed a significant interaction between group and imagery task [F(1, 46) = 46, p < 0.001]. Further t-tests revealed that basketball athletes imagined basketball throws more clearly than they imagined volleyball serves (p < 0.001), whereas volleyball athletes imagined volleyball serves more clearly than they imagined basketball throws (p < 0.01) (**Figure 2B**). No significant main effects were found for group or task.

[1]http://www.fil.ion.ucl.ac.uk/spm

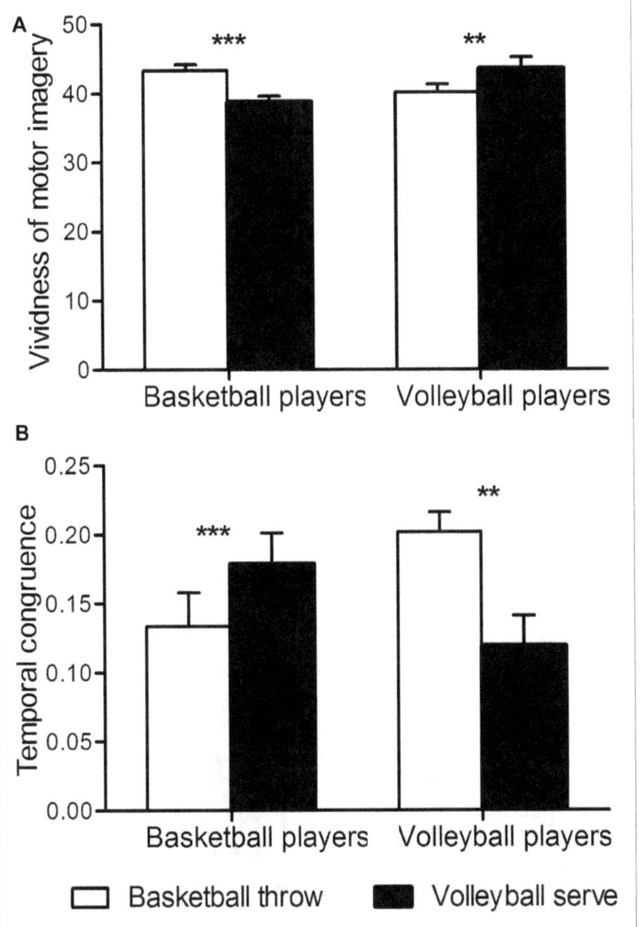

FIGURE 2 | Behavioral measures. **(A)** Temporal congruence. The ordinate shows temporal congruence. Congruence is expressed as [imagery time] minus [execution time] divided by [imagery time plus execution time]. **(B)** Vividness of motor imagery. $^{**}p < 0.01$; $^{***}p < 0.001$.

Expertise-Dependent Functional Activation of Motor Imagery

The differences in cortical activity between the two imagery tasks in the two groups of expert athletes were of more interest. *F* contrast revealed an interaction between these two main factors in the left putamen, the right insula, the left inferior parietal lobule, supplementary motor area and postcentral gyrus (**Table 2, Figures 3A–E**, left panel). The significant interaction was further investigated by examining the contrast values in the parameter estimate. Expert athletes showed less activation when imagining movements from their self-sport than when imagining movements from the other-sport, and there was a crossover pattern for the interaction between imagery task and group (**Figure 3**, right panel).

Parameter Analysis

Correlation analysis between behavioral measures and functional measures revealed a significant negative correlation in the left inferior parietal lobule ($r = -0285$, $p = 0.049$). No significant correlation was found for the left supplementary motor area

TABLE 2 | Expertise effect on motor imagery.

Brain area	Side	Cluster	MNI coordinate (mm)			*F*
			x	y	z	
Putamen	L	16	−27	−3	12	24.58
Insula	R	47	39	−27	21	25.28
Inferior parietal lobule	L	49	−48	−36	24	34.06
Supplementary motor area	L	125	0	−18	60	32.98
Postcentral gyrus	L	31	−15	−33	75	27.96

L = left. FDR-corrected to $p < 0.05$, extent threshold 15 voxels.

($r = -0.218$, $p = 0.137$), postcentral gyrus ($r = -0.129$, $p = 0.382$), putamen ($r = -0.143$, $p = 0.331$) and the right insula ($r = -0.043$, $p = 0.769$).

Discussion

The present study tested the neural efficiency hypotheses. Results showed that motor imagery performance was superior but cortical activation was decreased in athletes during imagining movements from their self-sport, suggesting a relatively facilitated motor simulation process for self-sport.

Expertise-Dependent Behavior of Motor Imagery

At the behavioral level, athletes showed better congruence in the time course between motor execution and motor imagery and greater vividness of motor imagery for the self-sport than for the other-sport. Both groups significantly overestimated the motor imagery duration for movements associated with the other-sport. This difference could be attributed to the extra effort required to represent the detailed movement components of unfamiliar movements (Guillot and Collet, 2005). The superior behavioral performance achieved in the self-sport indicated the presence of effective internal motor representation processes related to the self-sport (Guillot and Collet, 2005). Aspeculation is that this process is the mechanism underlying the effect of neural efficiency. This will be examined further in the next section from the neural representation level.

Expertise-Dependent Functional Activation of Motor Imagery

The experiment's factorial design revealed an interaction effect for group and task in the parietal-premotor cortical circuit. Besides, the left putamen and the right insula also showed the interaction effect. Neural activation in these regions was attenuated for the self-sport imagery compared with that for the other-sport imagery. This difference was interpreted as evidence of neural efficiency, i.e., motor imagery performance was superior for the self-sport, which required less energy consumption.

The findings of present study are consistent with those of a previous study which showed that there was left hemisphere dominance during the simulation of hand movements from a

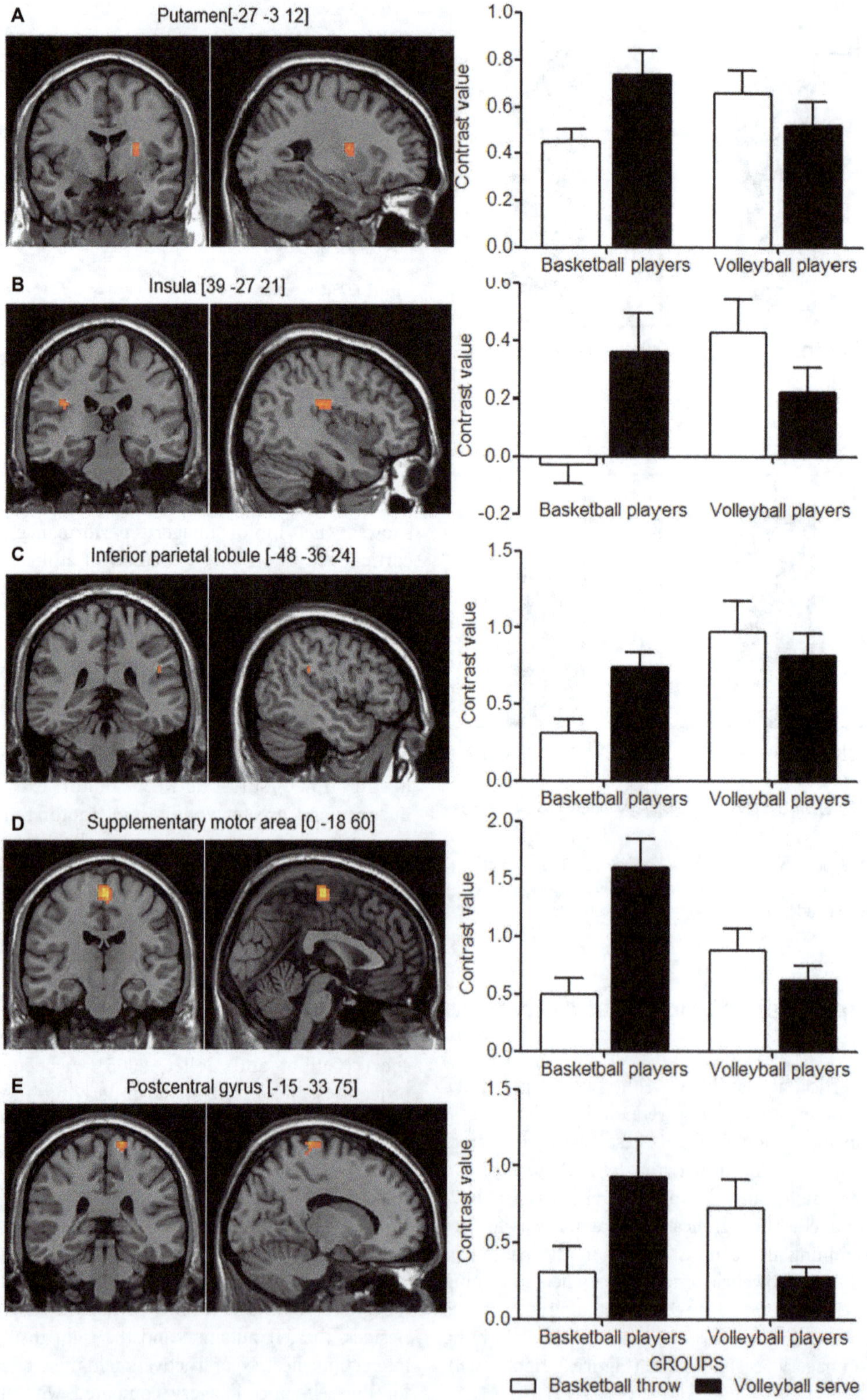

FIGURE 3 | Cortical areas showing interactions between group and motor imagery tasks. The left panel shows the cortical areas with activation in axial (z) and sagittal (x) views based on the interaction effect for group and motor imagery task. The right panel shows the mean contrast value for each activation cluster for each group in the two imagery tasks. **(A–E)** show the pair of left and right panels for each activation cluster of the interaction effect. White columns indicate basketball throws, and black columns indicate volleyball serves. Error bars indicate the standard error of the mean.

first person perspective (Lorey et al., 2009). This confirmed the embodied nature of the motor imagery paradigm used in the present study (i.e., the first-person perspective). This embodied process has in particular been associated with the left inferior parietal lobule. The inferior parietal lobule is a site associated with internal models and body representations (Macuga and Frey, 2011) that has been reported to be recruited when observing kinematic display of one's own movements (Bischoff et al., 2012) and during first-person perspective motor imagery (Lorey et al., 2009). The embodied simulation processes that occur in the inferior parietal lobule have also been emphasized by other studies (Keysers et al., 2004; Gallese, 2005). Furthermore, the inferior parietal lobule is related to the degree to which an action is embodied (Cross et al., 2006). The decreased activation during self-sport imagery is likely because that the internal representation of self-sport movements configured with the athletes' motor reservoirs that are shaped by long-term training and overpractice requires less neural resources to simulate the task. The inferior parietal lobule is also involved in pragmatic analysis related to action-oriented object manipulation (Jeannerod, 1994; Buccino et al., 2001) and codes for specific goals or intentions of motor acts (Fogassi et al., 2005). Together with the premotor areas, the parietal-premotor cortical circuit functions to build an integrated presentation of actions, objects acted on and locations toward which actions are directed (Gallese, 2005). Both tasks performed in the present study required participants to integrate their kinesthetic movements with their manipulation of the ball and to aim the ball at the target (basket/net). However, participants were more skilled in performing the integrated representation of the self-sport, which may have involved more efficient motor simulation and less neural effort.

The supplementary motor cortex is reported to be involved in motor planning, especially for the orderly performance of complex motor sequences (Hayes et al., 2012; Marchand et al., 2013). Patients with left supplementary motor area disorders showed impaired procedural learning (Ackermann et al., 1996). The activation in the supplementary motor area was also relatively lower when participants imagined movements from their self-sport relative to when they imagined movements from the other-sport. This finding is in accordance with that of Milton et al. (2007), who found that the level of supplementary motor area activity was lower in expert golfers than in novices. In the present study, both imagery tasks required coordination of different body parts to achieve a series of movements that were performed in a well-organized temporal order. Additionally, the supplementary motor area has been reported to play a leading role in the action-monitoring system that assesses ongoing actions and detects errors (Bonini et al., 2014) and to be involved in more extensive executive control activities, including reducing inference from irrelevant, distracting features in the environment (Nachev et al., 2008). The level of activation in the supplementary motor area was lower during imagery related to the self-sport, suggesting that the orderly representation of the movement components meant less effort and neural cost were needed (Shiffrin and Schneider, 1977).

The postcentral gyrus is classically associated with somatosensory processing (Iwamura et al., 1994; Tamè et al., 2016). This area is recruited even when athletes passively listen to sports sounds (Woods et al., 2014). Similar to the inferior parietal lobule and the supplementary motor cortex, the activation of the postcentral gyrus was also down-modulated for the self-sport. According to the somatosensory homunculus, this activation cluster was the trunk area. Trunk muscle function plays an important role in both sports but kinematic chains of the trunk differ (da Silva Santos et al., 2017; Sekiguchi et al., 2017). It is plausible that athletes from one domain were clearly aware of the different kinematic chains of the two different tasks and made different performance of them. Taken together, participants were able to generate automatic motor procedures related for self-sport as a result of long-term training. This may allow them to complete the motor task with least assistance from somatosensory inputs, resulting in a decrease in the activation of the postcentral gyrus. A similar reduction in cortical activation in the postcentral gyrus was observed in pianists, who may suppress sensory feedback to enable smooth and sequential motor behaviors (e.g., shifting from one key to another) (Oechslin et al., 2012).

Putamen, as part of the basal gangalia, supports willed, intentional movements (Groenewegen, 2003). In particular, putamen has been reported to be important for chucking movement sequences by concatenating movements at various stages (Wymbs et al., 2012). Chunking allows performance of a well learned motor sequence to be executed as a single unit of activity rather than multiple individual actions. Thus, decreased activity in putamen for self-sport imagery may reflect a more effective (chunked) representation that accompanies automatization as a result of extensive training for self-sport. Our findings were in line with a previous study which found training-related decrease in putamen even after a short time learning for a motor sequence task (Poldrack et al., 2005).

The right insula has been reported to be the seat of interoception (Critchley et al., 2004) or part of the pathway of interoceptive awareness (Khalsa et al., 2009). Either way, the right insula seems to play an important role in generating accurate predictions of the bodies' internal state in the next moment. The model of the body's future condition further instructs other brain areas to initiate actions that are more tailored to coming demands (Faull et al., 2018). It is plausible that predicting interception during other-sport imagery is more challenging than that of self-sport imagery, thus needs more efforts (increased activity in the right insula).

Relationship Between Behavioral and Functional Measures

A negative correlation was found between the behavioral measure and the functional measure for elite athletes. This finding suggests that greater neural efficiency underlies superior motor performance. In other words, better behavioral performance at less neural effort enables individuals to perform the internal processes associated with movements of high proficiency. This is plausible because well-established skills are believed to be based on automaticity and reduction in nonessential inputs of task-irrelevant processes (Logan and Crump, 2009; Rieger, 2012). Attention to such automatic processes can even undermine performance (Beilock et al., 2002). Neural efficiency may stem from the long-term training and be task-specific which enabled athletes to develop a focused and efficient organization of task-related neural networks.

Limitations

Our findings should be interpreted in light of the following limitations. The cross-sectional design of the present study, though articulate that neural efficiency is task-specific, is insufficient to impute that neural efficiency is training-induced. Further studies that randomly allocate naive participants to different sport interventions are expected to separate the effects of training and other confounding factors. Additionally, the correlation between behavioral measure and functional measure, although existed, was weak.

CONCLUSION

The present study revealed greater temporal congruence and vividness of motor imagery but attenuated activity in the parieto-premotor motor representation circuit and the insula interoceptive cortex when athletes imagined movements from the self-sport compared with when they imagined movements from the other-sport. Athletes were more effective in the representation of the motor sequences and the interoception of the motor sequences for their self-sport. The finding that elite athletes achieved superior behavioral performance with minimal neural energy consumption thus confirms the neural efficiency hypotheses.

ETHICS STATEMENT

The studies involving human participants were reviewed and approved by the ethics committee of Shanghai University of Sport. The patients/participants provided their written informed consent to participate in this study.

AUTHOR CONTRIBUTIONS

LZha concepted, drafted, and revised the work. FQ and HZ acquired and analyzed the data. LZho and MX concepted the work, intepreted the data, and revised the manuscript critically for important intellectual content. All authors approved the final version and agreed to be accountable for all aspects of the work.

REFERENCES

Ackermann, H., Daum, I., Schugens, M. M., and Grodd, W. (1996). Impaired procedural learning after damage to the left supplementary motor area (SMA). *J. Neurol. Neurosurg. Psychiatry* 60, 94–97. doi: 10.1136/jnnp.60.1.94

Arce-McShane, F. I., Hatsopoulos, N. G., Lee, J.-C., Ross, C. F., and Sessle, B. J. (2014). Modulation dynamics in the orofacial sensorimotor cortex during motor skill acquisition. *J. Neurosci.* 34, 5985–5997. doi: 10.1523/JNEUROSCI.4367-13.2014

Babiloni, C., Marzano, N., Infarinato, F., Iacoboni, M., Rizza, G., Aschieri, P., et al. (2010). "Neural efficiency" of experts' brain during judgment of actions: a high-resolution EEG study in elite and amateur karate athletes. *Behav. Brain Res.* 207, 466–475. doi: 10.1016/j.bbr.2009.10.034

Bakker, M., De Lange, F., Helmich, R. C., Scheeringa, R., Bloem, B. R., and Toni, I. (2008). Cerebral correlates of motor imagery of normal and precision gait. *NeuroImage* 41, 998–1010. doi: 10.1016/j.neuroimage.2008.03.020

Beilock, S. L., Carr, T. H., MacMahon, C., and Starkes, J. L. (2002). When paying attention becomes counterproductive: impact of divided versus skill-focused attention on novice and experienced performance of sensorimotor skills. *J. Exp. Psychol. Appl.* 8:6. doi: 10.1037//1076-898x.8.1.6

Bischoff, M., Zentgraf, K., Lorey, B., Pilgramm, S., Balser, N., Baumgartner, E., et al. (2012). Motor familiarity: brain activation when watching kinematic displays of one's own movements. *Neuropsychologia* 50, 2085–2092. doi: 10.1016/j.neuropsychologia.2012.05.009

Bonini, F., Burle, B., Liégeois-Chauvel, C., Régis, J., Chauvel, P., and Vidal, F. (2014). Action monitoring and medial frontal cortex: leading role of supplementary motor area. *Science* 343, 888–891. doi: 10.1126/science.1247412

Buccino, G., Binkofski, F., Fink, G. R., Fadiga, L., Fogassi, L., Gallese, V., et al. (2001). Action observation activates premotor and parietal areas in a somatotopic manner: an fMRI study. *Eur. J. Neurosci.* 13, 400–404. doi: 10.1046/j.1460-9568.2001.01385.x

Chang, Y., Lee, J. J., Seo, J. H., Song, H. J., Kim, Y. T., Lee, H. J., et al. (2011). Neural correlates of motor imagery for elite archers. *NMR Biomed.* 24, 366–372. doi: 10.1002/nbm.1600

Costanzo, M. E., VanMeter, J. W., Janelle, C. M., Braun, A., Miller, M. W., Oldham, J., et al. (2016). Neural efficiency in expert cognitive-motor performers during affective challenge. *J. Mot. Behav.* 48, 573–588. doi: 10.1080/00222895.2016.1161591

Critchley, H. D., Wiens, S., Rotshtein, P., Öhman, A., and Dolan, R. J. (2004). Neural systems supporting interoceptive awareness. *Nat. Neurosci.* 7:189. doi: 10.1038/nn1176

Cross, E. S., Hamilton, A. F. d. C., and Grafton, S. T. (2006). Building a motor simulation de novo: observation of dance by dancers. *NeuroImage* 31, 1257–1267. doi: 10.1016/j.neuroimage.2006.01.033

da Silva Santos, S., Krishnan, C., Alonso, A. C., and Greve, J. M. D. A. (2017). Trunk function correlates positively with wheelchair basketball player classification. *Am. J. Phys. Med. Rehabil.* 96, 101–108. doi: 10.1097/PHM.0000000000000548

Dale, A. M., and Buckner, R. L. (1997). Selective averaging of rapidly presented individual trials using fMRI. *Hum. Brain Mapp.* 5, 329–340. doi: 10.1002/(SICI)1097-0193(1997)5:5<329::AID-HBM1>3.0.CO;2-5

Decety, J. (1996). Do imagined and executed actions share the same neural substrate? *Cogn. Brain Res.* 3, 87–93. doi: 10.1016/0926-6410(95)00033-X

Decety, J., and Jeannerod, M. (1995). Mentally simulated movements in virtual reality: does Fitt's law hold in motor imagery? *Behav. Brain Res.* 72, 127–134. doi: 10.1016/0166-4328(96)00141-6

Eden, G., Joseph, J., Brown, H., Brown, C., and Zeffiro, T. (1999). Utilizing hemodynamic delay and dispersion to detect fMRI signal change without auditory interference: the behavior interleaved gradients technique. *Magn. Reson. Med.* 41, 13–20. doi: 10.1002/(SICI)1522-2594(199901)41:1<13::AID-MRM4>3.0.CO;2-T

Faull, O. K., Cox, P. J., and Pattinson, K. T. (2018). Cortical processing of breathing perceptions in the athletic brain. *NeuroImage* 179, 92–101. doi: 10.1016/j.neuroimage.2018.06.021

Fogassi, L., Ferrari, P. F., Gesierich, B., Rozzi, S., Chersi, F., and Rizzolatti, G. (2005). Parietal lobe: from action organization to intention understanding. *Science* 308, 662–667. doi: 10.1126/science.1106138

Friston, K. J., Holmes, A. P., Worsley, K. J., Poline, J. P., Frith, C. D., and Frackowiak, R. S. (1994). Statistical parametric maps in functional imaging: a general linear approach. *Hum. Brain Mapp.* 2, 189–210. doi: 10.1002/hbm.460020402

Gallese, V. (2005). Embodied simulation: from neurons to phenomenal experience. *Phenomenol. Cogn. Sci.* 4, 23–48. doi: 10.1007/s11097-005-4737-z

Genovese, C. R., Lazar, N. A., and Nichols, T. (2002). Thresholding of statistical maps in functional neuroimaging using the false discovery rate. *NeuroImage* 15, 870–878. doi: 10.1006/nimg.2001.1037

Grèzes, J., Armony, J. L., Rowe, J., and Passingham, R. E. (2003). Activations related to "mirror" and "canonical" neurones in the human brain: an fMRI study. *NeuroImage* 18, 928–937. doi: 10.1016/S1053-8119(03)00042-9

Grezes, J., and Decety, J. (2001). Functional anatomy of execution, mental simulation, observation, and verb generation of actions: a meta-analysis. *Hum. Brain Mapp.* 12, 1–19. doi: 10.1002/1097-0193(200101)12:1<1::AID-HBM10>3.0.CO;2-V

Groenewegen, H. J. (2003). The basal ganglia and motor control. *Neural Plast.* 10, 107–120. doi: 10.1155/NP.2003.107

Guillot, A., and Collet, C. (2005). Duration of mentally simulated movement: a review. *J. Mot. Behav.* 37, 10–20. doi: 10.3200/JMBR.37.1.10-20

Guo, Z., Li, A., and Yu, L. (2017). "Neural efficiency" of athletes' brain during visuo-spatial task: an fMRI study on table tennis players. *Front. Behav. Neurosci.* 11:72. doi: 10.3389/fnbeh.2017.00072

Hall, C. R., and Martin, K. A. (1997). Measuring movement imagery abilities: a revision of the movement imagery questionnaire. *J. Ment. Imag.* 21, 143–154.

Hanakawa, T., Immisch, I., Toma, K., Dimyan, M. A., Van Gelderen, P., and Hallett, M. (2003). Functional properties of brain areas associated with motor execution and imagery. *J. Neurophysiol.* 89, 989–1002. doi: 10.1152/jn.00132.2002

Hayes, S. J., Andrew, M., Elliott, D., Roberts, J. W., and Bennett, S. J. (2012). Dissociable contributions of motor-execution and action-observation to intermanual transfer. *Neurosci. Lett.* 506, 346–350. doi: 10.1016/j.neulet.2011.11.045

Holmes, C. J., Hoge, R., Collins, L., Woods, R., Toga, A. W., and Evans, A. C. (1998). Enhancement of MR images using registration for signal averaging. *J. Comput. Assist. Tomogr.* 22, 324–333. doi: 10.1097/00004728-199803000-00032

Iwamura, Y., Iriki, A., and Tanaka, M. (1994). Bilateral hand representation in the postcentral somatosensory cortex. *Nature* 369, 554–556. doi: 10.1038/369554a0

Jeannerod, M. (1994). The representing brain: neural correlates of motor intention and imagery. *Behav. Brain Sci.* 17, 187–202. doi: 10.1017/S0140525X00034026

Jeannerod, M. (2001). Neural simulation of action: a unifying mechanism for motor cognition. *NeuroImage* 14, S103–S109. doi: 10.1006/nimg.2001.0832

Keysers, C., Wicker, B., Gazzola, V., Anton, J.-L., Fogassi, L., and Gallese, V. (2004). A touching sight: SII/PV activation during the observation and experience of touch. *Neuron* 42, 335–346. doi: 10.1016/S0896-6273(04)00156-4

Khalsa, S. S., Rudrauf, D., Feinstein, J. S., and Tranel, D. (2009). The pathways of interoceptive awareness. *Nat. Neurosci.* 12:1494. doi: 10.1038/nn.2411

Logan, G. D., and Crump, M. J. (2009). The left hand doesn't know what the right hand is doing: the disruptive effects of attention to the hands in skilled typewriting. *Psychol. Sci.* 20, 1296–1300. doi: 10.1111/j.1467-9280.2009.02442.x

Lorey, B., Bischoff, M., Pilgramm, S., Stark, R., Munzert, J., and Zentgraf, K. (2009). The embodied nature of motor imagery: the influence of posture and perspective. *Exp. Brain Res.* 194, 233–243. doi: 10.1007/s00221-008-1693-1

Macuga, K. L., and Frey, S. H. (2011). Selective responses in right inferior frontal and supramarginal gyri differentiate between observed movements of oneself vs. another. *Neuropsychologia* 49, 1202–1207. doi: 10.1016/j.neuropsychologia.2011.01.005

Marchand, W. R., Lee, J. N., Suchy, Y., Garn, C., Chelune, G., Johnson, S., et al. (2013). Functional architecture of the cortico-basal ganglia circuitry during motor task execution: correlations of strength of functional connectivity with neuropsychological task performance among female subjects. *Hum. Brain Mapp.* 34, 1194–1207. doi: 10.1002/hbm.21505

Milton, J., Solodkin, A., Hluštík, P., and Small, S. L. (2007). The mind of expert motor performance is cool and focused. *NeuroImage* 35, 804–813. doi: 10.1016/j.neuroimage.2007.01.003

Nachev, P., Kennard, C., and Husain, M. (2008). Functional role of the supplementary and pre-supplementary motor areas. *Nat. Rev. Neurosci.* 9, 856–869. doi: 10.1038/nrn2478

Nakata, H., Yoshie, M., Miura, A., and Kudo, K. (2010). Characteristics of the athletes' brain: evidence from neurophysiology and neuroimaging. *Brain Res. Rev.* 62, 197–211. doi: 10.1016/j.brainresrev.2009.11.006

Neubauer, A. C., and Fink, A. (2009). Intelligence and neural efficiency. *Neurosci. Biobehav. Rev.* 33, 1004–1023. doi: 10.1016/j.neubiorev.2009.04.001

Oechslin, M. S., Van De Ville, D., Lazeyras, F., Hauert, C.-A., and James, C. E. (2012). Degree of musical expertise modulates higher order brain functioning. *Cereb. Cortex* 23, 2213–2224. doi: 10.1093/cercor/bhs206

Oldfield, R. C. (1971). The assessment and analysis of handedness: the Edinburgh inventory. *Neuropsychologia* 9, 97–113. doi: 10.1016/0028-3932(71)90067-4

Poldrack, R. A., Sabb, F. W., Foerde, K., Tom, S. M., Asarnow, R. F., Bookheimer, S. Y., et al. (2005). The neural correlates of motor skill automaticity. *J. Neurosci.* 25, 5356–5364. doi: 10.1523/JNEUROSCI.3880-04.2005

Rieger, M. (2012). Motor imagery in typing: effects of typing style and action familiarity. *Psychon. Bull. Rev.* 19, 101–107. doi: 10.3758/s13423-011-0178-6

Ruby, P., and Decety, J. (2001). Effect of subjective perspective taking during simulation of action: a PET investigation of agency. *Nat. Neurosci.* 4:546. doi: 10.1038/87510

Sekiguchi, T., Hagiwara, Y., Momma, H., Tsuchiya, M., Kuroki, K., Kanazawa, K., et al. (2017). Coexistence of trunk or lower extremity pain with elbow and/or shoulder pain among young overhead athletes: a cross-sectional study. *Tohoku J. Exp. Med.* 243:173–178. doi: 10.1620/tjem.243.173

Shiffrin, R. M., and Schneider, W. (1977). Controlled and automatic human information processing: II. Perceptual learning, automatic attending and a general theory. *Psychol. Rev.* 84, 127. doi: 10.1037/0033-295X.84.2.127

Sirigu, A., Cohen, L., Duhamel, J., Pillon, B., Dubois, B., Agid, Y., et al. (1995). Congruent unilateral impairments for real and imagined hand movements. *Neuroreport* 6, 997–1001. doi: 10.1097/00001756-199505090-00012

Sirigu, A., Duhamel, J.-R., Cohen, L., Pillon, B., Dubois, B., and Agid, Y. (1996). The mental representation of hand movements after parietal cortex damage. *Science* 273, 1564–1570. doi: 10.1126/science.273.5281.1564

Tamè, L., Braun, C., Holmes, N. P., Farnè, A., and Pavani, F. (2016). Bilateral representations of touch in the primary somatosensory cortex. *Cogn. Neuropsychol.* 33, 48–66. doi: 10.1080/02643294.2016.1159547

Vidoni, E. D., Acerra, N. E., Dao, E., Meehan, S. K., and Boyd, L. A. (2010). Role of the primary somatosensory cortex in motor learning: an rTMS study. *Neurobiol. Learn. Mem.* 93, 532–539. doi: 10.1016/j.nlm.2010.01.011

Wang, Z., Wang, S., Shi, F.-Y., Guan, Y., Wu, Y., Zhang, L.-L., et al. (2014). The effect of motor imagery with specific implement in expert badminton player. *Neuroscience* 275, 102–112. doi: 10.1016/j.neuroscience.2014.06.004

Woods, E. A., Hernandez, A. E., Wagner, V. E., and Beilock, S. L. (2014). Expert athletes activate somatosensory and motor planning regions of the brain when passively listening to familiar sports sounds. *Brain Cogn.* 87, 122–133. doi: 10.1016/j.bandc.2014.03.007

Wright, M. J., Bishop, D. T., Jackson, R. C., and Abernethy, B. (2011). Cortical fMRI activation to opponents' body kinematics in sport-related anticipation: expert-novice differences with normal and point-light video. *Neurosci. Lett.* 500, 216–221. doi: 10.1016/j.neulet.2011.06.045

Wu, Y., Zeng, Y., Zhang, L., Wang, S., Wang, D., Tan, X., et al. (2013). The role of visual perception in action anticipation in basketball athletes. *Neuroscience* 237, 29–41. doi: 10.1016/j.neuroscience.2013.01.048

Wymbs, N. F., Bassett, D. S., Mucha, P. J., Porter, M. A., and Grafton, S. T. (2012). Differential recruitment of the sensorimotor putamen and frontoparietal cortex during motor chunking in humans. *Neuron* 74, 936–946. doi: 10.1016/j.neuron.2012.03.038

Yamashiro, K., Sato, D., Onishi, H., Yoshida, T., Horiuchi, Y., Nakazawa, S., et al. (2013). Skill-specific changes in somatosensory-evoked potentials and reaction times in baseball players. *Exp. Brain Res.* 225, 197–203. doi: 10.1007/s00221-012-3361-8

Zhang, L. L., Pi, Y. L., Shen, C., Zhu, H., Li, X. P., Ni, Z., et al. (2018). Expertise level-dependent functionally plastic changes during motor imagery in basketball players. *Neuroscience* 380, 78–89. doi: 10.1016/j.neuroscience.2018.03.050

15

Strategy and Decision Making in Karate

Jérôme Frigout*[1], *Sophie Tasseel-Ponche*[2,3] *and Arnaud Delafontaine*[4,5]

[1] I3SP Laboratory, Department of Sports Science and Physical Education, Paris Descartes University, Paris, France,
[2] Médecine Physique et de Réadaptation, CHU Amiens-Picardie, Amiens, France, [3] EA 4559, Laboratoire de Neurosciences Fonctionnelles et Pathologies, Centre Universitaire de Recherche en Santé, CHU Sud, Amiens, France, [4] CIAMS, Université Paris-Sud, Université Paris-Saclay, Orsay, France, [5] CIAMS, Université d'Orléans, Orléans, France

***Correspondence:**
Arnaud Delafontaine
arnaud_94150@hotmail.fr

Karate will be included in the 2020 Summer Olympics in Tokyo as an additional sport. The inner logic of this activity includes a specific scoring system and way of modeling. Three hundred and nine bouts were observed in the competition context, which resulted in new perspectives on training and competition. The scoring of punches (43.7% of total scored points) and face kicks (37.9%) appears to be more significant ($p \leq 0.01$) than that of body kicks (15.3%, $p \leq 0.01$) and leg-sweeping (3.1%, $p = 0.31$). Penalties appear to be very significant and associated with victory when "scored" by the competitor against himself or herself ($p \leq 0.01$). Competitors must score points and penalties. This zero-sum game induces a simple rivalry, whose purpose is domination and which must rely on a predefined strategy and initiative. Karatekas have to make decisions, such as when taking the risk to score points and penalties, whether or not they lead the score. Karatekas may decide to expose or protect themselves, create situations, or simply remain realistic and adhere to the plan. The question of decision making, which is central to this work, forces us to focus our future work on the notions of expectations and self-fulfilling prophecies.

Keywords: karate, modeling, inner logic, strategy, decision making

INTRODUCTION

Karate is a traditional martial art that originated in Japan. It is also a sport that will make its first appearance in the Olympic Games programme in Tokyo 2020.

According to the 2016 Referee rules (FFKDA, 2016) of the French Karate and Related Sports Federation [*Fédération Française de Karaté et Disciplines Associées* (FFKDA, 2016)], the bouts are managed by a central referee, who applies penalties, and by four judges seated at the corner, who record the points awarded. The different types of scores are as follows: *Yuko* for a 1-point awarding punch, *Waza ari* for a 2-points awarding upper body kick, and *Ippon* for a 3-points awarding face kick or a leg-sweeping technique followed by a punch or a kick. In the case of a tie at the end of the regular time, the referee and judges grant a flag in favor of the winner (fighting spirit and strength, superiority of tactics, and techniques displayed, initiative of actions). For a point to be awarded, four criteria must be met (potential effect, awareness, timing, distance), and at least two flags must be raised in favor of the competitor's colors (blue or red); the four judges may simultaneously award points to each competitor (for instance, two flags for the competitor with the blue belt, i.e., *ao*, and two flags for the competitor with the red belt, i.e., *aka*). The central referee may impose penalties (category 1 for excessive contact, category 2 for prohibited behavior), which must be confirmed by the four judges. When points are awarded or penalties imposed, the bout will stop. Thus, the fight occurs in segments, and the competitors take their original positions before the bout resumes. If a competitor has a clear lead of eight points, the bout is stopped, and victory is awarded.

Three additional rules must be followed: The "ten-second" rule allows the referee to withdraw a competitor from the tournament who is knocked down, who fell, or who is thrown, and who does not get back up on his or her feet within a maximum of 10 s. In addition, the use of video review allows the coach, seated in the corner of the competitor, to request a review of a decision and be awarded points despite the observation and confirmation of the judges. Finally, the *senshu* rule (the competitor who has obtained the first unopposed score advantage at time-up), which is currently being tested in international competitions, has just been introduced for the very first time at the 2017 Open Paris Karate–Premier League, held between 27 and 29 January at the Pierre de Coubertin stadium.

The goal of our study is to determine whether, beyond potentially modeling karate competitions, it would be possible to issue coaching requirements. We assume that the existing literature on the scoring system in karate must be supplemented by issue related to the expectations of the coaches (Fantoni, 2016) and the relationships between the coaches and their competitors (K/Bidy and Escalie, 2016). What types of motor decisions could karatekas make during a competition in an ongoing bout and in their relationship with their coaches (Biéchy, 2012; Fantoni, 2016)?

To achieve this goal, the authors carried out observations during four selective competitions at the French district level (in the cities of Rungis, Thiais, and Orly, all located near Paris, in the Val-de-Marne Department), which may lead competitors to participate in national championships in their own categories in case they are successful (FFKDA, 2016). Additionally, two competitions at international level were observed: the Open Paris Karate–Premier League, which is a ranking competition that allows competitors to score points to be qualified for the 2020 Olympics in Tokyo.

For instance, **Table 1** shows quantitative information on a bout that occurred at the 2017 Open Paris Karate–Premier League, on January 29, during one final bout.

This bout analysis is clearly in favor of the results presented by Vidranski et al. (2015) concerning the significant differences between actions attempted and points scored in competitive karate.

Thanks to this type of observation, we were able to define a performance model in karate competitions (Frigout et al., 2017, p. 75) by using Biéchy's (2012, p. 38) work: the technical and tactical paradox, which requires finding the right balance between "*exposing, realism, protecting, creativity.*"

To this end, the coach must act as a researcher and try to be as objective as possible through observation.

Modeling in sports is the subject of several studies that have proven relevant: from Franks and Goodman (1986), who define the necessity of a systematic model and quantification, to Garganta (1998), who discusses game modeling in the context of better training, to Hughes et al. (2012) in the context of soccer.

TABLE 1 | Quantitative information on one final bout, 2017 Open Paris Karate–Premier League.

Anonymous final – 2017 Open Paris Karate-Premier League					
***Aka* (red color): victory 4**			***Ao* (blue color): defeat 1**		
Simultaneous actions	**Attempted**	**Scored**	**Simultaneous actions**	**Attempted**	**Scored**
Yuko	12	1/0	*Yuko*	14	1/0
Waza ari	3	0	*Waza ari*	1	0
Ippon	6	1/0	*Ippon*	5	0
Leg-sweeping *ippon*	0	0	Leg-sweeping *ippon*	4	0
Senshu	N/A	1	*Senshu*	N/A	0
Category 1	N/A	0	Category 1	N/A	0
Category 2	N/A	3	Category 2	N/A	0
Video review	1	0	*Video review*	1	1

These different works discuss how modeling "can be considered as a mediator between a theoretical and an empirical field (...) in order to analyse performance trends and to prioritize potential issue within the training structure" (Hughes et al., 2012, p. 403).

How should a coach choose a strategic training method specific to competition while implementing several tactical adaptation schemes? Should competitors try to simultaneously validate points to minimize both their gains and losses? Could the Nash (1950) be applied and used to model training sessions?

Let us remind ourselves that the *inner logic* (Parlebas, 2005) of sports relies, in regard to exclusive fighting sports, on the following relation: $R \cap S = \emptyset$ (Parlebas, 1986, p. 208). This relation reminds us that two opposing karatekas may not be simultaneously rivals and partners. This type of game where the scoring system is strictly contrary (Parlebas, 2005, p. 30) can be described by the following formula $M^{+} = \emptyset$. In a competition, karate is a zero-sum game (Rapoport, 1967). In addition, Nash (1950) provides evidence that there is no equilibrium in regard to pure strategy and that there is a need to rely on probabilities, i.e., a mixed strategy.

Thus, in relation to the new *senshu* rule mentioned in part 1, coaches and karatekas should not confuse an offensive with an initiative. Here, initiative in relation to formulating a strategy does not necessarily mean choosing to attack. Therefore, we must examine the notions of *decision making* and *rationality* (Shubik, 1971; Raïffa, 1973) and *expected utility* (Von Neumann and Morgenstern, 1944). These notions are linked to the concepts and possible scopes of game theory (Von Neumann and Morgenstern, 1944; Davis, 1973).

MATERIALS AND METHODS

Between January 24, 2016, and January 29, 2017, observations were carried out in real time by one of the authors, who is holder of a national degree (*BEES 2ème degré karaté*), by using and filling out the official FFKDA game sheets during the bouts.

The data collection method used by one of the authors is not subject to any objective errors, as the conclusions are supported thanks to the electronic device present in the competitions (computer, scoring and video screens, timer), which indicate, during and at the end of each fight, every element of the scoring: points scored, penalties, *senshu*, and in specific cases the victory by flag vote (when no points are scored).

Additionally, as karate fights are stopped to deal with points and penalties attributions, the scoring registered in the specific sheets was possible to make with no mistakes. Every time a point or a penalty had to be scored, the fight was stopped: at that precise time, the author used the scoring sheets.

This organization of karate competitions always uses these kinds of electronic devices. These facilitate the scoring for every observer (the coaches, of course, and also the authors).

The observations were made during six different competitions with various types of opponents, such as children, teenagers, adults and veteran athletes (more than 55 years old) of both genders. A significant proportion of international athletes, including the top eight ranking karatekas in the last world championships, in each weight division and of both genders (Linz, 2016), were observed for a total of 191 fights. In addition, 118 bouts in the children, teenage and veteran categories for both genders were examined. A total of 148 bouts in the male category and 161 bouts in the female category were attended. A total of 618 observations in 309 bouts were made of competitors involved in a fight.

Four competitions were followed in the national categories (October 9, 2016, in Rungis, during which 66 observations were made of children; January 15–22, 2017, in Thiais, during which 80 observations were made of teenagers and seniors and 66 of children; January 29, 2017, in Orly, during which 24 observations were made of veteran athletes) and 2 competitions in the international categories (January 24, 2016, and January 28, 2017, at the Open Paris Karate–Premier League, during which six observations and 376 observations were made of seniors athletes). The study complied with the standards established by the Declaration of Helsinki. The participants were fully informed about the protocol before participating in this study and signed an informed consent form.

The experiment was approved by the local ethics committee of the University Paris-Saclay (affiliations: EA 4532; CIAMS, Université Paris-Sud., Université Paris-Saclay, 91405 Orsay, France; CIAMS, Université d'Orléans, 45067 Orléans, France).

These observations represented a total of 38.187% of national categories, including children, veteran athletes, teenagers and adults (seniors), and a total of 61.812% of adult (senior) international categories (**Table 2**).

Observations were made of the different components of the scoring system and, in particular, the data that the judges and referees validate as part of this system: the date and location of the event, the observer, the category (age, gender, weight), the belt (blue or red), the points scored (simultaneously or separately), the category 1 or category 2 penalties, the possible flags (in case of a tie at time-up), the total number of points scored, the victory or defeat (including before time-up in case of a lead of at least 8 points between competitors), the potential disqualifications, the potential injuries, and the *senshu* (first unopposed point advantage).

The observations carried out during bouts between the abovementioned categories enabled us to determine whether the scoring system may significantly model karate techniques in competitions and the quest for performance and whether coaches and athletes should include additional data in their practice sessions on the basis of a performance model and regular observations: those related to the inner logic of the activity and their consequences for the purposes of scoring or achieving a flag. The significance threshold was set at $p < 0.05$. A chi2 test was performed over a series of the karatekas involved in competitions with Sphinx IQ2®, a quantitative data processing software.

RESULTS

The results described in the tables below specify the number of competitors involved. The losing competitor appears before the/symbol and the winner after. **Table 3** presents an overview of the points and penalties scored in relation to victory.

This table first shows the maximum number of occurrences by type of points scored and presents a significant link with the victory or loss. It appears that the number of points scored, expressed as a number of occurrences, is highly correlated with the use of punches.

The difference of results by category (all categories and seniors only) reveals that the victory is achieved by obtaining the seventh point, no matter the technique used (the total number of points scored). This trigger, which implies an irrevocable win, can be expressed by significance $p \leq 0.01$ TS (Khi2 = 311.75; ddl = 15) for all categories and by $p = 0.00$ TS (Khi2 = 205.26; ddl = 12) for the seniors only.

The results that relate to bouts won before time-up (8-point gap between the two competitors) show a significant difference between all the bouts observed and those with only seniors involved. The percentage of bouts won before time-up, which is low overall (10.7%), decreases even more (4.8%) in regard to seniors.

As for the type of points scored, and given that each technique grants a different number of points, we observe that punches account for 43.7% of points scored, body kicks for 15.3%, face kicks for 37.9% and leg-sweeping techniques followed by a kick or a punch when the opponent has fallen for 3.1%. Such information shows that punches and face kicks validate 4/5th of the points scored and that leg-sweeping techniques only represent a low percentage of total points scored.

This table also shows how category 2 penalties (prohibited behavior: grabbing without engaging in combat, escaping or stalling, exiting the competition area) are frequently used by competitors who have a significant advantage in the score to keep the opponent from engaging in viable combat or scoring back. These penalties are used by competitors until receiving three penalties (the fourth one means that they will be disqualified). A particular case, entitled *Mubobi*, is a warning about self-endangerment (for instance, a competitor who throws themselves at the opponent, by exposing his or her face to a counterattack without being able to block or avoid it). For seniors only, category 1 (a single penalty), i.e., excessive contacts and forbidden

TABLE 2 | Informations concerning the categories of competitors observed.

Categories	Male children	Female children	Male teenager	Female teenager	Male senior	Female senior	Male veteran	Female veteran	Total
Age	6–11	6–11	12–17	12–17	18–34	18–34	35+	35+	NA
National competitions	88	44	32	38	10	0	24	0	236
Weight categories (in kg)	Po −30 Po −25 Pu −35 Be −30 Be −40	Po −25 Po −30 Po −35 Pu −30	Mi −45 Mi −50 Ju −55 Ju −76 Ju +76 Ju Open	Mi −45 Mi −50 Ju −59 Ju +59	Se −84	/	Ve −75 Ve −84 Ve +84	/	NA
International competitions	0	0	0	0	142	240	0	0	382
Weight categories (in kgs)	/	/	/	/	Se −75 Se −84 Se +84	Se −50 Se −55 Se −61 Se −68 Se +68	/	/	NA

Poussin (6–7) = Po/Pupille (8–9) = Pu/Benjamin (10–11) = Be/Minime (12–13) = Mi/Cadet (14–15) = Ca/Junior (16–17) = Ju/Senior (18–34) = Se/Veteran (35+) = Ve

TABLE 3 | Points and penalties scored in relation to victory.

Points	0	1	2	3	4	5	6	7	8	9	10	11	*p*
Yuko	193/41 VS	71/74 VS	34/60 VS	7/51 VS	1/36 VS	1/23 VS	2/11 VS	0/5 VS	0/3 VS	0/1 VS	0/2 VS	0/2 VS	$p \leq 0.01$

Khi2 = 211.87; ddl = 11

S, significant; FS, few significant; NS, non-significant; VS, very significant

xxx/xxx = occurrences scored by *ao/aka* (the two opponents)

Points	0	1	2	3	4	*p*
Waza ari	285/256 VS	10/40 VS	4/7 VS	0/5 VS	0/1 VS	$p \leq 0.01$

Khi2 = 27.58; ddl = 4

Points	0	1	2	3	*p*
Ippon	293/214 VS	15/69 VS	0/22 VS	1/4 VS	$p \leq 0.01$

Khi2 = 70.82; ddl = 3

Points	0	1	*p*
Leg-sweeping ippon	306/303 NS	3/6 NS	$p = 0.31$

Khi2 = 1.01; ddl = 1

Penalties	0	1	2	3	4	*p*
Category 1	264/253 NS	45/56 NS* 14/23 VS**	12/17 NS	6/6 NS	3/0 FS	$p = 0.17$ *All categories **Seniors only

Khi2 = 6.44; ddl = 4

Not significant relation with Khi2, but correlation between the number of penalties and victory

Penalties	0	1	2	3	4	*p*
Category 2	154/140 NS	155/169 NS	87/107 FS	39/69 VS	6/0 S	$p \leq 0.01$

Khi2 = 20.87; ddl = 4

Among the six competitors disbarred, two were for endangerment (*mubobi*) which resulted in injuries

techniques, also shows a significant link to victory. These results (**Table 4**) also highlight a small number of injuries (two in seniors) as well as a small proportion of disqualified competitors (those who received four penalties), both in categories 1 and 2.

The results that we observed for potential points simultaneously scored by the two competitors are not significant: $p = 0.85$ NS for punches (Khi2 = 0.32; ddl = 2), $p = 0.16$ NS for body kicks (Khi2 = 2.01; ddl = 1), $p = 0.16$ NS for face kicks

TABLE 4 | Points simultaneously scored and the *senshu* rule in relation to victory.

Points simultaneously scored	0	1	2	p
Yuko	295/292 NS	11/13 NS	3/4 NS	$p = 0.85$
Waza ari	307/309 NS	2/0 NS		$p = 0.16$
Ippon	307/309 NS	2/0 NS		$p = 0.16$
Leg-sweeping ippon				∅

***Yuko* Khi2 = 0.32; ddl = 2/*Waza ari* Khi2 = 2.01; ddl = 1/*Ippon* Khi2 = 2.01; ddl = 1**

Flag rule	0	1	2	3	4	5	p
120 bouts analyzed	302/292 VS	3/0 VS	4/0 VS	0/4 VS	0/3 VS	0/10 VS	$p \leq 0.01$
***Senshu* rule**							
189 bouts analyzed	0/9 VS						$p \leq 0.01$

Flag rule Khi2 = 24.17; ddl = 5

Columns indicates the flag vote number (0 means inequality of scores at the end of bouts. 1 to 5 means draws at the end of bouts, and so flag votes)

Senshu rule Khi2 = 9.22; ddl = 2

Only nine bouts finished with draws and so victories due to *senshu* advantage

(Khi2 = 2.01; ddl = 1), and no occurrences for leg-sweeping techniques followed by a kick or a punch when the opponent has fallen. This is due to the number of points simultaneously scored, which is too low compared to all the points scored over all the competitions and bouts observed.

As for the *senshu* rule, we observed the following: before the rule was applied, only one competitor won his bout with the flags with a 0–0 score and another one only with the flags for an x–x score. A total of 120 bouts were analyzed in this case. With the *senshu* rule, no victory was awarded with the flags for an x-x score (a 0–0 draw or a draw with *senshu* scored simultaneously) and nine wins awarded with *senshu* for an x-x score. A total of 189 bouts were analyzed in the context of the application of this new rule. Additionally, no competitor lost this *senshu* advantage by being penalized in the last 15 s of the bout (this situation forfeits the *senshu* of the competitor who scores it). When *senshu* is awarded, at the end of a fight in an x–x situation (draw), the winner is the one who scored first, that is to say, he or she who obtained the *senshu* advantage. Each of these rules appears to be very significant in the way that it is applied: $p \leq 0.01$ TS (Khi2 = 24.17; ddl = 5) for the flag rule in the case of a tie, and $p = 0.01$ TS (Khi2 = 9.22; ddl = 2) for the *senshu* rule and the application of the first unopposed point advantage in the case of a tie.

DISCUSSION

Several profiles of karatekas, whether male or female, are likely to win and have repeatedly done so. The karatekas can engage in offensive, defensive or countering tactics.

Points Scored

There is a strong correlation between the number of *yuko* and victory. The more *yuko* a competitor wins, the larger the victory will be. This tendency reveals a possible paradox between fighting techniques that are based on single or cyclical (over two punches or kicks) actions and the tendencies observed, which show the significance of punches. What if the karateka had to combine two or three punches or kicks, just as boxers do, and only cease his or her sequenced cyclical actions and take his or her original position when the referee stops the bout?

In this scoring system, we notice that from 7 *yuko*, victory becomes certain in our entire sample. This certainty of scoring 7 *yuko* or more happened in this study to only 13 competitors (see **Table 3**). A *yuko* is a trigger in itself, both in terms of losses and gains.

Being awarded *waza ari* shows an even stronger correlation with winning than *yuko*. Surprisingly, the victory percentage is higher for 1 *waza ari* than for 2. From 3 *waza ari* scored, victory becomes certain. However, very few of these *waza ari* are scored. This could be explained by the body protection system the competitors use by placing their guards with their arms close to their bodies, which protects from body kicks and enables the opponent to counter the attack or to strike back. This could also be explained by the strong expectations of the referees and judges as to the scoring criteria (potential effect, awareness, timing, distance) or by a combination of these factors.

While only one competitor who was awarded 1 *ippon* lost in the entire sample of this study, managing to score with face kicking techniques significantly tends to lead to victory. This is something that coaches know in terms of points scored (3), and this imposes complex and hard work during physical training for athletes on one-foot postures when not protected against counterattacks or leg-sweeping techniques. This is also true for an *ippon* awarded for a leg-sweeping technique, which may lead to a loss in 33% of cases. This fact cannot be due to the risk of the technique itself, for if the *ippons* were scored, there would be no possibility of counterattacks because the bouts are stopped by the referee to score points. Rather, this must be due to other more complex relationships (i.e., were the sweeps tried as a desperate technical resource when a losing athlete tried to win back a losing match by earning the higher number of points with a single technique?).

In relation to the number of points scored, the results hold, yet again, few surprises: the more points that are scored, the most likely a victory is. A switch can be noted at 2 points. Defeat is then just as likely to occur as victory. A win becomes a certainty from 7 points, but there was 1 occurrence of 67 loses with at least 8 points (10–15). However, this result is significant.

Penalties

Observing category 1 penalties (for excessive contact) independently does not show any significant link with victory, except for the fact that the fourth penalty results in the competitor being disqualified. Further, the likelihood of victory for a disqualified competitor is zero.

Observing these penalties as a whole, as **Table 3** summarizes, is more interesting. Even if the link is not significant for khi2, there is an actual relation between the data. Victories are more or less frequent depending on the number of excessive contact penalties. The more contact penalties that are scored, the more victories that are obtained. Of course, the number decreases at 4 because of the resulting disqualification. However, the number of affected individuals is not high, as these penalties are moderately rare. As these components are not significant, looking for excessive contacts is not necessary, and we would rather elaborate on significant criteria that tend to lead to victory. By only examining the seniors and category 1 penalties (excessive contacts), it appears that contact penalties do not help competitors win, except for those who only receive penalty.

As for category 2 penalties (prohibited behavior), they become intricately linked to victory from the third penalty imposed. The penalties are not prior to the third strike and, because of the disqualification rule, automatically result in defeat when reaching the fourth penalty.

In all the results observed, only two competitors were disqualified because of prohibited behavior (exposing without protecting, called *mubobi*), which resulted in injuries. These two injuries affected karatekas who threw themselves into an offensive without protection to catch-up and who were hit by their opponents. These specific cases are among the few disabling actions authorized in karate competition (knock-out). In such circumstances, scoring a point requires meeting the four criteria (potential effect, awareness, timing, distance), as described in part 1, for the competitor who hit the wounded competitor. This is a situation that may happen to a led competitor. Thus, no tactics can effectively provoke the *mubobi* situation, which is almost always an accident, in which the motor control of one of the karateka is overwhelmed by an irrational action of the opponent.

Points Scored Simultaneously, Flags and *Senshu*

While karate is a zero-sum game (Rapoport, 1967), as Parlebas (2005) specifies, karate may also be exercised, in certain circumstances, according to a cautious strategy, based on observing and waiting for the opponent's moves. Attempting to minimize one's gains for the purposes of minimizing one's losses becomes a mostly defensive strategy. Can this be done?

If we agreed that such an exercise has already enabled an athlete to rise to the top of the world (for example : Nadége Aït-Ibrahim, karate World champion in 2012) or continental (for example : Anne-Laure Florentin, karate European champion in 2017) championships, i.e., that a Nash (1950) can be reached between two offensive strategies in a zero-sum game, the result would be considered suboptimal (Parlebas, 2005, p. 35) according to game theory.

Indeed, two of the rules of karate competitions result in cooperative strategies, thus becoming not significant: first, the stopping of the bout to award points to the first unopposed point advantage becomes a material standard, contrary to scoring simultaneous points, which, as we observed, is too rare of a situation to lead to any modeling that coaches and athletes could use. Scoring points during simultaneous actions is not enough to ensure a victory. Observations tend to lead to a contrary statement, although there are too few cases for that to be significant. Finally, the introduction of the *senshu* rule did not materially change the competitors' behavior by making them unflinching attackers. However, recent studies on the number of valid points scored in karate competition point to the fact that having to balance the risk of obtaining a double advantage with the first unopposed score versus the fact that the opponent could be the one who obtains the valid score if the attack is not precise enough and is counterattacked has led to a delay in the moment of the first combat attacking actions.

In addition, the low number of points scored during the bout should not hide the reality of interactions between the opponents: many decisions are made and many actions are attempted by competitors concerning "*realism, creativity, exposing, protecting*" (Biéchy, 2012) during fighting situations.

Points were scored by attacking, defending, or counterattacking, and very few of the points were awarded simultaneously.

Given the quantitative information described in **Table 1** of this article as to the bout between *Aka* (red color) competitor and *Ao* (blue color) competitor, we can highlight that *Aka* acts depending on what the scoring system analyzed considered significant (types of points, use of penalties, win at time-up) and is able to determine the errors that *Ao* makes (overuse of leg-sweeping techniques, failure to rely on penalties). *Aka* is well known for his *ippon* technics. Did *Ao* want to counter *Aka*'s work by using *ippon leg-sweeping* technics to prevent him from scoring with face kicks (even if he failed trying to do so)? Such quantitative information allows us to assume that there is a need for competitors to multiply social and motor actions. At that level of competition (finals of an international tournament), *Ao*'s fighting approach does not seem *realistic* enough and leads him to *expose* himself in vain. In contrast, *Aka*'s strategy, which is more appropriate considering the significance of the scoring system used, is closely related to the types of karatekas who often win. Additionally, in any combat, the technical level of both contestants might not be the same, and so one of them might have a clear advantage over the other, which cannot be reversed by any tactic.

The bout that we observed is a good representation of a zero-sum game, in which seeking an equilibrium between gains and losses is suboptimal.

These results may also be cross-checked with previous results from soccer (Hughes et al., 2012). Five purposes were discussed: "*movement analysis, educational use for coaches and players, tactical evaluation, database and technical evaluation.*" In comparison with the present work, the player roles were studied with educational and performance purposes, and we present the competitor roles concerning "*realism, creativity, exposing, protecting.*" Additionally, the significant results we present in this article concerning the scoring system in competitive karate and consequently the strategies that we propose next may be the first approach to identifying the Key Performance Indicators (KPI) used by Hughes et al. (2012). Indeed, further work may be engaged in to create a useful KPI for karate competitors.

Taekwondo researchers and trainers have already started working on modeling to "*provide objective data on competitive behavior*" (Menescardi et al., 2019). Their study focuses on technical and tactical behaviors and the regulations that need to be made concerning their inclusion in trainings, and of course, in bouts. The researchers assess that psychologists and coaches may help trainees pattern visualization plan sessions during training and thus elaborate on the tactical strategies to be used during competitions.

These previous studies may be of help for the continuation of this work.

On the basis of interactive logic, and as Conte and Lukonaitiene (2018) discussed regarding basketball and the case of different strategies, as to whether a team is winning or losing a match, we make some proposals that are the result of Biéchy's interpretations, in which penalties may be scored by a competitor because he or she has not yet scored 3 penalties (**Table 5**).

We also propose some different tactics when penalties may not be scored again by a competitor because this competitor has already scored 3 penalties (**Table 6**).

Before the end of the bout, when 15 s remain, the referee announces *Atoshi baraku.* This period immediately before the end of the fight is very important in terms of tactics, because *senshu* advantage can be lost during this period. The result of the fight could be reversed, and the competitors cannot avoid combat, which – to a certain extent – might give some small advantage to the competitor who is losing the fight, as his or her opponent is forced to confront the fight. Avoiding combat (retreats without effective counter, holds, clinches, or exits from the area) during *Atoshi baraku* is penalized with a category 2 penalty (3rd degree, or 4th if the competitor already scored 3 penalties, which means disqualification) and with the loss of this *senshu* advantage.

It appears, indeed more than ever, that the definition of strategies and the determination of possible tactical schemes occurs in the relationship between the trainer and the trainee and that the trainers rely on *rationality* (Shubik, 1971) in deciding how to train the trainee and compete.

For us, the main question to be asked is that regarding decision making, which was raised by Raïffa (1973). Coaches should help the trainees reach the relevant control and performance levels (Le Scanff and Legrand, 2004), i.e., to work toward improving their self-esteem. Self-esteem leads to the ability to set goals for oneself. Optimizing technical and tactical work for the purposes of reaching a certain level of performance will be, in close collaboration with the coach, one of the tools (Le Scanff, 2003)

TABLE 5 | Possible strategic options when penalties may still be scored by a competitor.

Current situation	Penalties	Possible strategic actions
Leading competitor: suppressing valid touch surfaces	Category 1: less than three penalties imposed	– Defending + face punch (*jodan uchi*)
	Category 2: less than three penalties imposed	– Grabbing (+defending with face punch – *jodan uchi*) – Exiting the area + counter face kick (*jodan geri*)
	Atoshi baraku (last 15 s): less than three penalties imposed	– Defending + grabbing + face punch (*jodan uchi*) – Exiting the area + counter body or face kick (*chudan geri* or *jodan geri*)
Led competitor: entering – exiting – re-entering the touch distance	Category 1: less than three penalties imposed	– Attacking with a face or body punch (*jodan uchi* or *chudan uchi*) + attacking (free technics) – Attacking with a face or body punch (*jodan uchi* or *chudan uchi*) + defending
	Category 2: less than three penalties imposed	– Attacking (free technics) + defending + grabbing
	Atoshi baraku: less than three penalties imposed	– Same tactic as above

Vocabulary used by referees (FFKDA, 2016): *jodan uchi* (face punch), *chudan uchi* (body punch), *jodan geri* (face kick), *chudan geri* (body kick), leg-sweeping technique
Strategic possible actions: attacking (attempt to hit an opponent by taking the initiative), counter (create an attack in an opponent attack to regain initiative and score points by hitting first), defending (block, dodge, parry an attack), existing the area (getting out the fighting area to win time, and cause a change of strategy of the opponent that he/she does not rationally decide), and grabbing (grab an opponent in order to prevent him/her to produce an attack/counter-attack that may score points).

TABLE 6 | Possible strategic options when penalties may not be scored because three are already scored.

Leading competitor: suppressing valid touch surfaces	Category 1: three penalties imposed	– Defending with body punch (*chudan uchi*) – Defending with face kick (*jodan geri*)
	Category 2: three penalties imposed	– Counter-attacking with face kick (*jodan geri*)
	Atoshi baraku: three penalties imposed	– Counter-attacking with body kick (*chudan geri*)
Led competitor: entering – exiting – re-entering the touch distance	Category 1: three penalties imposed	– Attacking (free technics) + defending on two sequenced height levels (mixing face and body technics)
	Category 2: three penalties imposed	– Same tactic as above
	Atoshi baraku: three penalties imposed	– Same tactic as above

Vocabulary used by referees (FFKDA, 2016): *jodan uchi* (face punch), *chudan uchi* (body punch), *jodan geri* (face kick), *chudan geri* (body kick), leg-sweeping technique
Strategic possible actions: attacking (attempt to hit an opponent by taking the initiative), counter (create an attack in an opponent attack to regain initiative and score points by hitting first), and defending (block, dodge, parry an attack).

for managing emotions and stress in the context of practice and in the bouts themselves. In this context, the trainer will have to work toward helping the trainee acquire new skills in relation to expectations, prophecies and a possible Pygmalion effect, as Fantoni (2016) showed. Determining the potential expectations of the coach will be a factor in the decision making for the athletes and will allow them to avoid the "*motor suicide*" obstacle (Fantoni, 2016, p. 155).

There are indeed "*interactive dynamics*" (K/Bidy and Escalie, 2016, p. 61) to be implemented by the trainer and the trainee once modeling is included in the practice process, in order to "*schedule ordinary training sessions*" and create a performance project.

According to Menescardi et al. (2019), "*objective data regarding successful behavioral patterns, (...) are important for coaches and psychologists to train and develop psychological strategies to prepare athletes. For instance, they can be used to individualize training sessions, including visualization of specific combat situations. (...) Coaches may use these findings for specific tasks related to technical-tactical improvement of scoring effectiveness.*"

The results of our analysis enable us to understand that an equilibrium between gains and losses is not relevant in a karate competition. As a zero-sum game, domination prevails.

The scoring system described in our analysis reveals that there is a need for karatekas to understand the wide variety of actions that can be used to score points. If competitors have to score points with punches as well as with face kicks, karatekas will have to make decisions depending on their opponent's level and will have to wonder if *realism* is to be favored over *creativity* or if they should rather *expose* or *protect* themselves. Far from being ignored and poorly considered, both categories of penalties should be used. Competitors must be acquainted with a possible scoring knockout if their opponents expose themselves. In all these different fighting scenarios, the sport is a lasting game, where the trainee has to expect fierce struggles that are rarely won before time-up.

CONCLUSION

The presentation of the technical and tactical paradox (which requires finding the right balance between "*exposing, realism, protecting, creativity*") in the context of the analysis of 309 karate bouts clearly indicates suggestions for coaches and athletes, for both training sessions and competitions, to avoid unsuccessful situations and to perform by winning fights, thanks to successful behavioral choices. The paradox concept is used to expose how the apparently sound principles of tactical options such as "*exposing, realism, protecting, creativity,*" which reason from acceptable premises, may be opposed to some of the techniques used to score and how this could lead to a conclusion that seems logically unacceptable or self-contradictory. These strategic choices are presented in this study. However, to pursue this research in future work, we could try establishing key performance indicators (KPI) to make the coach-trainee relationship even more efficient on the basis of significant technical and tactical decisions, leading to rationality. These future analyses may be realized for different competition issues and in different contexts, from national to international contexts and for different categories (age, sex, level).

ETHICS STATEMENT

The studies involving human participants were reviewed and approved by the University of Paris-Saclay (EA 4532, CIAMS, Université Paris-Sud, Université Paris-Saclay, Orsay, France; CIAMS, Université d'Orléans, Orléans, France). The patients/participants provided their written informed consent to participate in this study.

AUTHOR CONTRIBUTIONS

JF designed the study and collected, analyzed, and interpreted the data. JF, ST-P, and AD drafted and revised the manuscript and tables and gave the final approval.

REFERENCES

Biéchy, J.-P. (2012). *Approche Systémique de la Performance Sportive. Systemic Approach to Sport Performance.* Paris: Amphora.

Conte, D., and Lukonaitiene, I. (2018). Scoring strategies differentiating between winning and losing teams during FIBA EuroBasket Women 2017. *Sports* 6:50. doi: 10.3390/sports6020050

Davis, M. D. (1973). *La Théorie des Jeux. Game Theory.* Paris: Armand Colin.

Fantoni, C. (2016). *Attentes, Prises de Décisions Motrices et Performances. Impact des Prophéties Autoréalisatrices (PA) Sur les Choix D'étudiants STAPS Soumis à un Dilemme en Action Motrice. Expectations, Motor Decision-Making and Performance. Impact of Self-Fulfilling Prophecies (PA) Considering STAPS Students Choices Subject to a Dilemma in Motor Action.* dissertation thesis. Université Paris 5 Descartes: Paris, FR.

FFKDA (2016). *Règlement D'arbitrage. Arbitration Rules.* Montrouge: Fédération Française de Karaté et Disciplines Associées.

Franks, I. M., and Goodman, D. (1986). A systematic approach to analyzing sports performance. *J. Sports Sci.* 4, 49–59. doi: 10.1080/02640418608732098

Frigout, J., Laporte, R., and Lepresle, A. (2017). Modelling and scoring system in karate. *Olympika* 26, 73–92.

Garganta, J. (1998). "Tactical modelling in soccer: a critical view," in *Notational Analysis of Sport IV*, eds M. Hughes, and F. Tavares, (Porto: Centre for team sports studies), 58–64.

Hughes, M., Caudrelier, T., James, N., Redwood-Brown, A., Donnelly, I., Kirkbride, A., et al. (2012). Moneyball and soccer - an analysis of the key performance indicators of elite male soccer players by position. *J. Hum. Sport Exerc.* 7, 402–412. doi: 10.4100/jhse.2012.72.06

K/Bidy, J., and Escalie, G. (2016). Analyser la dynamique interactive entre un entraîneur et une athlète de haut niveau pour optimiser les situations d'entraînement. Contribution d'un programme de recherche en anthropologie culturaliste. *Recherche et formation* 81, 51–64. doi: 10.4000/rechercheformation.2619

Le Scanff, C. (2003). *Manuel de Psychologie du Sport. 2. L'Intervention Auprès du Sportif. Sport Psychology Manual. 2. Intervention with the Athlete.* Paris: Revue EPS.

Le Scanff, C., and Legrand, F. (2004). *Psychologie. L'essentiel en Sciences du Sport. Psychology. The Essentials in the Sciences of Sport.* Paris: Ellipses.

Menescardi, C., Falco, C., Estevan, I., Ros, C., Morales-Sánchez, V., and Hernández-Mendo, A. (2019). Is it possible to predict an athlete's behavior? The use of polar coordinates to identify key patterns in Taekwondo. *Front. Psychol.* 10:1232. doi: 10.3389/fpsyg.2019.01232

Nash, J. (1950). Equilibrium points in n-person games. *Proc. Natl. Acad. Sci. U.S.A.* 36, 48–49. doi: 10.1073/pnas.36.1.48

Parlebas, P. (1986). *Eléments de Sociologie du Sport. Elements of Sociology of Sport.* Paris: Presses Universitaires de France.

Parlebas, P. (2005). Modélisation dans les jeux et les sports. Mathématiques et sciences humaines. Modelization in games and sports. *Math. Hum. Sci.* 170, 11–45.

Raïffa, H. (1973). *Analyse de la Décision. Decision. Analysis: Introductory Lectures on Choices Under Uncertainty.* Paris: Dunod.

Rapoport, A. (1967). *Combats, Débats et Jeux. Combats, Games and Debates.* Paris: Dunod.

Shubik, M. (1971). The dollar auction game: a paradox in noncooperative behavior and escalation. *J. Confl. Resolut.* 15, 109–111. doi: 10.1177/002200277101500111

Vidranski, T., Sertić, H., and Jukić, J. (2015). Technical and tactical aspects that differentiate winning and losing performances in elite male karate fighters. *Coll. Antropol.* 39, 95–102.

Von Neumann, J., and Morgenstern, O. (1944). *Theory of Games and Economic Behavior.* Princeton: Princeton University Press.

16

Heart Rate Kinetics and Sympatho-Vagal Balance Accompanying a Maximal Sprint Test

Jorge L. Storniolo*, Roberto Esposti and Paolo Cavallari

Human Physiology Section, Department of Pathophysiology and Transplantation, University of Milan, Milan, Italy

****Correspondence:***
Jorge L. Storniolo
jorge.lopes@unimi.it

When a maximal sprint starts, heart rate (HR) quickly increases. After the exercise ends, HR keeps high for seconds before recovering with a roughly exponential decay. Such decay and its time constant (τ_{off}) have been widely studied, but less attention was devoted to the time delay (t_{delay}) between sprint end and HR decay onset. Considering the correlation between sympatho-vagal balance and performance, as well as the occurrence of heart failure in cardiopaths during the post-exercise phase, we evaluated sympatho-vagal balance before and after sprint, trying to correlate it with both t_{delay} and τ_{off}. R-R intervals, recorded in 24 healthy adults from 5 min before to 5 min after a 60-m sprint-test (from Storniolo et al., 2017, with permission of all authors), were re-processed to extract HR variability power (LF and HF) in the low- and high-frequency ranges, respectively. The sympatho-vagal balance, evaluated in pre-test resting period $(LF/HF)_{REST}$ and at steady-state recovery $(LF/HF)_{RECOV}$, was correlated with t_{delay} and τ_{off}. Both $(LF/HF)_{REST}$ and $(LF/HF)_{RECOV}$ had a skewed distribution. Significant rank correlation was found for $(LF/HF)_{REST}$ vs. τ_{off} and for $(LF/HF)_{RECOV}$ vs. both τ_{off} and t_{delay}. The difference $(LF/HF)_{RECOV-REST}$ had a normal distribution and a strong partial correlation with t_{delay} but not with τ_{off}. Thus, a long t_{delay} marks a sympathetic activity that keeps high after exercise, while a high sympathetic activity before sprint leads to a slow recovery (high τ_{off}), seemingly accompanying a poor performance.

Keywords: R-R variability, heart rate recovery, maximal exercise, autonomic nervous system, human

INTRODUCTION

Current studies have widely reported the role of heart rate (HR) kinetics after exercise in predicting health issues such as cardiac disease, heart failure, and sudden death (Imai et al., 1994; Aeschbacher et al., 2016; Qiu et al., 2017). It is well known (Task Force of the European Society of Cardiology the North American Society of Pacing Electrophysiology, 1996) that the analysis of HR variability (HRV) needs a steady-state HR kinetic, or at least a linear trend of the signal, in order to reliably calculate variability indices like the SD of R-R intervals and the root mean square of successive differences (in the time domain), or the spectral components of HRV (in the frequency domain).

Concurrently, the specific analysis of the HR decay in the recovery phase from exercise has been as well accepted as a marker of the sympatho-vagal balance (Dimkpa, 2009; Billman, 2011). The advantage of this approach, compared to traditional HRV analysis consists of the possibility of calculating these parameters directly from HR time course (Peçanha et al., 2014; Watson et al., 2017). However, it should be taken into account that some studies reported controversial results when the analysis was restricted to a short part of the decay (commonly no more than 60 s), due to the non-linearity of the signal (Michael et al., 2017).

HRV is acknowledged as an indicator of the cardiac sympathetic and parasympathetic control (Task Force of the European Society of Cardiology the North American Society of Pacing Electrophysiology, 1996). In particular, the fraction of the total power in the low-frequency range (LF, 0.04–0.15 Hz) reflects the sympathetic drive, while the fraction in the high-frequency range (HF, 0.15–0.4 Hz) unveils the parasympathetic drive through the *vagus* nerve. Accordingly, the LF/HF ratio quantifies the sympatho-vagal balance (Malliani et al., 1991). This balance has been shown to undergo significant changes at exercise transitions (basal to exercise to recovery) where its effects may be appreciated by rapid changes in HR (Michael et al., 2017). Fast feedbacks from muscle mechanoreceptors contribute to initial parasympathetic withdrawal as well as to its reverse process upon the exercise cessation (Pierpont et al., 2000; Dupuy et al., 2012). However, the speed of the process may vary in response to different factors, such as the exercise type and intensity, as well as the posture adopted in the baseline and recovery periods (Coote, 2010). It is also worth noting that a low LF/HF ratio, reflecting a generally high vagal tone, has been shown to be associated with a better cardiac adaptation to daily life exercise or activities (Peçanha et al., 2014).

HRV tests do not require expensive apparatuses, besides reliable HR monitors capable of beat-by-beat acquisition. However, its evaluation in exercise protocols commonly needs at least 25 min, spanned among baseline, exercise, and recovery acquisitions (Storniolo et al., 2017). Indeed, a quite long exercise is required to reach a stationary HR, from which HRV frequency distribution is calculated. However, it has been recently shown (Storniolo et al., 2017) that the maximal oxygen consumption, which correlates to the individual's adaptation to strenuous exercise, may be predicted also by measuring the HR decay after a 60-m sprint exercise, which is so short that the metabolic rate could not even approach the steady-state value.

In this perspective, we reprocessed HR data before, during, and after such sprint test, seeking for parameters of post-exercise HR kinetics that could correlate with sympatho-vagal balance, assessed through HRV frequency analysis in the pre-exercise and full-recovery periods. Should our search be fruitful, an important index could be easily derived from HR monitor data to estimate the individual adaptation to everyday life exercises. Among the HR recovery parameters, we considered the constant of the mono-exponential decay (τ_{off}), which is considered an indicator of higher aerobic and anaerobic power as estimated from different running protocols (Otsuki et al., 2007; Borresen and Lambert, 2008; Storniolo et al., 2017). Besides, we evaluated the period of time (t_{delay}) for which the HR plateaus between the exercise cessation and the onset of the exponential decay. Such delay in HR decrease has been observed in different physiological markers after exercises, including blood lactic acid concentration and oxygen consumption (Margaria, 1976; Bailey et al., 2018). Actually, t_{delay} in HR recovery has been repeatedly observed in the literature; nevertheless, many authors simply discarded it as a "confounding factor" for the kinetics analysis of HR exponential decay (Buchheit et al., 2007; Peçanha et al., 2014).

It is noteworthy to emphasize that t_{delay} is particularly evident after strenuous exercise, but to our knowledge, it was never correlated to sympatho-vagal balance, or discussed in physiological terms. Thus, given the proven correlation between the sympatho-vagal balance and the exercise performance (Michael et al., 2017), we evaluated HRV before and after a maximal sprint test, trying to correlate the sympatho-vagal balance with both t_{delay} and τ_{off}. Our hypothesis states that these parameters (particularly t_{delay}) might be associated with the sympatho-vagal balance since parasympathetic reactivation is notably impaired after high exercise intensity.

MATERIALS AND METHODS

Heart rate data analyzed in this study were originally collected by Storniolo et al. (2017), who also extracted the onset of the HR mono-exponential decay after exercise and its time-constant τ_{off}. Here HR data were re-processed, with kind permission of all co-authors, so as to measure HRV in pre-exercise and full-recovery periods, and correlate it with the time interval between the exercise end and the onset of HR decay, here called t_{delay}. Details of population parameters and data acquisition are thus reported in brief (for all details, see Storniolo et al., 2017).

Subjects

Out of the 25 subjects who attended the Storniolo et al. (2017) study, we excluded data from one subject whose t_{delay} was larger than the population mean + 2 SD. The resulting sample was composed of 24 subjects (7 women and 17 men, 25.0 ± 5.0 years, 1.77 ± 0.08 m height, 71.9 ± 8.5 kg body mass; mean ± SD). They were physically active, being involved either in recreational activity, or in amateur sport activity with a maximum of three sessions per week.

Experimental Protocol

Subjects performed a 60-m maximal sprint accomplished on an outdoor athletic track. They were instructed to get at the experimental session in a relaxed and fully hydrated state. In addition, they were told to avoid alcohol (24 h) and caffeine (6 h) intake before the test. Subjects were asked to perform the sprint at their best.

Data Acquisition

The 60-m maximal sprint trial was preceded by a short warm-up (5 min with jogging and stretching) and 10 min of resting period, 5 min in a seated and 5 min in a standing position. HR was recorded beat-by-beat throughout the 5 min of standing rest, the running phase and the 5 min of standing recovery, using a HR monitor with transmitter belt (Polar S410, Kempele, Finland). All tests were performed at the same time of the day (10–11 am) to limit the influences of circadian rhythm on muscle performance and HR response/variability (Task Force of the European Society of Cardiology the North American Society of Pacing Electrophysiology, 1996).

Sympatho-Vagal Balance

HRV was separately evaluated into the first 3 min of the standing rest and in the last 3 min of the recovery phases. R-R intervals were pre-processed so as to exclude those falling outside $\pm$ 2 SD with respect of the mean R-R duration, then the R-R time sequence was resampled at 10 Hz with spline interpolation. The RMS Power Spectral Density was extracted by the Least-Squares autoregressive method, setting the order parameter to the value that minimized the Akaike information criterion (Task Force of the European Society of Cardiology the North American Society of Pacing Electrophysiology, 1996).

The fractions of the total power in the LF and HF bands (LF: 0.04–0.15 Hz and HF: 0.15–0.40 Hz, approximately) were evaluated as the area under the respective spectral peaks, identified by means of the valleys between them. Then the ratio of LF/HF power was calculated before the sprint [$(LF/HF)_{REST}$] and at late recovery [$(LF/HF)_{RECOV}$], so as to evaluate the sympatho-vagal balance in the two phases (Malliani et al., 1991); the higher the ratio, the higher the sympathetic drive. The difference $(LF/HF)_{RECOV-REST}$ was also determined.

STATISTICS

Shapiro-Wilk test was used to assess the normal distribution of the data. Linear associations between $(LF/HF)_{RECOV-REST}$ with t_{delay} and τ_{off} were evaluated by Pearson partial correlation coefficients. Spearman's rank-order correlation was instead applied for $(LF/HF)_{REST}$ and $(LF/HF)_{RECOV}$ because their distribution deviated from normality. Statistical significance was granted at $p < 0.05$.

RESULTS

An example of HR time course during standing rest, 60-m sprint, and standing recovery is illustrated in **Figure 1**. It is apparent that HR started to rise in advance of the 60-m sprint, as the subject was readying itself to the effort. It is also apparent that after the end of the sprint, it took more than 1 min for the HR to regain a steady state. Thus, the last 2 min of standing rest and the first 2 min after sprint end were excluded from HRV analysis. Note that the HR exponential decay started about 10 s later than the end of the sprint (t_{delay}), a value that covered about 1/3 of the decay time-constant (τ_{off}). In the experimental sample, t_{delay} resulted to be 8.50 $\pm$ 1.98 s (mean $\pm$ SD), while τ_{off} was 27.85 $\pm$ 6.83 s. The 60-m sprint lasted 9.76 $\pm$ 1.37 s.

Figure 2 illustrates, in the experimental sample, the correlations between each of the HRV-based indicators of sympatho-vagal balance [$(LF/HF)_{REST}$, $(LF/HF)_{RECOV}$, and $(LF/HF)_{RECOV-REST}$] and the two parameters characterizing of HR recovery (t_{delay} in panel A, and τ_{off} in panel B). Since $(LF/HF)_{REST}$ and $(LF/HF)_{RECOV}$ significantly deviated from the normal distribution, Spearman's rank correlations (ρ) were calculated for these variables. Pearson's partial correlations (r) was instead used for $(LF/HF)_{RECOV-REST}$. A significant positive correlation between $(LF/HF)_{REST}$ and τ_{off} ($\rho = 0.42$, $p = 0.043$) was found, but not with t_{delay} ($\rho = -0.19$, $p = 0.37$); note, however, that this last correlation had a negative trend. Instead, $(LF/HF)_{RECOV}$ had a significant positive correlation with both t_{delay} ($\rho = 0.43$, $p = 0.035$) and τ_{off} ($\rho = 0.44$, $p = 0.030$). Therefore, while τ_{off} seems more linked to the sympatho-vagal balance in the rest and recovery time periods separately, t_{delay} seems to be a better indicator of the change in sympatho-vagal balance between these two periods. Indeed, the opposite ρ that $(LF/HF)_{RECOV}$ and $(LF/HF)_{REST}$ had with such delay resulted in a strong Pearson's partial correlation between the difference $(LF/HF)_{RECOV-REST}$ and t_{delay} ($r = 0.60$, $p = 0.002$), while the partial correlation with τ_{off} was at all marginal ($r = -0.038$, $p = 0.86$; **Figures 2A,B**).

DISCUSSION

In this study, we aimed to highlight the importance of t_{delay}, a representative parameter of the post-exercise HR recovery, as an important variable to assess the sympatho-vagal balance in that phase. In this aim, two time-domain parameters of the fast HR recovery after a maximal sprint-test (t_{delay} and τ_{off}) were tested for correlation with the HRV LF/HF ratio, at baseline before the sprint and at late recovery. To our knowledge, the present study is the first that correlates t_{delay} to sympatho-vagal balance and discusses it in physiological terms.

It was found that t_{delay} is a good candidate for indicating the changes in sympatho-vagal balance between resting baseline and late recovery, while τ_{off} seems more linked to the sympatho-vagal balance in each period separately. Indeed, τ_{off} was positively correlated with the sympatho-vagal balance both at rest and at late recovery; thus, it cannot be used to discriminate whether (i) the subject has an overall prevalence for the sympathetic vs. parasympathetic drive, or (ii) he strongly increases his sympathetic drive only after the exercise; in fact, τ_{off} would be high in both cases. On the contrary, the strong partial correlation between t_{delay} and $(LF/HF)_{RECOV-REST}$ clearly witnesses that t_{delay} selectively identifies a subject with problems in recovering his sympatho-vagal balance after a strenuous exercise.

Although t_{delay} has been frequently reported in the literature, it has been often dismissed from analysis due to the difficulty in inquiring the specific chemical dynamics involved during this period (Zhang et al., 2014). Besides that, the persistence of an high HR immediately after the end of an intense exercise might also depend on the high respiratory frequency (Pierpont et al., 2000; Borresen and Lambert, 2008). In accordance with Pierpont et al. (2000), a sustained tachycardia influenced by a high respiratory frequency may indicate a sympathetic predominance, despite the known re-activation of the parasympathetic system, during the fast phase of recovery. Even though some authors (Buchheit et al., 2007; Peçanha et al., 2014) excluded the very first seconds before the start of HR decay, so as to pinpoint the mono-exponential trend, such exclusion may hide part of the autonomic regulation of HR. Considering that a delayed HR recovery has been associated with the healthy and training status of the subject (Borresen and Lambert, 2008), it is of interest to understand whether this delay is secondary to a delayed HR decay (long t_{delay}) and/or a slower exponential phase (long τ_{off}).

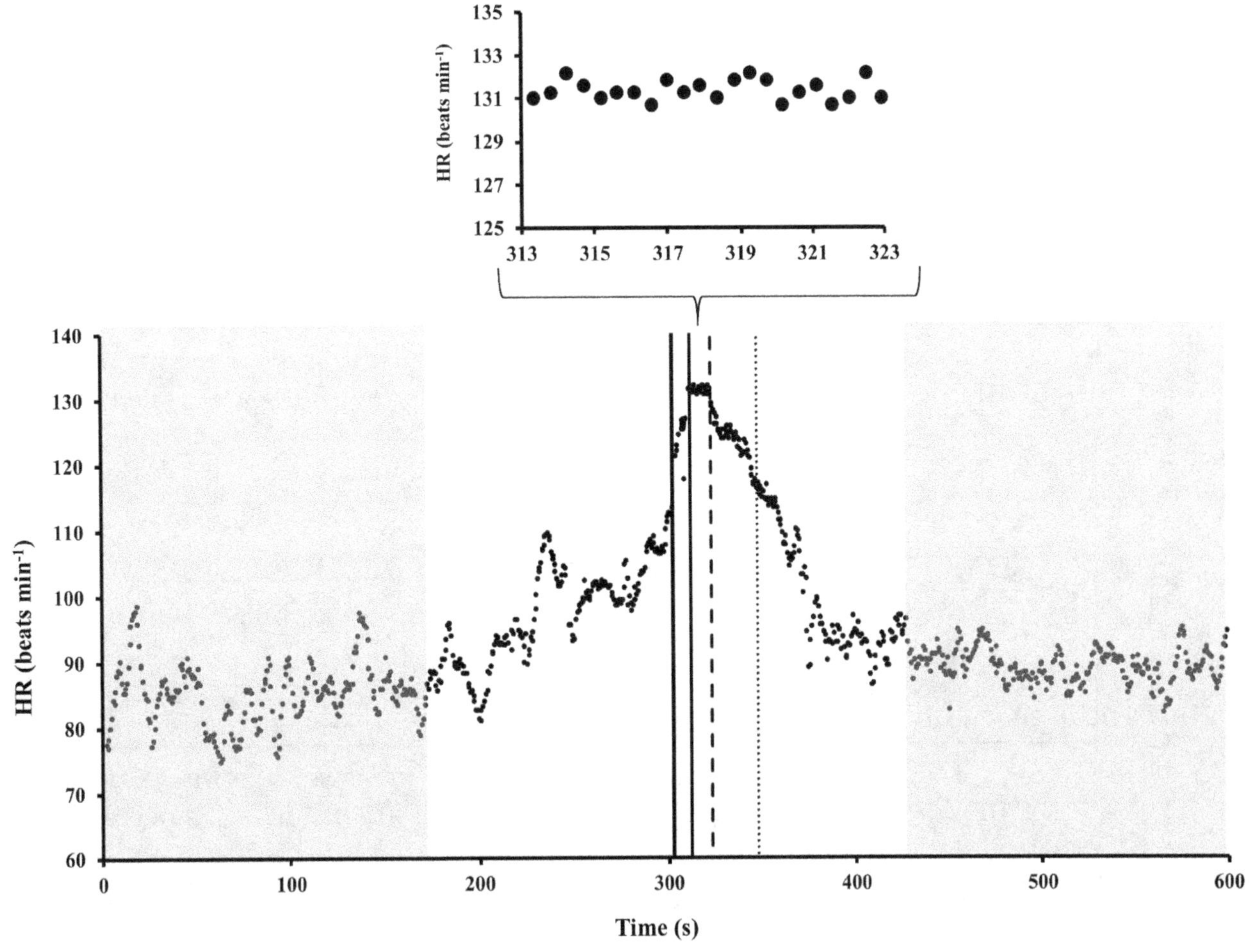

FIGURE 1 | Example of heart rate (HR) time course during standing rest, 60-m sprint, and standing recovery (redrawn from Storniolo et al., 2017). Shadow gray areas represent the time periods for HR variability analysis. It is apparent that in those periods HR was stationary. Solid vertical lines mark the start and end of the sprint. Dashed line marks the onset of HR exponential decay; thus, its distance from the last solid line represents t_{delay}. Dotted line is set at the time in which the HR decay was 63% completed, so that its distance from dashed line represents τ_{off}.

Moreover, it should be noted that "t_{delay}" after strenuous exercise has been previously reported not only for HR but also for other physiological markers, such as the lactic acid concentration in the blood, the oxygen uptake and the ventilation (Di Prampero et al., 1973; Margaria, 1976; Bailey et al., 2018). In fact, it is well known that during the exercise recovery phase, the muscle has to pay for the oxygen debt contracted at the beginning. When the load is kept below the maximum aerobic power, the oxygen debt is limited to that needed for phosphocreatine resynthesis, and the oxygen uptake (and the correlated variables) starts to decay as soon as the exercise ends. Instead, when the anaerobic threshold is crossed, also the lactic acid production should be added; therefore, the oxygen uptake should keep high for some seconds, so as to pay the lactacid debt. In this case, the oxygen uptake (and the correlated variables) shows a delayed exponential decay, which may be seen as a clipped exponential curve. Such curve would theoretically decrease immediately after the exercise, starting from the oxygen energetic equivalent of the load, but actually, it is clipped at the maximum oxygen uptake allowed by the cardiopulmonary limits. Acknowledging the correlation between the kinetics of oxygen uptake and HR, the statement mentioned above might explain the HR persistence after intense exercise. Considering that (i) the cardiac output is the product of stroke volume and HR, and that (ii) in exercises exceeding ~60% of individual's maximum HR the stroke volume stops raising, it follows that HR remains the only responsible for covering the need of a high perfusion after strenuous exercise (Zhang et al., 2014). In this perspective, our sprint exercise apparently crossed the anaerobic threshold; thus, no wonder that we could observe the clipping in HR recovery. It is then clear that the persistence of a high HR should be associated with a high sympathetic drive, influenced by the "payment" of the lactacid debt.

Notably, the delay in oxygen uptake recovery has been shown to be prolonged in heart failure individuals (Bailey et al., 2018). It is also known that a slow HR decay after exercise can be a good predictor of sudden deaths correlated to heart diseases (Huang et al., 2013; Bailey et al., 2018). In this regard, Huang et al. (2013) showed that in

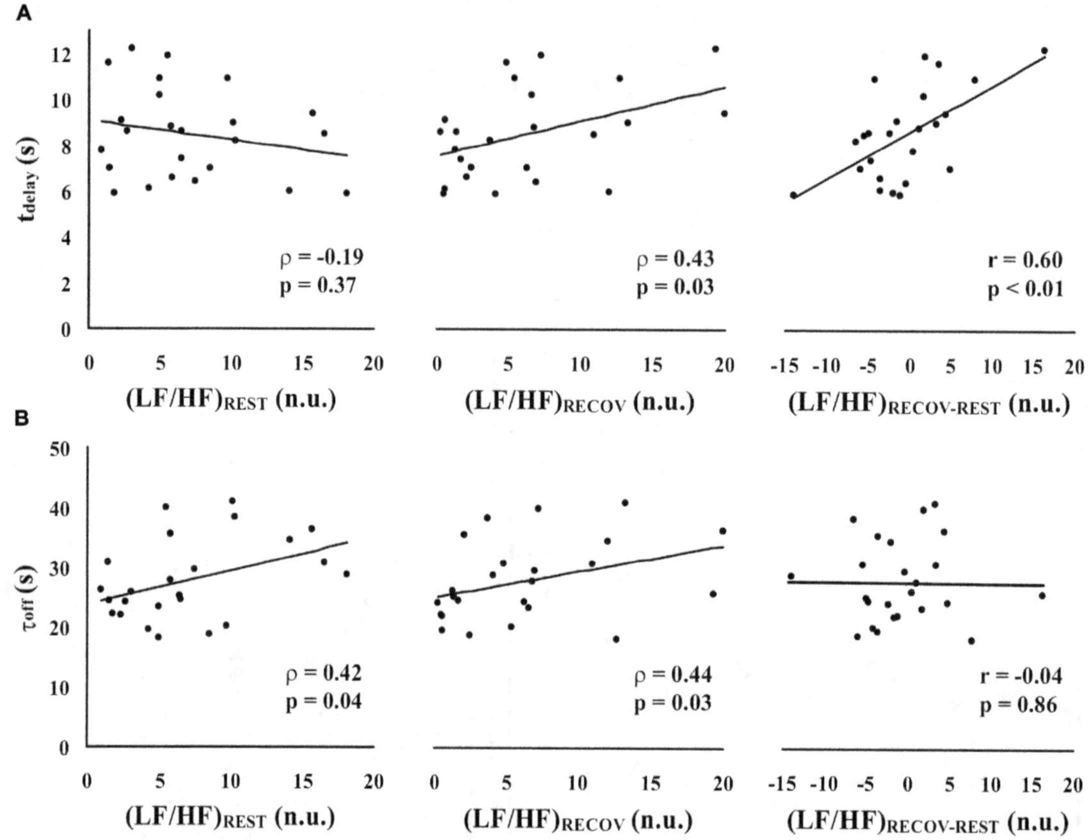

FIGURE 2 | Spearman's rank correlations (ρ) and Pearson's partial correlations (r) between each of the HRV-based indicators of sympatho-vagal balance [$(LF/HF)_{REST}$, $(LF/HF)_{RECOV}$, and $(LF/HF)_{RECOV-REST}$] and the parameters characterizing the time-course of HR recovery [t_{delay} in panel **(A)**, and τ_{off} in panel **(B)**].

elderly, in women, and in patients with normal chronotropic response during exercise, the slower the return of HR to baseline values, the higher is the probability of a vagal deficit. As justified in section "Introduction," our protocol may ensure the identification of potential risks in individuals attending the sprint test, with the advantage of a short-time requirement (approximately 10 min) and of the easiness of the measuring apparatus.

A short comment deserves the heterogeneous composition of the tested sample. Actually, we spanned on purpose different ages, training statuses, and days within the infradian cycle of interest (menstruation in women, see Schmalenberger et al., 2019, and testosterone seasonal secretion changes in men, see Smith et al., 2013). Indeed, all these aspects affect both HRV and exercise performance, therefore contributing to enhancing the inter-subject variability. In this way we effectively strengthened the reliability of the observed correlations.

A final note deserves the linkage between sympatho-vagal balance and training/emotional status. Our results also highlighted a predominance of the sympathetic drive [$(LF/HF)_{REST} > 1$, average HR ~81 bpm] during pre-exercise rest, although we excluded the elevated HR values that preceded the sprint, thus limiting HRV analysis to the first 3 min of rest. Such result may come from the fact that subjects were resting in the orthostatic position, which promotes a higher sympathetic activation even in no exercise situations (Buchheit et al., 2009). However, this could also be linked to the emotional status related to mind-body preparation for the sprint (Choi et al., 2017). Indeed, it has been recognized how emotional factors, such as anxiety, can influence the sympatho-vagal balance mainly during stress situations (ChuDuc et al., 2013). From this perspective, Sanchéz-Conde et al. (2019) reported a high sympathetic drive in nurse students before their first clinical activities, associated with high subjective stress responses. The reason for such a behavior, as discussed by those authors, was the lack of habituation to the emotional stress of the work. Indeed, more experience could bring more adaptation, like in high-level sports athletes who show a lower sympathetic drive despite the stress situation preceding the competitions. Finally, such sympathetic predominance among our participants could also represent their sub-optimal fitness status. Indeed, the positive correlation we found between $(LF/HF)_{REST}$ and τ_{off} is in agreement with Danieli et al. (2014), who showed that the higher vagal predominance at rest in athletes vs. control subjects correlates with a faster HR recovery after sub-maximal exercise. In this regard, it was also reported that τ_{off} correlates with maximal aerobic capacity (Boullosa et al., 2014; Storniolo et al., 2017), a "gold standard" for assessing fitness level. As a whole, these observations stress the importance of a good preparation, both in terms of fitness and in terms of emotion control, to attain a fast recovery after strenuous exercise. Besides an appropriate physical training, it has been reported that mind activities, as yoga and meditation, drive improvements in parasympathetic reactivation through slow breathing techniques, without requiring the same energy expenditure of physical exercises (Adhana et al., 2013).

CONCLUSION

These results confirm our hypothesis that t_{delay} is a significant marker for the autonomic nervous system recovery after a sprint test. Still, further studies are needed to elucidate whether a diverse range of running intensities may influence the t_{delay} and τ_{off}, as well as the autonomic cardiac control.

AUTHOR CONTRIBUTIONS

PC conceived the study. JS collected the data. JS, RE, and PC analyzed the data, drafted the manuscript, and revised the final version.

ACKNOWLEDGMENTS

Many thanks to Prof. Alberto Minetti and Dr. Gaspare Pavei for their kind permission to reprocess data from Storniolo et al. (2017).

REFERENCES

Adhana, R., Gupta, R., Dvivedi, J., and Ahmad, S. (2013). The influence of the 2:1 yogic breathing technique on essential hypertension. *Indian J. Physiol. Pharmacol.* 57, 38–44.

Aeschbacher, S., Bossard, M., Ruperti Repilado, F. J., Good, N., Schoen, T., Zimny, M., et al. (2016). Healthy lifestyle and heart rate variability in young adults. *Eur. J. Prev. Cardiol.* 23, 1037–1044. doi: 10.1177/2047487315623708

Bailey, C. S., Wooster, L. T., Buswell, M., Patel, S., Pappagianopoulos, P. P., Bakken, K., et al. (2018). Post-exercise oxygen uptake recovery delay: a novel index of impaired cardiac reserve capacity in heart failure. *JACC Heart Fail.* 6, 329–339. doi: 10.1016/j.jchf.2018.01.007

Billman, G. E. (2011). Heart rate variability – a historical perspective. *Front. Physiol.* 2:86. doi: 10.3389/fphys.2011.00086

Borresen, J., and Lambert, M. (2008). Autonomic control of heart rate during and after exercise: measurements and implications for monitoring training status. *Sports Med.* 38, 633–646. doi: 10.2165/00007256-200838080-00002

Boullosa, D. A., Barros, E. S., del Rosso, S., Nakamura, F. Y., and Leicht, A. S. (2014). Reliability of heart rate measures during walking before and after running maximal efforts. *Int. J. Sports Med.* 35, 999–1005. doi: 10.1055/s-0034-1372637

Buchheit, M., Al Haddad, H., Laursen, P. B., and Ahmaidi, S. (2009). Effect of body posture on postexercise parasympathetic reactivation in men. *Exp. Physiol.* 94, 795–804. doi: 10.1113/expphysiol.2009.048041

Buchheit, M., Laursen, P. B., and Ahmaidi, S. (2007). Parasympathetic reactivation after repeated sprint exercise. *Am. J. Physiol. Heart. Circ. Physiol.* 293, H133–H141. doi: 10.1152/ajpheart.00062.2007

Choi, K. H., Kim, J., Kwon, O. S., Kim, M. J., Ryu, Y. H., and Park, J. E. (2017). Is heart rate variability (HRV) an adequate tool for evaluating human emotions? – A focus on the use of the International Affective Picture System (IAPS). *Psychiatry Res.* 251, 192–196. doi: 10.1016/j.psychres.2017.02.025

ChuDuc, H., NguyenPhan, K., and NguyenViet, D. (2013). A review of heart rate variability and its applications. *APCBEE Procedia* 7, 80–85. doi: 10.1016/j.apcbee.2013.08.016

Coote, J. H. (2010). Recovery of heart rate following intense dynamic exercise. *Exp. Physiol.* 95, 431–440. doi: 10.1113/expphysiol.2009.047548

Danieli, A., Lusa, L., Potocnik, N., Meglio, B., Grad, A., and Bajrovic', F. F. (2014). Resting heart rate variability and heart rate recovery after submaximal exercise. *Clin. Auton. Res.* 24, 53–61. doi: 10.1007/s10286-014-0225-2

Di Prampero, P. E., Peeters, L., and Margaria, R. (1973). Alactic O2 debt and lactic production after exhausting exercise in man. *J. Appl. Physiol.* 34, 628–632. doi: 10.1152/jappl.1973.34.5.628

Dimkpa, U. (2009). Post-exercise heart rate recovery: an index of cardiovascular fitness. *J. Exerc. Physiol.* 12, 10–22.

Dupuy, O., Mekary, S., Berryman, N., Bherer, L., Audiffren, M., and Bosquet, L. (2012). Reliability of heart rate measures used to assess post-exercise parasympathetic reactivation. *Clin. Physiol. Funct. Imaging* 32, 296–304. doi: 10.1111/j.1475-097X.2012.01125.x

Huang, W. L., Chang, L. R., Kuo, T. B., Lin, Y. H., Chen, Y. Z., and Yang, C. C. (2013). Gender differences in personality and heart-rate variability. *Psychiatry Res.* 209, 652–657. doi: 10.1016/j.psychres.2013.01.031

Imai, K., Sato, H., Hori, M., Kusuoka, H., Ozaki, H., Yokoyama, H., et al. (1994). Vagally mediated heart-rate recovery after exercise is accelerated in athletes but blunted in patients with chronic heart-failure. *J. Am. Coll. Cardiol.* 24, 1529–1535. doi: 10.1016/0735-1097(94)90150-3

Malliani, A., Pagani, M., Lombardi, F., and Cerutti, S. (1991). Cardiovascular neural regulation explored in the frequency domain. *Circulation* 84, 482–492. doi: 10.1161/01.CIR.84.2.482

Margaria, R. (1976). *Biomechanics and Energetics of Muscular Exercise.* Oxford: Oxford University Press, 50–52.

Michael, S., Graham, K. S., and Davis, G. M. (2017). Cardiac autonomic responses during exercise and post-exercise recovery using heart rate variability and systolic time intervals - a review. *Front. Physiol.* 8:301. doi: 10.3389/fphys.2017.00301

Otsuki, T., Maeda, S., Iemitsu, M., Saito, Y., Tanimura, J., Sugawara, R., et al. (2007). Postexercise heart rate recovery accelerates in strength-trained athletes. *Med. Sci. Sports Exerc.* 39, 365–370. doi: 10.1249/01.mss.0000241647.13220.4c

Peçanha, T., Silva-Junior, N. D., and De Moraes Forjaz, C. L. (2014). Heart rate recovery: autonomic determinants, methods of assessment and association with mortality and cardiovascular diseases. *Clin. Physiol. Funct. Imaging* 34, 327–339. doi: 10.1111/cpf.12102

Pierpont, G. L., Stolpman, M. D., and Gornick, C. C. (2000). Heart rate recovery post-exercise as an index of parasympathetic activity. *J. Auton. Nerv. Syst.* 80, 169–174. doi: 10.1016/S0165-1838(00)00090-4

Qiu, S., Cai, X., Sun, Z., Li, L., Zuegel, M., Steinacker, J. M., et al. (2017). Heart rate recovery and risk of cardiovascular events and all-cause mortality: a meta-analysis of prospective cohort studies. *J. Am. Heart Assoc.* 6:e005505. doi: 10.1161/JAHA.117.005505

Sanchéz-Conde, P., Beltrán-Velasco, A. I., and Clemente-Suárez, V. J. (2019). Influence of psychological profile in autonomic response of nursing studentsin theirfirst hospital clinical stays. *Physiol. Behav.* 207, 99–103. doi: 10.1016/j.physbeh.2019.05.008

Schmalenberger, K. M., Eisenlohr-Moul, T. A., Würth, L., Schneider, E., Thayer, J. F., Ditzen, B., et al. (2019). A systematic review and meta-analysis of within-person changes in cardiac vagal activity across the menstrual cycle: implications for female health and future studies. *J. Clin. Med.* 8:1946. doi: 10.3390/jcm8111946

Smith, R. P., Coward, R. M., Kovac, J. R., and Lipshultz, L. I. (2013). The evidence for seasonal variations of testosterone in men. *Maturitas* 74, 208–212. doi: 10.1016/j.maturitas.2012.12.003

Storniolo, J. L., Pavei, G., and Minetti, A. E. (2017). A "wearable" test for maximum aerobic power: real-time analysis of a 60-m sprint performance and heart rate off-kinetics. *Front. Physiol.* 8:868. doi: 10.3389/fphys.2017.00868

Task Force of the European Society of Cardiology the North American Society of Pacing Electrophysiology (1996). Heart rate variability: standards of measurement, physiological interpretation, and clinical use. *Circulation* 93, 1043–1065. doi: 10.1161/01.CIR.93.5.1043

Watson, A. M., Brickson, S. L., Prawda, E. R., and Sanfilippo, J. L. (2017). Short term heart rate recovery is related to aerobic fitness in elite intermittent sport athletes. *J. Strength Cond. Res.* 31, 1055–1061. doi: 10.1519/JSC.0000000000001567

Zhang, Y., Haddad, A., Su, S. W., Celler, B. G., Coutts, A. J., Duffield, R., et al. (2014). An equivalent circuit model for onset and offset exercise response. *Biomed. Eng. Online* 13:145. doi: 10.1186/1475-925X-13-145

17

Anxiety and Emotional Intelligence: Comparisons between Combat Sports, Gender and Levels using the Trait Meta-Mood Scale and the Inventory of Situations and Anxiety Response

María Merino Fernández[1,2], Ciro José Brito[3]*, Bianca Miarka[3,4]* and Alfonso Lopéz Díaz-de-Durana[1]**

[1] Department of Sports, Faculty of Physical Activity and Sport Sciences-INEF, Universidad Politécnica de Madrid (UPM), Madrid, Spain, [2] Faculty of Health Sciences, Universidad Francisco de Vitoria (UFV), Madrid, Spain, [3] Faculty of Physical Education and Sport, Federal University of Juiz de Fora, Juiz de Fora, Brazil, [4] Laboratory of Psychophysiology and Performance in Sports & Combats, School of Physical Education and Sport, Federal University of Rio de Janeiro, Rio de Janeiro, Brazil

***Correspondence:**
María Merino Fernández
m.merino76@hotmail.com
Ciro José Brito
cirojbrito@gmail.com
Bianca Miarka
miarkasport@hotmail.com
Alfonso Lopéz Díaz-de-Durana
alfonso.lopez@upm.es

The present study compared emotional intelligence and anxiety between six combat sports of lower, intermediate and high-level female and male athletes. The sample was composed by 444 athletes (age: 24.7 ± 8.8 years, body mass: 72.4 ± 12.1 kg, height: 1.82 ± 0.3 m, and practice time: 13.1 ± 7.4 years) separated by sex (male *n* = 273, female *n* = 171) from different combat sports (jiu-jitsu *n* = 142, judo *n* = 137, karate *n* = 57, kendo *n* = 63, taekwondo *n* = 25, and freestyle wrestling *n* = 20) of three levels (high-level *n* = 57, intermediate *n* = 137 and low-level *n* = 142). Inventory of situations and anxiety response (ISRA) provided an independent evaluation for the three systems: cognitive, motor and physiological, as well as a total with four factors of analysis (anxiety before the evaluation, interpersonal, phobic and before habitual, and daily situations). Trait Meta-Mood Scale (TMMS-24) verified emotional intelligence scales. Descriptive results are demonstrated by percentage or median (first quartile Q1; third quartile Q3), Kruskal-Wallis and Mann-Whitney tests were conducted to compare groups, $p \leq 0.05$. The main results demonstrated 10% more total anxiety for wrestling and judo compared to the other groups ($p \leq 0.05$). Female athletes showed 15% more anxiety than men, while emotional attention demonstrated 10% better results for women. Significant differences were observed between high- versus low-level athletes in the total anxiety with 85 (44; 143) versus 122 (69; 186) of ISRA index and emotional repair with 30 (25; 34) versus 27 (22; 32) of TMMS-24 index. Emotional intelligence seems to be higher in female and in higher level, while anxiety appears to be prevalent in judo and wrestling, low-level and in female athletes. These outcomes provide support for the hypothesis that emotional abilities are an important contributor to emotional intelligence, particularly differentiating high level athletes than other levels. Results can be incorporated into strategies for reducing anxiety and improving emotional intelligence, considering particularities of gender and level groups.

Keywords: mood, martial arts, psychology, sports, sexual and gender disorders, anxiety

INTRODUCTION

Anxiety is a sensation of uneasiness and worry, typically generalized and unfocused as an overreaction to a condition that is only subjectively seen as intimidating (Brandt et al., 2018; Tahtinen and Kristjansdottir, 2018). This feeling has been an essential concept for sports psychology and has demanded intensive investigation in combat sports for its effects on championship performance in karate (Friesen et al., 2018), judo (Matsumoto et al., 2000; Interdonato et al., 2013), kendo (Usui et al., 2018), jiu-jitsu (Andreato et al., 2014), taekwondo (Maloney et al., 2018), and wrestling (Bawa, 2010). Despite such well-known concern, martial arts and combat sports practices that originally bring philosophical aspects are supposed to assist practitioners in self-control, an aspect of inhibitory control, as the ability to regulate one's emotions, thoughts, and behavior in the face of anxieties and impulses.

One of the major difficulties confronting the researcher of combat sports in anxiety studies is the assessment of situational anxiety response or state anxiety. This assessment has been showed using behavioral (Tiric-Campara et al., 2012), physiological (Capranica et al., 2017), and/or with self-report techniques (Cerin and Barnett, 2011; Coswig et al., 2018). A variety of self-report procedures in combat sports has been used with a practical degree of success. A collective instrument to measure anxiety is the item response scale, in which the total item scores replied in the "anxious" way is the quantity of anxiety (Cheng and McCarthy, 2018). Preceding authors have developed anxiety traits questionnaires that were especially tailored to sports and was denominated as the sport competition anxiety test (SCAT) used in karate (Terry and Slade, 1995) and judo with higher values for female than male athletes (Wong et al., 2006; Interdonato et al., 2013). Recently, comparisons of mood states, using the Brunel Mood Scale (BRUMS), associated with outcomes achieved by female and male athletes in high-level judo and Brazilian jiu-jitsu (BJJ) championships demonstrated that female judo athletes had higher depression and vigor index than BJJ athletes (Brandt et al., 2019), while the logistic regression revealed that higher levels of anger and tension increased athletes' chances of performing well in a match by 23% and 13%, respectively (Brandt et al., 2019). Overall, authors observed a significant relationship between mood state and sports performance (Brandt et al., 2019).

Presently, two different lines of study can be found in meta-mood combat sports research. The first one is focused on insightful experience of mood as state, as BRUMS (Wong et al., 2006; Brandt et al., 2019). Much of this investigation is concerned in investigating how a fighter's thoughts may be affected by his/her mood state, and in considerate the various types of mood regulation (Jin, 1992; Terry and Slade, 1995). In addition, the second line is interested in more stable affective capacities that people routinely use to experience their feelings and moods (Salovey et al., 1995; Filaire et al., 2011; Espinoza-Venegas et al., 2015). This approach is denominated trait-meta mood research for which Salovey et al. (1995) developed the Trait Meta-Mood Scale (TMMS). In the present article we focused on this latter approach in combat sports, using a brief description of the TMMS-24, its three dimensions (Attention, Clarity, and Repair). Consequently, coaching staff and athletes should monitor athletes' mood and anxiety states to ensure that they are in optimal condition to perform and use psychological interferences to care athlete's preparation. However, more studies have compared gender differences, anxiety, and emotional intelligence levels between martial arts practice and combat sports.

Researchers recognize that any measure of sport anxiety must take into consideration cognitive anxiety (negative thoughts, worry) and somatic anxiety (physiological response) (Terry and Slade, 1995). The Competitive State Anxiety Inventory (CSAI-2) considers the difference between Anxiety state (i.e., momentary anxiety) and Anxiety trait (i.e., chronic anxiety) and distinguishes between cognitive and somatic anxiety (Smith et al., 2006). The CSAI-2 verified effects of anxiety in novice karate performers on visual search strategy, changing their peripheral narrowing or increasing susceptibility to peripheral distractors in response to taped offensive karate sequences (Williams and Elliott, 1999). Using CSAI-2, preceding authors demonstrated that cognitive and somatic anxiety were higher in interregional compared to regional judo championships with positive associations with cortisol (Filaire et al., 2001). Bringing together the behavioral and interactive approaches in the development of the Anxiety Situation and Response Inventory – ISRA (Miguel-Tobal and Cano-Vindel, 2002), an Inventory in the Situation-Response format, designed to assess the frequency with which manifests itself in a series of cognitive responses, physiological and motor disorders before different situations (i.e., of evaluation, interpersonal, phobic, and of the daily life). The ISRA psychometric properties, concerning convergent validity, as well as their capacity for discrimination, both between groups with various anxiety disorders, as between anxiety and depression (Miguel-Tobal and Cano-Vindel, 2002). Several adaptations of the original inventory have also been elaborated, oriented toward the valuation of anxiety in highly specific contexts, such as anxiety for medical revisions and to value the eagerness of the pilots of the Air Force (Miguel-Tobal and Cano-Vindel, 2002).The practical applications of these psychological instruments in combat sports are important to incorporate self-regulation strategies.

Self-regulation of anxiety plays an essential role in competitive and professional combat sport (Diamond, 2012; Breitschuh et al., 2018). During championship, for example, it is important to stick to one's competition plan and not give up when it gets tough but rather to mobilize additional energy (Alsamir Tibana et al., 2019). Self-regulation of anxiety is similarly a required condition for maintaining practice during long and exhausting periods of training that require concentration (Finkenberg et al., 1992; Lakes et al., 2013). This is particularly crucial if the training is under conditions of high demand and, in itself is not very motivating, but nevertheless active (Jin, 1992; Matsumoto et al., 2000). The contributions of preceding studies have shown anxiety as an eminent problem in different combat sports (Terry and Slade, 1995; Williams and Elliott, 1999; Tiric-Campara et al., 2012; Interdonato et al., 2013). However, the actual psychological distance between points or scores on these scales is typically unknown, while the Interval Scale of Anxiety Response

Scale (ISAR) can provide a sensitive instrument for measuring situational anxiety (Heaton et al., 2007).

Therefore, the aim was to compare emotional intelligence and anxiety between six combat sports of lower, intermediate and high-level female and male athletes. Based on these assumptions, our first hypothesis suggested that those athletes who perform combat sports and have a higher performance would show higher emotional intelligence and lower anxiety levels, measured by the ISRA than athletes of combat sports with a lower performance. The second hypothesis is regarding gender differences, being that female who train and compete in combat sports will have higher anxiety scores than male, as measured through the ISRA.

MATERIALS AND METHODS

Study Design

Present study is a cross-sectional study. We applied a descriptive method in which anxiety and emotional intelligence in athletes were analyzed according to their competitive levels. As dependent variables we used: emotional intelligence and anxiety; and as independent variables: competitive levels (low, medium and high) and gender (male and female). The measures were carried out in two situations: (a) competitions when the athletes were in qualification procedures and weighing (24-h before the competition); and (b) during national trainings. All measurements were performed by a single researcher, with ISRA applied first, followed by the TMMS-24. The aims and risks of the study were informed to the participants and they signed the Informed Consent Form. This protocol was approved by the Research Ethics Committee of the University in which it was performed.

Sample

The following inclusion criteria were applied: (a) be ≥15 years of age, (b) to practice and compete in jiu-jitsu, judo, karate, kendo, taekwondo and wrestling (≥5 years). 1,400 questionnaires were applied to carry out the study, of which 922 were returned, and 476 were rejected because they presented incomplete information, therefore the final sample was composed by 444 athletes (age: 24.7 ± 8.8 years, body mass: 72.4 ± 12.1 kg, height: 1.82 ± 0.3 m, and practice time: 13.1 ± 7.4 years) separated by sex (female = 171, male = 273) from different combat sports (Jiu-jitsu = 142, judo = 137, karate = 57, kendo = 63, taekwondo = 25, and freestyle wrestling = 20) of three levels (high level = 57, intermediate = 137, and lower level = 142). Regarding performance, the athletes were classified as: (a) low (compete, but without regional medals; female = 59 and male = 126); (b) medium (compete and own regional and national medals; female = 80 and male = 112); and (c) high (they compete and were classified in the top 5 in the continental or world championships; female = 33 and male = 36).

Measurements

The Trait Meta-Mood Scale (TMMS-24) (Salovey et al., 1995) or Emotional Intelligence Scale translated into Spanish (Fernández-Berrocal et al., 2004) was used. This inventory consists of 24 items that are subdivided into three subscales or dimensions: (a) emotional attention; (b) emotional clarity; and (c) emotional repair. The score for each of these subscales is classified into three ranges. For the emotional perceived subscale, the middle score range (22–32 in male; 25–35 in female) indicates adequate emotional attention, and scores in the high (>33 in male; >36 in female) or low (<21 in male; <24 in female) range indicate that emotional attention should be improved. In contrast, for the clarity subscale, scores in the low range indicate a need for improvement (<25 in male, <23 in female), those in the middle range (26–35 in male; 24–34 in female) indicate adequate clarity, and those in the high range (>36 in male; >35 in female) indicate excellent emotional clarity. Likewise, in the emotional repair subscale, low scores (<23 in male and female) indicate the need for improvement, scores in the middle range (24–35 in male, and 24–34 in female) indicate adequate repair, and high scores (>36 in male, >35 in female) indicate excellent emotional repair. In the questionnaire, individuals must rate each of their responses on a Likert scale from one to five points to indicate their level of agreement. The total score is obtained by adding the responses from each sub-scale, each of which ranges from eight to 40 points.

ISRA

Inventory of situations and anxiety responses provides an independent evaluation for the three response systems: cognitive, motor and physiological, as well as a total. It also includes four factors of analysis: anxiety before the evaluation (FI), interpersonal (F-II), phobic (F-III), and before habitual and daily situations (FIV). This enabled us to develop a profile of individual reactivity and measurements followed preceding protocol (Miguel-Tobal and Cano-Vindel, 2002). The athlete had to indicate the frequency with which each one of the anxiety responses appears in the proposed situation according to a Likert scale of 5 points. The original version of the ISRA was used consisting of 224 items in an open situation. These items are composed of an interaction of 22 situations and 24 responses. We obtained direct scores and subsequently calculated a percentile that offers a scale for each subject in each of the measures. The objective of passing this inventory was to see how the anxiety of the subjects was distributed in terms of the triple response system (motor, physiological, and cognitive) and to observe their general anxiety. Regarding the factors that it offers us, we consider the FI to be important since it measures the anxiety before the evaluation. In any case, the others were analyzed to see if there were any other differences. In the case of athletes, one of the factors that is indicated as causing anxiety is precisely the fear of being evaluated or doing it badly and failing (factor I of the ISRA measures the anxiety before the evaluation).

To estimate the internal reliability coefficient of the questionnaire items, the reliability used the Cronbach's alpha (a) coefficient, since an analysis based on internal consistency of the items (Artioli et al., 2010; Molanorouzi et al., 2014). The coefficient "alpha" is the designation of the statistical procedure using scales with Likert type items and this method was used because the responses to the items are distributed by an ordinal scale (Shojima and Toyoda, 2002; Okada, 2015). The methods based on the internal consistency of the items tend to supplant the stability-based coefficients, thus requiring higher than or equal to 0.70 (Moret et al., 1993; Sun et al., 2007). The reliability of the TMMS-24 instrument for the Spanish subscales were Emotional Attention $\alpha = 0.90$, Emotional Clarity $\alpha = 0.90$, and Emotional Repair $\alpha = 0.86$ (Fernández-Berrocal et al., 2004). In addition, the spanish version of the Inventory of Situations and Responses of Anxiety (ISRA) (Miguel-Tobal and Cano-Vindel, 2002). The reliability of the TMMS-24 instrument for the Spanish subscales were $\alpha = 0.87$ cognitive, $\alpha = 0.85$ physiological, and $\alpha = 0.74$ motor responses of anxiety (Martínez-Sánchez et al., 1995; Ziv and Lidor, 2013).

Statistical Analysis

Descriptive data is presented as median [25th percentile; 75th percentile] values and the Kruskal-Wallis One-way Analysis of Variance and pairwise Mann-Whitney tests were conducted to compare ISRA frequencies between groups. For the Kruskal-Wallis, the effect size was calculated as $ES = \sqrt{(chi^2/N)}$, where chi^2 is derived from the Kruskal-Wallis test results and N is the total number of observations (Rosenthal and DiMatteo, 2001). For the Mann-Whitney test, the effect size was calculated as $r = Z/\sqrt{N}$, where Z is derived from the Mann-Whitney test results and N is the total number of observations, and ES was interpreted as follows: small ($r = 0.1$), medium ($r = 0.3$), or large ($r = 0.5$). The significance level of $p \leq 0.05$ was used. All analyses were conducted using SPSS 20.0 for Windows.

RESULTS

Descriptive analysis of ISRA and TMMS-24 between combat sports are shown in **Table 1**. Jiu-jitsu athletes demonstrated lower values of cognitive anxiety than judo ($p = 0.26$) or kendo athletes ($p = 0.033$). The Judo group showed higher cognitive anxiety than karate ($p = 0.005$), and karate presented lower levels of cognitive anxiety than kendo ($p = 0.006$). Kendo was different from taekwondo ($p = 0.047$). Judo athletes presented higher ISRA T than Jiu-jitsu ($p = 0.040$) or kendo athletes ($p = 0.005$), while karate presented lower values of total anxiety than kendo ($p = 0.021$) and wrestling ($p = 0.038$).

The Jiu-jitsu group showed similar results of total anxiety from karate ($p = 0.17$), kendo ($p = 0.21$), taekwondo ($p = 0.65$), and wrestling ($p = 0.19$). Judo presented similar results of total anxiety when compared with kendo ($p = 0.57$), taekwondo ($p = 0.38$), and wrestling ($p = 0.87$). Karate presented similar results for total anxiety as taekwondo ($p = 0.19$). Total anxiety comparison for kendo, taekwondo and wrestling did not present a significant effect ($p = 0.532$ and $p = 0.85$). Similar results of total anxiety were observed between jiu-jitsu ($p = 0.52$), karate ($p = 0.20$), taekwondo ($p = 0.37$) and wrestling ($p = 0.87$); judo and kendo ($p = 0.75$), taekwondo ($p = 0.49$), and wrestling ($p = 0.28$).

Judo had higher motor anxiety than karate ($p = 0.015$) and Jiu-jitsu ($p = 0.047$), and karate had lower motor anxiety than wrestling ($p = 0.015$). Jiu-jitsu had similar motor anxiety to karate ($p = 0.32$), kendo ($p = 0.42$), taekwondo ($p = 0.85$), and wrestling ($p = 0.069$); karate was similar to kendo ($p = 0.13$) and taekwondo ($p = 0.60$), while kendo was similar to taekwondo ($p = 0.44$) and wrestling ($p = 0.14$); in addition, taekwondo and wrestling were similar ($p = 0.056$).

Judo demonstrated higher interpersonal anxiety than jiu-jitsu ($p = 0.016$) and karate ($p = 0.007$). Kendo showed higher values of interpersonal anxiety than karate ($p = 0.038$). Judo and wrestling presented a higher result of phobic anxiety than jiu-jitsu ($p = 0.02$ and $p = 0.019$). Jiu-jitsu presented similar results to karate ($p = 0.35$), kendo ($p = 0.2$), taekwondo ($p = 0.69$), and wrestling ($p = 0.20$). Judo had similar results of interpersonal anxiety when compared to kendo ($p = 0.32$), taekwondo ($p = 0.32$), and wrestling ($p = 0.91$). Karate demonstrated similar results for interpersonal anxiety when compared with taekwondo ($p = 0.44$) and wrestling ($p = 0.65$), and taekwondo had similar results of interpersonal anxiety as wrestling ($p = 0.7$). Wrestling presented higher phobic anxiety than karate ($p = 0.026$) and taekwondo ($p = 0.03$).

Jiu-jitsu presented similar result of phobic anxiety when compared with karate ($p = 0.88$), kendo ($p = 0.52$), and taekwondo ($p = 0.95$). Judo presented similar results for phobic anxiety to karate ($p = 0.056$), kendo ($p = 0.19$), taekwondo ($p = 0.15$), and wrestling ($p = 0.34$). Karate and taekwondo presented similar results ($p = 0.98$). No effects in TMMS-24 comparisons were observed between combat sports when compared to emotional attention ($p = 0.54$), clarity ($p = 0.39$) and emotional repair ($p = 0.90$). A descriptive analysis of ISRA and TMMS-24 between levels are in **Table 2**.

High level athletes presented lower values than lower level athletes in cognitive anxiety ($p = 0.002$), motor anxiety ($p = 0.028$), physiological anxiety ($p = 0.039$), total anxiety ($p = 0.003$), before the evaluation ($p = 0.024$), interpersonal anxiety ($p = 0.01$) and before everyday situations ($p = 0.031$). Regarding the interaction between level and combat sport groups, a main effect was observed in karate athletes ($X^2 = 6.468$, df = 2, $p = 0.039$), high level karate group had lower motor anxiety than the intermediate athletes ($p = 0.032$).

In addition, high level athletes presented lower values than intermediate athletes for total anxiety ($p = 0.028$), before the evaluation ($p = 0.003$) and phobic anxiety ($p = 0.011$). Concerning the interaction between level and combat sports, a main effect was observed in phobic anxiety of karate athletes ($X^2 = 6.193$, df = 2, $p = 0.045$), where high level group demonstrated lower phobic anxiety values than the intermediate athletes ($p = 0.045$). Significant differences in TMMS-24 comparisons between levels were observed in clarity ($X^2 = 7.444$, df = 2, $p = 0.024$) with higher scores for the high level group versus the low level group ($p = 0.013$), and in emotional repair ($X^2 = 12.794$, df = 2, $p = 0.002$) with lower scores to the low level group when compared with the intermediate group ($p = 0.003$) and high level group ($p = 0.002$). Regarding the interaction between level and combat sport groups, significant differences were observed in emotional repair ($X^2 = 8.943$, df = 2, $p = 0.011$) jiu-jitsu athletes presented lower values in lower level group than the intermediate athletes ($p = 0.01$), kendo also demonstrated differences between levels in emotional repair ($X^2 = 7.362$, df = 2, $p = 0.025$) with higher emotional repair on high level group

TABLE 1 | Descriptive and inferential analysis of combat sports anxiety and emotional intelligence comparisons (median, first, and third quartiles).

Factors	Jiu-jitsu	Judo	Karate	Kendo	Taekwondo	Wrestling	Statistical Inference			
	μ (25th; 75th)	μ (25th; 75th)	μ (25th; 75th)	μ (25th; 75th)	μ (25th; 75th)	μ (25th; 75th)	X^2	df	*P*	ES
ISRA C	55 (30; 70)	62 (35; 89)	44.0 (25.5; 68.5)	59 (38; 93)	66 (31; 80.5)	57.5 (35.5; 65.8)	134.245	5	0.04	0.17
ISRA M	24 (11; 43)	30 (12; 63)	20 (9.5; 39.5)	28 (10; 49)	22 (10.5; 40.5)	47 (27; 55)	10875	5	0.09	0.16
ISRA F	27 (12; 50)	29 (13; 58)	21 (9.5; 40)	24 (12; 48)	32 (11.5; 58.5)	39.5 (12.8; 55)	56.901	5	0.46	0.11
ISRA T	108 (56; 161)	125 (60; 214)	85 (45.5; 147)	113 (73; 181)	107 (56.5: 190.5)	153.5 (92.5; 171)	113.352	5	0.08	0.16
I F1	47 (25; 74)	60 (28; 88)	51 (22.5; 70)	48 (32; 78)	49 (28.5; 79.5)	56.5 (33.3; 77)	6.183	5	0.42	0.12
I F2	10 (4; 19)	13 (5; 27)	8 (4.5; 14.5)	10 (6; 21)	9 (3; 30.5)	18.5 (4.8; 22)	1167	5	0.09	0.16
I F3	14 (4; 30)	22 (6; 43)	13 (3; 30.5)	14 (4; 33)	13 (5.5; 31)	32 (23.5; 40.8)	115.400	5	0.07	0.16
I F4	5 (2; 16)	9 (3; 20)	6 (2.5; 13.5)	7 (3; 18)	7 (2.5; 14.5)	13.5 (3.3; 29)	8.600	5	0.23	0.13
IE 1	23 (19; 27)	23 (19; 28.5)	22 (18; 27)	21 (17; 29)	22 (18; 26)	21.5 (15.3; 25.8)	536	5	0.53	0.06
IE 2	28 (23; 32)	26 (22; 31)	30 (23; 32)	28 (23; 32)	31 (24; 33)	29.5 (20; 33)	6.284	5	0.39	0.07
IE 3	29 (25; 32)	28 (24; 33)	30 (25; 33)	26 (25; 32)	27 (23.5; 33)	28.5 (18.3; 36.3)	2.164	5	0.90	0.06

ISRA C, cognitive anxiety; ISRA M, motor anxiety; ISRA F, physiological anxiety; ISRA T, total anxiety; I F1, anxiety before the evaluation; I F2, interpersonal anxiety; IF 3, phobic anxiety; I F4, anxiety before habitual and daily situation; IE 1, emotional attention; IE 2, clarity; IE3, emotional repair; μ, median; 25th, 1st quartile; 75th, 3rd quartile; X^2, Chi-square; df, degrees of freedom; P, P calculated; ES, effect size.

TABLE 2 | Descriptive and inferential analysis of different levels anxiety and emotional intelligence comparisons (median, first, and third quartiles).

Factors	High level	Intermediate level	Low level	Statistical inferences			
	μ (25th; 75th)	μ (25th; 75th)	μ (25th; 75th)	X^2	df	*P*	ES
ISRA C	41 (22; 65.5)	54 (33; 80)	62 (35; 87)	11.524	2	0.003	0.16
ISRA M	21 (9.5; 30)	27 (10; 52)	28 (13; 53)	7.183	2	0.028	0.13
ISRA F	21 (10; 36)	26 (12; 51)	30 (13.5; 54.5)	6.225	2	0.044	0.12
ISRA T	85 (44.5; 143)	116 (60; 179)	122 (69; 186.5)	11.101	2	0.004	0.16
I F1	37 (24; 63)	52 (30; 79)	56 (27; 82.5)	7.448	2	0.024	0.13
I F2	6 (3; 15.5)	11 (5; 22)	12 (5; 25)	14.326	2	0.001	0.18
I F3	12 (3; 29.5)	15 (4; 35)	20 (6; 41)	7.531	2	0.023	0.13
I F4	5 (1; 12.5)	6 (3; 17)	8 (3; 17)	4.588	2	0.101	0.10
IE 1	22 (17; 27)	14 (19; 28)	22 (17.5; 27)	5.390	2	0.68	0.01
IE 2	30 (25; 32)	27 (23; 32)	27 (22; 32)	7.444	2	0.024	0.12
IE 3	30 (25; 34.5)	30 (25; 33)	27 (22; 32)	12.794	2	0.003	0.14

ISRA C, cognitive anxiety; ISRA M, motor anxiety; ISRA F, physiological anxiety; ISRA T, total anxiety; I F1, anxiety before the evaluation; I F2, interpersonal anxiety; IF 3, phobic anxiety; I F4, anxiety before habitual and daily situation; IE 1, emotional attention; IE 2, clarity; IE3, emotional repair; μ, median; 25th, 1st quartile; 75th, 3rd quartile; X^2, Chi-square; df, degrees of freedom; P, P calculated; ES, effect size.

compared with the lower level athletes (p = 0.025). Karate athletes demonstrated significant effects in emotional attention when compared level groups ($X^2 = 6.537$, df = 2, $p = 0.038$), high level athletes presented higher emotional attention than the lower level group (p = 0.034). No effects in emotional attention (p = 0.068) were observed. Descriptive analysis of ISRA and TMMS-24 between male and female athletes are in **Table 3**.

Female athletes presented higher cognitive, motor, physiological and total anxiety than male athletes (p = 0.001). Significant differences in TMMS-24 comparisons between genders were observed in clarity, with higher values for female compared with male ($p < 0.001$). When observed the interaction between sex and level groups in TMMS-24, comparisons indicated differences in the clarity dimension ($X^2 = 6.073$, df = 2, $p = 0.048$) with higher values by female and male high-level than female low-level athletes ($p = 0.044$). No effects were observed in clarity ($p = 0.95$) and emotional repair ($p = 0.57$) between male and female combat athletes.

DISCUSSION

This study examined the associations between important factors in the field of sports psychology (i.e., anxiety and emotional intelligence), comparing emotional intelligence and anxiety between six combat sports of lower, intermediate and high-level female and male athletes. The main results demonstrated higher values of cognitive and motor anxieties in judo, taekwondo and kendo than for jiu-jitsu, wrestling and karate groups. Judo athletes demonstrated higher phobic and interpersonal anxieties than the other groups. No difference in emotional intelligence was observed between modalities, which may suggest that anxiety is more associated with other factors such as gender

TABLE 3 | Descriptive and inferential analysis of gender anxiety and emotional intelligence comparisons (median, first, and third quartiles).

Factors	Female	Male	Statistical inferences			
	μ (25th; 75th)	μ (25th; 75th)	*U*	*Z*	*P*	ES
ISRA C	68 (43; 88)	46 (27; 71)	16833	4.997	0.001	0.24
ISRA M	35 (20; 55)	20 (8; 45.3)	16963	4.899	0.001	0.23
ISRA F	34 (20; 55)	20 (10; 45)	17597	4.419	0.001	0.21
ISRA T	138 (95; 194)	90 (48; 158.5)	16587	5.183	0.001	0.25
I F1	63 (38; 85)	42.5 (22.8; 68)	15932	5.680	0.001	0.27
I F2	10 (6; 25)	10 (4; 21)	21075	1.784	0.07	0.08
I F3	25 (6; 41)	13 (4; 31)	19109	3.274	0.001	0.16
I F4	10 (4; 18)	5 (1; 15)	1833.5	3.869	0.001	0.18
IE 1	24 (20; 28)	21 (17; 27)	1941.5	3.417	0.001	0.16
IE 2	27 (23; 32)	28 (23; 32)	23.646	1.323.2	0.62	0.06
IE 3	29 (24; 33.8)	29 (24; 33)	22.811	1.323.4	0.57	0.06

ISRA C, cognitive anxiety; ISRA M, motor anxiety; ISRA F, physiological anxiety; ISRA T, total anxiety; I F1, anxiety before the evaluation; I F2, interpersonal anxiety; IF 3, phobic anxiety; I F4, anxiety before habitual and daily situation; IE 1, emotional attention; IE 2, clarity; IE3, emotional repair; μ, median; 25th, 1st quartile; 75th, 3rd quartile; X^2, Chi-square; df, degrees of freedom; P, P calculated; ES, effect size.

and competitive level. Our data showed an inverse relationship between anxiety levels and expertise in combat sports practices, while females revealed higher anxiety than male athletes for all the analyzed variables. On the other hand, females demonstrated higher scores in emotional attention than male athletes, but both groups were classified as having low emotional attention, while high-level athletes showed better (classified as adequate) clarity and emotional repair than low-level athletes. Self-knowledge about the emotions, feelings, and moods together with the skill domain can help an athlete improve their performance (Cerin and Barnett, 2011; Tiric-Campara et al., 2012).

Emotional intelligence of applied psychology suggested the existence of three major conceptual models: (i) a transverse section of interrelated emotional and social competencies, abilities, and facilitator that influence intelligent behavior, called emotional clarity; (ii) a wide range of competencies and abilities that increase work performance, called emotional attention; and (iii) the ability to perceive, understand, manage, and regulate one's emotions, as well as the emotions of others, called emotional repair (Espinoza-Venegas et al., 2015). Despite the importance of emotional intelligence in combat sports, few studies have been conducted with this theme (Filaire et al., 2011).

Recently, in a randomized controlled trial, the effects of karate versus a mind-based stress reduction intervention on well-being and cognitive functioning in older adults demonstrated that both methods showed only small training effects concerning the assessed emotional and cognitive parameters (Jansen et al., 2017). This emotional self-control associated with anxiety levels has not been studied in different combat sports practices and in adults who are competitors in different levels until now. Assuming that combat sports present particular philosophies empirically associated with emotional control, it is significant to verify associations between expertise and controlled levels of anxiety.

The symptoms of anxiety can be recognized on different levels (Cheng and McCarthy, 2018), such as Cognitive (i.e., by a thought process), Somatic (i.e., by a physical response) and Behavioral (i.e., by patterns of behavior). For instance, a preceding report found that winning male college taekwondo athletes showed higher self-confidence and lower cognitive and somatic anxiety than their losing counterparts (Chapman et al., 1997). Although different studies have already verified the state and trait anxiety in combat sports, no studies have compared the symptoms of anxiety and emotional intelligence scale in different combat modalities.

Our gender comparisons shown larger effect sizes of anxiety variables and significant differences; female athletes had ~35% more total anxiety than males who had ~30% less cognitive anxiety characterized by indecision, sense of confusion, feeling heavy, negative thoughts, poor concentration, irritability, fear, forgetfulness, loss of confidence, and other negative factors. Furthermore, female presented ~60% more physiological and ~60% more motor anxieties. Female participants presented common indications of physiological anxiety such as increased blood pressure, respiration rate, sweating, adrenaline surge, needing to urinate, muscular tension, trembling, incessant talking and sleeplessness. In addition, motor anxiety was characterized by lethargic movements, inhibited posture and uncontrolled motor feeling. Females also had high scores of interpersonal and phobic anxieties which could be associated with presented symptoms. This outcome is consistent with an earlier study that suggested significant differences between male and female athletes during a judo championship (Interdonato et al., 2013).

To the author's knowledge, TMMS-24 was measured here for the first time in combat sports, with gender differences in emotional attention set shifting ability. Female athletes with higher total anxiety and worrisome thoughts did not associate difficulty in anxiety with emotional attention capacity; on the contrary, these results suggest that activation caused by anxiety may increase emotional attention. Although this study demonstrated that female athletes were related to anxiety and worry, it remains unclear whether female anxieties are related to a generalized mechanism of emotion repair. Regarding emotional intelligence differences between the level groups, TMMS-24 for the high-level group demonstrated ~40% less total anxiety and

~10% more clarity and repair than the low-level group. This result demonstrated that emotional intelligence and expertise are associated in combat sports, as well as the anxiety reduction, especially cognitive anxiety, which is associated with negative thoughts, poor concentration, fear and loss of confidence. Coco et al. (2019) indicated that judo turns out to be a sport discipline useful to male athletes control their aggressiveness and to try of overcoming their limits. Another study recently showed a positive association between religious beliefs with anxiety in competitive judo athletes (Moghadam et al., 2015).

Although such settings have greater external validity, the variables of interest are more difficult to control and measure than in a laboratory environment. Present study indicated as a limitation the fact that information collected was a cross-sectionally design, occurring during an over short period of time, it did not show a long-term profile of combat athletes. No effects of age, body mass, height or practice time were observed in present research. However, preceding reports indicated that a rapid weight loss is associated with high anger, confusion and greater total mood disturbance at the official weigh-in in Mixed Martial Arts athletes (Brandt et al., 2018). Recently, findings indicated the association between obesity and hyperactivity and anxiety among female school students in Japan (Suzuki et al., 2019). Future studies would do longitudinal studies, conducting several observations of the same athletes over a period of time in combat sports, verifying the relationship between anxiety, emotional intelligence, and anthropometric factors.

The benefit of a longitudinal study is that researchers would be able to detect developments or changes in the anxiety and emotional intelligence characteristics of the combat sports over a year or during sequential championships, principally comparing levels of anxiety. Our study ensured that participants were of the same age range; even so, it is important to point out a limitation for non-comparisons between combat outcomes during championships. Preceding research indicated that better performance during judo championships was associated with significantly lower levels of cognitive anxiety or higher levels of confidence (Filaire et al., 2001). Chiodo et al. (2011) also demonstrated significantly higher post-match scores emerged for anger-hostility and depression-dejection, whereas the reverse was observed for vigor-activity. In particular, results discriminated observed parameters between different competition levels of each single combat sport and highlighted significant findings in jiu-jitsu, judo, karate and kendo. This approach clarified the findings of present study, as preceding reports indicated that different attention could emerge in the same combat sport group, because taekwondo athletes who train with different approaches had different session-RPE quantifying loads (Lupo et al., 2017).

Our results indicated higher values of cognitive and motor anxieties in judo, taekwondo and kendo than in other groups. These findings highlight that judo athletes demonstrated higher phobic and interpersonal anxieties than other modalities. Recent judo rules changes have reduced male combat time to 4 minutes and moments of low-intensity combat time during the approach and gripping time before the attack (Miarka et al., 2016; Brito et al., 2017). A recent study has shown blood lactate rates associated with a protective role against fatigue toward frontal cortex and defined worse performances in backward memory capacity by conditioning strategic ability of the athletes (Coco et al., 2019). Recent study in rodents compellingly supports the knowledge that the projection of neurons extending from the CA1 region of the hippocampus and from the subiculum to the prefrontal cortex, denoted to the H-PFC pathway, that is critically involved in aspects of cognition associated to the executive function, as to the repair (Godsil et al., 2013). Simultaneously, it is becoming evident that judo fighter suffering from depression, and post-traumatic stress could display structural anomalies and unusual functional coupling within the hippocampal–prefrontal circuit (Godsil et al., 2013). This overlap might similarly be intertwined with the pathway's evident susceptibility to stress and with its relationship to the amygdala, associated with anxiety and mood disorders (Kirkbride et al., 2012) in judo/Brazilian jiu-jitsu (Brandt et al., 2019) and MMA athletes (Brandt et al., 2018). In consequence, the H-PFC pathway could be a potentially crucial element of the anxiety in judo athletes.

Present study did not observed effects of interventions able to reduce anxiety levels and it could offer a specific target for therapeutic intervention in future studies. Furthermore, it has been shown that anxiety and stress responses to stressful motivations take account of coping strategies (Ursin, 1988). Coping depends on a positive response outcome expectancy, which again depends on a high emotional intelligence; our results of emotional clarity and repair were classified as adequate, while emotional attention had a low score. Filaire et al. (2001) indicated two styles of coping strategies that can be used when confronting an adverse event, being emotion-focused and problem-focused strategies, which could affect performance (Scanlan et al., 1991). The present findings help to create new strategies that can not only reduce the effects of anxiety, but also increase emotional intelligence, especially emotional attention, as well as creating strategies to reduce anxieties, particularly in judo, taekwondo and kendo. These modalities have meditation, as well as practicing forms that could be used as coping strategies for anxiety reduction and stress, especially in beginners and low-level competitive athletes.

Future studies could incorporate other measures, considering the limitations of the present study, as the answers that it gathers in the cognitive, physiological and motor systems allow only to obtain a general level of information, and little differentiated, of the existence of anxiety, since the sampling of responses that it contemplates is reduced; Practical applications could use our data, trying also to assess differential profiles of situational reactivity, since it does not take into account the continuous process of subject-situation-response interaction, and; in the clinical setting, to adapt the treatment to the specificity of the gender profiles of the specific combat sport and level that elicits emotional responses.

In fact, this study proposed a unique approach to characterizing the anxiety and emotional intelligence in gender, level, and combat sports. The presented results demonstrated higher values of cognitive and motor anxieties in judo, taekwondo and kendo, while judo athletes revealed higher phobic and interpersonal anxieties than other modalities. The findings indicated an inverse relationship between anxiety levels and expertise in combat sports, while females revealed higher anxiety than male athletes in all analyzed variables. Female athletes revealed higher emotional attention than male athletes, but both groups were classified with low emotional attention, while high-level athletes showed better and adequate clarity and emotional repair than the low-level athletes. These findings can be used in combination with the extensive knowledge of sport physiology as a means to support psychological preparation for combat sports, considering particularities of gender and level groups.

ETHICS STATEMENT

Ethical review and approval was not required for the study on human participants in accordance with the local legislation

AUTHOR CONTRIBUTIONS

MF and AD conceived, planned, and carried out the study. CB and BM realized statistical analysis and wrote the manuscript with input from all authors.

ACKNOWLEDGMENTS

We thank all athletes, coaches, and federations for allowing and contributing to the accomplishment of this work.

REFERENCES

Alsamir Tibana, R., Manuel Frade de Sousa, N., Prestes, J., da Cunha Nascimento, D., Ernesto, C., Falk Neto, J. H. et al. (2019). Is perceived exertion a useful indicator of the metabolic and cardiovascular responses to a metabolic conditioning session of functional fitness? *Sports* 7:E161. doi: 10.3390/sports7070161

Andreato, L. V., Franzói de Moraes, S. M., Del Conti Esteves, J. V., Luiz Miranda, M., Jacques Pastório, J., Pastório, E. J. et al. (2014). Psychological, physiological, performance and perceptive responses to brazilian Jiu-jitsu combats. *Kinesiology* 46, 44–52.

Artioli, G. G., Scagliusi, F., Kashiwagura, D., Franchini, E., Gualano, B., and Junior, A. L. (2010). Development, validity and reliability of a questionnaire designed to evaluate rapid weight loss patterns in judo players. *Scand. J. Med. Sci. Sports* 20:e0177-87. doi: 10.1111/j.1600-0838.2009.00940.x

Bawa, H. S. (2010). Personality hardiness, burnout and sport competition anxiety among athletics and wrestling coaches. *Br. J. Sports Med.* 44(Suppl. 1), i57–i58. doi: 10.1136/bjsm.2010.078725.193

Brandt, R., Bevilacqua, G. G., Coimbra, D. R., Pombo, L. C., Miarka, B., and Lane, A. M. (2018). Body weight and mood state modifications in mixed martial arts: an exploratory pilot. *J. Strength Cond. Res.* 32, 2548–2554. doi: 10.1519/JSC.0000000000002639

Brandt, R., Bevilacqua, G. G., Crocetta, T. B., Monteiro, C., Guarnieri, R., Hobold, E., et al. (2019). Comparisons of mood states associated with outcomes achieved by female and male athletes in high-level judo and brazilian jiu-jitsu championships: psychological factors associated with the probability of success. *J. Strength Cond. Res.* doi: 10.1519/JSC.0000000000003218 [Epub ahead of print],

Breitschuh, S., Schone, M., Tozzi, L., Kaufmann, J., Strumpf, H., Fenker, D., et al. (2018). Aggressiveness of martial artists correlates with reduced temporal pole grey matter concentration. *Psychiatry Res. Neuroimag.* 281, 24–30. doi: 10.1016/j.pscychresns.2018.08.001

Brito, C. J., Miarka, B., de Durana, A. L. D., and Fukuda, D. H. (2017). Home advantage in judo: analysis by the combat phase, penalties and the type of attack. *J. Hum. Kinet.* 57, 213–220. doi: 10.1515/hukin-2017-0062

Capranica, L., Condello, G., Tornello, F., Iona, T., Chiodo, S., Valenzano, A., et al. (2017). Salivary alpha-amylase, salivary cortisol, and anxiety during a youth taekwondo championship: an observational study. *Medicine* 96:e7272. doi: 10.1097/MD.0000000000007272

Cerin, E., and Barnett, A. (2011). Predictors of pre-and post-competition affective states in male martial artists: a multilevel interactional approach. *Scand. J. Med. Sci. Sports* 21, 137–150. doi: 10.1111/j.1600-0838.2009.01006.x

Chapman, C., Lane, A. M., Brierley, J. H., and Terry, P. C. (1997). Anxiety, self-confidence and performance in tae-kwon-do. *Percept. Mot. Skills* 85, 1275–1278. doi: 10.2466/pms.1997.85.3f.1275

Cheng, B. H., and McCarthy, J. M. (2018). Understanding the dark and bright sides of anxiety: a theory of workplace anxiety. *J. Appl. Psychol.* 103, 537–560. doi: 10.1037/apl0000266

Chiodo, S., Tessitore, A., Cortis, C., Cibelli, G., Lupo, C., Ammendolia, A., et al. (2011). Stress-related hormonal and psychological changes to official youth Taekwondo competitions. *Scand. J. Med. Sci. Sports* 21, 111–119. doi: 10.1111/j.1600-0838.2009.01046.x

Coco, M., Di Corrado, D., Ramaci, T., Di Nuovo, S., Perciavalle, V., Puglisi, A., et al. (2019). Role of lactic acid on cognitive functions. *Phys. Sportsmed.* 47, 329–335. doi: 10.1080/00913847.2018.1557025

Coswig, V. S., Miarka, B., Pires, D. A., da Silva, L. M., Bartel, C., and Del Vecchio, F. B. (2018). Weight regain, but not weight loss, is related to competitive success in real-life mixed martial arts competition. *Int. J. Sport Nutr. Exerc. Metab.* doi: 10.1123/ijsnem.2018-0034 [Epub ahead of print],

Diamond, A. (2012). Activities and programs that improve children's executive functions. *Curr. Dir. Psychol. Sci.* 21, 335–341. doi: 10.1177/0963721412453722

Espinoza-Venegas, M., Sanhueza-Alvarado, O., Ramírez-Elizondo, N., and Sáez-Carrillo, K. (2015). A validation of the construct and reliability of an emotional intelligence scale applied to nursing students. *Rev. Lat. Am. Enfermagem.* 23, 139–147. doi: 10.1590/0104-1169.3498.2535

Fernández-Berrocal, P., Extremera, N., and Ramos, N. (2004). Validity and reliability of the Spanish modified version of the trait meta-mood scale. *Psychol. Rep.* 94, 751–755. doi: 10.2466/pr0.94.3.751-755

Filaire, E., Larue, J., and Rouveix, M. (2011). Eating behaviours in relation to emotional intelligence. *Int. J. Sports Med.* 32, 309–315. doi: 10.1055/s-0030-1269913

Filaire, E., Maso, F., Sagnol, M., Ferrand, C., and Lac, G. (2001). Anxiety, hormonal responses, and coping during a judo competition. *Aggress. Behav.* 27, 55–63. doi: 10.1002/1098-2337(20010101/31)27:1<55::aid-ab5>3.0.co;2-h

Finkenberg, M. E., DiNucci, J. M., McCune, E. D., and McCune, S. L. (1992). Analysis of the effect of competitive trait anxiety on performance in Taekwondo competition. *Percept. Mot. Skills* 75, 239–243. doi: 10.2466/pms.1992.75.1.239

Friesen, A., Lane, A., Galloway, S., Stanley, D., Nevill, A., and Ruiz, M. C. (2018). Coach–Athlete perceived congruence between actual and desired emotions in karate competition and training. *J. Appl. Sport Psychol.* 30, 288–299. doi: 10.1080/10413200.2017.1388302

Godsil, B. P., Kiss, J. P., Spedding, M., and Jay, T. M. (2013). The hippocampal-prefrontal pathway: the weak link in psychiatric disorders? *Eur. Neuropsychopharmacol.* 23, 1165–1181. doi: 10.1016/j.euroneuro.2012.10.018

Heaton, L. J., Garcia, L. J., Gledhill, L. W., Beesley, K. A., and Coldwell, S. E. (2007). Development and validation of the Spanish interval scale of anxiety response (ISAR). *Anesth. Prog.* 54, 100–108. doi: 10.2344/0003-3006(2007)54\%5B100:davots\%5D2.0.co;2

Interdonato, G. C., Miarka, B., and Franchini, E. (2013). Analysis of pre-competitive and competitive anxiety in youth judoka. *Rev. Artes Marc. Asiát.* 8, 471–479.

Jansen, P., Dahmen-Zimmer, K., Kudielka, B. M., and Schulz, A. (2017). Effects of karate training versus mindfulness training on emotional well-being and cognitive performance in later life. *Res. Aging* 39, 1118–1144. doi: 10.1177/0164027516669987

Jin, P. (1992). Efficacy of Tai Chi, brisk walking, meditation, and reading in reducing mental and emotional stress. *J. Psychosom. Res.* 36, 361–370. doi: 10.1016/0022-3999(92)90072-a

Kirkbride, J. B., Errazuriz, A., Croudace, T. J., Morgan, C., Jackson, D., Boydell, J., et al. (2012). Incidence of schizophrenia and other psychoses in England, 1950–2009: a systematic review and meta-analyses. *PLoS One* 7:e31660. doi: 10.1371/journal.pone.0031660

Lakes, K. D., Bryars, T., Sirisinahal, S., Salim, N., Arastoo, S., Emmerson, N., et al. (2013). The healthy for life Taekwondo pilot study: a preliminary evaluation of effects on executive function and BMI, feasibility, and acceptability. *Ment. Health Phys. Act* 6, 181–188. doi: 10.1016/j.mhpa.2013.07.002

Lupo, C., Capranica, L., Cortis, C., Guidotti, F., Bianco, A., and Tessitore, A. (2017). Session-RPE for quantifying load of different youth taekwondo training sessions. *J. Sports Med. Phys. Fitness* 57, 189–194. doi: 10.23736/S0022-4707.16.06021-X

Maloney, M., Renshaw, I., Headrick, J., Martin, D. T., and Farrow, D. (2018). Taekwondo fighting in training does not simulate the affective and cognitive demands of competition: implications for behaviour and transfer. *Front. Psychol.* 9:25. doi: 10.3389/fpsyg.2018.00025

Martínez-Sánchez, F., Cano-Vindel, A., Precioso, C. C. J., García, J. A. S., Soria, B. O., and Del Valle, E. G. (1995). A first version of a brief aniety scale based on the inventory of situations and responses of anxiety (I.S.R.A.). *Ann. Psychol.* 11, 97–104.

Matsumoto, D., Takeuchi, M., Nakajima, T., and Iida, E. (2000). Competition anxiety, self-confidence, personality, and competition performance of American elite and non-elite judo athletes. *Res. J. Budo* 32, 12–21.

Miarka, B., Del Vecchio, F. B., Julianetti, R., Cury, R., Camey, S., and Franchini, E. (2016). Time-motion and tactical analysis of Olympic judo fighters. *Int. J. Perform. Anal. Sport* 16, 133–142.

Miguel-Tobal, J., and Cano-Vindel, A. (2002). *Inventario De Situaciones y Respuestas de Ansiedad (ISRA)*. Madrid: TEA Ediciones.

Moghadam, Z. P., Tojari, F., and Khodayari, A. (2015). Relationship practice religious beliefs and self-efficacy with competitive anxiety judo athletes. *J. Novel Appl. Sci.* 4, 987–991.

Molanorouzi, K., Khoo, S., and Morris, T. (2014). Validating the physical activity and leisure motivation scale (PALMS). *BMC Public Health* 14:909. doi: 10.1186/1471-2458-14-909

Moret, L., Mesbah, M., Chwalow, J., and Lellouch, J. (1993). Internal validation of a measurement scale: relation between principal component analysis, Cronbach's alpha coefficient and intra-class correlation coefficient. *Rev. Epidemiol. Sante Publique* 41, 179–186.

Okada, K. (2015). Bayesian meta-analysis of Cronbach's coefficient alpha to evaluate informative hypotheses. *Res. Synth. Methods* 6, 333–346. doi: 10.1002/jrsm.1155

Rosenthal, R., and DiMatteo, M. R. (2001). Meta-analysis: recent developments in quantitative methods for literature reviews. *Ann. Rev. Psychol.* 52, 59–82. doi: 10.1146/annurev.psych.52.1.59

Salovey, P., Mayer, J. D., Goldman, S. L., Turvey, C., and Palfai, T. P. (1995). "Emotional attention, clarity, and repair: exploring emotional intelligence using the trait meta-mood scale," in *Emotion, Disclosure, & Health*, ed. J. W. Pennebaker, (Washington, D.C.: American Psychological Association), 125–154. doi: 10.1037/10182-006

Scanlan, T. K., Stein, G. L., and Ravizza, K. (1991). An in-depth study of former elite figure skaters: III sources of stress. *J. Sport Exerc. Psychol.* 13, 103–120. doi: 10.1123/jsep.13.2.103

Shojima, K., and Toyoda, H. (2002). Estimation of Cronbach's alpha coefficient in the context of item response theory. *Shinrigaku Kenkyu* 73, 227–233. doi: 10.4992/jjpsy.73.227

Smith, R. E., Smoll, F. L., Cumming, S. P., and Grossbard, J. R. (2006). Measurement of multidimensional sport performance anxiety in children and adults: the sport anxiety scale-2. *J. Sport Exerc. Psychol.* 28, 479–501. doi: 10.1123/jsep.28.4.479

Sun, W., Chou, C. P., Stacy, A. W., Ma, H., Unger, J., and Gallaher, P. (2007). SAS and SPSS macros to calculate standardized Cronbach's alpha using the upper bound of the phi coefficient for dichotomous items. *Behav. Res. Methods* 39, 71–81. doi: 10.3758/bf03192845

Suzuki, Y., Ikeda, A., Maruyama, K., Sakamoto, N., Wada, H., and Tanigawa, T. (2019). The association between obesity and hyperactivity/anxiety among elementary school students in Japan. *Int. J. Behav. Med.* doi: 10.1007/s12529-019-09827-x [Epub ahead of print],

Tahtinen, R. E., and Kristjansdottir, H. (2018). The influence of anxiety and depression symptoms on help-seeking intentions in individual sport athletes and non-athletes: the role of gender and athlete status. *J. Clin. Sport Psychol.* 13, 1–31. doi: 10.1123/jcsp.2017-0028

Terry, P. C., and Slade, A. (1995). Discriminant effectiveness of psychological state measures in predicting performance outcome in karate competition. *Percept. Mot. Skills* 81, 275–286. doi: 10.2466/pms.1995.81.1.275

Tiric-Campara, M., Tupkovic, E., Mazalovic, E., Karalic, E., Biscevic, M., Djelilovic-Vranic, J., et al. (2012). Correlation of aggressiveness and anxiety in fighting sports. *Med. Arch.* 66, 116–121.

Ursin, H. (1988). "Expectancy and activation: an attempt to systematize stress theory," in *Neurobiological Approaches to Human Diseases*, eds D. Hellhammer, J. Florin, and I. Weiner, (Toronto: Hans Huber), 313–334.

Usui, N., Okumura, M., and Kudo, K. (2018). Expertise differences in movement switching in kendo players. *Int. J. Sport Health Sci.* 16, 19–26. doi: 10.5432/ijshs.201719

Williams, A. M., and Elliott, D. (1999). Anxiety, expertise, and visual search strategy in karate. *J. Sport Exerc. Psychol.* 21, 362–375. doi: 10.1123/jsep.21.4.362

Wong, R. S., Thung, J. S., and Pieter, W. (2006). Mood and performance in young malaysian karateka. *J. Sports Sci. Med.* 5, 54–59.

Ziv, G., and Lidor, R. (2013). Psychological preparation of competitive judokas - a review. *J. Sports Sci. Med.* 12, 371–380.

18

The Psychophysiological Effects of Different Tempo Music on Endurance versus High-Intensity Performances

Vittoria Maria Patania[1†], Johnny Padulo[2†], Enzo Iuliano[3], Luca Paolo Ardigò[4], Dražen Čular[1], Alen Miletić[1] and Andrea De Giorgio[3]*

[1] Faculty of Kinesiology, University of Split, Split, Croatia, [2] Department of Biomedical Sciences for Health, University of Milan, Milan, Italy, [3] Faculty of Psychology, eCampus University, Novedrate, Italy, [4] School of Exercise and Sport Science, Department of Neurosciences, Biomedicine and Movement Sciences, University of Verona, Verona, Italy

***Correspondence:**
Andrea De Giorgio
andrea.degiorgio@uniecampus.it

† These authors have contributed equally to this work

The use of music during training represents a special paradigm for trainers to stimulate people undertaking different types of exercise. However, the relationship between the tempo of music and perception of effort during different metabolic demands is still unclear. Therefore, the aim of this research was to determine whether high intensity exercise is more sensitive to the beneficial effects of music than endurance exercise. This study assessed 19 active women (age 26.4 ± 2.6 years) during endurance (walking for 10′ at 6.5 km/h on a treadmill) and high intensity (80% on 1-RM) exercise under four different randomly assigned conditions: no music (NM), with music at 90–110 bpm (LOW), with music at 130–150 bpm (MED), and with music at 170–190 bpm (HIGH). During each trial, heart rate (HR) and the rating of perceived exertion (RPE) were assessed. Repeated analysis of variance measures was used to detect any differences between the four conditions during high intensity and low intensity exercise. RPE showed more substantial changes during the endurance exercises (11%), than during high intensity exercise (6.5%), between HIGH and NM conditions. The metabolic demand during the walking exercise increased between NM and HIGH bpm conditions. This study indicates the benefits of music under stress conditions as well as during endurance and high intensity training. The results demonstrate that the beneficial effects of music are more likely to be seen in endurance exercise. Consequently, music may be considered an important tool to stimulate people engaging in low intensity physical exercise.

Keywords: training and testing, rating perception effort, exercise, RPE, sport

INTRODUCTION

The psychophysiological effects of music have been widely investigated in both psychology (De Giorgio et al., 2017; Benke et al., 2018; Innes et al., 2018; Padovan et al., 2018) and in exercise and sport related fields (Jarraya et al., 2012; Terry et al., 2012). The effects of exercise on the brain are well known (for a review see De Giorgio, 2017, De Giorgio et al., 2018a), but the effect that music has on exercise and its cerebral counterpart has only recently been investigated (Bigliassi et al., 2017; Tabei et al., 2017). It has been demonstrated that music is able to trigger behavioral changes, i.e., there is an underlying modification of brain function which can induce people to increase their exercise adherence and participation (Altenmüller and Schlaug, 2012). Music has also been demonstrated to be effective in reducing fatigue and its related symptoms (Jing and Xudong, 2008), in emotional regulation (Hou et al., 2017), in regulating affective arousal (Hutchinson et al., 2018) and in improving the efficacy of the motor system (Bigliassi et al., 2017).

However, music remains a subjective experience and De Nora (2000) discussed how people select music in a subjective manner to improve mood and energy levels during physical activity. Furthermore, the influence of music is also associated with both its intrinsic elements, such as rhythm and musicality and extrinsic factors emerging from cultural and extra-musical associations (Zatorre et al., 2007; Koc and Curtseit, 2009; Karageorghis et al., 2012). Listening to a particular type of music has been found to improve subjective experience during low, moderate, and high intensity exercise (De Nora, 2000; Karageorghis and Priest, 2012a,b; Karageorghis et al., 2012).

In the neurophysiological context, it has been demonstrated that music influences processes in the autonomic nervous system and can even be used to regulate blood pressure and heart rate (HR) (Schneck and Berger, 2006; Karageorghis and Priest, 2012a,b). The central nervous system is highly sensitive to musical cues and its reaction is diverse, involving muscle activation, attention, thoughts, behavior, and executive functions (Thaut, 2005; Thaut and Abiru, 2010; Altenmüller and Schlaug, 2013).

With respect to attention, listening to music during physical activity has been described in the literature as a dissociative cognitive strategy that enables a shift in attention away from subjective experiences of discomfort or pain (De Nora, 2000; Rodriguez-Fornells et al., 2012; Altenmüller and Schlaug, 2013). It has been shown that as the intensity of exercise increases, discomfort and related bodily sensations increase, eliciting a greater awareness of fatigue-related symptoms (Karageorghis and Priest, 2012a). Conversely, when people are exposed to environmental sensory cues such as music, colors, or videos, these cues can divert attention and modify both behavior and bodily discomfort sensations during exercise or other tasks (Karageorghis and Jones, 2014; De Giorgio et al., 2018a,b).

As mentioned previously, the literature describes the capacity of music to shift the focus away from feelings of discomfort and fatigue and this has been demonstrated through the assessment of the rating of perceived exertion (RPE). In particular, it has been found that reduced RPE with music is associated with low to moderate intensity exercise, but not high intensity exercise (Harmon and Kravitz, 2007; Karageorghis and Priest, 2012b). The authors proposed that music seems unable to divert attention during exercise that is overly intense with a high degree of bodily discomfort (for a review see Karageorghis and Priest, 2012a,b). Despite this, it was found that while the RPE during high intensity exercise remained the same with or no music (NM), participants experienced more positive mood profiles when listening to music, regardless of exercise intensity. The authors suggest that this could have occurred because although the participants knew that they were exercising hard, they were happier about the activity (Karageorghis and Priest, 2012a,b). In their literature review, Karageorghis and Priest (2012a,b) also highlighted the finding that trained athletes are less influenced by the effects of music compared to those who are untrained. This could be a result of the practice athletes have in diverting their attention away from bodily discomfort in any situation.

However, to the best of our knowledge there have been no studies to date that have linked the effect of two different exercise types on the RPE under different music conditions. This study investigated the RPE after low intensity and high intensity exercise, conducted under different music conditions.

Participants

Nineteen female participants ranging from 24 to 31 years old were enrolled for the present study. All participants regularly performed physical activity three to five times a week and a good proportion of the participants were involved in physical fitness. The following participant information was collected: mass, height, BMI (body mass index, obtained by dividing the weight in kg of the participant with the square of the height expressed in meters), training experience [endurance intensive effort and/or high intensity effort (Chamari and Padulo, 2015)], and maximal HR. The participants' data are reported in **Table 1**. All participants gave written informed consent following verbal and written explanations regarding the study. All methodological procedures were approved by the local Ethics Committee.

Socio-Demographic Variables and Enrolment Process

The participants were enrolled in different fitness centers located in Rome using a convenience sampling based on the following inclusion criteria: (1) female gender; (2) age between 18 and 35 years old; (3) at least 1 year of experience in fitness training (minimum three to five session of training per week; and (4) at least high school graduation. To assure the safety of the procedure and the correct interpretation of the data the following exclusion criteria were instead applied: (1) presence of relevant disease or other condition (temporary or permanent) incompatible with the proposed interventions; (2) history of relevant cardiopulmonary disease; (3) BMI > 25 kg/m^2; (4) presence of relevant disease or other condition (temporary or permanent) potentially influencing the physical performance of the participant. The participants were all volunteers and were invited for an individual appointment in a Sports Science Laboratory in order to explain them the procedure of the study and in order to collect the information via survey. The survey aimed to investigate and collect the data reported in **Table 1**, the adherence to the inclusion criteria, and the absence of exclusion criteria.

Procedures

Each participant was asked to perform two different training sessions: (1) walking at 6.5 km/h (endurance exercise) on a treadmill for 10 min to reach a steady state (Padulo et al., 2014) and (2) high intensity exercise on leg press machine based on the one repetition maximum test (1-RM) (Padulo et al., 2015). Each exercise test was performed four times by each participant under four different tempo music conditions.

TABLE 1 | Characteristics of participants.

	Mass (kg)	Height (cm)	BMI (kg/m^2)	Age (years)	Theoretical maximal HR (bpm)	Training experience	Training experience (years)
Participant 1	67.2	175	22.0	24	187	EIE	16
Participant 2	61.3	168	21.7	26	186	EIE	13
Participant 3	63.8	170	22.1	24	190	EIE	12
Participant 4	67.5	177	21.6	26	175	EIE	15
Participant 5	56.6	167	20.3	29	186	HIE	7
Participant 6	63.9	175	20.9	31	184	EIE	3
Participant 7	62.0	173	20.3	25	185	EIE	14
Participant 8	48.9	160	19.1	24	179	HIE	2
Participant 9	61.3	169	21.5	24	177	EIE	1
Participant 10	57.4	165	21.1	24	190	HIE	5
Participant 11	53.0	170	18.3	24	170	HIE	1
Participant 12	62.9	164	23.4	25	185	HIE	3
Participant 13	70.0	170	24.2	29	184	EIE	11
Participant 14	53.7	170	18.6	31	187	HIE	7
Participant 15	61.3	157	24.9	27	187	HIE	0.6
Participant 16	57.3	177	18.3	31	178	EIE	2
Participant 17	54.5	170	18.9	27	184	HIE	1
Participant 18	55.0	168	19.5	26	184	EIE	4
Participant 19	54.5	173	18.2	25	188	EIE	3
MEAN	59.58	169.37	20.78	26.42	183.47	–	6.35
SD	5.65	5.30	2.02	2.57	5.31	–	5.39

Mean and standard deviation (SD) for the anthropometric measures and the training experience. EIE, endurance intensive efforts; HIE, high intensity efforts.

TABLE 2 | Results with pairwise comparisons among the four music conditions.

Dependent variables	Music conditions	Mean	SD	95% CI		Pairwise comparisons			
				Lower	Upper	NM vs.	LOW vs.	MED vs.	HIGH vs.
aHRwalking (bpm)	NM	83.37	4.166	81.360	85.376	LOW: $p < 0.0001$	NM: $p < 0.0001$	NM: $p < 0.0001$	NM: $p < 0.0001$
	LOW	95.79	4.237	93.747	97.832	MED: $p < 0.0001$	MED: $p = 0.001$	LOW: $p = 0.001$	LOW: $p < 0.0001$
	MED	99.47	3.289	97.888	101.059	HIGH: $p < 0.0001$	HIGH: $p < 0.0001$	HIGH: $p < 0.0001$	MED: $p < 0.0001$
	HIGH	110.11	4.054	108.151	112.059				
pHRwalking (bpm)	NM	95.95	4.731	93.667	98.228	LOW: $p < 0.0001$	NM: $p < 0.0001$	NM: $p < 0.0001$	NM: $p < 0.0001$
	LOW	104.37	4.044	102.419	106.318	MED: $p < 0.0001$	MED: $p < 0.0001$	LOW: $p < 0.0001$	LOW: $p < 0.0001$
	MED	109.05	4.020	107.115	110.990	HIGH: $p < 0.0001$	HIGH: $p < 0.0001$	HIGH: $p < 0.0001$	MED: $p < 0.0001$
	HIGH	125.37	4.044	123.419	127.318				
RPEwalking (Borg's scale score)	NM	9.26	0.653	8.948	9.578	LOW: $p = 0.002$	NM: $p = 0.002$	NM: $p < 0.0001$	NM: $p < 0.0001$
	LOW	8.58	0.692	8.245	8.913	MED: $p < 0.0001$	MED: $p = 0.049$	LOW: $p = 0.049$	LOW: $p < 0.0001$
	MED	8.05	0.848	7.644	8.461	HIGH: $p < 0.0001$	HIGH: $p < 0.0001$	HIGH: $p = 0.045$	MED: $p = 0.045$
	HIGH	7.47	0.772	7.101	7.846				
1RMlp (kg)	NM	133.26	41.777	113.127	153.399	LOW: p not sign.	NM: p not sign.	NM: p not sign.	NM: p not sign.
	LOW	133.26	41.777	113.127	153.399	MED: p not sign.	MED: p not sign.	LOW: p not sign.	LOW: p not sign.
	MED	133.26	41.777	113.127	153.399	HIGH: $p < 0.0001$	HIGH: $p < 0.0001$	HIGH: $p < 0.0001$	MED: p not sign.
	HIGH	136.47	43.004	115.746	157.201				
RPElp (Borg's scale score)	NM	16.26	1.447	15.566	16.961	LOW: p not sign.	NM: p not sign.	NM: $p = 0.002$	NM: $p = 0.002$
	LOW	15.89	1.595	15.126	16.663	MED: $p = 0.002$	MED: p not sign.	LOW: p not sign.	LOW: $p = 0.011$
	MED	15.53	1.541	14.784	16.269	HIGH: $p < 0.0001$	HIGH: $p = 0.011$	HIGH: p not sign.	MED: p not sign.
	HIGH	15.21	1.228	14.618	15.803				

Mean and standard deviation (SD) and 95% confidence interval (95% CI) for the aHRwalking (average HR during walking at 6.5 km/h); pHRwalking (peak of HR during walking at 6.5 km/h); RPEwalking (RPE during walking at 6.5 km/h); 1RMlp (One-repetition maximum at leg press); and RPElp (RPE during 1-RM at leg press) on four conditions: NM (no music), LOW (music with bpm between 90 and 110), MED (music with bpm between 130 and 150), and HIGH (music with bpm between 170 and 190).

The order of the four music conditions was randomly assigned in a counterbalanced way. Subsequently, in the other four experimental sessions (each conducted under different music conditions) each participant individually performed the two exercise sessions. The participant's HR was recorded during each endurance session (10 min for each one) and at the end of the test, the participant's average HR and peak HR were then calculated. Furthermore, immediately after the walking exercise, the participant was asked to express their perception of fatigue as a value based on the Borg scale ($0 < 20$). On a different day, each participant was assessed with regard to their maximal repetitions during the leg-press exercise (Padulo et al., 2017; Migliaccio et al., 2018) and the 1-RM based on the Brzycki method was calculated at the same time (Padulo et al., 2015). To ensure standardization of the procedure the following method was used. The participant began the leg-press exercise with a load equivalent to their body weight (measured in the preliminary session) and performed the maximal number of repetitions. When the participant reached 10 repetitions with the selected weight, the exercise was stopped and 20 kg was added for a further attempt after four minutes of rest. When the participant was unable to perform more than 10 repetitions with the selected load, the respective 1-RM was calculated using the Brzycki equation: 1-RM theoretical = lifted load/[1.0278 − (0.0278 × repetitions performed)]. Immediately after the last try, the participant was once again asked to express their perception of fatigue as a value based on the Borg scale (CR $0 < 20$). The four tempo music conditions were: NM, with music at 90–110 bpm (LOW), with music at 130–150 bpm (MED), and with music at 170–190 bpm (HIGH). During each music condition, five pop songs were used with increasing bpm (e.g., in the MED condition, the first song had 132 bpm, the second had 136 bpm, the third had 141 bpm, the fourth had 143 bpm, and the last song had 148 bpm). All sessions were conducted in the same Sports Science Laboratory of the enrolment process, and similar environmental conditions at each session were ensured (temperature and relative humidity for each session ranging from 22 to 24°C and 25 to 27%, respectively). All the sessions under different music condition were performed one week apart each other to avoid the influence of fatigue of each session on the subsequent ones. A reminder was sent to each participant 2 days before each session in order to assure the correct adherence to the study planning. No dropout or unavailability of the participants occurred during the study.

Statistical Analysis

The Shapiro–Wilk test was used to evaluate the normality of the data distribution. Successively, multivariate analysis of variance with repeated measures (RM-MANOVA) was conducted to determine whether significant differences existed between the four different music conditions. This was considered as the factor of the analysis (named CONDITION). The following five variables were considered dependent variables: aHRwalking (average HR during walking at 6.5 km/h); pHRwalking (peak HR during walking at 6.5 km/h); RPEwalking (RPE during walking at 6.5 km/h); 1-RMlp (one-repetition maximum during leg-press); and RPElp (RPE during leg-press). The alpha test level for statistical significance was set at $p < 0.05$ and η_p^2 was calculated as the index of effect size. The Bonferroni correction was used for pairwise comparison of the four music conditions. The reliability of the external load time (10′ on treadmill/leg-press machine) was assessed by calculating the intra-class correlations coefficient (ICC), according to the literature (Weir, 2005). The SPSS statistical software package (Version 25.0; IBM) was used for all statistical analysis.

RESULTS

On leg-press exercise the 1-RM was 133.26 ± 41.78 kg with the starting load of 62.11 ± 4.19 kg and concluded with 4.21 ± 1.90 sets/3.32 ± 0.89 reps. The ICC for external load time (treadmill/leg-press) on the four conditions was >0.985 for high intensity and endurance exercises, respectively. The results of the RM-MANOVA indicated significant differences between the four conditions ($F_{13,6} = 94{,}152$; $p < 0.0001$; $\eta_p^2 = 0.995$). The univariate analysis showed significant differences with regard to all five dependent variables analyzed: aHRwalking ($F_{3,54} = 242.08$; $p < 0.0001$; $\eta_p^2 = 0.931$); pHRwalking ($F_{3,54} = 631.38$; $p < 0.0001$; $\eta_p^2 = 0.972$); RPEwalking ($F_{3,54} = 35.27$; $p < 0.0001$; $\eta_p^2 = 0.662$); 1-RMlp ($F_{3,54} = 39.54$; $p < 0.0001$; $\eta_p^2 = 0.687$); and RPElp ($F_{3,54} = 15.86$; $p < 0.0001$; $\eta_p^2 = 0.468$). The results obtained for each condition and the pairwise comparisons between the four conditions are reported in **Table 2** and **Figure 1**.

DISCUSSION

The results of this study support the findings of other studies regarding the effects of music on cognitive motor processes (Bianco et al., 2017; Mohammad Alipour et al., 2019). This study is the first to link the effect of music with RPE and HR under different music conditions. The effects of music involve both unconscious sub-cortical areas and conscious cortical stimulation and the responses are highly complex (Zatorre et al., 2007; Levitin and Tirovolas, 2009; Rodriguez-Fornells et al., 2012; Altenmüller and Schlaug, 2013). Music can stimulate the human brain to such an extent that to ignore it is more difficult than interaction (Zatorre et al., 2007; Levitin and Tirovolas, 2009).

As mentioned previously, music perception involves both cortical and sub-cortical areas, but it has an effect on the whole brain. Music influences emotional responses (i.e., the limbic system), associate/automatic movements (i.e., the basal ganglia), coordination (i.e., the cerebellum), and the organization and planning of movements (motor, pre-motor, and supplementary motor areas). The rhythmic patterns of music facilitate error correction and the execution of movements (Levitin and Tirovolas, 2009). Indeed, repeated movements seem to be related to the phases between pulse music beats, stimulating a feedback/forward loop (Todd et al., 2002; Levitin and Tirovolas, 2009). In addition to the involvement of the whole brain, music also affects the whole body and this influence

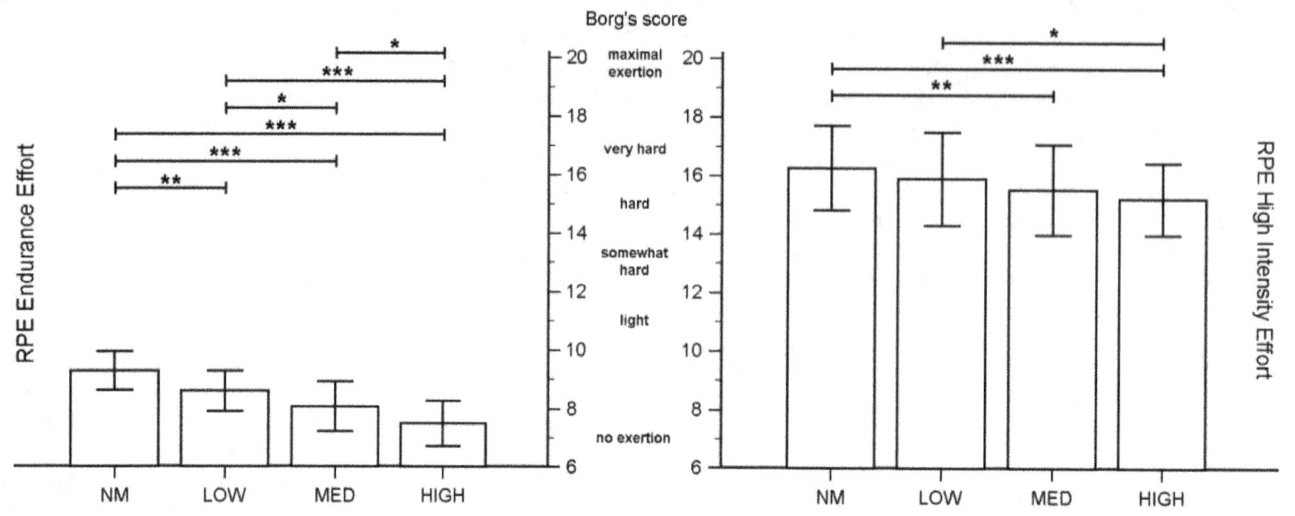

FIGURE 1 | Rating of perceived exertion (RPE) in both exercises during the four conditions. *$p < 0.05$; **$p < 0.01$; ***$p < 0.001$.

occurs through physiological arousal mediated by sub-cortical structures and bodily rhythms such as walking, breathing, and HR (Schneck and Berger, 2006; Levitin and Tirovolas, 2009; Altenmüller and Schlaug, 2013). Previous studies have demonstrated that music regulates processes in the autonomic nervous system and can be used to regulate the cardiovascular system with regard to both HR and blood pressure (Harmon and Kravitz, 2007; Murrock and Higgins, 2009; Karageorghis and Priest, 2012a,b). Bodily activation is very important in feeling fatigue, as signals traveling from the body toward the brain inform the latter on the effort in progress, modulating physical activity as a result. These signals capture conscious attention and can change behavioral responses relating to exercise adherence. Becomes These signals capture conscious attention and can change behavioral responses (De Giorgio, 2016) also relating to exercise adherence. However, music can be considered a useful tool in regulating the intensity of physiological arousal and subjective experiences in order to improve levels of physical activity and exercise participation (De Nora, 2000; Zatorre et al., 2007; Karageorghis and Priest, 2012a,b; Altenmüller and Schlaug, 2013). Indeed, in the context of sport and exercise performance, De Nora (2000) discussed how music can be strategically chosen in order to induce physio-psychological responses that lead to better performance, experience, and adherence to exercise as well as regulating mood and shifting attention away from discomfort (De Nora, 2000). Our investigation showed the differences in the effects of listening to music during high intensity and low intensity exercise (i.e., endurance exercise). Endurance exercise seems more sensitive to external stimuli (Van Cutsem et al., 2017) due to the mental fatigue and perception of effort involved in endurance exercise. High intensity training (i.e., explosive effort) seems characterized by an all-out approach that is powered primarily by metabolic pathways through muscular simulation without the use of oxygen (Van Cutsem et al., 2017). As such, "anaerobic" high intensity training requires fewer decision-making processes compared to endurance exercise, due to the all-out strategy and the intrinsically shorter duration (Van Cutsem et al., 2017).

This study presents some limitations. First, the results refer to a physically trained adult female population. Consequently, these results need to be confirmed for other populations such as male subjects, untrained people, older people, or adolescents. Furthermore, music cannot be described only using tempo, but also other characteristics need to be considered such as lyrics, melody, and genre. These characteristics were not considered in this study, but they could influence the performance of the participant. Also, the preference of the participants concerning their musical preferences were not collected and considered in the present study. Finally, the effect in the different moments of the same exercise was not considered as in previous study (Di Cagno et al., 2016).

CONCLUSION

This study indicates the benefits of listening to music under physical stress conditions as well as during endurance and high intensity training. The results of this study demonstrate that the beneficial effects of music are more apparent for endurance exercise. Consequently, music may be considered an important tool to stimulate people engaging in physical exercise. The finding of this study underlines the efficacity of the tempo of music in improving the performance and simultaneously reducing the RPE during the exercises. With this in mind, it is important to understand how this music influence can be used to improve training load and performance in trained people, but also the risk of an "altered" RPE during the exercise (both endurance and high intensity) needs to be clarified.

ETHICS STATEMENT

The studies involving human participants were reviewed and approved by the local Ethics Committee. The patients/participants provided their written informed consent to participate in this study.

AUTHOR CONTRIBUTIONS

VP, JP, and AD: conceptualization and writing. JP and EI: methodology and formal analysis. EI and LA: validation. DČ, AM, and VP: investigation. LA, DČ, and AM: resources. EI: data curation. AD and JP: review and editing. AD: supervision.

REFERENCES

Altenmüller, E., and Schlaug, G. (2012). "Music, brain, and health: exploring biological foundations of music's health effects," in *Music, Health & Wellbeing*, eds R. A. R. MacDonald, G. Kreutz, and L. Mitchell, (Oxford: Oxford University Press), 12–24.

Altenmüller, E., and Schlaug, G. (2013). Neurologic music therapy: the beneficial effects of music making on neurorehabilitation. *Acoust. Sci. Technol.* 34, 5–12. doi: 10.1250/ast.34.5

Benke, G., Dimitriadis, C., Zeleke, B. M., Inyang, I., McKenzie, D., and Abramson, M. J. (2018). Is exposure to personal music players a confounder in adolescent mobile phone use and hearing health studies? *J. Int. Med. Res.* 46, 4527–4534. doi: 10.1177/0300060518760700

Bianco, V., Berchicci, M., Perri, R. L., Quinzi, F., and Di Russo, F. (2017). Exercise-related cognitive effects on sensory-motor control in athletes and drummers compared to non-athletes and other musicians. *Neuroscience* 30, 39–47. doi: 10.1016/j.neuroscience.2017.07.059

Bigliassi, M., Karageorghis, C. I., Wright, M. J., Orgs, G., and Nowicky, A. V. (2017). Effects of auditory stimuli on electrical activity in the brain during cycle ergometry. *Physiol. Behav.* 177, 135–147. doi: 10.1016/j.physbeh.2017.04.023

Chamari, K., and Padulo, J. (2015). 'Aerobic and Anaerobic' terms used in exercise physiology: a critical terminology reflection. *Sports Med. Open* 1:9.

De Giorgio, A. (2016). From emotional education to collaborative intelligence. *Espressivamente.* 1, 16–41. ISSN 2239-4044.

De Giorgio, A. (2017). The roles of motor activity and environmental enrichment in intellectual disability. *Somatosens. Mot. Res.* 34, 34–43. doi: 10.1080/08990220.2016

De Giorgio, A., Dante, A., Cavioni, V., Padovan, A. M., Rigonat, D., Iseppi, F., et al. (2017). The IARA Model as an integrative approach to promote autonomy in COPD patients through improvement of self-efficacy beliefs and illness perception: a mixed-method pilot study. *Front. Psychol.* 8:1682. doi: 10.3389/fpsyg.2017.01682

De Giorgio, A., KuvaČić, G., Milić, M., and Padulo, J. (2018a). The brain and movement: How physical activity affects the brain. *Monten. J. Sports Sci. Med.* 7, 63–68. doi: 10.26773/mjssm.180910

De Giorgio, A., Sellami, M., Kuvacic, G., Lawrence, G., Padulo, J., Mingardi, M., et al. (2018b). Enhancing motor learning of young soccer players through preventing an internal focus of attention: the effect of shoes colour. *PLoS One* 13:e0200689. doi: 10.1371/journal.pone.0200689

De Nora, T. (2000). *Music in Everyday Life*. Cambridge: Cambridge University Press.

Di Cagno, A., Iuliano, E., Fiorilli, G., Aquino, G., Giombini, A., Menotti, F., et al. (2016). Effects of rhythmical and extra-rhythmical qualities of music on heart rate during stationary bike activities. *J. Sport Med. Phys. Fit.* 56, 1226–1231.

Harmon, N. M., and Kravitz, L. (2007). The beat goes on: the effects of music on exercise: a review of the research on the ergogenic and psychophysical impact of music in an exercise program. *IDEA Fit. J.* 4, 72–77.

Hou, J., Song, B., Chen, C. A. N., Sun, C., Zhou, J., Zhu, H., et al. (2017). Review on neural correlates of emotion regulation and music: implications for emotion dysregulation. *Front. Psychol.* 8:501. doi: 10.3389/fpsyg.2017.00501

Hutchinson, J. C., Jones, L., Vitti, S. N., Moore, A., Dalton, P. C., and O'Neil, B. J. (2018). The influence of self-selected music on affect-regulated exercise intensity and re- membered pleasure during treadmill running. *Sport Ex. Perf. Psychol.* 7, 80–92. doi: 10.1037/spy0000115

Innes, K. E., Selfe, T. K., Kandati, S., Wen, S., and Huysmans, Z. (2018). Effects of mantra meditation versus music listening on knee pain, function, and related outcomes in older adults with knee osteoarthritis: an exploratory Randomized Clinical Trial (RCT). *Evid. Based Complement. Alternat. Med.* 2018:7683897. doi: 10.1155/2018/7683897

Jarraya, M., Chtourou, H., Aloui, A., Hammouda, O., Chamari, K., Chaouachi, A., et al. (2012). The effects of music on high-intensity short-term exercise in well trained athletes. *Asian J. Sports Med.* 3, 233–238.

Jing, L., and Xudong, W. (2008). Evaluation on the effects of relaxing music on the recovery from aerobic exercise-induced fatigue. *J. Sports Med. Phys. Fit.* 48, 102–106.

Karageorghis, C. I., and Jones, L. (2014). On the stability and relevance of the exercise heart rate–music-tempo preference relationship. *Psychol. Sport Exerc.* 15, 299–310. doi: 10.1016/j.psychsport.2013.08.004

Karageorghis, C. I., and Priest, D. L. (2012a). Music in the exercise domain: a review and synthesis (part I). *Int. Rev. Sport Exerc. Psychol.* 5, 44–66. doi: 10.1080/1750984X.2011.631026

Karageorghis, C. I., and Priest, D. L. (2012b). Music in the exercise domain: a review and synthesis (part II). *Int. Rev. Sport Exerc. Psychol.* 5, 67–84. doi: 10.1080/1750984X.2011.631027

Karageorghis, C. I., Terry, P. C., Lane, A. M., Bishop, D. T., and Priest, D. L. (2012). The BASES expert statement on use of music in exercise. *J. Sports Sci.* 30, 953–956. doi: 10.1080/02640414.2012.676665

Koc, H., and Curtseit, T. (2009). The effects of music on athletic performance. *Ovidius University Ann. Series Phys. Educ. Sport Sci. Movement Health* 9, 43–47.

Levitin, D. J., and Tirovolas, A. K. (2009). Current advances in the cognitive neuroscience of music. *Ann. N. Y. Acad. Sci.* 1156, 211–231. doi: 10.1111/j.1749-6632.2009.04417.x

Migliaccio, G. M., Dello Iacono, A., Ardigò, L. P., Samozino, P., Iuliano, E., Grgantov, Z., et al. (2018). Leg press vs. smith machine: quadriceps activation and overall perceived effort profiles. *Front. Physiol.* 23:1481. doi: 10.3389/fphys.2018.01481

Mohammad Alipour, Z., Mohammadkhani, S., and Khosrowabadi, R. (2019). Alteration of perceived emotion and brain functional connectivity by changing the musical rhythmic pattern. *Exp. Brain Res.* 237, 2607–2619. doi: 10.1007/s00221-019-05616-w

Murrock, C. J., and Higgins, P. A. (2009). The theory of music, mood and movement to improve health outcomes: discussion paper. *J. Adv. Nurs.* 65, 2249–2257. doi: 10.1111/j.1365-2648.2009.05108.x

Padovan, A. M., Oprandi, G. M., Padulo, J., Bruno, C., Isoardi, M., Gulotta, F., et al. (2018). A novel integrative approach to improve the quality of life by reducing pain and kinesiophobia in patients undergoing TKA: the IARA Model. *Muscles Ligaments Tendons J.* 8, 93–103. doi: 10.11138/mltj/2018.8.1.093

Padulo, J., Chamari, K., and Ardigò, L. P. (2014). Walking and running on treadmill: the standard criteria for kinematics studies. *Muscles Ligaments Tendons J.* 14, 159–162.

Padulo, J., Laffaye, G., Chaouachi, A., and Chamari, K. (2015). Bench press exercise: the key points. *J. Sport Med. Phys. Fit.* 55, 604–608.

Padulo, J., Migliaccio, G. M., Ardigò, L. P., Leban, B., Cosso, M., and Samozino, P. (2017). Lower limb force, velocity, power capabilities during leg press and squat movements. *Int. J. Sports Med.* 38, 1083–1089. doi: 10.1055/s-0043-118341

Rodriguez-Fornells, A., Rojo, N., Amengual, J. L., Ripollès, P., Altenmüller, E., and Münte, T. F. (2012). The involvement of audio-motor coupling in the music- supported therapy applied to stroke patients. *Ann. N. Y. Acad. Sci.* 1252, 282–293. doi: 10.1111/j.1749-6632.2011.06425.x

Schneck, D. J., and Berger, D. S. (2006). *The Music Effect: Music Physiology and Clinical Applications*. London: Jessica Kingsley.

Tabei, K. I., Satoh, M., Ogawa, J. I., Tokita, T., Nakaguchi, N., Nakao, K., et al. (2017). Physical exercise with music reduces gray and white matter loss in the frontal cortex of elderly people: the mihama-kiho scan project. *Front. Aging Neur.* 7:174. doi: 10.3389/fnagi.2017.00174

Terry, P. C., Karageorghis, C. I., Mecozzi Saha, A., and D'Auria, S. (2012). Effects of synchronous music on treadmill running among elite triathletes. *J. Sci. Med. Sport* 15, 52–57. doi: 10.1016/j.jsams.2011.06.003

Thaut, M. H. (2005). *Rhythm, music, and the brain*. London: Routledge.

Thaut, M. H., and Abiru, M. (2010). Rhythmic auditory stimulation in rehabilitation of movement disorders: a review of current research. *Music Perc.* 27, 263–269. doi: 10.1525/MP.2010.27.4.263

Todd, N., Lee, C., and O'Boyle, D. (2002). A sensorimotor theory of temporal tracking and beat induction. *Psychol. Res.* 66, 26–39. doi: 10.1007/s00426010007

Van Cutsem, J., Marcora, S., De Pauw, K., Bailey, S., Meeusen, R., and Roelands, B. (2017). The effects of mental fatigue on physical performance: a systematic review. *Sports Med.* 47, 1569–1588. doi: 10.1007/s40279-016-0672-0

Weir, J. P. (2005). Quantifying test-retest reliability using the intra-class correlation coefficient and the SEM. *J. Strength Cond. Res.* 19, 231–240. doi: 10.1519/15184.1

Zatorre, R. J., Chen, J. L., and Penhune, V. B. (2007). When the brain plays music: auditory-motor interactions in music perception and production. *Nat. Rev. Neur.* 8, 547–558. doi: 10.1038/nrn2152

19

A Qualitative Study on Pre-Performance Routines of Diving: Evidence from Elite Chinese Diving Athletes

Qiang Yao[1], *Feng Xu*[2]* *and Jiabao Lin*[2]

[1] *Department of Physical Education, Beijing Language and Culture University, Beijing, China,* [2] *College of Economics and Management, South China Agricultural University, Guangzhou, China*

***Correspondence:**
Feng Xu
xufeng@scau.edu.cn

Pre-performance routines (PPRs) are essential motor skills prior to a competition for athletes. But we believe that a specific kind of sport has its own PPRs. Using a qualitative research design, this study conducted in-depth interviews with 14 elite Chinese athletes in competitive diving and their coaches as well as observed and analyzed the behaviors of 13 athletes during diving competitions. The results showed that the divers' PPRs were constituted of four components (psychological skills, pace setting, mastering competition progress, and behavioral strategies), which could be divided into 20 core categories, with the entire diving process divided into three sections and ten stages, including 13 subcategories in off-platform, 12 subcategories in on-platform and the diving stage. Thus, patterns in the PPRs for divers were established and a clear and comprehensive picture of the diving process, as well as the psychological characteristics and behavioral patterns of athletes during the process, were obtained. The findings entail implications for developing PPRs for diving athletes and future studies on PPRs in other competitive diving and other sports.

Keywords: Chinese athletes, diving, grounded theory, pre-performance routines, qualitative research

INTRODUCTION

Pre-performance routines (PPRs) are pre-arranged sequential thoughts and actions that help athletes stabilize and control their thoughts, emotions, and behaviors prior to a competition (Singer, 2002; Cotterill, 2010). Relevant studies and sports-related research tend to refer to PPRs as a plan, a strategy, a protocol, a technique, and even a ritual (e.g., Cohn et al., 1990; Foster et al., 2006; Lonsdale and Tam, 2008; Mesagno et al., 2019). PPRs involve a variety of psychological skills and behavioral responses, which are widely adopted in different sports; particularly, they are most commonly adopted in the preparation stage of self-paced events involving technical performance (e.g., Lonsdale and Tam, 2008; Clowes and Knowles, 2013). Scholars have suggested that PPRs are extremely important for high-performing or elite athletes; the motor skills of these athletes tend to be over-learned and the operation of the expected movements becomes mechanized, whereby they are executed without conscious attention (Cotterill, 2010). They are thus faced with an increased likelihood of being disturbed by internal and external non-task-related stimuli, which may negatively affect their athletic performance (Beauchamp et al., 1996; Jackson and Baker, 2001; Mesagno et al., 2015). The use of cognitive and behavioral procedures helps these athletes avoid interference and ensures smooth performance in the competition.

Singer (2002) conducted a general analysis of the pre-performance state in self-paced events and concluded that it should include the following steps: (1) self-regulation of thoughts and emotions to a status compatible with the expected movements; (2) narrow, dedicated, and sustained concentration; (3) attainable ideal self-efficacy; (4) appropriate distribution of activated locations in the brain to ensure a quiet mind; (5) maximal focus on the target (frequency and duration) to channel the direction of attention; (6) generating a set of simplified routine behaviors prior to and during the competition; and (7) automatic activation of the above processes to allow effortless, effective, and successful performance in the competition. The ultimate goal is to use the aforementioned steps to create individualized consistent PPRs that can be performed automatically regardless of the situation. The purpose of such routines is to ensure that athletes are continually in their best emotional state with high self-expectations, confidence, and concentration prior to and during the competition. Such self-regulatory techniques are essential as they are the driving force of athletes' performance during the competition, helping them control and regulate their emotions, thoughts, and attention to remain focused and self-controlled, and to ensure a state of flow (Jackson and Baker, 2001; Cotterill, 2010).

It is evident that athletes who have better motor skills and are able to perform effortlessly during competitions have more advantages than their opponents; however, it is a challenge to ensure effortless performance on a consistent basis during competitions. In order to achieve an optimal performance state, it may be a prerequisite to develop and master a set of effective PPRs. Systematic studies on athletes who could effectively perform PPRs have yielded that, regardless of being a conscious or subconscious behavior, PPRs are associated with motor skills, of which they have become an integral part. To a certain degree, PPRs directly affect athletes' readiness for their performance and results (Cotterill, 2010; Macnamara et al., 2016). Singer (2002) proposed a general five-step PPR approach applicable to different sports. However, empirical results showed that the proposed model was not specific and detailed enough to provide practical guidance for any given sport. Therefore, it would be theoretically and practically more useful if research could target PPRs with consideration of the characteristics of a specific sport.

The research interest of the present study is competitive diving. Patterns in PPRs in the context of diving have not been thoroughly studied. Since China is one of the leading nations in the sport of diving, this study recruited elite diving athletes and coaches of the Chinese national and provincial teams as research subjects. The qualitative research method was adopted to conduct comprehensive and in-depth investigations, interviews, and observations with the subjects. By analyzing their competition experience and behavioral patterns, a set of PPRs for diving was constructed in order to facilitate relevant studies and improve PPR interventions in the sport of diving.

MATERIALS AND METHODS

Research Subjects

Among the 14 athletes interviewed, 6 were from the national diving team and 8 from a provincial diving team. Among the 8 provincial athletes, 4 had previously been selected for the national team. Among the 4 remaining provincial athletes, 2 had previously received the title of "international professional athlete," and 2 had been granted the title of "national professional athlete." The athletes' mean age was 23 years (min = 15 and max = 39), with experience spanning, on average, 14 years as a professional athlete (min = 7 and max = 22). These athletes had collectively won 18 Olympic gold medals (two of them had won five Olympic gold medals each), 1 Olympic silver medal, and 6 gold medals in diving at the World Aquatics Championships. Three of the athletes had won two Olympic championships (see **Table 1**).

Six coaches (2 male and 4 female) were interviewed, among whom three currently coach in the national team and two had prior experience as a coach for the national team (**Table 2**).

Statistical Analysis Software

The QSR Nvivo 7.0 qualitative analysis software package was used to analyze the data collected during the interviews, while the data collected from the video recordings and observations were analyzed using Noldus' The Observer 6.0 behavioral analysis software package.

Data Collection

Collection of Interview Data

The purpose of this study was to identify PPRs for diving based on an investigation of Chinese elite diving athletes and their coaches. Based on the research objectives, a semi-structured interview outline was drafted. Next, a team of experts who are providing psychological services to the diving team preparing for the coming Olympic Games (experts, including a professor, a doctoral student, and two postgraduate students of athletic psychology) were invited to examine the coverage and contents of the drafted outline. The final outline was updated based on their suggestions and comments. A Behavioral Event Interview (BEI) was used to identify the characteristics of the skills mastered by the interviewed athletes during competitions. Data related to diving competitions were collected through interviews with the athletes, to determine their behaviors, moods, and psychological strategies at different stages of the diving competitions, as well as through interviews with their corresponding coaches. The interview outlines included items designed to collect the athletes' BEI data, behaviors during diving competitions, and viewpoints from their coaches.

In addition, a pilot study, based on the drafted outline, was conducted by the present researcher to interview two national team gymnastics athletes to improve the operational skills required for the interviews. The interviews were conducted face-to-face by the present author; the average duration was approximately 30 min, and all interviews were recorded.

TABLE 1 | Basic information of the interviewed athletes.

	Gender		Category		Professional level		# of Olympic gold medals	# of Olympic silver medals	Years of service	
	Male	Female	Platform diving	Springboard diving	International level	National level			<14	≥14
National athlete (*n* = 6)	4	2	2	4	6	0	5	1	1	5
Provincial athlete (*n* = 8)	3	5	2	6	6	2	0	0	7	1

TABLE 2 | Basic information of the interviewed coaches.

	Gender		Professional title		Years of service		Best achievement as a coach		
	Male	Female	National coach	Senior coach	<40	≥40	# of Olympic champion coached as the head coach	# of Olympic 1st runner-up coached as the head coach	# of Olympic champion coached as the 1st coach
Coach of the national team (*n* = 3)	2	1	2	1	2	1	2	1	0
Coach of the provincial team (*n* = 3)	0	3	2	1	1	2	1	0	2

Collection of Observed Data

The collection of observed data was completed by three people: the first person used a digital video camera to record the behavior of all participating athletes prior to ascending the platform or springboard (off-platform). The second person used a digital video camera to record the behavior of the participating athletes when they were on the platform or springboard (on-platform). The third person was expected to take a video camera and move between the various athletes' zones (such as coaches' stand, locker rooms, and warm-up areas) to observe and collect information that was not within the coverage of the other cameras.

Data Analysis

Analysis of the Interview Data

Grounded theory involves the development of a new theory based on raw data, to guide the development of theory driven by qualitative research (Glaser, 2001; Charmaz, 2006). The strategy proposed by grounded theory and the method of constructing theory using qualitative data have been widely applied to different fields and disciplines. Based on the results of comparative analysis, Charmaz (2006) suggested that we should regard grounded theory and corresponding methods as a set of principles and practices, rather than prescriptions or packaged procedures. On that account, a grounded-theory perspective that emphasizes the flexible use of coding guidelines is suitable for addressing the research questions of the present study. Therefore, this theory was employed as the data analysis method, based on the following process: open coding, axial coding, and selective coding were primarily applied; then, key behaviors were identified and a PPR model was developed. The coding system was developed strictly following the qualitative research process. First, two of the present researchers participated in the analysis of all of the collected data independently and established a preliminary coding table according to standard theoretical definitions in psychology. Next, a group discussion was conducted to resolve any disagreement on themes and groupings of behaviors until consensus was reached. Following the construction of the preliminary coding table, the researchers referred to the principles of thematic analysis and combined themes based on their similarities, so as to establish a more complex second-level coding table. Specifically, each theme was compared to each of the other themes, so that any themes with a similar meaning were combined, and themes with contrasting meanings were separated. Following the group discussion, the two researchers consistently agreed on the coding system to be applied.

All records of the interviews were first transcribed by the researcher. Next, the transcripts were checked against the records to ensure the accuracy of the information. Another member of the research team was also invited to conduct a second check of the transcripts to compare them against the records. The verified information was then imported into QSR Nvivo 7.0.

Analysis of the Observed Data

The recorded videos were imported into Noldus' The Observer 6.0. Firstly, the researcher conducted a preliminary coding table for the data, according to the research purpose. Next, a group discussion was conducted to resolve any disagreement on the theme and grouping of the behavior until a consensus was reached.

Test for Validity

The five types of validity standards include descriptive validity, interpretive validity, theoretical validity, generalizability, and evaluative validity and triangulation methods were used test the validity of the data.

Firstly, four strategies, used to improve the descriptive validity of the data, were adopted during the data collection process: (1) the interviewer ensured that the recording equipment was functional during the interview; (2) the transcriber ensured that the interviews had been transcribed verbatim; (3) the initial coding (components and categories) were sent to the interviewees for verification, and their suggestions were considered to ensure the accuracy of the terms; (4) finally, both athletes and coaches were interviewed to ensure that the collected data from the two groups complemented one another.

Secondly, two strategies were adopted to improve the interpretive validity of the data: (1) a group of experts, specialized in psychology, was recruited to provide suggestions and guidance throughout the entire research process, from preparation to implementation of the research; (2) during the transcription and coding process, the researcher maintained close communication with the interviewees (athletes and coaches) for advice and suggestions.

Thirdly, expert meetings were organized at each data analysis stage, and the OG-P experts were invited to evaluate the accuracy of the data coding.

Fourthly, the research results were sent to some interviewees, who confirmed that the results accurately reflected their situation and presented some abstract concepts in a more tangible manner, as well as confirming that the results could be internally generalized. This study also received recognition from target readers and relevant professionals, following communication with them; the constructed PPRs achieved acceptable external generalizability.

Fifthly, the researcher comprehensively reviewed and studied existing research and related theories on PPRs, from home and abroad, to gain a full understanding of the technical, psychological, and competitive characteristics of diving. In addition, the researcher also investigated the background of the interviewees in terms of years of service as an athlete or coach, as well as educational background. Expert meetings were held throughout the entire research process to improve its evaluative validity.

Lastly, triangulation, which refers to the use of different data sources, methods, analyses, and theories as a means of ensuring the accuracy of research results, was adopted. In this study, the findings from the interviews were further verified during the observation process, and the findings from the observations were compared with those from the interviews to ensure that the findings from the two methods matched, confirmed, and supplemented one another. Moreover, the study not only included athletes as interviewees but also coaches. During the observation process, both horizontal and vertical comparisons were conducted.

RESULTS AND ANALYSIS

Due to the word count restriction, the original quotes of the interviewees were only included for a limited number of topics.

Results of the Interviews

The analysis of the interview results with the athletes and coaches yielded four components and 16 categories of PPRs, as presented in **Table 3**.

Results of the Observation

Observation Results Off-Platform

The analysis of the behavior of 13 athletes off-platform showed that the athletes tended to exhibit the following behaviors: (1) climbing out of the pool to salute the referee and the audience; (2) listening to or checking the announced score of the dive; (3) showering with hot water and then drying off; (4) returning to the rest zone to rest; (5) warming up; (6) looking for the coach; (7) imitating the moves of the dive; (8) showering; and (9) waiting for their turn of the next dive. In addition, following a comparison between the observed behavior and the results of the interviews, three additional categories related to behavioral strategies emerged as follows: (1) climbing out of the pool to salute the referee and the audience; (2) listening to or checking the announced score of the dive; and (3) showering with hot water and then drying. These three categories were considered supplementary to the findings of the interviews.

Observation Results On-Platform

The analysis of the behavior of 13 athletes on-platform showed that the athletes tended to exhibit the following behaviors: (1) physical arousal behavior, such as clenching the fists, treading water, shaking and swinging the legs, bending the knees, rotating the head, and twisting the neck; (2) adjusting the springboard (springboard diving); (3) imitating the moves of the dive (platform diving); (4) throwing the towel; (5) adjusting breathing; (6) listening to the broadcast and the starting signal prior to beginning their dive; (7) habitual behavior, such as rubbing hands, squeezing wrists, touching hips, and rubbing face; (8) standing still; and (9) diving. A comparison of the observed categories with the results of the interview yielded one additional category related to behavioral strategies: standing still.

Observation of an Individual Case On-Platform

With the development of technological counseling services for the Olympic diving team, and the in-depth investigation of the present study, it was determined that certain associations existed between the behavior of outstanding athletes on the diving platform and their performance during competition. For that reason, the present researchers conducted an investigation on the behaviors of key athletes from the national team during major competitions. The athletes' habitual behaviors on the diving platform were categorized into movements of the hands, body, and head (including facial expressions). Physical arousal behavior on the platform was divided into upper limb movement and lower limb movement. In addition, habitual behavior that frequently occurred in the same dive group and the order of the movement of each action were analyzed and summarized. Cognitive processes and the stress levels of the athletes accompanying these frequently occurring habitual behaviors were further verified based on observation results and interviews. Since the goal of the present study was not to develop PPRs for a specific athlete or to establish a relationship between PPRs and competition performance, only the data of Athlete 5 (Olympic champion), who performed behavior 5253B in 10 major competitions, were presented and analyzed. The relationship between the frequency of the habitual

TABLE 3 | List of the components and categories of the PPRs collected through the interviews.

	Interviewees/meaning unit	Athlete (*n* = 14)			Total number of meaning unit	Coach (*n* = 6)			Total number of meaning unit
Component	**Category**	**On-platform**	**Off-platform**	**Total**		**On-platform**	**Off-platform**	**Total**	
Psychological Skills	Visualizing the moves of the dive	14	7	14	62	6	3	6	10
	Adjusting breathing	14	3	14	23	2	0	2	2
	Self-talk	5	2	5	13	0	0	0	0
	Concentrating	4	0	4	4	2	/	2	2
Pace setting	Pace setting	6	3	6	9	2	2	3	4
Mastering competition progress	Using the other participating athletes as a reference for the progress of the competition	/	8	8	11	/	4	4	4
	Listening to the broadcast and the starting signal prior to beginning their dive	7	/	7	10	1	/	1	1
Behavioral strategies	Warming up	0	14	14	21	0	6	6	11
	Habitual behavior	5	0	5	5	2	0	2	3
	Avoiding watching the dive of other athletes	/	4	4	4	/	2	2	2
	Imitating the moves of the dive	4	10	10	16	2	6	6	8
	Throwing the towel	2	/	2	2	1	/	1	1
	Adjusting the springboard (springboard diving)	5	/	5	5	4	/	4	9
	Looking for the coach	/	14	14	15	/	6	6	6
	Showering	/	9	9	9	/	2	2	2
	Resting	/	14	14	14	/	6	6	10

Unless specified otherwise, "on-platform" refers to the time period during which the athletes were on the platform or springboard, and "off-platform" refers to the time period during which the athletes were not on the platform or springboard.

behaviors, length of time standing still, and achievements in each competition are presented in **Table 4** and **Figure 1**. More data and behavioral analysis information on other athletes are not included in this paper, due to the word limit.

The frequency of habitual behavior of AI5 ranged between 4 and 7 times and the duration of standing still time ranged between 3 and 6 s prior to performing 5253B. In addition, the resulting score of the performance appeared to be higher when the frequency of the habitual behavior was 6 or 7 times and the duration of the standing still time ranged between 4 and 6 s.

TABLE 4 | Analysis of the on-platform behaviors of AI5 prior to performing 5253B.

	Scores	On-platform habitual behavior	Standing still (second)
Competition 1	93.8	5	4
Competition 2	96.9	7	4
Competition 3	102	6	4
Competition 4	96.9	7	6
Competition 5	95.2	6	4
Competition 6	91.5	5	3
Competition 7	90	4	3
Competition 8	97.4	6	5
Competition 9	95.6	7	4
Competition 10	98.3	6	4

A further interview with AI5 showed that the habitual behavior was usually accompanied by self-talk, intense concentration, and adjustment of breathing, while standing still was accompanied by visualizing the moves of the dive.

Analysis of Athlete 5's behaviors on the diving platform resulted in conclusions regarding their corresponding characteristics and patterns. In addition, different athletes tended to show unique behavioral characteristics and patterns on the diving platform prior to their dives. The characteristics and patterns not only provide the basis for constructing PPRs but also serve as a key reference for coaches and athletes to develop personalized PPRs. It should be emphasized that some of the habitual behaviors on the diving platform were associated with

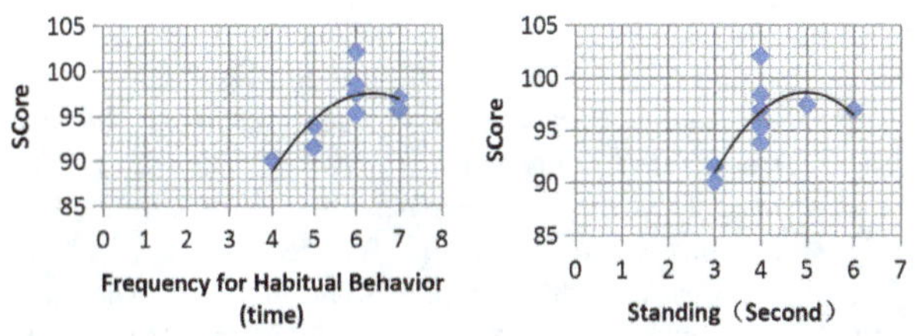

FIGURE 1 | Scatter plots of the relationship between scores and on-platform behaviors of interviewee 5 prior to performing 5253B.

athletes' psychological skills during the competition. Therefore, it is of great importance to elucidate such a relationship prior to developing PPRs.

Patterns in the Diving PPRs

The off-platform diving PPRs included the following:

(1) Psychological skills: (a) visualizing the moves of the dive, (b) adjusting breathing, and (c) self-talk; (2) pace setting; (3) mastering competition progress: (a) using the other participating athletes as a reference for the progress of the competition; (4) behavioral strategies: (a) climbing out of the pool to salute the referee and the audience; (b) listening to or checking the announced score of the dive; (c) showering with hot water and then drying the body; (d) returning to the rest zone to rest; (e) standing up and warming up; (f) looking for the coach; (g) imitating the moves of the dive; and (h) showering the body.

The on-platform diving PPRs included the following:

(1) Psychological skills: (a) visualizing the moves of the dive, (b) adjusting breathing, (c) self-talk, and (d) concentrating; (2) pace setting; (3) mastering competition progress: (a) listening to the broadcast and the starting signal prior to beginning their dive; (4) behavioral strategies: (a) physical arousal behavior, (b) adjusting the springboard (springboard diving), (c) imitating the moves of the dive (platform diving), (d) throwing the towel, (f) habitual behavior, and (g) standing still.

In order to present the distribution of the components and categories of the PPRs during the diving competition more clearly, the diving process was divided into three parts (**Figure 2**) and 10 stages. Each diving competition consisted of five (women's competition) or six (men's competition) such cycles. In light of the findings obtained through the interviews and observations, combined with the three-part model of the diving process, the diving PPRs were constructed (**Figure 3**).

Analysis of the Patterns in the Diving PPRs

Pace Setting

The category "pace setting" is involved in all parts of the diving PPRs, including the pace of off-platform preparation, the pace of on-stage preparation, and the pace of the dive. Pace setting during the competition is a very important step to ensure effective self-regulation during the competition. One of the interviewees explained "pace setting" as follows:

> *The behavior of athletes with more experience in competitions lends itself to a certain pace. For example, the usual pace during the Olympic Games is approximately one behavior per minute. The progress of the competitions is usually controlled by the corresponding TV stations, as they need time to broadcast other information, such as advertisements. There is a sense of rhythm in terms of when the athlete should ascend the stairs, when the broadcast announces the scores, when to adjust the springboard, when to throw the towel, when the broadcast announces his/her name, when to step onto the springboard, and when to jump (Coach Interviewee 1).*

Off-Platform Preparation

Stage 1: resting

During this stage, athletes use various strategies of self-regulation, such as visualizing the moves of the dive, adjusting breathing, self-talk, listening to music, and chatting with others, to rest. Other self-regulation strategies include not watching the dives of the other athletes and trying to avoid receiving information related to the performance of other athletes.

Stage 2: receiving the coach's instructions

When the athletes are preparing for the next dive, the coach usually gives instructions related to the essentials of the next dive and the moves that they should pay attention to. The athletes usually reinforce their understanding of the instructions by imitating or visualizing the moves of the dive. It was also found that the sequence of stage 2 and 3 (warm up) depends on the personal habits of the athletes rather than being fixed. Specifically, some of investigated athletes went directly to their coaches for instruction following the rest stage, while other athletes preferred to warm up prior to receiving instructions from their coach.

Stage 3: warm up

During this stage, common warm-up activities are carried out; the athletes tend to apply imitation and visualization of the dive moves to activate their body and mind and reinforce the essentials of the dive. In addition, athletes are required to shower and test the water to prepare their body for diving into the water. The time spent on showering and water temperature testing was believed by the interviewees to have a certain impact on the preparation of the dive.

Stage 4: waiting to ascend the platform/springboard

At this stage, the athlete waits for the completion of the previous athlete's dive prior to ascending the platform/springboard. Since the wait is usually not very long, the athlete is required to be alert and aware of when the previous athlete has completed the dive and he/she is able to ascend the platform/springboard. Therefore, the athletes tend to be nervous during this stage and usually adopt self-talk and breathing regulation to assist self-regulation.

Stage 10: transition and feedback following the dive

This stage is a transition stage between two dives. A certain number of behaviors is expected from the athletes, such as climbing out of the pool to salute the referee and the audience, listening to or checking the announced score of the dive, showering with hot water and then drying the body, looking for the coach, returning to the rest zone, putting on clothes, and resting. One other important aspect at this stage is to forget the result of the previous dive, regardless of it being good or bad, and swiftly adjust oneself for the next dive. One of the interviewees described this stage as follows:

> *Regardless of the result of the previous dive, [I] try not to think about it, but rather [I] clear my mind and try to calm down. Usually [my] heart beats fast during this time period, [so I] go and find a place to sit and rest (Athlete Interviewee 2).*

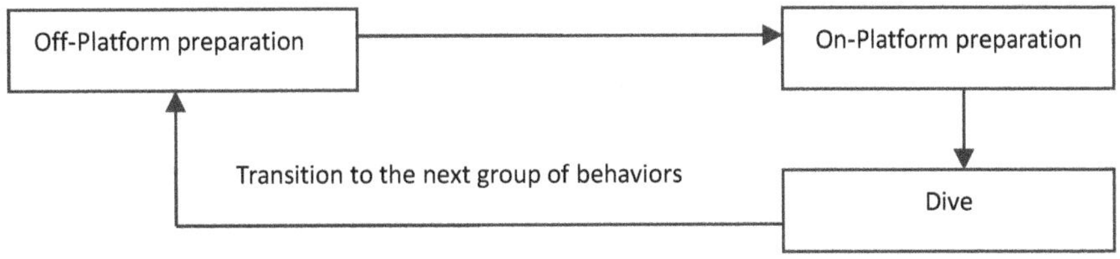

FIGURE 2 | The three diving stages.

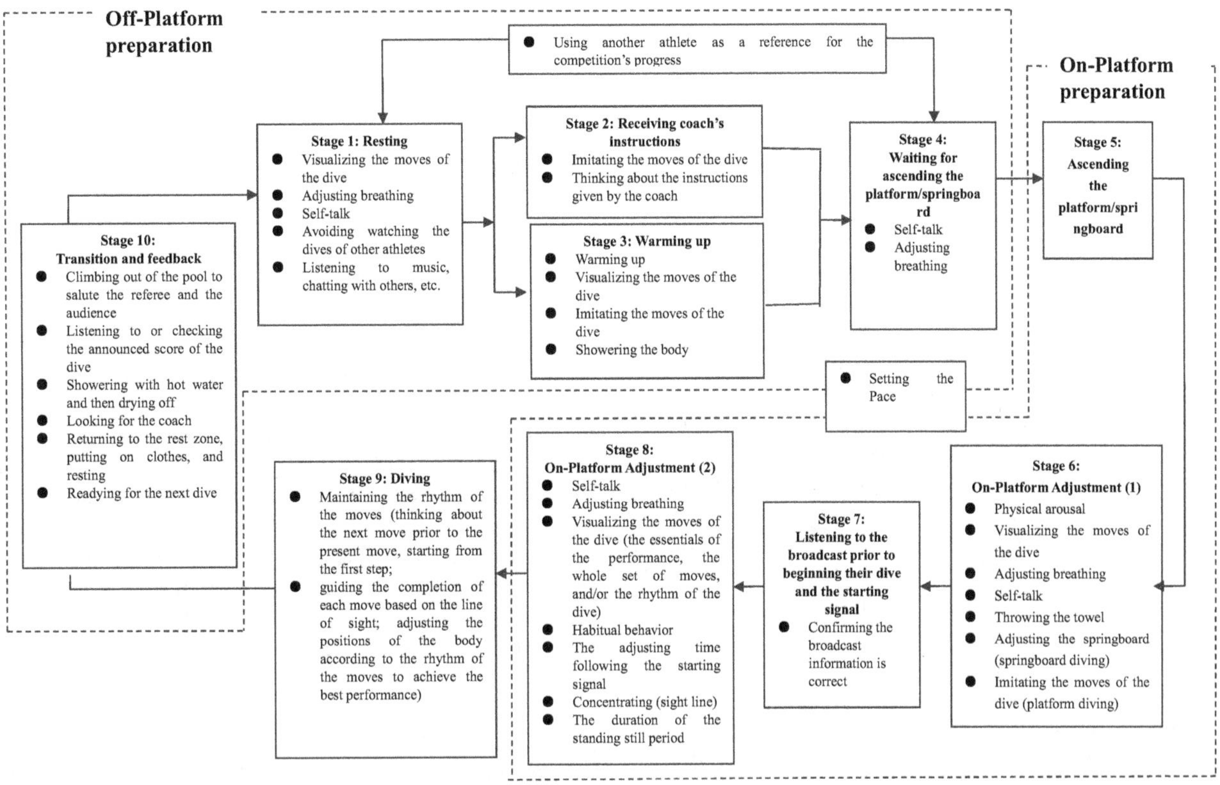

FIGURE 3 | The diving PPRs.

On-Platform Preparation

Stage 5: ascending the platform/springboard

This stage is a transition phase between off-platform and on-platform preparation. The ascent is usually too brief to allow for any other moves to be executed.

Stage 6: on-platform adjustment (1)

Athletes' appearance on the platform/springboard is similar to actors' appearance on the stage of theaters. Moving from "backstage" to being in front of the audience is likely to generate feelings of nervousness. Young and inexperienced athletes are likely to feel dizziness. In order to avoid potential negative effects of such pressure, athletes usually adopt strategies such as getting physically aroused, imitating the moves of the dive, and adjusting their breathing to alleviate the tension and ready themselves for the dive.

Stage 7: listening to the broadcast and the starting signal

At this stage, the athlete is expected to check the accuracy of the broadcast and the information displayed on the big screen. If the information does not match his/her personal information, he/she is supposed to raise his/her hand and ask for a correction. If no errors are identified in the broadcast and on the big screen, he/she is supposed to begin the dive after receiving the starting signal.

Stage 8: on-platform adjustment (2)

Although this stage lasts less than 1 min, it greatly affects the athletes' performance. The results showed that athletes tended to adopt self-regulation strategies such as self-talk, visualizing the moves of the dive, adjusting breathing, and concentrating. Habitual behaviors also occur during this stage and are usually accompanied by self-talk, concentrating, and adjustment of breathing, while standing still is usually accompanied by visualizing the moves of the dive.

Stage 9: diving

Very few interviewees mentioned self-regulation during this stage. In addition, the self-regulation strategies described by them appeared to be more abstract and highly personalized. Some examples of the responses are as follows:

> *[I] think about the essentials of a move prior to executing it. [I] find a good rhythm for the moves, such as [counting] "1, 2, 3" and complete the dive following my own pace. When [I] feel that a move was not executed smoothly, [I] try to think of ways to save it (Athlete Interviewee 8).*

> *[I] begin to think about the essentials of the moves after I take the first step, because that's when you develop the sense for the dive and think about what should be done (Athlete Interviewee 2).*

> *Once I stand there, the moves become a conditioned reflex in my mind. Once I jump, my mind automatically recalls which move/position is the most important to the dive and how I can optimize my performance. Maybe it's because I have been a diver for a long time that all the moves have become conditioned reflexes to me (Athlete Interviewee 4).*

DISCUSSION

Methodology

The advantage of qualitative research lies in the fact that it provides a profound, vivid, and comprehensive description of an object or phenomenon. The distinguishing characteristic of grounded theory is that researchers generally have no theoretical hypothesis prior to the research, but rather establish the theory using a bottom-up approach, by compiling and summarizing the concepts and propositions from the original data. The purpose of this study was to elucidate the PPRs of diving. It was expected that the findings would objectively present the experience of senior diving athletes in China and their existing PPRs and patterns so as to construct a PPR model for athletic diving. The choice of research methods in research generally depends on the research question and objectives. Considering the research questions and objectives of this study, the traditional quantitative research paradigm did not appear to fit the needs of the study. Therefore, the researcher chose the qualitative approach, combining interviews and observations (behavior analysis), to achieve the research objectives.

Nevertheless, there were certain limitations to the methodology of the study. Firstly, since this study mainly focused on the psychological training, behavioral strategies, and behavioral cues prior to and during past diving competitions, the responses of the interviewees were based on memory; hence, certain deviations from reality may have existed. Secondly, following the interviews, the researcher found that some of the concepts and responses required supplementary information for further clarification. Multiple rounds of interviews could have resolved the problem; however, due to several reasons, only a few of the interviewees were re-interviewed in this study. Thirdly, due to restriction of resources, the researcher was not able to conduct on-spot observations and timely interviews for each competition. The majority of the behaviors were recorded by video cameras and analyzed following the competition. Information that was not covered by the cameras was not included, which hindered in-depth revelations of the athletes' behaviors. Fourthly, only four interviewees were platform diving athletes (two males and two females). This was due to the fact that the majority of the platform-diving athletes were much younger, rendering it difficult to conduct in-depth interviews.

Research Content

Based on the five-step PPRs and related theory, as proposed by Singer et al., combined with the characteristics of the competitive sport of diving and diving athletes, this study divided the diving process into 10 stages and constructed a model of PPRs of diving. The off-platform preparation (stages 1, 2, 3, 4, and 10) in this study corresponded to the stages of "evaluating," "feedback," and "readying" of the five-step routines; the on-platform preparation (stages 5, 6, 7, and 8) corresponded to the stages of "imaging" and "focusing"; while diving (stage 9) corresponded to the stage of "starting the competition with a peaceful mind." In addition, this study also uncovered the behaviors, mental tactics, and patterns of top athletes in China during different stages of competition and proposed the concept of "pace-setting" of the competition, which was a dominant factor throughout the entire PPRs. Maintaining an appropriate rhythm for each movement during off-platform preparation, on-platform preparation, and the diving process was found to be a key measure in ensuring effective self-control and smooth performance during the competition itself. The model proposed in this study clearly and comprehensively revealed the diving process and the psychological and behavioral patterns of top diving athletes during the competition process, so that developers of PPRs, and other athletes, could accurately grasp the requirements of the competition process. However, in reality, the sequence and connection between some stages are not fixed, and athletes are required to adjust their preparation sequence according to their personal habits. Moreover, when applying the model to design PPRs for diving athletes, the specific behavioral procedures should be determined with consideration of the individual characteristics of each athlete. Training on psychological skills, such as how to adjust breathing, self-talk, visualizing the moves of the dive, and concentrating, should be provided to athletes on a regular basis to improve their ability to use the skills; the athletes should also frequently test and modify the skills with practical application.

Developing personalized PPRs that can be easily mastered by athletes is a difficult task. Each athlete has their own unique characteristics. In order to uncover the indicators and habitual behaviors suitable for each athlete, it is necessary to conduct in-depth interviews, repeated observation of large quantities of video recordings, and careful observation of the training and competition process, followed by further verification. In addition to collecting responses and viewpoints from the head coach, team coach, teammates, and athletes, it is also necessary to conduct research and analysis into the personality and characteristics of individual athletes. Furthermore, in the process of designing PPRs for diving athletes, it is also necessary to regularly conduct psychological skills training for athletes, such breathing control, use of self-talk, visualization of the moves of the dive, and concentration, so as to raise their ability to use these critical skills, and to continuously test and revise these skills during application.

The findings of the study also showed that some habitual behaviors (such as hand movements and hand-body movements) during the on-platform stage were accompanied by psychological skills (such as self-talk, concentrating, and adjustment of breathing), while standing still and looking forward and downward were accompanied by visualizing the moves of the dive. Uncovering the relationship between such behaviors and psychological skills is very important for the formulation of PPRs. It is likely that the PPRs of individual dives and synchronized group dives share some common characteristics as well as distinctive stages.

The present research mainly focused on the PPRs of individual dives; hence, the constructed model is suitable for individual diving athletes in the divisions of platform and springboard diving. However, the study did not collect or analyze data related to two-person synchronized dive teams. Since the PPR routines of synchronized diving are also important to the development of the sport, it is suggested that future studies include subjects from this area of the sport.

CONCLUSION

Based on the five-step PPRs and related theory proposed by Singer et al., combined with the characteristics of the competitive sport of diving and diving athletes, this study divided the diving process into 10 stages and constructed a model for diving PPRs. The model revealed the behaviors and psychological strategies and patterns of top diving athletes in China during various stages of the competition. In addition, the concept of competition "pace-setting" was proposed.

Off-platform preparation consisted of 13 categories, including: (1) visualizing the moves of the dive; (2) adjusting breathing; (3) self-talk; (4) pace setting; (5) tracking progress using other athletes as a reference; (6) climbing out of the pool to salute the referee and the audience; (7) listening to or checking the announced score of the dive; (8) showering with hot water and then drying off; (9) returning to the rest zone to rest; (10) standing up and warming up; (11) imitating the moves of the dive; (12) looking for the coach; and (13) showering.

On-platform preparation consisted of 12 categories, including: (1) visualizing the moves of the dive; (2) adjusting breathing; (3) self-talk; (4) concentrating; (5) pace setting; (6) listening to the broadcast and starting signal prior to the dive; (7) physical arousal behavior; (8) adjusting the springboard (springboard diving); (9) imitating the moves of the dive (platform diving); (10) throwing the towel; (11) habitual behavior; and (12) standing still.

The third part is diving. The three parts are connected to one another, forming a closed behavioral cycle that clearly and comprehensively demonstrates the diving process as well as the psychological characteristics and behavioral patterns of the athletes during the diving competitions. At the same time, "pace-setting" is the key to organically connecting various stages throughout the process of PPRs and clearly and comprehensively demonstrating the diving process, psychological characteristics, and behavioral patterns of top athletes during such a process. This research mainly focused on PPRs of individual diving divisions; hence, the constructed model is suitable for individual diving athletes in the divisions of platform and springboard diving.

ETHICS STATEMENT

The studies involving human participants were reviewed and approved by the Beijing Normal University. The ethics committee waived the requirement of written informed consent for participation.

AUTHOR CONTRIBUTIONS

QY designed the study. All authors analyzed the data, wrote and revised the manuscript, contributed to the manuscript revision, and approved the submitted version.

ACKNOWLEDGMENTS

We express our deepest thanks to all the elite Chinese diving athletes and coaches involved in our study.

REFERENCES

Beauchamp, P. H., Halliwell, W. R., Fournier, J. F., and Koestner, R. (1996). Effects of cognitive-behavioral psychological skills training on the motivation, preparation, and putting performance of novice golfers. *Sport Psychol.* 10, 157–170. doi: 10.1123/tsp.10.2.157

Charmaz, K. (2006). *Constructing Grounded Theory: A Practical Guide through Qualitative Analysis.* Thousand Oaks, CA: Sage Publications.

Clowes, H., and Knowles, Z. (2013). Exploring the effectiveness of pre-performance routines in elite artistic gymnasts: a mixed method investigation. *Sci. Gym. J.* 5, 27–40.

Cohn, P. J., Rotella, R. J., and Lloyd, J. W. (1990). Effects of a cognitive-behavioral intervention on the preshot routine and performance in golf. *Sport Psychol.* 4, 33–47. doi: 10.1123/tsp.4.1.33

Cotterill, S. T. (2010). Pre-performance routines in sport: current understanding and future directions. *Int. Rev. Sport Exerc. Psychol.* 3, 132–153. doi: 10.1080/1750984x.2010.488269

Foster, D. J., Weigand, D. A., and Baines, D. (2006). The effect of removing superstitious behavior and introducing a pre-performance routine on basketball free-throw performance. *J. Appl. Sport Psychol.* 18, 167–171. doi: 10.1080/10413200500471343

Glaser, B. G. (2001). *The Grounded Theory Perspective: Conceptualization Contrasted with Description.* Mill Valley, CA: Sociology Press.

Jackson, R. C., and Baker, J. S. (2001). Routines, rituals, and rugby: a case study of aworld class goal kicker. *Sport Psychol.* 15, 48–65. doi: 10.1123/tsp.15.1.48

Lonsdale, C., and Tam, J. T. M. (2008). On the temporal and behavioural consistency of pre-performance routines: an intra-individual analysis of elite basketball players' free throw shooting accuracy. *J. Sports Sci.* 26, 259–266. doi: 10.1080/02640410701473962

Macnamara, B. N., Moreau, D., and Hambrick, D. Z. (2016). The relationship between deliberate practice and performance in sports: a meta-analysis. *Perspect. Psychol. Sci.* 11, 333–350. doi: 10.1177/1745691616635591

Mesagno, C., Beckmann, J., Wergin, V. V., and Gröpel, P. (2019). Primed to perform: comparing different pre-performance routine interventions to improve accuracy in closed, self-paced motor tasks. *Psychol. Sport Exerc.* 43, 73–81. doi: 10.1016/j.psychsport.2019.01.001

Mesagno, C., Hill, D. M., and Larkin, P. (2015). Examining the accuracy and in-game performance effects between pre- and post-performance routines: a mixed methods study. *Psychol. Sport Exerc.* 19, 85–94. doi: 10.1016/j.psychsport.2015.03.005

Singer, N. R. (2002). Pre-performance state, routines, and automatidty: what does it take to realize expertise in self-paced events? *J. Sport Exerc. Psychol.* 24, 359–375. doi: 10.1123/jsep.24.4.359

20

Former Road Cyclists Still Involved in Cycling Report Lower Burnout Levels than those who Abandoned this Sport

Fabrizio Sors[1,2,3], David Tomé Lourido[4], Stella Damonte[3], Ilaria Santoro[2,3], Alessandra Galmonte[1], Tiziano Agostini[2] and Mauro Murgia[2]**

[1] Department of Medicine, Surgery and Health Sciences, University of Trieste, Trieste, Italy, [2] Department of Life Sciences, University of Trieste, Trieste, Italy, [3] Department of Medical Area, University of Udine, Udine, Italy, [4] Faculty of Psychology, National Distance Education University, Madrid, Spain

***Correspondence:**
Fabrizio Sors
fsors@units.it
Mauro Murgia
mmurgia@units.it

Despite the numerous benefits associated with sport practice, many children and adolescents end up quitting it year after year, with a stable dropout rate between 10 and 19 years of age. Among the causes of sport abandonment, the scientific literature highlights the presence of burnout as a fundamental factor. In this regard, the aim of the present study was to investigate the levels of the three components of sport burnout–emotional and physical exhaustion, reduced sense of accomplishment, and sport devaluation–reported by a sample of young (former) athletes, depending on whether their sport abandonment was relative (i.e., change to another sport modality) or definitive. In particular, participants were former agonist road cyclists, who have been divided into three groups on the basis of what they did after abandoning road bicycle racing, namely: (a) those still involved in cycling, either in a different specialty (e.g., mountain bike) or with a different role (e.g., coach for kids); (b) those who started practicing a different sport; and (c) those who definitively abandoned sports. The general hypothesis was that, with respect to those who changed sport and those who definitively abandoned it, those still involved in cycling would report experiencing lower levels of the three burnout components during the last year practicing it. To test this hypothesis, the Athlete Burnout Questionnaire (ABQ; Raedeke and Smith, 2001) was administered to 85 young former road cyclists. The results seem to support the hypothesis for two out of the three components, namely, emotional and physical exhaustion and sport devaluation; on the other hand, for reduced sense of accomplishment, no difference among the three groups emerged. Further research is needed to deepen the understanding of such processes, also in relation with other relevant constructs; yet, the results of the present study should already raise the awareness of sport organizations on the need to deal with this and related phenomena by adopting appropriate strategies to ensure the well-being of young athletes, thus trying to reduce early dropout.

Keywords: burnout, cycling, sport abandonment, young athletes, emotional/physical exhaustion, reduced sense of accomplishment, sport devaluation

INTRODUCTION

The practice of physical activity and sports has been considered as a healthy habit for many decades (e.g., Tušak and Blatnik, 2014; Di Corrado, 2017; Petralia et al., 2018; Coco et al., 2019). Currently, there is consolidated evidence about how increasing exercise promotes self-esteem and cognitive functioning, as well as relieving depression levels in children and adolescents (Biddle et al., 2019). As long as the training load is appropriate for the maturation level of minors, it is unlikely that negative consequences for young athletes–such as injuries–can occur (McKay et al., 2019). However, despite the benefits undoubtedly associated with sport practice, many children and adolescents end up abandoning it year after year, with a stable dropout rate between 10 and 19 years of age (Møllerløkken et al., 2015). Crane and Temple (2015) conducted a systematic review on the issue of youth abandonment in organized sports, identifying five major areas related to it: lack of fun; perception of competence; social pressures; competitive priorities; and physical factors, such as maturation and injuries. Among the causes of sport abandonment, the scientific literature highlights the presence of burnout as a fundamental factor (e.g., Gustafsson et al., 2014; Isoard-Gautheur et al., 2016a; Larner et al., 2017).

The conceptualization of burnout arises in the clinical setting (Freudenberger, 1974). However, it is of great importance to contextualize it also in the sports environment; indeed, although most athletes do not experience this syndrome to a significant degree, it can lead to serious consequences for the physical and mental well-being of people who practice sports (Eklund and DeFreese, 2015). Burnout was defined in the sports context by Raedeke (1997), through a three-dimensional conceptualization, characterizing this syndrome by emotional and physical exhaustion, reduced sense of accomplishment, and sport devaluation. As a complement to this sports burnout model, and seeking to create a valid and reliable instrument, Raedeke and Smith (2001) developed the Athlete Burnout Questionnaire (ABQ) to measure the three postulated dimensions. This scale has shown good validity and reliability properties in different languages and cultural contexts (e.g., Arce et al., 2012).

In addition to the aforementioned sport abandonment, burnout syndrome has a series of negative consequences, such as depressed mood, psychological stress, or negative affect (De Francisco et al., 2016; Gustafsson et al., 2017a). The causes of burnout syndrome and the consequent abandonment of sports practice in young athletes are often related either with dispositional variables such as low levels of resilience and fear of failure (Gustafsson et al., 2017b; Sorkkila et al., 2019) or with motivational variables, linked to the non-satisfaction of the athlete's basic psychological needs (Sorkkila et al., 2018; Lonsdale et al., 2009). Concerning the latter, according to the self-determination theory (Ryan and Deci, 2017), intrinsic motivation would be determined by the satisfaction of the psychological needs of autonomy, perceived competence, and relatedness with others. Such postulations have been corroborated in the sports context (Gustafsson et al., 2017a), with the observation that when athletes have a high intrinsic motivational profile, they have lower levels of burnout (Gustafsson et al., 2018a). In a complementary way, other researchers postulate that sport motivation is also determined by the achievement goal theory (Nicholls, 1984; Ames, 1995); in particular, intrinsic motivation would be linked to the task goals–those goals depending on the athlete's effort–rather than to the ego goals, whose achievement is related to comparison with others in a range of superiority–inferiority (Lochbaum et al., 2016; Balaguer et al., 2017). The establishment of task-oriented goals, as well as of an empowering climate that favors athletes' self-determination, is related to a lower presence of burnout (Lonsdale and Hodge, 2011; Vitali et al., 2014).

The fact that athletes are able to maintain a high intrinsic motivation–through the satisfaction of basic psychological needs and effort goals–depends also on other variables, such as family and/or coach support, which become crucial to prevent burnout (Isoard-Gautheur et al., 2016b; Ingrell et al., 2018). Focusing on the effects that these variables have on young athletes, it was found that those who receive greater social support from their team or have higher levels of sports competence and autonomy have lower levels of burnout and higher levels of intrinsic motivation (DeFreese and Smith, 2013; Rottensteiner et al., 2015; Jowett et al., 2016). On the other hand, the absence of fun or the establishment of ego goals is closely related to the presence of burnout symptoms, as well as to sport dropout (Gardner et al., 2017; Sorkkila et al., 2018).

To contribute to this line of research, the aim of the present study is to investigate the levels of the three components of sport burnout–emotional and physical exhaustion, reduced sense of accomplishment, and sport devaluation–reported by a sample of young (former) athletes, depending on whether their sport abandonment was relative (i.e., change to another sport modality) or definitive. Specifically, as concerns relative sport abandonment, we separately considered those who remained in the same sport–either in a different specialty or with a different role (e.g., as coaches for kids)–and those who started practicing a different sport. No previous studies investigated burnout with a similar approach; however, it is reasonable to put forward the general hypothesis that, with respect to those who changed sport and those who definitively abandoned it, those who remained in the same sport would report experiencing lower levels of the three burnout components during the last year practicing the specialty they then abandoned. As previous research highlighted a potential role of gender in quitting physical activity (e.g., Labbrozzi et al., 2012; Crane and Temple, 2015), we also tested for gender differences in reported burnout levels (regardless of the sport activity participants have undertaken after abandoning the specialty they practiced).

MATERIALS AND METHODS

Participants

Eighty-five former agonist road cyclists (40 females, 45 males) were recruited as participants. At the moment of data collection, their age ranged between 18 and 25 years (M = 20.49, SD = 1.71). On average, they abandoned road bicycle racing when they were 16.35 years old (SD = 1.45); on average, the abandonment occurred 4.62 years (SD = 1.71) before data collection.

Participants were divided into three groups on the basis of what they did after abandoning road bicycle racing: (a) those still involved in cycling, either in a different specialty (e.g., mountain bike) or with a different role (e.g., coach for kids); (b) those who started practicing a different sport; and (c) those who definitively abandoned sports. From now on, the three groups will be called "Cycling other" ($N = 33$), "Different sport" ($N = 29$), and "No sport" ($N = 23$), respectively. **Table 1** summarizes the descriptive data of the three groups; as can be noticed, the groups did not differ in terms of age at data collection, age at road bicycle racing abandonment, and years between abandonment and data collection.

Informed consent was obtained from each participant prior to the beginning of the data collection. The protocol was approved by the Ethics Committee of the University of Trieste, and the study was carried out in accordance with its recommendations.

Questionnaire and Procedure

The ABQ (Raedeke and Smith, 2001) is a self-report inventory consisting of 15 items, equally distributed among the three subscales of emotional and physical exhaustion, reduced sense of accomplishment, and sport devaluation. In the present study, the Italian translation used by Vitali et al. (2014) was administered. With respect to the original version, we modified the general request to refer to the last year participants practiced road bicycle racing, that is, "Thinking about your last year practicing road bicycle racing, rate how often you experienced the following situations"; accordingly, the tense of all items was changed from present to past. Items were to be answered like in the original version, that is, on a five-point Likert scale, with the following anchors: (1) almost never, (2) rarely, (3) sometimes, (4) frequently, and (5) almost always. For each participant, the score of each subscale corresponds to the average of the responses given to the five items characterizing it.

In addition, participants were asked to specify the following information: their sex, their current age, and their age when they abandoned road bicycle racing, the year they abandoned road bicycle racing, and what they did at a sport level after abandoning road bicycle racing.

For data collection, a digital survey was prepared by means of Google Forms, including both the ABQ and the personal questions mentioned above. Such a survey was preceded by the description of relevant information about the study, to allow participants to express their informed consent. The form was structured in such a way that when consent was expressed, the browser automatically redirected to the survey; on the other hand, when consent was denied, the browser automatically redirected to a standard exit page.

As concerns the procedure, in a preliminary phase, young former road cyclists from the Italian regions of Friuli Venezia Giulia and Veneto were contacted and informally asked for their availability to participate to the study. Those who agreed (>98%) were sent the link to the form described above.

TABLE 1 | Descriptive data of the three groups of participants.

Group	Sex	Age at data collection (M ± SD)	Age at road bicycle racing abandonment (M ± SD)	Years between abandonment and data collection (M ± SD)
Cycling other	F = 12, M = 21	20.67 ± 1.65	16.64 ± 1.25	4.58 ± 1.46
Different sport	F = 15, M = 14	20.48 ± 2.05	16.00 ± 1.63	4.97 ± 1.95
No sport	F = 13, M = 10	20.26 ± 1.32	16.39 ± 1.44	4.26 ± 1.71

Statistical Analyses

Preliminarily, we calculated Cronbach's alpha for each subscale of the ABQ. Then, to address the main research question of the study, a multivariate analysis of variance (MANOVA) was conducted, considering each of the three subscales of the ABQ in relation with what participants did after abandoning road bicycle racing; *post hoc* comparisons were run using the least significant difference (LSD) correction. Finally, to investigate for potential gender differences in reported burnout levels, another MANOVA was performed, considering each of the three subscales of the ABQ in relation with gender. The analyses were run using the statistical software SPSS 25.0 for Windows.

RESULTS

Cronbach's alpha values were 0.87 for emotional/physical exhaustion, 0.81 for reduced sense of accomplishment, and 0.80 for sport devaluation.

With regard to the main research question, the MANOVA revealed a significant main effect for the subscales "emotional and physical exhaustion" [$F(2,82) = 3.96$; $p < 0.05$; $\eta^2 = 0.09$; power = 0.70] and "sport devaluation" [$F(2,82) = 4.16$; $p < 0.05$; $\eta^2 = 0.09$; power = 0.72]. Conversely, the analysis did not reveal a significant value for the main effect of the subscale "reduced sense of accomplishment" [$F(2,82) = 0.11$; $p = 0.90$].

As for emotional and physical exhaustion, the *post hoc* analyses highlighted: (a) a significant difference between the group *Cycling other* and the group *Different sport*, with lower levels for the former group ($p < 0.05$; *Cycling other*: M = 1.68, SD = 0.62; *Different sport*: M = 2.22, SD = 0.91); (b) a significant difference between the group *Cycling other* and the group *No sport*, with lower levels for the former group ($p < 0.05$; *No sport*: M = 2.11, SD = 0.89); and (c) no difference between the group *Different sport* and the group *No sport* ($p = 0.88$).

As for reduced sense of accomplishment, the *post hoc* analyses revealed no difference in the three comparisons between pairs of groups (*Cycling other* versus *Different sport*: $p = 0.81$; *Cycling other* versus *No sport*: $p = 0.80$; *Different sport* versus *No sport*: $p = 0.64$). In particular, the scores for each condition were the following: *Cycling other*: M = 3.28, SD = 0.80; *Different sport*: M = 3.23, SD = 0.84; and *No sport*: M = 3.34, SD = 0.94.

As for sport devaluation, the *post hoc* analyses highlighted: (a) a significant difference between the group *Cycling other* and the group *Different sport*, with lower levels for the former group

($p < 0.05$; *Cycling other*: M = 2.00, SD = 0.82; *Different sport*: M = 2.48, SD = 0.93); (b) a significant difference between the group *Cycling other* and the group *No sport*, with lower levels for the former group ($p < 0.05$; *No sport*: M = 2.67, SD = 1.00); and (c) no difference between the group *Different sport* and the group *No sport* ($p = 0.45$). All results are summarized in **Figure 1**.

With regard to the potential gender differences in reported burnout levels, the MANOVA revealed no differences between females and males in any of the subscales (emotional/physical exhaustion: $p = 0.21$; reduced sense of accomplishment: $p = 0.08$; sport devaluation: $p = 0.60$). In particular, for emotional/physical exhaustion, the score for females was M = 1.86, SD = 0.75, while for males, M = 2.09, SD = 0.89; for reduced sense of accomplishment, the score for females was M = 3.11, SD = 0.94, while for males, M = 3.43, SD = 0.72; for sport devaluation, the score for females was M = 2.40, SD = 1.05, while for males, M = 2.29, SD = 0.84.

DISCUSSION

The aim of the present study was to investigate the levels of the three components of sport burnout–emotional and physical exhaustion, reduced sense of accomplishment, and sport devaluation–reported by a sample of young (former) athletes, depending on whether their sport abandonment was relative or definitive. The general hypothesis was that, with respect to those who changed sport and those who definitively abandoned it, those who remained in the same sport (in a different specialty or with a different role) would report experiencing lower levels of the three burnout components during the last year practicing the specialty they then abandoned. The results seem to support this hypothesis for two out of the three components, namely, emotional and physical exhaustion and sport devaluation. Indeed, the group *Cycling other*–that is, former agonist road cyclists still involved in cycling, either in a different specialty (e.g., mountain bike) or with a different role (e.g., coaches for kids)–reported experiencing lower levels of these two components during the last year practicing road bicycle racing with respect to both those who started practicing a different sport from cycling and those who definitively abandoned sports. Instead, for reduced sense of accomplishment, no difference among the three groups emerged. Interestingly, between the groups of those who changed sport and those who definitively abandoned it, no difference emerged also for the other two components. Moreover, as a secondary result, no gender differences emerged in any of the three burnout components.

There are two potential explanations for the main results. On the one hand, we can speculate that, during the last year practicing road cycling, participants had actually experienced the different burnout levels they have reported in the present study, and (also) based on these, they decided to remain in cycling or to abandon it. On the other hand, we can speculate that such differences did not actually exist, but the fact of remaining in cycling versus abandoning it has influenced participants' memories about the burnout levels experienced during the last year practicing road cycling, with a softening effect for those who remained in cycling and a worsening effect for those who abandoned it. Of course, it is also possible–and reasonable–to think about a combination of these two explanations: some differences in burnout levels may have actually existed (contributing to the decision of remaining in cycling or not), and they could have been magnified by the subsequent experiences of participants.

As for the first potential explanation (i.e., the actual experience of different burnout levels), the establishment of a sport identity specifically associated with cycling might have occurred. The establishment of such an identity would be promoted by the satisfaction of the basic psychological needs in that sport in particular and by the resulting intrinsic motivation (Reifsteck et al., 2016). As children and adolescents play a particular sport, they develop an identity associated with their role as an athlete, as part of their self-concept (Brewer et al., 1993). However, if this identity is mono-dimensional–focusing only on sport practice and excluding other personal aspects–when sport abandonment occurs, it can lead to the suffering of psychiatric symptoms and burnout, both in young people and in adults (Giannone et al., 2017; Chang et al., 2018; Gustafsson et al., 2018b). As a consequence, especially for children and adolescents, on the one hand, it is essential to develop an identity as an athlete that allows them to feel competent and autonomous and maintain positive relationships with their peers; on the other hand, to prevent negative consequences in case of sport abandonment (either relative or definitive), such an identity should not be mono-dimensional, being preferably focused on their overall development as athletes rather than exclusively linked to their competence in a specific sport (Coakley, 1992). To evaluate the appropriateness of this interpretation, future studies aimed at investigating similar issues should take into consideration the potential mediating effects that the (non-)satisfaction of basic psychological needs could have on burnout levels. From a broader perspective, in future studies, former athletes from sports other than cycling should also be involved, in order to evaluate the degree of generalizability of the results that emerged from the present investigation. In particular, it would be interesting to see whether, when considering also former athletes from other sports, the absence of a difference concerning reduced sense of accomplishment, as well as the absence of a difference between those who changed sport and those who definitively abandoned it, is confirmed.

As for the second potential explanation (i.e., the influence of participants' subsequent experiences on their memories), there are two aspects to be considered in this regard. On the one hand, it is well known that explicit memory is reconstructive, namely, people's current thoughts and feelings influence the recall of their past thoughts and feelings (e.g., Levine, 1997; Ross and Newby-Clark, 1998); in particular, memories of emotional states are updated in light of subsequent experience (e.g., Safer et al., 2002; for a review, see Levine and Safer, 2002). On the other hand, people typically exaggerate the intensity of past emotions, overestimating the intensity of both the positive and negative emotions actually experienced (e.g., Wirtz et al., 2003; for a review, see Levine et al., 2006). In light of these two mechanisms–which are not mutually exclusive–and considering the fact that

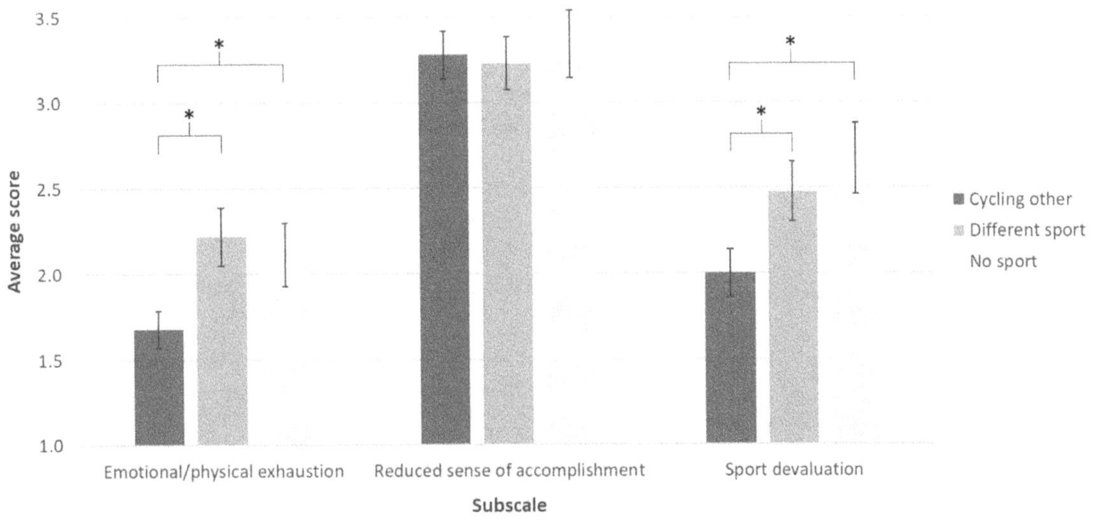

FIGURE 1 | Average scores of the three groups for the three subscales of the Athlete Burnout Questionnaire (ABQ); error bars show the standard error of the mean; $*p < 0.05$.

both those who remained in cycling and those who abandoned it had experienced negative emotions during their last year practicing road cycling, it is reasonable to hypothesize that all participants overestimated such negative emotions, but those still involved in cycling did it to a minor extent with respect to those who abandoned this sport. The experimental design used in the present study did not allow us to test this hypothesis; to evaluate its appropriateness, future studies on this topic should adopt a design typically used to investigate memories of emotional states, with repeated measurements during and after the event(s) of interest. However, identifying in advance athletes who are willing to abandon the sport they are practicing is not easy; a possible strategy is to start "monitoring" some teams toward the end of a sport season to identify the missing athletes at the beginning of the new one, so that the first measurement can occur only a couple of months after the abandonment (relative or definitive).

To sum up, the present study revealed that former agonist road cyclists still involved in cycling (either in a different specialty or with a different role) reported that they had experienced lower levels of emotional and physical exhaustion and sport devaluation during the last year practicing this specialty, with respect to both those who started practicing a different sport and those who definitively abandoned it. Interestingly, the presence of differences in these two burnout components, as well as the absence of differences in reduced sense of accomplishment, is coherent with a recent study by Gerber et al. (2019), which highlighted greater emotional/physical exhaustion and sport devaluation in young elite athletes reporting high compared to low burnout symptoms. A reasonable explanation for the results observed in our study is that some differences in burnout levels actually existed (contributing to the decision of remaining in cycling or not), and these differences have been magnified by the subsequent experiences of participants. Further research is needed to deepen the understanding of such processes, also in relation with other relevant constructs, like for example, the (non-)satisfaction of basic psychological needs. The secondary result of the absence of gender differences in the reported burnout levels suggests that burnout itself would not contribute to gender differences in the early dropout phenomenon.

Interestingly, the present study adds to the literature of psychology in the domain of cycling; previous psychological studies addressed other aspects related to cycling, such as mood (e.g., Murgia et al., 2016), recovery–stress balance (e.g., Filho et al., 2013, 2015), attentional focus (e.g., Bertollo et al., 2015; di Fronso et al., 2018), and psychobiosocial states (e.g., Robazza et al., 2017). As concerns psychobiosocial states, other studies highlighted their potential role as mediators of the relationship between the perceived motivational climate by young athletes and their motivation to continue playing sports (e.g., Bortoli et al., 2009, 2011, 2014); thus, psychobiosocial states also could be taken into consideration by future studies aiming to better understand the role of burnout in sport abandonment.

From an applied perspective, the results of the present study highlight two important aims to be pursued by sport organizations to prevent young athletes from experiencing negative emotions potentially leading to burnout and, consequently, to sport abandonment (relative or definitive): on the one hand, avoiding the exasperation of emotional and physical components of sport practice, and on the other hand, maintaining positive and meaningful feelings associated to it. It is quite intuitive that in this process, among all the figures populating sport organizations, a key role is played by the coaches; however, in dealing with these issues, young athletes may significantly benefit also from the interventions and the support provided by sport psychologists. From a broader perspective, findings deriving from studies on similar issues should raise the awareness of sport organizations on the need to deal with this and related phenomena by adopting appropriate strategies to ensure the well-being of young athletes, thus trying to reduce early dropout.

ETHICS STATEMENT

The studies involving human participants were reviewed and approved by the Ethics Committee of the University of Trieste. The patients/participants provided their written informed consent to participate in this study.

AUTHOR CONTRIBUTIONS

FS, IS, and MM conceived the idea. FS, DT, SD, IS, AG, TA, and MM designed the study. FS, SD, and AG prepared the digital form for data collection. SD recruited participants and collected the data. FS, MM, and TA analyzed the data. FS, DT, and MM wrote the first draft of the manuscript. SD, IS, AG, and TA revised the manuscript.

REFERENCES

Ames, C. (1995). "Achievement goals, motivational climate, and motivational processes," in *Motivation in Sport and Exercise*, ed. G. C. Roberts, (Champaign, IL: Human Kinetics Books), 161–176.

Arce, C., De Francisco, C., Andrade, E., Seoane, G., and Raedeke, T. (2012). Adaptation of the athlete burnout questionnaire in a spanish sample of Athletes. *Spanish J. Psychol.* 15, 1529–1536. doi: 10.5209/rev_sjop.2012.v15.n3.39437

Balaguer, I., Stebbings, J., Appleton, P. R., and Duda, J. L. (2017). "Towards more empowering and less disempowering environments in youth sport: Theory to evidence-based practice," in *Sport Psychology for Young Athletes*, eds C. J. Knight, C. G. Harwood, and D. Gould, (New York, NY: Routledge), 81–93. doi: 10.4324/9781315545202-8

Bertollo, M., di Fronso, S., Filho, E., Lamberti, V., Ripari, P., Reis, V. M., et al. (2015). To focus or not to focus: is attention on the core components of action beneficial for cycling performance? *Sport Psychol.* 29, 110–119. doi: 10.1123/tsp.2014-0046

Biddle, S. J. H., Ciaccioni, S., Thomas, G., and Vergeer, I. (2019). Physical activity and mental health in children and adolescents: an updated review of reviews and an analysis of causality. *Psychol. Sport Exerc.* 42, 146–155. doi: 10.1016/j.psychsport.2018.08.011

Bortoli, L., Bertollo, M., Comani, S., and Robazza, C. (2011). Competence, achievement goals, motivational climate, and pleasant psychobiosocial states in youth sport. *J. Sports Sci.* 29, 171–180. doi: 10.1080/02640414.2010.530675

Bortoli, L., Bertollo, M., Filho, E., and Robazza, C. (2014). Do psychobiosocial states mediate the relationship between perceived motivational climate and individual motivation in youngsters? *J. Sports Sci.* 32, 572–582. doi: 10.1080/02640414.2013.843017

Bortoli, L., Bertollo, M., and Robazza, C. (2009). Dispositional goal orientations, motivational climate, and psychobiosocial states in youth sport. *Personal. Individ. Differ.* 47, 18–24. doi: 10.1016/j.paid.2009.01.042

Brewer, B. W., Van Raalte, J. L., and Linder, D. E. (1993). Athletic identity: hercules' muscles or Achilles heel? *Int. J. Sport Psychol.* 24, 237–254.

Chang, W. H., Wu, C.-H., Kuo, C.-C., and Chen, L. H. (2018). The role of athletic identity in the development of athlete burnout: the moderating role of psychological flexibility. *Psychol. Sport Exerc.* 39, 45–51. doi: 10.1016/j.psychsport.2018.07.014

Coakley, J. (1992). Burnout among Adolescent Athletes: A Personal Failure or social problem? *Sociol. Sport J.* 9, 271–285. doi: 10.1123/ssj.9.3.271

Coco, M., Guerrera, C. S., Di Corrado, D., Ramaci, T., Maci, T., Pellerone, M., et al. (2019). Personality traits and athletic young adults. *Sport Sci. Health* 15, 435–441. doi: 10.1007/s11332-019-00551-3

Crane, J., and Temple, V. (2015). A systematic review of dropout from organized sport among children and youth. *Eur. Phys. Educ. Rev.* 21, 114–131. doi: 10.1177/1356336X14555294

De Francisco, C., Arce, C., Vílchez, M. P., and Vales, Á (2016). Antecedents and consequences of burnout in athletes$erceived stress and depression. *Int. J. Clin. Health Psychol.* 16, 239–246. doi: 10.1016/j.ijchp.2016.04.001

DeFreese, J. D., and Smith, A. L. (2013). Teammate social support, burnout, and self-determined motivation in collegiate athletes. *Psychol. Sport Exerc.* 14, 258–265. doi: 10.1016/j.psychsport.2012.10.009

Di Corrado, D. (2017). Biological underpinnings of mood and the role of physical exercise. *Sport Sci. Health* 13, 461–468. doi: 10.1007/s11332-017-0374-5

di Fronso, S., Tamburro, G., Robazza, C., Bortoli, L., Comani, S., and Bertollo, M. (2018). Focusing attention on muscle exertion increases EEG coherence in an endurance cycling task. *Front. Psychol.* 9:1249. doi: 10.3389/fpsyg.2018.01249

Eklund, R. C., and DeFreese, J. D. (2015). Athlete burnout: what we know, what we could know, and how we can find out more. *Int. J. Appl. Sports Sci.* 27, 63–75. doi: 10.24985/ijass.2015.27.2.63

Filho, E., di Fronso, S., Forzini, F., Agostini, T., Bortoli, L., Robazza, C., et al. (2013). Stress/recovery balance during the girobio: profile of highly trained road cyclists. *Sport Sci. Health* 9, 107–112. doi: 10.1007/s11332-013-0153-x

Filho, E., di Fronso, S., Forzini, F., Murgia, M., Agostini, T., Bortoli, L., et al. (2015). Athletic performance and recovery–stress factors in cycling: an ever changing balance. *Eur. J. Sport Sci.* 15, 671–680. doi: 10.1080/17461391.2015.1048746

Freudenberger, H. J. (1974). Staff burn-out. *J. Soc. Issues* 30, 159–165. doi: 10.1111/j.1540-4560.1974.tb00706.x

Gardner, L. A., Magee, C. A., and Vella, S. A. (2017). Enjoyment and behavioral intention predict organized youth sport participation and dropout. *J. Phys.Activ. Health* 14, 861–865. doi: 10.1123/jpah.2016-0572

Gerber, M., Brand, R., Antoniewicz, F., Isoard-Gautheur, S., Gustafsson, H., Bianchi, R., et al. (2019). Implicit and explicit attitudes towards sport among young elite athletes with high versus low burnout symptoms. *J. Sports Sci.* 37, 1673–1680. doi: 10.1080/02640414.2019.1585313

Giannone, Z. A., Haney, C. J., Kealy, D., and Ogrodniczuk, J. S. (2017). Athletic identity and psychiatric symptoms following retirement from varsity sports. *Int. J. Soc.Psychiatry* 63, 598–601. doi: 10.1177/0020764017724184

Gustafsson, H., Carlin, M., Podlog, L., Stenling, A., and Lindwall, M. (2018a). Motivational profiles and burnout in elite athletes: a person-centered approach. *Psychol. Sport Exerc.* 35, 118–125. doi: 10.1016/j.psychsport.2017.11.009

Gustafsson, H., DeFreese, J., and Madigan, D. J. (2017a). Athlete burnout: review and recommendations. *Curr.Opin. Psychol.* 16, 109–113. doi: 10.1016/j.copsyc.2017.05.002

Gustafsson, H., Martinent, G., Isoard-Gautheur, S., Hassmén, P., and Guillet-Descas, E. (2018b). Performance based self-esteem and athlete-identity in athlete burnout: a person-centered approach. *Psychol. Sport Exerc.* 38, 56–60. doi: 10.1016/j.psychsport.2018.05.017

Gustafsson, H., Sagar, S. S., and Stenling, A. (2017b). Fear of failure, psychological stress, and burnout among adolescent athletes competing in high level sport. *Scand. J. Med. Sci. Sports* 27, 2091–2102. doi: 10.1111/sms.12797

Gustafsson, H., Hancock, D. J., and Côté, J. (2014). Describing citation structures in sport burnout literature: a citation network analysis. *Psychol. Sport Exerc.* 15, 620–626. doi: 10.1016/j.psychsport.2014.07.001

Ingrell, J., Johnson, U., and Ivarsson, A. (2018). Developmental changes in burnout perceptions among student-athletes: an achievement goal perspective. *Int. J. Sport Exerc. Psychol.* 17, 509–520. doi: 10.1080/1612197x.2017.1421679

Isoard-Gautheur, S., Guillet-Descas, E., and Gustafsson, H. (2016a). Athlete burnout and the risk of dropout among young elite handball players. *Sport Psychol.* 30, 123–130. doi: 10.1123/tsp.2014-0140

Isoard-Gautheur, S., Trouilloud, D., Gustafsson, H., and Guillet-Descas, E. (2016b). Associations between the perceived quality of the coach–athlete relationship and athlete burnout: an examination of the mediating role of achievement goals. *Psychol. Sport Exerc.* 22, 210–217. doi: 10.1016/j.psychsport.2015.08.003

Jowett, G. E., Hill, A. P., Hall, H. K., and Curran, T. (2016). Perfectionism, burnout and engagement in youth sport: the mediating role of basic psychological needs. *Psychol. Sport Exerc.* 24, 18–26. doi: 10.1016/j.psychsport.2016.01.001

Labbrozzi, D., Bucci, I., Bortoli, L., Bertollo, M., Doria, C., and Robazza, C. (2012). Age-related differences in actual and perceived levels of physical activity in adolescent girls. *Percept. Mot. Skills* 114, 723–734. doi: 10.2466/06.10.13.PMS.114.3.723-734

Larner, R. J., Wagstaff, C. R. D., Thelwell, R. C., and Corbett, J. (2017). A multistudy examination of organizational stressors, emotional labor, burnout, and turnover in sport organizations. *Scand. J. Med. Sci. Sports* 27, 2103–2115. doi: 10.1111/sms.12833

Levine, L. J. (1997). Reconstructing memory for emotions. *J. Exp. Psychol. Gen.* 126, 165–177. doi: 10.1037/0096-3445.126.2.165

Levine, L. J., and Safer, M. A. (2002). Sources of bias in memory for emotions. *Curr. Dir. Psychol. Sci.* 11, 169–172. doi: 10.1111/1467-8721.00193

Levine, L. J., Safer, M. A., and Lench, H. C. (2006). "Remembering and misremembering emotions," in *Judgments Over Time: The Interplay of Thoughts, Feelings, and Behaviors*, eds L. J. Sanna, and E. C. Chang, (New York, NY: Oxford University Press), 271–290. doi: 10.1093/acprof:oso/9780195177664.003.0015

Lochbaum, M., Kazak-Çetinkalp, Z., Graham, K.-A., Wright, T., and Zazo, R. (2016). Task and ego goal orientations in competitive sport. *Kinesiology* 48, 3–29. doi: 10.26582/k.48.1.14

Lonsdale, C., and Hodge, K. (2011). Temporal ordering of motivational quality and athlete burnout in elite sport. *Med.Sci. Sports Exerc.* 43, 913–921. doi: 10.1249/mss.0b013e3181ff56c6

Lonsdale, C., Hodge, K., and Rose, E. (2009). Athlete burnout in elite sport: a self-determination perspective. *J. Sci.* 27, 785–795. doi: 10.1080/02640410902929366

McKay, C. D., Cumming, S. P., and Blake, T. (2019). Youth sport: friend or Foe? *Best Pract. Res. Clin. Rheumatol.* 33, 141–157. doi: 10.1016/j.berh.2019.01.017

Møllerløkken, N. E., Lorås, H., and Pedersen, A. V. (2015). A systematic review and meta-analysis of dropout rates in youth soccer. *Percept. Mot. Skills* 121, 913–922. doi: 10.2466/10.pms.121c23x0

Murgia, M., Forzini, F., Filho, E., di Fronso, S., Sors, F., Bertollo, M., et al. (2016). How do mood states change in a multi-stage cycling competition? Comparing high and low performers. *J. Sports Med.Phys. Fitn.* 56, 336–342.

Nicholls, J. G. (1984). Achievement motivation: conceptions of ability, subjective experience, task choice, and performance. *Psychol. Rev.* 91, 328–346. doi: 10.1037/0033-295X.91.3.328

Petralia, M. C., Coco, M., Maci, T., Minissale, C., De Pasquale, C., D'Orto, G., et al. (2018). Successfully aging. Choice of life or life that choices?. *Acta Med. Mediter.* 34, 107–111. doi: 10.19193/0393-6384_2018_1_18

Raedeke, T. D. (1997). Is athlete burnout more than just stress? a sport commitment perspective. *J. Sport Exerc. Psychol.* 19, 396–417. doi: 10.1123/jsep.19.4.396

Raedeke, T. D., and Smith, A. L. (2001). Development and preliminary validation of an athlete burnout measure. *J. Sport Exerc. Psychol.* 23, 281–306. doi: 10.1123/jsep.23.4.281

Reifsteck, E. J., Gill, D. L., and Labban, J. D. (2016). "Athletes" and "exercisers": understanding identity, motivation, and physical activity participation in former college athletes. *Sport Exerc. Perform. Psychol.* 5, 25–38. doi: 10.1037/spy0000046

Robazza, C., Forzini, F., di Fronso, S., and Bertollo, M. (2017). "Recovery-stress balance and psychobiosocial states monitoring of road cyclists," in *Sport, Recovery, and Performance: Interdisciplinary Insights*, eds M. Kellmann, and J. Beckmann, (London: Routledge), 63–73. doi: 10.4324/9781315268149-5

Ross, M., and Newby-Clark, I. R. (1998). Construing the past and future. *Soc. Cogn.* 16, 133–150. doi: 10.1521/soco.1998.16.1.133

Rottensteiner, C., Tolvanen, A., Laakso, L., and Konttinen, N. (2015). Youth athletes' motivation, perceived competence, and persistence in organized team sports. *J. Sport Behav.* 38, 1–18.

Ryan, R. M., and Deci, E. L. (2017). *Self-Determination Theory. Basic Psychological Needs in Motivation, Development and Wellness.* New York, NY: Guilford Press.

Safer, M. A., Levine, L. J., and Drapalski, A. (2002). Distortion in memory for emotions: the contributions of personality and post-event knowledge. *Personal. Soc. Psychol. Bull.* 28, 1495–1507. doi: 10.1177/014616702237577

Sorkkila, M., Aunola, K., Salmela-Aro, K., Tolvanen, A., and Ryba, T. V. (2018). The co-developmental dynamic of sport and school burnout among student-athletes: the role of achievement goals. *Scandi. J. Med. Sci. Sports* 28, 1731–1742. doi: 10.1111/sms.13073

Sorkkila, M., Tolvanen, A., Aunola, K., and Ryba, T. V. (2019). The role of resilience in student-athletes' sport and school burnout and dropout: a longitudinal person-oriented study. *Scand., J. Med. Sci. Sports* 29, 1059–1067. doi: 10.1111/sms.13422

Tušak, M., and Blatnik, P. (2014). Health impact of running, psychological factor of marathon success, and flow states. *Med. Športa* 1, 52–57.

Vitali, F., Bortoli, L., Bertinato, L., Robazza, C., and Schena, F. (2014). Motivational climate, resilience, and burnout in youth sport. *Sport Sci. Health* 11, 103–108. doi: 10.1007/s11332-014-0214-9

Wirtz, D., Kruger, J., Scollon, C. N., and Diener, E. (2003). What to do on spring break? The role of predicted, on-line, and remembered experience in future choice. *Psychol. Sci.* 14, 520–524. doi: 10.1111/1467-9280.03455

21

Mental Imagery Skills in Competitive Young Athletes and Non-Athletes

Donatella Di Corrado[1], Maria Guarnera[1], Claudia Savia Guerrera[2], Nelson Mauro Maldonato[3], Santo Di Nuovo[2], Sabrina Castellano[2] and Marinella Coco[4]*

[1] Department of Human and Social Sciences, Kore University, Enna, Italy, [2] Department of Formative Processes, University of Catania, Catania, Italy, [3] Department of Neuroscience and Reproductive and Odontostomatological Sciences, University of Naples Federico II, Naples, Italy, [4] Department of Biomedical and Biotechnological Sciences, University of Catania, Catania, Italy

***Correspondence:**
Donatella Di Corrado
donatella.dicorrado@unikore.it

Mental imagery is a fully immersive multi-sensory procedure that associates as numerous senses to create a mental image and process it without the presence of external stimuli. In the sport situation, imagery has been designated as the state in which people imagine themselves while effecting abilities to deal with the forthcoming duty or improve performance. Methodical analyses have revealed that imagery increases performance in motor tasks. This study aims at observing not the vividness of image but the cognitive abilities useful for the inspection, maintenance, generation, and manipulation of dissimilar classes of images, investigating modifications in mental imagery skills in competitive athletes and non-athletes. Participants were competitive athletes (*n* = 48) and non-athletes (*n* = 48) between the ages of 8 and 13 years (M_{age} = 10.50, *SD* = 1.73). The athletes had a minimum of 5 years of training skill in the sport. They completed the Mental Imagery Test (MIT). Competitive athletes showed higher scores on mental imagery skills than non-athletes. The study contributed to increase the exploration in the definite area of mental imagery, supplying an added support for the pluridimensional nature of mental imagery and for its practicality in motor and sport sciences.

Keywords: mental imagery, children, athletes, sport, cognitive performance

INTRODUCTION

Mental imagery is the reproduction of perceptual experience (Kosslyn et al., 2001; Pearson, 2007) across multisensory ways and the processing of images in the absence of external stimuli. Mental imagery is a significant element in human functioning.

In the sport situation, imagery has been designated as the state in which people imagine themselves while effecting abilities to deal with the forthcoming duty or improve performance. Imagery may be a consequence from both thoughtful and unconscious recall procedures; an individual sees an image, or experiences a movement as an image, without experiencing the real thing through a process. Imagery plays a significant role in this context, improving performance in motor tasks (Di Corrado et al., 2014, 2019).

It is usually assessed in relations of its mental and emotional characteristics, as well as motivational competence (Cumming and Williams, 2012). Owing to the gains of imagery, it is, nowadays, included in numerous mental skills line-ups, in addition to physical preparation.

Goals leading to positive psychological outcomes. In contrast, martial arts players who feel that they are not part of the team, often gets negative feedback from peers and coaches, and have no choice in the decision-making, their motivation to perform the behavior tends to be less self-determined (externally regulated) and concurrently impair their self-regulation capacity resulting to negative consequences such as decrease in self-satisfaction, self-confidence and commitment. Therefore, a relationship exists between self-management and psychological outcomes. That is, the use of self-management may facilitate athletes' psychological responses and it may function to regulate different dimensions (i.e., psychosocial, physical, and tactical) of athletes' sports participation, thus influencing not only their behaviors but also their cognitive states.

For the last few decades, various researchers have focused on exploring both traditional and new forms of martial arts (e.g., Green and Svinth, 2010) examining athletes' employment of self-management and its associated outcomes. While martial arts can be described in several ways, we define martial arts as combat or self defense techniques with the use of either bare hands/feet or weapons (bow and arrow, stick, and sword). Martial arts can be categorized in various approaches such as armed with weapon or unarmed, traditional or modern, or practice orientation (combat or spiritual). Hence, each form of martial arts may fall into several categories depending on the established criteria such as: armed with weapon (encing-foil, épée, and saber swords, archery (bow and arrow), kumdo (wooden stick) vs unarmed (judo, taekwondo, and wrestling); traditional (ssireum-Korea, taekwondo-Korea, and judo-Japan) vs modern (kumdo; fencing; archery; and mixed martial arts); or combat (archery; wrestling, boxing) vs spiritual (hapkido, aikido, and tai chi; Green and Svinth, 2010; Cynarski, 2019). In South Korea, scholars have been interested in martial arts education and its importance in a practitioners' life and well-being (Kim J. et al., 2011; Choi, 2017). Further, due to the rise of competitive martial arts, researchers have shown increased interest in examining this topic such as concept of self-management of Korean athletes from various martial arts for they achieved many sporting successes in various international competitions particularly in the Olympic Games such as archery, taekwondo, judo, wrestling (Greco-Roman and freestyle), fencing, and boxing. These martial arts sports have made consistent and significant contributions to South Korea's Olympic dominance accounting for 63% of the total medals won in the Summer Olympic Games (Olympic Games, 2021). For instance, Choi et al. (2009) reported that a high level of self-control is an essential psychological characteristic for taekwondo practitioners to achieve higher skill levels in techniques related to the martial arts and higher self-confidence. Similarly, competitive players in ssireum, judo, and wrestling with high levels of self-confidence, performance, and task orientation were found to frequently employ different self-management strategies (Han, 2008; Kim and Chun, 2010; Kim et al., 2015). Lim et al. (2015) found taekwondo athletes who practiced self-management positively influenced their sport commitment and exercise satisfaction.

Furthermore, qualitative studies provide evidences about the effectiveness of self-management in improving sport performance of athletes. Park (2000) described that training hard, yelling, singing, listening to music, and ignoring the actual date of competition were some thought- and emotional-regulating strategies employed by a judo athlete who won a gold medal in the Olympics. Lim and O'Sullivan (2016) did a case study about the effect of a systematic mental skills program on the psychological state and performance of a taekwondo Olympian and found positive changes in the athlete's psycho-emotional condition and behaviors. Increased physical effort, positive mentality, self-confidence, decreased negative thoughts, anxiety level, and perceived stress, and improved competition performance style were observed after employing several strategies to regulate the player's feelings, thoughts and actions. They reported that a systematic mental skills program helped the player how to better control the stressors of competition that subsequently facilitated the taekwondo athlete's gold medal success in the Olympic Games.

Based on the results, the authors of these cited studies concluded that self-management may play a determinant role in practitioners' psychological characteristics. Specifically, the self-management of martial arts practitioners might be the main influential factor of their exercise self-confidence, satisfaction, and commitment (Huh, 2003; Han, 2008; Chun, 2011; Kim, 2015; Kim and Cho, 2017; Kim and Kim, 2018). Here, we define satisfaction as cognitive evaluation of one's athletic participation (Riemer and Chelladurai, 1998) while commitment is a person's motivational desire and determination to continue sports participation (Scanlan et al., 1993).

Notwithstanding, despite the multitude of studies verifying the relationships between athletes' self-management and exercise self-confidence, satisfaction, and commitment, no attempt has been made to systematically investigate these variables and consolidate the findings in the literature through a meta-analytic approach. We believe that a meta-analysis on the relationships between self-management and these psychological characteristics in the sports field could serve to bridge theoretical knowledge and practical implications; specifically, the provision of systematic data can help coaches/sports psychologists to identify/develop effective training interventions targeted at the development of athletes' self-management skills—thereby potentially helping enhance athletes' psychological well-being. Such a study could also serve to provide additional knowledge on the self-management phenomenon, thus enriching interdisciplinary literature on the topic in general and South Korea in particular. Likewise, a greater understanding of this phenomenon—and its benefits—can help athletes with no access to professional sports/mental coaches by providing information on specific aspects of their training that they can directly modify; this could potentially help them achieve an optimal psychological state, which could, in turn, allow for longer sports participation and higher performance.

Accordingly, this study aimed to meta-analyze studies on the relationships between athletes' self-management and exercise self-confidence, satisfaction, and commitment. The following are the research questions of this study: (1) What are the overall effect sizes (ES) of the relationships among self-management and the outcome variables (i.e., exercise self-confidence, satisfaction, and

Various overlying terms have been utilized to refer to several sides of mental imagery in sports (Hale et al., 2005; Cumming and Ramsey, 2009; Collet et al., 2013). Morris et al. (2005) proposed that a further complete description of sports imagery is "*the intentional or unintentional conception or regeneration of an experience produced from memorial information, concerning quasi-affective and quasi-sensorial features that may occur in the absence of the tangible stimulus antecedents usually associated with the real experience*" (p. 19).

Within the mental mode, kinesthetic (i.e., perceptual involvement of the body while executing a movement) and visual (i.e., what a person sees) are the most usual sensory tested mentally approaches of creating images (Guarnera et al., 2016).

However, imagery is a complex construct. In the several explorations of mental imagery, researchers have investigated equally *imagery use* and *imagery ability*. The capability of creating vivid images is different from the competence in controlling and manipulating the created images (Morris et al., 2005). Cognitive psychology designed instruments to measure imagery ability into two aspects: controllability, i.e., "*manipulate mentally an image in precise way*" (Guillot and Colle, 2010; Pirrone and Di Nuovo, 2014), and vividness, i.e., "*the sensory richness of an image*" (Murphy, 2005). Murphy and Martin (2002) defined imagery use as the "*use of imagery to reach a variety of cognitive, behavioral, and affective changes*" (p. 418). Hall et al. (1998) underline that images address distinct motivational and cognitive aspects, both on a common and definite level. Consequently, differentiations in the use of imagery occur: cognitive specific (e.g., movements), cognitive general (e.g., tactics), motivational general, motivational specific (e.g., aims), motivational general–affective (e.g., anxiety), and motivational general–mastery (e.g. self-confidence).

In addition to the aforementioned considerations, the model of imagery suggested by Kosslyn et al. (2006) established which cognitive procedures are required in order to generate the configurations of behavior related with the everyday use and experience of mental imagery (Slotnick et al., 2012). These processes consist of generation, inspection, maintenance, and manipulation of visual images, in the lack of visual input. In detail, generation is the ability to generate mental representations deprived of a perceived stimulus. Maintenance is the capacity to maintain images in the short-term memory. Inspection describes the capacity to explore a generated image to interpreting a spatial property or an object-based characteristic of the image. Manipulation is the capacity to modify a mental image in some manner. Individuals can manipulate, transform, or rotate objects in visual imagery much like real objects, in their mind (Pearson and Kosslyn, 2013). This component of "controllability" of the images has been less studied in athletes.

Although previous investigation on mental imagery has principally concentrated on adult athletes, fewer studies have examined the young athlete population. Ashby (1983) have showed that imagery ability does not grow completely until 7 years of age. Parker and Lovell (2009) discovered high improvement in imagery ability in athletes between 7 and 17 years of age. Regarding the imagery use, previous studies showed that young athletes, competing at different levels, obviously use all components of imagery (Munroe-Chandler et al., 2007a; Parker and Lovell, 2012).

Comparing athletes' imagery with that of non-athletes, Isaac and Marks (1994) investigated whether distinctions in movement and visual imagery vividness can be assessed in 16 different sporting disciplines. Results showed that elite athletes had significantly higher vivid imagery than non-athlete controls. Williams and Davids (1995) compared the soccer knowledge base of three groups of participants: highly skilled, lower skilled, and controls (who had never played the game). Results showed that the highly skilled participants scored considerably higher than the others did on the ability to recognize and recall soccer movements. Moreau et al. (2011) investigated whether the level of expertise in a particular sport is related to better motor performance and spatial abilities, such as mental rotation, in particular. The findings indicated that young elite athletes reported consistent high performance in the spatial ability.

In a research on high school athletes, Godoy-Izquierdo et al. (2007) described more levels of imagery in elite athletes compared with non-elite ones. Mohammadzadeh and Sami (2014) investigated some psychological skills such as motivation, imagery, arousal, focus, self-confidence, and goal setting of elite and non-elite volleyball players (N = 60). Regarding imagery as the usage of all the senses to recreate or make an experience in mind, the results indicated that elite volleyball players had superior performance than non-elite ones.

Nevertheless, little investigation has been conducted on younger athletes comparing imagery—i.e., perception without present stimuli—with other cognitive abilities (e.g., spatial perception and visual memory).

The aim of the current study is to investigate the ability of children to engage in visual and spatial mental imagery (image maintenance, image inspection, image generation, and image manipulation), and to compare these processes between athletes and non-athletes (8–13 years of age). This age range has been selected as it is recommended that children aged 7 and over can form kinesthetic and transformational images (Piaget and Inhelder, 1971). In fact, although in disagreement with Piaget's theory, much research has demonstrated that under certain conditions, children younger than 7 years of age can transform visual mental images (Quaiser-Pohl et al., 2010; Guarnera et al., 2017, 2019). There is general agreement that children over 7 years of age improve their imagery ability, as they move from perceptual to conceptual activity (Munroe-Chandler et al., 2007b).

We expected athletes to show greater ability in controlling mental images than non-athletes.

MATERIALS AND METHODS

Participants and Procedure

The participants Were competitive athletes (n = 48) and non-athletes (n = 48) Between the ages of 8 and 13 years. the groups Were matched so they Had the same mean and standard deviation (M_{age} = 10.50, SD = 1.73, t = 0).

The athletes had a minimum of 5 years of training skill in the sport, and they were all associates of sport clubs. These athletes had different competitive sport backgrounds (e.g., soccer, karate, gymnastics, dance, and handball). Their hours of exercise per week ranged from 3.0 to 21.5 h (M = 7.39, SD = 3.41). Forty-eight students who had no experience in any sport represented control participants. Participants did not obtain before mental abilities or imagery training. Measurements were carried in clusters of four participants. Athletes were tested in an isolated place near the training accommodations. The control group was from dissimilar classes and was tested in a separate place near the school at the end of the educational activities. Prior to the beginning of the study, ethical approval was granted from the first author's university ethics committee. The study obtained ethical permission from the University Enna Kore Internal Review Board for psychological research (September 26, 2019).

Before starting the protocol, parents signed a consent form, and were informed about the processes of the study and the anonymity of their answers, in accordance with the Declaration of Helsinki.

Measures

Imagery Assessment

A sequence of tasks evaluating mental imagery skills including maintenance, inspection, generation, and manipulation of different categories of images was administered. Eight tasks are incorporated in the Mental Imagery Test (MIT) and standardized for usage in childhood (Di Nuovo et al., 2014):

Visualizing letters

The individuals are invited, without seeing the stimuli and spending only imagination, to say which upper-case letters have curled parts (e.g., A, P, or R; not L, M, or N).

Brooks "F" test

With their imagination, the individuals are asked to walk along the delineation of a large upper-case letter F earlier viewed for 30 s on a reproduced card. The individual is asked to say whether the limits encountered when moving from the lower left corner in a counter-clockwise direction are external or internal.

Clock

The task necessitates imagining a clock with hands indicating 10 min past 10:00, then imagining the clock reproduced in a mirror and saying what time the mirrored clock will show after 10 min.

Cube

The image of a large cube is shown for 30 s; it is collected of nine small cubes per face (3 × 3), and the external faces are colored. After the stimulus is detached, the subject is asked to state how many small cubes have three, two, one, or none external (colored) faces.

Subtraction of parts

A digital display with the number 88 collected of small segments is shown for 10 s. Then, another digital display with designated segments of a two-digit number is shown for 10 s. The individual is asked to imagine what two-digit number will remain after deducting the parts of the new figure from the figure with all digits seen beforehand.

Mental exploration of a map

The individual is presented with a map of an island, with a house, a church, a lake, and a wood located on it. The instructions ask to look with attention at the map, staring at the distances among the elements located. After the map is detached, the individual is asked to answer four questions about the comparative distance between couples of the earlier seen components.

Imagined paths

The individual is asked to imagine a small ball moving in dissimilar directions, succeeding a suggested path in the imagined space, and saying if at the end of the route the ball will end up above or below the initial point, or at the similar level.

Mental representation of shapes of objects

The individual hears the names of 20 concrete objects (e.g., bottle, pizza, candle, tower, and bed) and is asked to imagine them and select if the object has a taller or larger form.

A total score of mental imagery can be found by the sum of the scores in the single subtests. Cronbach's alpha for this

TABLE 1 | *T*-test results.

Variables		Controls	Athletes	*T*	P
Mental imagery abilities					
Visualizing letters	M	10.02	11.88	−6.22	< 0.001
	SD	2.04	0.33		
Brooks "F" test	M	4.10	7.44	−6.43	< 0.001
	SD	2.42	2.66		
Clock	M	1.29	0.08	5.00	< 0.001
	SD	1.62	0.40		
Cube	M	1.15	1.71	−1.40	0.17
	SD	1.53	2.33		
Subtraction of parts	M	5.04	10.04	−8.65	< 0.001
	SD	3.23	2.37		
Mental exploration of a map	M	4.00	5.23	−4.64	< 0.001
	SD	1.49	1.08		
Imagined paths	M	4.29	7.48	−6.03	< 0.001
	SD	2.56	2.62		
Mental representation of shapes of objects	M	14.13	18.54	−7.24	< 0.001
	SD	4.12	0.94		
Memory and visual perception					
Forward digit-span	M	3.87	5.10	−4.07	< 0.001
	SD	1.95	0.75		
Backward digit-span	M	1.88	3.79	−7.56	< 0.001
	SD	1.45	0.99		
Visual–spatial memory test	M	2.29	15.35	−16.39	< 0.001
	SD	2.93	4.68		
Memory of objects	M	5.12	6.63	−5.73	< 0.001
	SD	1.67	0.70		
Memory of position of objects	M	6.15	9.56	−6.30	< 0.001
	SD	3.05	2.20		
Mirror reproduction of spatial position	M	9.58	15.31	−6.38	< 0.001
	SD	5.80	2.25		

score of imagery is 0.75. A confirmatory factor analysis showed the monodimensionality of the measure containing the eight tasks, in a sample of 556 participants aged 8 to 13 years (chi-square = 186.28, $p < 0.01$; Root Mean Square Error of Approximation (RMSEA) = 0.09, $p < 0.01$; Comparative Fit Index (CFI) = 0.90; Standardized Root Mean (SRM) = 0.05; Goodness of Fit Index (GFI) = 0.93 (Di Nuovo et al., 2014).

The selection of the tasks, resulting from the preceding literature on mental imagery, was designed at expressing all the functions implicated in imagery, agreeing to the classification proposed by Pearson et al. (2013).

Comparison Tasks

With the aim of discriminating mental imagery abilities from those based on memory and visual perception—without necessitating active generation and/or alteration of mental images—some other cognitive standardized tasks are proposed.

Forward and backward digit span

The individual hears gradually increasing digit series, and has to repeat them in direct or backward order. Verbal working memory is implicated in these attentive tasks.

Memory of objects and of position of objects

The individual, after seeing seven concrete objects for 30", is invited to evoke as many of them as possible in a free recall. Subsequently, the individual has to recall the position in a matrix of six objects before seen for 30".

Visual–spatial memory test

Individuals are presented for 10" with a matrix in which a number of cells are completed and, after, are required to recall where they were located using a blank matrix. Six matrices are presented, and completed cells increase gradually from 2 to 4.

The tasks of memory of position, for both objects and matrices, necessitate a passive maintenance of spatial position in working memory and, consequently are useful to differentiate this skill from active elaboration of mental images.

Mirror reproduction of spatial position

The individual is requested to copy a model in a mirror position, though really seeing the model. This task of copy includes spatial perception without active alteration of images.

Statistical Analyses

Differences between the two groups of participants were assessed by t-test comparisons. Moreover, Pearson correlational analyses were completed to explore possible existing relationships between mental imagery abilities, and memory and visual perception within each group of participants. Statistical analyses were performed using SPSS version 23 Statistical Software Package for Windows (SPSS Inc., Chicago, IL, United States).

RESULTS

Preliminary, for the global score of imagery, we verified that the general difference due to the gender was non-significant: males' mean = 53.27, SD = 13.74; females' mean = 53.15, SD = 12.24; $t = 0.05$; $p = 0.96$. For this reason, the subsequent analyses were carried out without taking into account gender.

The analyses of differences in the performances of controls and athletes in the specific tasks are shown in **Table 1**.

Results showed high significant differences in all mental imagery abilities (except the "cube" test) and, in memory and visual perception with athletes. The only task showing a different trend is "clock," the performance being better in the control group.

In addition, the difference in the total score of imagery is highly significant: for the athletes group, mean = 62.40, SD = 7.13; for the controls group, mean = 44.02, SD = 10.74; $t = -9.87$, $p < 0.001$.

Correlational analyses between imagery tasks and perceptual and memory tests were performed separately for the two groups of athletes and controls (**Tables 2, 3**). Bonferroni confidence interval adjustments were used throughout.

Results showed that the mental imagery performances are differently correlated with perceptual and memory ones. As for

TABLE 2 | Pearson correlation matrix between imagery subtest and perceptual and memory tasks—athletes.

Athletes	Forward digit-span	Backward digit-span	Visual–spatial memory test	Memory of objects	Memory of position of objects	Mirror reproduction of spatial position
Visualizing letters	0.31*	0.11	0.27	0.16	0.27	0.08
Brooks "F" test	0.19	0.13	0.38**	0.01	0.27	0.19
Clock	0.25	0.15	0.14	0.11	0.14	−0.08
Cube	−0.10	0.32*	−0.08	−0.07	−0.09	0.15
Subtraction of parts	0.32*	0.22	0.05	0.32	0.14	0.37**
Mental exploration of a map	0.05	0.07	−0.02	0.34*	0.16	−0.10
Imagined paths	0.37**	0.34*	0.22	0.22	0.00	0.42***
Mental representation of shapes of objects	0.25	0.37**	0.21	0.22	0.27	0.35*

*$p < 0.05$, **$p < 0.01$, ***$p < 0.001$.

TABLE 3 | Pearson correlation matrix between imagery subtest and perceptual and memory tasks—controls.

Controls	Forward digit-span	Backward digit-span	Visual-spatial memory test	Memory of objects	Memory of position of objects	Mirror reproduction of spatial position
Visualizing letters	0.26	−0.09	0.32*	0.16	0.10	0.24
Brooks "F" test	0.45***	0.30*	0.60***	0.48***	0.60***	0.10
Clock	−0.07	−0.04	0.08	−0.06	−0.01	0.01
Cube	−0.25	−0.07	0.29*	0.08	0.17	0.06
Subtraction of parts	0.31*	0.55***	−0.09	0.32*	0.04	0.32*
Mental exploration of a map	0.25	0.20	0.34*	0.42***	0.35**	0.31*
Imagined paths	0.49***	0.49***	0.46***	0.63***	0.57***	0.32*
Mental representation of shapes of objects	0.56***	0.61***	0.30*	0.61***	0.62***	0.57***

*$p < 0.05$, **$p < 0.01$, ***$p < 0.001$.*

group differences, an interesting exception to the general trend is the "clock" task, which is positively (although not significantly) correlated with memory and perception tasks in athletes, while in the control group, these correlations are null or inverse.

DISCUSSION

The present study aimed to assess the ability of children to engage in visual and spatial mental imagery (image maintenance, image inspection, image generation, and image manipulation), and to compare these processes between athletes and non-athletes.

Results showed high significant differences in all mental imagery abilities (except the "cube" test) and, in memory and visual perception with athletes. According to Moreau et al. (2011), imagery ability is known to be closely related to visual perception and to be determinant in learning, memory, and motor processes.

The only task showing a different trend is "clock": the performance being better in the control group. This suggests that image maintenance abilities depend on stimulus complexity, according to previous research (e.g., Kosslyn, 1994; Frank et al., 2016). Children are better able to recall an image with specific features than an image with a more abstract pattern (Simonsmeier and Buecker, 2017). We, therefore, determine that the image generation task reasonably plays a significant role in reversal ability: the ability to form an image of another interpretation and impose this imagined assembly onto the figure.

Correlational analyses showed that the mental imagery performances are differently correlated with perceptual and memory ones. In the group of young athletes, the significant correlations are few and with lower size, indicating that in this group, the imagery functions are more independent from perception and memory than in non-athletes, and this independence could justify the overall better performance. We know that having solid mental imagery is an advantage to resolving visual and spatial tasks; nevertheless, our results propose that persons might use diverse cognitive approaches to resolve the similar visual memory task.

An interesting exception to this general trend is the "clock" task, which is positively correlated with memory and perception tasks in athletes (not significantly, although the size of the correlation with the forward digit span is relevant, i.e., 0.25), while in the control group, these correlations are null or inverse. In this task, the performance of the group of athletes is worse than that of the non-athletes; it could be influenced by the integration between memory and perceptual abilities, differently from controls. In fact, this task—being the most difficult—requires more than others to join visualizing and remembering the position in the space (of the hands of the visualized clock) and, therefore, an integration between imagery and other cognitive function, less present in the group of athletes as demonstrated in the other tasks. Probably, the young athletes are less able in the clock task for their less familiarity with analogical clocks, since they have more practice with digital clocks (e.g., for monitoring functioning during training and performances). For the same reason, in this task, the influence of the perceptual and memory abilities is more relevant in the athletes.

Despite the strengths of the current study, which include novel findings for a young population, there are several limitations that should be noted. For one, the ability of children to engage in visual and spatial mental imagery could be resulted with a longitudinal design. The relationship between the variables could be identified through since to start sport. Future research should investigate the mechanism more specifically, for example, investigating the association between cognitive-specific imagery ability and learning development of athletes.

CONCLUSION

In conclusion, it can be determined that imagery seems to be an instinctive psychological ability, which grows in early years of life. This finding is in line with previous studies, which showed that children often use imagery to acquire skills in a natural way (Wolmer et al., 1999; Munroe-Chandler et al.,

2007a). Consequently, to improve learning, performance, and other results related with imagery (such as self-efficacy, anxiety regulation, and cognition), athletes and coaches should incorporate the regular practice of mental imagery in their training programs.

ETHICS STATEMENT

The studies involving human participants were reviewed and approved by the University Enna Kore Internal Review Board for psychological research (September 26, 2019). Written informed consent to participate in this study was provided by the participants' legal guardian/next of kin.

AUTHOR CONTRIBUTIONS

DD, MG, SD, and MC contributed to the conception and design of the study. CG and SC were responsible for testing. MC, MG, SD, DD, and NM were responsible for data collection and statistical analysis. DD, MG, and MC were responsible for drafting and finalization of the manuscript. All authors contributed to manuscript revision and approved the submitted version.

REFERENCES

Ashby, A. A. (1983). Developmental study of short-term memory characteristics for kinesthetic movement information. *Percept. Mot. Skills* 57, 649–650. doi: 10.2466/pms.1983.57.2.649

Collet, C., Di Rienzo, F., El Hoyek, N., and Guillot, A. (2013). Autonomic nervous system correlates in movement observation and motor imagery. *Front. Hum. Neurosci.* 7:415. doi: 10.3389/fnhum.2013.00415

Cumming, J., and Ramsey, R. (2009). "Sport imagery interventions," in *Advances in Applied Sport Psychology: A Review*, eds S. Mellalieu and S. Hanton (London, UK: Routledge), 5–36.

Cumming, J., and Williams, S. E. (2012). "The role of imagery in performance," in *Handbook of Sport and Performance Psychology*, ed. S. Murphy (New York, NY: Oxford University Press), 213–232.

Di Corrado, D., Guarnera, M., and Quartiroli, A. (2014). Vividness and transformation of mental images in karate and dance. *Percept. Mot. Skills* 119, 764–773. doi: 10.2466/22.24.PMS.119c30z6

Di Corrado, D., Guarnera, M., Vitali, F., Quartiroli, A., and Coco, M. (2019). Imagery ability of elite level athletes from individual vs. team and contact vs. no-contact sports. *PeerJ* 7:e6940. doi: 10.7717/peerj.6940

Di Nuovo, S., Castellano, S., and Guarnera, M. (2014). *Mental Imagery Test.* Florence: Hogrefe.

Frank, C., Land, W. M., and Schack, T. (2016). Perceptual-cognitive changes during motor learning: the influence of mental and physical practice on mental representation, gaze behavior, and performance of a complex action. *Front. Psychol.* 6:1981. doi: 10.3389/fpsyg.2015.01981

Godoy-Izquierdo, D., Vélez, M., and Godoy, J. (2007). "Results of a seasonal-period psychological skills training in football young-players," in *Proceedims of the 12th European Congress of Sport Psychology*, Halkidiki.

Guarnera, M., Faraci, P., Commodari, E., and Bucchieri, S. (2017). Mental imagery and school readness. *Psychol. Rep.* 120, 1058–1077. doi: 10.1177/0033294117717262

Guarnera, M., Pellerone, M., Commodari, E., Valenti, G. D., and Buccheri, S. L. (2019). Mental images and school learning: a longitudinal study on children. *Front. Psychol.* 10:2034. doi: 10.3389/fpsyg.2019.02034

Guarnera, M., Stummiello, M., Cascio, M. I., and Di Corrado, D. (2016). Vividness and transformation of mental images in karate. *Int. J. Kinesiol. Sports Sci.* 4, 10–17. doi: 10.7575/aiac.ijkss.v.4n.3p.10

Guillot, A., and Colle, C. (2010). *The Neurophysiological Foundations of Mental and Motor Imagery.* Oxford: Oxford University Press.

Hale, B. D., Seiser, L., Mcguire, E. J., and Weinrich, E. (2005). "Mental imagery," in *Applying Sport Psychology: Four Perspectives*, eds J. Taylor and G. Wilson (Champaign, IL: Human Kinetics), 117–136.

Hall, C., Mack, D. E., and Paivio, A. (1998). Imagery use by athletes: development of the sport imagery questionnaire. *Int. J. Sport Psychol.* 29, 73–89. doi: 10.1037/t52953-000

Isaac, A. R., and Marks, D. F. (1994). Individual differences in mental imagery experience: developmental changes and specialization. *Br. J. Psychol.* 85, 479–500. doi: 10.1111/j.2044-8295.1994.tb02536.x

Kosslyn, S. M. (1994). *Image and Brain.* Cambridge, MA: MIT Press.

Kosslyn, S. M., Ganis, G., and Thompson, W. L. (2001). Neural foundations of imagery. *Nat. Rev. Neurol.* 2, 635–642. doi: 10.1038/35090055

Kosslyn, S. M., Thompson, W. L., and Ganis, G. (2006). *The Case for Mental Imagery.* New York: Oxford University Press.

Mohammadzadeh, H., and Sami, S. (2014). Psychological skills of elite and non-elite volleyball players. *Ann. Appl. Sport Sci.* 2, 31–36. doi: 10.18869/acadpub.aassjournal.2.1.31

Moreau, D., Mansy-Dannay, A., Clerc, J., and Guerrién, A. (2011). Spatial ability and motor performance: assessing mental rotation processes in elite and novice athletes. *Int. J. Sport Psychol.* 42, 525–547.

Morris, T., Spittle, M., and Watt, A. P. (2005). *Imagery in Sport.* Campaign, IL: Human Kinetics.

Munroe-Chandler, K., Hall, C., Fishburne, G. J., O, J., and Hall, N. (2007a). The content of imagery use in youth sport. *Int. J. Sport Exerychol.* 5, 158–174. doi: 10.1080/1612197X.2007.9671817

Munroe-Chandler, K., Hall, C., Fishburne, G. J., and Strachan, L. (2007b). Where, when, and why young athletes use imagery: an examination of developmental differences. *Res. Q. Exerc. Sport* 78, 103–116. doi: 10.1080/02701367.2007.10599408

Murphy, L., and Martin, K. (2002). "The use of imagery in sport," in *Advances in Sport Psychology*, ed. T. S. Horn (Champaign, IL: Human Kinetics), 405–439.

Murphy, S. M. (2005). "Imagery: inner theater becomes reality," in *The Sport Psych Handbook*, ed. S. M. Murphy (Champaign, IL: Human Kinetics), 128–151.

Parker, J. K., and Lovell, G. P. (2009). Characteristics affecting the use of imagery: a youth sports academy study. *J. Imagery Res. Sport Phys. Activ.* 4, 1–15. doi: 10.2202/1932-0191.1034

Parker, J. K., and Lovell, G. P. (2012). Age differences in the vividness of youth sport performers imagery ability. *J. Imagery Res. Sport Phys. Activ.* 7, 1–13. doi: 10.1515/1932-0191.1069

Pearson, D. G. (2007). Mental imagery and creative thought. *Proc. Br. Acad.* 147, 187–212. doi: 10.5871/bacad/9780197264195.003.0009

Pearson, D. G., Deeprose, C., Wallace-Hadrill, S. M. A., Burnett Heyes, S., and Holmes, E. A. (2013). Assessing mental imagery in clinical psychology: a review of imagery measures and a guiding framework. *Clin. Psychol. Rev.* 33, 1–23. doi: 10.1016/j.cpr.2012.09.001

Pearson, J., and Kosslyn, S. M. (2013). Mental imagery. *Front. Psychol.* 4:198. doi: 10.3389/fpsyg.2013.00198

Piaget, J., and Inhelder, B. (1971). *Mental Imagery in the Child.* New York, NY: Basic Books.

Pirrone, C., and Di Nuovo, S. (2014). Can playing and imagining aid in learning mathematics? An experimental study of the relationships among building-block play, mental imagery, and arithmetic skills. *Appl. Psychol. Bull.* 62, 30–39.

Quaiser-Pohl, C., Rohe, A., and Amberger, T. (2010). The Solution strategy as an indicator of the developmental stage of pre-school children's mental-rotation ability. *J. Individ. Differ.* 31, 95–100.

Simonsmeier, B. A., and Buecker, S. (2017). Interrelations of imagery use, imagery ability, and performance in young athletes. *J. Appl. Sport Psychol.* 29, 32–43. doi: 10.1080/10413200.2016.1187686

Slotnick, S. D., Thompson, W. L., and Kosslyn, S. M. (2012). Visual memory and visual mental imagery recruit common control and sensory regions of the brain. *Cogn. Neurosci.* 3, 14–20. doi: 10.1080/17588928.2011.578210

Williams, A. M., and Davids, K. (1995). Declarative knowledge in sport: a by-product of experience or a characteristic of expertise? *J. Sport Exerc. Psychol.* 17, 269–275. doi: 10.1123/jsep.17.3.259

Wolmer, L., Laor, N., and Token, P. (1999). Image control from childhood to adolescence. *Percept. Mot. Skills* 89, 471–485. doi: 10.2466/pms.1999.89.2.471

22

Stress and Coping in Esports and the Influence of Mental Toughness

Dylan Poulus, Tristan J. Coulter, Michael G. Trotter and Remco Polman*

School of Exercise and Nutrition Sciences, Queensland University of Technology, Brisbane, QLD, Australia

Correspondence:
Dylan Poulus
dylan.poulus@gmail.com

This study explored stress and coping in electronic sports (esports) athletes and the influence of mental toughness (MT), as defined by two prominent conceptualizations: the 4/6Cs and Mental Toughness Index (MTI) frameworks. Participants were 316 esports athletes, ranked in the top 40% of one of five major esports: Defense of the Ancients 2, League of Legends (LoL), Counter Strike: Global Offensive, Overwatch and Rainbow Six: Siege. Participants completed the MTI, Mental Toughness Questionnaire 6 (MTQ6), Stress Appraisal Measure, and Brief COPE inventory. Results showed that MT (via both MT frameworks) was associated with perceived control, and MTQ6 subscales were associated with stress intensity. Mental toughness (both frameworks) was associated with the selection of more problem-focused and emotion-focused coping strategies and less avoidance coping strategies. The results indicate there is some overlap between the MT and stress-coping process in high-performing traditional sports and competitive esports athletes. These results suggest that esports athletes could benefit from sports psychology interventions designed for traditional sports athletes. Finally, the MTQ6 and MTI had low shared variance (20%), suggesting that the two questionnaires appear to measure different aspects of MT.

Keywords: electronic sport, threat, challenge, control, intensity appraisal

INTRODUCTION

Electronic sports (esports) is the term used to describe the casual or organized playing of video games in a way that provides professional or personal development to the player (Pedraza-Ramirez et al., 2020). While there is still definitional debate around what is an esport and what is a video game, this study will be adopting the definition proposed by Pedraza-Ramirez et al. (2020). Esports is beginning to see increased attention from researchers (Reitman et al., 2019). One topic of interest and debate has been the comparison esports has with traditional sports (Bányai et al., 2018). This debate mainly centers on whether esports can be classified as a "sport" and if its players can be treated as traditional "athletes." Jenny et al. (2017) identified that esports fitted well within the sociological and philosophical definitions of sport (e.g., it involves play, competition, and skill). Total prize pools for esports competitions are predicted to reach more than US $413 million by 2020 (Goldman Sachs, 2018). In 2019, the Defense of the Ancients 2 (DOTA 2) major tournament, "The International 9," had a total prize pool of US $34 million, with the winning side (Team OG) collecting US $15 million (*The International, 2020*). Growth in viewership and prize pools has led to the development of professional players/teams competing in regular professional esports leagues (Taylor, 2012). Furthermore, talent development pathways for esports players are becoming more common with a number of governments and American (Conditt, 2016) and Australian student sporting portfolios (Lace, 2019) now recognizing esports athletes. As such, it would be important to examine some of the psychological factors that might determine success in esports.

On a psychological level, it has been suggested that the competitive and cooperative nature of esports requires similar mental skills as traditional sports (Murphy, 2009; Campbell et al., 2018). Supporting this idea, Himmelstein et al. (2017) qualitatively examined the mental skills and obstacles encountered by five League of Legends (LoL) athletes. To achieve optimal performance, 11 mental skills were identified (e.g., staying in the moment, utilizing preperformance routines, adapting to competition). Himmelstein et al. (2017) also identified four ways esports athletes acquired their skills (i.e., setting goals, analyzing performance, practicing individual skill, and maintaining a growth mindset). Smith et al. (2019), through interviews, investigated the stressors experienced and the associated coping strategies used by seven professional esports competitors. The associated coping strategies identified in the data supported the existing stress-coping literature (Polman, 2012). Emotion-focused (EFC), problem-focused (PFC), avoidance (AC), approach, and appraisal coping strategies were all employed by esports athletes (Smith et al., 2019). The studies by Himmelstein et al. (2017) and Smith et al. (2019) are limited by small samples sizes. Toth et al. (2019) explored esports players of different skill levels on tests of cognitive functioning. Results showed that elite esport athletes (based on in-game rankings) displayed faster response times and higher accuracy for simple choice reaction time stimuli (control trials), but that there were no differences between groups in cognitive inhibition. Clearly there is a need for more research on the psychological determinants of success for esports players (Pedraza-Ramirez et al., 2020).

A factor that has been shown to influence performance in sport is the way athletes cope with stressors they encounter (Lazarus, 2000). Considering esports has some similarities to traditional sport, it is timely to examine the stress and coping process in esports athletes to explore whether performance and well-being could be enhanced through established or new psychological interventions or training programs (Polman et al., 2018). An athlete's ability to cope with stress has been shown to be important to success in traditional sport (Lazarus, 2000; Polman, 2012). The main framework adopted by researchers has been the cognitive–motivational–relational theory of stress and coping (Lazarus, 2000). According to this framework, appraisal of stressors, coping, and consequences are viewed as a dynamical and recursive process between the individual and his/her environment. Specifically, the person appraises events through primary (something at stake) and secondary (available coping options in relation to the event) appraisals (Lazarus, 2000). Following appraising an event as stressful, an individual invokes a voluntary coping response to manage the stress. Coping responses have been identified as falling into three common, higher-order dimensions (Nicholls and Polman, 2007): PFC (strategies aimed at changing stressful situation), EFC (strategies to regulate emotions associated with a stressful situation), and AC (physical or cognitive efforts to disengage from the stressor).

Studies have indicated that stable personality factors can directly or indirectly influence the stress-coping process (Polman et al., 2010). A disposition considered to be influential in sporting success is mental toughness (MT) (Coulter et al., 2018). There is ongoing debate around the conceptualization and definition of mental toughness (Gucciardi et al., 2015). This debate largely stems from two main perspectives that have recently emerged in the sport psychology literature.

The first perspective originated in Clough et al.'s (2002) work, who proposed the 4/6Cs model of MT. This model builds on Kobasa's (1979) conceptualization of hardiness, a stress buffering personality trait. Based on interviews with coaches, athletes, and sport psychologists, Clough and colleagues added *confidence* (interpersonal and in one's ability) to Kobasa's (1979) three-factor hardiness construct: challenge, commitment (to one's goals), and control (emotions and life). From this 4/6C model, Clough et al. (2002) developed a 48-item Mental Toughness Questionnaire (MTQ-48). While the MTQ-48 has been used extensively in the literature, several research teams have reported equivocal results about its psychometric properties (Gucciardi, 2017). To improve the factorial validity of the MTQ-48, Kawabata et al. (under review) recently refined the MTQ-48 to create a statistically and conceptually rigorous six-item multidimensional model of the 4/6Cs – the Mental Toughness Questionnaire 6 (MTQ6).

The second notable approach to the conceptualization and psychometric assessment of MT derives from qualitative methods to understand people's perceptions of MT and its core attributes. Gucciardi et al. (2015) recently synthesized this body of research to identify several core properties of MT. Based on this work, the Mental Toughness Index (MTI) was developed (Gucciardi et al., 2015), which assesses seven core constructs: generalized self-efficacy, buoyancy, success mindset, optimistic style, context knowledge, emotion regulation, and attention regulation. According to Gucciardi et al. (2015), the MTI is a unidimensional measure that treats MT as a trait construct with state-like properties (i.e., it can fluctuate across time and context).

While similarities and differences exist across the two conceptualizations of MT, the current study aims to incorporate both perspectives into its research design, as an opportunity to explore the relationships and comparative explanatory impact the two perspectives have with stress and coping. In addition, the team-based nature of many esports requires its athletes to engage in interpersonal interactions. The 4/6C model (via the MTQ6) includes an interpersonal aspect to being mentally tough (interpersonal confidence), hence the decision to include it in the current study.

The relationship between MT and the stress and coping process has been researched in traditional sport. A study by Kaiseler et al. (2009) found that higher levels of MT were associated with lower levels of perceived stress and higher levels of emotional control. Furthermore, Nicholls et al. (2008) found that athletes who were more mentally tough used more PFC strategies and less AC strategies. Nicholls et al. (2012) also found that an athlete's perception of challenge and threat was associated with one's perceived control of the stressor. Higher levels of control were associated with perceiving the stressor as a challenge, and lower levels of control were associated with perceiving the stressor as a threat.

To better understand the relationship between MT and the stress and coping process in competitive esports players, this study will target players in the top 40% of their chosen esport. Esports games that use an in-game ranking system calculate players' level of competence. The top 40% of competitors (according to in-game ranking) represents a large ability range and is more likely to capture players who play regularly and at a higher competency level. Esports players from five major team based esports will be selected in this study: DOTA 2, LoL, Counter Strike: Global Offensive (CS: GO), Overwatch (OW), and Rainbow Six: Siege (R6) (Pedraza-Ramirez et al., 2020). The games were chosen because of their popularity, prize pool (tournaments), in-game ranking system, and accessibility of participants (Goldman Sachs, 2018; Pedraza-Ramirez et al., 2020). Each of the five esports explored in this study have a competitive or ranked game play mode where an in-game ranking system sorts players into rankings based on their in-game competence.

The aim of the present study is to examine stress and coping in competitive esports athletes and explore how this regulatory process may be influenced by MT. To that end, it is predicted that esports athletes with higher MT scores will report lower levels of stress intensity and higher levels of perceived control, see stressors more as a challenge than a threat, and use more PFC and less EFC and AC (e.g., Nicholls et al., 2008, 2012; Kaiseler et al., 2009). Esports athletes who scored higher MT (total and item) will have higher levels of achievement (determined by in-game rank). Finally, the potential similarities or differences across the two MT conceptualizations were explored; no explicit *a priori* predictions were made.

METHODS

Participants

Participants were 316 esports athletes (283 Males, 33 Female) aged 18–41 ($M = 22.61$, $SD = 4.35$). **Table 1** provides descriptive statistics for gender, age, in-game rank, percentile group, and the frequency of professional players for each esports game. **Table 2** shows the distribution of participants' in-game ranks across each of their chosen esports and how in-game ranking was standardized and grouped into achievement levels across esports for statistical analysis.

Measures

Demographics

The first part of the questionnaire pack for this study included completion of some demographic information including type of esport played, in-game ranking, age, and gender. The questionnaire allowed only players in the top 40% of their chosen esports (as determined by self-reported in-game rank) and players who played on a desktop computer, to continue through the questionnaire. In-game rank cutoffs were as follows: DOTA 2 ≥ Archon 3, LoL ≥ Silver 1, CS: GO ≥ Master Guardian 1, OW ≥ Platinum 1, R6 ≥ Gold3 (**Table 2**). No participants who met the in-game ranking cutoff were excluded. Players were also asked if they had ever competed in a professional esports tournament.

Stress Appraisal

To measure how esports athletes appraise stress, participants were asked to report a stressor that they recently encountered while playing their esport. On analog scales, participants rated the intensity of the stressor (Kowalski and Crocker, 2001) (1 = not stressful, 10 = extremely stressful), how much control they felt they had over the situation (1 = no control at all, 10 = full control), how much of a threat they felt the situation was (1 = not at all threatening, 10 = extremely threatening), and how challenging they felt the situation was (1 = not at all challenging, 10 = extremely challenging) (Kaiseler et al., 2012; Britton et al., 2019).

Coping

Coping was assessed by using the 28-item Brief COPE inventory (Carver, 1997). Using a four-point scale, the Brief COPE assesses how a participant has been dealing with the stressors in his/her life. The Brief COPE has 14 factors that can be classified into three higher-order dimensions: PFC, EFC, and AC coping (Dias et al., 2012). The Brief COPE has good psychometric properties (Carver, 1997). In the current study, reliability for 13 of the 14 factors was satisfactory (**Table 3**). Although one of the scales of the Brief COPE did not reach acceptable levels of internal consistency, it was included in the statistical analysis because estimates of internal consistency have limited applicability when assessing psychometric properties of measures of coping

TABLE 1 | Frequency of gender, average age, average in-game rank, and frequency of professional players by esport game.

Esport	Gender		Average age		Level of competition		Average in-game rank
	Male	Female	Mean	*SD*	Professional	Nonprofessional	
DOTA 2 (*n* = 18)	18	0	21.67	4.20	2	16	Ancient 1
LoL (*n* = 118)	105	13	23.78	4.61	8	110	Platinum 2
CS: GO (*n* = 61)	56	5	21.38	3.60	16	45	Distinguished Master Guardian
OW (*n* = 84)	71	13	22.75	4.47	6	78	Diamond
R6 (*n* = 35)	33	2	21.00	3.05	8	27	Platinum 2
Total (*n* = 316)	283	33	22.61	4.35	40	276	-

TABLE 2 | In-game ranking standardized into achievement level groups across esports.

DOTA 2			League of legends			Counterstrike: global offensive			Overwatch			Rainbow six: siege		
Group	**Rank**	**Percentage**	**Group**	**Rank**	**Percentage**	**Group**	**Rank**	**Percentage**	**Group**	**Rank**	**Percentage**	**Group**	**Rank**	**Percentage**
5	Archon 4	(58.17–63.61)	5	Silver 1	(56.3–62.18)	5	Master Guardian 1	(66.61–74.16)	5	Platinum (>2588)	60.0–77.7	5	Gold 3	(64.89–73.64)
5	Archon 5	(63.61–68.96)	5	Gold 5	(62.18–73.62)	4	Master Guardian 2	(74.16–80.77)	4	Diamond	77.8–91.2	4	Gold 2	(73.64–81.81)
5	Legend 1	(68.96–74.11)	4	Gold 4	(73.62–79.26)	3	Master Guardian Elite	(80.77–86.01)	2	Master		3	Gold 1	(81.81–88.06)
4	Legend 2	(74.11–78.73)	4	Gold 3	(79.26–83.28)	3	Distinguisher Master Guardian	(86.01–90.16)	2	Grandmaster		3	Platinum 3	(88.06– 95.52)
4	Legend 3	(78.73–82.78	3	Gold 2	(83.28–85.92)	2	Legendary Eagle		1	Top 500		2	Platinum 2	
3	Legend 4	(82.78–86.24)	3	Gold 1	(85.92– 89.7)	2	Legendary Eagle Master					2	Platinum 1	
3	Legend 5	(86.24–89.19)	3	Platinum 5	(89.7–93.02)	2	Supreme Master First Class					1	Diamond	
3	Ancient 1	(89.19–91.60)	2	Platinum 4		1	The Global Elite							
2	Ancient 2		2	Platinum 3										
2	Ancient 3		2	Platinum 2										
2	Ancient 4		2	Platinum 1										
2	Ancient 5		2	Diamond 5										
2	Divine 1		1	Diamond 4										
2	Divine 2		1	Diamond 3										
2	Divine 3		1	Diamond 2										
1	Divine 4		1	Diamond 1										
1	Divine 5		1	Master										
1	Immortal		1	Challenger										

Achievement Level Groups	Ranking Percentage
5	~ 60–70
4	~ 70–80
3	~ 80–90

Note: The ranking percentages above were gather at below times and location.

DOTA 2	Based on June 2018	Cutoff rank: > Archon 3	https://www.esportstales.com/dota-2/seasonal-rank-distribution-and-mmr-medals
League of legends	Based on august 2018	Cutoff rank: > Silver 1	https://www.esportstales.com/league-of-legends/rank-distribution-percentage-of-players-by-tier
Counter strike	Based on August 2018 data	Cutoff rank: > Master Guardian 1	https://totalcsgo.com/ranks
Overwatch	Based on August 2018 (season 11)	Cutoff rank: Platinum (> 2588SR)	https://www.esportstales.com/overwatch/competitive-rank-distribution-pc-and-console
Rainbow six siege	Based on July 2018 data	Cutoff rank: > Gold 3	https://www.esportstales.com/rainbow-six-siege/seasonal-rank-distribution-and-percentage-of-players

TABLE 3 | Mean, standard deviation, Cronbach α for stressor appraisal, coping strategies, mental toughness index, and mental toughness questionnaire.

Stress appraisal	**Mean**	***SD***	α
Perceived stress intensity	6.42	2.27	
Perceived control	3.86	2.92	
Perceived threat	4.07	2.97	
Perceived challenge	6.19	2.62	
Coping strategies			
Problem-focused coping	**2.47**	**0.63**	**0.81**
Active coping	2.79	0.79	0.72
Use of instrumental support	2.03	0.88	0.70
Positive reframing	2.42	0.92	0.81
Planning	2.65	0.83	0.70
Emotion-focused coping	**2.23**	**0.49**	**0.75**
Use of emotional support	1.99	0.89	0.83
Venting	2.06	0.81	0.63
Humor	2.67	0.83	0.84
Acceptance	2.99	0.78	0.60
Self-blame	2.39	0.90	0.72
Religion	1.29	0.63	0.71
Avoidance coping	**1.64**	**0.45**	**0.68**
Self-distraction	2.47	0.89	0.61
Denial	1.37	0.61	0.53
Substance use	1.19	0.47	0.87
Behavioral disengagement	1.53	0.71	0.68
Mental toughness			
Mental Toughness Index (MTI)	**5.23**	**0.95**	**0.86**
Mental Toughness Questionnaire (MTQ6)	**4.18**	**0.37**	**0.61**
Challenge: Challenges usually bring out the best in me.	4.16	0.67	
Commitment: I don't usually give up under pressure.	4.29	0.63	
Emotional control: Even when under considerable pressure, I usually remain calm.	4.15	0.65	
Life control: I generally feel that I am in control of what happens in my life.	4.04	0.65	
Confidence in abilities: I am generally confident in my own abilities.	4.16	0.62	
Interpersonal confidence: I usually take charge of a situation when I feel it is appropriate.	4.33	0.62	

(Billings and Moos, 1981). Confirmatory factor analysis (CFA) was conducted, using AMOS 25, to explore the psychometric properties of the Brief COPE. This showed an excellent fit (CMIN/DF = 1.57, CFI = 0.95, RMSEA = 0.04, PCLOSE = 0.94).

Mental Toughness

The two MT questionnaires administered were the MTI (Gucciardi et al., 2015) and the MTQ6 (Kawabata et al., under review). The MTI has eight items and is scored on a seven-point Likert scale. The MTI has shown good psychometric properties across a range of independent samples (Gucciardi et al., 2015) and measures overall MT. CFA for the present sample showed a good fit (CMIN/DF = 1.55, CFI = 0.99, RMSEA = 0.04, PCLOSE = 0.66).

The MTQ6 has six items and is scored on a five-point scale. Initial results have shown good factorial structure for the MTQ6 (Kawabata et al., under review). In the current study, CFA showed an adequate fit (CMIN/DF = 2.76, CFI = 0.92, RMSEA = 0.08, PCLOSE = 0.12).

Procedure

The study received institutional ethical approval. Participants provided informed consent before participation in the study. Participants were recruited to the study through two methods, either online (n = 314) or in-person (n = 2) at esports events. Online participants were directed to a URL where they could complete the questionnaire pack (developed and managed by Qualtrics). The URL was distributed via email and online via social media (Twitter and Facebook) and YouTube.

Data Analysis

Esports classify their players into levels, based on a percentage range. The number of levels differs across esports. To standardize in-game ranking across five esports into achievement level, five group classifications were developed: level 1 = 99–100%, level 2 = 90–98%, level 3 = 89–80%, level 4 = 79–70%, and level 5 = 69–60% (**Table 2**). Before the main analysis, a Shapiro–Wilk test was used to examine the distribution of each variable. All study variables were normally distributed, and skewness and kurtosis were not breached. Cronbach α's and descriptive statistics were obtained for all study variables (**Table 3**). Pearson product-moment correlations between the variables were then calculated. Initial analysis compared differences between gender (Kaiseler and Polman, 2010) and game across stress appraisal, coping, and MT. No significant differences were found (all $P > 0.05$), and the data were collapsed across game and gender.

To determine whether MT was associated with perceived stressor intensity, stressor control, stressor threat, and stressor challenge, several separate linear regressions were run with the MTQ6 items (1–6), MTQ6 total, or MTI total, as predictor variables. To assess whether MT was associated with coping strategy selection, linear regressions were used. The 14 factors of the Brief COPE were entered as the dependent variables, whereas the MT measures represented the predictor variables. Similarly, regression analysis was conducted to explore the association between MT and coping at the dimensional level.

We first calculated Pearson product-moment correlations between the variable in this study. To investigate if achievement level was associated with participant's stressor appraisal and selection of coping strategies, a number of multivariate analyses of variance (MANOVAs) were run. In the instance of significant main or interaction effects, follow-up analysis of variance (ANOVA) was conducted. Analyses of variance were conducted to explore if achievement level was associated with participants' total MT levels. *Post hoc* comparisons were conducted using Sidak.

RESULTS

Correlation Analysis of Study Variables

The means, standard deviations, and Cronbach α for stressor appraisal, coping strategies (dimensional and strategy level), and both MT questionnaires are reported in **Table 3**. The results of the correlational analysis of the study variables are shown in **Table 4**. Contrary to predictions, correlational analysis demonstrated that there was no association between overall MT level (both frameworks) and stressor intensity. However, there were small significant inverse relationships between MTQ6 dimensions, emotional control (r = -0.11), life control (r = −0.12), and stressor intensity. In terms of perceptions of control, only a small, significant positive correlation was identified with the MTI (r = 0.12).

For threat perceptions, a small significant inverse correlation with emotional control (r = −0.13) (MTQ6) was found, whereas for challenge perceptions, there was a negative correlation with MTQ6 total score (r = −0.11) and life control (r = −0.14). For PFC, there were small to moderate positive correlations with both the MTQ6 total (r = 0.26) and MTI (r = 0.35). In addition, small significant correlations were identified with challenge (r = 0.17), commitment (r = 0.18), confidence ability (r = 0.17), and interpersonal (r = 0.18) items of the MTQ6. Similarly, small significant inverse correlations were found between the MTQ6 total (r = −0.20), MTI (r = −0.27), and AC. The MTQ6's commitment (r = −0.22), emotional control (r = −0.15), confidence ability (r = −0.12), and confidence (r = −0.14) interpersonal items also showed small significant negative associations with AC. Finally, there were no associations between MT (both frameworks) and EFC (all $P > 0.05$). See **Table 4** for full results of the correlational analysis.

Associations Between Coping Strategies and MT Measures

Regression analysis was run to explore the association between coping strategies and the six items of the MTQ, the MTQ6 total score, and MTI total score (**Table 5**). The PFC strategy, active coping, was associated with commitment (β = 0.16), confidence ability (β = 0.13), and interpersonal confidence (β = 0.13), explaining 11% the variance in the use of this strategy. Similarly, MTQ6 and MTI total scores respectively explained 9% (β = 0.30) and 15% (β = 0.38) of the variance in active coping. The use of instrumental support was only predicted by the MTI, which explained 2% of the variance in using instrumental support as a coping strategy. Higher levels of positive reframing and planning were also associated with higher levels of total MTQ6 (2%, β = 0.14; and 7%, β = 0.27) and MTI (4%, β = 0.20; and 10%, β = 0.31). Higher levels of challenge (β = 0.12) and interpersonal confidence (β = 0.17) also predicted increased use of the coping strategy planning (9%).

Regarding EFC, acceptance was the only strategy associated with MT. In particular, the MTQ6 (5%, β = 0.24) and MTI (2%, β = 0.14) showed small but significant associations. In addition, challenge (β = 0.13) and emotional control (β = 0.16) (MTQ6) had a significant positive association with acceptance (7%). No associations were observed between the MTQ6 items, MTQ6 total, MTI, and the EFC strategies venting, humor, self-blame, or religion.

For AC, self-distraction (β = −0.15) was negatively associated with MTI total score (2%), whereas substance use and behavioral disengagement were negatively associated with both MTQ6 (2%, β = −0.16; and 6%, β = −0.24, respectively) and MTI (2%, β = −0.13; and 12%, β = −0.35) scores. Also, commitment (β = −0.17) (MTQ6) was associated with substance abuse

TABLE 4 | Correlational analysis of the study variables.

Stress appraisal measure	Stressor intensity	Stressor control	Stressor threat	Stressor challenge	Problem-focused coping	Emotion-focused coping	Avoidance coping
Stressor intensity							
Stressor control	−0.24*						
Stressor threat	0.44*	−0.19*					
Stressor challenge	0.48*	−0.13*	0.39*				
Coping strategies							
Problem-focused coping	0.08	0.21*	0.24*	35			
Emotion-focused coping	0.11*	0.04	0.19*	0.10	0.57*		
Avoidance coping	0.18*	−0.07	0.08	0.08	0.08	0.43*	
MTQ6 total	−0.08	0.05	0.07	−0.11*	0.26*	0.10	−0.20*
MTQ 1 – challenge	0.04	0.05	0.02	0.02	0.17*	0.07	0.02
MTQ 2 – commitment	−0.02	0.05	0.00	−0.09	0.18*	0.03	−0.22*
MTQ 3 – emotional control	−0.11*	0.05	−0.13*	−0.09	0.11	0.07	−0.15*
MTQ 4 – life control	−0.12*	−0.01	−0.07	−0.14*	0.09	0.04	−0.08
MTQ 5 – confidence in abilities	−0.01	0.00	−0.00	−0.05	0.17*	0.09	−0.12*
MTQ 6 – interpersonal control	−0.06	0.04	−0.07	−0.04	0.18*	0.06	−0.14*
MTI total	−0.06	0.12*	0.02	−0.01	0.35*	0.08	−0.27*
Game rank	0.16	0.03*	0.56	0.19	0.49	0.61	0.27

*$p < 0.05$.

TABLE 5 | Regression analysis to explore the association between mental toughness and coping strategies.

Construct	Construct – MTQ6 (Items 1–6)			Construct – MTQ6 Total			Construct – MTI		
Coping strategies	R^2	$F(6, 309)$ =	Six MTQ 6 (1–6) – β significant predictors	R^2	$F(1, 314)$ =	Six MTQ 6 total – β significant predictor	R^2	$F(6, 309)$ =	Six MTI total – β significant predictor
Problem-focused coping	0.07	4.02**		0.7	22.04**	0.26**	0.12	42.30**	0.36**
Active coping	0.11	6.45**	Q2 = 0.16**; Q5 = 0.13*; Q6 = 0.13*	0.9	30.96**	0.3**	0.15	54.16**	0.38**
Use of instrumental support	0.01	0.336		0.00	1.28		0.02	6.1*	0.14*
Positive reframing	0.02	1.16		0.02	6.09*	0.14*	0.04	13.18**	0.201**
Planning	0.09	5.19**	Q1 = 0.12*; Q6 = 0.17**	0.70	24.56**	0.27**	0.10	33.12**	0.31**
Emotion-focused coping	0.01	0.70		0.01	3.14		0.01	2.02	
Use of emotional support	0.02	1.21		0.01	2.79		0.01	2.54	
Venting	0.04	1.98		0.01	2.12		0.01	1.59	
Humor	0.02	1.24		0.01	3.24		0.00	0.41	
Acceptance	0.07	3.89**	Q1 = 0.13*; Q3 = 0.16**	0.05	18.88**	0.24**	0.02	5.81*	0.135*
Self-blame	0.01	0.64		0.00	0.02		0.00	0.03	
Religion	0.01	0.42		0.00	0.02		0.01	3.01	
Avoidance coping	0.08	4.63**	Q1 = 0.14**; Q2 = −0.20**	0.40	12.44**	-0.2	0.07	24.87**	-0.27**
Self-distraction	0.02	1.15		0.01	1.99		0.02	7.2**	-0.15**
Denial	0.02	1.19		0.01	1.71		0.00	1.37	
Substance use	0.04	2.33*	Q2 = −0.17**	0.20	5.9*	-0.16*	0.02	5.75*	-0.13*
Behavioral disengagement	0.10	5.43**	Q2 = −0.21**; Q6 = −0.16**	0.06	18.63**	-0.24**	0.12	42.84**	-0.35**

*$p < 0.05$; **$p < 0.01$.

(4%), whereas commitment (β = −0.21) and interpersonal confidence (β = −0.16) (MTQ6) were associated with behavioral disengagement (10%). There was no association between MT and denial. **Table 5** provides details of the regression analysis.

Influence of Achievement Level on MT, Stressor Appraisal, and Coping

Multivariate analyses of variance were used to test the influence of achievement level on MT, stressor appraisal, and coping (**Table 6**). Perceived stressor control was influenced by achievement level. Although there was a trend for higher-achieving players to perceive more control over the stressor, *post hoc* comparisons only showed that the 99th–100th percentile scored significantly higher than the 70th–80th percentile in levels of perceived control. There was no association between achievement level, perceived stressor intensity, threat, and challenge. Similarly, at both the strategy (Wilks' λ = 0.80, P = 0.36, η_p^2 = 0.05) and dimensional (Wilks' λ = 0.96, P = 0.45, η_p^2 = 0.01) levels, coping was not influenced by rank.

Achievement level was significantly influenced by MTQ6 items. *Post hoc* comparisons showed lower challenge scores for the 60th–70th percentile group compared to the 90th–99th and 99th–100th percentile groups. For commitment, the 80th–90th percentile group scored lower compared to the 90th–99th and the 99th–100th percentile groups.

One-way ANOVA showed significant differences between achievement level and both MTQ6 and MTI totals. *Post hoc* comparisons only showed that, for the MTI total, the 99th–100th and 80th–90th percentile participants scored higher than the 60th–70th percentile group.

There was a significant positive correlation between MTQ6 total and MTI (r = 0.45). The MTI positively correlated with all items of the MTQ6, except for life control. However, the shared

TABLE 6 | MANOVA between achievement level and stressor appraisal, coping strategies, Mental Toughness Index, and mental toughness questionnaire.

MANOVA	**Wilks'**	p	η_p^2
Stress appraisal	0.91	0.74	0.02
Coping dimensions	0.96	0.45	0.01
Coping strategies	0.80	0.36	0.05
MTQ6 item (1–6)	0.86	0.17	0.04
ANOVA	$F(4, 277)$	p	η_p^2
MTQ6 total	2.70	0.03	0.04
MTI	4.14	0.003	0.06

variance between the MTQ6 and MTI was only 20% and lower between the items of the MTQ6 and MTI. See **Table 7** for full results of the correlational analysis.

DISCUSSION

The main purpose of this study was to examine stress and coping in esports athletes and explore how this regulatory process is influenced by MT. Results suggest that the MTI was associated with perceived control, and MTQ6 subscales were associated with stress intensity. Furthermore, MT was associated with how stress was perceived as being a challenge or threat (both inversely) and the selection of coping strategies.

Association Between Stress Appraisal and MT

Results did not support the *a priori* prediction that esports athletes with higher overall levels of MT would report lower levels of stress intensity and higher levels of stress control. This observation contradicts previous findings by Kaiseler et al. (2009) and Levy et al. (2012), who found that higher levels of MT, using the MTQ-48, were associated with lower levels of perceived stress. This result might be explained due to esports athletes experiencing different types of stressors to traditional sports athletes (Nicholls and Polman, 2007). For example, esports athletes in the present study reported technical issues and antisocial behavior as stressors that have not been reported previously, however, further research is needed to understand this. Providing partial support for this study's prediction, small significant negative associations were observed between emotional control and life control and stress intensity, indicating that esports athletes, with higher levels of emotional control, rated the intensity of the self-reported stressor lower. It appears that only those esports athletes, who reported to have higher levels of emotional control, were able to reduce the intensity of the perceived stressor.

In support of the initial hypothesis, a positive association was observed between overall MT (MTI) and stress control. Similar to previous findings (Kaiseler et al., 2009; Levy et al., 2012), those esports athletes higher in MT (MTI) reported more control over the self-reported stressor. Literature on MT has described more mentally tough people as having an unshakable faith in their abilities to control their own destiny and an increased ability to remain in control under pressure (Clough et al., 2002; Nicholls et al., 2008). The result here appears to match this description of mentally tough people and suggest that more mentally tough esports athletes have increased levels of perceived control over a stressor.

The present study did not support previous findings (Kaiseler et al., 2009; Levy et al., 2012) and the *a priori* prediction that MT would be associated with lower threat and higher challenge appraisal. There was only a small negative correlation between emotional control and threat perception. In addition, overall score of the MTQ6 and the life control subscale had a negative association with challenge. Previous studies have found athletes with higher overall MT perceive stressors more as a challenge than a threat (Nicholls et al., 2012). First, the present findings suggest that the relationship between challenge and threat appraisal is not dichotomous (Britton et al., 2019). Esports athletes appear to appraise stressors as both a threat and challenge at the same time. This finding might be explained through the use of a single item to measure threat and challenge. Second, differences in threat and challenge perception between esports and traditional sports athletes could be explained due to the online nature of esports. Nonprofessional play is largely done online through ranked or competitive play; players may not be able to choose all their teammates. Players are often randomly grouped with different teammates (this varies between esports), and the only outcome at stake is their in-game rank. When playing in a professional tournament, often in front of a live audience for a cash prize, the stakes could be comparable to traditional sports. This study, having less professionals (n = 40) than nonprofessional (n = 276) players, could account for the difference in threat and challenge perceptions.

Associations Between Stress Coping and MT

Correlational and regression analysis showed support for the hypothesis that PFC, at both the dimensional and strategy levels (active coping, use of instrumental support, positive reframing, and planning), was positively associated with total MT (both frameworks). Higher levels of the MTQ6 subscales commitment,

TABLE 7 | Correlational analysis the mental toughness inventory, mental toughness questionnaire 6 total, and mental toughness questionnaire 6 subscales.

Construct	MTQ6 total	MTQ 1 challenge	MTQ 2 commitment	MTQ 3 emotional control	MTQ 4 life control	MTQ 5 confidence in abilities	MTQ 6 interpersonal confidence
MTQ6 TOTAL							
MTQ 1 – challenge	0.60**						
MTQ 2 – commitment	0.62**	0.33**					
MTQ 3 – emotional control	0.59**	0.24**	0.35**				
MTQ 4 – life control	0.52**	0.06	0.08	0.17**			
MTQ 5 – confidence in abilities	0.61**	0.19**	0.21**	0.17**	0.31**		
MTQ 6 – interpersonal control	0.57**	0.24**	0.20**	0.11	0.20**	0.28**	
MTI total	0.45**	0.33**	0.41**	0.18**	0.10	0.25**	0.30**

**p < 0.05.

confidence in abilities, and interpersonal confidence predicted increased active coping, and higher levels of challenge and interpersonal confidence predicted increased planning. These results are consistent with previous research, which has shown that mentally tough athletes are more likely to use PFC strategies, suggesting that esports athletes in the top 40% cope with stressors similarly to high-performing sports athletes and that mentally tougher esports athletes appear to want to actively deal with their stressors (Nicholls et al., 2008).

Like previous research, mentally tougher esports athletes reported less use of AC and AC strategies (e.g., self-distraction, substance use, and behavioral disengagement; Nicholls et al., 2008; Kaiseler et al., 2009). Such associations were also observed for some of the factors of MT (MTQ6). Specifically, higher levels of commitment were associated with less substance use and behavioral disengagement, and interpersonal confidence with less use of behavioral disengagement. This finding suggests that athletes who have lower levels of MT, and who employ more AC strategies, may be less skillful and may not perform as well as athletes with higher levels of MT. These results also suggest that competitive esports and sports athletes with high levels of MT (both frameworks) cope similarly by employing less AC strategies.

Contrary to the hypothesis, MTI, MTQ6 total, challenge, and emotional control all positively predicted the use of acceptance (EFC strategy). This observation suggests that acceptance could be important for competitive esports athletes. The use of acceptance could be explained through the match-making algorithm used in solo queue. When playing ranked or competitive play, many factors can be out of the player's control, which includes teammates, opponents, and character selection. Although these issues might result in stress, being able to accept that these factors are beyond a players control could be associated with performing more highly in esports.

Because this is the one of the first studies exploring stress and coping in an esports population, scores obtained for the Brief COPE were compared to those obtained in the sport domain. To this end, Dias et al. (2010) explored coping in a team sport setting using the Brief COPE. At the dimension level, traditional sports athletes reported the use of more PFC and EFC, and on a strategy level, they reported a higher use of instrumental and emotional support. Such differences between traditional sport and esports might be due to the fast-paced nature of esports. As such, esports athletes might have less time to invoke PFC strategies. Also, esports athletes used more acceptance and self-distraction strategies compared to the team athletes in Dias et al. (2010) study. These differences could be explained by the online nature of esports requiring acceptance or ignoring of stressors to perform at the highest level.

Associations Between MT and Achievement Level

The current study found partial support for the notion that achievement level was associated with MT. In particular, those with higher ranks tended to have higher total and subscale MT scores, with a number of significant differences for challenge and commitment (MTQ6). Similar to traditional sport, these findings suggest there could be an association between esports performance and MT levels (Cowden, 2016). It would appear that those who are more successful esports athletes have higher levels of MT.

Similarities and Differences Between the MTQ6 and MTI8

There were interesting similarities and differences that emerged from the results of the MTQ6 and MTI. Regression analysis shows that both MT measures predicted the use PFC and AC at a dimensional level, and active coping, planning, acceptance, substance use, and behavioral disengagement at a strategy level. Correlational analysis from the MTQ6 and MTI showed differences in stress appraisal. The MTQ6 was associated with perceived stressor intensity, threat, and challenge, whereas the MTI was associated only with perceived stressor control. Mixed results are not surprising considering each questionnaire represents a different, yet partly similar, framework. Furthermore, correlational analysis showed that the MTQ6 and MTI had low shared variance (20%). This would suggest that the two questionnaires measure different aspects of MT. Overall, these findings represent the ongoing debate surrounding the conceptualization of MT.

Practical Implications

While further research is needed, the findings of the present study could be beneficial for sport psychologists working with esports athletes. Interventions to increase emotional control may help lower perceived stress intensity, potentially improving performance and quality of life. Furthermore, results suggest that acceptance coping is an important strategy used by esports players. Esport athletes who more effectively utilize acceptance coping may better deal with stressors caused by factors outside of their control (i.e., teammates and opponents). Based on the notion the esports athletes are more likely to report the use of PFC strategies and less AC strategies, it would be suggested that coaches, team managers, and/or sport psychologists help their athletes to actively deal with the stressors they experience, although future research should examine coping effectiveness.

Limitations and Future Research Direction

The present study is not without limitations. A cross-sectional design was used, meaning that causality cannot be inferred. The constructs were measured using self-reported questionnaires. Data collected were retrospective and collected from players only in the top 40% of their esport, which limits the generalizability of the findings. Moreover, stress appraisal was assessed in relation to one specific stressful event, and the potential baseline differences in stress reactivity were not controlled for. One coping strategy measured by the Brief COPE showed low reliability, however, it was included in the analysis because previous research has indicated that estimates of internal consistency have limited applicability when assessing psychometric properties of measures of coping (Billings and Moos, 1981). Standardizing rankings across games means that the study could not control for differences in skill distribution or game difficulty between esports. Future research could investigate the relationship between MT and stress coping in one game and across all game ranks (Pedraza-Ramirez et al., 2020). In addition, it could be beneficial to explore how esports athletes cope over time and across multiple stressful events.

CONCLUSION

The present study suggests that MT may influence the stress and coping process in esports athletes. There is an overlap between the MT and stress-coping processes in traditional sports and esports athletes. These similarities appeared more in the selection of coping rather than the appraisal process. This result suggests that esports athletes could benefit from traditional sports psychology interventions in MT and stress coping and that further research is required into the psychological determinants of success for esports athletes. Finally, low correlations between the MTQ6 and MTI – representing two of the fundamental and most popular models of MT in current literature – indicate that further debate is encouraged on how best to conceptualize MT.

ETHICS STATEMENT

The studies involving human participants were reviewed and approved by the Queensland University of Technology Office of Research Ethics and Integrity. The patients/participants provided their written informed consent to participate in this study.

AUTHOR CONTRIBUTIONS

The study was designed by DP, TC, and RP. The data were collected by DP and MT. The data were analyzed by DP and RP. The manuscript was written by DP, TC, and RP. All authors read and approved the manuscript.

REFERENCES

Bányai, F., Griffiths, M. D., Király, O., and Demetrovics, Z. (2018). The psychology of esports: A systematic literature review. *J. Gambl. Stud.* 35, 351–365. doi: 10.1007/s10899-018-9763-1

Billings, A. G., and Moos, R. H. (1981). The role of coping responses and social resources in attenuating the stress of life events. *J. Behav. Med.* 4, 139–157. doi: 10.1007/BF00844267

Britton, D. M., Kavanagh, E., and Polman, R. (2019). Validating a self-report measure of student athletes' perceived stress reactivity: Associations with heart-rate variability and stress appraisals. *Front. Psychol.* 10:1083. doi: 10.3389/fpsyg.2019.01083

Campbell, M. J., Toth, A. J., Moran, A. P., Kowal, M., and Exton, C. (2018). "Chapter 10 - eSports: a new window on neurocognitive expertise?," in *Progress in Brain Research*, Vol. 240, eds S. Marcora, and M. Sarkar, (Amsterdem: Elsevier), 161–174. doi: 10.1016/bs.pbr.2018.09.006

Carver, C. S. (1997). You want to measure coping but your protocol's too long: consider the brief cope. *Int. J. Behav. Med.* 4:92. doi: 10.1207/s15327558ijbm0401_6

Clough, P., Earle, K., and Sewell, D. (2002). "Mental toughness: The concept and its measurement," in *Solutions in Sport Psychology*, (London: Thomson), 32–43.

Conditt, J. (2016). *UC Irvine Debuts the First Public College Esports Arena in the US. Engadget*. California: The University of California.

Coulter, T. J., Mallett, C. J., and Singer, J. A. (2018). A three-domain personality analysis of a mentally tough athlete. *Eur. J. Pers.* 32, 6–29. doi: 10.1002/per.2129

Cowden, R. G. (2016). Mental toughness, emotional Intelligence, and coping effectiveness: An analysis of construct interrelatedness among high-performing adolescent male athletes. *Percept. Mot. Skills* 123, 737–753. doi: 10.1177/0031512516666027

Dias, C., Cruz, J. F., and Fonseca, A. M. (2010). Coping strategies, multidimensional competitive anxiety and cognitive threat appraisal: differences across sex, age and type of sport. *Serb. J. Sports Sci.* 4, 23–31.

Dias, C., Cruz, J. F., and Fonseca, A. M. (2012). The relationship between multidimensional competitive anxiety, cognitive threat appraisal, and coping strategies: A multi-sport study. *Int. J. Sport Exerc. Psychol.*10, 52–65. doi: 10.1080/1612197X.2012.645131

Goldman Sachs, (2018). *eSports: From Wild West to Mainstream*. New York, NY: Goldman Sachs.

Gucciardi, D. F. (2017). Mental toughness: progress and prospects. *Curr. Opin. Psychol.* 16, 17–23. doi: 10.1016/j.copsyc.2017.03.010

Gucciardi, D. F., Hanton, S., Gordon, S., Mallett, C. J., and Temby, P. (2015). The concept of mental toughness: tests of dimensionality, nomological network, and traitness. *J. Pers.* 83, 26–44. doi: 10.1111/jopy.12079

Himmelstein, D., Liu, Y., and Shapiro, J. L. (2017). An exploration of mental skills among competitive league of legend players. *Int. J. Gam. Comput. Media. Simulat.* 9, 1–21. doi: 10.4018/IJGCMS.2017040101

Jenny, S. E., Manning, R. D., Keiper, M. C., and Olrich, T. W. (2017). Virtual(ly) athletes: Where esports fit within the definition of "Sport". *Quest* 69, 1–18. doi: 10.1080/00336297.2016.1144517

Kaiseler, M., Polman, R., and Nicholls, A. (2009). Mental toughness, stress, stress appraisal, coping and coping effectiveness in sport. *Pers. Individ. Differ.* 47, 728–733. doi: 10.1016/j.paid.2009.06.012

Kaiseler, M., Polman, R. C. J., and Nicholls, A. R. (2012). Effects of the big five personality dimensions on appraisal coping, and coping effectiveness in sport. *Eur. J. Sport Sci.* 12, 62–72. doi: 10.1080/17461391.2010.551410

Kaiseler, M. H., and Polman, R. C. J. (2010). "Chapter 5: Gender and coping in sport: Do male and female athletes cope differently?," in *Coping in Sport: Theory, Methods, and Related Constructs*, Ed. A. R. Nicholls, (New York, NY: Nova Science Publishers), 77–94.

Kobasa, S. C. (1979). Stressful life events, personality, and health: An inquiry into hardiness. *J. Pers. Soc. Psychol.* 37, 1–11. doi: 10.1037/0022-3514.37.1.1

Kowalski, K. C., and Crocker, P. R. (2001). Development and validation of the Coping Function Questionnaire for adolescents in sport. *J. Sport Exerc. Psychol.* 23, 136–155. doi: 10.1123/jsep.23.2.136

Lace, T. (2019). *Dylan Poulus - QUT Tigers - Australia's First University Esports Program*. New York, NY: Esports Insider.

Lazarus, R. S. (2000). How emotions influence performance in competitive sports. *Sport Psychol.* 14, 229–252. doi: 10.1123/tsp.14.3.229

Levy, A., Nicholls, A., and Polman, R. (2012). Cognitive appraisals in sport: The direct and moderating role of mental toughness. *Int. J. Appl. Psychol.* 2, 71–76. doi: 10.5923/j.ijap.20120204.05

Murphy, S. (2009). Video games, competition and exercise: A new opportunity for sport psychologists? *Sport Psychol.* 23, 487–503. doi: 10.1123/tsp.23.4.487

Nicholls, A. R., and Polman, R. C. J. (2007). Coping in sport: A systematic review. *J. Sports Sci.* 25, 11–31. doi: 10.1080/02640410600630654

Nicholls, A. R., Polman, R. C. J., and Levy, A. R. (2012). A path analysis of stress appraisals, emotions, coping, and performance satisfaction among athletes. *Psychol. Sport Exerc.* 13, 263–270. doi: 10.1016/j.psychsport.2011.12.003

Nicholls, A. R., Polman, R. C. J., Levy, A. R., and Backhouse, S. H. (2008). Mental toughness, optimism, pessimism, and coping among athletes. *Pers. Individ. Differ.* 44, 1182–1192. doi: 10.1016/j.paid.2007.11.011

Pedraza-Ramirez, I., Musculus, L., Raab, M., and Laborde, S. (2020). Setting the scientific stage for esports psychology: A systematic review. *Int. Rev. Sport Exerc. Psychol.* 0, 1–34. doi: 10.1080/1750984X.2020.1723122

Polman, R. (2012). "Elite athletes' experiences of coping with stress," in *Coping and Emotion in Sport*, 2nd Edn, eds J. Thatcher, M. Jones, and D. Lavallee, (Abington: Routledge), 284–301. doi: 10.4324/9780203852293_chapter_13

Polman, R., Trotter, M., Poulus, D., and Borkoles, E. (2018). *eSport: Friend or foe? In Joint International Conference on Serious Games.* Cham: Springer, 3–8.

Polman, R. C. J., Clough, P. J., and Levy, A. R. (2010). "Personality and coping in sport: The big five and mental Toughness," in *Coping in Sport: Theory, Methods, and Related Constructs*, ed. A. R. Nicholls (New York, NY: Nova Science Publishers), 79–93.

Reitman, J. G., Anderson-Coto, M. J., Wu, M., Lee, J. S., and Steinkuehler, C. (2020). Esports research: a literature review. *Games Cult.* 15, 32–50. doi: 10.1177/1555412019840892

Smith, M. J., Birch, P. D., and Bright, D. (2019). Identifying stressors and coping strategies of elite esports competitors. *Int. J. Gam. Comput. Med. Simulat.* 11, 22–39. doi: 10.4018/ijgcms.2019040102

Taylor, T. L. (2012). *Raising the Stakes: E-Sports and the Professionalization of Computer Gaming.* Cambridge, MA: MIT Press.

Toth, A. J., Kowal, M., and Campbell, M. J. (2019). The color-word stroop task does not differentiate cognitive inhibition ability among esports gamers of varying expertise. *Front. Psychol.* 10:2852. doi: 10.3389/fpsyg.2019.02852

23

Antidepressant Drugs and Physical Activity: A Possible Synergism in the Treatment of Major Depression?

Claudia Savia Guerrera[1,2†], Giovanna Furneri[1,2†], Margherita Grasso[3,4†], Giuseppe Caruso[3], Sabrina Castellano[2], Filippo Drago[1], Santo Di Nuovo[2] and Filippo Caraci[3,4]*

[1] Department of Biomedical and Biotechnological Sciences, University of Catania, Catania, Italy, [2] Department of Educational Sciences, University of Catania, Catania, Italy, [3] Department of Laboratories, Oasi Research Institute – IRCCS, Troina, Italy, [4] Department of Drug Sciences, University of Catania, Catania, Italy

***Correspondence:**
Filippo Caraci
carafil@hotmail.com

† These authors share first authorship

Major depressive disorder (MDD) is a severe mental illness that affects 5–20% of the general population. Current antidepressant drugs exert only a partial clinical efficacy because approximately 30% of depressed patients failed to respond to these drugs and antidepressants produce remission only in 30% of patients. This can be explained by the fact that the complex pathophysiology of depression has not been completely elucidated, and treatments have been mainly developed following the "monoaminergic hypothesis" of depression without considering the key role of other factors involved in the pathogenesis of MDD, such as the role of chronic stress and neuroinflammation. Chronic stress acts as a risk factor for the development of MDD through the impairment of neurotrophins signaling such as brain-derived neurotrophic factor (BDNF) and transforming-growth-factor-β1 (TGF-β1). Stress-induced depressive pathology contributes to altered BDNF level and function in MDD patients and, thereby, an impairment of neuroplasticity at the regional and circuit level. Recent studies demonstrate that aerobic exercise strongly increases BDNF production and it may contribute as a non-pharmacological strategy to improve the treatment of cognitive and affective symptoms in MDD. Here we will provide a general overview on the possible synergism between physical activity and antidepressants in MDD. Physical activity can synergize with antidepressant treatment by rescuing neurotrophins signaling in MDD patients, promoting neuronal health and recovery of function in MDD-related circuits, finally enhancing pharmacotherapeutic response. This synergism might be particularly relevant in elderly patients with late-life depression, a clinical subgroup with an increased risk to develop dementia.

Keywords: depression, physical activity, stress, affective symptoms, cognition, brain-derived neurotrophic factor, transforming-growth-factor-β1

INTRODUCTION

Major depressive disorder (MDD) is a severe and a common mental illness affecting more than 264 million people worldwide (Gbd 2017 Disease and Injury Incidence and Prevalence Collaborators, 2018). The World Health Organization (WHO) describes depression, also indicated as MDD or clinical depression, as a mental disorder characterized by sleep and appetite disturbances, variation of mood, loss of energy, and psychomotor retardation[1].

Among the different hypotheses that have been proposed to explain MDD pathophysiology, the "monoaminergic hypothesis" has been initially validated with the development of monoaminergic antidepressants. Based on this hypothesis an impairment of monoaminergic systems [serotonin (5-HT), noradrenaline, and dopamine] has been considered a primary event for the onset of affective and cognitive symptoms in MDD (Hirschfeld, 2000; Hamon and Blier, 2013). Therefore, the majority of antidepressant drugs have been developed according to this hypothesis, representing a useful therapeutic tool (Lopez-Munoz and Alamo, 2009); unfortunately around 30% of depressed patients are considered treatment resistant (Caraci et al., 2018a), probably because emerging additional factors involved in the pathophysiology of MDD, such as chronic stress and neuroinflammation, should be considered (Caraci et al., 2018b). The pathological effects of stress on hippocampus have contributed to the development of the so-called "neurotrophic hypothesis" according to which neurotrophic factors play a key role in the etiology of depression (Altar, 1999; Duman and Li, 2012; Jaggar et al., 2019). This hypothesis suggests that depression derives from decreased neurotrophic support resulting in neuronal atrophy, decreased hippocampal neurogenesis, and loss of glial cells (Duman and Monteggia, 2006). A hyperactivation of the hypothalamic-pituitary-adrenal (HPA) axis has been found in the 50% of depressed patients (Krishnan and Nestler, 2008) and several evidences identify chronic stress, linked to an impairment of neurotrophins such as brain-derived neurotrophic factor (BDNF) and transforming-growth-factor-β1 (TGF-β1) (Caraci et al., 2018b), as a risk factor for the development of MDD (Pittenger and Duman, 2008; Caraci et al., 2010). A significant decrease of BDNF levels has been demonstrated in animal models of depression stress-induced (Berry et al., 2012) as well as in depressed patients (Angelucci et al., 2005). Likewise, a decrease of TGF-β1 levels has been observed in hippocampus and cortex of animal models of depression (Yu et al., 2011); furthermore, several studies carried out in depressed patients have demonstrated that plasma TGF-β1 levels are reduced and correlate with depression severity (Myint et al., 2005; Rush et al., 2016). A chronic treatment with first- and second-generation antidepressants rescues BDNF levels in different preclinical models of depression (Duman and Monteggia, 2006), while selective serotonin reuptake inhibitors (SSRIs) drugs and the new multimodal antidepressant vortioxetine are able to reverse the depressive-like phenotype and memory deficits induced by amyloid-β (Aβ) in mice by the rescue of TGF-β1 (Torrisi et al., 2019). Furthermore, antidepressant drugs exert immunoregulatory effects reducing the production of pro-inflammatory cytokines and stimulating the synthesis of TGF-β1 in depressed patients (Sutcigil et al., 2007).

Noteworthy, it has been shown that epigenetic mechanisms such as DNA methylation, microRNAs, and histone modifications are able to influence the development of depression (Lin and Tsai, 2019) and, with specific regard to BDNF, their altered activity can in turn affect the expression and the activity of this neurotrophic factor (Hing et al., 2018).

Several studies have demonstrated that aerobic exercise (AE) could represent a non-pharmacological strategy to improve the treatment of depression, decreasing, at the same time, the burden of somatic comorbidity of this pathology (Mura and Carta, 2013; Josefsson et al., 2014). Since the 1980s, several papers have reported on the beneficial effects played by exercise and physical activity in the treatment of depression, effects comparable to those of antidepressants (Martinsen et al., 1985; Babyak et al., 2000; Belvederi Murri et al., 2018; Lopez-Torres Hidalgo, 2019). This increased interest in this field has led to the proposal that physical exercise may serve as an alternative or integrative approach in combination with monoaminergic drugs for the treatment of MDD (Martinsen, 2008).

In the present review we will provide a general overview on the possible synergism between physical activity and antidepressants in treatment of MDD, analyzing the possible benefits of physical activity both at a neurobiological level and clinical level focusing in particular on the treatment of affective and cognitive symptoms in MDD.

THE PATHOPHYSIOLOGY OF DEPRESSION: THE ROLE OF NEUROTROPHIC FACTORS AND THE POSSIBLE IMPACT OF PHYSICAL ACTIVITY

MDD shows a complex pathophysiology that has been only partially elucidated in the last 10 years (Caraci et al., 2018a). Chronic stress, reduced synaptic plasticity, impairment of adult hippocampal neurogenesis, and hippocampal neurodegeneration along with the well-known dysregulation of the monoaminergic system contribute to explain the pathophysiology of MDD (Jaggar et al., 2019; Vu, 2019). Epidemiological studies support the pivotal role played by chronic stress in MDD (Pittenger and Duman, 2008); in fact, the exposure to stressful life events contributes to the development of this disease (Czeh and Lucassen, 2007). Chronic stress leads to an impaired negative feedback of glucocorticoids (GR) on the activity of HPA axis, which results in elevated cortisol levels (de Kloet et al., 2005). Excess of GR is able to induce neuronal death at hippocampal level (Yu et al., 2008) as well as dysfunctional changes in the prefrontal cortex (PFC), two regions critically involved in the cognitive symptoms of depression (Krishnan and Nestler, 2008). Stress also exerts its effects by reducing the synthesis of factors essential for neuronal homeostasis such as BDNF

[1]https://www.who.int/health-topics/depression#tab=tab_1

(Nowacka and Obuchowicz, 2013), a neurotrophin fundamental for the maintenance of dendritic spines (Vigers et al., 2012), the regulation of adult hippocampal neurogenesis (Vilar and Mira, 2016), cognitive and mood-related behavior and aging (Castren and Kojima, 2017). Reduced levels of BDNF have been connected to dendritic atrophy, neuronal apoptosis, and inhibition of neurogenesis in MDD (Nowacka and Obuchowicz, 2013). Stress decreases BDNF concentrations in hippocampus and PFC of animal models of depression (Smith et al., 1995; Duman and Monteggia, 2006; Filho et al., 2015), in line with the reduced expression of this neurotrophic factor observed at cortical, hippocampal, and peripheral level of depressed patients (Thompson Ray et al., 2011; Reinhart et al., 2015). Stress exposure also leads to an impairment of TGF-β1 signaling in different brain regions (hippocampus, cortex, and hypothalamus) (You et al., 2011; Caraci et al., 2015). This impairment has been connected to the onset of a depressive-like phenotype in mice (Torrisi et al., 2019). Lastly, a correlation between reduced TGF-β1 plasma levels, depression severity, and treatment resistance in MDD has been proved (Sutcigil et al., 2007; Caraci et al., 2018a).

In addition to HPA axis hyperactivation, immune system dysregulation and neuroinflammation play a central role in the pathophysiology of depression (Caraci et al., 2010), underlining the great impact of immune system activation on the central nervous system and in particular on the overall activity of monoaminergic systems (Caraci et al., 2018a). An increase of two well-known pro-inflammatory cytokines, called interleukin (IL)-1β and tumor necrosis factor-α (TNF-α), as well as a decrease of anti-inflammatory cytokines (e.g., IL-10, IL-4, and TGF-β1) have been observed in hippocampus and cortex of animal models of depression (You et al., 2011) and MDD patients (Farooq et al., 2017; Caruso et al., 2019).

Antidepressant drugs, such as sertraline and fluoxetine, exert immunomodulatory effects, reducing the production of pro-inflammatory cytokines and stimulating the synthesis of TGF-β1 in depressed patients (Sutcigil et al., 2007; Maes et al., 2016; Caraci et al., 2018a). Furthermore, the ability of some antidepressant drugs to induce the synthesis and the release of BDNF and TGF-β1 has been demonstrated both *in vitro* and *in vivo* studies (Caraci et al., 2010), suggesting that the long time required for BDNF restore could, at least in part, contributes to explain the therapeutic latency (2–4 weeks) of these drugs (Racagni and Popoli, 2010). Recent studies have demonstrated the rapid and long-lasting antidepressant effects of TGF-β1 as well as the key role of TGF-β1 released from microglia in mediating the antidepressant activity of (R)-ketamine (10 mg/kg) in a mouse model of depression (Zhang et al., 2020). (R)-ketamine is a novel drug under study for treatment-resistant MDD patients. Interestingly this drug rescued the expression of TGF-β1 and its receptors in the PFC and hippocampus, whereas inhibition of TGF-β1 signaling (i.e., SB431542) or neutralizing antibody of TGF-β1 blocked the antidepressant effects of (R)-ketamine, thus suggesting the essential and novel role of TGF-β1 as antidepressant.

According to the neurotrophic hypothesis of depression, which could be the impact of physical activity on the neurobiology of depression considering recent evidence in MDD patients?

Physical activity as an add-on strategy to the traditional treatment of depression is able to reduce the relapse risk, increase adherence to pharmacological treatment, and promote the management of side effects with a 60–80% of success (Neumeyer-Gromen et al., 2004; Silveira et al., 2013; **Figure 1**).

Interestingly a recent study conducted by Murri et al. (2018), has demonstrated that physical exercise, in combination with the SSRI sertraline, reduces affective symptoms and psychomotor retardation in MDD. Furthermore, the beneficial effects of AE as an add-on strategy in the treatment of moderate to severe depression has been shown in a study carried out by Imboden et al. (2019), considering different psychological and biological variables (e.g., BDNF, HPA axis activity, cognitive symptoms) besides depression severity.

Physical activity exerts beneficial effects on pre- and postnatal brain development (Gomes da Silva and Arida, 2015), stimulates neurogenesis and synaptic plasticity by increasing BDNF synthesis and release (Walsh and Tschakovsky, 2018), and reduces HPA axis hyperactivation (Nabkasorn et al., 2006). In particular, it has been proposed, as a proof of muscle-brain crosstalk, that irisin, produced during exercise through the cleavage of fibronectin type III domain-containing protein 5 (FNDC5) membrane protein and able to cross the blood-brain barrier, induces BDNF expression at brain level, which in turn will lead to an increased hippocampal neurogenesis, and therefore to enhanced learning, memory, and mood (Pedersen, 2019). With regard to TGF-β1, the plasma concentration of this neurotrophin increases in response to exercise (1 h of treadmill running) (Heinemeier et al., 2003). In a different study enrolling healthy people and Parkinson subjects, the immunomodulatory effects of moderate intensity on plasma neurotrophins levels was investigated (Szymura et al., 2020). Szymura et al. (2020) demonstrated that after completion of the 12 weeks training program the concentration of TGF-β1 as well as of other neurothophic factors (nerve growth factor and BDNF) were found to be increased only in training groups. Furthermore, in a study considering a total of 29 athletes, the serum levels of TGF-β1 were higher in athletes with high relative Vo_2peak (relVo_2peak) values, a measure of the athletes' cardiovascular fitness and aerobic endurance, compared to low relVo_2peak (Weinhold et al., 2016). No studies have been conducted yet in MDD patients to assess whether SSRIs can synergize with AE to increase TGF-β1 signaling, although preliminary available evidence suggests the existence of common biological targets.

All together, the above mentioned evidence suggests a synergistic effect between AE and antidepressant drugs for the treatment of depression (**Figure 2**), reducing the cognitive deficits that compromise the working activities of MDD patients and influence their relapse risk (Albert et al., 2016). This synergism might be particularly relevant in elderly patients with late-life depression (LLD), a clinical sub-group with an increased risk to develop dementia, improving patients' cognitive outcomes (Neviani et al., 2017).

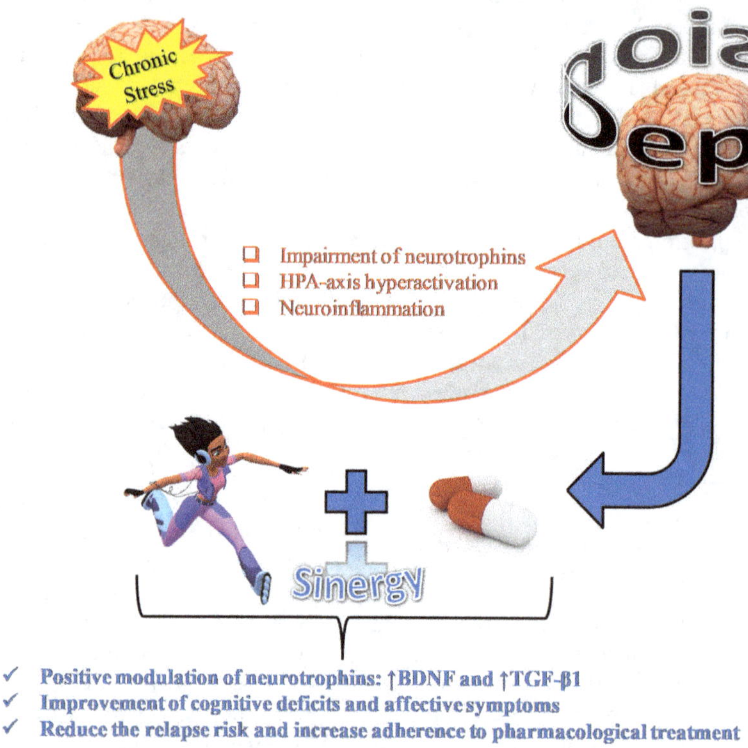

FIGURE 1 | Physical activity as an add-on treatment strategy to antagonize stress-induced depression.

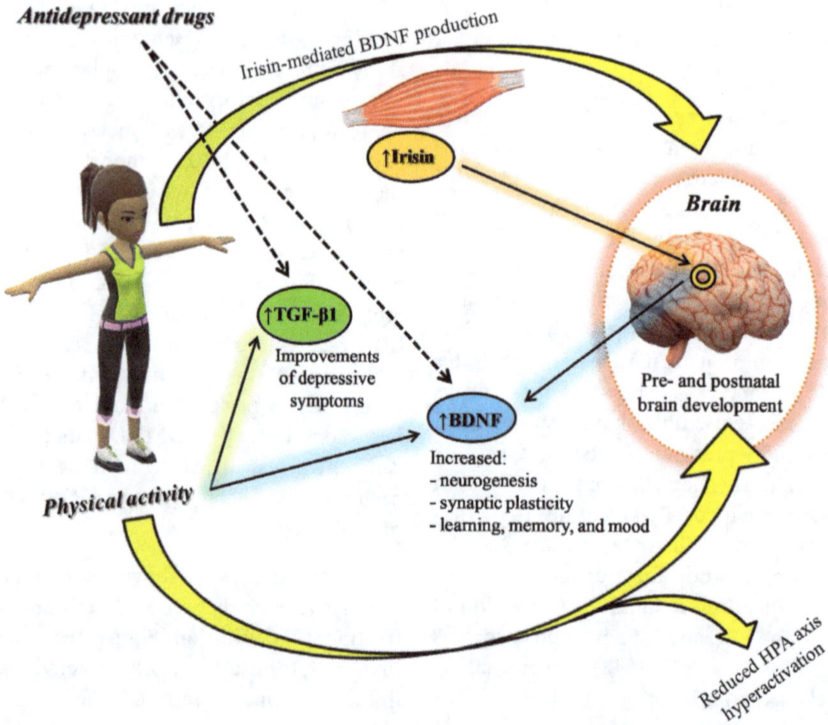

FIGURE 2 | Synergic effect between physical activity and antidepressants: positive modulation of neurotrophic factors.

IMPACT OF PHYSICAL ACTIVITY ON AFFECTIVE SYMPTOMS IN MDD

Apart from biological and genetic risk factors (Hammen, 2018), physical inactivity has been identified as a risk factor for the development of depression (Adamson et al., 2016; Hammen, 2018). Along this line different studies have shown that physical activity is able to provide mental health benefits in patients with severe mental illness, reducing depressive symptoms and improving social and cognitive functions (Rosenbaum et al., 2014). In a recent global systematic review and meta-analysis including 69 studies, Vancampfort et al. (2017) have examined sedentary behavior and levels of physical activity in patients with MDD or other severe mental disorders. After the analysis of the studies, it was clear as the physical activity was connected to health benefits in healthy controls while the level of activity as well as the related benefits were low in people with severe mental illnesses (Vancampfort et al., 2017). Indeed, as confirmed in different studies, regular physical activity of moderate intensity, such as walking or cycling, is enough to give significant benefits for health and plays a protective role in preventing different mental disorders (Ashdown-Franks et al., 2019); whereas lack of exercise represents a major cause of chronic diseases, including depression (Booth et al., 2012). Several studies have focused their attention on the potential benefits of physical activity to prevent the development of this disease. The "HUNT Cohort Study" investigated whether exercise provides protection against new-onset depression, the importance of both intensity and amount of physical activity and existing associations between them (Harvey et al., 2018). The results based on a healthy cohort of 33,908 adults followed for 11 years suggested that regular leisure-time exercise of any intensity provides protection against future depression development. Very recently Bennie et al. (2020) showed in a study employing a large sample (23,635) of German adults that AE is associated with a lower likelihood of depressive symptoms severity, as assessed by eight-item Patient Health Questionnaire depression scale (PHQ-8). In a case report published by Büyükturan et al. (2017), AE was able to improve physical conditions and to dramatically decrease depressive symptoms (sadness, anhedonia, reluctance to getting out of house, memory complaints) in a 76 years old female patient. Before enrollment in the study, she followed a 6-months treatment with antidepressants without getting any improvement. She followed a special 4-weeks exercise program consisting of 10 min warm-up (jogging, breathing, upper, and lower extremity active exercises), 20–25 min flexibility, balance and strengthening exercise, and 10 min cool-down exercise periods.

It has been shown that regular physical activity is able to reduce sleep disturbances (Chen et al., 2010) and improve somatic, affective, and cognitive symptoms in depressed patients, especially by enhancing the psychological health and social relationships (Babyak et al., 2000). Netz (2017), by the analysis of different randomized controlled trials in which physical exercise and pharmacologic treatment were compared, found in all studies considered, except one, that patients performing physical activity as an adjunctive treatment for depression have a significant improvement of depressive symptoms and a better clinical response after the exercise period.

An additional meta-analysis, carried out by Kvam et al. (2016), shows as different types of exercise (e.g., walking, running, cycling) could represent a viable adjunct treatment in combination with antidepressants. They demonstrate that the effects of exercise as an independent treatment were evident, with maximum efficacy showed when compared to no intervention, suggesting that physical activity may represent an alternative approach in non-responder patients.

As discussed above, a regular physical activity is also able to reduce depressive symptoms by different neurobiological mechanisms. In fact, it can increase monoaminergic neurotransmission (Stenman and Lilja, 2013), reduce cortisol levels simultaneously increasing hippocampal neurogenesis (Rethorst et al., 2009; Blake, 2012; Niwa et al., 2016), and increase β-endorphin and BDNF levels (Ernst et al., 2006). Since in the brain, neurons are a significant source of BDNF, whose synthesis occurs in regions fundamental for emotional and cognitive functions (Sasi et al., 2017), these preliminary evidence suggests that physical activity, when performed in combination with pharmacological antidepressant treatment, may improve affective symptoms in MDD patients.

IMPACT OF PHYSICAL EXERCISE ON COGNITIVE SYMPTOMS IN MDD

MDD could be considered as the most common mental illness among elderly people with an estimated prevalence ranging from 4.6 to 9.3% (Luppa et al., 2012). Rates of MDD are by and large lower in healthy community-dwelling elderly people than in younger adult populations, in a range from 1 to 3% (Kessler et al., 2010). However, these rates can increase on the basis of increasing medical and psychiatric comorbidity as well as in relation to various social conditions (Espinoza and Kaufman, 2014). LLD, occurring in people with an age $\geq$60 years, is often associated to cognitive dysfunction (Taylor, 2014). Cognitive dysfunction can affect one or multiple cognitive domains such as attention, working memory, verbal fluency, visuospatial abilities, and executive function (Murrough et al., 2011). Furthermore, this clinical sub-group presents a higher risk to develop dementia, in particular Alzheimer's disease and vascular dementia (Caraci et al., 2010; Diniz et al., 2013). LLD clinical manifestations are individual suffering, increased morbidity, premature mortality, and greater healthcare utilization (Diniz et al., 2013; Meijer et al., 2013), compromising the geriatric patients' life quality (Morimoto et al., 2015). Moreover, LLD is a condition often accompanied by significant impairment in physical and social functioning as well as disability (Blazer, 2003; Chang et al., 2016). Longitudinal studies have shown that LLD worsens the outcomes of physical illnesses and the likelihood of frailty in elderly people (Butters et al., 2008; Vaughan et al., 2015). Research community has focused its attention on physical exercise as a potential non-pharmacological treatment to improve cognitive function in depressed elderly patients. Since 1990s, several studies have been carried out to demonstrate the efficacy of physical exercise as an intervention for clinical depression in these patients (Dupuis and Smale, 1995; Blumenthal et al., 1999). In a randomized controlled trial, Singh et al. (2001) demonstrated the effectiveness of a 20 weeks physical exercise program as a long-term treatment for clinical depression in elderly patients. The same year, in a different study, the effectiveness of a structured exercise program on specific areas of cognitive functioning (e.g., attention, concentration, executive processes, figural memory) compared to antidepressants treatment has been proved (Khatri et al., 2001). In 2012, Bridle et al. (2012) showed that structured physical exercise tailored to individual ability reduces depression severity in older people with clinically significant symptoms of depression. More recently, Heinzel et al. (2015) demonstrated that all investigated types of physical exercise, such as AE, resistance training, dancing, and alternative forms of exercise (Qi Gong and Tai Chi), may serve as a feasible and additional intervention for depression in elderly people. This preliminary evidence was strengthen by a meta-analysis of randomized controlled trials carried out by Schuch et al. (2016), suggesting that previous meta-analyses have underestimated the benefits of exercise and therefore structural physical exercise should be considered as a routine component of the management of depression in older adults.

This evidence shows how physical exercise could improve the effectiveness of pharmacological treatments in elderly depressed patients (Mura and Carta, 2013; Murri et al., 2015). An improvement in memory and executive functions that persists for up to 24 months was demonstrated in elderly depressed patients who followed an integrative approach consisting of combined physical activity and pharmacological treatment (Bragin et al., 2005). Murri et al. (2015), in a study of 24 weeks employing 121 primary care patients (>65 years) with major depression, demonstrated the synergism between the antidepressant sertraline and two different types of physical exercise in improving the outcomes related to LLD. In particular, a higher remission rate (primary outcome) was observed for the higher intensity, progressive AE plus sertraline group (81%), showing an increment of +8% (and shorter time to remission) and +36% compared to lower-intensity, non-progressive exercise plus antidepressant and sertraline alone, respectively.

Neviani et al. (2017) performed secondary analyses on data from the Safety and Efficacy of Exercise for Depression in Seniors study, a trial comparing the effectiveness of sertraline, in the absence or in the presence of progressive or non-progressive exercise. The results of 121 patients (mean age 75 years) showed improvements of Montreal Cognitive Assessment (MoCA) total scores and visuospatial/executive functions for sertraline plus progressive exercise group, showing how the addition of aerobic, progressive exercise to antidepressant drug treatment may offer significant advantages over standard treatment with regard to cognitive abilities and disability (Neviani et al., 2017).

CONCLUSION

Physical activity stimulates neurogenesis and synaptic plasticity through BDNF synthesis and release, induces physiological changes in endorphine and monoamine levels, increases the plasma concentration of TGF-β1, and reduces cortisol levels; it can also act as an "anti-inflammatory factor" increasing IL-10 levels and suppressing TNF-α production, hus exerting "antidepressant-like effects". Therefore, we can assert that physical activity modulates many mechanisms and systems involved in the pathophysiology of depression. Physical activity has also proved able to act on the core symptoms of depression, decreasing sadness, anhedonia, and sleep disturbances, improving metabolic control and cognitive functions such as attention and concentration, and also decreasing the risk of depression and dementia development. Lastly, different clinical trials have highlighted the effects of physical activity as add-on treatment for MDD patients with moderate to severe depression, underlining the existing synergism between AE and the traditional pharmacological treatment. This synergism might be particularly relevant in elderly patients with LLD, a clinical sub-group characterized by an increased risk to develop dementia.

AUTHOR CONTRIBUTIONS

All authors listed have made a substantial, direct and intellectual contribution to the work, and approved it for publication.

REFERENCES

Adamson, B. C., Yang, Y., and Motl, R. W. (2016). Association between compliance with physical activity guidelines, sedentary behavior and depressive symptoms. *Prev. Med.* 91, 152–157. doi: 10.1016/j.ypmed.2016.08.020

Albert, U., Brugnoli, R., Caraci, F., Dell'Osso, B., Di Sciascio, G., Tortorella, A., et al. (2016). Italian psychiatrists' perception on cognitive symptoms in major depressive disorder. *Int. J. Psychiatry Clin. Pract.* 20, 2–9. doi: 10.3109/13651501.2015.1093147

Altar, C. A. (1999). Neurotrophins and depression. *Trends Pharmacol. Sci.* 20, 59–61. doi: 10.1016/s0165-6147(99)01309-1307

Angelucci, F., Brene, S., and Mathe, A. A. (2005). BDNF in schizophrenia, depression and corresponding animal models. *Mol. Psychiatry* 10, 345–352. doi: 10.1038/sj.mp.4001637

Ashdown-Franks, G., Sabiston, C. M., and Stubbs, B. (2019). The evidence for physical activity in the management of major mental illnesses: a concise overview to inform busy clinicians' practice and guide policy. *Curr. Opin. Psychiatry* 32, 375–380. doi: 10.1097/yco.0000000000000526

Askari, J., Saberi-Kakhki, A., Taheri, H., Yassini, S. M., and Hassanbeigi, A. (2019). The effect of aerobic exercise on various symptoms of depression: the mediating role of quality of life. *Sport Sci. Health* 1–8. doi: 10.1007/s11332-019-00601-w

Babyak, M., Blumenthal, J. A., Herman, S., Khatri, P., Doraiswamy, M., Moore, K., et al. (2000). Exercise treatment for major depression: maintenance of therapeutic benefit at 10 months. *Psychosom. Med.* 62, 633–638. doi: 10.1097/00006842-200009000-200009006

Belvederi Murri, M., Ekkekakis, P., Magagnoli, M., Zampogna, D., Cattedra, S., Capobianco, L., et al. (2018). Physical exercise in major depression: reducing the mortality gap while improving clinical outcomes. *Front. Psychiatry* 9:762. doi: 10.3389/fpsyt.2018.00762

Bennie, J. A., Teychenne, M., and Tittlbach, S. (2020). Muscle-strengthening exercise and depressive symptom severity among a nationally representative sample of 23,635 German adults. *J. Affect. Disord.* 266, 282–287.

Berry, A., Bellisario, V., Capoccia, S., Tirassa, P., Calza, A., Alleva, E., et al. (2012). Social deprivation stress is a triggering factor for the emergence of anxiety- and depression-like behaviours and leads to reduced brain BDNF levels in C57BL/6J mice. *Psychoneuroendocrinology* 37, 762–772. doi: 10.1016/j.psyneuen.2011.09.007

Blake, H. (2012). Physical activity and exercise in the treatment of depression. *Front. Psychiatry* 3:106. doi: 10.3389/fpsyt.2012.00106

Blazer, D. G. (2003). Depression in late life: review and commentary. *J. Gerontol. Ser. A* 58, M249–M265.

Blumenthal, J. A., Babyak, M. A., Moore, K. A., Craighead, W. E., Herman, S., Khatri, P., et al. (1999). Effects of exercise training on older patients with major depression. *Arch. Intern. Med.* 159, 2349–2356.

Booth, F. W., Roberts, C. K., and Laye, M. J. (2012). Lack of exercise is a major cause of chronic diseases. *Compr. Physiol.* 2, 1143–1211. doi: 10.1002/cphy.c110025

Bragin, V., Chemodanova, M., Dzhafarova, N., Bragin, I., Czerniawski, J. L., and Aliev, G. (2005). Integrated treatment approach improves cognitive function in demented and clinically depressed patients. *Am. J. Alzheimer Dis. Dement.* 20, 21–26.

Bridle, C., Spanjers, K., Patel, S., Atherton, N. M., and Lamb, S. E. (2012). Effect of exercise on depression severity in older people: systematic review and meta-analysis of randomised controlled trials. *Br. J. Psychiatry* 201, 180–185. doi: 10.1192/bjp.bp.111.095174

Butters, M. A., Young, J. B., Lopez, O., Aizenstein, H. J., Mulsant, B. H., Reynolds, C. F. III, et al. (2008). Pathways linking late-life depression to persistent cognitive impairment and dementia. *Dialog. Clin. Neurosci.* 10:345.

Büyükturan, Ö, Naharcı, M., and Kırd, N. (2017). Effects of aerobic exercise in an older adult with chronic major depressive disorder who untreated with pharmacotherapy. *Ann. Yoga Phys. Ther.* 2:1019.

Caraci, F., Calabrese, F., Molteni, R., Bartova, L., Dold, M., Leggio, G. M., et al. (2018a). International union of basic and clinical pharmacology CIV: the neurobiology of treatment-resistant depression: from antidepressant classifications to novel pharmacological targets. *Pharmacol. Rev.* 70, 475–504. doi: 10.1124/pr.117.014977

Caraci, F., Spampinato, S. F., Morgese, M. G., Tascedda, F., Salluzzo, M. G., Giambirtone, M. C., et al. (2018b). Neurobiological links between depression and AD: the role of TGF-beta1 signaling as a new pharmacological target. *Pharmacol. Res.* 130, 374–384. doi: 10.1016/j.phrs.2018.02.007

Caraci, F., Copani, A., Nicoletti, F., and Drago, F. (2010). Depression and Alzheimer's disease: neurobiological links and common pharmacological targets. *Eur. J. Pharmacol.* 626, 64–71. doi: 10.1016/j.ejphar.2009.10.022

Caraci, F., Gulisano, W., Guida, C. A., Impellizzeri, A. A., Drago, F., Puzzo, D., et al. (2015). A key role for TGF-beta1 in hippocampal synaptic plasticity and memory. *Sci. Rep.* 5:11252. doi: 10.1038/srep11252

Caruso, G., Fresta, C. G., Grasso, M., Santangelo, R., Lazzarino, G., Lunte, S. M., et al. (2019). Inflammation as the common biological link between depression and cardiovascular diseases: Can carnosine exert a protective role?. *Curr. Med. Chem.* doi: 10.2174/0929867326666190712091515 [Epub ahead of print].

Castren, E., and Kojima, M. (2017). Brain-derived neurotrophic factor in mood disorders and antidepressant treatments. *Neurobiol. Dis.* 97(Pt B), 119–126. doi: 10.1016/j.nbd.2016.07.010

Chang, S. C., Pan, A., Kawachi, I., and Okereke, O. I. (2016). Risk factors for late-life depression: a prospective cohort study among older women. *Prev. Med.* 91, 144–151. doi: 10.1016/j.ypmed.2016.08.014

Chen, K. M., Chen, M. H., Lin, M. H., Fan, J. T., Lin, H. S., and Li, C. H. (2010). Effects of yoga on sleep quality and depression in elders in assisted living facilities. *J. Nurs. Res.* 18, 53–61. doi: 10.1097/JNR.0b013e3181ce5189

Czeh, B., and Lucassen, P. J. (2007). What causes the hippocampal volume decrease in depression? Are neurogenesis, glial changes and apoptosis implicated? *Eur. Arch. Psychiatry Clin. Neurosci.* 257, 250–260. doi: 10.1007/s00406-007-0728-720

de Kloet, E. R., Joels, M., and Holsboer, F. (2005). Stress and the brain: from adaptation to disease. *Nat. Rev. Neurosci.* 6, 463–475. doi: 10.1038/nrn1683

Diniz, B. S., Butters, M. A., Albert, S. M., and Dew, M. A. (2013). Late-life depression and risk of vascular dementia and Alzheimer's disease: systematic review and meta-analysis of community-based cohort studies. *Br. J. Psychiatry* 202, 329–335. doi: 10.1192/bjp.bp.112.118307

Duman, R. S., and Li, N. (2012). A neurotrophic hypothesis of depression: role of synaptogenesis in the actions of NMDA receptor antagonists. *Philos. Trans. R. Soc. Lond. B Biol. Sci.* 367, 2475–2484. doi: 10.1098/rstb.2011.0357

Duman, R. S., and Monteggia, L. M. (2006). A neurotrophic model for stress-related mood disorders. *Biol. Psychiatry* 59, 1116–1127. doi: 10.1016/j.biopsych.2006.02.013

Dupuis, S. L., and Smale, B. J. (1995). An examination of relationship between psychological well-being and depression and leisure activity participation among older adults. *Soc. Leisure* 18, 67–92.

Ernst, C., Olson, A. K., Pinel, J. P., Lam, R. W., and Christie, B. R. (2006). Antidepressant effects of exercise: evidence for an adult-neurogenesis hypothesis? *J. Psychiatry Neurosci.* 31, 84–92.

Espinoza, R., and Kaufman, A. H. (2014). Diagnosis and treatment of late-life depression. *Psychiatric Times* 31, 18–18.

Farooq, R. K., Asghar, K., Kanwal, S., and Zulqernain, A. (2017). Role of inflammatory cytokines in depression: Focus on interleukin-1beta. *Biomed. Rep.* 6, 15–20. doi: 10.3892/br.2016.807

Filho, C. B., Jesse, C. R., Donato, F., Giacomeli, R., Del Fabbro, L., da Silva Antunes, M., et al. (2015). Chronic unpredictable mild stress decreases BDNF and NGF levels and Na(+),K(+)-ATPase activity in the hippocampus and prefrontal cortex of mice: antidepressant effect of chrysin. *Neuroscience* 289, 367–380. doi: 10.1016/j.neuroscience.2014.12.048

Gbd 2017 Disease and Injury Incidence and Prevalence Collaborators (2018). Global, regional, and national incidence, prevalence, and years lived with disability for 354 diseases and injuries for 195 countries and territories, 1990-2017: a systematic analysis for the Global Burden of Disease Study 2017. *Lancet* 392, 1789–1858. doi: 10.1016/S0140-6736(18)32279-7

Gomes da Silva, S., and Arida, R. M. (2015). Physical activity and brain development. *Expert. Rev. Neurother.* 15, 1041–1051. doi: 10.1586/14737175.2015.1077115

Hammen, C. (2018). Risk factors for depression: an autobiographical review. *Annu. Rev. Clin. Psychol.* 14, 1–28. doi: 10.1146/annurev-clinpsy-050817-084811

Hamon, M., and Blier, P. (2013). Monoamine neurocircuitry in depression and strategies for new treatments. *Prog. Neuropsychopharmacol. Biol. Psychiatry* 45, 54–63. doi: 10.1016/j.pnpbp.2013.04.009

Harvey, S. B., Overland, S., Hatch, S. L., Wessely, S., Mykletun, A., and Hotopf, M. (2018). Exercise and the prevention of depression: results of the HUNT cohort study. *Am. J. Psychiatry* 175, 28–36. doi: 10.1176/appi.ajp.2017.16111223

Heinemeier, K., Langberg, H., and Kjaer, M. (2003). Exercise-induced changes in circulating levels of transforming growth factor-beta-1 in humans: methodological considerations. *Eur. J. Appl. Physiol.* 90, 171–177. doi: 10.1007/s00421-003-0881-888

Heinzel, S., Lawrence, J. B., Kallies, G., Rapp, M. A., and Heissel, A. (2015). Using exercise to fight depression in older adults. *Geropsychiatry* 28, 149–162.

Hing, B., Sathyaputri, L., and Potash, J. B. (2018). A comprehensive review of genetic and epigenetic mechanisms that regulate BDNF expression and function with relevance to major depressive disorder. *Am. J. Med. Genet. B Neuropsychiatr. Genet.* 177, 143–167. doi: 10.1002/ajmg.b.32616

Hirschfeld, R. M. (2000). History and evolution of the monoamine hypothesis of depression. *J. Clin. Psychiatry* 61(Suppl. 6), 4–6.

Imboden, C., Gerber, M., Beck, J., Eckert, A., Pühse, U., Holsboer-Trachsler, E., et al. (2019). Effects of aerobic exercise as add-on treatment for inpatients with moderate to severe depression on depression severity, sleep, cognition, psychological well-being, and biomarkers: study protocol, description of study population, and manipulation check. *Front. Psychiatry* 10:262. doi: 10.3389/fpsyt.2019.00262

Jaggar, M., Fanibunda, S. E., Ghosh, S., Duman, R. S., and Vaidya, V. A. (2019). The neurotrophic hypothesis of depression revisited: new insights and therapeutic implications. *Neurobiol. Depress* 367, 43–62.

Josefsson, T., Lindwall, M., and Archer, T. (2014). Physical exercise intervention in depressive disorders: meta-analysis and systematic review. *Scand. J. Med. Sci. Sports* 24, 259–272. doi: 10.1111/sms.12050

Kessler, R. C., Birnbaum, H., Bromet, E., Hwang, I., Sampson, N., and Shahly, V. (2010). Age differences in major depression: results from the national comorbidity survey replication (NCS-R). *Psychol. Med.* 40, 225–237. doi: 10.1017/s0033291709990213

Khatri, P., Blumenthal, J. A., Babyak, M. A., Craighead, W. E., Herman, S., Baldewicz, T., et al. (2001). Effects of exercise training on cognitive functioning among depressed older men and women. *J. Aging Phys. Activ.* 9, 43–57.

Krishnan, V., and Nestler, E. J. (2008). The molecular neurobiology of depression. *Nature* 455, 894–902. doi: 10.1038/nature07455

Kvam, S., Kleppe, C. L., Nordhus, I. H., and Hovland, A. (2016). Exercise as a treatment for depression: a meta-analysis. *J. Affect. Disord.* 202, 67–86. doi: 10.1016/j.jad.2016.03.063

Lin, E., and Tsai, S. J. (2019). Epigenetics and depression: an update. *Psychiatry Investig.* 16, 654–661. doi: 10.30773/pi.2019.07.17.2

Lopez-Munoz, F., and Alamo, C. (2009). Monoaminergic neurotransmission: the history of the discovery of antidepressants from 1950s until today. *Curr. Pharm. Des.* 15, 1563–1586. doi: 10.2174/138161209788168001

Lopez-Torres Hidalgo, J. (2019). Effectiveness of physical exercise in the treatment of depression in older adults as an alternative to antidepressant drugs in primary care. *BMC Psychiatry* 19:21. doi: 10.1186/s12888-018-1982-1986

Luppa, M., Sikorski, C., Luck, T., Ehreke, L., Konnopka, A., Wiese, B., et al. (2012). Age- and gender-specific prevalence of depression in latest-life–systematic review and meta-analysis. *J. Affect. Disord.* 136, 212–221. doi: 10.1016/j.jad.2010.11.033

Maes, M., Nowak, G., Caso, J. R., Leza, J. C., Song, C., Kubera, M., et al. (2016). Toward Omics-based, systems biomedicine, and path and drug discovery methodologies for depression-inflammation research. *Mol. Neurobiol.* 53, 2927–2935. doi: 10.1007/s12035-015-9183-9185

Martinsen, E. W. (2008). Physical activity in the prevention and treatment of anxiety and depression. *Nord. J. Psychiatry* 62(Suppl. 47), 25–29. doi: 10.1080/08039480802315640

Martinsen, E. W., Medhus, A., and Sandvik, L. (1985). Effects of aerobic exercise on depression: a controlled study. *Br. Med. J.* 291:109. doi: 10.1136/bmj.291.6488.109

Meijer, A., Conradi, H. J., Bos, E. H., Anselmino, M., Carney, R. M., Denollet, J., et al. (2013). Adjusted prognostic association of depression following myocardial infarction with mortality and cardiovascular events: individual patient data meta-analysis. *Br. J. Psychiatry* 203, 90–102. doi: 10.1192/bjp.bp.112.111195

Morimoto, S. S., Kanellopoulos, D., Manning, K. J., and Alexopoulos, G. S. (2015). Diagnosis and treatment of depression and cognitive impairment in late-life. *Ann. N. Y. Acad. Sci.* 1345:36.

Mura, G., and Carta, M. G. (2013). Physical activity in depressed elderly. A systematic review. *Clin. Pract. Epidemiol. Ment. Health* 9, 125–135. doi: 10.2174/1745017901309010125

Murri, M. B., Amore, M., Menchetti, M., Toni, G., Neviani, F., Cerri, M., et al. (2015). Physical exercise for late-life major depression. *Br. J. Psychiatry* 207, 235–242.

Murri, M. B., Ekkekakis, P., Menchetti, M., Neviani, F., Trevisani, F., Tedeschi, S., et al. (2018). Physical exercise for late-life depression: effects on symptom dimensions and time course. *J. Affect. Disord.* 230, 65–70. doi: 10.1016/j.jad.2018.01.004

Murrough, J. W., Iacoviello, B., Neumeister, A., Charney, D. S., and Iosifescu, D. V. (2011). Cognitive dysfunction in depression: neurocircuitry and new therapeutic strategies. *Neurobiol. Learn. Mem.* 96, 553–563.

Myint, A. M., Leonard, B. E., Steinbusch, H. W., and Kim, Y. K. (2005). Th1, Th2, and Th3 cytokine alterations in major depression. *J. Affect. Disord.* 88, 167–173. doi: 10.1016/j.jad.2005.07.008

Nabkasorn, C., Miyai, N., Sootmongkol, A., Junprasert, S., Yamamoto, H., Arita, M., et al. (2006). Effects of physical exercise on depression, neuroendocrine stress hormones and physiological fitness in adolescent females with depressive symptoms. *Eur. J. Public Health* 16, 179–184. doi: 10.1093/eurpub/cki159

Netz, Y. (2017). Is the comparison between exercise and pharmacologic treatment of depression in the clinical practice guideline of the american college of physicians evidence-based? *Front. Pharmacol.* 8:257. doi: 10.3389/fphar.2017.00257

Neumeyer-Gromen, A., Lampert, T., Stark, K., and Kallischnigg, G. (2004). Disease management programs for depression: a systematic review and meta-analysis of randomized controlled trials. *Med. Care* 42, 1211–1221. doi: 10.1097/00005650-200412000-200412008

Neviani, F., Belvederi Murri, M., Mussi, C., Triolo, F., Toni, G., Simoncini, E., et al. (2017). Physical exercise for late life depression: effects on cognition and disability. *Int. Psychogeriatr.* 29, 1105–1112. doi: 10.1017/s1041610217000576

Niwa, A., Nishibori, M., Hamasaki, S., Kobori, T., Liu, K., Wake, H., et al. (2016). Voluntary exercise induces neurogenesis in the hypothalamus and ependymal lining of the third ventricle. *Brain Struct. Funct.* 221, 1653–1666. doi: 10.1007/s00429-015-0995-x

Nowacka, M., and Obuchowicz, E. (2013). BDNF and VEGF in the pathogenesis of stress-induced affective diseases: an insight from experimental studies. *Pharmacol. Rep.* 65, 535–546. doi: 10.1016/s1734-1140(13)71031-71034

Pedersen, B. K. (2019). Physical activity and muscle-brain crosstalk. *Nat. Rev. Endocrinol.* 15, 383–392. doi: 10.1038/s41574-019-0174-x

Pittenger, C., and Duman, R. S. (2008). Stress, depression, and neuroplasticity: a convergence of mechanisms. *Neuropsychopharmacology* 33, 88–109. doi: 10.1038/sj.npp.1301574

Racagni, G., and Popoli, M. (2010). The pharmacological properties of antidepressants. *Int. Clin. Psychopharmacol.* 25, 117–131. doi: 10.1097/YIC.0b013e3283311acd

Reinhart, V., Bove, S. E., Volfson, D., Lewis, D. A., Kleiman, R. J., and Lanz, T. A. (2015). Evaluation of TrkB and BDNF transcripts in prefrontal cortex, hippocampus, and striatum from subjects with schizophrenia, bipolar disorder, and major depressive disorder. *Neurobiol. Dis.* 77, 220–227. doi: 10.1016/j.nbd.2015.03.011

Rethorst, C. D., Wipfli, B. M., and Landers, D. M. (2009). The antidepressive effects of exercise: a meta-analysis of randomized trials. *Sports Med.* 39, 491–511. doi: 10.2165/00007256-200939060-200939064

Rosenbaum, S., Tiedemann, A., Sherrington, C., Curtis, J., and Ward, P. B. (2014). Physical activity interventions for people with mental illness: a systematic review and meta-analysis. *J. Clin. Psychiatry* 75, 964–974. doi: 10.4088/JCP.13r08765

Rush, G., O'Donovan, A., Nagle, L., Conway, C., McCrohan, A., O'Farrelly, C., et al. (2016). Alteration of immune markers in a group of melancholic depressed patients and their response to electroconvulsive therapy. *J. Affect. Disord.* 205, 60–68. doi: 10.1016/j.jad.2016.06.035

Sasi, M., Vignoli, B., Canossa, M., and Blum, R. (2017). Neurobiology of local and intercellular BDNF signaling. *Pflugers. Arch.* 469, 593–610. doi: 10.1007/s00424-017-1964-1964

Schuch, F. B., Vancampfort, D., Rosenbaum, S., Richards, J., Ward, P. B., Veronese, N., et al. (2016). Exercise for depression in older adults: a meta-analysis of randomized controlled trials adjusting for publication bias. *Braz. J. Psychiatry* 38, 247–254.

Silveira, H., Moraes, H., Oliveira, N., Coutinho, E. S., Laks, J., and Deslandes, A. (2013). Physical exercise and clinically depressed patients: a systematic review and meta-analysis. *Neuropsychobiology* 67, 61–68. doi: 10.1159/000345160

Singh, N. A., Clements, K. M., and Singh, M. A. (2001). The efficacy of exercise as a long-term antidepressant in elderly subjects: a randomized, controlled trial. *J. Gerontol. A Biol. Sci. Med. Sci.* 56, M497–M504. doi: 10.1093/gerona/56.8.m497

Smith, M. A., Makino, S., Kvetnansky, R., and Post, R. M. (1995). Stress and glucocorticoids affect the expression of brain-derived neurotrophic factor and neurotrophin-3 mRNAs in the hippocampus. *J. Neurosci.* 15(3 Pt 1), 1768–1777.

Stenman, E., and Lilja, A. (2013). Increased monoaminergic neurotransmission improves compliance with physical activity recommendations in depressed patients with fatigue. *Med. Hypotheses* 80, 47–49. doi: 10.1016/j.mehy.2012.10.007

Sutcigil, L., Oktenli, C., Musabak, U., Bozkurt, A., Cansever, A., Uzun, O., et al. (2007). Pro- and anti-inflammatory cytokine balance in major depression: effect of sertraline therapy. *Clin. Dev. Immunol.* 2007:76396. doi: 10.1155/2007/76396

Szymura, J., Kubica, J., Wiecek, M., and Pera, J. (2020). The immunomodulary effects of systematic exercise in older adults and people with Parkinson's Disease. *J. Clin. Med.* 9:184. doi: 10.3390/jcm9010184

Taylor, W. D. (2014). Clinical practice. Depression in the elderly. *N. Engl. J. Med.* 371, 1228–1236. doi: 10.1056/NEJMcp1402180

Thompson Ray, M., Weickert, C. S., Wyatt, E., and Webster, M. J. (2011). Decreased BDNF, trkB-TK+ and GAD67 mRNA expression in the hippocampus of individuals with schizophrenia and mood disorders. *J. Psychiatry Neurosci.* 36, 195–203. doi: 10.1503/jpn.100048

Torrisi, S. A., Geraci, F., Tropea, M. R., Grasso, M., Caruso, G., Fidilio, A., et al. (2019). Fluoxetine and vortioxetine reverse depressive-like phenotype and memory deficits induced by abeta1-42 oligomers in mice: a key role of transforming growth factor-beta1. *Front. Pharmacol.* 10:693. doi: 10.3389/fphar.2019.00693

Vancampfort, D., Firth, J., Schuch, F. B., Rosenbaum, S., Mugisha, J., Hallgren, M., et al. (2017). Sedentary behavior and physical activity levels in people with schizophrenia, bipolar disorder and major depressive disorder: a global systematic review and meta-analysis. *World Psychiatry* 16, 308–315. doi: 10.1002/wps.20458

Vaughan, L., Corbin, A. L., and Goveas, J. S. (2015). Depression and frailty in later life: a systematic review. *Clin. Intervent. Aging* 10:1947.

Vigers, A. J., Amin, D. S., Talley-Farnham, T., Gorski, J. A., Xu, B., and Jones, K. R. (2012). Sustained expression of brain-derived neurotrophic factor is required for maintenance of dendritic spines and normal behavior. *Neuroscience* 212, 1–18. doi: 10.1016/j.neuroscience.2012.03.031

Vilar, M., and Mira, H. (2016). Regulation of neurogenesis by neurotrophins during adulthood: expected and unexpected roles. *Front. Neurosci.* 10:26. doi: 10.3389/fnins.2016.00026

Vu, D. (2019). Molecular mechanism of depression: a narrative review of the leading neurobiological theories of depression. *Austr. Med. Stud. J.* 9.1.

Walsh, J. J., and Tschakovsky, M. E. (2018). Exercise and circulating BDNF: Mechanisms of release and implications for the design of exercise interventions. *Appl. Physiol. Nutr. Metab.* 43, 1095–1104. doi: 10.1139/apnm-2018-2192

Weinhold, M., Shimabukuro-Vornhagen, A., Franke, A., Theurich, S., Wahl, P., Hallek, M., et al. (2016). Physical exercise modulates the homeostasis of human regulatory T cells. *J. Allergy Clin. Immunol.* 137, 1607–1610. doi: 10.1016/j.jaci.2015.10.035

You, Z., Luo, C., Zhang, W., Chen, Y., He, J., Zhao, Q., et al. (2011). Pro- and anti-inflammatory cytokines expression in rat's brain and spleen exposed to chronic mild stress: involvement in depression. *Behav. Brain Res.* 225, 135–141. doi: 10.1016/j.bbr.2011.07.006

Yu, S., Holsboer, F., and Almeida, O. F. (2008). Neuronal actions of glucocorticoids: focus on depression. *J. Steroid Biochem. Mol. Biol.* 108, 300–309. doi: 10.1016/j.jsbmb.2007.09.014

Yu, T., Guo, M., Garza, J., Rendon, S., Sun, X. L., Zhang, W., et al. (2011). Cognitive and neural correlates of depression-like behaviour in socially defeated mice: an animal model of depression with cognitive dysfunction. *Int. J. Neuropsychopharmacol.* 14, 303–317. doi: 10.1017/s1461145710000945

Zhang, K., Yang, C., Chang, L., Sakamoto, A., Suzuki, T., Fujita, Y., et al. (2020). Essential role of microglial transforming growth factor-beta1 in antidepressant actions of (R)-ketamine and the novel antidepressant TGF-beta1. *Transl. Psychiatry* 10:32. doi: 10.1038/s41398-020-0733-x

24

What Brings out the Best and Worst of People with a Strong Explicit Achievement Motive? The Role of (Lack of) Achievement Incentives for Performance in an Endurance Task

Julia Schüler* and Wanja Wolff

Department of Sport Science, University of Konstanz, Konstanz, Germany

***Correspondence:**
Julia Schüler
julia.schueler@uni-konstanz.de

An explicit achievement motive is intuitively related to good performance. In contrast, the present paper directs attention to conditions where individuals with a strong explicit achievement motive display poor performance. We hypothesized that participants with a strong achievement motive perform worse in a bicycle ergometer task when task instructions lack achievement incentives than when the instructions include achievement incentives. Furthermore, we expected that, when achievement incentives are lacking, they show even worse performance than participants with a weak achievement motive. For the latter, we assumed that they are relatively unaffected by the achievement incentive content of the instructions. In a within-subject experimental design ($N = 55$) with two blocks (achievement incentives vs. lack of achievement incentives; each block consisted of three trials), our hypotheses were partly supported. The lack of achievement incentives brought out the worst (regarding performance), but the presence of achievement incentives did not bring out the best of participants with a strong achievement motive. In the discussion, we suggest how to improve future experimental achievement settings and reflect the results within the framework of the differentiation into implicit and explicit motives.

Keywords: explicit achievement motive, motives, incentives, motor performance, underperformance

INTRODUCTION

That a strong achievement motive, defined as "the capacity to derive satisfaction from the autonomous mastery of challenging tasks" (Schultheiss, 2008, p. 603), which in turn encourages people to seek out situations that allow measuring one's standards of excellence (McClelland et al., 1953), is associated with high performance is not only intuitively plausible but also supported by research in sports (Elbe et al., 2005; Wegner et al., 2014; Gröpel et al., 2016) and in several other domains of life, for example, at the workplace (e.g., Andrews, 1967; McClelland and Franz, 1992), in learning contexts (e.g., McKeachie, 1961; O'Connor et al., 1966; Dahme et al., 1993; Schultheiss and Köllner, 2014), and in research laboratories with a broad variety of achievement tasks (to name but a few examples: Thurstone, 1937; Lowell, 1952; Biernat, 1989; Puca and Schmalt, 1999; Fodor and Carver, 2000; Brunstein and Hoyer, 2002; Brunstein and Maier, 2005; Pang, 2010).

In the present paper, we focus on *explicit* achievement motive, which has to be differentiated from *implicit* achievement motive due to differences in the behavior it influences, in the incentives that arouse the motives, and in motive development, to name a few examples. (For a detailed differentiation into implicit and explicit motives, see McClelland et al., 1989; see also discussion below.) The explicit achievement motive is a consciously represented part of one's self-concept ("I am a person for whom it is important to perform well," "It is important for me to demonstrate good performance"). According to previous theoretical considerations, the explicit achievement motive is highly relevant for performance in general (McClelland, 1980; Brunstein and Maier, 2005), as well as for performance in the sports and exercise context (Elbe and Wenhold, 2005; Elbe et al., 2005).

Motivation researchers share the view that the link between achievement motivation and performance stems from the interaction between the person's achievement motive and characteristics of the situation (e.g., performance feedback), which is associated with the possibility to satisfy the achievement motive and, as a result, promises the experience of positive affects (for achievement: feelings of pride, being satisfied because one acts in accordance with one's self-concept) (Brunstein and Heckhausen, 2008). In brief, the achievement motive is aroused by corresponding achievement incentives (Beckmann and Heckhausen, 2018a,b; McClelland, 1980).

The explicit achievement motive is incited in situations in which *social* incentives are present. Social incentives are characteristics of the situation such as demands and expectations that come from outside the task (e.g., from experimenters, teachers, coaches) rather than from the task itself (activity incentives) (for details about social and activity incentives, see McClelland et al., 1989). Further typical social achievement incentives, which we will also utilize in our study, are *verbal stimuli*. Bargh et al. (2001), for example, found that achievement-related words such as "win," "master," and "achieve" enhance performance. Also supporting this so-called "behavioral priming effect" (see also Breidebach and Gruber, 2019), Engeser et al. (2016) used excerpts from mathematics (Experiment 1) and language (Experiment 2) schoolbooks and found that semantic achievement primes enhanced performance in an arithmetic task and an anagram task, respectively. Following our line of argumentation that verbal stimuli leave *implicit* motives unaffected, the implicit achievement motive did not moderate the priming effect. In another series of studies, Engeser and Baumann (2014) found that verbally presented achievement primes indeed arouse explicit, but not implicit, achievement motivation (for further examples of achievement motive priming, see Breidebach, 2012, 2017).

A further example of verbal stimuli is achievement-related instructions in an experiment (McClelland et al., 1953; French, 1958). In the present study, we use task instructions for our experimental manipulation that stress the personal importance of performing well and demonstrating one's competence.

The *presence* of achievement incentives is one "side" of the achievement motive × incentive interaction. But what about the other side of the interaction: How do people behave, when achievement incentives are *absent*? When social extrinsic incentives are missing, and when people do not feel responsible for the performance outcome (e.g., when performance depends on a device's technical properties rather than on their performance; see calibration task below), then achievement behavior is not stimulated, and people with a strong achievement motive might perform even worse than people with weak achievement motives. The reason is that the explicit motives are built on the self-image of a person: "It operates as a cognitive regulator that shapes voluntary behavior in accordance with a person's motivational self-view, mainly through its influence on cognitively based choices and explicit responses to social–extrinsic cues" (Brunstein and Maier, 2005, p. 206). One possible choice or explicit response is to put no effort in tasks that do not satisfy the achievement motive, for example, in a task without individual performance feedback, because this makes it impossible to assess and demonstrate one's ability. In accordance with most motivation theories' assumption, that goal characteristics and needs have a direct (McClelland et al., 1953; Wigfield and Eccles, 2000) or indirect (Brehm and Self, 1989; Wright, 2008) crucial role for investing energy in goal pursuit, people with a strong achievement motive are effective in effort regulation in the sense that they put the effort in tasks that are "worth" it (worth concerning motive-satisfying potential). When performance has consequences for one's self-concept as an achievement-oriented and successful person, more effort should be mobilized to achieve high performance (Brunstein and Maier, 2005; Gendolla and Richter, 2010). They do not, however, waste time and effort in tasks that are "worthless" (= unable to satisfy the achievement motive). In sum, we assume that a strong achievement motive is associated with strategic effort investment. In contrast, for people with a weak achievement motive, achievement incentives are irrelevant, and their task performance might depend more strongly on other factors (e.g., compliance with the experimenter's instructions).

In the present study, we experimentally designed instructions that either contain (achievement condition) or lack (calibration condition) achievement incentives to test the following interaction hypotheses concerning motor performance in a strenuous motor task: Participants with a strong achievement motive are expected to perform worse in an experimental condition that lacks achievement-related incentives than in a condition that includes achievement incentives. We furthermore assume that when a condition is void of achievement incentives, they perform even worse than participants with a weak achievement motive. When achievement incentives are present, they should perform better than the latter. We chose an endurance task (cycling on a bicycle ergometer) because physical performance can be accurately and continuously measured, and performance can be visualized to participants in real time. Further, as physical exertion creates a strong sense of effort, strategic effort investment (i.e., pacing) occurs even during short experimental tasks. We varied the difficulty of the endurance task (low, moderate, and hard levels of load) referring to an established power table (Coggans power table)[1] and

[1] https://www.trainingpeaks.com/blog/power-profiling/

exploratorily examined whether load influences the hypothesized effect reported above.

MATERIALS AND METHODS

Participants

Fifty-five students (31 women) from different faculties of a German university with a mean age of 23.67 years (SD = 5.09) participated in an experiment that was announced as a study that allegedly tested emotional well-being during an ergometer endurance task. We recruited participants using a university-internal platform, postings on blackboards, and advertisement in lectures. As exclusion criteria, we defined consumption of caffeine and tobacco less than 2 h before the experiment and alcohol or other drug intakes less than 12 h before the experiment. Further exclusion criteria were lower limb injuries and strenuous workouts in the last 12 h. Participants were informed that they will receive 10 Euros and that the study will last about 1 h.

Procedure

The study design and material (e.g., information sheet, debriefing form) met the standards of the Ethics Committee of the authors' university and were in line with the Declarations of Helsinki (World Medical Association, 2013). Participants were tested individually in a laboratory at the authors' university. After being greeted by a female experimenter, participants read the information sheet and filled in the informed consent form. Then their height and body weight were assessed. While the experimenter prepared the bicycle ergometer (e.g., chose a load profile that fit participant characteristics, e.g., profile for men and women depending on body weight; see below), participants filled in a questionnaire containing the achievement motive measure (Unified Motive Scale, UMS, Schönbrodt and Gerstenberg, 2012) and a questionnaire that was used to test a hypothesis irrelevant for the present research (Self-Regulation Scale, Schwarzer et al., 1999)[2].

After that, the experimenter adjusted the parameters on the bicycle according to the participants' comfort (i.e., pedal and crank arm are parallel to the floor, while the knee and shank are perpendicular to the floor). Participants were then asked to start pedaling to familiarize themselves with the bike. They learned that they are expected to practice maintaining a given cadence that allegedly will be computed later from their individual scores (in fact, all cadences were 70 rpm) and tried it out during a familiarization phase. The cadence was displayed continuously on a screen in front of the participants while they were pedaling. The given cadence was clearly marked by a line so that participants could continuously observe deviations from the target cadence. It was explained that being precise – that is, keeping a specified cadence of 70 rpm – represents good performance. This should also include the reverse conclusion that poor performance is indicated by deviations from cadence (no matter whether higher or lower scores were achieved). A warm-up phase lasting 3 min followed. Participants were requested to inform the experimenter in case of any pain or discomfort during the course of the test and had the opportunity to ask questions about the whole procedure.

Then the actual test that consists of two blocks with three levels of load started. The first block consisted of half of the participants in the calibration condition and the other half in the achievement condition (random assignment to the order of condition). After a 5 min break, the groups received the respective other condition. The experimental conditions were implemented using written instructions for the cycling task. The achievement instructions contained positive evaluations of performance (which is a scoring category for the achievement motive in Winter's scoring manual, Winter, 1994) (e.g., "optimal cadence," "accuracy of your performance") that unambiguously can be attributed to participants (it is about "YOUR individual performance"). As the incentive for people with a strong achievement motive is "to do something better" (McClelland, 1985), they need a tool to assess performance, for example, by receiving feedback on how well they are doing. In accordance with these theoretical considerations, previous research supported that people with a strong (implicit and explicit) achievement motive benefit more from feedback than participants with weak achievement motives (Fodor and Carver, 2000; Brunstein and Maier, 2005). We, therefore, announced an "individual performance log" in the instructions of the achievement condition. In contrast, in the calibration task, performance was framed as an accuracy assessment of the ergometer. With this, we intended to make participants feel responsible for their performance outcome in the achievement, but not in the calibration, condition (for a similar procedure, see McClelland et al., 1949). The concrete instructions for the achievement and calibration conditions are displayed in **Table 1**.

The two ergometer blocks consisted of three levels of loads (low, moderate, hard) lasting 2 min each with a break of 1 min between each run. We used the Coggans power table[3] to determine gender-specific power/weight (p/w) ratios for the low, moderate, and hard load levels. Female participants had to pedal at a p/w ratio of 1.6 for the easy, 2.1 for the moderate, and 2.6 for the hard load levels, and male participants pedaled at 2.4, 3, and 3.6 p/w for the easy, moderate, and hard levels. The loads were calibrated in such a way that even untrained participants would be able to complete 2 min of the hard load. After the cycling part, the participants answered two questions checking whether they were aware of the hypotheses (What do you think was the real aim of the study? How do you think the two sessions were connected?). No participant realized the study's intention. Then they stated whether they consumed any drugs, caffeine, or alcohol prior to the study (exclusion criteria). They then received a debriefing form and their payment and were thanked and dismissed.

[2]Further variables were assessed that are not relevant for the present research question (weight, height, perceived exertion).

[3]https://www.trainingpeaks.com/blog/power-profiling/

TABLE 1 | Wording for the achievement and calibration conditions in the two separated blocks of the experiment.

	Block 1: Achievement		Block 2: Calibration
1.1	Let's start with the test.	2.1	The ergometer needs a new calibration. Like this, we can be sure about the accuracy of the ergometer.
1.2	First of all, we will do three runs with different levels of difficulty	2.2	We are again performing three runs with different levels.
1.3	With these runs, we will measure the accuracy of YOUR task PERFORMANCE.	2.3	We will perform the same as before. But this time, we will test the ERGOMETER instead of you.
1.4	We can measure your performance accurately in the course and compare it to the rest of the participants.	2.4	This time, we are measuring the accuracy of our ergometer. We have to calibrate the ergometer to make sure it measures accurately.
1.5	Here you can see your personal performance line, which we have calculated for you during the pre-test (warming-up). The optimal cadence per minute for you is 70. This line here displays the 70 rpm cadence line. Your task is to keep the cadence of 70 rpm as constant as possible around (above or below) this line. Like this, we can exactly figure out your precision of riding a specific cadence. Go for it!	2.5	Here you can see a calibration profile presented by the software of the ergometer. The cadence is 70 rpm. This line here displays the 70 rpm cadence line. Your task is to keep the cadence of 70 rpm as constant as possible around (above or below) this line. Like this, we can figure out the accuracy of our ergometer. The calibration is starting soon!
1.6	*Afterward, you will receive your individual performance log. Here, you can see an example of an ergometer protocol. The performance log will look like this. It shows your performance over time and in comparison to the other participants.	2.6	*This time, this will be the test report for the ergometer. So, we will get a log with the deviation of the ergometer from its calibration line. Roughly the same will be our performance log for the ergometer. It shows the deviation of the ergometer compared to the calibration line.

*The numbering is just for illustration of the experimental manipulation; participants read a running text. *A profile example was presented to show how the participant's profile (/the bicycle ergometer's profile) could look at the end. Participants were told that they would receive a printed version of their own profile (/the ergometer's profile) at the end of the study.*

Measures

We used a German version of the Unified Motive Scale (UMS-10, 54 items, Schönbrodt and Gerstenberg, 2012) that assesses a broader range of self-attributed motives. Reports about the UMS reliability and validity can be found in Schönbrodt and Gerstenberg (2012); see also Sariyska et al. (2019). The **achievement motive** scale, which is relevant for our research question, consists of two statements (i.e., "I am appealed by situations allowing me to test my abilities, "My goal is to do at least a little bit more than anyone else has done before"), which require an agreement rating on a six-point rating scale ranging from 1, strongly disagree, to 6, strongly agree, and eight goals (e.g., "continuously improve myself," "personally producing work of high quality," "opportunities to take on more difficult and challenging goals and responsibilities," "personally doing things better than they have been done before," "opportunities to create new things," "projects that challenge me to the limits of my ability," "continuously new, exciting, and challenging goals and projects," "maintaining high standards for the quality of my work"), which require an importance rating (1, not important to me, to 6, extremely important to me).

We used a Cyclus2 ergometer (by RBM Elektronik-automation GmbH, Leipzig, Germany) to assess **motor performance**. Cycling data were measured at a sampling rate of 2 Hz and with a set true gear ratio of 53/14. Participants were asked to keep the cadence as close as possible to around 70 rpm. In asking participants to keep this pre-defined cadence, we used accuracy rather than a "the more the better" (e.g., higher cadence indicates better performance) criterion of performance. We therewith ensured that the participants could not overspend themselves at the beginning (and have to abort their participation in the rest of the experiment due to physical exhaustion). In addition to these laboratory experimental reasons, motor precision is important to be analyzed, because it is crucial for an accurate execution of movement, which is important for injury prevention (for a similar reasoning, see Hirsch et al., 2020, March 17). A further reason is that motor response precision requires high exertion of self-control. Manohar et al. (2015, p. 1707) called this fact "cost of control," which means that exerting control to improve response precision itself comes at a cost (the costs to attenuate a proportion of intrinsic neural noise) (Giboin et al., 2019). Furthermore, keeping a specific cadence comes closer to Brunstein and Maier (2005) findings that the explicit achievement motive predicts the continuation of a task (keep on going) rather than the performance itself (e.g., peak performance).

Our choice of the level of cadence that we asked participants to keep (70 rpm) was based on studies that analyzed what cadence non-cyclists prefer when they are free to choose (Whitty et al., 2009). Non-cyclists freely chose levels of the cadence of about 80 rpm that they report to be comfortable, which, however, were significantly higher than the most economical cadence (in terms of metabolic economy, 50 rpm). Cycling at a cadence above or below the most economical cadence of 50 rpm was experienced as strenuous, indicated by higher ratings of perceived effort (RPEs). We chose a cadence (70 rpm) that deviates from the expected preferred cadence of 80 rpm, to ensure that participants were not likely to automatically gravitate to our target cadence.

In our experiment, deviations from a cadence of 70 rpm were squared and averaged for each load and condition. Thus, higher scores in "Cadence" represent poorer performance.

RESULTS

Description of Data and Their Relationships

Table 2 depicts means and standard deviations for participants' motor performance (Cadence) for the achievement goal and calibration conditions, each for an overall score and for low,

TABLE 2 | Means and standard deviations (in brackets) for Cadence for the Achievement and Calibration Conditions separated for different levels of load.

	Achievement condition				Calibration condition			
Load	**Overall**	**Low**	**Moderate**	**Hard**	**Overall**	**Low**	**Moderate**	**Hard**
Cadence	2.27	2.24	2.13	2.45	4.07	2.97	4.14	5.09
	(4.21)	(3.95)	(4.37)	(4.32)	(8.82)	(5.66)	(9.1)	(11.7)

Cadence means squared deviations from a cadence of 70 rpm, and thus, higher scores mean poorer performance.

moderate, and hard loads. The achievement motive (M = 3.48, SD = 0.723) is positively correlated with deviation from cadence in the achievement condition (r = 0.31, p = 0.021) as well as in the calibration condition (r = 0.38, p = 0.004). Cadence scores of both conditions were highly related with $r = 0.37, p < 0.005$.

Testing the Hypotheses

To test the hypothesis that participants with a strong achievement motive perform worse in the calibration condition than in the achievement condition (goal conditions were nested within participants), we conducted a hierarchical multi-level regression analysis using the statistical software R (R Core Team, 2017) and the lme4 package (Bates et al., 2015). We chose a hierarchical multi-level model to better account for the fact that people differ but that these differences do not stem from the experimental manipulation. The regression model was built by sequentially adding predictors after an intercept-only model, and its random intercept had been specified (*baseline model*). To create the *main effect model*, we added the single predictors (Condition, ACHmotive) to the baseline model with Condition allowed to vary between participants. The *interaction model* consists of the single predictors and the two-way interaction (Condition × ACHmotive). This procedure allowed us to compare all stages of model specification and figure out whether the interplay between ACHmotive and Condition can explain variance in addition to the single variables.

The interaction model summary showed that the ACHmotive significantly [b = 1.538, $t(53)$ = 2.371, p = 0.021, d = 0.320] and the interaction marginally [b = 2.755, $t(53)$ = 1.973, p = 0.054, d = 0.266] predicted performance. Condition was not a significant predictor [b = −7.800, $t(53)$ = −1.571, p = 0.122, d = 0.212]. An ANOVA testing the *main effect model* against the *interaction model* revealed a significant effect [$\chi^2(1)$ = 3.898, p = 0.048] indicating that the interaction model significantly improved the fit over the main effect model. **Figure 1** illustrates the nature of the interaction.

In accordance with the hypothesis, participants with a strong achievement motive (blue lines and dots) performed worse in the calibration than in the achievement condition. Also as expected, in the calibration condition, they performed worse than participants with a weak motive (red lines and dots). Unexpectedly, however, participants with strong and weak achievement motives did not significantly differ in the achievement condition.

Exploratory Analyses

To examine whether the load of the task (easy, moderate, high) could improve the fit of the model, we examined a *main effect model* (Condition, ACHmotive, Load), a *two-way interactions model* (main effect model plus the three two-way interactions), and a *three-way interaction model* (two-way interaction model plus Condition × Load × ACHmotive interaction). Neither the three-way interaction nor the two-way interactions were significant[4].

DISCUSSION

We aim to make use of the primacy effect (Ebbinghaus, 1913; Murdock, 1962) and start our discussion with the results that support our hypotheses. A hierarchical linear regression analysis revealed that considering the interaction between incentive content of task instruction and participants' achievement motive contributes to explain performance. The interaction itself was only marginal, but the interaction model contributes significantly when compared to the main effect model. To sum, although we assumed this interaction effect to be stronger, it is a least partly in conformity with the fundamental hypothesis in motive research that motives interact with characteristics of the situation to predict behavior (Brunstein and Heckhausen, 2008). However, the pattern of the interaction only partly supported our assumptions. In line with the hypotheses, participants with a strong achievement motive performed worse in an experimental condition that lacks achievement incentives (calibration condition) than in a condition that includes achievement incentives (achievement condition). Also as expected, in the calibration condition, they performed worse than participants with weak achievement motives. This supports our assumption that people with strong achievement motives perform badly when the effort that has to be invested in a task is not worth the effort because it does not promise motive satisfaction. We speculate that this "lazy" behavior is a clever strategy to invest one's effort efficiently, for example, by not "wasting" it on an unrewarding task (but saving energy for highly rewarding tasks).

Also in accordance with our hypotheses, people with a weak achievement motive, who are not dispositionally interested in demonstrating performance, showed relatively robust performance across the two experimental conditions. Their performance behavior was fully in line with the instructions given by the experimenter. It seems that agreeableness and

[4]We conducted a power analysis (using GPower 3.1; Faul et al., 2009) for a design with lower statistical power (no multi-level design). This analysis for an ANOVA with repeated measures testing a 2 (condition vs. achievement) * 3 (easy vs. moderate vs. high) design (effect size = 0.25, alpha = 0.05, power = 0.80) revealed an ideal sample size of 44 participants (actual power: 0.9557).

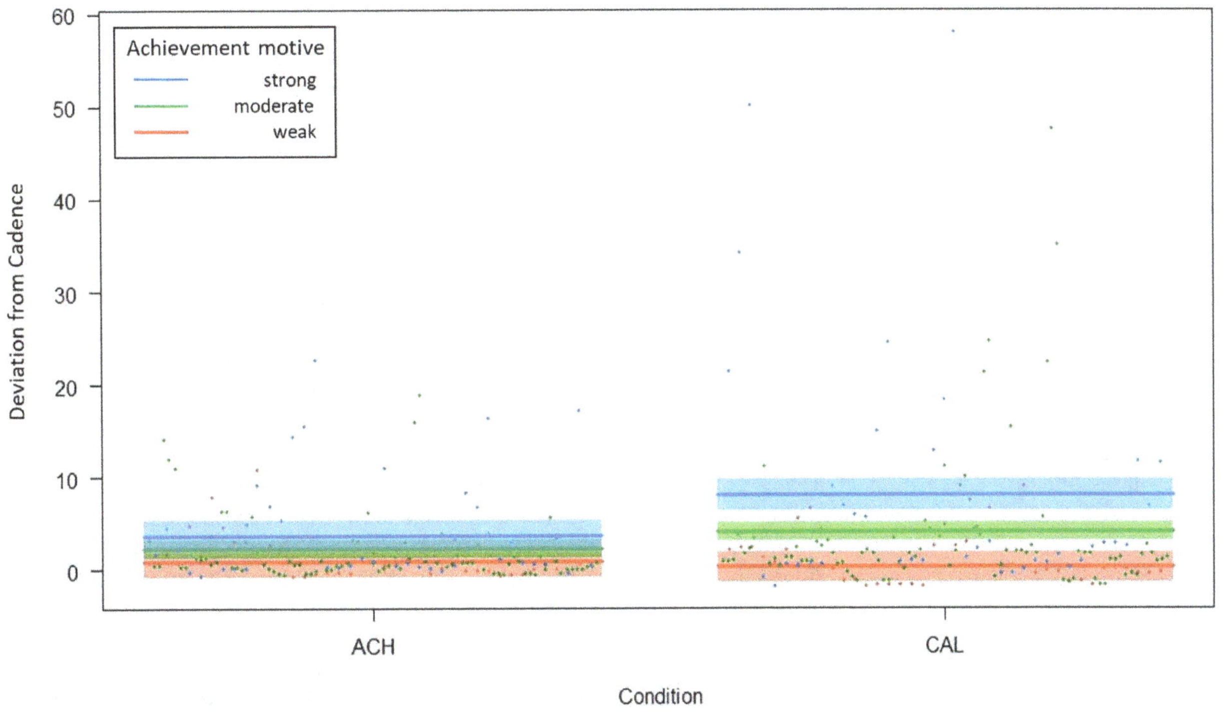

FIGURE 1 | Illustration of the Condition × Achievement Motive interaction. Note. Cadence means squared deviations from a cadence of 70 rpm, and thus, higher scores mean poorer performance. ACH: Achievement condiction, CAL: calibration conditions.

compliance with experimental instructions had guided their behavior. This is in contrast to participants with a strong achievement motive who appear to have regulated their effort depending on the incentive content of the instructions. Unexpectedly, the assumption made for the achievement condition was not supported by the data. Here, participants with a strong achievement motive did not perform better than participants with a weak achievement motive. An obvious reason is that participants with a weak achievement motive performed extremely well (very small deviations from cadence), and surpassing this level is virtually impossible. However, people with strong achievement motives should at least show the same performance. One explanation why they don't might be that - although we derived the components of the task instructions theoretically - we failed to create an experimental setting that incites the explicit achievement motive well. It might be that announcing an individual performance log did not directly promise to fulfill the desire to demonstrate one's performance. We should have extended the announcement by adding the information that their ergometer protocol would be published and therefore would be visible for others. Furthermore, as has been shown in the literature of achievement goal priming, using words as primes is not always effective (Harris et al., 2013). In addition, the effects of self-set goals might outweigh those of the priming, or stronger effects would be revealed from field rather than from laboratory settings (Chen et al., 2020).

It could also be that we did not only fail to incite the achievement motive in the achievement condition but that we even demotivated people with a strong achievement motive (as the positive correlation between achievement motive and deviation from cadence would support) by accidentally restricting their autonomy. Although the following considerations about autonomy and achievement motive refer to the implicit achievement motive, they could also apply to the explicit achievement motive: The incentive for people with a strong achievement motive is the autonomous mastery of challenging tasks (McClelland et al., 1953). As pointed out by Schultheiss (2008, p. 603), however, if people with a strong achievement motive "cannot chose and solve such tasks on their own terms, but are given explicit advice and direction on how to do it, they are likely to leave the field and invest no effort in the task" (see also Spangler, 1992). Reconsidering the instructions in the achievement condition, we might have put too much pressure on them by clearly directing them ("Your task is to keep the cadence of 70 rpm") and by demonstrating control by announcing that the experimenter monitors compliance with the instruction ("We can exactly figure out your precision of riding a specific cadence"). Future studies should give people with a strong explicit achievement motive more scope to choose the challenging task themselves. Most importantly, speculations about if and how the experimental manipulation had worked can be simply avoided by manipulations checks (e.g., asking participants how motivated they felt in each condition).

Furthermore, physical performance is only one single aspect of one's capability, and some (rather untrained) participants with strong achievement motives might not feel incited by this domain-specific performance setting. To avoid possibly domain-specific arousal of the achievement motive, we suggest adding the information to future study instructions that showing good performance in this endurance task is known to be an indicator of good performance in other domains of life (academia, workplace).

Limitations and Further Research Tasks

Our research leaves further open research questions that we aim to address in the following. In our study, we assessed explicit achievement motives because they are known to be triggered by social achievement incentives such as expectations from the experimenter, coaches, sport education teachers, and fitness instructors. However, next to the explicit achievement motive, the implicit achievement motive (unconsciously represented, based on affects), which is characterized by the enjoyment of challenging tasks and the anticipation of feeling proud after success (McClelland et al., 1953; Brunstein and Heckhausen, 2008), also plays a crucial role in sport performance (Gröpel et al., 2016). Implicit and explicit motives differ, among other things, in the incentives (social vs. activity incentives) that trigger them and lead to motive-relevant behavior. On the theoretical level, there is a clear-cut differentiation in regard to what type of incentives arouse which type of motive. Experimentally (and in everyday life), it is challenging to create incentives that map perfectly on this differentiation. Social and activity incentives cannot easily be isolated from each other. In the present laboratory study, it is highly probable that not only the result of the motor task motivated people to perform well or to save energy (explicit incentive) but also characteristics of the task itself. People with a strong *implicit* achievement motive might have been also attracted by, for example, the possibility to exceed their physical comfort zones and master a physically challenging task, regardless of the outcome of the activity (and therefore also regardless of being in the achievement or control group). We did not assess the implicit achievement motive and therewith cannot control for its influence on performance. A second way in which the implicit achievement motive might have undermined the hypothesized results is by being incongruent with the explicit achievement motive. The disconcordance between implicit and explicit motives causes impairment of well-being and motivation (Brunstein et al., 1998; Brunstein, 2010; Schüler, 2010) and requires self-control (Kehr, 2004; Schüler et al., 2019). However, all these are crucial for high performance in a strength endurance task.

Schüler (2010) took an even more extended perspective and examined the interplay between implicit and explicit achievement motives as well as achievement incentives. She found that achievement motive incongruence exerted stronger negative effects when individuals act in situations in which achievement incentives are present and arouse the conflict between the two motives. For the present study, this applies to the achievement condition but not the calibration condition. In brief, it might be that motive incongruence undermined the expected results only in the achievement condition (in which we found unexpected results) and left performance in the control condition (in which we found expected results) unaffected. Schüler (2010), however, analyzed effects on flow experience, and it is pure speculation (although theoretically plausible) that her findings also apply to motor performance. If we briefly accept this speculation as true, it still has to be explained why in the achievement condition, the motive incongruence reduced performance of people with a strong explicit achievement motive (and a weak implicit motive, Type 1 of motive incongruence) but not performance of people with a weak explicit achievement motive (and a strong implicit achievement motive, Type 2 of motive incongruence), who maintained their performance (see **Figure 1**). This can only be answered with another speculation. If a strong explicit achievement motive is not supported by the energy that is exerted in connection with a high implicit motive (Type 1 of incongruence), but this "energizing function" of implicit motives (McClelland et al., 1953) is needed for a strenuous endurance task, performance should be reduced. Type 2, in contrast, is characterized by a high implicit motive that remains unsatisfied, because a corresponding high explicit motive is lacking that elicits achievement-relevant behavior. In our laboratory session, however, the "achievement behavior" (holding a specific cadence) is pre-defined by the experimenter rather than initiated by the explicit achievement motive. The explicit achievement motive might not come into play here, and thus, the negative effects of this type of incongruence might therefore not be evinced. This explanation, however, is built on two speculations and has to be tested empirically.

Also, in reality, sport and exercise settings probably require a mixture of "respondent behavior" (McClelland, 1980) triggered by explicit motives and "operant behavior" triggered by implicit motives so that high standards of excellence can be achieved. Performance in a marathon race, for example, depends on the choice to participate in a large city marathon, for example, to fulfill the expectations of the running group and to demonstrate one's high-performance capacity to the public (social incentives, respondent behavior), and it depends on activity-inherent incentives, such as liking to run and enjoying that one's performance improves over time, that ensure long-term adherence to one's training program (activity incentives, operant behavior). Therefore, one imperative for future research is to assess behavior in settings that are closer to sports reality and allow, for example, spontaneously generated behavior (operant behavior) and examine its interplay with respondent behavior. Furthermore, more complex incentive patterns (e.g., social and activity incentives) and the assessment and arousal of implicit and explicit achievement motives have to be considered to overcome the artificiality of the laboratory and to better understand the complex interplay of implicit and explicit motives.

A further task for future research is to assess the mechanism that we assume to underlie the underperformance of people with strong achievement motives. The "worth" of performance behavior outcome can be assessed by asking participants how much they value the calibration task and the achievement task, respectively. Additionally, the willingness to invest effort has to be assessed with objective measures (cardiovascular effort indicators) or by assessing the self-reported willingness to invest effort.

In recent years, there has been a growing interest in studying the relationship between effective leadership and the ethical behavior of the leader (Kaptein, 2019; Gamarra and Girotto, 2021). For this reason, models oriented toward the ethical dimension of team leadership have recently emerged, such as what has been termed "authentic leadership," (Avolio and Gardner, 2005; Gardner et al., 2005a; Moriano et al., 2011). Walumbwa et al. (2008) which posit that authentic leadership comprises four related dimensions: self-awareness, internalized moral perspective, relational transparency, and balanced processing.

Self-awareness refers to the extent which a leader possesses accurate self-knowledge and uses that knowledge to demonstrate he or she is cognizant of their impact on others. Internalized moral perspective pertains to the degree in which a leader's behavior is directed by and is congruent with their personal values and moral standards. It represents a form of self-regulation which allows leaders to engage in ethical conduct even against external pressures. Relational transparency is a leader's presentation of their true thoughts and emotions in an open and transparent manner (vs. being fake or manipulative), while balanced processing is evident when a leader objectively considers and analyzes all relevant information before making decisions (Walumbwa et al., 2008).

Various contextually different studies have shown that authentic leadership is related to the well-being of the leader (Baron, 2012; Gatling and Harrah, 2014; Weiss et al., 2018), additionally improving followers' behavior, satisfaction, and performance (Walumbwa et al., 2008; Caza et al., 2010). In the realm of sports, it has been associated with higher levels of competence and perceived justice on the part of the coach (González-Ponce, 2018), as well as increased satisfaction, enjoyment and cohesion among the team (Bandura and Kavussanu, 2018), as well as greater team cohesion; a relationship mediated by trust and sacrifice (Bandura et al., 2019). A study by McDowell et al. (2018) involving basketball players, the positive team climate presented a mediating effect between authentic leadership and psychological capital and player commitment.

Two of the most influential approaches to sports leadership have been: Leadership Behaviors Model of Sport Leadership (Smoll et al., 1978; Smoll and Smith, 1989) and Multidimensional Model of Sport Leadership (Chelladurai, 1978, 1990, 2007). There have been several programs aimed at training coaches in sports leadership skills which predominantly follow these approaches. One of the pioneers and most widely used is Coach Effectiveness Training (CET), by Smith et al. (1979), which aims to facilitate positive behavior on the part of coaches; likewise, to improve interactions with their athletes. Several studies have supported the usefulness of CET, resulting in more effective coach behaviors and better interactions (Sousa et al., 2008). Based on CET, the Mastery Approach to Coaching (MAC) (Smith et al., 2007; Smoll and Smith, 2009) emphasizes the importance of a task-oriented climate as generated by the coach rather than results-oriented. In this line, the MAC also recommends that coaches avoid post-error punishment and punitive technical instruction (Smoll and Smith, 2010; Vella and Perlman, 2014) in order to facilitate positive athletic behavior and promote a task-oriented climate.

The Transformational Leadership Approach to Coaching (TLAC) is another proposed approach to developing leadership skills. In essence, transformational leaders promote autonomous actions, pursuing the personal growth of athletes, as well as task cohesion, the satisfaction of needs, and intrinsic motivation Vella and Perlman, 2014). In youth sport contexts, the TLAC has been implemented with the aim of facilitating positive developmental outcomes among athletes (Vella et al., 2012, 2013) and has been employed to facilitate high performance among Olympic athletes as well (Din and Paskevich, 2013).

The convenience of this study is due to the influence that the coach has on the athletes, and also, putting in value the positive effects that authentic leadership has on athletes (Bandura and Kavussanu, 2018), it could be considered transcendent to seek ways to develop this style of leadership and observe the effects on different variables associated with the abilities to lead by the coach and how it affects the athletes.

The objective of this study was to investigate the effect of an authentic sports leadership training program on several variables affecting both the coaches participating in the program and their players. The efficacy of this intervention was tested by both coaches and their players using a before and after study design. Authentic coach leadership, perceived justice, coach competence, and collective efficacy was evaluated by the coaches. The same variables (excluding coach self-efficacy) along with the satisfaction with the coach and perceived need satisfaction was evaluated by the players. As a result, two main hypotheses were developed:

1. From the perspective of the coaches, it is expected that those coaches who received the training program (experimental group) will show a significant increase in the evaluation of their levels of authentic coach leadership, perceived justice, coach competence (total competence, motivation, decision-making, teaching and instruction of skills, and character influence), coach self-efficacy, and collective efficacy after the intervention in comparison with before, whereas no changes will be found in those coaches who did not receive the intervention (control group).

2. From the evaluation of the players, it is expected that those players whose coaches have received the training program (experimental group) will show an increase in their perception of their coach's authentic leadership, perceived justice, coach competence (total competence, motivating, decision-making, teaching and instruction of skills, and character influence), collective efficacy, satisfaction with the coach, and coach support of their basic psychological needs (competence, autonomy, and relatedness).

CONCLUSION

To make use of the recency effect (Ebbinghaus, 1913; Murdock, 1962), we would like to close with a positive statement. Experimenters, coaches, sport education teachers, and fitness instructors can easily assist people by paying careful attention to the instructions they give. Although our study has not figured out what brings out the best from people with a strong achievement motive, it shows what instructions should be avoided because they harm people with a strong achievement motive. Practitioners in the sport context, for example, are recommended to avoid task instructions that do not contain any achievement incentives. They might function for some people who might exercise only to meet the expectations of others (in our study, people with a weak achievement motive who complied with instructions of the experimenter) but would discriminate against people with a strong achievement motive. But also for the former, the longer-term perspective does not look good: According to Self-Determination Theory (Deci and Ryan, 1985), external regulation (perform a behavior because somebody else wants me to do it) and introjected regulation (do it because you feel obligated) are less good predictors for the maintenance of sport and exercise over a longer time (for an overview, see Hagger and Chatzisarantis, 2008). We encourage researchers and people in the applied setting to consider individual differences in motives. This might help to better understand phenomena such as the assumed unwillingness to invest effort and the underperformance of people who are expected to perform well.

ETHICS STATEMENT

The studies involving human participants were reviewed and approved by Ethical committee of University of Konstanz. The patients/participants provided their written informed consent to participate in this study.

AUTHOR CONTRIBUTIONS

JS and WW conceived the study design, conducted the study, and performed the statistical analyses together. JS wrote the first draft of the manuscript. WW revised and finalized the manuscript.

REFERENCES

Andrews, J. D. W. (1967). The achievement motive and advancement in two types of organizations. *J. Pers. Soc. Psychol.* 6, 163–168. doi: 10.1037/h0024689

Bargh, J. A., Lee-Chai, A., Barndollar, K., Gollwitzer, P., and Trötschel, R. (2001). The automated will: nonconscious activation and pursuit of behavioral goals. *J. Pers. Soc. Psychol.* 81, 1014–1027. doi: 10.1037/0022-3514.81.6.1014

Bates, D., Maechler, M., Bolker, B., and Walker, S. (2015). Fitting linear mixed-effects models using lme4. *J. Stat. Softw.* 67, 1–48. doi: 10.18637/jss.v067.i01

Beckmann, J., and Heckhausen, H. (2018a). "Motivation as a function of expectancy and incentive," in *Motivation and Action*, eds J. Heckhausen and H. Heckhausen (Cham: Springer), 163–220.

Beckmann, J., and Heckhausen, H. (2018b). "Situational determinants of behavior," in *Motivation and Action*, eds J. Heckhausen and H. Heckhausen (Cham: Springer), 113–162.

Biernat, M. (1989). Motives and values to achieve: different constructs with different effects. *J. Pers.* 57, 69–95. doi: 10.1111/j.1467-6494.1989.tb00761.x

Brehm, J. W., and Self, E. A. (1989). The intensity of motivation. *Annu. Rev. Psychol.* 40, 109–131. doi: 10.1146/annurev.ps.40.020189.000545

Breidebach, G. (2012). *Bildungsbenachteiligung: Warum die Einen Nicht Können Und Die Anderen Nicht Wollen [Educational Disadvantage: Why Some Can't and Some Won't]*. Hamburg: Kovac.

Breidebach, G. (2017). *Mosk - Training zur Förderung von Motivation und Selbstkonzept [Mosk - Training to Promote Motivation and Self-Concept.]* Hamburg: Kovac.

Breidebach, G., and Gruber, N. (2019). Erfolgssicherheit und -gewissheit (esg) – Konstitution einer "Hoffnung auf Erfolg"-Subkategorie im Rahmen des Auswertungsschlüssels nach Heckhausen zur Steigerung der Güte des TAT [sureness and certainty of success (esg) – development of a "hope of success" subcategory for the coding system of Heckhausen to increase the quality of the TAT]. *Diagnostica* 65, 75–85. doi: 10.1026/0012-1924/a000215

Brunstein, J. C. (2010). "Implicit motives and explicit goals: the role of motivational congruence in emotional well-being," in *Implicit Motives*, eds O. C. Schultheiss and J. C. Brunstein (Oxford: Oxford University Press), 347–374.

Brunstein, J. C., and Heckhausen, H. (2008). "Achievement motivation," in *Motivation and Action*, eds J. Heckhausen and H. Heckhausen (Cambridge: Cambridge University Press), 137–183.

Brunstein, J. C., and Hoyer, S. (2002). Implizites versus explizites Leistungsstreben: Befunde zur Unabhängigkeit zweier Motivsysteme [implicit versus explicit achievement motivation: findings on the independence of two motivational systems]. *Z. Pädagog. Psychol.* 16, 51–62. doi: 10.1024//1010-0652.16.1.51

Brunstein, J. C., and Maier, G. W. (2005). Implicit and self-attributed motives to achieve: two separate but interacting needs. *J. Pers. Soc. Psychol.* 89, 205–222. doi: 10.1037/0022-3514.89.2.205

Brunstein, J. C., Schultheiss, O. C., and Grässmann, R. (1998). Personal goals and emotional well-being: the moderating role of motive dispositions. *J. Pers. Soc. Psychol.* 75, 494–508. doi: 10.1037/0022-3514.75.2.494

Chen, X., Latham, G. P., Piccolo, R. F., and Itzchakov, G. (2020). An enumerative review and a meta-analysis of primed goal effects on organizational behavior. *Appl. Psychol.* 44, 1–38. doi: 10.1111/apps.12239

Dahme, G., Jungnickel, D., and Rathje, H. (1993). Güteeigenschaften der achievement motives scale (ams) von Gjesme und Nygard (1970) in der deutschen Übersetzung von Göttert und Kuhl: Vergleich der Kennwerte norwegischer und deutscher Stichproben [validation data for the achievement motives scale (ams) by Gjesme and Nygard (1970) in the german version by Göttert and Kuhl: comparison of the data from the norwegian and the german samples]. *Diagnostica* 39, 257–270.

Deci, E. L., and Ryan, R. M. (1985). *Intrinsic Motivation and Self-Determination in Human Behavior*. New York, NY: Plenum Press.

Ebbinghaus, H. (1913). *On Memory: A Contribution to Experimental Psychology*. New York, NY: Teacher College.

Elbe, A.-M., and Wenhold, F. (2005). Cross-cultural test-control criteria for the achievement motives scale-sport. *Int. J. Sport Exerc. Psychol.* 3, 163–177. doi: 10.1080/1612197X.2005.9671765

Elbe, A.-M., Wenhold, F., and Müller, D. (2005). Zur Reliabilität und Validität der achievement motive scale-sport [On the reliability and validity of the achievement motive scale-sport]. *Z. Sportpsychol.* 12, 57–68. doi: 10.1026/1612-5010.12.2.57

Engeser, S., and Baumann, N. (2014). Does achievement motivation mediate the semantic achievement priming effect? *J. Exp. Psychol. Gen.* 143, 1861–1874. doi: 10.1037/a0036864

Engeser, S., Baumann, N., and Baum, I. (2016). Schoolbook texts: behavioral achievement priming in math and language. *PLoS One* 11:e015049. doi: 10.1371/journal.pone.0150497

Faul, F., Erdfelder, E., Buchner, A., and Lang, A. G. (2009). Statistical power analyses using G*Power 3.1: tests for correlation and regression analyses. *Behav. Res. Methods* 41, 1149–1160. doi: 10.3758/brm.41.4.1149

Fodor, E. M., and Carver, R. A. (2000). Achievement and power motives, performance feedback, and creativity. *J. Res. Pers.* 34, 280–306. doi: 10.1006/jrpe.2000.2289

French, E. G. (1958). "Some characteristics of achievement motivation," in *Motives in Fantasy, Action, and Society*, ed. J. W. Atkinson (Princeton, NJ: Van Nostrand), 270–277.

Gendolla, G. H. E., and Richter, M. (2010). Effort mobilization when the self is involved: some lessons from the cardiovascular system. *Rev. Gen. Psychol.* 14, 212–226. doi: 10.1037/a0019742

Giboin, L.-S., Gruber, M., Schüler, J., and Wolff, W. (2019). Investigating performance in a strenuous physical task from the perspective of self-control. *Brain Sci.* 9:317. doi: 10.3390/brainsci9110317

Gröpel, P., Wegner, M., and Schüler, J. (2016). Achievement motive and sport participation. *Psychol. Sport Exerc.* 27, 93–100. doi: 10.1016/j.psychsport.2016.08.007

Hagger, M., and Chatzisarantis, N. (2008). Self-determination theory and the psychology of exercise. *Int. Rev. Sport Exerc. Psychol.* 1, 79–103. doi: 10.1080/17509840701827437

Harris, C. R., Coburn, N., Rohrer, D., and Pashler, H. (2013). Two failures to replicate high-performance-goal priming effects. *PLoS One* 8:e72467. doi: 10.1371/journal.pone.0072467

Hirsch, A., Bieleke, M., Schüler, J., and Wolff, W. (2020). Implicit theories about athletic ability modulate the effects of if-then planning on performance in a standardized endurance task. *Int. J. Environ. Res. Public Health* 9:2576.doi: 10.31234/osf.io/exwnf

Kehr, H. M. (2004). Implicit/ explicit motive discrepancies and volitional depletion among managers. *Pers. Soc. Psychol. Bull.* 30, 315–327. doi: 10.1177/0146167203256967

Lowell, E. L. (1952). The effect of need for achievement on learning and speed of performance. *J. Psychol.* 33, 31–40. doi: 10.1080/00223980.1952.9712815

Manohar, S. G., Chong, T. T.-J., Apps, M. A. J., Batla, A., Stamelou, M., Jarman, P. R., et al. (2015). Reward pays the cost of noise reduction in motor and cognitive control. *Curr. Biol.* 25, 1707–1716. doi: 10.1016/j.cub.2015.05.038

McClelland, D. C. (1980). "Motive dispositions: the merits of operant and respondent measures," in *Review of Personality and Social Psychology*, ed. L. Wheeler (Beverly Hills, CA: Sage Publishing House), 10–41.

McClelland, D. C. (1985). *Human Motivation.* Glenview: Scott, Foresman & Co.

McClelland, D. C., Atkinson, J. W., Clark, R. A., and Lowell, E. L. (1953). *The Achievement Motive.* New York, NY: Appleton-Century-Crofts.

McClelland, D. C., Clark, R. A., Roby, T. B., and Atkinson, J. W. (1949). The projective expression of needs. Iv. The effect of the need for achievement on thematic apperception. *J. Exp. Psychol.* 39, 242–255. doi: 10.1037/h0062969

McClelland, D. C., and Franz, C. E. (1992). Motivational and other sources of work accomplishments in mid-life: a longitudinal study. *J. Pers.* 60, 679–707. doi: 10.1111/j.1467-6494.1992.tb00270.x

McClelland, D. C., Koestner, R., and Weinberger, J. (1989). How do self-attributed and implicit motives differ? *Psychol. Rev.* 96, 690–702. doi: 10.1037/0033-295X.96.4.690

McKeachie, W. J. (1961). "Motivation, teaching methods, and college learning," in *Nebraska Symposium on Motivation*, ed. M. R. Jones (Lincoln: University of Nebraska Press), 111–142.

Murdock, B. B. (1962). The serial position effect of free recall. *J. Exp. Psychol.* 64, 482–488. doi: 10.1037/h0045106

O'Connor, P. A., Atkinson, J. W., and Horner, M. A. (1966). "Motivational implications of ability grouping in schools," in *A Theory of Achievement Motivation*, eds J. W. Atkinson and N. T. Feather (New York, NY: Wiley).

Pang, J. S. (2010). "Content coding methods in implicit motive assessment: standards of measurement and best practices for the picture story exercise," in *Implicit Motives*, eds O. C. Schultheiss and J. C. Brunstein (Oxford: Oxford University Press).

Puca, R. M., and Schmalt, H. D. (1999). Task enjoyment: a mediator between achievement motives and performance. *Motiv. Emot.* 23, 15–29. doi: 10.1023/A:1021327300925

R Core Team (2017). *R: A Language and Environment for Statistical Computing.* Vienna: R Foundation for Statistical Computing.

Sariyska, R., Lachmann, B., Cheng, C., Gnisci, A., Sergi, I., Pace, A., et al. (2019). The motivation for facebook use – is it a matter of bonding or control over others? Evidence from a cross-cultural study. *J. Individ. Differ.* 40, 26–35. doi: 10.1027/1614-0001/a000273

Schönbrodt, F. D., and Gerstenberg, F. X. R. (2012). An irt analysis of motive questionnaires: the unified motive scales. *J. Res. Pers.* 46, 725–742. doi: 10.1016/j.jrp.2012.08.010

Schüler, J. (2010). Achievement incentives determine the effects of achievement-motive incongruence on flow experience. *Motiv. Emot.* 34, 2–14. doi: 10.1007/s11031-009-9150-4

Schüler, J., Zimanyi, Z., and Wegner, M. (2019). Paved, graveled, and stony paths to high performance: theoretical considerations on self-control demands of achievement goals based on implicit and explicit motives. *Perform. Enhanc. Health* 7:100146. doi: 10.1016/j.peh.2019.100146

Schultheiss, O. C. (2008). "Implicit motives," in *Handbook of Personality: Theory and Research*, 3rd Edn, eds O. P. John, R. W. Robins, and L. A. Pervin (New York: Guilford Press), 603–633.

Schultheiss, O. C., and Köllner, M. (2014). "Implicit motives and the development of competencies: a virtuous-circle model of motive-driven learning," in *International Handbook of Emotions in Education*, eds R. Pekrun and L. Linnenbrink-Garcia (New York: Taylor and Francis/Routledge), 73–95.

Schwarzer, R., Diehl, M., and Schmitz, G. C. (1999). *The Self-Regulation Scale.* Available online at: http://userpage.fu-berlin.de/~health/selfreg.htm (accessed May 12, 2020).

Spangler, W. D. (1992). Validity of questionnaire and TAT measures of need for achievement: two meta-analyses. *Psychol. Bull.* 112, 140–154. doi: 10.1037/0033-2909.112.1.140

Thurstone, L. L. (1937). Ability, motivation, and speed. *Psychometrika* 2, 249–254. doi: 10.1007/BF02287896

Wegner, M., Sieber, V., and Schüler, J. (2014). "Implicit motives of elite athletes, sport students, and non-sport students: power, affiliation, and achievement," in *Motivation: Psychology, Strategies and Impact on Performance*, ed. R. Morisson (New York, NY: Nova Publishers), 109–124.

Whitty, A. G., Murphy, A. J., Coutts, A. J., and Watsford, M. L. (2009). Factors associated with the selection of the freely chosen cadence in non-cyclists. *Eur. J. Appl. Physiol.* 106, 705–712. doi: 10.1007/s00421-009-1071-0

Wigfield, A., and Eccles, J. S. (2000). Expectancy-value theory of achievement motivation. *Contemp. Educ. Psychol.* 25, 68–81. doi: 10.1006/ceps.1999.1015

Winter, D. G. (1994). *Manual for Scoring Motive Imagery in Running Text (version 4.2).* Ann Arbor, MI: University of Michigan.

World Medical Association. (2013). World medical association declaration of helsinki: ethical principles for medical research involving human subjects. *JAMA* 310, 2191–2194. doi: 10.1001/jama.2013.281053

Wright, R. A. (2008). Refining the prediction of effort: brehm's distinction between potential motivation and motivation intensity. *Soc. Pers. Psychol. Compass* 2, 682–701. doi: 10.1111/j.1751-9004.2008.00093.x

25

Memory Reactivation and its Effect on Exercise Performance and Heart Rate

*Abhishek G. Dhawan**

Agricultural Development Trust, Baramati, India

Correspondence:
Abhishek G. Dhawan
abhishek27099@gmail.com

Neuronal ensemble and brain plasticity both play an important role in memory consolidation and subsequently memory reactivation. To date, many studies have been designed to study the effect of exercise, heart-rate variability, and other factors on brain plasticity and memory. Here, we present a case study in which we have demonstrated the effect of neuronal ensemble and memory formed during High-intensity aerobic training (VO2 max) and Target Heart-Rate (THR) training and the effect of reactivation of same memory on THR and performance. Of note is the fact that the reactivation and recreation of memory stimulus learned and formed during High-intensity training, such as place, time, odor, and other conditions, can elevate the THR to the same previous peak zone even at low intensity. This demonstrates that reactivation of previously acquired memory or using the stimulation from the neuronal ensemble of consolidated memory during the specific event of training may exert similar physiological effects on exercise or the body to those that are learned during the memory acquisition phase. Hence, as exercise has an effect on memory, the memories may have an effect on exercise performances.

Keywords: neuronal ensemble, memory reactivation, THR, peak heart rate, exercise, aerobic

INTRODUCTION

Memories play an important role in cognitive as well as functional behavior. Exercise and memories have been an important part of studies in recent years. The effects of exercise on memory consolidation, Neurogenesis, and Neuroplasticity have been observed on a different scale. The paradoxical relationship has not been thoroughly observed or studied. The memory consolidation and reactivation incorporate neuro-cortical paradigms as well as physiological shifts. As motor and sensory inputs play an important role in memory formation, the studies on memory reactivation and its physiological effects on biological systems need to be understood as part of learning during memory encoding. To begin the case study, we have created an overview of the fundamentals of exercise and memory.

MEMORY AND NEURONAL ENSEMBLE

The memory is a collection of neurons and can be classified as declarative, procedural, or cognitive memory. The basic unit of memory in the brain is depicted as an Engram. An Engram is a unit of cognitive facts inside the brain, theorized to be representative of how memories are stored as biophysical or biochemical changes in response to sensory stimuli (Ungerleider et al., 2002; Herz et al., 2004; Moehring, 2019). The formation of memory is not just the acquisition of information, but it is more profoundly a three-step process: acquisition, consolidation, and reactivation. The neurons involved in memory formation are populated across the brain space, forming a neuronal ensemble. A neuronal ensemble (Qin et al., 1997; Sutherland and McNaughton, 2000) is a population of nervous system cells involved in a particular neural computation where computation could be a complete path of a different set of neurons involved in memory. Memory is often imbued with multisensory richness; the recall of an event can be endowed with the sights, sounds, and smells of its prior occurrence (Musso et al., 1999; Ramachandran and Rogers-Ramachandran, 2000; Flor et al., 2013). All types of sensory inputs are encoded in memory learned during acquisition. Memory Consolidation is the process of stabilizing a memory trace after the initial acquisition and making it available for long term archive and reactivation (Moorman and Miner, 1997; Lundborg, 2000; Banks, 2016). It is usually considered to consist of two specific processes: synaptic consolidation and systemic consolidation. It can be considered an interplay between multiple cortical brain regions, and it has a prominent role in the hippocampus.

The reactivation of memory triggers the whole path of an ensemble: neurons that wire together fire together. The retrieving of these memories involve the reactivation of neural ensembles that were established during learning (Kolb and Whishaw, 1998; Lane et al., 2009; Flor et al., 2013). The well set of an experiment performed using optogenetics demonstrates that reactivation of a set of neurons reactivates the same encoded emotional set (Laubach et al., 2000; Critchley et al., 2002; Sumbre et al., 2008; Smith et al., 2009). Any trigger to the partial sensory group may trigger the whole set of the ensemble, resulting in the complete retrieval of state or emotion.

When it comes to exercise, in this context, we have looked at aerobic exercise. *Aerobic exercise* mainly involves aerobic energy-generating process or exercise that involves primarily aerobic or free oxygen metabolic processes. This aerobic exercise could be categorized ranging from low intensity to high intensity. High-intensity exercises involve the peak performance of cardiorespiratory capacity. Peak Heart rate involves reaching above 85% of one's cardio capacity depending on age (Stiedl et al., 2004; Mahncke et al., 2006).

Training Methods and Settings

The person involved in the case study was a 28-year-old male with a BMI of 20. The program was adapted for Target heart rate (THR) training by High-intensity Interval training-based treadmill running. The training aimed to achieve the THR in peak HR for the maximum time possible, thus improving VO2 max (Tayler et al., 2013; Thomas et al., 2016). The device used to track the Heart rate and Program data was a Fitbit Charge 2. The case study divided training into five phases, namely, the initial training phase, training phase, peak phase, weight training/detraining phase, and memory reactivation phase.

The maximum aerobic capacity or max heart rate (HR) was calculated by a formula created by Nes et al. (2013): $HRmax = 211 - (0.64 \times age)$, which is 193 bpm. The peak zone or maximum THR to peak zone (i.e., 85% and above of the maximum aerobic capacity) is >85% of 193. The training type used was High-Intensity Interval training (HIIT). High-intensity Interval training is built upon alternating between short, high-intensity bursts of energy with slower recovery phases throughout a single workout. Initially starting with steady-state cardio, this method gradually progresses to HIIT. It starts with an initial warm-up phase followed by alternating high-intensity running and slow walking recovery bursts; lastly, there is a cool-down phase. The aerobic detraining phase was achieved by inducing weight training. The weight training work out was low to mid-intensity weight training.

The main parameters considered for evolution were the heart rate zone and graph, the number of steps per exercise session, the calories burnt, and the duration of the exercise. The conditions set for training were considered to be the timing of training and the intensity of the treadmill, including speed in km/hr and inclination. The training was done in the morning session. Before training, the subject was regularly exercising/running for 20–30 min a day for 6 months. The average foot stride was of 2.5ft. The average room temperature varied from (22 ± 2) Celsius in winter to (31 ± 3) Celsius in summer. The activity tracker data report consists of the date, time, HR graph, Calorie burn graph, step count, HR zone, etc.

CASE STUDY

Initial Training

This consisted of 5 km running on a treadmill within approximate 40 (±5) min. The initial warm-up burst was 3 KM/Hr to 6 KM/Hr walk for 5–7 min. The maximum speed of highest intensity per burst was 12 KM/Hr with every burst of 1 min, and the lowest was 6 KM/Hr for a low-intensity bout with every burst of 1 min. Total High- and Low-intensity alternating bursts was on average 25–29 min. The last 2–3 min phase consisted of the cool down. As shown in **Figure 1**, the average step count was (5,200 ± 400) steps per exercise session, summating to an average of 5 km on the ground running. The average calorie burn was (400 ± 30) calories. The peak heart zone (85 to 100 percent of the maximum HR) maintained was 4 (±2 min). The maximum maintained zone was the cardio zone (70 to 84 percent of your maximum heart rate). This training was varied to 4–5 days a week for nearly 7 months. The treadmill inclination varied by 2% (±1).

Peak Phase

After the initial training, the peak performance stage was reached. As shown in **Figure 2**, the average step count was 5,600 (±500) steps per exercise session, resulting in an average of 5.5 (±0.5) km on the ground running. The average calorie burn was 470/±30 calories. The enhancement to VO2 Max was seen. The peak heart zone (85 to 100 percent of your maximum heart rate) that was maintained for 15 min (±4). The maximum maintained zone was the peak heart rate zone. The cardio zone was maintained for an average 15 (±4) min (70 to 84 percent of your maximum heart rate). All treadmill training parameters were, on average, the same as the initial phase.

Post Peak Phase

After the peak performance stage was reached, the subject maintained a regular training schedule for 3–4 days a week,

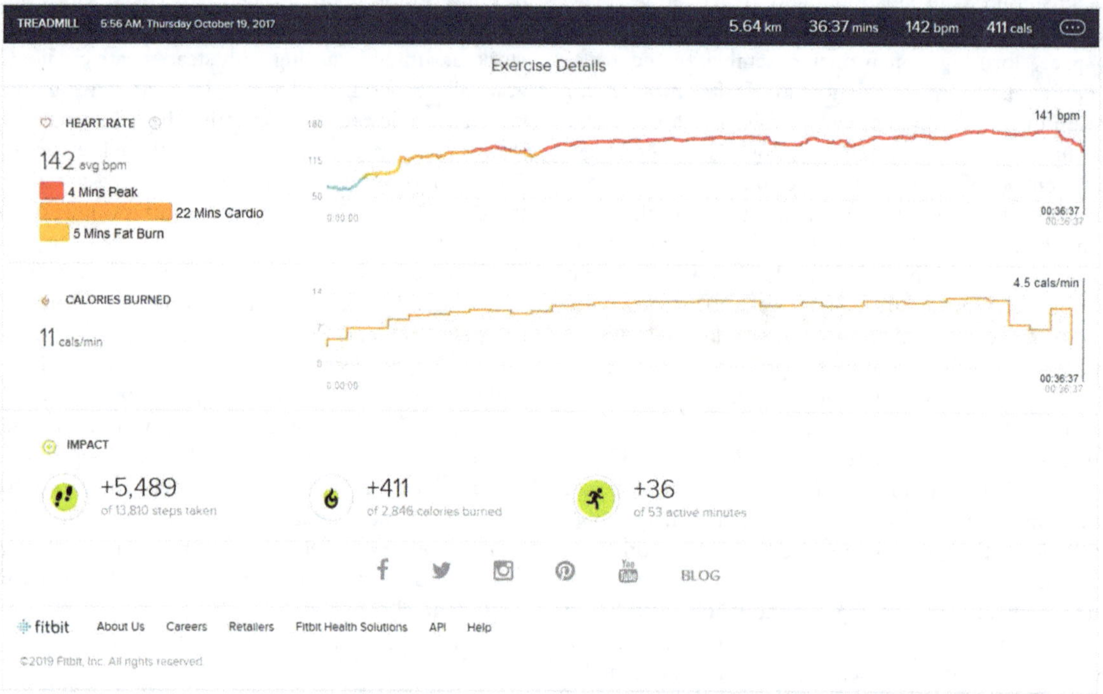

FIGURE 1 | Analysis report during one of the initial training months.

FIGURE 2 | Analysis report during one of the Peak phase achieved months.

with a reduction in treadmill training parameters concerning the intensity of bursts, number of bursts per exercise, and high burst time duration. The main aim of the schedule was to maintain the peak heart performance achieved during training. As shown in **Figure 3**, the maintained VO2 Max was seen. The peak heart zone (85–100% of your maximum heart rate) maintained was 14 min

FIGURE 3 | Analysis report during on one of the days of the maintenance phase months after months of peak phase being achieved.

(±4). The maximum maintained zone was the peak heart rate zone. The cardio zone was maintained for an average of 16 (±4) min (70 to 84% of your maximum heart rate).

Weight Training Phase/Aerobic Detraining

Following continuous induction of high-intensity aerobic exercise for almost 1.5 years, remarkable weight loss (10 ± 0.5 Kg) and subsequent muscle loss was seen. So, the partial detraining from aerobic exercise and added weight training was achieved. Weight training consisted of 2 days of weight training followed by cardio training for 1 day and a following 2 days of weight training. Weight training was low to mid intensity supplemented by a protein diet with 1–1.2 gm protein per kg in the natural form. No as shown in **Figure 4**, peak HR zone was maintained. The maximum HR zone maintained was the fat burn zone for an average of 22 (±10) min. Average exercise lasts for 40 min (±5). The average step count was 2,100 (±500) steps per exercise bout, coming to an average of 1.5 (±0.5) km. The average calorie burned was 250/±30 calories.

Memory Reactivation

This was very important phase to be noted. After 3 months of treadmill activity of regular steady sate jogging/walking was added at a speed of 6 km/Hr for just 10 min (±3) at the end of weight training without any HIIT or high intensity burst, the heart rate suddenly peaked to the peak HR zone. The place and the time spent on the treadmill were all similar stimuli to that used during peak HR training. There was no high inclination of increment in the speed to reach peak HR. As shown in **Figure 5**, even the average distance covered after 10 min on the treadmill was not more than the 1.2 km average, and that is despite the total steps taken being close to 3,000 in the whole session.

To cross verify whether this was the effect of memory reactivation, i.e., the same stimulus as time, odor, temperature, place, and equipment, four different settings were tested. First, the treadmill session was added to the first part of weight training. Second, we tested the effect of running the whole session outdoors or in a completely different environment. Third, we changed the treadmill environment by changing the complete stimulus other than that previously used. Last, we carried out reverification after a few months under the same stimulus.

In the first trial, the result was the same as with the stimulus that was used during training when added at the start of weight training instead of at the end; HR was easily raised to the peak zone. It was tested for an average of 15 min. The heart rate was triggered to reach toward the peak HR zone in just couple of minutes. During the weight training session, it varied in the fat burn zone.

As shown in **Figure 6**, during the second verification trial, the subject was made to run for 38 min (±2) in an outdoor non-similar stimulus environment with HIIT-type running. Of note was the fact that the heart rate remained in the cardio and fat burn zone and did not reach the peak HR. The distance was 4.6 km, and the step count was 4,870. Looking at distance covered, the step count, and the calorie burn graph, we can see that it was similar to the training or peak phase data, but changes in the environment resulted in different HR zones, and this was after nearly 5 months of aerobic partial detraining.

FIGURE 4 | Analysis report on one of the days during weight training phase.

FIGURE 5 | Analysis report on the addition of the same environment stimulus of treadmill jogging to weight training and HR raising to peak phase.

As shown in **Figures 7**, **8**, during the third verification trial, yjr subject was made to run for 12 min (±2) in a non-similar treadmill stimulus environment with HIIT-type running during his weight training session of an average of 37 min. The location, equipment, and environment (Rasch and Born, 2007) was changed completely.

FIGURE 6 | Analysis report on the addition of same environment stimulus of treadmill jogging at the start of weight training instead of the end of weight training and HR raising to peak phase.

FIGURE 7 | Analysis report on the addition of different environment stimulus in cardio training and HR not raising to the peak zone.

Of note was the fact that the heart rate remained in the cardio and fat burn zone and did not reach the peak HR.

In the fourth trial, the subject was weight trained in the same environment (Rasch and Born, 2007; Van Someren et al., 2011; Schedlbauer et al., 2015) after a few days of

FIGURE 8 | Analysis report on the addition of different environment stimuli to weight training and the HR not raising above the peak zone.

FIGURE 9 | Analysis report reactivation of memory/environment stimulus during weight training and HR raising to peak zone, similarly to how it does during the memory acquisition phase.

discontinuation with the addition of cardio training at the end of session, i.e., a similar treadmill stimulus environment with slow jogging of 6 km/Hr during the weight training session with the same place, time, equipment, etc, As shown in **Figure 9**, the heart rate was easily raised to the peak zone. It was tested for 12 min average. Heart rate was triggered to reach the peak HR zone in just a couple of minutes.

DISCUSSION

From this case study, it is of note that whenever the subject was in an environment (Rasch and Born, 2007; Wimmer and Büchel, 2015; Yanagisawa et al., 2016) that was similar to during training, the physiological response—in this case, the peak heart rate—was elevated to the same intensity zone, i.e., peak HR even with less or minimal physical effort, which was quite unexpected. The loss of efficiency after detraining was an expected factor that was observed in outdoor running after detaining, but the above result is opposite when it comes to peak HR during simple walking/jogging after weight training under the same stimulus. After partial detraining or weight training of about 6 months, aş seen in second trial, the subject was not easily able to reach peak HR in a non-stimulus environment. The distinguishable thing is that, when the subject is confronted with same stimulus, even after same detraining phase, the subject was easily able to reach the peak HR. This is indicative of the predictable idea that the memory or neuronal reactivation may have physiological effects on the body that can extend to exercise performance. Many recent studies have linked the effect of memory reactivation to the physical responses (Hall et al., 1990; Flor et al., 2013; Banks, 2016) of body. Some studies, including that of V. S. Ramchandran et al., demonstrate that the pain acquired in disease and its memory during the pain phase have the same trigger effect, even after amputation of that part, e.g., phantom limbs (Gottfried et al., 2004; Flor, 2008) (the physiological effect of memory and pain). Brain plasticity is an important aspect of human physiological adaption (Rasch et al., 2007; Guan et al., 2016; Forte et al., 2019). Neural plasticity plays an important role in making the adaption of training into reflexes. Rigorous training for days results in improved cognitive reserve and elevated neuronal synaptic plasticity (Aglioti et al., 1994). Many recent studies have correlated the link between olfactory and other stimulus during memory consolidation to memory reactivation (Banks, 2016) by same stimulus (Armstrong and Maresh, 1998; Nyberg et al., 2000; Herz et al., 2004). The more intense the training, the stronger its memory formation. Fear or stress memories activate sympathetic responses in the body that include HR, dilation of the pupil, etc. (Cotman and Berchtold, 2002; Chamine and Oken, 2016; Corder et al., 2019), and, correlating all the above literature, it can be said that the memory reactivation could trigger the same physiological responses consolidated during acquisition. This demonstrates that reactivation of previously acquired memory or using stimulation of neuronal ensemble of consolidated memory during the specific event of training may exert similar physiological effects on exercise or the body that are learned during memory acquisition phase. Hence, as exercise has effect on memory, the memories may have an effect on exercise performances.

ETHICS STATEMENT

The studies involving human participants were reviewed and approved by Agricultural Development Trust. The patients/participants provided their written informed consent to participate in this study.

AUTHOR CONTRIBUTIONS

The author confirms being the sole contributor of this work and has approved it for publication.

REFERENCES

Aglioti, S., Bonazzi, A., and Cortese, F. (1994). Phantom lower limb as a perceptual marker of neural plasticity in the mature human brain. *Proc. R. Soc. Lond. B* 25, 5273–5278. doi: 10.1098/rspb.1994.0039

Armstrong, L. E., and Maresh, C. M. (1998). Effects of training, environment, and host factors on the sweating response to exercise. *J. Sports Med. Phys. Fitness* 19 (Suppl. 2):S103–S105. doi: 10.1055/s-2007-971969

Banks, D. (2016). What is brain plasticity and why is it so important? *Neuroscience.*

Chamine, I., and Oken, B. S. (2016). Aroma effects on physiologic and cognitive function following acute stress: a mechanism investigation. *J. Altern Compl. Med.* 22, 713–721. doi: 10.1089/acm.2015.0349

Corder, G., Ahanonu, B., Grewe, B. F., Wang, D., Schnitzer, M. J., and Scherrer, G. (2019). An amygdalar neural ensemble that encodes the unpleasantness of pain. *Science* 363, 276–281. doi: 10.1126/science.aap8586

Cotman, G. W., and Berchtold, N. C. (2002). Exercise: a behavioral intervention to enhance brain health and plasticity. *Trends Neurosci.* 25, 295–301. doi: 10.1016/S0166-2236(02)02143-4

Critchley, H. D., Mathias, C. J., and Dolan, R. J. (2002). Fear conditioning in humans: the influence of awareness and autonomic arousal on functional neuroanatomy. *Neuron* 33, 653–663. doi: 10.1016/S0896-6273(02)00588-3

Flor, H. (2008). Maladaptive plasticity, memory for pain and phantom limb pain: review and suggestions for new therapies. *Exp. Rev. Neurotherap.* 8, 809–818. doi: 10.1586/14737175.8.5.809

Flor, H., Diers, M., and Andoh, J. (2013). The neural basis of phantom limb pain. *Trends Cognit. Sci.* 17, 307–308. doi: 10.1016/j.tics.2013.04.007

Forte, G., Favieri, F., and Casagrande, M. (2019). Heart rate variability and cognitive function: a systematic review. *Front. Neurosci.* 13:710. doi: 10.3389/fnins.2019.00710

Gottfried, J. A., Smith, A. P. R., Rugg, M. D., and Dolan, R. J. (2004). Remembrance of odors past: human olfactory cortex in cross-modal recognition memory. *Neuron* 42, 687–695. doi: 10.1016/S0896-6273(04)00270-3

Guan, J. S., Jiang, J., Xie, H., and Liu, K. L. (2016). How does the sparse memory "engram" neurons encode the memory of a spatial–temporal event? *Front. Neural Circ.* 10:61. doi: 10.3389/fncir.2016.00061

Hall, E. J., Flament, D., Fraser, C., and Lemon, R. N. (1990). Non-invasive brain stimulation reveals reorganized cortical outputs in amputees. *Neurosci. Lett.* 116, 379–386. doi: 10.1016/0304-3940(90)90105-I

Herz, R. S., Eliassen, J., Beland, S., and Souza, T. (2004). Neuroimaging evidence for the emotional potency of odor-evoked memory. *Neuropsychologia* 42, 371–378. doi: 10.1016/j.neuropsychologia.2003.08.009

Kolb, B., and Whishaw, I. Q. (1998). Brain plasticity and behavior. *Ann. Rev. Psychol.* 49, 43–64. doi: 10.1146/annurev.psych.49.1.43

Lane, R. D., McRae, K., Reiman, E. M., Chen, K., Ahern, G. L., and Thayer, J. F. (2009). Neural correlates of heart rate variability during emotion. *NeuroImage* 44, 213–222. doi: 10.1016/j.neuroimage.2008.07.056

Laubach, M., Wessberg, J., and Nicolelis, M. A. L. (2000). Cortical ensemble activity increasingly predicts behaviour outcomes during learning of a motor task. *Nature* 405, 567–571. doi: 10.1038/35014604

Lundborg, G. (2000). Brain plasticity and hand surgery: an overview. *J. Hand Surg.* 25, 242–252. doi: 10.1054/jhsb.1999.0339

Mahncke, H. W., Connor, B. B., Appelman, J., Ahsanuddin, O. N., Hardy, J. L., Wood, R. A., et al. (2006). Memory enhancement in healthy older adults using a brain plasticity-based training program: a randomized, controlled study. *Proc. Natl. Acade. Sci. U.S.A.* 103, 12523–12528. doi: 10.1073/pnas.0605194103

Moehring, F. (2019). A neural ensemble in the amygdala makes pain unpleasant. *Pain Res. Forum.*

Moorman, C., and Miner,. A. S. (1997). The impact of organizational memory on new product performance and creativity. *J. Marketing Res.* 34, 91–106. doi: 10.1177/002224379703400108

Musso, M., Weiller, C., Kiebel, S., Müller, S. P., Bülau, P., and Rijntjes, M. (1999). Training-induced brain plasticity in aphasia. *Brain* 122, 1781–1790. doi: 10.1093/brain/122.9.1781

Nes, B. M., Janszky, I., Wisløff, U., Støylen, A., and Karlsen, T. (2013). Age-predicted maximal heart rate in healthy subjects: The HUNT fitness study. *Scand. J. Med. Sci. Sports.* 23, 697–704. doi: 10.1111/j.1600-0838.2012.01445.x

Nyberg, L., Habib, R., McIntosh, A. R., and Tulving, E. (2000). Reactivation of encoding-related brain activity during memory retrieval. *Proc. Natl. Acad. Sci. U.S.A.* 97, 11120–11124. doi: 10.1073/pnas.97.20.11120

Qin, Y. L., Mcnaughton, B. L., Skaggs, W. E., and Barnes, C. A. (1997). Memory reprocessing in corticocortical and hippocampocortical neuronal ensembles. *Philos. Trans. R. Soc. Lond. B* 35, 1525–1533. doi: 10.1098/rstb.1997.0139

Ramachandran, V. S., and Rogers-Ramachandran, D. (2000). Phantom limbs and neural plasticity. *Arch. Neurol.* 57, 317–320. doi: 10.1001/archneur.57.3.317

Rasch, B., and Born, J. (2007). Maintaining memories by reactivation. *Curr. Opin. Neurobiol.* 17, 698–703. doi: 10.1016/j.conb.2007.11.007

Rasch, B., Büchel, C., Gais, S., and Born, J. (2007). Odor cues during slow-wave sleep prompt declarative memory consolidation. *Science* 315, 1426–1429. doi: 10.1126/science.1138581

Schedlbauer, A. M., Copara, M. S., Watrous, A. J., and Ekstrom, A. D. (2015). Multiple interacting brain areas underlie successful spatiotemporal memory retrieval in humans. *Sci. Rep.* 4:6431. doi: 10.1038/srep06431

Smith, G. E., Housen, P., Yaffe, K., Ruff, R., Kennison, R. F., Mahncke, H. W., et al. (2009). A cognitive training program based on principles of brain plasticity: results from the Improvement in Memory with Plasticity-based Adaptive Cognitive Training (IMPACT) Study. *J. Am. Geriatr. Soc.* 57, 594–603. doi: 10.1111/j.1532-5415.2008.02167.x

Stiedl, O., Tovote, P., Ogren, S. O., and Meyer, M. (2004). Behavioral and autonomic dynamics during contextual fear conditioning in mice. *Auton Neurosci.* 115, 15–27. doi: 10.1016/j.autneu.2004.07.006

Sumbre, G., Muto, A., Baier, H., and Poo, M. (2008). Entrained rhythmic activities of neuronal ensembles as perceptual memory of time interval. *Nature* 456, 102–106. doi: 10.1038/nature07351

Sutherland, G. R., and McNaughton, B. (2000). Memory trace reactivation in hippocampal and neocortical neuronal ensembles. *Curr. Opin. Neurobiol.* 10, 180–186. doi: 10.1016/S0959-4388(00)00079-9

Taya, F., Sun, Y., Babiloni, F., Thakor, N., and Bezerianos, A. (2015). Brain enhancement through cognitive training: a new insight from brain connectome. *Front. Syst. Neurosci.* 9:44. doi: 10.3389/fnsys.2015.00044

Tayler, K. K., Tanaka, K. Z., Reijmers, L. G., and Wiltgen, B. J. (2013). Reactivation of neural ensembles during the retrieval of recent and remote memory. *Curr. Biol.* 23, 99–106. doi: 10.1016/j.cub.2012.11.019

Thomas, R., Johnsen, L. K., Geertsen, S. S., Christiansen, L., Ritz, C., Roig, M., et al. (2016). Acute exercise and motor memory consolidation: the role of exercise intensity. *PLoS ONE* 11:e0159589. doi: 10.1371/journal.pone.0159589

Ungerleider, L. G., Doyon, J., and Karni, A. (2002). Imaging brain plasticity during motor skill learning. *Neurobiol. Learn. Memory* 78, 553–564. doi: 10.1006/nlme.2002.4091

Van Someren, E. J. W., Van Der Werf, Y. D., Roelfsema, P. R., Mansvelder, H. D., and Lopes da Silva, F. H. (2011). Slow brain oscillations of sleep, resting state and vigilance. *Prog. Brain Res.* 193, 3–15. doi: 10.1016/b978-0-444-53839-0.00001-6

Wimmer, G. E., and Büchel, G. (2015). Pain to remember: a single incidental association with pain leads to increased memory for neutral items one year later. *Front. Syst. Neurosci.* 9:44. doi: 10.1101/035212

Yanagisawa, T., Fukuma, R., Seymour, B., Hosomi, K., Kishima, H., Shimizu, T., et al. (2016). Induced sensorimotor brain plasticity controls pain in phantom limb patients. *Nat. Commun.* 7:13209. doi: 10.1038/ncomms13209

Permissions

All chapters in this book were first published by Frontiers; hereby published with permission under the Creative Commons Attribution License or equivalent. Every chapter published in this book has been scrutinized by our experts. Their significance has been extensively debated. The topics covered herein carry significant findings which will fuel the growth of the discipline. They may even be implemented as practical applications or may be referred to as a beginning point for another development.

The contributors of this book come from diverse backgrounds, making this book a truly international effort. This book will bring forth new frontiers with its revolutionizing research information and detailed analysis of the nascent developments around the world.

We would like to thank all the contributing authors for lending their expertise to make the book truly unique. They have played a crucial role in the development of this book. Without their invaluable contributions this book wouldn't have been possible. They have made vital efforts to compile up to date information on the varied aspects of this subject to make this book a valuable addition to the collection of many professionals and students.

This book was conceptualized with the vision of imparting up-to-date information and advanced data in this field. To ensure the same, a matchless editorial board was set up. Every individual on the board went through rigorous rounds of assessment to prove their worth. After which they invested a large part of their time researching and compiling the most relevant data for our readers.

The editorial board has been involved in producing this book since its inception. They have spent rigorous hours researching and exploring the diverse topics which have resulted in the successful publishing of this book. They have passed on their knowledge of decades through this book. To expedite this challenging task, the publisher supported the team at every step. A small team of assistant editors was also appointed to further simplify the editing procedure and attain best results for the readers.

Apart from the editorial board, the designing team has also invested a significant amount of their time in understanding the subject and creating the most relevant covers. They scrutinized every image to scout for the most suitable representation of the subject and create an appropriate cover for the book.

The publishing team has been an ardent support to the editorial, designing and production team. Their endless efforts to recruit the best for this project, has resulted in the accomplishment of this book. They are a veteran in the field of academics and their pool of knowledge is as vast as their experience in printing. Their expertise and guidance has proved useful at every step. Their uncompromising quality standards have made this book an exceptional effort. Their encouragement from time to time has been an inspiration for everyone.

The publisher and the editorial board hope that this book will prove to be a valuable piece of knowledge for researchers, students, practitioners and scholars across the globe.

List of Contributors

Aleksandra Samełko and Anna Kuk
Department of Pedagogy and Psychology of Physical Culture, Józef Piłsudski University of Physical Education in Warsaw, Warsaw, Poland

Monika Guszkowska
Department of Occupational Therapy, Józef Piłsudski University of Physical Education in Warsaw, Warsaw, Poland

Chunxiao Li
School of Physical Education and Sports Science, South China Normal University, Guangzhou, China

Chee Keng John Wang, Koon Teck Koh, Kwang San Steven Tan, Shern Meng Tan and Wee Boon Ang
National Institute of Education, Nanyang Technological University, Singapore, Singapore

Liang Han Wong and Huat Neo Connie Yeo
Physical, Sports and Outdoor Education Branch, Ministry of Education, Singapore, Singapore

Francisco Cano-Noguera, Ricardo José Ibáñez-Pérez, Francisco Cavas-García and Alfonso Martínez-Moreno
INGESPORTFI Research Group, Department of Physical Activity and Sports, University of Murcia, Murcia, Spain

Diego Soto Garcia
Department of Physical and Sports Education, Universidad de León, León, Spain

Juan Antonio García Herrero
Department of Didactics of Musical, Plastic and Body Expression, University of Salamanca, Salamanca, Spain

Rodrigo Jesús Carcedo
Department of Developmental and Educational Psychology, University of Salamanca, Salamanca, Spain

Mario Sánchez García
Education Faculty, Pontifical University of Salamanca, Salamanca, Spain

Karolina Kostorz
Department of Theory and Methodology of Physical Education, The Jerzy Kukuczka Academy of Physical Education in Katowice, Katowice, Poland
Department of Pedagogy, Psychology and Sociology, The Jerzy Kukuczka Academy of Physical Education in Katowice, Katowice, Poland

Krzysztof Sas-Nowosielski
Department of Theory and Methodology of Physical Education, The Jerzy Kukuczka Academy of Physical Education in Katowice, Katowice, Poland

Junyi Zhou
School of Physical Education and Sport Sciences, Fujian Normal University, Fuzhou, China
Provincial University Key Laboratory of Sport and Health Science, Fujian Normal University, Fuzhou, China
Key Laboratory of Kinesiological Evaluation General Administration of Sport of China, Fujian Normal University, Fuzhou, China

Guodong Zhang, Xin Chen, Yun Li, Liya Guo and Bing Li
Key Lab of Physical Fitness Evaluation and Motor Function Monitoring of General Administration of Sports of China, College of Physical Education, Institute of Sports Science, Southwest University, Chongqing, China

Luxia Xiao
Center for Mental Health Education, School of Psychology, Southwest University, Chongqing, China

Zi Yan
Health Sciences Department, Merrimack College, North Andover, MA, United States

Detlef H. Rost
Key Lab of Physical Fitness Evaluation and Motor Function Monitoring of General Administration of Sports of China, College of Physical Education, Institute of Sports Science, Southwest University, Chongqing, China
Department of Child and Youth Psychology, Faculty of Psychology, Philipps-University Marburg, Marburg, Germany

David L. Neumann
School of Applied Psychology, Griffith University, Gold Coast, QLD, Australia

Sepehr Jalali, Sian E. Martin and Kielan Yarrow
Department of Psychology, City, University of London, London, United Kingdom

Tandra Ghose
Department of Psychology, Technische Universität Kaiserslautern, Kaiserslautern, Germany

Richard M. Buscombe
School of Health Sport and Bioscience, University of East London, London, United Kingdom

Joshua A. Solomon
Centre for Applied Vision Science, City, University of London, London, United Kingdom

Fabrizio Sors
Department of Medicine, Surgery and Health Sciences, University of Trieste, Trieste, Italy
Department of Life Sciences University of Trieste, Trieste, Italy
Department of Medical Area, University of Udine, Udine, Italy

Alessandra Galmonte
Department of Medicine, Surgery and Health Sciences, University of Trieste, Trieste, Italy

Tiziano Agostini and Mauro Murgia
Department of Life Sciences, University of Trieste, Trieste, Italy

Vittoria Parisi
Department of Medical Area, University of Udine, Udine, Italy

Ilaria Santoro
Department of Life Sciences, University of Trieste, Trieste, Italy
Department of Medical Area, University of Udine, Udine, Italy

David Tomé Lourido
Department of Psycho-Socio-Educational Analysis and Intervention, University of Vigo, Vigo, Spain
Faculty of Psychology, National Distance Education University, Madrid, Spain

Marinella Coco
Department of Biomedical and Biotechnological Sciences, University of Catania, Catania, Italy

Andrea Buscemi
Study Center of Italian Osteopathy, Horus Social Cooperative, Catania-Ragusa, Italy

Valentina Perciavalle
Department of Educational Sciences, University of Catania, Catania, Italy

Tiziana Maci
Independent Researcher, Catania, Italy

Gianluca Galvano and Antonio M. F. Scavone
U.O.C. Diagnostic Imaging, Interventional Radiology and Neuroradiology, Garibaldi Hospital, Catania, Italy

Vincenzo Perciavalle
Faculty of Human and Society Sciences, Kore University of Enna, Enna, Italy

Donatella Di Corrado
Faculty of Human and Society Sciences, Kore University of Enna, Enna, Italy
Department of Human and Social Sciences, Kore University, Enna, Italy

Raúl Baños
Department of Physical Education and Sports Science, Autonomous University of Baja California, Ensenada, Mexico

Antonio Baena-Extremera and María del Mar Ortiz-Camacho
Department of Didactic of Corporal Expression, Faculty of Education Sciences, University of Granada, Granada, Spain

Sophia D. Papadopoulou
Department of Physical Education and Sport Science, Laboratory of Evaluation of Human Biological Performance, Aristotle University of Thessaloniki, Thessaloniki, Greece

Sousana K. Papadopoulou
Department of Nutritional Sciences and Dietetics, International Hellenic University, Thessaloniki, Greece

Thomas Rosemann and Beat Knechtle
Institute of Primary Care, University of Zurich, Zurich, Switzerland

Pantelis T. Nikolaidis
Exercise Physiology Laboratory, Nikaia, Greece

Lanlan Zhang and Liangjun Zhou
Department of Leisure Sports and Management, Guangzhou Sport University, Guangzhou, China

Fanghui Qiu
Department of Physical Education, Qingdao University, Qingdao, China

Hua Zhu
Department of Biological Science and Medical Engineering, Beihang University, Beijing, China

Mingqiang Xiang
Department of Sport and Health, Guangzhou Sport University, Guangzhou, China

Jérôme Frigout
I3SP Laboratory, Department of Sports Science and Physical Education, Paris Descartes University, Paris, France

Sophie Tasseel-Ponche
Médecine Physique et de Réadaptation, CHU Amiens-Picardie, Amiens, France
EA 4559, Laboratoire de Neurosciences Fonctionnelles et Pathologies, Centre Universitaire de Recherche en Santé, CHU Sud, Amiens, France

Arnaud Delafontaine
CIAMS, Université Paris-Sud, Université Paris-Saclay, Orsay, France
CIAMS, Université d'Orléans, Orléans, France

Jorge L. Storniolo, Roberto Esposti and Paolo Cavallari
Human Physiology Section, Department of Pathophysiology and Transplantation, University of Milan, Milan, Italy

María Merino Fernández
Department of Sports, Faculty of Physical Activity and Sport Sciences-INEF, Universidad Politécnica de Madrid (UPM), Madrid, Spain
Faculty of Health Sciences, Universidad Francisco de Vitoria (UFV), Madrid, Spain

Alfonso Lopéz Díaz-de-Durana
Department of Sports, Faculty of Physical Activity and Sport Sciences-INEF, Universidad Politécnica de Madrid (UPM), Madrid, Spain

Ciro José Brito
Faculty of Physical Education and Sport, Federal University of Juiz de Fora, Juiz de Fora, Brazil

Bianca Miarka
Faculty of Physical Education and Sport, Federal University of Juiz de Fora, Juiz de Fora, Brazil Laboratory of Psychophysiology and Performance in Sports & Combats, School of Physical Education and Sport, Federal University of Rio de Janeiro, Rio de Janeiro, Brazil

Vittoria Maria Patania, Dražen Čular and Alen Miletić
Faculty of Kinesiology, University of Split, Split,Croatia

Johnny Padulo
Department of Biomedical Sciences for Health, University of Milan, Milan, Italy

Enzo Iuliano and Andrea De Giorgio
Faculty of Psychology, eCampus University, Novedrate, Italy

Luca Paolo Ardigò
School of Exercise and Sport Science, Department of Neurosciences, Biomedicine and Movement Sciences, University of Verona, Verona, Italy

Qiang Yao
Department of Physical Education, Beijing Language and Culture University, Beijing, China

Feng Xu and Jiabao Lin
College of Economics and Management, South China Agricultural University, Guangzhou, China

Fabrizio Sors
Department of Medicine, Surgery and Health Sciences, University of Trieste, Trieste, Italy
Department of Life Sciences, University of Trieste, Trieste, Italy
Department of Medical Area, University of Udine, Udine, Italy

Stella Damonte
Department of Medical Area, University of Udine, Udine, Italy

Ilaria Santoro
Department of Life Sciences, University of Trieste, Trieste, Italy
Department of Medical Area, University of Udine, Udine, Italy

Maria Guarnera
Department of Human and Social Sciences, Kore University, Enna, Italy

Claudia Savia Guerrera
Department of Formative Processes, University of Catania, Catania, Italy
Department of Biomedical and Biotechnological Sciences, University of Catania, Catania, Italy of Educational Sciences, University of Catania, Catania, Italy

Nelson Mauro Maldonato
Department of Neuroscience and Reproductive and Odontostomatological Sciences, University of Naples Federico II, Naples, Italy

Filippo Drago
Department of Biomedical and Biotechnological Sciences, University of Catania, Catania, Italy

Dylan Poulus, Tristan J. Coulter, Michael G. Trotter and Remco Polman
School of Exercise and Nutrition Sciences, Queensland University of Technology, Brisbane, QLD, Australia

Giovanna Furneri
Department of Biomedical and Biotechnological Sciences, University of Catania, Catania, Italy
Department of Educational Sciences, University of Catania, Catania, Italy

Sabrina Castellano and Santo Di Nuovo
Department of Educational Sciences, University of Catania, Catania, Italy
Department of Formative Processes, University of Catania, Catania, Italy

Giuseppe Caruso
Department of Laboratories, Oasi Research Institute - IRCCS, Troina, Italy

Margherita Grasso and Filippo Caraci
Department of Laboratories, Oasi Research Institute - IRCCS, Troina, Italy
Department of Drug Sciences, University of Catania, Catania, Italy

Julia Schüler and Wanja Wolff
Department of Sport Science, University of Konstanz, Konstanz, Germany

Abhishek G. Dhawan
Agricultural Development Trust, Baramati, India

Index

www.ingramcontent.com/pod-product-compliance
Lightning Source LLC
LaVergne TN
LVHW060941220926
848485LV00015B/1209